"Robert Darnton is one of the world's greatest historia............ ....
book: a huge social and cultural portrait of Paris in the build-up to the French Revolution. Every chapter brims with life and colour, from newspapers and sex scandals
to philosophers and hot air balloons. Step by step he shows how the revolutionary
momentum mounted, reaching a crescendo with the storming of the Bastille. A
titanic work."   —Dominic Sandbrook, *Sunday Times*

"Lucidly argued and entertaining. . . . Darnton's book is a very fine account of how
18th-century Parisians received and interpreted public events, putting them on the
road to revolution."   —Tony Barber, *Financial Times*

"*The Revolutionary Temper* is vintage Darnton. Written in his strikingly clear
prose, argued with cogency, craft and conviction, and drawing on a lifetime of distilled research, . . . *The Revolutionary Temper* offers a superlative description of the
febrile volatility of opinion through the last half century of the *ancient regime,* as
many Parisians reacted—sometimes viscerally, sometimes wittily, and sometimes in
despair—to the problems faced by the monarchy. It works best as a vivid account of
what it must have felt like for many inhabitants of the city to find themselves caught
up in collective political turbulence—then to discover that they were on the cusp of
a new age."   —Colin Jones, *Times Literary Supplement*

"Darnton provides a sweeping account of succeeding events from the Parisian perspective, encompassing disastrous wars, struggles over Enlightenment ideas, fights
for religious toleration and crazes for all manner of new phenomena, such as hot
air balloons and mesmerism. . . . No one is better placed to uncover this world and
bring it to life than Robert Darnton, a historian who[se] pathbreaking studies
on 18th-century literature and the cultural impact of the Enlightenment . . . have
inspired a generation of historians. *The Revolutionary Temper* is the culmination of
Darnton's output and, like all his works, it is very readable."
                                    —Marisa Linton, *History Today*

"This book is the culmination of a lifetime of scholarly research, enhanced by an
intuitive understanding of the French mood. Short chapters stand alone as delight-
fully intriguing stories about a society in turmoil. Brought together, they explain
how the French eventually turned to revolution. This book is, quite simply, a feast,
but one that, thanks to superb storytelling, is easy to digest."
                                    —Gerard DeGroot, *Times* (UK)

"[Darnton] somehow combines acuity and erudition with an unbounded zest for literary performance. His energy seems palpable on every page.... It is hard to imagine a more engaging introduction to the intellectual currents of 18th-century France."

—John Adamson, *Literary Review*

"*The Revolutionary Temper* is a richly researched, ambitious and fascinating history. It asks a big question in a novel way." —Camilla Cassidy, *Sunday Telegraph*

"*The Revolutionary Temper* is a book that convincingly reframes the French Revolution—and Darnton's synthesis of scholarly rigor with style, brevity and wit is a singular achievement." —Madoc Cairns, *Observer*

"[An] exhilarating book . . . deep, rich and enthralling."

—Kathryn Hughes, *Guardian*

"What did Parisians think and gossip, sing and obsess about over the decades before the storming of the Bastille? In *The Revolutionary Temper*, Robert Darnton paints a sumptuous mural of the eighteenth-century mind. With the *Encyclopédie*, with manned balloons in the air, reason seemed on a roll. With posters, pamphlets, and public readings, the written word appeared supreme. A few vicious libels, some stock market manipulation, a lurid adultery trial, one notorious diamond necklace, any number of court intrigues, skyrocketing bread prices and plunging temperatures combined, among other elements, to shake a nation to its core. A rich, beautifully crafted book that plants the reader in a Paris that feels at all times electric."

—Stacy Schiff, author of *The Revolutionary: Samuel Adams*

"Standing at the summit of Robert Darnton's towering intellectual career, *The Revolutionary Temper* plunges the reader into the coffee shops, workrooms, and alleys of prerevolutionary Paris. Following the traces of songs and rumors, insults and discontent, Darnton allows us to eavesdrop, almost miraculously, on whispers nearly two and a half centuries old. Here is the hive mind of ordinary people in extraordinary times, as they shake loose the thought and feeling of ages past, and decide—slowly, and then all at once—to begin the world anew."

—Jane Kamensky, author of *A Revolution in Color*

THE
REVOLUTIONARY
TEMPER

• THE •
REVOLUTIONARY
TEMPER

PARIS, 1748–1789

ROBERT DARNTON

W. W. NORTON & COMPANY
Independent Publishers Since 1923

For information about permission to reproduce selections
from this book, write to Permissions, W. W. Norton & Company, Inc., 500 Fifth
Avenue, New York, NY 10110

For information about special discounts for bulk purchases,
please contact W. W. Norton Special Sales at
specialsales@wwnorton.com or 800-233-4830

Manufacturing by Lakeside Book Company
Book design by Brooke Koven
Production manager: Anna Oler

ISBN 978-1-324-08642-0 pbk.

W. W. Norton & Company, Inc.
500 Fifth Avenue, New York, N.Y. 10110
www.wwnorton.com

W. W. Norton & Company Ltd.
15 Carlisle Street, London W1D 3BS

10 9 8 7 6 5 4 3 2 1

To Susan

CONTENTS

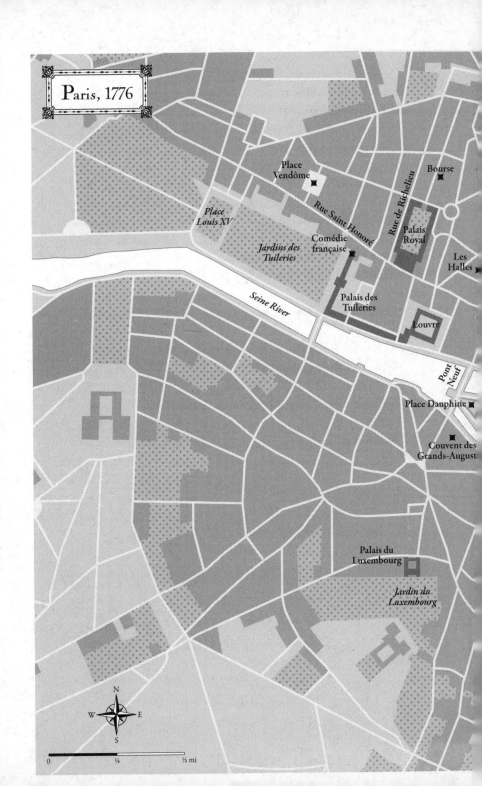

Paris, 1776

To live over other people's lives is nothing unless we live over their perceptions, live over the growth, the change, the varying intensities of the same—since it was by these things they themselves lived.

—Henry James as cited in Leon Edel, *Henry James: A Life*

Il semble que certaines réalités transcendantes émettent autour d'elles des rayons auxquelles la foule est sensible. C'est ainsi que, par exemple, quand un événement se produit, quand à la frontière une armée est en danger, ou battue, ou victorieuse, les nouvelles assez obscures qu'on reçoit et d'où l'homme cultivé ne sait pas tirer grand'chose, excitent dans la foule une émotion qui le surprend et dans laquelle, une fois que les experts l'ont mis au courant de la véritable situation militaire, il reconnaît la perception par le peuple de cette "aura" qui entoure les grands événements et qui peut être visible à des centaines de kilomètres.

It seems that certain transcendent realities emit from themselves beams of light that are picked up by the crowd. Thus it is, for example, that when an event occurs, when at the border an army is in danger, or is defeated, or wins a victory, the rather obscure news that one receives and that a cultivated man can't make much sense of, arouses in the crowd an emotion that surprises him and in which, once the experts have made him aware of the actual military situation, he recognizes the perception by the common people of that "aura" which surrounds great events and which can be visible at a distance of hundreds of kilometers.

—Marcel Proust, *À l'ombre des jeunes filles en fleurs*

INTRODUCTION

AN EARLY INFORMATION SOCIETY
AND COLLECTIVE CONSCIOUSNESS

E VENTS DO NOT come naked into the world. They come clothed—in attitudes, assumptions, values, memories of the past, anticipations of the future, hopes and fears, and many other emotions. To understand events, it is necessary to describe the perceptions that accompany them, for the two are inseparable. This book tells the story of how Parisians experienced the sequence of events that extended from the end of the War of the Austrian Succession (1740–1748) to the taking of the Bastille in 1789.

"Event history" has been deprecated for decades by professional historians—the leaders of the "Annales school" in France dismissed it as a thin veneer covering the deep structures of the past—but it is undergoing a revival, and it can be reworked, I believe, not simply as a record of what happened but as a way to understand how people made sense of happenings.[1] Their responses provide clues to public opinion, which has often been studied by historians, and also to something deeper: collective consciousness.

That something, I admit, is difficult to pin down with words. Social scientists frequently use related terms such as mentality, worldview, climate of opinion, and Zeitgeist, although, as explained below, "collective consciousness" emerged long ago in the work of Durkheim as a favorite concept among sociologists. I have adapted it under another name, "revolutionary temper," to characterize the way Parisians responded to the events that swept through their lives from 1748 to 1789. By "temper," I mean a frame of mind fixed by experience in a manner that is analogous to the "tempering" of steel by a process of heating and cooling.[2]

Paris underwent many changes during the eighteenth century, in its population, geography, and physical appearance. Thanks to research by a new generation of social and economic historians, we now can trace accompanying changes in Parisians' everyday surroundings, even of their diet, dress, furniture, shopping habits, amusements, and reading. Although the living conditions colored their general outlook on life, their sense of the direction taken in public affairs did not derive directly from their environment or their books. It developed in response to the news they received. I hope to allow for the influence of socioeconomic conditions and literature, but I will concentrate on the flow of information at street level—on the reports of events and of reactions to events as conveyed by the contemporary media.

So much happened during the four decades before the Revolution that, to avoid drowning the reader in detail, I have had to be selective. Rather than narrating an uninterrupted sequence, I have chosen four especially dense periods (1748–1754, 1762–1764, 1770–1775, 1781–1786) and then have concentrated on events from 1787 up to the storming of the Bastille. The narrative is meant to show how Parisians apprehended the course of events in a way that made them ready to take the great leap into a revolution in 1789.

I have limited the story to Paris, although much of it applies to the rest of France.[3] To wander through the provinces would be to lose the narrative thread in an overabundance of detail. Paris itself was a complex world, composed of many neighborhoods, each with its own identity, and an enormous, expanding population, differentiated by endless degrees of wealth and status. Intermixing increased in the second half of the century, when haberdashery in secondhand finery made it difficult to read "quality" by dress, and plebeians rubbed shoulders with patricians in theaters and public gardens. Yet Parisians retained an acute awareness of social standing, and they consistently differentiated between the "little people" (*le menu peuple, les petites gens*) at the bottom of society and *les grands* at the top. *Les grands* had access to Versailles: hence the expression "*la cour et la ville*," which indicated the connection between court and capital reserved for the great. For most Parisians, especially the "little people," Versailles was an alien world, and politics was the king's business, transacted in his name by ministers, courtiers, and power brokers among *les grands.* Yet word about the power plays leaked from Versailles, and it converged with all sorts of other news in the information system of Paris. In order to follow the ebb and flow of information among ordinary Parisians, I will avoid recounting events such as ministerial intrigues that took place beyond their range of vision, except insofar as they were reworked as rumors in salons, cafés, wineshops, street corners, and marketplaces.

I have relied primarily on diaries, correspondence, gazettes, and informal newssheets known as *nouvelles à la main.* Each has its limitations, and none provides a clear window into the past. In recounting events, the sources often describe how Parisians in general reacted to them, but there were no Parisians-in-general. Remarks about what "tout Paris" was saying usually were limited to a well-informed elite. The "on" in references to *"on dit"*—a common way of describing general opinion—did not usually extend deep into the world of artisans and shopkeepers; and when the talk referred explicitly to the common people, it often revealed more about the observers than the observed. There is no unmediated view of collective consciousness, which must be understood by inferences and interpretive leaps, supported by all the available evidence strung out over an adequate stretch of time.

While acknowledging the difficulties in this approach to history, I would like to emphasize its strengths. The sources about the flow of information in eighteenth-century Paris are extraordinarily rich. We can reconstruct conversations in cafés, pick up news in underground gazettes, listen to the running commentary of street songs, and visualize power as it was displayed in processions and festivals. We often say that we live in an age of information, as if this were something new. Yet every period of history is an age of information, each in its own way, and in the eighteenth century, Paris was saturated with information transmitted by a multimedia system peculiar to its time and place.[4]

Consider the Tree of Cracow, a large chestnut tree in the northern part of the garden in the Palais-Royal at the heart of Paris. Every day, *"nouvellistes de bouche"* (oral newsmongers) gathered under it to exchange the latest news by word of mouth. Ambassadors reportedly sent agents to pick up information or implant it, while ordinary people stopped by to satisfy their curiosity. "Craque" in slang meant false news, and the tree's branches supposedly made a cracking sound whenever a *nouvelliste* got things blatantly wrong.[5] Some of the listeners scribbled notes about the latest reports and declaimed from them to groups that gathered in other meeting places— the nearby Café du Caveau and Café de Foy, certain benches in the Luxembourg Gardens and the gardens of the Tuileries, wineshops, dinner tables, and salons. Tucked in sleeves and waistcoat pockets, the notes were confiscated by the police when they frisked prisoners in the Bastille. They can still be seen in the Bastille archives, fragments of the information that stirred up talk two and a half centuries ago. The conversations themselves can be followed, café by café, in reports by police spies, which were often written in dialogue form.

Other kinds of newsmongers transformed the notes into "*nouvelles à la main*" or manuscript newsletters, which circulated "*sous le manteau*" (under the cloak). At least thirty-one *nouvellistes* produced gazettes of this kind during the last decades of the Ancien Régime. Although they were illegal, the police knew all about them, frequently vetted them, and even produced bulletins of their own, so insatiable was the demand for information in a society that lacked modern newspapers—that is, printed periodicals with reports about politics and public affairs. France's first daily, the *Journal de Paris*, did not appear until 1777. It was heavily censored and contained nothing that would upset anyone in the government or church while the official *Gazette de France*, produced for many years by the ministry for foreign affairs, carried little more than notices issued by the powers in Versailles.

For local information, Parisians consulted a newssheet, *Annonces, affiches et avis divers*, which carried advertisements and short articles on all sorts of nonpolitical subjects.[6] For international news, they read French-language newspapers printed in the Low Countries, the Rhineland, and Avignon, which then was a papal enclave in the Comtat Venaissin. The foreign journals circulated widely, especially during the forty years after 1745, when their number increased from fifteen to eighty-two.[7] Although effectively censored (the police could cut off their distribution through the mail), they contained a great deal of news from around the world, including the revolutionary colonies of America; and their Parisian correspondents often wrote extensive dispatches.[8]

The information system of the Ancien Régime blended news from oral, manuscript, and printed sources. How this happened is illustrated best by the salon of Marie-Anne Doublet, a group known as "*la paroisse*" (the parish) that met every Saturday in Mme Doublet's apartment in the Marais district. To prepare for the meeting, one of her valets went around the servants' quarters of the neighborhood gathering gossip. He entered the information in two registers kept for the salon, one for news that seemed reliable, the other for dubious rumors. As the "parishioners" arrived, they consulted the registers, added reports of their own, and then gathered around a table for discussion and supper. Servants later made digests of the news that the group deemed credible. Copies circulated for sale, and copies of the copies spread in widening circles throughout France and much of Europe. A version first appeared in print in 1777 and was extended in edition after edition to thirty-six volumes by 1789 under the title *Mémoires secrets pour servir à l'histoire de la république des lettres en France*. The authorities knew all about the activities of the parish and at one point threatened to shut Mme Doublet up in a convent. Yet her primitive newsroom survived, and it left its mark on the news it produced— worldly, gossipy, spiced with witticisms about actresses and men about town, full of reviews of plays, books, and art exhibits, sympathetic to the Voltairean strain of the Enlightenment, and in political matters slanted in favor of the Parlement of Paris.[9]

While news and information of all kinds derived from word of mouth, Parisians inhabited a world where media overlapped and intersected. No boundaries separated communication by sounds and sights, whether in talk, writing, printing, or images. Rumor, for example, shaded off from casual gossip to seditious *bruits publics* (public noises). The extent of the variations can be gauged from the terminology of the time: *commérage, potin, ragot, on dit, rumeur, murmure, tapage, bruit public*. Witticisms took many forms such as the *bon mot, épigramme*, and *pont neuf*; and after being improvised in a verbal exchange, they often appeared in print. The manner and the tone of the exchanges inflected their meaning and effectiveness. Ridicule was a powerful weapon, as indicated by common remarks about the importance of getting laughter on one's side ("*mettre les rieurs de son côté*").

So was sentiment. In fact, the growth of *sensiblerie* during the second half of the century was accompanied by a shift in rhetoric. Just as Rousseau challenged the dominance of Voltaire, laughter gave way to tears. The change in tone showed up especially in court cases that attracted so much attention that they became "affairs," as in the Calas Affair, the Diamond Necklace Affair, and the Kornmann Affair, which stirred passions and spread them through a broad public.

An element of theatricality pervaded the arguments of lawyers and of talk in general, whenever it attracted a crowd. Individuals declaimed pamphlets at street corners and read them aloud in cafés. On occasion, the readings turned into performances with elaborate scenarios: After being read to an audience, a pro-government tract was sometimes put on trial, accused of a crime, condemned, and burned. Messages were conveyed by all sorts of gestures and even by clothing. Well-dressed men sometimes sported buttons on their waistcoats with images about current events, and women wore bonnets that evoked the themes of pamphlets. During the American Revolution, society ladies had elaborate coiffures "à la Philadelphie" and "à l'Indépendance."

Words also traveled by means of music. Nearly all Parisians carried in their heads a common repertory of tunes, at least a dozen, I have calculated. Nearly everyone could hum favorites such as "Les Pendus" ("The Hanged") and "Réveillez-vous belle endormie" ("Wake Up Beautiful Sleeper"). Every week and nearly every day, a wit, sometimes someone from the lower classes, composed a new verse to an old tune, making fun of a public figure or commenting on a current event. Collectors copied the latest songs into scrapbooks known as *chansonniers*. The eighteenth-century Chansonnier Clairambault in the Bibliothèque nationale de France runs to fifty-eight volumes. A *chansonnier* in the Bibliothèque historique de la ville de Paris contains 641 songs and poems in thirteen thick volumes merely for the period 1745–1752. Singers with fiddles or hurdy-gurdies begged for pennies in the streets, and artisans often sung at work—as Charles-Simon Favart did while kneading dough in his father's pastry shop before he was discovered and became the best-known author of comic operas.[10]

The most popular songs, attributed to fictitious authors such as "Bel-humeur, chanteur de Paris" ("Good Humor, Parisian Singer") and "Baptiste dit le divertissant" ("Baptiste, Known as the Amuser"), were printed as pamphlets, sometimes with their musical annotation. The music can also be identified from contemporary "keys." Therefore, one can recover something of the sound along with the words of street songs. Although they covered all kinds of subjects, especially drink and love, the songs conveyed so much information about current events that they functioned as oral newspapers. They were powerful enough in 1749 to precipitate the fall of the Maurepas ministry.

Some oral performances were known as publications. After all the major wars—in 1749, 1763, and 1783—peace was "published" by an enormous parade with drums and trumpets, which marched through the entire city and stopped at appointed places, where a herald read out a royal proclamation declaring the end of hostilities. Performances in general conveyed messages to Parisians, because the church and the state paraded themselves before the public on feast days and celebrations such as royal weddings. Royal funerals and "entrées" into Paris provided a way of acting out the importance of *les grands*. They required careful preparation, and they often went wrong. The misperformance of a ceremony meant to demonstrate dignity and power undermined the public respect for authority. Parisians sometimes took the staging of ceremonies into their own hands, drawing on patterns of riotous behavior familiar from the carnivals of Mardi Gras. At critical moments, they protested by dressing up straw men to imitate ministers, paraded the mannequins through the streets, staged mock trials, and burned them. In 1788 the bonfires led to rioting that nearly turned into a popular uprising.

These modes of communication did not require a high rate of literacy to be effective. Yet most Parisians, including the great majority of adult males, could read fairly well, and they read their way around the city, deciphering posters, commercial notices, signs, and graffiti. Their exposure to printed matter varied enormously, as did the act of reading itself. Everyone encountered posters, which could be crude, handwritten messages or printed manifestoes. If attached to walls with enough pressure and powerful glue, they could leave a readable impression after being removed by the police. All Parisians could understand the message of prints, whether or not they could read the captions. Workshops along the rue Saint Jacques churned out engravings of public figures, events such as sea battles, and facetious episodes known as "canards." The semiliterate also took in texts through their ears, because reading was often done aloud before groups in cafés, salons, and settings known as "lieux publics." These public places included the gardens of the Palais-Royal, the Tuileries, and the Luxembourg Palace, where Parisians liked to stroll and, as mentioned, *nouvellistes* held forth. The Palais-Royal was also a *"lieu privilégié"*— that is, an area under the autonomous jurisdiction of its owner, the Duc d'Orléans—so the police could not raid its bookstalls and cafés without clearance from its *gouverneur*. Peddlers hawked all kinds of printed material—government edicts, judicial memoirs (*factums*), pamphlets, chapbooks, and engravings—everywhere in the city. They kept Parisians informed about the latest publications by their cries—and also by the *way* they cried: if they were peddling best sellers, they belted out their sales pitch; if they were distributing decrees about new taxes, they barely raised their voices, because crowds sometimes vented their anger at the government by beating up the peddlers who hawked its edicts.

The raucous side of the information system flared up during crises and did not stifle everyday activities such as silent reading by isolated individuals. Many Parisians frequented the well-appointed bookshops of the Latin Quarter, bought books in popular genres such as travel and history, and read them quietly at home. By 1765, the most important works of the Enlightenment had appeared, and they were generally tolerated by the authorities, unless they advocated atheism or attacked the monarchy. The government secretly protected the sale of Diderot's *Encyclopédie* in its relatively inexpensive quarto editions during the late 1770s, and they reached a broad public of lawyers, doctors, administrative officials, and landowners. Nothing suggests that the state had abandoned its official values, as expressed, for example, by the oath Louis XVI took during his coronation in 1775. (He swore to exterminate heretics and to uphold the Orders of the Holy Ghost and of Saint Louis, but in 1787 he would agree to granting civil rights to Calvinists.) The last great Enlightenment tract, *Histoire philosophique et politique des établissements et du commerce des Européens dans les deux Indes* by Guillaume-Thomas Raynal (with large contributions by Diderot), was condemned and burned in 1781. But the increased toleration of unorthodox works indicates the extent to which the regime accommodated new ideas, and the diffusion of the books shows that those ideas penetrated deeply into the upper and middle strata of society. They won many adherents among the elite whose privileges they challenged. *"Tout Paris"* turned out to celebrate Voltaire when he returned to the city in 1778 after many years of exile. His apotheosis confirms that his crusade against *"l'infâme"* (religious bigotry, intolerance, and injustice) had won the sympathy of Parisians in general.[11]

Although the history of books provides plenty of surmises about attitudes and values among the reading public, it does not open up a way for arguments that lead directly from the publishing of books to their sales, reading, and absorption in the consciousness of readers. Yet research on the illegal sector of the book trade offers insights into the way books "took," because it shows how they were imbedded in the surrounding information system. Prohibited books were known in the underground trade as *"livres philosophiques"*—and to the police as *"marrons"* (chestnuts) or simply *"mauvais livres."* They contained a good deal of philosophy, especially the atheistic variety developed in the circle of the Baron d'Holbach, along with pornography and seditious libel. The best sellers in this sector were *"libelles"*—scandalous attacks on ministers, royal mistresses, and the king himself. They proliferated in many periods of French history, notably the uprisings of 1648–1653 known as the Fronde and the Regency of 1715–1723, and they were especially popular during the 1770s and 1780s. *"Libelles"* often looked imposing, as in the case of the four-volume *Vie privée de Louis XV,* which can be read as a detailed history of France from 1715 to 1774; but if examined closely, they can be seen to be composed of episodes, known at the time as anecdotes, which were combined to form a narrative. The same anecdote, often word for word, appears in several works, because the authors lifted material from one another and from common sources like gossip and *nouvelles à la main.* More than plagiarism, the libelling was a matter of rampant intertextuality, in which the basic unit was not the book but the anecdote—that is, a nugget of information that could be moved around and inserted wherever it would fit. Anecdotes traveled so widely that they became lodged in many imaginations.[12]

Not all *"livres philosophiques"* were built in this manner, nor did books in general conform to the same structure, but most of them contained ingredients derived from other segments of the information system, whether oral, written, or printed. Different media reinforced each other and sent ripples through every sector of the Parisian population. Although we cannot trace all the messages, we can follow them well enough to see how the system functioned. In recounting events and the perception of events, therefore, this book is meant to reveal the way an early information society operated.

Although the information often took the form of factual reports, the facts were infused with meaning—not morals attached to stories but implicit ways of making sense of the subject. For example, Siméon-Prosper Hardy, a middle-class bookseller, frequently recorded the price of bread, which was the basis of most Parisians' diets, in his diary. Sometimes he merely jotted down the current price, but in April 1775 he noted a sequence of price increases, which constituted a warning about hunger among the "little people." They understood the increases as a violation of a norm— a just price of 8 or 9 sous for a four-pound loaf—and they responded, as Hardy observed, with "*murmures*" and even riots, which were known as "*émotions populaires*." In fact, Paris exploded in an "*émotion*" on May 3, 1775, when rioters sacked nearly every bakery in the city. Steven Kaplan, the preeminent authority on the bread question, argues that the obsession with dearth belonged to a collective "subsistence consciousness."[13]

Current historians often use such phrases, including "the collective imaginary" and "the collective memory."[14] The usage derives, directly or indirectly, from efforts by sociologists and anthropologists to explain how we make our way in a world that is already organized and invested with meaning independently of our existence. Without pretending to offer a discourse on method, I should make explicit some of the connections between their theories and the kind of history I am attempting to write.

Emile Durkheim defined collective consciousness as "the totality of the beliefs and sentiments common to the average members of the same society," and he emphasized its existence as "a fixed system that has a life of its own."[15] That view, which prioritizes the social over the individual realm of experience, helps to account for the collective "*murmures*" and "*émotions*" mentioned by Hardy. Durkheim also used a complementary notion of "*sensibilité collective*," yet his abstract formulations do not convey the immediacy and emotional power of such experience.

Durkheim's rival, Gabriel Tarde, tried to show how common sentiments actually operate by discussing the example of reading. In late nineteenth-century Paris, he noted, readers often consulted newspapers in cafés, where they became available at about the same time every day. The readers, like the newspapers, favored different political parties, yet they had a sense that others, whatever their opinions, were reading at the same time, and therefore they were conscious of participating in a collective experience.[16] Benedict Anderson applied a similar argument to the development of nationalism in colonial societies. By reading books and especially newspapers, individuals felt united with persons they had never seen in an "imagined community," which underlay the transformation of a colonial state into a national state.[17] I believe that Parisian readers, despite their different opinions about particular issues, developed a similar sense of community, which they identified as a nation, by 1789. The feeling of participation in a common experience extended far beyond the experience of reading and even the limits of literacy. Virtually everyone in Paris shared the shock of the police kidnappings and riots of 1750; deplored the slaughter provoked by the attempt to celebrate the dauphin's wedding to Marie-Antoinette in 1770; and marveled at the first balloon flights in 1783–1784.

Parisians also shared an implicit sense of reality that lay behind those events. Sociologists have found it difficult to evoke this collective sentiment, which they sometimes describe as the social construction of reality. But by close study of social interaction, Erving Goffman shows how it can occur. In any encounter, he argues, we play roles, both as actors and audience, and this improvised behavior follows an implicit script, which determines what is actually going on, whether it is ordering a meal in a restaurant or participating in a political rally. "My aim," he explained in *Frame Analysis*, "is to try to isolate some of the basic frameworks of understanding available in our society for making sense out of events."[18] I find that Goffman's concept of dramaturgy works as a way to interpret the violent events of 1788, which were staged and performed according to a common frame of meaning.[19]

Max Weber made the social dimension of meaning the focus of his sociology. He used a complex German term, *Sinnzusammenhang* (the hanging together of meaning), to express the fundamental character of culture[20]—which the American anthropologist, Clifford Geertz, put aptly in English: "Believing with Max Weber, that man is an animal suspended in webs of significance he himself has spun, I take culture to be those webs, and the analysis of it to be therefore not an experimental science in search of law but an interpretive one in search of meaning." Although that approach does not involve a specific methodology, it entails teasing out meaning in concrete cases, as the "natives" construed it; and in practice, it leads to the study of events. Geertz quotes Weber: "Events are not just there and happen, but they have a meaning and happen because of that meaning."[21]

For my part, I am convinced by Weber's argument filtered through Geertz. It is compatible with the work of other anthropologists such as E. E. Evans-Pritchard, Victor Turner, and Mary Douglas—and also with the cultural history developed by Jacob Burckhardt, Johan Huizinga, and Lucien Febvre, who taught by example rather than by theory. With their help, I think it possible to show how the French Revolution happened—not by tracing a clear line of causality, but by narrating events in such a way as to describe the emergence of a revolutionary temper that was ready to destroy one world and construct another.

PART ONE

The
Mid-Century Crisis,
1748–1754

1

War and Peace

G LOBAL EVENTS touched daily life in eighteenth-century Paris
only glancingly and on rare occasions. What little we know
from sources like diaries and police archives suggests that most
people went about their business without much concern for international
affairs, yet they shared a general awareness of changes in the outside world.
The War of the Austrian Succession, 1740–1748, offers an opportunity to
study the way news about war and peace reached Parisians and how they
made sense of it. Although the history of the war is too complex to be discussed here, the flow of information can be understood by examining two
related events: the Battle of Lawfeld, which was the last major engagement
of the war, and the proclamation of the Peace of Aix-la-Chapelle, which
brought the war to an end.[1]

The battle took place at the village of Lawfeld near Maastricht on the
morning of July 2, 1747. News of it first came in the form of two notes
from Louis XV, who had witnessed the fighting from the headquarters
of the French commander, the *maréchal* Maurice de Saxe. By 12:30 in the
afternoon, the French had driven the main force of the Allies (British,
Hanoverians, Hessians, and Dutch under the command of the Duke of
Cumberland, George II's youngest son) from the village. Soon afterward,
Louis dictated the notes from conquered territory, and a page galloped
off with them to Versailles. In the first note, consisting of only a few sentences, he informed the dauphin of a French victory. He occupied the very

spot where Cumberland had commanded the enemy troops a few hours earlier, he said, and concluded by mocking Cumberland's boast that he would eat his boots if he did not defeat the French: "I think this duke is most upset. I don't know what he will eat now."[2] Louis addressed the second note to the queen, adopting a more formal tone: "The Day of the Virgin [the Day of the Visitation of the Blessed Virgin, July 2] has been most favorable for us. The heretics have been struck by all our blows. I have just won a complete victory against my enemies."[3] The notes arrived in Versailles at two o'clock in the morning on July 5, and copies of them were circulating in Paris a few days later.

Messages from the army arrived soon afterward. The first, also dated July 2, contained a sixteen-page list of casualties—officers sabered, shot, trampled, and mauled—and it was but the first of several lists that circulated, each one looking less triumphant than its predecessors. A series of reports, somewhat confused and contradictory, recounted details of the fighting. One, dated July 3 and sent by courier from the nearby camp of Tongres, described two unsuccessful assaults on the main enemy battalions followed by a third, which forced Cumberland to retreat from the village amidst "horrible carnage." Yet the enemy retired in excellent order, it noted, and the estimate of casualties was about the same on both sides—7,000 to 8,000 killed and 5,000 wounded. A second report, dashed off on July 5, confirmed that account. A third, undated, went into more detail, stressing Saxe's masterful command; and a fourth revealed that the enemy had regrouped in such a strong position outside Maastricht that the summer campaign could not be continued, although the French would lay siege to Bergen op Zoom.[4]

An official account of the battle, printed with a royal privilege and dated July 13, construed it as a glorious victory commanded by the king. By then Parisians knew that the *maréchal* de Saxe, not Louis XV, had directed the attack, and they had reason to be skeptical of the casualty report—10,000 lost by the Allies, 5,000 by the French—because the French-language gazettes published outside France were beginning to arrive, and they told a different story. As the Dutch Republic had abandoned its neutral stance and sided with Britain in 1747, the *Gazette d'Amsterdam* treated the French as the enemy. In its first dispatches on Lawfeld, it stressed the severity of the French losses and the strong position of the

Allied forces under the protective cannon of Maastricht, without indicating who had won the battle. Its Paris correspondent sent word that the French claimed a victory, but later articles cast that in doubt—and how, in fact, were victory and defeat to be determined? The French had occupied the battlefield, the *Gazette* acknowledged, but according to some measurements, they had not won the battle. The English reported 4,000 killed and wounded as opposed to 10,000 of the French. The Allies had captured nine flags and seven standards, the French only two standards. The count of captured cannon and drums also favored the Allies, who, moreover, occupied such a favorable position that they blocked the French advance and threatened to counterattack at any moment. Seen from Amsterdam, the result of the battle was ambiguous, and in some ways it looked as though the Allies had prevailed.[5]

Police spies noted that the foreign gazettes were widely read in Paris and that some Parisians—those with enough money and leisure to frequent cafés—had doubts about the government's claim of victory.[6] The police took great pains to keep track of public opinion. They also tried to influence it by distributing bulletins about the progress of the war in cafés and by subsidizing their own gazetteers.[7] But the café talk drew on other sources, not only Dutch journals but letters from individuals located near the action. The first letters about Lawfeld arrived on July 11, and they indicated that the French had lost twice as many men as the Allies. That was a heavy price to pay for occupying the battlefield, according to the police reports on the café conversations: "That is to say that according to them [café commentators], we won the battlefield and they won the battle."[8] The Parisian barrister Edmond-Jean-François Barbier wrote in his journal in July, "The court and the town have not been happy with this engagement, whose result is only a battlefield that cost more than six thousand men."[9]

The difficulty of determining who won the Battle of Lawfeld applied on a larger scale to the entire war. Parisians paid special attention to the fighting north of France's border in the Austrian Netherlands. It conformed to warfare of the kind that had prevailed under Louis XIV—that is, sieges of fortresses and fortified cities combined with occasional, large-scale battles. The sieges required months of digging trenches and undermining redoubts until at last the enemy could be overwhelmed by an attack or forced to capitulate. The *batailles rangées* pitted densely packed rows of troops on both sides. Muskets took a long time to load (a soldier had to tear open a cartridge with his teeth, pour some powder in the pan of the flintlock, pour the rest down the barrel followed by a bullet, and tamp the bullet down with a ramrod before he could pull the trigger), and they had little accuracy (they could rarely hit a target at a distance of a hundred yards). Therefore, a line of musketeers in tight formation fired all at once at their officer's command in the general direction of the enemy, reloaded while a line behind them fired, and advanced until ordered to stop and fire another volley. Then, when they closed in on the enemy, they charged with their bayonets and tried to win in hand-to-hand combat (the *mêlée*) or to force a retreat. It was this kind of fighting that made the French win (or lose) at Lawfeld and that produced such heavy casualties.

Nouvellistes under the Tree of Cracow in the Palais-Royal and at certain benches in the Luxembourg and Tuileries gardens discussed these tactics, claiming to have inside information from witnesses or military sources. They traced battle lines on the ground with their canes and debated questions of strategy on a continental scale. One self-appointed expert was known as the "abbé Thirty Thousand Men," because he constantly argued that the French could take London if they shipped 30,000 troops across the Channel.[10] Others held forth about troop movements in Italy and Germany. For the most part, however, the *nouvellistes* concentrated on campaigns in the Low Countries. The lines they drew in the dirt illustrated the advance of the main French forces under the *maréchal* de Saxe, year after year, fortress after fortress: Menin, Ypres, the great victory at Fontenoy (May 11, 1745), Tournai, Ghent, Oudenarde, Bruges, Dendermonde, Antwerp, the Battle of Rocoux (another victory, October 11, 1746), Liège, the Battle of Lawfeld (July 2, 1747), and Bergen op Zoom. By the end of the summer campaign in 1747, Saxe had conquered the Austrian Netherlands and seemed to have a clear road into the Dutch Republic. To those who followed the news in Paris, it made a gripping story, which raised the possibility of winning territory that Louis XIV had failed to conquer during nearly fifty years of fighting.

Yet Saxe's campaigns occurred in only one sector, barely one hundred miles wide, in a series of conflicts that stretched over much of the globe, involved a dozen sovereign states, and extended from 1740 to 1748. "The War of the Austrian Succession," as it came to be called, was a misnomer for a struggle that can be considered a world war—perhaps the first world war, unless the War of the Spanish Succession, 1701–1715, deserves that title. The dynastic aspect remained important, of course, and contemporaries talked about the fighting as if it pitted Louis of France and Frederick of Prussia against Maria Theresa of Austria and George of England along with their assorted allies.[11] The personalization of the warfare made it seem comprehensible, as if it were a great game played on a chessboard the size of Europe, but that view looked archaic if seen from the perspective of the action on the high seas and colonies. In North and South America, the Atlantic and Pacific, the Mediterranean and Caribbean, the English Channel and the coast of India, fleets, convoys, and privateers waged constant battles. In the end, especially after the second Battle of Finistère (October 14, 1747), the British established naval supremacy, laying the basis of a colonial and commercial empire.

Reports of the overseas warfare appeared in the gazettes, and café sophisticates discussed them, but most Parisians, if they followed foreign affairs at all, concentrated on the fighting nearby in the Low Countries, where Saxe scored his victories. They were appalled, therefore, as soon as they learned about the preliminaries to the Peace of Aix-la-Chapelle, to discover that Louis XV had agreed to return everything France had won at such expense and suffering. In exchange, he received virtually nothing. He got back Louisbourg, a fortress on Cape Breton Island, while he surrendered Madras, a greater prize, to the British. To ordinary Parisians with an uncertain grasp of geography, the global readjustment in the balance of power, insofar as they were aware of it, mattered less than the sacrifice of the fortresses in Flanders.[12]

Most Parisians, moreover, experienced the war as hardship inflicted on their daily lives in the form of increased taxes, scarcer goods, and higher prices. The *dixième*, a special tax levied since 1741 to support the war, fell on virtually all revenue, although the clergy negotiated an exemption (it paid a sizeable *don gratuit* or free gift to the Crown in order to maintain its privileges).[13] Salaries were exempt; so, laborers did not suffer directly, but the *dixième* was a bitter blow to rentiers, merchants, artisans, and shopkeepers. Heavy tariffs were levied on consumer goods that entered Paris, and surtaxes were added to the tariffs in March 1745, October 1747, and March 1748, when the head tax (*capitation*) was also increased. Meanwhile, prices had risen, particularly on bread. In March 1748, Barbier noted in his journal, "Everything necessary to sustain life, food, wood, candles, upkeep, is generally unaffordable."[14]

Peace did not bring immediate relief. By May 1748, Parisians knew the fighting had stopped, and the treaty of Aix-la-Chapelle, signed on October 18, 1748, formally brought the war to an end; but the king did not proclaim peace until nine months later. The proclamation, like many events under the Ancien Régime, was a theatrical affair acted out in the streets of Paris in a ceremony called "*la publication de la paix*"—publication being understood in the contemporary sense of "rendering public" or making something generally known.[15]

At dawn on February 12, 1749, cannonades from the Invalides, the Bastille, and the château de Vincennes summoned magistrates and guildsmen to assemble at the Hôtel de Ville dressed in their finest costumes and accompanied by drummers and flag bearers.[16] They formed a cortege led by detachments of soldiers, some on horse, some on foot, interspersed by drummers and fife players. Next came several rows of magistrates and a large corps of musicians, carrying drums, fifes, trumpets, bugles, cymbals, oboes, and other wind instruments. At the heart of the procession, on magnificent horses, rode the Roi d'armes, a court official, and six royal heralds in livery and plumed hats. The lieutenant general of police and the prévôt des marchands (Paris's chief municipal official) followed, outfitted in splendid uniforms, mounted on horses draped in velvet cloth with gold braiding, and accompanied by six lackeys wearing specially designed livery. After them marched a long cavalcade of municipal officers and guildsmen in two columns arranged by rank as ordained by a decree. A troop from the Watch (*guet à pied* and *guet à cheval*) brought up the rear, making a procession of eight hundred persons in all.

The cortege paraded through the city and stopped at thirteen appointed places, including the Halles, the Place Maubert, and other locations where the common people gathered. At each stop, fanfares alerted the neighborhood, and the musicians played. The Roi d'armes ordered a herald to read out the royal proclamation of the peace—not the text of the treaty, which ran to seventy-nine pages, but a declaration that hostilities had ceased and that safe travel and commerce were assured among the subjects of the former belligerents. Then a soldier summoned the people in the street to shout *Vive le roi*, and the cortege moved on to the next stop. After a long day of parading, the participants retired to a feast in the Hôtel de Ville set off by fanfares and cannonades.

On the following day, all shops were closed and a Te Deum was celebrated in Notre Dame. An "illumination générale" lit up Paris that evening. Every house was required to display a *lampion*, and candles burned in many windows. At eight in the evening, a fireworks display dazzled an enormous crowd crammed into the Place de Grève. When the spectators began to disperse, however, they got blocked in a bottleneck, panicked, and stampeded. A dozen persons were crushed to death. Despite this disaster, large groups piled into a dance hall built specially for the occasion on the Quai Pelletier near the Hôtel de Ville. Two orchestras played; wine flowed from four fountains; and sausages, cuts of turkey, mutton, and bread were distributed, all of it free and intended primarily for "the little people." Dancing, drinking, and eating also took place at twenty-five other sites scattered through the city. For two days and nights, Parisians gave themselves over to celebrating the peace, but what did they make of it?

The most revealing commentary occurs in Barbier's journal. During the parade, he noted, many people refused to cry *Vive le roi*. "The common people in general are not happy with this peace, which, however, they badly needed," he explained. "It is reported that in les Halles, the market women say, when they quarrel with each other, 'You are as stupid as the peace.'"[17] Police spies picked up similar remarks. And the Marquis d'Argenson noted in his journal that the peace celebrations had backfired because so many people were trampled to death during the fireworks. Parisians blamed the tragedy on the government: "People revert to superstition and prophesies as pagans used to do. They say, 'What is augured by such a peace, which was celebrated with such general horrors?'"[18]

The global conflict left no happy memories among Parisians in 1748, because the tide in the flow of information had turned against the government. Parisians did not enjoy any satisfaction at having won the war after the fighting stopped; and they sensed that they had lost the peace, despite the cannonading, parading, Te Deums, fireworks, dancing, and free wine and food offered them at the time of its "publication." In fact, the very notions of winning and losing got lost in the fog of war, and the year ended in an atmosphere of discontent.

2

A Prince Is Mugged
by Order of the King

IN ADDITION TO restoring the balance of power throughout Europe, the Treaty of Aix-la-Chapelle was intended to solve a diplomatic problem embodied by a person: Charles Edward Stuart, later known as "Bonnie Prince Charlie" and already a legend among Parisians in 1748 as the most intrepid and dashing of the many royal personages occupying or claiming thrones. The throne he claimed was that of Great Britain, which, he maintained, belonged by right of succession to his father, known in France as Jacques III and in Britain as the Pretender. As the first-born heir to his father, he demanded to be acknowledged as the Prince of Wales and not, as the Britons put it, the Young Pretender. Parisians called him "le Prince Édouard" and celebrated him, both as a man-about-town and as the champion of a lost cause, who had dared against impossible odds to attempt the conquest of their English enemy in 1745. He posed a problem for the restoration of peace, because he refused to leave France.[1]

The treaty committed Louis XV to recognize the Hanoverian line as the legitimate rulers of Great Britain and therefore bound him to expel Prince Édouard from France, where he had been given asylum. To Parisians, or at least those who followed the rise and fall of monarchs, that provision was outrageous. The prince's grandfather, James II of England and Ireland (also James VII of Scotland), had taken refuge in France after being driven out of his kingdom by the Glorious Revolution of 1688. Louis XIV had treated him with full honors as a fellow monarch, residing with his court in the Château de Saint-Germain-en-Laye. To be sure, France had recognized the Hanoverians in 1718 as part of the settlement following the wars of Louis XIV, but it supported Prince Édouard's attempt to restore the Stuart line by invading Scotland in July 1745.

Parisians followed news of the invasion as best they could from the French gazettes published in the Netherlands and whatever they could pick up in cafés and salons. Judging from the entries in Barbier's journal, they found the story riveting. Édouard set out with two ships, lost one, and landed in Scotland with only seven supporters. Two months later he had established himself with a force of 17,000 men in Edinburgh and had proclaimed his father king of Scotland and Ireland. Barbier expected the father to abdicate, so Édouard would become king; and in December, when his army was reported to be within thirty leagues (ninety miles) of London, it looked as if George II was doomed. A long silence followed. Word arrived that the Duke of Cumberland had left Flanders with 12,000 troops in a desperate attempt to save the Crown, and this diversion made it possible for the *maréchal* de Saxe to take Brussels on February 23, 1746. For several months Parisians struggled to sort out contradictory reports— some had Édouard retreating to the Highlands; some claimed relief was on its way from France; some even anticipated a Jacobite revolt in London. Finally, on May 17, Paris learned of a disaster: Cumberland had crushed Édouard's forces on April 16 at Culloden, near Inverness.

For the next three months, various "*bruits*" (rumors) spread tales of spectacular episodes. Édouard was reported to be hiding in the Highlands and dashing from island to island in the Hebrides, just beyond the reach of his pursuers, sometimes alone, sometimes in disguise, and saved time and again by humble folk who refused to be tempted by the reward of 30,000 pounds placed on his head. He escaped at last on a small French frigate, and on October 28 he appeared to tremendous applause in the royal box of the Paris Opera. Although he had failed to conquer Britain, Barbier noted, Édouard had won the hearts of Parisians by his heroism, suffering, and "bravura." "The public will be unhappy if this prince is sacrificed."[2]

Yet the Treaty of Aix-la-Chapelle did sacrifice him. It could not do otherwise, because peace could not be restored unless France recognized the Hanoverian succession. Louis XV did what he could to soften the blow. According to the gazettes, he met privately with Édouard, offered advice about stoically accepting fate, and presented a gift of a table service worth 300,000 L. (At that time a semiskilled worker usually made one livre a day; the livre, which was the main unit of currency, is abbreviated here as L.; it contained 20 sous, and each sous was worth 12 deniers.) Édouard, however, would not be moved, although his father, who had retired to Rome, ordered him to submit to the peace settlement. In July 1748, Édouard produced a manifesto asserting that his father, as James III, was still king of Britain. All the events since 1688 made no difference, he claimed, speaking as "Régent de la Grande Bretagne," because the passage of time had no bearing on legitimacy and the fundamental constitution of the state. The Paris police managed to confiscate the manifesto in the printer's shop and to keep their intervention secret, because they worried about provoking a reaction among Édouard's many supporters in Paris. But a second edition soon appeared, and the police learned that it had been read aloud in the café de Viseux, rue Mazarine, where it was available to everyone on the counter. In August 1748, as the diplomats neared agreement on the final terms of the treaty in Aix-la-Chapelle, Édouard had a notice printed and pinned to their doors, warning them to avoid any settlement that would violate his right to the throne of Great Britain.[3]

According to the gazettes that circulated in Paris, the French foreign minister, in the name of the king, requested Édouard to leave France in November. The prince refused, and then the king sent the Duc de Gesvres, a friend of Édouard's and an important Court official, to make a personal appeal. According to rumors that spread through Paris, Édouard told the duke that he always carried two loaded pistols in his pockets. If anyone arrived with an order for his expulsion, he would shoot that person with the first pistol and kill himself with the second. The Dutch gazettes reported that Louis would have to resort to violence, and Parisians prepared themselves for a dramatic "event." Meanwhile, Édouard cut quite a figure in Paris, along with a retinue of Scottish and English Jacobites who had survived the adventure of 1745. He appeared every day in theaters or at the Opera, and strolled conspicuously in the Tuileries gardens, much to the Parisians' delight and perhaps, as some suspected, because he was courting popular support that could be turned against Versailles.

At 5 o'clock on December 10, soon after he descended from his carriage to attend a performance at the Opera, Prince Édouard was accosted by a major of the Gardes Françaises, who informed him that the king had ordered his arrest. Instantly, six soldiers, disguised as civilians, surrounded him. According to reports that circulated soon afterward, two of them grabbed his arms, and the others seized his legs, lifting him off the ground. While holding him in the air, they bound his arms to his body with silk ropes in order to prevent him from using his pistols. They carried him to an adjoining courtyard, removed the two pistols and his sword, then dispatched him in a carriage to the dungeon of Vincennes. A detachment of Gardes and the Mounted Watch *(guet à cheval)*, which had been waiting nearby in the Place des Victoires, accompanied the carriage, and soldiers stationed all along the route held their muskets ready, bayonets attached. Three companions of the prince who had accompanied him to the Opera were taken to the Bastille. Another detachment of the Gardes Françaises surrounded the town house that served as the prince's headquarters. They arrested thirty-three of his other retainers who also disappeared into the Bastille. More than a thousand soldiers participated in the operation. Everything was prepared carefully in advance and took place rapidly in order to avoid provoking a riot by Édouard's many admirers.[4]

After five days of confinement in the dungeon, Édouard left for an unknown destination. An official escort took him as far as Pont de Beauvoisin at the border with Savoy, and then the prince disappeared. Some of the more savvy gossips known as *"politiques"* asserted he would set up court in Fribourg, Switzerland; others placed him in Rome or in Avignon, which was papal territory, but everyone agreed that he would have to take up residence outside France. In January 1749 he was given a hero's reception in Avignon; he was later spotted in Venice; and he eventually settled in Rome, fading from the limelight, as Parisians shifted their attention to other subjects, including a rhinoceros, the first ever seen in France, which was exhibited at the foire Saint-Germain in March 1749.

In the winter of 1748–1749, however, Édouard was the talk of the town, despite the orders of the police, who told café owners to stifle conversations about him. Half of Paris wept over his unhappy fate, according to the *Courrier d'Avignon*. Parisians went over every detail of his arrest and expulsion, venting resentment at the heavy hand of Louis XV. The king had reneged on a sacred commitment, they complained. He had failed to send the support that would have made the difference between victory and defeat in Scotland. Then, after profiting from the diversion created by the Scottish uprising, he had caved in to the demands of the enemy in the peace negotiations and had executed them with a brutality unworthy of a monarch. Édouard in defeat was more of a king than Louis in victory.

That theme stood out in a flood of poems, songs, epigrams, and prints that contrasted Édouard's heroism with Louis's fecklessness.[5] For example,

O Louis! Vos sujets de douleur abattus,	*O Louis! Your subjects crushed with pain,*
Respectent Édouard captif et sans couronne:	*Respect Édouard as a captive without a crown:*
Il est roi dans les fers, qu'êtes vous sur le trône?	*He is a king in chains, what are you on the throne?*

Édouard's expulsion epitomized the disaster of the peace settlement, according to several poems:

Peuple jadis si fier, aujourd'hui si servile,
Des princes malheureux vous n'êtes plus l'asile.
Vos ennemis vaincus aux champs de Fontenoy
A leurs propres vainqueurs ont imposé la loi.

(You people once so proud, today so servile, / No longer are you the refuge of unhappy princes. / Your enemies, defeated on the field of Fontenoy, / Now impose the law on their own conquerors.)

In a more popular vein, a burlesque poster pretended to be an order by George II commanding Louis, his obedient servant, to deliver Édouard to the pope. The savagery of Édouard's expulsion made it seem especially outrageous, and it demonstrated how Louis had debased himself by letting George II dictate the terms of the peace.[6]

This message made the complexities of the peace settlement intelligible to Parisians who did not follow international relations closely. It reduced foreign affairs to personal antagonisms: George vs. Louis vs. Édouard.

Even to the more sophisticated—the "politiques" and café regulars—
Louis XV's behavior appeared in a new light, influenced by other personal
circumstances. Louis had acquired the title of "le Bien-Aimé" in 1744,
when all of France prayed for his recovery from a dangerous illness near
the front lines in Metz and then rejoiced when he survived and returned
in good health to Versailles. But that high point in the public's affection
for him declined as the war inflicted increasing hardship in the daily life
of Parisians. On the few occasions when he appeared in Paris, the people
refused to cry *Vive le roi* (Long live the king). Normally, when he traveled from Versailles to the château of Compiègne and his favorite hunting grounds, he stopped in Paris near the Porte Saint Denis to receive a
salute from the Gardes Françaises and to greet his subjects, while cannon
boomed from Vincennes, the Bastille, and the Invalides. In August 1749,
however, he avoided this traditional ceremony, and he did so again in June
1750, touching off rumors among Parisians. Did he fear he might provoke
a riot by the discontented? they wondered. Or did he want to demonstrate
his scorn for their refusal to express devotion? Louis's visits to Paris then
became increasingly rare. When he came to attend a mass at Notre Dame
in November 1751, he was met with a stony silence in the streets. By then
he had had a road built so that he could make a detour around Paris when
he traveled to Compiègne.[7]

The growing hostility of Parisians to the king fed on the taxes and the
economic suffering imposed on them by the war, but it had another, more
insidious source. From 1732 until 1744, Louis had taken as his mistress
three (some said four) of the daughters of the Marquis de Nesle, one after
another. Although the French had long ago grown accustomed to royal
mistresses and acknowledged the *maîtresse en titre* as a fixture in the court,
they considered sex with sisters as a form of incest. Moreover, Louis himself viewed his extramarital relations as sinful, although he pursued them
as avidly as his hunting, and he admitted his sins to his confessor. The confessor would not grant him absolution unless he renounced adultery, and
without absolution Louis could not take communion. Although he dismissed the Duchesse de Châteauroux, the youngest of the de Nesle sisters,
for a few weeks after his illness in 1744, Louis soon took up with her again
and in 1745, after she had died, moved on to Madame de Pompadour.

By then, his unshriven state had become notorious. Although he attended mass, he no longer took communion, and he therefore lacked the necessary grace to administer the royal touch. By touching subjects who suffered from scrofula, French kings were believed to cure the disease known as *le mal du roi* (the King's Evil). They supposedly acquired this power through the religious rites at their coronation, and they traditionally exercised it after Easter mass by touching the sick lined up in the Grande Galerie of the Louvre. Having failed to *faire ses Pâques* (take communion on Easter), Louis had lost this sacred power.[8]

The loss affected all his subjects, not merely those with scrofula. In 1750, the French hoped the pope would declare a Jubilé or period of collective penitence and remission of sins, which usually occurred once every twenty-five years. But word had spread that the Jubilé would be canceled as a punishment inflicted on all of them for the king's exclusion from the sacrament of communion. One *nouvelliste* published a letter from a correspondent who vilified Louis for depriving his people of the Jubilé: "It is monstruous that all of France should be deprived of it, because the king, by his own fault, is not in a state to receive this grace [holy communion]."[9] The general resentment was expressed in some of the crudest poems:

Louis le mal-aimé	*Louis the badly loved,*
Fais ton Jubilé,	*Make your Jubilé,*
Quitte ta putain	*Give up your whore*
	[Mme de Pompadour]
Et donne-nous du pain.[10]	*And give us bread.*

This was strong stuff, and it circulated among the common people. Although the police rarely identified the authors of the poems, in one case they discovered that an attack on the king had been written by a Madame Dubois, the wife of an obscure shopkeeper. She began her verse by expressing consternation about the Jubilé:

Nous n'aurons point de Jubilé.	*We won't have a Jubilé.*
Le peuple en est alarmé.	*The people are alarmed about it.*

And ended with a crude reference to the king's sexual sins:

Le pape en est ému, l'Église s'en offense.	*The pope is moved, the Church offended,*
Mais ce monarque aveuglé,	*But this blinded monarch,*
Se croyant dans l'indépendance	*Believing himself independent,*
Rit du Saint Père et f—[fout] en liberté.[11]	*Laughs at the Holy Father and fucks in liberty.*

In fact, Pope Benedict XIV promulgated a bull extending a Jubilé to all Catholics in 1751, and the rites began to be celebrated in Paris on March 29. By then, however, the sacred character of Louis's kingship had been damaged. In 1749, the Marquis d'Argenson noted that a miscarriage of the dauphine was seen by the common people as God's punishment for the king's sins,[12] and a police spy reported the following conversation in a wigmaker's shop:

> This officer [Jules-Alexis Bernard] while visiting the wigmaker Gaujoux, recited in the presence of M. d'Azémard, an invalided officer, a written attack on the king, which accused His Majesty of allowing himself to be led by ignorant and incapable ministers and of having made a shameful and dishonorable peace that gave up all the conquered territory.... [Also] that the king, who had consorted with the three sisters, scandalised his people by his conduct and would bring upon himself all sorts of misfortune if he did not mend his ways, ... [and] that the king had not taken Easter communion and would bring upon the kingdom the curse of the Lord.

The abduction of Prince Édouard marked a turning point in the relations between Parisians and the king. It belonged to the general discontent with the war and the peace. Parisians reacted by withholding cries of *Vive le roi*, and Louis responded by avoiding Paris altogether. At the same time, his inability to take communion sapped his sacramental power. He lost his royal touch, and in losing it, he lost contact with the people of Paris.

3

Songs Bring Down the Government

PARISIANS TOOK THE NEWS in through their ears. They heard it sung in the streets. Every day, wits improvised new words to old tunes, and the messages flew through the air, serving in effect as sung newspapers. Ministers in Versailles and police inspectors in Paris understood the power of songs and kept track of them, for the French state, as the Parisian wit Nicolas Chamfort put it, was "an absolute monarchy tempered by songs."[1] On April 24, 1749, songs brought down the governing ministry: that was the conclusion reached by observers at the time,[2] and it can be taken as an indication of the way sound infused the mental landscape of Parisians in the eighteenth century.

Entire populations share a repertory of tunes attached to lullabies, religious hymns, Christmas carols, ballads, love songs, drinking songs, battle songs—and, today, the pervasive jingles of commercials and popular recordings. In the eighteenth century, as explained in the Introduction, Parisians carried around in their heads a common corpus of tunes, and many of them composed new words to the best-known tunes as a way of making fun of prominent persons or commenting on current events. The music served as a mnemonic device and a medium to spread messages throughout the city, where street singers could be heard everywhere and people commonly sang at social gatherings and at work. Some Parisians scribbled the latest verses on scraps of paper, which were passed around, declaimed, and sung in public places. Collectors copied the verses in albums known as *chansonniers*, which contain so many texts that particular songs can be followed as they evolved in response to current events. Contemporaries also produced "keys" with the musical scores to the most popular songs, identified by their titles or first lines. It is possible, therefore, to reconstruct the way the songs sounded—that is, allowing for variations in the mode of singing and irregularities in the survival of the evidence, we can hear, at least approximately, fragments of the past.[3]

Without going into the musicological aspect of this research, one can identify the most common tunes and the words attached to them. The half dozen melodies that appear most frequently in the *chansonniers* during the 1740s are:

"Dirai-je mon Confiteor"
("Shall I say my Confiteor" [a confessional prayer]), also known as
"Quand mon amant me fait la cour" ("When my lover courts me")
"Réveillez-vous, belle endormie"
("Awake, beautiful sleeper"), also known as "Quand le péril est
agréable" ("When the peril is agreeable")
"Lampons"
("Drink up")
"Les Pantins"
("The Puppets")
"Biribi"
(Biribi, a game of chance)
"La Coquette sans le savoir"
("The Coquette who does not know it")

Each of these tunes carried a string of comments on current events during the mid-century years. The first provides the best example of how the commentary worked.[4] In its conventional form it is a plaintive love song. I have located nine satirical versions of it, each with a refrain that mocks Louis XV as a feckless, clueless ruler:

Ah! Le voilà, ah! le voici	*Ah! There he is, ah! here he is*
Celui qui n'en a nul souci.	*He who does not have a care.*

The first verse attacks the king and Madame de Pompadour:

Qu'une bâtarde de catin	*That a bastard strumpet*
A la cour se voit avancée,	*Should get ahead in the court,*
Que dans l'amour et dans le vin	*That in love or in wine,*
Louis cherche une gloire aisée,	*Louis should seek easy glory,*
Ah! Le voilà, ah! Le voici	*Ah! There he is, ah! here he is,*
Celui qui n'en a nul souci.	*He who does not have a care.*

The next verses ridiculed the queen, the dauphin, the *maréchal* de Saxe, and the most prominent ministers. Then, as time passed, the song evolved, growing from six to twenty-three verses, which can be dated from notes in the margins and allusions to events such as the peace negotiations at Aix-la-Chapelle, the resistance to the *vingtième* tax, and the notorious cuckolding of the tax farmer La Popelinière by the *maréchal* de Richelieu, who had a secret door built through La Poplinière's town house so he could get access to the wife's bedroom. Each version differs slightly from the others, indicating variations in the process of oral transmission, which extended from August 1747 to February 1749. Taken together, the verses provided a widespread indictment of the people in power and the system itself.

Of course, Parisians had enjoyed making fun of *les grands* for more than a century, and much of the ridicule was produced by the courtiers themselves in the endless battles to gain traction and bring down rivals in Versailles. A contemporary description shows that verse spread from the top down as well as from the bottom up:

A dastardly courtier puts them [slanderous rumors] into rhyming couplets and, by means of lowly servants, has them planted in market halls and street stands. From the markets they are passed on to artisans, who, in turn, relay them back to the noblemen who had composed them and who, without losing a moment, take off for the Oeil-de-Boeuf [a meeting place in the Palace of Versailles] and whisper to one another in a tone of consummate hypocrisy: "Have you read them? Here they are. They are circulating among the common people of Paris."[5]

During critical periods such as the four years after the War of the Austrian Succession, these ephemera could inflict serious damage. One song in particular precipitated a fundamental shift of power within the government. The second of the tunes cited above, "Réveillez-vous, belle endormie," also originated as a love song, then turned into a slanderous attack on a duchess, and finally brought down Jean-Frédéric Phélypeaux, Comte de Maurepas, the most powerful minister in Versailles, on April 24, 1749. Although it created a scandal that shocked and fascinated Parisians, it required some hearing between the lines:[6]

Par vos façons nobles et franches,	*By your noble and free manner,*
Iris, vous enchantez nos coeurs.	*Iris, you enchant our hearts.*
Sur nos pas, vous semez des fleurs,	*On our path you strew flowers,*
Mais ce sont des fleurs blanches.	*But they are white flowers.*

On the evening before the poem began to circulate, Maurepas had attended a dinner in the *petits appartements* of Versailles, where the king often retired to enjoy himself in privacy. Only two persons, Mme de Pompadour and her cousin, Mme d'Estrades, were present in addition to Louis and Maurepas. In a gallant gesture, Mme de Pompadour distributed some white hyacinths, which she had picked herself, to her dinner companions. Far from being lyrical, however, the reference to white flowers (*fleurs blanches*) in the song indicated venereal disease, *flueurs*, in menstrual discharge. The royal mistress, the song said, had given the king VD. Even to a public hardened by obscene songs at the time of the Regency (1715–1723) and the Fronde (1648–1653, the civil war precipitated by the Parlement of Paris and the nobility), this was going too far. The king dismissed Maurepas and exiled him to his country estate.

Maurepas was the prime suspect in the scandal, because he had firsthand knowledge of the hyacinth episode and he frequently distributed songs or even composed them himself. He renewed his supply from reports provided by the Paris police and used it to amuse the king and undermine his enemies. His stock of songs, transcribed into the forty-five volumes of the Chansonnier *Maurepas* now in the Bibliothèque nationale de France, provides a rich source of information about singing as an ingredient of politics in the eighteenth century. Well-informed about his passion for songs, contemporaries were convinced that they had caused his downfall. As Barbier put it, "One is absolutely convinced that the poems and the songs that greatly offended the king and that are said to have been sung before him at suppers, are the cause."[7]

Of course, Parisians realized that there was more to this event than the nasty song about Mme de Pompadour. As minister of the navy and of the Maison du roi, which included the Département de Paris and control of the Paris police, Maurepas dominated the government. He had been a minister for twenty-six years (he first entered the government in 1718 at age seventeen) and seemed unmovable. Yet he built his power base around the queen and the dauphin, and did not get on well with royal mistresses, notably Mme de Pompadour, who became aligned with his rival, the Comte d'Argenson, minister of war. According to rumors, Maurepas fostered the spread of the anti-Pompadour songs and poems known as Poissonnades in reference to her unfortunate maiden name, Poisson (fish). If he could demonstrate to the king that Mme de Pompadour was reviled by Parisians, some suspected, he might get Louis to turn her in for a mistress aligned with his own court faction. To cover his trail, Maurepas supposedly attributed the Poissonnades to another of his enemies, the *maréchal* de Richelieu, an ally of d'Argenson and Pompadour. Richelieu discovered the plot and revealed it to the king just as the song about the white flowers began to circulate.

This version of Maurepas's fall owed a great deal to the rumor mill of the court and the baroque character of politics in Versailles. Parisians, who had little contact with that alien world, could not be certain about what lay behind Maurepas's fall, but they knew that songs precipitated it and that the result was a realignment of power. In the subsequent reallocation of ministries, d'Argenson added the Paris Department to his dossier as war minister and therefore gained control of the police reports about the Parisian *bruits*, *on dits*, and *pont neufs* that Maurepas had fed to Louis. He then unleashed a campaign by the police to silence songs, using his new power to consolidate the support of Mme de Pompadour.

Soon after the fall of Maurepas, the police received an order from d'Argenson to arrest the author of a poem. Their only clue was its first line: "Monstre dont la noire furie" ("Monster whose black fury"). The monster was Louis XV, and the poem belonged to a surge of new verse attacking the king and Mme de Pompadour. A spy eventually turned up a medical student who possessed a copy of the poem. Under interrogation in the Bastille, he confessed that he had got it from a priest, who was arrested and said he had got it from another priest, who was arrested and said he had got it from a third priest . . . and so on, until the police had filled the Bastille with fourteen suspects, mainly students and young abbés.

Along the way, the police uncovered the trail of five other poems and songs, which had been copied, memorized, declaimed, and sung in various settings, including a lecture room in the Collège du Plessis, where a young professor, Pierre Sigorgne, dictated a poem to his students, who then shared copies with their classmates. Sigorgne was the first professor in the University of Paris to teach Newtonian physics, which he had expounded in a treatise, *Institutions newtoniennes* (1747). One of his students sent a copy of the poem to a friend inside a book, Diderot's *Lettre sur les aveugles*, an illegal, irreligious tract. Diderot was arrested for writing it in July 1749 at the same time as the police were hunting down the fourteen purveyors of the songs and poems, although he had no connection to them. He was then deep into work as editor of the *Encyclopédie*, whose first volume was due to appear in 1751, and his publishers, who had invested enormous sums in that enterprise, used all the influence they could muster to get him out of prison in the dungeon of Vincennes. The police therefore turned up all sorts of elements that were fermenting in Parisian culture— Newtonianism, Encyclopedism, and libertine freethinking as well as hostility to the king and his mistress—when they dug into the "Affair of the Fourteen," as they called it.

D'Argenson paid no heed to the broader dimension of the case. To him, as he put it in a letter to Nicolas René Berryer, the lieutenant general of police, much of the poetry "seems to me as to you to smell of the pedantry in the Latin quarter."[8] Little abbés and students had no importance because he was after larger game. In other letters to Berryer, he said that he had discussed the affair with the king, who took great interest in it. He urged Berryer to push on with the investigation: "You must not, Monsieur, let loose of the thread since we now have it in our grasp. On the contrary, we must strive to follow it up to its origin, as high as is possible."[9]

D'Argenson hoped to implicate Maurepas's partisans, who still wielded influence at the height of the power system and threatened to engineer Maurepas's return. They used songs and poems as weapons in the continuing struggle to dominate the government, and d'Argenson fought back by suppressing the poetry.

The police eventually gave up the hunt. They never found the author of "Monster whose black fury," perhaps because the poem was a collective creation that evolved in the telling rather than the product of a particular individual. After several months in the Bastille, the fourteen were released and sentenced to exile. They had no idea of the machinations that had taken place above their heads, far off in Versailles. Nor did most Parisians. Yet the police repression—a matter of abducting individuals from cafés and breaking into their apartments—aroused a great deal of attention and indignation. Although it could not be mentioned in newspapers, it was treated as an important event in private journals. The Marquis d'Argenson (not to be confused with the Comte d'Argenson, the war minister, who was his brother) noted in his journal that everyone around him had memorized the songs and poems, which he took to be symptomatic of a dangerous divide between the people of Paris and their rulers in Versailles. "I observe in the public and in select company talk that shocks me, an open contempt for the government and a profound discontent with it," he wrote. "Songs and satires are pouring down everywhere."[10]

Although the Affair of the Fourteen turned out to be nothing more than an episode in the endless struggle of court politics, it left a mark in Parisian memories. The abbé Morellet, who had belonged to Sigorgne's entourage as a student, described it in vivid detail fifty years later, and it was depicted as a turning point of Louis XV's reign in a clandestine best seller, *Vie privée de Louis XV*, published in 1781.[11] The songs themselves became absorbed in the general body of contestatory verse that went back to the Fronde, and they covered the entire range of topics that obsessed Parisians in the mid-century years. Many, as mentioned, protested against the treatment of Prince Édouard. Others condemned the peace settlement, the taxes, and the decadence of the court.

Mme de Pompadour provided a favorite target. While some songs derided her appearance (flat chest, yellowish skin, tainted teeth) without making political comments, several deplored her power over the ministers and attributed Maurepas's fall to her influence. Thus a Poissonnade composed to the tune of a drinking song and addressed to Maurepas:

On dit que Madame Catin,	*It's said that Madam Slut,*
Qui vous mène si beau train	*Who leads you by the nose*
Et se plaît à la culbute,	*And is pleased by [the*
	ministry's] collapse,
Vous procure cette chute.	*Was the one who caused your fall.*
Lampons, lampons,	*Drink up, drink up,*
Camarades, lampons.*¹²*	*Comrades, drink up.*

Far from challenging the principle of the monarchy, the songs condemned Pompadour for demeaning the majesty of the throne and attacked Louis for being an unworthy monarch:

Elle ordonne, il souscrit, humilié, soumis.
Aux genoux d'une femme on voit tomber Louis.
Et jaloux d'assouvir sa passion brutale,
Il profane à ses pieds la Majesté Royale.¹³

(She commands, he accepts, humiliated, submissive. / One sees Louis fall to the ground before a woman, / And determined to satisfy his brutal passion, / He profanes the Royal Majesty at her feet.)

The songs attacked Louis directly as "un roi fainéant, lâche, faible, imbécile"¹⁴ ("a feckless king, lazy, weak, imbecilic"). They conveyed a general feeling of disgust with the reign rather than an ideological message:

Les grands seigneurs s'avilissent,	*The great lords are making*
	themselves vile,
Les financiers s'enrichissent,	*The financiers are getting rich,*
Tous les Poissons s'agrandissent	*All the Fish are growing big.*
C'est le règne des vauriens.	*It's the reign of*
	the good-for-nothings.

Yet some went so far as to threaten regicide:

> Louis prend garde à ta vie.   *Louis beware of your life.*
> Il est encore des Ravaillac à Paris.[15] *There still are Ravaillacs in Paris.*

(François Ravaillac was the assassin of Henry IV.)

Contemporaries like the Marquis d'Argenson detected sedition in such singing, but they looked back to 1648 rather than forward to 1789. No one could foresee the French Revolution in 1749, and no one today should view the songs as a sound track leading unproblematically to the past. Even if we can sing them ourselves to the tunes of the time, they merely provide clues as to what was in the air in eighteenth-century Paris, not unmediated access to the consciousness of eighteenth-century Parisians. At the very least, however, we can see that Parisians considered songs a power to be reckoned with, powerful enough in 1749 to bring down the government.

4

Saints Are Sent to Hell

RARELY, IF EVER, had Parisians witnessed such an outpouring of grief and indignation: A line of mourners, 10,000 strong, stretched across the Latin Quarter from the church of Saint-Etienne-du-Mont to the chapel of the Collège de Beauvais on June 22, 1749. They grieved over the death of Charles Coffin, the former principal of the college, rector of the university, and a devout Jansenist, revered for his piety and considered by some to be a saint. They fumed with anger at the archbishop of Paris, who had issued an order for the dying to be refused the last sacraments unless they produced a certificate attesting to their rejection of Jansenism—or, more precisely as will be explained, that they confessed to a priest who accepted the anti-Jansenist papal bull *Unigenitus*.[1]

Most French Catholics believed that salvation depended on the performance of the last rites. Some (not in Paris but in large parts of the South) belonged to associations of penitents, who rehearsed deathbed scenes so they would be prepared to renounce sin and resist the temptations of the devil at the supreme moment when salvation and damnation hung in the balance. To be denied extreme unction and absolution of sins was, in the eyes of the faithful, to be exposed to the danger of hellfire. The curate in Coffin's parish, Father Bouettin, had obeyed the archbishop's order with ruthless intransigence. By withholding the Viaticum (the eucharist given with extreme unction) from Coffin, it could be said that he had barred the way to grace and sent a saint to hell.

The mourners, who included a great many priests, magistrates, and students, were not inclined to take such a simplified view. No one, they knew, could be certain about Coffin's fate in the afterlife, although some priests claimed that his refusal to renounce Jansenism meant he had been damned. But the mourners shared a widespread resentment about the refusal of sacraments, an issue that cut to the heart of Catholicism as a faith lived out in the lives of ordinary Parisians.

Jansenism had gone through several phases since it became attached to the name of Cornelius Jansen, a theologian from Leuven, whose *Augustinus* (1640) reworked the austere, Augustinian strain in Catholicism. Seventeenth-century French Jansenists such as Antoine Arnauld and Pasquier Quesnel developed a dark, tragic vision of the human condition. Man was inherently sinful, they argued, and salvation came through grace, a nearly unattainable infusion of the Holy Spirit that had to be "efficacious" as well as "sufficient," meaning it could not be earned or deserved. They scorned the casuistry of their enemies, the Jesuits, for being soft on sin, while the Jesuits attacked them as heretics, hardly different in their theology from Protestants. Taking their inspiration from Thomas Aquinas (and ultimately from Aristotle), the Jesuits offered a more positive view of the world, which included the frequent practice of confession, absolution, and communion. They participated actively in secular affairs, often as advisors to kings and courtiers. The Jansenists tended to withdraw from the world, sometimes in ascetic communities like the Abbey de Port-Royal outside Paris, from which Pascal launched his *Lettres provinciales* (1656–1657), a devastating attack on Jesuitism. Unlike the Jesuits, they never constituted a separate order, and even refused to be identified as Jansenists, a label that could easily come loose in theological debates.

By the time Pascal's generation had died out, Jansenism had lost its sharp, theological edge and had spread through the lower clergy and professional classes as a general ethos, characterized by austere piety and political activism. The politics were connected with the thirteen parlements of France, particularly the Parlement of Paris, whose area of jurisdiction as a high court covered nearly half the kingdom. Although the parlements functioned primarily as appellate courts (*cours souveraines*), they exercised police powers and participated in the legislative process. Royal edicts did not become effective as laws until they had been entered in the register of the parlement where they applied. If a parlement objected to an edict, it could delay registering it and protest by remonstrating.

The back-and-forth of remonstrances, royal responses, and "iterative" remonstrances, accompanied by high-flown oratory in contentious cases, stirred up a great deal of dust. But the king could always force registration in a ceremony known as a *lit de justice*; for, as the parlements conceded in obsequious "humble representations," the king was absolute and his will was law. The parlements also insisted, however, that an edict might express the king's momentary will, which could be "surprised," perhaps by an erring minister, as opposed to his long-term will, which by its nature conformed to the fundamental laws of the monarchy. Those laws remained implicit and varied according to different parlementary pronouncements, but at a minimum they included the Salic Law, which determined the succession to the Crown by the eldest male heir, and the prohibition against alienating any part of the kingdom. The parlements frequently invoked the fundamental laws to justify their opposition to particular edicts.[2]

The Parlement of Paris, located in the Palais de justice at the center of the city, generated a subculture of its own. It included a Grand'Chambre, composed of the most distinguished elderly magistrates; five Chambres des enquêtes (reduced to three in 1756); and one Chambre des requêtes. Important cases were pleaded before the Grand'Chambre, while the lesser chambers handled subordinate functions. All the magistrates owned their offices and therefore could not be removed—a crucial condition for maintaining an independent judiciary and therefore liberty, according to Montesquieu. They were also nobles, members of the *noblesse de robe* as opposed to the nobles of the sword (*noblesse d'épée*), who descended from the feudal nobility. The robes themselves—some in deep black velvet with ermine trim, others brilliant red for attending high mass—expressed their superior standing, which the magistrates displayed in many processions. Although the nobles of the sword looked down on the *parlementaires*, they often intermarried and closed ranks to defend their fiscal privileges. The Parlement of Paris had nearly 250 members, including bailiffs and other officers. It employed hundreds of clerks, who had their own informal organization, the *basoche*, which sometimes staged mock ceremonies and rowdy protests. About six hundred lawyers pleaded cases before the Parlement, and all sorts of hangers-on—notaries, scriveners, booksellers, even doctors and apothecaries—did business within its precinct. Two other "sovereign" courts—the Chambres des comptes for fiscal affairs and the Cour des aides for adjudicating tax cases—also occupied the Palais de justice, which was a complex of buildings grouped around six courtyards under the tower of the Sainte Chapelle. The total population of this bustling legal world came to about 40,000 persons.[3]

Many of the magistrates and lawyers were educated by Jansenists, notably in Coffin's Collège de Beauvais. They became a powerful force within the Parlement of Paris during the 1720s and 1730s, when the controversy over Jansenism within the Gallican Church spilled into politics, eventually pitting the Parlement against the archbishop of Paris and the government. The disputes centered on *Unigenitus*, a papal bull or "constitution" issued at the urging of Louis XIV in 1713, which branded as heresy 101 propositions from Quesnel's *Réflexions morales sur le Nouveau Testament* (first complete edition, 1692), a fundamental Jansenist text. Jansenists who opposed the bull hoped to find support in the Parlement and ultimately to have it reversed by appealing to a general council of the church. They became known as *appellants*, while their opponents, led by Jesuits and powerful prelates, were called *constitutionnaires*. Papal bulls did not have the force of law in France until they were issued as a royal edict registered in the parlements. The Parlement of Paris had registered *Unigenitus* in 1714 only with the reservation that it had to be unanimously accepted by France's bishops. Some bishops refused to do so because they had Jansenist sympathies. Moreover, the French Church did not accept the supreme authority of the pope, and therefore the Jansenists claimed that *Unigenitus* was not an article of faith for French Catholics. By 1732 the Jansenist "party" in the Parlement came to about sixty magistrates, nearly one-fourth of the total members. When Jansenist issues arose, they often won the support of the other magistrates by claiming to defend the autonomy of the Gallican Church.

At the same time, a popular variety of Jansenism grew up among the common people of Paris, bearing traits of revivalist movements that went back to the Middle Ages.[4] It spread through the city from the church of Saint-Médard in the poor and densely populated faubourg de

Saint-Marcel. François de Pâris, a deacon of the Oratory of Saint Magloire and a devout Jansenist, died in 1727 after dedicating his life to serving the poor, living in poverty himself, and mortifying his flesh by extreme measures—a hairshirt reinforced with sharp, iron wires; a diet reduced to one daily meal of little more than soup and bread; a bed consisting of an overturned armoire. At his funeral in the church of Saint-Médard, an illiterate, destitute widow touched his bier and prayed for his intercession to cure a paralyzed arm. It was immediately healed. Soon afterward, others were cured from all kinds of diseases and infirmities by touching the dirt on his grave or, later, a marble slab erected over it. While lying on the slab, some broke into convulsions, flailing about and shrieking as if possessed by the power that wrought the cures. Word of the miracles reached all corners of Paris. The ill and the penitent poured into the graveyard of Saint-Médard, and they included some aristocrats and priests from other parishes, who added respectability to the extravagant scenes. The archbishop of Paris at that time, Louis-Antoine de Noailles, who had known Pâris and shared his commitment to Jansenism, named a commission to investigate the cures, and its preliminary results were positive. To many Parisians, Pâris was a saint, who performed miracles as saints had done since the early days of the church.

To the government, however, the religious enthusiasm threatened to get out of hand—and also to spread Jansenism. The Jansenist party within the Parlement of Paris supported testimony in favor of the cures and also opposed attempts by the new archbishop, a determined *constitutionnaire* who succeeded Noailles in 1729, to purge Jansenist curates under his jurisdiction. Pamphleteers took up the cause of the "convulsionaries," as did the *Nouvelles ecclésiastiques*, an underground Jansenist weekly with a growing readership. Faced with so much division and dissent, the government, acting in the name of the king, decided to close the churchyard of Saint-Médard on January 27, 1732. Although the police avoided violence, they could not prevent a surge of protests, which included an epigram posted on the churchyard fence that became the most famous antiroyal witticism of the century:

De par le roi,   *By order of the king,*
Défense à Dieu,   *God is forbidden*

De faire miracles,　　　　　　*To perform miracles*
En ce lieu.　　　　　　　　　*In this location.*

The defiance of the king's authority rode on a wave of religious fervor, which rose from the poorest sectors of Paris and carried with it some segments of the elite. By celebrating miracles, Parisians expressed indignation at the abuse of power, both ecclesiastical and royal, in an idiom of their own.

The spiritual element in the protests soon turned sour, however. The convulsionaries continued to meet in private and developed sectarian tendencies along with extreme practices. Some underwent beatings and flagellation, drove sharp objects into their bodies, vented chiliastic fantasies of the Last Judgment, and, in one extreme, antinomian group, indulged in sexual orgies. By 1736, some of the most prominent Jansenists had disowned all connection with the convulsionaries. Many sectarians disappeared into the Bastille and then into exile. Their movement never had much coherence, either as a doctrine or an organization, and it eventually dissipated. Yet it had a powerful appeal to Parisians at the bottom of the social order, and it challenged the authority of those at the top. It therefore had an affinity with the more serious challenge that came from the Jansenists who protested against the refusal of sacraments to Charles Coffin.

The protest was aimed against Christophe de Beaumont, the devout and rigidly orthodox archbishop of Paris, who was even more inflexible in his opposition to Jansenism than his predecessor. In 1749 Beaumont ordered the priests in his diocese to refuse to administer the sacraments to anyone who did not confess to an orthodox priest. In practice, the order was used against notorious Jansenists who could not produce a document called a *billet de confession*, which certified that they received the sacraments from a priest who adhered to the bull. Most Parisians had little interest in the fine points of theology. If asked to explain the difference between sufficient and efficacious grace, they probably would have shrugged their shoulders. But deathbed rites touched everyone, and many ordinary Catholics were outraged at the refusal of extreme unction to a person on the brink of death who was struggling to attain salvation. Stories circulated about Jansenists who died unshriven after a life of piety and were even denied burial in sacred ground. Nearly every week the *Nouvelles ecclésiastiques* published accounts of Jansenists who died as martyrs. The scenario was always the same: Suffering horribly from the last stages of disease, barely able to talk or think clearly, they were hounded by priests who demanded adherence to theological propositions and then exulted in abandoning them to their fate. Bouettin, who had refused the viaticum to Coffin, was denounced by the journal for exceptional cruelty. Behind him stood the archbishop, and behind the archbishop, the king.

After Coffin's death, his nephew appealed to the Parlement requesting reparations for Bouettin's refusal of the sacraments.[5] He received support from four "consultations" signed by sixty lawyers, who argued that the affair came within the Parlement's jurisdiction over secular disturbances in Paris and its role as "protector and conserver of the rights of citizens." The consultations were printed and fed a great deal of agitation—described as "great noise," "murmurs," and "greatly agitated spirit"—among the Parisian public.[6] Before the Parlement could take action, the king evoked the affair to himself as the supreme authority in matters of justice, and he quashed the consultations on the grounds that they disturbed public tranquility.

Having recently clashed with the government over the *vingtième* and other issues, the Parlement backed down; but in December 1750 Coffin's nephew, then twenty-eight years old, contracted a deadly disease. He, too, refused to accept *Unigenitus*, and therefore Bouettin denied him access to the sacraments. The nephew was a magistrate in the Châtelet court (a Parisian court under the Parlement's jurisdiction), which appealed to the archbishop to intervene. Beaumont refused, the Châtelet appealed to the Parlement, and the Parlement summoned Bouettin to justify his conduct. After much resistance, Bouettin appeared but insisted that he would only obey the orders of the archbishop. The Parlement responded by decreeing his arrest and imprisoning him overnight in the Conciergerie. Shaken by the experience, Bouettin was severely interrogated by the magistrates on the next day and released with a symbolic fine of 3 L. as punishment. A compliant curate was found to administer the last rites to young Coffin, who made an edifying death on January 9. He, too, received a long funeral procession from the church of Saint-Étienne-du-Mont before being buried next to his uncle. The double deaths of the Coffins aroused a great deal of angry talk among Parisians and dramatized the refusal of sacraments as an issue that made Jansenism a political force.[7]

The Parlement followed up its triumph over Bouettin with remonstrances denouncing the refusal of sacraments. Then, after the king rejected the remonstrances, it defied his authority in a related affair, which concerned the Hôpital-Général, a group of institutions that sheltered some of the Parisian sick and poor while serving as a prison for prostitutes and criminals. Archbishop Beaumont tried to purge Jansenists from the Hôpital's administration, and the king, who reportedly could not bear even to hear the word "Jansenist," issued a declaration on March 24, 1751, giving Beaumont full control of the Hôpital and excluding *appellants* from it. The Parlement retorted by remonstrances and then, in the face of Louis's intransigeance, iterative remonstrances, which invoked the fundamental laws of the kingdom in a manner that, to observers like the Marquis d'Argenson, indicated an ambition to transform France into a constitutional monarchy.[8]

By September, the disagreement over the Hôpital had escalated into a major crisis. The common people, suffering from a severe rise in the price of bread after a bad harvest, backed the Parlement and even expressed Jansenist sympathies. They did not indicate any interest in *Unigenitus*, but they supported the Jansenist administrators of the Hôpital and were often heard to mutter curses against the king and Mme de Pompadour. For lack of funds, the Hôpital had to turn many of its poor inmates out into the street. In November while en route to a service in Notre Dame, the dauphin and dauphine passed a crowd of 2,000 women in the street who screamed at them, "Give us bread, we are dying of hunger!"[9] The street patrols were doubled in order to prevent riots. In a confrontation with the Parlement on November 24, the king evoked the Hôpital affair. He demanded to see the minutes of the court's deliberations and then, in a scornful gesture, stuffed them into his pocket. The Parlement responded by suspending its functions. Lawyers supported it by going on strike, and the administration of justice ground to a halt. After secret negotiations and two days of debate, the Parlement decided on December 3 to retreat by registering the decree that had evoked the dispute. That decision finally put the Hôpital affair to rest, but to some Parisians it looked like a dress rehearsal for a more serious conflict, because the larger issue of the refusal of sacraments would not go away.

For the next two years the *constitutionnaire* clergy, backed by the archbishop, continued to deny extreme unction to Jansenists, and the deathbed scenes, reported in rumors and pamphlets as well as the *Nouvelles ecclésiastiques*, reinforced the general feeling that the church was exposing its saintliest members to an uncertain afterlife. Many cases were appealed to the Parlement, which claimed authority over the temporal affairs of the clergy along with the right to intervene in the policing of Paris. After the Coffin scandal, the case that whipped up most indignation concerned Ignace Lemère, a Jansenist who had retired on a small pension in Bouettin's parish of Saint-Etienne-du-Mont. Like Coffin, Lemère was respected for scholarship as well as piety, having spent most of his life in a priory translating religious works from the Greek. He lived austerely, fighting off ill health and studying scripture. A stroke paralyzed part of his body in 1749, and another attack in April 1752 brought him, at age 75, to death's door. After he requested the sacraments, Bouettin appeared at his bedside, demanding a *billet de confession*. For five weeks, the "pitiless inquisitor" harrangued Lemère about the necessity of accepting the bull *Unigenitus*, according to the account in the *Nouvelles ecclésiastiques*. Bouettin even tried to get him to admit that deacon Pâris was currently undergoing punishment in hell. Suffering from gangrene and too weak to debate, Lemère made negative gestures with his hands. As he sank into his last agony, Bouettin consulted the archbishop and returned with a firm refusal to administer extreme unction.

On March 23 the Parlement intervened. It summoned Bouettin for another interrogation; and when he insisted that he was following the archbishop's instructions, it passed à decree ordering Beaumont to have the sacraments administered within twenty-four hours. Faced with an open conflict between the secular and spiritual powers, the king annulled the decree and evoked the case. The Parlement, aware that Lemère could not hold out much longer, sent a delegation to protest that decision. Touched by its account of Lemère's desperate state, Louis dispatched a priest to perform the last rites. By the time he arrived, however, Lemère had succumbed to the gangrene. He died unshriven, surrounded by lay witnesses praying for his soul.

Because of the urgency, the Parlement remained in session late into the night. When it learned of Lemère's death, it decreed the arrest of Bouettin and adjourned at four in the morning. Bouettin went into hiding; the king also annulled this decree, which had been trumpeted in the streets; and Paris erupted in angry discussions. Nearly 10,000 mourners followed Lemère's coffin to the cemetery of Saint-Étienne-du-Mont on March 29. After a great deal of heated oratory, the Parlement then voted to make remonstrations. While it prepared the text, the lawyers of Paris refused to plead cases, and justice was again suspended. The remonstrances, printed by the Parlement and reprinted in the Dutch gazettes, protested that the partisans of *Unigenitus* were creating a schism within the Gallican Church that threatened the monarchy itself. They denied the validity of *Unigenitus* as an article of faith and condemned the use of it as a pretext for refusing to administer the sacraments to the dying. The king's reply was moderate enough for some Parisians to suspect that he secretly supported the Parlement's stand against the archbishop. They felt confirmed in that view on April 18, when the Parlement issued a decree forbidding the refusal of sacraments for lack of a *billet de confession*. The decree was printed overnight and distributed everywhere in Paris. It was even pasted on the walls of the archbishop's palace as a way to goad him. According to Barbier and the Marquis d'Argenson, Parisians now were united behind the Parlement and were turning against the king.[10]

Louis's position remained unclear for several weeks. He appointed a commission to resolve the ecclesiological issues, but it failed to reach any conclusion, and eventually he rejected the Parlement's decree of April 18. Meanwhile, *constitutionnaire* clergy continued to deny the sacraments to suspected Jansenists. As case after case came to their attention, the anger of Parisians threatened to boil over, and the Parlement resolved to take action.[11] In December 1752, Sister Antoinette Fournera, an aged member of a Jansenist community, the Maison de Sainte-Agathe, fell seriously ill and requested the last sacraments. The Maison was located in the parish of Saint-Médard, where the curates, appointed by the archbishop, had done their best to stamp out the remnants of the convulsionary sect. They had refused to administer extreme unction to four of the sisters in the Maison before Sister Antoinette made her request, and the current curate, Père Hardy-Levaré, was unbending: no *billet de confession*, no sacraments. Sister Antoinette barely summoned up the strength to resist. The next day she lost consciousness; the Maison summoned Père Hardy; he refused to give her extreme unction; and she died.

Soon afterward, Sister Perpétue, 79, an equally devout member of the Maison, suffered a stroke of apoplexy. She made the same request and received the same answer. At that point, the Parlement intervened by decreeing Hardy-Levaré's arrest. Although he was absent, one of his two vicars appeared before the Parlement and testified that Hardy-Levaré had followed a command from the archbishop. The Parlement then passed a decree ordering Beaumont to have the sacraments administered immediately, as Perpétue was in danger of dying. The archbishop refused, saying he was responsible only to God. After a second attempt to constrain Beaumont, the Parlement ordered the confiscation of his temporal belongings and took steps to bring him to trial—a complicated procedure because he was a peer of the realm and as such could only be tried before his fellow ducs et pairs, who sat with the Grand'Chambre but rarely attended its sessions. The king headed off this threat by forbidding the convocation of the peers. Meanwhile, the Parlement decreed the arrest of Hardy's two vicars and ordered other priests to administer the sacraments to Perpétue. Then, unexpectedly, she began to recover. The king dispatched some agents with a *lettre de cachet* (an extrajudicial, royal order) to carry her off in a *chaise à porteurs* to a convent, where she was kept in confinement. Having already denounced the "intolerable despotism" of the archbishop, the Parlement now protested against the "abduction" of a frail, sick, and elderly subject by an arbitrary order of the king. It voted to make more remonstrances, and then Louis quashed the affair by evoking it.[12]

Information about each of these episodes, spread by the *Nouvelles ecclésiastiques* and word of mouth, illustrated the larger issues of ecclesiastical and royal power. Parisians followed the events with enormous interest. Street peddlers hawked royal edicts and parlementary remonstrances within everyone's hearing. The texts were posted at street corners, where people gathered to read and discuss them. Remonstrances from the provincial parlements—especially those from Rouen, Toulouse, and Aix-en-Provence—circulated widely and sometimes outdid the protests from the Parlement of Paris in the violence of their language. Songs and prints amplified the messages. Sister Perpétue became something of a celebrity and *lettres de cachet*, a favorite subject of denunciation. According to the

Marquis d'Argenson, sympathy for what passed as Jansenism extended to "the little people and produces violent agitation among them." It was not a matter of doctrine but repugnance at the cruelty of denying virtuous Christians the possibility of making a good death—that is, of receiving the last sacraments and absolution of sin before entering the afterlife. When a group of fishmongers saw Archbishop Beaumont crossing the Pont Neuf in a carriage, they shouted at him, "That bugger should be drowned. He wants to prevent us from receiving the Church's sacraments."[13] A hundred market women from the Halles formed a guard at the church of Saint Eustache to prevent Beaumont from removing its Jansenist curate. The Parlement continued to intervene in cases of refusal of sacraments throughout its vast area of jurisdiction. It ordered the arrest of two priests in Abbeville, fined the bishop of Orléans 6,000 L., and confiscated the furniture of a curate in Troyes. Above all, it set out to bring together the arguments for its side of the conflicts in a full-scale, formal protest, which came to be known as the *grandes remontrances* because the text, when printed, formed a veritable treatise, 164 pages long.

Although it took nearly three months of debate for the Parlement to draft the *grandes remontrances*, summaries of their twenty-two main articles began to circulate in January 1753, alerting Parisians to a powerful attack on arbitrary power, both in the church and the state. The full text appeared in print after the Parlement voted to adopt the remonstrances on April 9. It was produced at an enormous pressrun (6,000 copies in-quarto and 10,000 in-duodecimo) and sold out immediately. Several reprints followed, along with pirated editions, which varied in price from 9 L. to 2 L., 10 s., and installments also appeared in the *Gazette d'Utrecht*. The reading public therefore had at its disposal an official defense of "the legitimate liberty of citizens," full of legal arguments and supporting documentation, which went over all the issues raised during the last three years. The remonstrances denied the legitimacy of *Unigenitus* as an article of faith, condemned the use of *billets de confession*, and contested the king's authority to put himself above the law—the "fundamental laws" of the monarchy—by evoking cases.[14]

Louis agreed to consider a summary of the twenty-two articles, but he refused to read the remonstrances themselves and insisted instead that the Parlement register a decree he had issued on February 22, which forbade it to intervene in cases involving the refusal of sacraments. A line had thus been drawn, and Parisians waited to see if the Parlement would cross it. On May 5 the chambers of Enquêtes and Requêtes voted to go on strike, and the Grand'Chambre said it would continue to sit but only to handle affairs of state; then it refused to register the edict of February 22. On the night of May 8–9, Louis dispatched musketeers with *lettres de cachet* to send the members of the lower chambers into exile and to imprison four of their most outspoken leaders. The Grand'Chambre protested and was punished by being transferred to Pontoise, where it continued to function, although all normal legal business came to a halt. Secret negotiations during the summer came to nothing. The Crown set up a temporary court composed of senior officials (*conseillers d'état* and *maîtres des requêtes*) to handle cases in September, but the Parisian lawyers refused to plead before it. As the Grand'Chambre remained intransigent, it was exiled to Soissons. To replace the entire Parlement, the Crown then created a *chambre royale*, filled with the officials, yet it, too, failed to function, owing to the strike of the lawyers. Despite on-and-off negotiations, the stalemate continued until September 1754, when the king finally recalled the Parlement and imposed a "law of silence," forbidding all parties to raise issues connected with *Unigenitus*, particularly the refusal of sacraments.

The reaction of Parisians to this protracted crisis is difficult to assess. Most of them had no sympathy with Archbishop Beaumont, but they suffered from hard times—severe weather, unemployment, and high prices of consumer goods, particularly bread. According to the Marquis d'Argenson, eight hundred jobless workers succumbed to hunger and exposure in February and March 1753. They died unshriven, in miserable attics, and no one raised an alarm about their access to the sacraments, although the Jansenists were then mobilizing protests about the treatment of Sister Perpétue. A good harvest brought relief that summer, but unemployment remained a problem. The suspension of legal activities meant that 20,000 persons—clerks, bailiffs, and all sorts of underlings and domestic servants—lost their jobs, according to Barbier. In May 1753, he noted a "spirit of revolt,"[15] and d'Argenson found the situation as explosive as in 1648, during the uprising of the Fronde.

A year later, however, Barbier considered Paris tranquil, despite occasional moments of "fermentation." The carnival season had been celebrated without incidents, and no one seemed to remember poor Per-pétue.[16] Parisians rejoiced at the return of the Parlement. Although they had deplored Louis's fecklessness—he cared for nothing but hunting and women, according to "bad talk" picked up by the police—they applauded his intervention to restrain the clergy and restore the administration of justice. By September 4, 1754, when the Parlement registered the declaration of the "law of silence," Parisians generally supported the king. They had had enough of the religious feuding.

Beaumont, as unbending as ever in his commitment to orthodoxy, broke the "law of silence" in December by ordering the refusal of the last sacraments to a linen maid who served Jansenist priests and shared their faith. The king promptly exiled Beaumont to his residence outside Paris and reaffirmed the requirement of silence, much to the delight of the common people in Paris. By then, d'Argenson concluded, the archbishop had lost his last grip on the loyalty of Parisians, and *Unigenitus* was dead, "annihilated."[17] In fact, the bull would continue to provoke controversy for another decade. But d'Argenson had correctly diagnosed a shift in the nature of the debate. Just as the Jansenists had appealed over the head of the archbishop to a general council of the church, so had the Parlement defied the king by courting the public. The religious conflict led to a political conclusion, according to d'Argenson: "The nation is above kings."[18] Few Parisians would go that far, but they were learning to speak a new language, which derived notions of liberty and constitutional constraint from an idiom steeped in convictions about the sacraments and salvation.

5

The People Seize the City

THE STREETS OF PARIS were always full of children—urchins, who had nowhere else to go, and the sons and daughters of the poor, who had nowhere else to play, as their families lived in cramped quarters, rarely more than a room or two. In the last months of 1749, the children began to disappear from the streets. At first, Parisians paid little attention. The urchins were a nuisance, and Paris was overrun with beggars, driven by the general misery in the surrounding region. The police received orders in November to round up beggars, confine them in prisons, and release them to the countryside—or, as rumor had it, pack them off in shipments to Tobago and the Mississippi, where labor was needed to develop a supposed (but nonexistent) silk industry. In May 1750, however, some children of artisans and bourgeois did not return to their families after playing in the street, leaving school, or being sent on errands. Word spread that they had been kidnapped by the police and that they, too, might disappear across the Atlantic. Paris exploded in the most violent riots anyone had known, an uprising that overwhelmed the police and that lasted, off and on, for a week. At its height, for a few hours on May 23, Paris was in the hands of the crowd.[1]

The riots followed rumors that police agents in civilian disguise were prowling through the city in search of children from five to ten years old whom they lured into carriages, which carried them off to prisons and an uncertain fate. On May 16, a child cried out from a carriage in the faubourg Saint Antoine near the Pont Marie. A woman heard it and called for help; workmen poured out of the surrounding shops; they seized the carriage, rescued the child, and thrashed his captor—a disguised police agent—and several soldiers who were assisting him. Crowds then pursued other police agents, and rioting spread throughout the faubourg. Although calm returned on the next day, wild talk followed in the wake of the violence. Some said that the police, with help from the military, received a bonus for every child they could capture for shipment to Mississippi. Others claimed that the police held the children for ransom, using as a pretext the earlier orders for eliminating mendicancy. Then a story spread that the children would be bled to death in order to supply a blood-bath for a prince who suffered from leprosy. Pure blood from innocent children served as a cure for leprosy, according to a legend connected with the conversion of Emperor Constantine and also with the Massacre of the Innocents under Herod.

More rumors circulated during the next few days along with some apparently reliable reports. Police agents and their spies were said to receive 15 L. for every child they captured and to charge 100 L. for every one they returned to its parents. Barbier, who dismissed the bloodbath talk as a myth, thought it likely that the kidnappings were being used to colonize the Mississippi, and he also believed that the police—and particularly the soldiers (*archers*) employed to carry out their orders—were capable of extorting ransom. On May 22, riots called *émotions populaires* broke out after incidents in several parts of the city. A crowd at the Porte Saint-Denis chased a suspected kidnapper into the house of a *commissaire* (local police official) and damaged it badly by throwing stones. In the faubourg Saint-Germain, two men seized the son of a coachman. The boy screamed; his father ran into the street, shouting for help; and the kidnappers, pursued by the neighbors, ran for their lives. One of them tried to save himself inside a rotisserie shop. Brandishing a skewer, a worker attempted to hold back the crowd; but it stormed past him and sacked the entire building, while the Night Watch, unable to stop the violence, let it rampage, and two persons were killed. In another incident, some soldiers disguised as civilians grabbed a boy returning from school at the quai des Morfondus. The boy's classmates ran after them, calling for help, and a crowd gave chase. After releasing the boy, one of the kidnappers tried to save himself inside the house of another *commissaire*. The crowd surrounded it, threw stones through all its windows, and was about to burn it down when the Mounted Watch (*guet à cheval*) arrived and, after much negotiation, restored calm. The *commissaire* with his family and the kidnapper escaped from the attic and across the roofs of the adjoining buildings.

On the following day in response to a report of an attempted abduction, a large crowd gathered at the Butte Saint-Roch. In search of kidnappers, it stormed across northern Paris to the rue Saint Honoré, where someone recognized a police spy named Labbé. The crowd pursued him into the house of a locksmith, where he hid in a room on the fourth floor. The locksmith, terrified by the violence, set him loose; and after another wild chase, Labbé ran into the house of a *commissaire* opposite the church of Saint-Roch. A soldier of the Watch fired at the pursuers from an outer gateway of the house. In a fury, the crowd then smashed through the gate and stormed into the courtyard, heaving stones through windows and threatening to set the house on fire unless Labbé was released. The *commissaire* surrendered him; the rioters beat him to death; and they dragged his body up the rue Saint-Honoré to the town house of the lieutenant general of police, Nicolas René Berryer, which effectively served as police headquarters for the entire city. After depositing the body at the front door, they shouted that they would kill Berryer, too, but he escaped out the back and hid in the nearby Jacobin convent.

While the rioters struggled to break inside Berryer's house, several brigades of the Watch, both mounted and foot, arrived in time to force them back into the street, where 10,000 persons had gathered. Cavalry from the Gardes Françaises and Gardes Suisses then appeared and galloped into the crowd, swinging their sabers. The cavalry charge dispersed the riot, although groups of protesters continued to roam through the city until late at night. Ten to fifteen persons were killed, and many rioters were imprisoned. They had to be punished, Barbier remarked, even though the rioting was understandable, given the provocation that ignited it: The government needed to assert its authority and to prevent Parisians from developing an awareness of their power because for a short time they had indeed taken over the city. The Marquis d'Argenson had the same reaction: "The common people now are under no constraint and can dare to do anything with impunity.... When the common people fear nothing, they are everything."[2]

The Watch, reinforced by a heavy deployment of regular soldiers, regained control of Paris on the next day, but the atmosphere remained charged with anger. People spoke openly about their hatred of the police, the ministers, Mme de Pompadour, and the king. They said they wanted to massacre Berryer and "eat his heart."[3] Although he did not dare appear in public for several days, he was summoned by the Parlement and assured it that the police had never ordered the abduction of any children. The Parlement then published an edict that denied the kidnapping rumors, yet announced that any parents whose children had disappeared could get them back by applying to the police. It also conducted an investigation of the riots, which turned up information that some soldiers employed by the police had indeed abducted children of "good bourgeois" and held them for ransoms of 60, 90, or 150 L. Barbier confided to his journal that he knew of a barrel maker who had paid a police official 60 L. to get back his kidnapped son.[4] By the end of May, the prevailing view among Parisians was that many kidnappings had occurred and that the police had participated in them.

In June, two soldiers on a visit to Orléans said, as a prank, that they had come to seize children. A crowd formed, turned violent, and beat one of them to death. The other was later condemned to be whipped, branded, exposed in the marketplace, and sent to the galleys for nine years.[5] Smaller riots broke out in other cities. In Paris, rumors circulated that the populace planned to march on Versailles and burn down the palace, and soldiers were dispatched to guard the route. On June 8, for the first time, the king avoided Paris while traveling from Versailles to Compiègne. As mentioned, he had a dirt road cut through fields that were being harvested, touching off more angry talk among peasants and Parisians. Meanwhile, the Parlement pursued its investigation of the May riots. It arrested forty suspects, including some soldiers as well as rioters, all of them from the lower ranks of the common people. The entire city buzzed with discussions of the crisis and waited anxiously for the magistrates to reach a verdict.[6]

On August 1 the Parlement sentenced three of the prisoners—a porter, a collier, and a secondhand furniture dealer—to be hanged. An enormous crowd gathered to witness the executions two days later in the Place de

Grève. To prevent another uprising, the authorities deployed 1,500 soldiers in the Place and lined the nearby streets with two regiments of the Gardes Françaises. The sympathy of the crowd went out to the condemned because, as Barbier remarked, the *émotion populaire* had expressed both horror at the kidnappings and fury at the police. When the collier mounted the scaffold—he was a handsome man who had beaten a soldier in a hand-to-hand fight—the crowd cried, "Grace!" The executioner paused for a moment, signaling to the collier that he should descend a few steps. But contrary to everyone's hopes and expectations, no messenger arrived with a last-minute reprieve. The soldiers pushed back the crowd, injuring some with their bayonets and intimidating the others. The collier was hanged, followed by his two companions, and the crowd dispersed.

By that time, the road to Compiègne had acquired the name of "the path of the revolt," and the king had had it paved. He would not expose himself to the Parisians, he declared, because they had called him a Herod.[7]

6

The Politics of Tax Avoidance

ALTHOUGH THEY had learned to live with all sorts of taxes and tariffs, Parisians held to an archaic view that the king should pay for his affairs from his own income. He possessed vast estates, and he should draw on them to finance the ordinary business of the state. True, war created exceptional burdens on the royal treasury. Therefore, it could be funded by "extraordinary" taxes, but they should not be applied in peacetime.[1] A *dixième* tax levied in 1741 on the revenue of all subjects (in principle at a rate of one-tenth, although in practice it varied), plus heavy borrowing, had made it possible for Louis to get through the War of the Austrian Succession—barely, because the controller general of finances, Jean-Baptiste de Machault d'Arnouville, a tough, thick-skinned minister, had warned Louis that the state was teetering on the brink of bankruptcy. Peace, Parisians assumed, would bring relief, from various indirect taxes as well as the *dixième*, which Louis had promised to revoke as soon as the war ended. Yet Machault extended the *dixième* until January 1750, long after the fighting had stopped, and in May 1749 the Crown imposed a new tax, the *vingtième*, which also would be collected on the revenue of all subjects, including the clergy and the nobility, and would continue indefinitely. Parisians therefore faced something new, a measure that would become a staple of life in modern society: a permanent income tax.[2]

Proposals to transform the tax system had existed for decades. The best known of them appeared as a book, *La Dîme royale* (1706), by the great military engineer Sébastien Le Prestre de Vauban. In order to relieve the tax burden on the poor and to rescue the state's finances during the desperate last years of Louis XIV's reign, Vauban advocated the creation of a single tax on all agricultural and industrial output, annulling the exemptions of the church and the nobility. The book was produced clandestinely and promptly banned. Its ideas could not be tolerated, not merely because they threatened economic interests, but also because they were incompatible with a deeply ingrained view of the world. Most Frenchmen assumed that the law should fall unequally on the population, as men and women (especially women) were born unequal and were intended by God to remain that way. The social order was built on privilege—a concept derived from the Latin *leges privatae* (private law), meaning that some persons should enjoy rights and immunities denied to others. In principle, therefore, the clergy and nobility, who constituted the privileged orders, should not pay taxes.

In practice, a complex system had evolved, which subjected nobles to considerable direct taxation, while imposing the heaviest burden on commoners.[3] Although a head tax (*capitation*) fell on all subjects when it was first levied in 1695, some nobles avoided most of it by negotiating special arrangements, and the church gained exemption from it in 1710 by agreeing to pay a "free gift" (*don gratuit*) to the Crown. The other direct tax, *la taille*, fell only on commoners, who were scorned by their social superiors as *taillables*. The inequality of the system was compounded by the way it was administered, because outlying provinces known as *pays d'états* contracted with the Crown to pay lump sums, which they gathered themselves through their own governing bodies called provincial estates. The church determined the amount of its *don gratuit* by a vote of its General Assembly, which met every five years and was dominated by its "first order" of prelates and wealthy abbots. It negotiated the sum with the government and collected it by raising funds on its extensive properties. Indirect taxes were collected by a private corporation, the General Tax Farm, which also contracted with the Crown to advance funds and kept a large proportion of what it raised. Rickety, leaky, and inefficient, the system appeared to be on the verge of collapse, especially when it had to bear the weight of war; but so many vested interests profited from it that it held up, even when threatened by a minister determined on reform.

When the government submitted the edict for the *vingtième* to be registered, the Parlement of Paris dug in its heels. Many of its members were already enfuriated by the refusal of sacraments to Jansenists, and they expected to reinforce their support among the common people by taking a strong stand on the tax issue. Several magistrates made vehement speeches denouncing a perpetual tax, levied in peacetime, just when the poor needed relief from their misery. Instead of squeezing more money from his subjects, they argued, the king should cut back on expenditures. At this time Parisians were gossiping about Louis's extravagances—the horses (he was said to possess 2,100), the *châteaux* (the gift of Bellevue to Mme de Pompadour was evaluated at 7 million livres), and the pensions (a cabinetmaker supposedly received an annuity of 4,000 L. for producing an exquisite *chaise percée* (toilet stool) for the favorite, whose own annuities were reportedly worth 1.8 million).[4] In an era when a semiskilled laborer made one livre a day, those sums seemed outrageous. On May 18 all the chambers of the Parlement gathered in the Grand'Chambre to vote on a proposal to make remonstrances against the *vingtième*, and it carried by a large majority—106 against 49.

As the Marquis d'Argenson saw it while scribbling comments on daily events in his journal, this was a dangerous moment. The Parlement could exploit the incipient bankruptcy of the state, refuse all taxation, mobilize the common people, precipitate an uprising, and force the king to convoke the Estates General, which might lead to a "revolution."[5] D'Argenson was given to jeremiads, however. He probably was looking backward to catastrophes in the seventeenth century, and, despite the parallel with the events of 1789, he did not prophesy the coming of the French Revolution. The parlementary crisis arrived as he had anticipated, yet it turned out to be surprisingly mild. Machault had prepared a strong response to the Parlement's vote, which the king delivered on the following day. It consisted of two stern sentences: Louis would not modify any aspect of the edict for the *vingtième*, and it must be registered immediately. Then, to the consternation of the Parisian public, the Parlement complied. It was all over in a few days. Machault had scored a "great coup," and the Parlement also agreed to register an edict for a loan of 36 million livres. Parisians had no explanation for this docility, although some suspected machinations in hidden corridors of power.[6]

By retreating before Machault's demands, the Parlement of Paris undercut resistance in the provincial parlements. But the controller general now faced more formidable opposition in the provincial estates and the clergy. Among the former, the estates of Languedoc and Brittany defended their exemptions most vehemently. Machault had the Languedoc assembly dissolved and counted on the royal intendants—the strong right arm of the central administration in the provinces—to organize the collection of the *vingtième* in all the *pays d'états*.

The church, however, posed a greater problem, because the Crown had often acknowledged its immunity from taxation, and it had consistently succeeded in protecting its enormous wealth by use of the *don gratuit*. The government could not even calculate the extent of its income, because each diocese collected its own funds, usually in kind. In many places, especially in the north, a "décimateur" of the church would drive a cart through the peasants' fields at harvest time and take one out of every fifteen or so sheaths of wheat (the rate of this *dîme* varied greatly but rarely came to one-tenth). By the time the grain had been sold and the funds distributed—a complex process dominated by the upper clergy in bodies known as *bureaux diocésains*—it was difficult to determine the sum that could be made available at the level of the diocese, to say nothing of the Gallican Church as a whole. The General Assembly of the Clergy would settle on a figure for the *don gratuit* in negotiations with the government during its quinquennial meetings, but that amount bore little relation to the value and productivity of the church's property. Machault planned to undermine the entire system by levying the *vingtième* directly and in kind on all ecclesiastical property at a rate of 5 percent of its actual production. How he could accomplish such a feat was not spelled out in the edict for the *vingtième*. It was left for preliminary negotiations with the agents who represented the church between the meetings of its General Assembly, and then for a settlement with the General Assembly that opened on May 25, 1750.

Parisians had little information about the power struggles that occurred behind the scenes. Rumors indicated that Machault had the backing of the king and Mme de Pompadour, although he had run into the opposition of well-connected prelates in the court. Sessions of the General Assembly took place behind closed doors in the convent of the Grands Augustins in

Paris. Despite leaks and gossip, the public did not get a clear view of the conflict until August 17, when the king issued a declaration that revealed Machault's demands. In place of a *don gratuit*, the Crown would accept payments of 1.5 million livres a year for five years, ostensibly to set up a fund to retire the clergy's debts, although the government would control the money, which would in effect be a tax. The Crown also required every holder of a benefice to declare its value as a property and the income it produced. The declarations would have to arrive within six months, and their accuracy could be verified by government officials. While supplying an immediate infusion of cash, therefore, the church would no longer be able to hide its riches behind the vast institutional structure that made it virtually a state within the state. The Crown would acquire crucial information, and it soon would be able to tax the clergy directly.[7]

Faced with this threat, the General Assembly voted to send remonstrances to the king, protesting that it could not permit the secular state to levy taxes on "property consecrated to God."[8] On September 18, Louis, advised by Machault, took a firm stand against the clergy's resistance. He dispatched Louis Phélypeaux, Comte de Saint-Florentin, the secretary of state in charge of religious affairs, to the Assembly with a letter addressed to its president, the cardinal de la Rochefoucauld. After reading it, the cardinal said the Assembly needed time to deliberate on a reply. Saint-Florentin insisted that the king had demanded an immediate answer. He was then invited to wait in a separate room. After two hours, he left for dinner, then returned and waited another two hours, while the Assembly struggled to reach a decision. Finally, at 6:00 in the evening, he was given a letter containing the Assembly's resolution, which denied that the king had a right to tax church property. After going outside the assembly hall to read the letter, Saint-Florentin returned with a package that he handed to la Rochefoucauld. It contained ready-prepared *lettres de cachet* or royal orders dissolving the Assembly and sending the bishops back to their dioceses. A subsequent edict ordered each bishop to produce his allotted share of the first installment of 1.5 million livres.[9]

As the Marquis d'Argenson observed, an ultimatum had been issued, the stakes were high, and Machault had acted so aggressively that Parisians talked about a "coup d'État" against the church.[10] Pamphlets began to stir up public opinion. One, simply entitled *Lettres*, mocked the clergy's claim to derive its tax exemptions from its high spiritual mission. Another, *La Voix du sage et du peuple* by Voltaire, made the same point, dismissing the distinction between the temporal and spiritual powers as "a leftover from vandalous barbarism." Voltaire also aligned tax reform with the mission of the *philosophes*—a matter of destroying superstition and reinforcing the king's power to promote the general good.[11] A long tract, *Procès-verbal de tout ce qui s'est passé depuis le jour que l'Assemblée du Clergé a commencé à ce qu'elle a été rompue*, became an instant best seller.[12]

Machault tried to wear down the resistance of the clergy throughout the winter of 1750–1751. He persuaded a few bishops to accept taxation and even seized some property of the bishop of Metz. Then he entered into negotiations with the church's agents and some prelates led by the archbishop of Paris, Christophe de Beaumont. Parisians did not know what outcome to expect, because Machault had a reputation for toughness, while the church leaders could draw on powerful contacts in court. Eventually, as the deadline of February 17 for the declarations of church property was about to expire, they learned that Machault had accepted an "accommodation," which in fact was a defeat. The clergy agreed to come up with a *don gratuit* worth half of what it had contributed in place of the old *dixième*, and there would be no more question of evaluating its property and enforcing a direct tax on its income. "M. de Machault is ill with despair," the Marquis d'Argenson reported. Tired of the pressure from the court—and even, it was rumored, of sex with Mme de Pompadour—the king had withdrawn his support for the controller general.[13]

In fact, the negotiating and politicking resumed, and went through several phases in the last six months of 1751, as Machault gained some ground and then lost it again in the perpetual struggle to win the king's favor. The conflict over the *vingtième* was also complicated by the Jansenist controversy and an increasingly hostile atmosphere in Paris. Parisians, still struggling under harsh economic conditions, exchanged seditious remarks, reported by the police as "bad talk" ("mauvais discours") and by d'Argenson as a call for a revolt, which, he feared, could be triggered by the assassination of the king.[14] Finally, on December 23, Louis issued an edict that suspended the payment of the *vingtième* and left the church in charge of its own finances, free from the threat of taxation and empowered in its General Assemblies to extract advantageous terms for *dons gratuits*.[15]

Although Parisians had not expressed sympathy for the clergy, they turned against Machault, associating him with the arbitrary power of the king. Handwritten notes circulated in December, saying, "Cut down the king, hang Pompadour, break Machault on the wheel."[16] They may have merely vented anger at the state's efforts to raise taxes, but they illustrated Machault's failure to mobilize support for a more equitable system of taxation. In the end, he had to concede defeat and left the Contrôle général to become minister of the navy in August 1754. The *vingtième* continued to exist, and the nobility paid a significant portion of it (14.5 percent in Languedoc), but the clergy had defanged it, and tax evasion, embodied as privilege, remained a basic principle of the political order.

Looking back over the mid-century years, d'Argenson remained convinced that France had entered a severe crisis, yet few Parisians shared that view. Although they complained about taxation, deplored the treatment of Prince Édouard, and often sympathized with the suffering of Jansenists denied the sacraments, they did not see connections among such disparate events. Memories would remain, but the discontent would not cohere into a general sense of hostility to the regime for another twenty years.

7

The World of Knowledge Is Mapped and Suppressed

INFORMATION ABOUT the peace, the antipolice riots, the quarrels over Jansenism, and other major events reached virtually everyone in Paris, but did Parisians know that they were living in the age of Enlightenment (*le siècle des Lumières*), as it came to be called? The Enlightenment was not an event. It was, as Diderot put it, a movement to "change the common way of thinking."[1] Ways of thinking involve ideas, values, attitudes, and turns of mind—historical phenomena of great importance but distressing elusiveness because they cannot be pinned down easily in time. Yet Diderot and his fellow philosophers—the *philosophes*, as they were known—attempted to change minds by writing books, and books are concrete objects whose history can be traced. The publication of the *philosophes'* works touched off so much scandal and debate that it marked the emergence of the Enlightenment as a force in public life. Of course, the Enlightenment was more than an attempt to conquer public opinion, and it cannot be reduced to the history of books. But the appearance of its key works constituted a series of events that captured the public's attention and indicated a decisive shift in the marketplace of ideas.

An extraordinary series of works burst into print during the mid-century years: Montesquieu's *De l'Esprit des lois* in 1748, the first volume of Buffon's *Histoire naturelle* in 1749, Condillac's *Traité des systèmes* in

1749, Rousseau's *Discours sur les sciences et les arts* in 1750, the Prospectus to the *Encyclopédie* in 1750, its first volume in 1751, and Voltaire's *Le Siècle de Louis XIV* in 1751. Radical philosophical tracts had circulated in manuscript for the first half of the century, and a few books by the *philosophes*— Montesquieu's *Lettres persanes* (1721) and Voltaire's *Lettres philosophiques* (1734)—had made a splash. But most of the basic Enlightenment works became available to the public all at once within four years. Rarely, if ever, in the history of publishing did such an explosion take place.

The *Encyclopédie* was the most notorious of those works, and it aroused so much controversy that it came to be identified with the Enlightenment itself.[2] Its editors, Denis Diderot and Jean le Rond d'Alembert, became public figures. They recruited as collaborators a great many eminent *philosophes*—Voltaire, Rousseau, Montesquieu (his article *Goût* was published after his death in 1755), d'Holbach, Turgot, Toussaint, Marmontel, Morellet, Duclos, and Quesnay among a total of nearly two hundred contributors. However, many of these had not yet become well known in 1750 (Turgot and Morellet were then students preparing ecclesiastical careers), and many, like Voltaire, joined the group after the *Encyclopédie* became notorious as the flagship of *philosophie*. Between 1748 and 1753, Joseph d'Hémery, the police inspector in charge of the book trade, kept track of all the authors he could find in Paris. He built files on 501 of them, noting which ones posed some kind of danger to the church and state. Diderot, who in 1749 had been imprisoned in Vincennes for his *Lettre sur les aveugles*, appeared in the files as "a boy ["garçon"; Diderot was then thirty-seven] who is full of wit but is extremely dangerous." D'Hémery took note of twenty-two writers who contributed to the *Encyclopédie*, although he usually did not mention their connection with it. He paid relatively little attention to them and to the *philosophes* in general—that is, writers who challenged orthodox values and were considered to be freethinkers. He did not use the word *philosophe*, nor did he refer to the Enlightenment as a coherent phenomenon. In fact, he expressed sympathy for talented authors, particularly Montesquieu, Rousseau, and d'Alembert, whom he described as "a man who is charming from his character and wit." He also wrote a sympathetic report about the *Encyclopédie*'s main publisher, André-François le Breton, who was a wealthy and respected leader of the booksellers' guild.

D'Hémery's principal concern was Jansenism, which, as we have seen, was the most contentious public issue at that time.

Although the Enlightenment had not aroused much of a storm before 1748, most of its works could not appear legally in France. They contained too many unorthodox ideas to win approval by a royal censor and an official privilege, the early-modern equivalent of copyright, which gave a member of the booksellers' guild an exclusive right to publish a book. The books of the *philosophes* were usually printed in publishing centers like Amsterdam and Geneva and distributed inside France through an extensive underground trade. By 1750, this trade produced such a boom among foreign publishers that the government department in charge of publishing, the *Direction de la librairie*, favored issuing informal approvals called tacit permissions, which permitted the publication in France of books that did not qualify for a privilege yet did not flagrantly violate official standards. In 1750 Chrétien-Guillaume de Lamoignon de Malesherbes, then twenty-nine years old, became director of the book trade. He sympathized with the ideas of the *philosophes*, and he also had a keen sense of the economic interests at stake in the publication of their works. Therefore, he loosened the state's control of the book trade in several ways, particularly the use of tacit permissions. His period in office, from 1750 to 1763, coincided with the golden years in the publishing of Enlightenment works.

When the prospectus for the *Encyclopédie* appeared in November 1750, it created a stir. It announced a monumental work, which would encompass the entire world of learning and order it in a new manner. As illustrated by a large diagram at the core of its long and learned text, the prospectus argued that all the arts and sciences could be envisaged as parts of a tree of knowledge. They had developed organically in accordance with the three faculties of the mind: reason (disciplines related to philosophy), memory (historical disciplines), and imagination (the fine arts). Although perfectly legal—the *Encyclopédie* had a privilege and a strong endorsement by a censor—the prospectus challenged an older view of learning, which made theology the queen of the sciences. It was an elegant work in itself, not a handout like most prospectuses but a pamphlet printed at an unusually large run of 8,000 copies. Its handsome paper and type served as samples for the quality of the eight volumes of text that it promised to deliver, along with two volumes of plates, by December 1754, at a cost to subscribers of 280 L. That turned out to be a spectacular case of false advertising. The text would eventually run to seventeen volumes, completed in 1765, and the plates would come to eleven volumes, issued from 1762 to 1772, while the subscription price would rise to 980 L. In retrospect, the publishers could defend themselves by invoking the need to adjust to circumstances—that is, the scandals and storms that transformed the *Encyclopédie* from a stately reference work to the main *machine de guerre* of the French Enlightenment.

The first whiff of scandal appeared before the first volume was published. In its January 1751 issue, the Jesuit periodical, *Mémoires de Trévoux*, attacked the prospectus by suggesting that its most important feature, the tree of knowledge and accompanying commentary, had been plagiarized from Francis Bacon. In fact, Diderot, the author of the prospectus, had acknowledged Bacon's influence but stressed the enormous advances in the world of learning since Bacon's time. He went over them at length and then used the diagram to describe their relation to the operations of the mind. Although Bacon featured the same three faculties in his version of the tree of knowledge, he accompanied it with a separate tree, which showed how "Divine Learning" derived from revelation. Diderot's vision of knowledge looked suspiciously secular. He gave "Revealed Theology" a place on his tree, but he consigned it to a small branch close to "Black Magic."

When the first volume of the *Encyclopédie* appeared on July 1, 1751, it confirmed those suspicions. The Jesuits continued to heap criticism on the *Encyclopédie* in nearly every issue of their journal for the next fifteen months. Aside from attacking irreligion, they had their own encyclopedia to defend, the *Dictionnaire de Trévoux*, first published in 1704 and reworked in 1752 in nine folio volumes, making it as extensive as the book envisaged in Diderot's prospectus. More important than the commercial rivalry was the claim of Diderot and d'Alembert to include all the arts, sciences, and crafts (*métiers*) in their encyclopedia and to do so by enlisting allies who could provide the most up-to-date, expert information. The prospectus offered to make all knowledge accessible in a way that would satisfy anyone who wanted information about virtually anything. And to the horror of the Jesuits, who viewed themselves as the guardians of orthodoxy, this modern summa would be produced by a band of *philosophes*.

The "Preliminary Discourse," written by d'Alembert and printed at the beginning of volume I, incorporated this argument—along with a revised text of the prospectus—in an exposition of the philosophy behind the *Encyclopédie*. Despite its alphabetical organization, d'Alembert explained, the *Encyclopédie* was far more than a compilation of information about everything from A to Z. It was a "mappemonde" or map of the world of knowledge that revealed the contours and boundaries of everything knowable. The drawing of boundaries, illustrated by the tree of knowledge, was crucial, because true philosophy recognized the limits of what could be known. All ideas were derived from sense impressions, and they were worked on by reflection in a manner that led from concrete experience to abstractions such as natural law and knowledge of God. Locke, modernized by Condillac, showed how that process took place, but this argument raised the danger of deism because it eliminated revelation. D'Alembert fobbed off that difficulty by acknowledging revelation, somewhat parenthetically, as a historical fact made accessible by the faculty of memory.

Shifting from epistemology to history, d'Alembert then took up the way ideas were perfected as they passed from philosopher to philosopher and spread through all the arts and sciences. It was a heroic story, which gave the leading roles to men of letters. Four great forefathers—Bacon, Descartes, Newton, and Locke—laid the foundation of modernity. Then came bold innovators such as Galileo, Harvey, and Bayle. And their work was currently being perfected by Condillac, Voltaire, Rousseau, and others—that is, the *Encyclopédistes* or the "société de gens de lettres" announced on the title page of the *Encyclopédie*, which also presented itself as a "dictionnaire raisonné," acknowledging reason as its central principle. The *Encyclopédistes* therefore claimed to have drawn the definitive map of knowledge, excluding everything outside the reach of reason. Although d'Alembert was too cautious to say so explicitly, they had expelled Catholic dogma from the world of the knowable and shouldered out the old cartographers, who mainly belonged to the church. In describing the new *mappemonde*, d'Alembert invoked an ideal type, who embodied the best qualities of the *Encyclopédistes*. He was the "*Philosophe*" (d'Alembert used the upper case), the only person who had a commanding view of the intellectual landscape.[3]

By this time, the figure of the *philosophe* was well known to the reading public. *Le Philosophe*, a tract from 1743 that was incorporated in volume XII of the *Encyclopédie* and later reprinted by Voltaire, had defined his characteristics: engagement in the world and an outlook that was worldly—a respect for facts, rejection of superstition (particularly Christian dogma, though this passage was cut from the text reprinted in the *Encyclopédie*), adherence to the guiding principle of reason, and commitment to be a useful and law-abiding member of society.[4] That formula excluded more than it included because it left out the clergy and their followers among the elite. Taken together, the prospectus and the *Discours préliminaire* suggested that men of a certain stripe were trying to seize power in the world of letters, a domain where they located the driving force of history.

That threat did not become apparent to contemporaries for some time, despite the constant attacks published in the *Mémoires de Trévoux*. The *Mercure*, France's most widely read literary journal, greeted the first volume of the *Encyclopédie* as "the beginning of one of the greatest works that has ever been undertaken." It praised the *Discours préliminaire* as a "masterpiece" and applauded the "philosophical spirit" that pervaded the text.[5] For the next two and a half years it continued to print favorable reviews and extracts. However, a more serious periodical, the *Journal des savants*, warned its readers that the *Encyclopédie* was dangerous. The *Discours préliminaire* opened the way to irreligion by adopting the epistemology of Locke. Its secular approach to ethics led to "fearful consequences," and it showed little regard for the established truths of Christianity.[6] D'Alembert was able to defend his position in a powerful foreword to volume three published in November 1753. But by that time the very existence of the *Encyclopédie* was threatened by a spectacular scandal.

On November 18, 1751, the abbé Jean-Martin de Prades successfully defended a thesis for a theological degree in the Sorbonne. The examiners did not read it carefully or perhaps not at all, because it was printed in the standard format of one page, but unlike most theses it went on for 8,000 words and therefore had to be printed in very small type. They passed it without hesitation, but then word spread that it contained heretical propositions. De Prades was known to be a friend of Diderot, and Diderot was said to have put him in charge of all the theological articles in the *Encyclopédie*. (In fact, de Prades wrote the article "Certitude," and his friend the abbé Yvon handled most of the theology.) According to some rumors, Diderot had actually written the thesis, hoping to get a stamp of approval by the faculty of theology for ideas that he was slipping into the *Encyclopédie*. De Prade's text was said (correctly) to contain passages that corresponded closely to the *Discours préliminaire* and to include all sorts of heresies—for example, the proposition that knowledge is derived solely from the senses, that revealed religion was compatible with natural religion or deism, that there were chronological inconsistencies in the Bible, and that the miracles of Christ were comparable to those of Esculapius, the Roman god of medicine. After raking over those arguments in several contentious faculty meetings, the professors of the Sorbonne condemned the thesis, punished its examiners, and expelled de Prades. The Parlement, which was defending Jansenists at this time, asserted its orthodoxy by decreeing de Prades's arrest. He escaped to Holland and then, thanks to Voltaire's recommendation, to employment as a reader to Frederick II in Berlin. While following his fate from the Dutch gazettes and gossip in cafés, Parisians were treated to the spectacle of irreligion seeping into the faculty of theology and theologians stumbling over themselves in an attempt to sweep it out.[7]

The scandal might have dissipated if Archbishop Beaumont had not thrown oil on the flames by issuing an episcopal decree (*mandement*) on January 31, which was distributed in all parishes and hawked through the streets. In it, he fulminated against de Prades's arguments in so much detail as to make them known and comprehensible to Parisians who had no familiarity with such abstract propositions. Beaumont also associated the arguments with the *Encyclopédie* and therefore brought it, too, within the range of the Parisians' attention. Barbier considered this publicity unwise: "This *Encyclopédie* is still a book that is rare, expensive, and abstract, one that can only be read by intelligent people and lovers of science. The number of them is small.... Why issue an episcopal decree, which circulates, makes all of the faithful curious, and instructs them about the reasoning that philosophers can apply to religion, whereas the only thing necessary for the bulk of the faithful is their catechism, and they have neither the time nor the intelligence to read anything else.... This decree is being actively hawked in Paris, is available at a cheap price, and even shopkeepers buy it. This can do more harm than good to religion."[8]

The persecution of de Prades, according to Barbier, was actually the opening salvo of a campaign against the *Encyclopédie* led by the Jesuits. The Marquis d'Argenson also was convinced that they wanted to take over the *Encyclopédie*, using powerful protectors at court, notably Jean-François Boyer, the former bishop of Mirepoix, who oversaw the allotment of benefices and had ready access to the king. Not to be outdone, the Jansenists blasted the *Encyclopédie* in their *Nouvelles ecclésiastiques*. They described it as the culmination of a wave of incredulity, for which they had a ready explanation: the long-term effects of the bull *Unigenitus*. Then the Parlement threatened to follow up its decree against de Prades by prohibiting the *Encyclopédie*.[9]

By February 1752, the polemics and politics had become so heated that the state decided to intervene. An edict passed by the Conseil d'État on February 7 and posted all over Paris six days later condemned the first two volumes of the *Encyclopédie* for "several maxims that tend to destroy royal authority, to establish a spirit of independence and revolt . . . and to lay the foundation for error, the corruption of morality, irreligion and disbelief."[10] That was strong language—so damning, in fact, that the Marquis d'Argenson took it as a sign of an "inquisition" at work to suppress all unorthodox ideas. He heard (wrongly) that Diderot had fled to escape a *lettre de cachet* for his imprisonment and that the *Encyclopédie* was doomed. Yet he also picked up a rumor that Malesherbes was determined to save it. Although the edict prohibited the sale of the first two volumes, they had already been distributed to the subscribers, and Diderot was permitted to continue on the successive volumes, working under Malesherbes's protection. The director of the book trade sympathized with the Encyclopedists, but his intervention in their favor also resulted from the responsibilities connected with his office. Committed to promoting the economic interests of publishers, he wanted to defend the *Encyclopédie* as an enterprise—the largest, in fact, that anyone in the booksellers' guild had ever known. And determined to uphold the authority of the king, he needed to head off the Parlement's attempt to assert power over the book trade by condemning the *Encyclopédie*. Another factor was political. The "devout party" in Versailles, led by Boyer, wanted to destroy the *Encyclopédie*, while a secular faction, gathered around Mme de Pompadour, protected it.[11]

Although well-informed contemporaries such as d'Argenson understood the power plays behind the scenes during the *Encyclopédie* crisis, most Parisians did not. Yet many of them became aware that a scandalous book had stirred up controversy, and the awareness spread as the scandal escalated at the end of the 1750s. That period lies outside the boundary of this chapter, but it should be mentioned here because of its relevance to the role of books as a force in the Enlightenment.

On January 5, 1757, an unemployed domestic servant, Robert François Damiens, rushed past the guards in Versailles and plunged a pocket knife, 8.1 centimeters long, into the right side of Louis XV. Although not seriously wounded, the king asked to receive extreme unction, and the kingdom fell into a crisis. Everyone in Paris wondered who had plotted the attempt—the Jesuits? (they had been condemned for the assassination of Henri IV); the Jansenists? (they had stirred up opposition to the king during the quarrels over the refusal of sacraments); the *philosophes*? (they reputedly had no respect for authority). In the end, despite torture and before being horribly drawn and quartered in a public spectacle, Damiens never revealed the name of any accomplice. But public authorities outdid themselves in an attempt to uncover a conspiracy and to demonstrate their loyalty by repressing any expression of critical convictions.

On April 16, 1757, the Crown decreed that anyone who published anything that merely tended to "stir up spirits" ("*émouvoir les esprits*") would be executed.[12] The book police seized everything suspicious. The Parlement ordered a bonfire of philosophic works and prepared to prohibit the *Encyclopédie* by appointing a committee to investigate it. To preempt action by the Parlement, the government banned the *Encyclopédie* outright—severely prohibited it this time by revoking its privilege and ordering the confiscation of its manuscripts and other materials. Then Malesherbes saved it again. He warned Diderot that the police would raid his workshop; and when Diderot asked where he could possibly stash all his books and papers, Malesherbes offered to hide them in his own *hôtel*.

While Diderot continued to work in secret, the enemies of the Encyclopedists unleashed a campaign to vilify them. Pamphlets depicted them as savage unbelievers ("Cacouacs") who were poisoning the body politic. Journals such as the *Année littéraire* pilloried them and deplored their works. A popular play at the Comédie française, *Les Philosophes* by Charles Palissot de Montenoy, held them up to ridicule. A member of the Académie française, Jacques Le Franc de Pompignan, denounced them at a public meeting of the Academy. In March 1759, Pope Clement XIII put the *Encyclopédie* on the Index and decreed that Catholics who owned a copy would be excommunicated if they did not turn it over to the church for burning. Far from being a literary squabble, the attacks threatened to drive the Enlightenment from the public sphere. Most *philosophes* retreated into silence. Many, including d'Alembert, withdrew from Diderot's team of collaborators. Yet Diderot soldiered on, and in 1765 the last ten volumes of text were published all at once, under a false address on the title page ("à Neufchastel, chez Samuel Faulche & Compagnie"), as if they had been produced abroad.

By then, the campaign against the *philosophes* had blown over. They had published more audacious works, including Rousseau's *Contrat social* (1762) and Voltaire's *Dictionnaire philosophique* (1764). While the period 1748–1751 represents the breakthrough of the French Enlightenment, the years covered by the publication of the *Encyclopédie*'s seventeen volumes, 1751–1765, coincide with the Enlightenment's full development. A few important works, such as d'Holbach's *Système de la nature* (1770) and Raynal's *Histoire philosophique et politique des établissements et du commerce des Européens dans les deux Indes* (1770), were published later, but the *Encyclopédie* can be said to have bookended the Enlightenment.

Yet the Enlightenment was greater than the battles of its books, and its greatest work, the *Encyclopédie*, served a larger purpose than spreading knowledge. The Enlightenment was a cause, a movement, a campaign to persuade people by appealing to their reason, and often to their emotions. It advocated values and ideas—the need for tolerance, the distrust of superstition, the importance of liberty, the power of reason to decode the laws of nature, the determination to hold institutions up to rational standards and to promote the general good. Although they disagreed in many ways, the *philosophes* shared a commitment to those convictions. Books served them as a means to give ideas life and to inject them into the bloodstream of society.

Seen in retrospect, however, the publication of the *Encyclopédie* raises a problem. Few Parisians could afford to buy it. The subscription price to the first edition, originally set at 280 L., eventually came to 980 L., and sets sometimes sold on the market for 1,400 L.—a lifetime's wages for a common laborer. The pressrun came to 4,225 copies, and many of them were sold outside France. Later editions, published from 1777 to 1782, had larger pressruns and lower prices— 225 L. for the octavo published at a run of 5,500.[13] Some people probably consulted copies owned by friends or made available for a fee in reading clubs (*cabinets littéraires*), but it seems unlikely that many Parisians ever laid eyes on the text, despite the many editions.

How then did they get to know the *Encyclopédie*? Not by plowing through seventeen folio volumes but rather through fragments that turned up here and there, in talk as well as print. Periodicals such as the *Mercure* published extensive extracts. The Prospectus circulated widely and was reprinted in the *Discours préliminaire*, which itself was reprinted by d'Alembert in his *Mélanges de littérature, d'histoire et de philosophie* in 1753. In a preface to the *Mélanges*, d'Alembert explained that he was republishing the *Discours* in order to make it available to those who could not obtain a copy of the *Encyclopédie*. The thesis of the abbé de Prades, reprinted to exploit the *succès de scandale*, contained whole paragraphs from the *Discours*, and, as we have seen, Archbishop Beaumont's diatribe against the thesis publicized d'Alembert's arguments very effectively. Diderot defended the *Encyclopédie* in pamphlets aimed against the Jesuits (*Lettre de M. Diderot au R. P. Berthier, Jésuite*, 1751) and the Jansenists (*Suite de l'Apologie de M. l'abbé de Prades*, 1752). And the enemies of the *Encyclopédie*—polemicists like Abraham-Joseph de Chaumeix—attacked it so incessantly as to keep it in the public eye.

Many Parisians therefore learned about the *Encyclopédie* without having read a word of it. They got to know it above all because it provoked scandals—the de Prades affair, the prohibitions of 1752 and 1759, and the persecution by public authorities, from the King's Council to the Parlement, the General Assembly of the Clergy, and the pope. Nothing worked better than official opprobrium, expressed in edicts, *mandements*, sermons, posters, and the bawling of street peddlers, to spread the knowledge that a new force had been set loose in the world: *Encyclopédisme*. A book had given birth to an "ism," and the book, as observers like Barbier remarked, became the talk of the town. Parisians may not have understood its finer points—its advocacy of Lockean empiricism as opposed to Cartesian innate ideas, for example. But they heard enough to grasp a fundamental message: a group of *philosophes* had mapped the world of knowledge, and the authorities had tried, unsuccessfully, to destroy the map.

PART TWO

The
Expanding Public Sphere,
1762–1764

8

The Peace Is Rained Out

WHEN THE Seven Years' War began in 1756, Parisians did not know what to call it. (It acquired its name much later and is often referred to as the French and Indian War in North America, where hostilities began in 1754.) They had no idea that it would rage on until 1763, nor did they have a clear sense of what it was about. Their traditional enemy, Habsburg Austria, had become an ally, while their previous ally, Prussia, had turned into an enemy, and other European powers joined the fighting on so many fronts, as diplomats made and unmade alliances, that it looked like chaos. Moreover, the reports available in journals like the *Gazette de Leyde* made the scramble on the continent seem small when read along with dispatches that arrived from all over the world, where a new power system dominated by Great Britain was confusedly taking shape.

The newsmongers under the Tree of Cracow in the Palais-Royal did their best to trace the movements of armies by drawing lines with their canes on the ground, but the action took place far away from France. Instead of focusing on border fortresses as they had done during the War of the Austrian Succession, they tried to follow armies marching across central Europe and doing battle in places with unpronounceable names like Zorndorf and Schweidnitz. The French forces fought mainly in western Germany and did badly, beginning with the Battle of Rossbach on

November 5, 1757, when Frederick II of Prussia defeated a French army twice the size of his own. Subsequent defeats inflicted on the French by smaller forces—Krefeld (June 23, 1758), and Minden (August 1, 1759)—made France's generals appear incompetent, especially when compared with the spectacular victories of Frederick, which were applauded by some Parisians, including his admirers among the *philosophes*.[1]

Greater losses piled up overseas—in North America, the Carribean, Africa, India, even in the Philippines—as well as off the French coast, where the British victory at Quiberon Bay (November 20–21, 1759) made the French navy look even worse than its army. By November 1762, when the preliminaries of the peace were signed, Parisians could measure the extent of France's humiliation. They had lost Canada, the left bank of the Mississippi, Louisiana, which went to Spain, and, effectively, India, while receiving back the conquered islands of Guadaloupe and Martinique. Despite the loss of millions in expenses and thousands of lives, they had gained nothing on the continent, and Britain had extended its empire on a global scale.

Although there was so little to celebrate, Parisians looked forward to the festivities that were, as required by tradition, to accompany the proclamation of the peace. Most of them had no interest in places like Canada, which Voltaire described as "a few acres of snow" ("quelques arpents de neige") in 1756. They had hailed the maréchal de Saxe as a herculean conqueror in 1748, but they had nothing good to say in 1762 about the Prince de Soubise, the Comte de Clermont, and the maréchal de Contades who had led their troops into spectacular defeats. The Seven Years' War produced few heroes. It brought increased taxes, especially the second and third *vingtièmes* levied in 1756 and 1760. And contrary to expectation, the taxes continued to be collected after the fighting stopped, while the official declaration of the peace was delayed until June 1763. Unlike the ceremony of 1749, it was spread out over three days and transformed into a celebration of Louis XV.

In 1755 the architect Ange-Jacques Gabriel won a competition to design a large square in the western sector of the city to be called the Place Louis XV (today Place de la Concorde). The city of Paris commissioned the eminent sculptor Edmé Bouchardon to produce a giant equestrian statue of the king, which would be erected in the center of the Place. Combined with the parade to publish the peace and the drinking and dancing in the streets, the inauguration of the statue was supposed to express the Parisians' devotion to their king, and the celebration would come to a climax with a spectacular fireworks display on the banks of the Seine opposite the new Place. In a world where parading and visual spectacles commanded everyone's attention, the three-day celebration promised to be a major event.

Although Bouchardon died nearly a year before the statue was erected, he completed everything but its pedestal. It stood 39 feet (pedestal included) above the ground, dwarfing everything around it. Louis appeared in a toga, as if he were a Roman emperor, although he had just lost an empire. Pasquinades mocking the statue did not bode well for its reception, but its transportation to the Place was hailed as a great feat of engineering. It weighed thirty tons, and the danger of damaging it meant that it had to be winched, inch by inch, from Bouchardon's studio, a distance that could be covered in fifteen minutes by foot and that required three days of hauling by specially designed machines. Enormous crowds followed its progress and applauded its erection on the pedestal by more elaborate machinery on February 23. The hero of the day was not the king but a sieur Lherber, "auteur des machines" from the École royale des ponts et chaussées, who masterminded the operation. During the process, the police arrested several persons for "indecent talk" about the king and Mme de Pompadour. Once in place, the statue became a target for verse pasted on the pedestal and quoted in conversations. One derided its equestrian character:

Grotesque monument, infâme piédestal!
Les vertus sont à pied, le vice est à cheval.

(Grotesque monument, infamous pedestal! / The virtues go on foot, vice rides horseback.)

Another referred to the hollow interior beneath the statue's bronze surface:

Il est ici comme à Versailles;   *He is the same here as at Versailles;*
Il est sans coeur et sans entrailles![2]   *He is without a heart or entrails!*

The celebration of the peace did not take place until four months after the erection of the statue, despite the growing impatience of the public. Parisians had been looking forward not merely to fireworks and free wine but to the end of the wartime taxes, which were supposed to expire at the time of the peace's publication. In late May, however, they learned that new taxes would be levied on articles of consumption such as salt and wine. Word also spread that the three days of festivities would cost a million livres, of which half would be devoted to the fireworks. On June 20, when at last the fête began and all shops were closed, Paris was not in a happy mood.[3]

The ceremonies opened with the dedication of the statue. A magnificent parade of officials from the Hôtel de Ville mounted on horses and followed by retainers in bright, new livery, circled the Place Louis XV, and each person saluted the statue as he passed in front of it. Although the official *Gazette de France* reported cheering from the crowd, Barbier noted in his journal that the spectators remained silent. At sunset that evening, the festivities for the common people opened in the Tuileries Garden, lit up splendidly by torches and girandoles. Crowds descended on serving stations for free cervelas, bread, and wine; and people started dancing to the music of orchestras situated at different locations in the garden. Feasting and dancing also occurred at other sites throughout the city. But within thirty minutes, a thunderstorm struck. The torches were extinguished in a heavy downpour, the music stopped, and everyone slouched home, soaked to the bones.[4]

The publication of the peace took place on the next day very much as it had occurred on February 12, 1749. For nine hours, a gigantic parade of dignitaries marched through the city, stopping at fourteen squares and marketplaces, where, to the blasts of trumpets and the beating of drums, heralds read out the royal proclamation. The final day of the festivities featured a Te Deum in Notre Dame. The king did not attend it, but he came "in cognito," or unofficially, with members of the court, to watch the fireworks, which were designed to bring the celebration to a spectacular end. Although fireworks in the eighteenth century had little color other than orange, Parisians loved them. When the city organized celebrations, they turned out by the thousands to gape at the rocket displays and land-based illuminations developed by expert firemasters (*artificiers*). The wealthy rented specially built platforms along the Seine in order to enjoy the best view of what promised to be the greatest spectacle ever on June 22—a *feu de joie* on the river and a *grande illumination* on the Place Louis XV. At 2:30, however, rain began to fall once more. It turned into another downpour with thunder and lightning that continued for nearly two hours. An enormous crowd, which had come early to get the best places, was drenched yet remained until 9:30, when the first part of the display began. It was judged to be "fairly good" as a prelude to the main event, but the climax never came. The firemasters had failed to cover their material, which was soaked so badly during the rainstorm that nothing would ignite. The crowd trudged home. Those in carriages became trapped in a three-hour traffic jam caused by a rush to see what little could be seen of a private illumination staged successfully for her guests by Madame de Pompadour from the garden of her Paris residence in the nearby Elysée Palace. In the aftermath of the fiasco, some of the *artificiers* were sent to prison.[5]

To commemorate the events, the Comédie italienne, which had recently merged with the Opéra comique, commissioned Charles Simon Favart, France's favorite author of light dramas, to produce a musical, *Les Fêtes de la paix*, which, in light of the theatricality that permeated the whole celebration, came across as a play-within-the-play. The stage depicted the Place Louis XV, where soldiers were holding back a crowd that wanted to see the statue of the king. Before things could get out of hand, the royal herald (Roi d'armes) appeared and sang an aria, thereby publishing the peace. He then ordered the soldiers to permit the people to admire the statue, but unaccountably no one appeared—an odd turn in the plot that some considered "an uncalled-for and even punishable epigram," although it probably was nothing more than a mistake by the director. Later scenes featured songs and dances that the audience found detestable. Written off as "miserable" after its first performance, *Les Fêtes de la paix* was a spectacular flop, like the entire, three-day celebration and like the peace itself. Louis appeared as a failure, on a pedestal, on a stage, and on display before the theater of public opinion.[6]

9

A Big Idea Goes Bust

A FTER THE WAR, Parisians all agreed that they could not bear any more taxation. The second and third *vingtièmes*, on top of the accumulated load of other taxes, had been accepted as temporary measures required to pay for the fighting, yet they had been inadequate, and the war was financed primarily by loans, creating an enormous deficit. No one knew the extent of the state's debt, which like all government affairs was a secret reserved to the king and his council, but everyone considered it so large as to be unmanageable. Reform of the fiscal system appeared to be impossible after the failure of Machault's attempt to create an effective land tax, so there seemed to be no escape, other than bankruptcy, from the financial dilemma. In May 1763, however, an anonymous pamphlet appeared that promised to provide a solution.[1]

The pamphlet, *Richesse de l'Etat*, took Paris by storm and stirred up an enormous debate about royal finances. It contained only eight pages organized around one big idea: The complex, expensive, and unjust system of taxation should be replaced by a single tax on wealth, which would be apportioned among the top two million property owners according to a graduated scale. They would be divided into twenty classes of 100,000 each. Those in the poorest class would pay only one *écu* (3 L.) a year, and the amount would increase in accordance with the estimated wealth in each class, culminating in 730 L. to be paid by the richest 100,000 persons in the kingdom. A simple table showed that the sums would add up to 698,366,666 L. A few indirect taxes such as customs duties and an impost on tobacco would be retained, adding another 42 million. The total would come to an annual income of 740 million, nearly three times the 250 million that the Crown currently received, according to the author's estimate. That would be enough to retire the debt and maintain the king magnificently, while relieving most of his subjects from an intolerable burden.

Similar ideas had appeared in earlier publications, notably *Théorie de l'impôt* (1760) by Victor de Riqueti, Marquis de Mirabeau, which had led to the author's imprisonment and exile. *Richesse de l'Etat*, however, arrived at just the right moment, when the public was primed for a debate about fiscal measures and the government, led by Étienne François, Duc de Choiseul, was willing to tolerate it. The pamphlet had a beguiling simplicity. It presented its argument in a straightforward manner, eschewing theory and insisting on practicality. Like many of his contemporaries, the author assumed, wrongly, that France's population had declined since the end of the seventeenth century. He estimated that it came to 16 million and wrote off 14 million as incapable of paying significant taxation, although the current system squeezed more out of them than they could afford. The only ones to suffer from the single-tax system would be the tax farmers (*fermiers généraux*), who collected huge sums in indirect taxes and kept most of it for themselves. The author referred to them as "blood suckers,"[2] although in general he did not adopt a polemical tone. His was the voice of reason; he avoided any hint of contentiousness, as if his proposal did not challenge the social order. It was based on wealth, he insisted, not "dignities," meaning that many aristocrats would pay less than rich merchants, but they would pay, nonetheless. Their tax privileges would simply disappear. So, too, would those of the clergy, although the author skirted the subject of ecclesiastical wealth so carefully as to leave that question hanging. He also implicitly abolished the tax-collecting function of the provincial estates without saying so. And to make everything look easy, he proposed that the system be voluntary: individuals would declare their wealth, presumably to their local intendant, and their position within the twenty classes would be recorded in a modified version of the *capitation* roll, which would be perfected as it evolved. The author referred favorably several times to the parlements, and contemporaries took him to speak as a *parlementaire*. He was soon identified as Roussel de la Tour, a counselor in the Parlement of Paris.

Barbier noted in June that *Richesse de l'Etat*, reprinted in edition after edition, had been discussed everywhere in Paris: "Everyone in the public had it in their hands; even the common people argue about it and desire its execution."[3] He found it persuasive, and so did the author of the *Mémoires secrets*, who hailed it as a "patriotic dream" that expressed "the wish of the nation."[4] The *Gazette de Leyde* reviewed *Richesse de l'Etat* favorably and also stressed the enthusiastic response it received, which, in the *Gazette*'s view, represented something new in public life: a debate about financial and administrative issues, taking place openly with the tacit approval of the government. Friedrich Melchior Grimm, whose private literary news-letter reached two dozen monarchs and grandees in northern Europe, remained unconvinced by the pamphlet, but he, too, observed that it dominated all conversations in the spring and summer of 1763. It also touched off responses, refutations, refutations of the refutations, and sim-ilar proposals, which Grimm followed for the rest of the year, doling out comments, most of them negative, as if he were charting a major current in the world of letters. For twelve months, from May 1763 until April 1764, the French witnessed an open debate about state finances.[5]

Although this "epidemic" of pamphleteering may not have spread far beyond the reading public, it set a new tone for the discussion of public affairs. The forty or so pamphlets that appeared in the wake of *Richesse de l'Etat* expressed a view that anyone could have a say on the sensitive issue of tax reform. "Everyone can discuss it, since the permission to do so has been given," wrote one pamphleteer. "Everyone today is occupied with the reform of the government and is giving lessons to the minis-ters," proclaimed another. A third simply jumped into the debate because "I have an itch to write." Many of the authors spoke to their readers in direct, somewhat folksy language, describing themselves as ordinary citizens—a seventy-three-year-old notary, a barber-surgeon, a clerk with a modest income of 600 L. a year. They should not be taken literally (one claimed to write in the person of Voltaire's Candide), because some were narrators invented by anonymous scribblers, who often wrote to promote vested interests such as the Parlement, the government, or the financiers themselves. But the majority, those that supported some variation of the proposal in *Richesse de l'Etat*, expressed a disturbing consensus. The taxation system could not be repaired, they concluded. Over the years, as controllers general came and went, imposing one measure on top of another, the common people had been taxed beyond their ability to pay. To add yet another tax, such as the new *vingtième* proposed by the government in April, would make things worse. A swarm of "financiers" siphoned off the taxes they were supposed to collect for the king. Various *receveurs* and *trésoriers* pocketed most of the direct taxes, and *fermiers* of the Tax Farm kept at least two-thirds of the duties on consumer goods. The system had become so dysfunctional that it had to be scrapped, destroyed from top to bottom, and replaced by something new. What France needed, the pamphleteers agreed, was one big idea, which would provide the foundation for constructing a freshly designed administrative system.[6]

Richesse de l'Etat answered that need, according to many of the pamphlets, which either endorsed it or proposed variations on the theme of a single-tax system. One writer, who described himself as a "true patriot," argued for a system based on landholding: Take the total acreage of the kingdom, subtract for the nonarable land, divide by the population, and you come up with a basic tax of 5 sous per *arpent* (0.84 acres). The taxpayers should be separated into classes, according to the amount of land they own; and in place of current privileges, their status should be expressed by dress: the lowest class could be permitted to wear silk; the next, gold embroidery; the next could carry a sword; and the top class could display a coat of arms. Another author, writing as a "patriot financier," devised a similar system: All landowners would pay at the same rate according to a nationwide cadastre, which would take account of discrepancies in the productivity of their holdings. To compensate for the loss of their privileges, noblemen in the military would receive an increase in salary, and the clergy would subtract an appropriate sum from its *don gratuit*. A third reformer appealed to "the patriot public" by designing a single tax based on wealth that would spare the sensitivities built into the current system by being collected separately for nobles, bourgeois, artisans, and peasants, although everyone would have to pay. A pamphleteer who identified himself as a "good patriot" and another who wrote as a "good citizen," proposed a "tithe," which would fall equally on everyone and be distributed through local assemblies or farmed out to the highest bidder.[7]

Although most of the pamphlets amounted to only a few pages and the exposition of a single, cure-all proposal, a few contained sophisticated arguments about what was beginning to be recognized as an "economic science" or "physiocracy." Inspired especially by François Quesnay's *Tableau économique* (1758), the physiocrats attempted, statistics at hand, to analyze the operations of an economy in systematic fashion. They claimed that all wealth derived from agriculture, dismissing urban manufacturing and trade as unproductive. Governments should promote free trade in grain, they argued, because the circulation of grain, like blood in the body, would enrich the entire country. The debate about tax reform gave the physiocrats an opportunity to float their ideas, which they had often expressed in an abstract and abstruse manner, before a general public. Two of them, Samuel du Pont de Nemours and Nicolas Baudeau, jumped into the controversy aroused by *Richesse de l'Etat*. Dupont's *Réflexions sur l'écrit intitulé Richesse de l'Etat* politely took Roussel to task for overestimating France's wealth and the ability of most classes to pay for the reduction of the state debt but praised the proposal to create a cadastre of landed property. Baudeau's *Idées d'un citoyen sur l'administration des finances du roi* was a large-scale treatise, aimed at "the patriotic public" and arguing for a single "royal subsidy" to replace all the current taxes. It was a radical proposal, Baudeau conceded, but "the entire nation desires at present the total overthrow of the present administration."[8]

The strongest argument against *Richesse de l'Etat* came from a notorious enemy of the *philosophes*, Jacob Nicolas Moreau.[9] While disputing the feasibility of a single tax, he objected above all to its egalitarian effect. Nobles would be taxed in the same way as commoners, creating a state based on wealth rather than time-honored "dignities." Moreau couched his argument as a dialogue between an abbé and an aristocrat, who tossed off witticisms at the expense of naïve reformers.[10] The pamphleteers who rebutted Moreau found his tone even more offensive than his ideas. By resorting to "mockery and irony," they objected, he demonstrated his incapacity to address a question of "patriotism" that had aroused "the wish of the nation."[11] A great deal of the debate had to do with tone and language. Roussel had not used terms like "nation" and "patriot," although in a sequel to *Richesse de l'Etat* he referred to "citizens" rather than "subjects."[12] But his followers adopted a new vocabulary. Words like "patriot" appeared on nearly every page of their pamphlets, and their idiom conveyed a general demand for equality—not social leveling but equal treatment in taxation by the state, and since the tax system extended through the entire society, favoring some and oppressing others, they opened a way to challenge the sociopolitical order as a whole.

The debate riveted the attention of Parisians because it took place at the height of another conflict between the Parlement and the Crown. As Moreau observed, *Richesse de l'Etat* appeared just before the *lit de justice* of May 31, in which Louis XV forced the Parlement to register some extremely unpopular financial measures. The pressure to relieve the state's debt had been building up since November 1759 when a tough, new controller general, Henri-Léonard-Jean-Baptiste Bertin, took office. As the income from the established taxes, especially the first and second *vingtièmes*, proved woefully inadequate, he levied a third *vingtième*, doubled the *capitation*, and added a surtax known as *sols pour livre* to the indirect taxes collected by the General Farm. Although he presented them in February 1760 as temporary expedients to finance the war, he extended them after the declaration of peace. Two edicts of April 1763 decreed that the third *vingtième* and the doubled *capitation* would end in January 1764, but the first two *vingtièmes* would continue for another six years, and a *cadastre général* or survey of all landed property would lay the basis for more effective taxation, even though the exemptions of the nobility and clergy would, in principle, be respected. To Parisian commentators, *Richesse de l'Etat* represented an attempt by the Parlement to block the taxes and to appeal to the citizenry with an alternative system.

The "immense deluge" of pamphlets kept this issue before the public for the rest of the year, while the Parlement resisted the edicts with its main weapon: *remontrances, nouvelles remontrances,* and *itératives remontrances.* The parlementary texts, which circulated in print from April through July, provided a legalistic framework to the public debate and also served as propaganda on their own. Parisians discussed the tax issue intensely, according to Barbier. They kept returning to the same theme: extraordinary taxes, forced on the population to support the war, had no legitimacy in peacetime, yet the king had rammed them through the Parlement. No one shouted *Vive le roi* when he came to preside over the *lit de justice* in Paris, and much of the talk in the following days was about "depredations"—that is, extravagant court expenditures, such as a fête presided over by Mme de Pompadour at the royal château of Choisy on June 13–16 with command performances by the Opéra, the Comédie française, and the Comédie italienne.[13]

In the summer of 1763, the opposition to Bertin's taxes shifted to the provincial parlements, led by the Parlement of Rouen, which produced remonstrances on July 16 that outdid those of the Parlement of Paris in the violence of their rhetoric.[14] The April edicts threatened to transform temporary, wartime taxes into a permanent system, the most oppressive in the history of the monarchy, the Rouennais protested. The edicts violated the natural rights of liberty and property, yet nothing indicated they were necessary. To justify them, the king should submit accounts of income and expenses to the Parlement for investigation—and the Rouennais spoke as if they were expressing the demands of all the parlements united as classes of a single body. The entire revenue system, they insisted, should be replaced with a new regime, based on a single, equitable tax.

Within three days, printed copies of the Rouen remonstrances were circulating in Paris, stirring up more angry talk. The king dispatched the Duc d'Harcourt in his capacity as lieutenant general of Normandy to bring the Parlement of Rouen to heel. It refused to deliberate in his presence and forbade officials to collect the new taxes within its area of jurisdiction. In a decree dated August 18, it spoke out again as one division of a supposed Parlement de France. It claimed to share the legislative power of the Crown and to be responsible to the nation. This text, printed with related material, caused a great stir in Paris, according to Barbier, who interpreted it as a direct attack on the authority of the king.[15] Although the government prohibited the publication of further remonstrances, they continued to arrive from many parlements—Dijon, remonstrances voted on August 13; Besançon, September 5; Grenoble, September 7; Bordeaux, September 7; Toulouse, September 13; and Pau, September 15. While refusing to register the April decrees, the parlements defied the emissaries of the king who tried to enforce his will. Dramatic scenes took place in the parlements of Grenoble and Toulouse, while another confrontation in Rouen led to the collective resignation of the magistrates.

By November, the "great fermentation" had reached such a point that the government agreed to negotiate.[16] It had now come under the domination of the Duc de Choiseul, minister of war, and his cousin, the Duc de Choiseul-Praslin, minister of foreign affairs, leaving Bertin exposed. Although Parisians heard only rumors about the realignment of power in Versailles, those who followed politics considered the Choiseuls as friendly to the parlements. It came as no surprise, therefore, that the government tried to restore peace by announcing a new policy on November 21. It withdrew the April edicts, suspended the cadastre, and agreed to collect the second *vingtiéme* only until the end of 1767. Bertin withdrew from the Contrôle général, and he was replaced by Clément Charles François de Laverdy, a member of the Paris Parlement. It looked like a government retreat and even like a replay of Machault's failure to reform the tax system in 1749–1750.

As a further means of pacifying the parlements, the edict of November 21 invited them to investigate possibilities of putting the state's finances on a sound basis. A few weeks later, the most outspoken of the fiscal pamphlets, *L'Anti-financier*, announced how that could be done. The proposal was not new. In fact, the author, a parlementary lawyer named Edme-François Darigrand, merely reworked the themes of *Richesse de l'Etat*, particularly the need for a single tax to replace all the current taxes. But he denounced the abuses of the General Tax Farm with a ferocity that made Roussel's condemnation look mild, and he advanced a radical argument to empower the Parlement of Paris. The Parlement represented the nation, he claimed, and had done so since the origin of the monarchy, when the king shared power with an assembly of the people. According to the fundamental laws of the kingdom, the king could not raise a new tax without the Parlement's consent, no matter what the pressure from "despotic ministers." Louis should therefore follow the Parlement's lead, abolish the Farm, remake the fiscal apparatus of the state, and impose "a simple and unique tax."[17]

The police immediately began to confiscate copies of *L'Anti-financier* from bookstores, which, as Barbier observed, drove up the price and made the public desire it all the more.[18] On January 4, Darigrand disappeared into the Bastille. Pamphlets continued to appear, but the government's capitulation of November 21 had taken the wind out of the controversy. On March 28, 1764, the king decreed that no further publications on state finance would be permitted, except reflections that the parlementary magistrates, in their wisdom, might propose.[19] The big Idea was dead.

10

The Jesuits Are Crushed

IN THE CAST of bogeymen who haunted Parisians' imaginations, the Jesuits played a leading role. Their enemies, especially the Jansenists, made them out to be the supreme villains of the eighteenth century: Jesuits lurked behind thrones, whispering evil advice to monarchs; they educated youth in the ways of immorality (casuistry, probabilism, jesuitry); they blindly followed orders from their "general" in Rome, who ruled over them like a despot over slaves; they sacrificed the interest of France, and especially the Gallican Church, to the global ambitions of their Order; and they advocated regicide—in fact, they were responsible for the assassinations of Henri III and Henri IV, and they had inspired Damiens's attempt to murder Louis XV, which would have brought the dauphin, a champion of their cause, to power. Parisians picked up these notions from loose talk about conspiracies, from pamphlets, and from the weekly issues of the *Nouvelles ecclésiastiques*, a well-informed and inexhaustible source of Jansenist propaganda.[1]

Yet the Jesuits maintained a powerful and respectable presence in France. They taught the elite in 111 *collèges* or secondary schools, notably Louis-le-Grand in Paris, where Voltaire had been one of their naughtiest and most brilliant students. Founded as the Collège de Clermont in 1563, it was an imposing edifice in the heart of Paris on the rue Saint Jacques. Among many other institutions, the Jesuits ran twenty-one seminaries and thirteen residences for their members. Since the early seventeenth century they had been *directeurs de conscience* as confessors to the kings. Louis XV's confessor since 1753, Philippe Onuphre Desmarets, intervened at crucial moments such as the crisis following Damiens's attack; and despite the Jesuits' reputation for condoning immorality, he refused to sanction Louis's relations with Mme de Pompadour. The Jesuits exercised considerable power in the court through the *dévot* party, which included the queen, the dauphin, and the chancellor, Lamoignon de Blancmesnil. In 1760, a large majority of bishops favored the Jesuits, as the Jansenists had been purged from the upper clergy during the previous four decades. At that time, for most Parisians, the idea that the Jesuits could be driven out of the kingdom was unthinkable. Five years later the Society of Jesus ceased to exist in France.[2]

Its destruction came to be known as the kind of event referred to in casual conversation as an *affaire*. Affairs occurred with increasing frequency during the second half of the eighteenth century, and they had a great impact on Parisians' view of public life. They usually crystallized around trials, where abstract issues came to life in courtroom dramas played out before large audiences and reported in gazettes. As mentioned, lawyers' briefs, known as *mémoires* and *factums*, were often printed and circulated like pamphlets, free from censorship because they were deemed to be part of the legal procedure, provided they bore a lawyer's signature.

L'affaire des Jésuites began in 1760, when commercial courts in Marseille and Paris ruled against the Jesuits in a bankruptcy case involving Père Antoine La Valette, who had developed an enormous trade in sugar and other colonial products from Martinique. Although committed in principle to nurture the spiritual life of the natives, he ran a slave plantation and exported its goods to France. On the eve of the Seven Years' War, English privateers captured five of his ships, making it impossible for him to honor bills of exchange that he had written to cover the Jesuits' debts and that he expected to redeem from the sale of his merchandise. He went bankrupt and threatened to drag down with him one of his creditors, the house of Lionci et Gouffre, which then tried to collect its debt, a matter of a million and a half livres, by suing La Valette's superior, the head of the Jesuit mission in Guadeloupe. The commercial courts found in favor of Lionci et Gouffre, and the Jesuits appealed to the Grand'Chambre of the Parlement of Paris. That was not a wise step because a "Jansenist party" had been gaining power in the Parlement since the early conflicts over the bull *Unigenitus* and the refusal of sacraments to Jansenist sympathizers. True, the elderly magistrates of the Grand'Chambre were known to be more moderate than the hotheads of the *Enquêtes* and *Requêtes*, and 104 of the total of 250 members in all the chambers had been educated in Louis-le-Grand. Moreover, bankruptcy cases did not attract much attention, so there was a possibility that this one could be settled without escalating into a full-scale affair.

Yet this case was different, not merely because it involved a monastic order, but because Parisians connected it with a spectacular string of events that had occurred two years earlier in Portugal. On September 3, 1758, an unknown assailant attempted to assassinate Portugal's king, Joseph I. The all-powerful prime minister of the Portuguese government, Sebastião José de Carvalho e Melo (made marquis of Pombal in 1769), blamed the attempt on the Jesuits and their allies in the upper aristocracy. After a special tribunal condemned the supposed conspirators, he staged some grisly executions and in September 1759 expelled all Jesuits from Portugal. The news from Portugal "became the subject of conversations in all of Paris," according to Barbier. It rekindled suspicions, fanned by the *Nouvelles ecclésiastiques*, that the Jesuits had inspired Damiens's attack on Louis XV, and stirred talk about driving them out of France. Jesuit fathers hardly dared appear in the street for fear of being insulted.[3]

The public hostility was still virulent when the trial opened on March 31, 1761. Large crowds packed into the Grand'Chambre and applauded wildly when lawyers for Lionci et Gouffre scored points. On May 8 the court condemned the Jesuit Order to pay 1,552,276 L. in damages. The joy of the audience—"excessive, even almost indecent"—spread throughout the city, where the Jesuits were "well hated," Barbier noted.[4] By this time, the issue had shifted to the larger question of the Jesuits' legitimacy as a monastic order inside France. Impassioned speeches by two magistrates, abbé Henri-Philippe de Chauvelin and Michel-Étienne Lepelletier de Saint Fargeau, led the Parlement to call for an investigation of the "constitutions" or statutes of the Order, and a memoir by a Jansenist lawyer for Lionci, Charlemagne Lalourcé, argued, with ample evidence, that it had never been legally established in the kingdom and therefore could be easily expelled.

To prevent the Parlement from overreaching its authority, the Crown ordered that the statutes be examined by a royal commission. The Parlement complied but managed to procure an additional copy of the statutes and to continue with its own investigation. In a first round of debates from July 3 to 7, it stressed the threat of the Jesuits, as agents of the pope, to the liberties of the French or Gallican Church. According to a declaration of 1682, those liberties excluded papal interference in the temporal affairs of the Gallican Church, which remained subject to the authority of the king. Chauvelin raised the stakes in the debate by a speech on July 8, which denounced the Jesuits for endorsing regicide (mainly in tracts published during the sixteenth and seventeenth centuries but reprinted right up to 1757); and he associated them with Damiens's attack on Louis XV, loading his rhetoric with so much pathos that he had everyone in tears.[5]

A printed version of Chauvelin's speech was soon circulating in Paris, and it was accompanied by a 155-page anthology of selections from Jesuit publications, arranged to make the reader's hair stand on end. Jesuits could justify anything, the anthology seemed to show; they had set out to subject the world to the tyranny of their general; they plotted and conspired everywhere; and if a prince stood in their way, they would arrange to have him eliminated. Among their many wicked manuals on ethics, *Theologia moralis* by Hermann Busembaum, first published in 1645, had gone through fifty editions right up to 1757, the year of Damiens's "execrable attack from which we still are groaning," and it proved that the Jesuits had never deviated from their commitment to regicide.[6] A deluge of pamphlets followed. *Idées générales des vices principales de l'institut des Jésuites* catalogued Jesuit vices. *Dénonciation des crimes et attentats des soi-disant Jésuites* warned about their political ambitions. Dozens of libels accused them of endless abominations, everything from sodomy to regicide. At a serious level, a two-volume *Histoire générale de la naissance et des progrès de la Compagnie de Jésus* by two determined Jansenists, Louis-Adrien Le Paige and Christophe Coudrette, provided an erudite, carefully documented survey of the Jesuits' rise to power, which served as an arsenal for arguments by the parlements. In fact, Le Paige coordinated the parlements' strategy, remaining hidden under the protection of the Prince de Conti. Parisians had no idea of the machinations behind the scenes, but they overwhelmingly supported the anti-Jesuit cause.[7]

While the ideological temperature rose, the government attempted to create a cooling-off period by ordering the Parlement to delay its decision about the Jesuits' statutes for a year. On August 6, however, the Parlement issued two aggressive edicts. First, it condemned twenty-four Jesuit works to be burned by the public executioner "as seditious, destructive of all principles of Christian morality, teaching a murderous and abominable doctrine not merely against the citizens' security of life but even against the sacred persons of sovereigns." Then it decreed that all Jesuit schools within its area of jurisdiction be closed by October 1. (The date was later extended until April 1, 1762.) The decree also forbade Jesuits to accept new members in their order, and it required all students and novices to withdraw from their schools and seminaries.[8]

This bold stroke stunned Parisians. They lined up to get copies of the decrees directly from the printing shop and bought out all that were hawked by peddlers. Most people approved of the Parlement's action, according to Barbier, although some worried that it undercut the king's authority, for the Jesuits had served as confessors to the royal family for two hundred years. Everyone who followed politics waited to see how Louis would react, expecting that he might annul the decrees and evoke the affair to his personal judgment. Yet he remained silent for several days, and the savviest members of the public—"the politiques" and "the reasoners," as Barbier called them—suspected that Choiseul, the dominant figure in the government, had little sympathy for the Jesuits and needed to appease the Parlement.[9] As recounted in the last chapter, the multiplication of taxes created enormous resentment, which the parlements, in the provinces as well as Paris, mobilized in opposition to Versailles. Desperate to raise funds through loans and new taxation, which required the registration of new edicts, the government could not afford to compound its political difficulties with a conflict over religion.

By the end of the month, it became clear that the king would not annul the decrees of August 6. He merely ordered the Parlement to suspend them for a year, and in registering his order, the Parlement proclaimed that it would extend the deadline for only six months, meaning that all Jesuit schools would close on April 1, 1762. To justify its resistance, it voted to send Louis extracts from the books it had burned as evidence of the threat posed by the Jesuits to all of his subjects and especially to himself, owing to the doctrine of regicide. When the texts were presented to the king, he reacted coolly, but he did not oppose the closing of the schools. Barbier concluded that Choiseul had now committed himself to the anti-Jesuit cause—for strategic reasons, as he had needed to persuade the Parlement to register an edict for a loan of 40 million livres. Large crowds attended the Parlement's sessions in August and September, and by the end of the year they were cheering victory over the Jesuits, who received a vote of support at a meeting of the upper clergy in November but remained thoroughly hated among the Parisians.[10]

The initiative in the anti-Jesuit campaign shifted to the provinces at the beginning of 1762. On February 12, the Parlement of Rouen took the radical step of expelling all Jesuits from the area of its jurisdiction. Their statutes were to be burned; they would have to vacate their residences within five months; and their property would be sold off. The government, taken by surprise, did not intervene. Other parlements—in Bordeaux, Grenoble, Metz, Besançon, and Rennes—followed suit by naming committees to investigate the statutes of the local Jesuit institutions in preparation for dissolving them. Their decrees were printed and read widely in Paris, where public sentiment now favored destroying the Jesuits altogether as an order within France. Rumors circulated that the king would come to their rescue before they were forced to close their schools, and on March 9 he issued a declaration indicating he would intervene in their favor. But when April 1 arrived, he had done nothing.

By then, the parents of the 150 boarders in Louis-le-Grand had already withdrawn their children, the Jesuit fathers had dismissed all their novices, and therefore the closing took place without incident. On April 23 the Parlement voted to sequester all Jesuit property. Six bailiffs arrived in carriages at Louis-le-Grand and the Jesuit residences. They put everything under seal; and when they did inventories, they discovered that the Jesuits had not lived in a style of monastic self-deprivation. The fathers had elegant furniture, and their larder contained "an astonishing amount of coffee."[11] The most valuable objects—vases, ornements, paintings—were advertised for sale in the *Petites affiches* and were auctioned off by December. But rumors circulated that prized possessions, including 20,000 L. worth of linens, and a great deal of cash had been secretly shipped out of the country. The Parlement ordered the lieutenant general of police to keep the Jesuit residences under surveillance and to station guards at the doors of Louis-le-Grand. Parisian gossip fed on reports of spectacular coups by the police. Agents in Lyons were said to have captured several wagons loaded with goods that the Jesuits had tried to sneak into Switzerland. Eighteen crates of silver were supposedly seized from another clandestine shipment. And more booty was expected to be confiscated by agents sent to stop smuggling to the papal enclave of Avignon. Reports also arrived about shady financial dealings—a loan business conducted by the fathers under assumed names and a real estate speculation done with the secret collaboration of a wine merchant. By May 1762 most Jesuits no longer dared to appear in the streets, and all of Paris, according to the *Gazette de Leyde*, talked about nothing but their expulsion.[12]

This activity attracted a great deal of attention. The bailiffs coming and going, the gutting of Louis-le-Grand, the advertisements and public auctions—everything proclaimed the downfall of an institution that had insinuated itself into the pinnacle of power and was identified with the monarchy through its confessors, who acted as the keepers of the king's conscience. Louis XV watched its demise, hesitated, took a few steps to protect it, and in the end did nothing. He dismissed Desmarets, his confessor, in April. In October, Barbier wrote, "The affair of the Jesuits has finished in Paris."[13]

In fact, the destruction of the Jesuits was an uneven process, which took place at different times in different parts of the kingdom. The Parlement of Paris suppressed the order within its jurisdiction on August 6, 1762, and by the end of 1763 most of the provincial parlements had done the same. When the Parisian Parlement took additional measures to drive all Jesuits out of the kingdom, the king issued an edict in November 1764 that dissolved the order but permitted its members to remain in France as secular priests subject to their local bishop and supported in many cases with a pension.

After losing the La Valette case, the Jesuits did not fight back in the courts. They attempted to rally support through pamphlets, but they also lost the battle to dominate public opinion. Their tracts, as Grimm observed, were drowned in the flood of hostile publications, and their best-known publication, *Remarques sur un écrit intitulé Compte rendu des constitutions des Jésuites*, convinced no one except their own partisans.[14]

The Parlement set the tone of the anti-Jesuit propaganda by publishing extracts from Jesuit works. *Extraits des assertions dangereuses et pernicieuses en tout genre que les soi-disants Jésuites ont, dans tous les temps et persévéramment, soutenues, enseignées et publiées dans leurs livres* was an impressive tome of 543 pages laid out in two columns, the original texts, mostly in Latin, on one side and the French translations on the other. It had all the prestige of an official publication, handsomely printed by Pierre-Guillaume Simon, the Parlement's printer, in accordance with a parlementary resolution that named a commission to collate the extracts with the original volumes and to attest to the accuracy of the translations. The text was divided into sections corresponding to the evils perpetrated by the Jesuits, such as "Probabilism," ninety-six pages; "Simony and Confidence, Blasphemy, Sacreligion," thirty-two pages; "Perjury, Fraud, False Witness," fifty-one pages; "Prevarication by Judges, Theft," forty-six pages; "Homicide," thirty-eight pages; and "Régicide," ninety-eight pages, the longest section. Snippets from manuals for confessors showed that the Jesuits considered theft permissible, or at most a venial sin, if the owner of an object did not make use of it or if a servant felt he was not adequately paid. Homicide was justifiable under some circumstances, although never by poisoning—unless the poison was transmitted from garments or the seat of a chair. And it was laudable, even heroic, for a subject to assassinate a king considered to be tyrannical.[15] In its commentary on the documents, the Parlement emphasized the Jesuits' commitment to regicide, and it also insisted on the general immorality of their teaching, which threatened to "break all the bonds of civil society in authorising theft, lies, betrayal, the most criminal impurity, and in general all passions and crimes."[16] Parisians found this message convincing, according to Grimm: "Everyone is struck by the dangerous and pernicious assertions of these old casuists. A holy horror has taken hold of the common people, and one is persuaded that the Jesuits spend their lives talking to their pupils about murders, assassinations, and abominations."[17]

The most effective of the many pamphlets against the Jesuits was *Compte rendu des constitutions des Jésuites* by Louis-René de Caradeuc de La Chalotais, an attorney general in the Parlement of Brittany.[18] It went through 12,000 copies within a month of its publication in February 1762, and continued to be reprinted many times along with an equally powerful sequel, *Second compte rendu*. La Chalotais's work carried conviction because of its moderate tone and carefully documented argument. The Jesuits were no worse in principle than other orders, it noted, because all monastic movements went into decline with the passage of time. What set the Jesuits apart was the nature of their mission. As their statutes demonstrated, they were not isolated in convents but dispatched into the secular world by a general in Rome, who demanded absolute obedience. They had no allegiance to the French monarchy and in fact no legal existence within France. True, the most extreme statements among their publications had appeared two hundred years ago, but the basic principles of their organization were reaffirmed in the two-volume work printed in 1757. Although they included many virtuous individuals who were dedicated to the vocation of teaching, they taught an antequated variety of scholasticism, and their manuals, from the sixteenth century to the present, propounded casuistry that made light of lying, stealing, conspiring, and a whole line of sins leading up to parricide and regicide. Two thousand Jesuits existed in France, ready to do anything ordered by their general, for his was the only authority they recognized. They perpetuated all the evils of the Inquisition: "fanaticism," "superstition," and "ignorance."[19]

Those were the favorite terms used by the *philosophes* in their attacks against the church. La Chalotais's rhetoric echoed theirs so clearly that some believed his text had actually been written by d'Alembert.[20] D'Alembert extolled it in a tract of his own published in 1765. By then, the Jesuits had been extinguished—not by the Jansenists, d'Alembert insisted, for they, too, were virtually dead, but by the *philosophes*. La Chalotais was one of them, as he had demonstrated by exposing religious fanaticism in all its forms, not merely Jesuitism. "It is actually philosophy that, by means of the magistrates, produced the death warrant of the Jesuits. Jansenism was merely the plaintiff in the case. The nation, with the *philosophes* at their head, wanted the annihilation of those fathers."[21] Voltaire had done his part two years earlier in a short pamphlet, *Balance Égale*, which listed all the accusations against the Jesuits and ostensibly refuted them, using such unconvincing arguments that they appeared guiltier than charged. He devoted half the pamphlet to the Jansenists and concluded that both camps were so iniquitous that the balance between them was equal.[22] For his part, d'Alembert considered the Jansenists more fanatical, but he

wrote them off as a spent force because they no longer occupied the public's attention. The extinction of the Jesuits, he concluded, was to be celebrated as a victory for *Philosophie.*

Of course, d'Alembert was promoting his own cause, and it seems
unlikely that most Parisians viewed the Jesuit Affair as a triumph of the
Enlightenment. Yet it came across as a blow to the church and perhaps
even the state. There was a new, disrespectful tone about religion in the
songs, rumors, jokes, and prints that circulated at street level in the early
1760s. The *Mémoires secrets* noted that many songs treated the upper clergy
"with the utmost contempt."[23] Pasquinades played on the theme of monas-
ticism and sodomy. Shopkeepers sold toy Jesuits made out of wax, which
could be made to retreat into a shell like a snail by pulling on a string. And
a great deal of gossip was stirred up by a hoax about a pamphlet, *Les Trois
Nécessités*, which did not exist, although the Conseil souverain of Alsace
condemned it to be burned. It supposedly announced an evil design to
bring down the regime by taking three necessary steps: first, the destruction of the Jesuits; second, the destruction of the church; and third, the
destruction of the monarchy. Grimm and others attributed the rumor to
Jesuits who wanted to alarm the public about the consequences of their
dissolution. Whatever its source, it had great shock value, perhaps because
some saw in it a grain of truth.[24]

The destruction of the Jesuits did indeed produce damaging consequences for the church. Louis XV mismanaged it so badly that the Crown
sustained collateral damage. And before he finally dissolved the Order,
the next affair, masterminded by Voltaire, would show that moral authority was shifting to the *philosophes*. The *philosophes*, however, did not maintain a united front. Voltaire's own authority was challenged from within
their ranks by a writer who mobilized emotions in a different key. Before
Voltaire appealed to the public in *Traité sur la tolérance* (1763), Rousseau
conquered it with *La Nouvelle Héloïse* (1761).

11

~

Rousseau Releases a Flood of Tears

AT THE APEX of Parisian society, far above the workshops, stores, and neighborhoods that made the city such a complex entity, stood an elite known as *le monde*. It was highly aristocratic, yet included wealthy commoners and even a few persons known primarily for their wit. It inhabited splendid town houses and went about town in carriages with footmen, stopping in salons and upscale cafés. While most of Paris was at work by dawn, the members of *le monde* lived according to a rhythm of their own, set by the time of meals—a late breakfast followed by some occupation (tax farmers might discuss reports; *rentiers* might tend to correspondence); dinner at 2:00, then amusement in a social gathering and entertainment in a theater or the opera, which normally began at 5:00; and supper, often at 10:00, and more socializing, frequently combined with gambling at card games, until late at night.

Members of *le monde* conformed to an ideal type. Voltaire defined it perfectly in a poem, "Le Mondain" (1736) where he mocked the Christian ideal of the Garden of Eden as a paradise.[1] Adam and Eve, he asserted, were filthy, ugly, vulgar, miserable, malnourished, and ignorant. By contrast, *le mondain* enjoyed all the good things in life, which Voltaire celebrated, speaking as a man of the world himself:

J'aime le luxe, et même la mollesse,
Tous les plaisirs, les arts de toute espèce,

La propreté, le goût, les ornements:
Tout honnête homme a de tels sentiments.

(I love luxury and even indolence, / All the pleasures, the arts of every kind, / Cleanness, taste, embellishments: / Every honnête homme has such sentiments.)

Far from being simply a sybarite, *le mondain* was an *honnête homme*—that is, he embodied an ideal, derived from the seventeenth century, of worldly uprightness, but his virtue was not Christian. Voltaire identified it with taste, politeness, the progress of the arts, and civilization itself, as he soon would describe it in his multivolume vision of world history, *Essai sur les moeurs*. He aimed the poem at the contrasting ideal of Christian asceticism. His *mondain* begins the day in a Parisian town house furnished elegantly with paintings and tapestry and overlooking a splendid garden. In the afternoon a gilded carriage whisks him to the opera. Then:

Allons souper. Que ces brillants services,
Que ces ragoûts ont pour moi de délices!

(Let's go to supper. These brilliant sittings, / These stews are a delight for me!)

The popping of corks sets off rounds of laughter in the company, which is as sparkling as its champagne. And the day ends with a conclusion:

Le paradis terrestre est à Paris

(The terrestrial paradise is in Paris.)

It was hardly a call to revolution, yet as Voltaire's admirers and enemies understood it, "Le Mondain," like all his other works, cut into the religious convictions that held the Ancien Régime together. It worked by wit, and it was aimed at the sector of the public where it could do most damage, the elite of the capital. No gentleman, Voltaire made clear, could accept the teachings of the Catholic Church. Christianity was bad taste.

The reading public had long been familiar with Voltaire's variety of irreligion when it was taken aback by a work that challenged his assumptions and exposed a vulnerable side of the Enlightenment: *Discours sur les sciences et les arts* (1750) by an obscure fellow traveler of the *philosophes*, Jean-Jacques Rousseau. Rousseau's background made him the antithesis of *le mondain*. The son of a watchmaker in the republic of Geneva, he had a latent Calvinist streak and too many rough edges to fit into the salon society of Paris. To the question of a prize-essay contest sponsored by the Academy of Dijon—"Has the revival of the arts and sciences contributed to making morals purer?"—he answered with an emphatic No! Literature, philosophy, the fine arts, the physical sciences, everything celebrated by Voltaire (who was not mentioned, though he was an implicit point of reference) had contributed to the increasing corruption of morals. The more sophisticated man became, the further removed he was from his original state of innocence.

The argument, conveyed by powerful rhetoric, made Rousseau a celebrity.[2] He took it further in *Discours sur l'origine et les fondements de l'inégalité parmi les hommes* (1755), which advocated equality of the sort he imagined in an original "newly born society," where man's natural inclination to goodness produced the flourishing of civic virtue, free from the corrupt influences of wealth and culture.[3] The public took this manifesto as an apology for a return to a primitive state of nature. Voltaire mocked it in a letter to Rousseau that circulated everywhere and soon was published in the *Mercure*: "Never has one used so much wit in trying to make us stupid. When one reads your book, one wants to walk on all four paws."[4]

From this point on, Voltaire and Rousseau appeared before the public as opposites, a pair of antithetical enemies. In fact, Rousseau's open opposition to Voltaire took place slightly later with the publication of his *Lettre à d'Alembert sur les spectacles* (1758), a work that also ruptured his relations with the entire group of *Encyclopédistes*, who had originally welcomed him into the world of letters. Rousseau took offense at d'Alembert's suggestion in the article on Geneva in volume seven of the *Encyclopédie* that Geneva shake off its Calvinist hostility to the arts and allow a theater to exist within its walls. D'Alembert had been prompted by Voltaire, whom he had recently visited in Geneva, where Voltaire was living in exile and staging private plays. The idea outraged Rousseau, who denounced it, writing as a "citizen of Geneva." What, among all the arts and sciences, he objected, could be more corrupting than the theater, where actors assumed fictitious personalities and audiences succumbed to immoral passions? In Paris, the theater was the playground of *le monde*. It represented the ultimate in worldliness and decadence. Genevans should treat it as a plague that would ravage their healthy, unsophisticated culture and destroy the moral foundation of their republic. They should retain their austere Calvinism, which served as a civil religion, holding the republic together. Instead of plays, they should have civic festivals, Spartan-like athletic contests, and collective celebrations of the harvest, where all would participate equally, both as players and spectators.

In pursuing this argument, Rousseau developed a view of culture as a political force that could sustain a democratic and egalitarian society (equality, as he understood it, would unite men, while women remained consigned to domestic life), but the public took it primarily as a critique of polite society in Paris. Rousseau turned his eloquence against "the man of the world," salons, sophistication, luxury, and ridicule, "the favorite arm of vice."⁵ When he broke with the *philosophes*, he deployed an antithetical mode of combat—a rhetoric of sentiment, which appealed to the heart by cutting through convention, as opposed to wit, which demeaned its targets by exposing them to derision.

Rousseau spelled out the political implications of his cultural critique in *Du Contrat social* (1762), but the public found that work hard going. To drive his point home, he needed to stir readers' emotions, touching them in their inner lives with another kind of narrative. He succeeded spectacularly with *La Nouvelle Héloïse* (1761). Historians of literature have rightly treated this book as a turning point in French culture, one that contributed mightily to the rise of romanticism. But Rousseau's contemporaries could not imagine the kind of writing that would captivate readers in the nineteenth century, and they found themselves in the face of a paradox: Rousseau had declaimed against the arts, yet he now appeared openly as the author of a novel—that is, of a work of art that belonged to the most dubious genre of literature, one considered to promote corruption, particularly among young women.

Moreover, *La Nouvelle Héloïse* is a love story, which has ingredients of libertinism, though it takes place in a small, Protestant, Swiss town.

Its heroine, Julie, is seduced by her tutor, Saint-Preux, who cannot marry her because he comes from a lower social rank. They exchange passionate letters (it is an epistolary novel) and finally settle into a spiritual *ménage à trois*. Having given her heart to Saint-Preux, Julie follows her father's instructions and gives her hand to Wolmar, a virtuous atheist (many readers considered such a creature an impossibility). Saint-Preux departs for adventures in the wicked outside world, beginning with Paris. Julie remains at Wolmar's side, although she does not share his disbelief, and presides over a happy family and a flourishing, bucolic estate. After ten years, Saint-Preux returns and receives a warm welcome, although Julie never fails in her faithfulness to Wolmar. In the end, she makes a noble death, heroic and supremely virtuous.

Rousseau addressed the paradox of his position as a novelist in two prefaces, which explained that novels were bad in themselves because they caused corruption, yet salutary in that they could inspire virtue among those already trapped in a corrupt society. He also added a further paradox: "This novel is not a novel."[6] Although he did not resolve it, he proclaimed that in place of artifice, the normal stuff of fiction, he was offering authenticity, genuine sentiment, which transpired directly to the reader from the letters in the text.

Thus instructed, readers discovered that *La Nouvelle Héloïse* opened up a new realm of experience, unmediated contact with emotion, as if the letters were written by real persons and they, the readers, took part in the epistolary exchanges. They responded with letters of their own, dozens of them, addressed to Rousseau, although they had never met him. This outpouring belonged to a wave of sentiment that was sweeping through Europe and was stimulated by other epistolary novels—Richardson's *Pamela*, which had appeared earlier (1740) and Goethe's *Sorrows of Young Werther*, which would be published later (1774). To call the response to *La Nouvelle Héloïse* fan mail is not to do it justice, because it expressed a new relationship between author and reader, as Rousseau recognized by preserving his readers' letters in a separate dossier, which he planned to publish. He never did so, but they can be consulted in a modern edition of his correspondence, which provides a rich record of his readers' responses.[7]

The letter writers expressed a conviction that the novel had penetrated their innermost selves: "Your divine works, Monsieur, are an all-consuming fire. They have penetrated my soul, fortified my heart, enlightened my mind." Some felt so moved that they could not contain themselves and had to stop in order to ingest the text in small, manageable doses. One reader hesitated for three days before he could bear to read a letter that, he anticipated, would announce the death of Julie: "It was necessary, however, to overcome my repugnance, and I never shed such delicious tears." Others raced through the six volumes several times, continually weeping "delicious tears."[8]

Of course, many earlier books, especially devotional tracts, had brought tears to the eyes of their readers,[9] but *La Nouvelle Héloïse* released a flood: "tears," "sweet tears," "tears that are sweet," "delicious tears," "tears of tenderness." One reader sobbed so vehemently that he cured himself of a severe cold. Others felt an irresistible need to communicate their experience to Rousseau: "It was imperative to choke up, to leave the book, to weep, to write to you that one was choked up and weeping." They were moved so deeply that they could not believe they had been reading fiction. "Oh Julie, oh Saint-Preux, oh Claire, oh Édouard! What globe do your souls inhabit, and how can I be united with you? Monsieur, those are the children of your heart; your wit could not have created them as they are; open this heart to me so that I may contemplate in real life the virtues whose mere image has made me shed such sweet tears."[10]

Many felt convinced that Julie and her companions were real persons. Their emotions told them so, because the letters gave such a powerful impression of heart-to-heart contact among the characters in the novel that they went straight to the hearts of its readers. "Many persons who have read your book and with whom I have talked assure me that it is a clever trick on your part," wrote a reader, who like most of the correspondents was unknown to Rousseau. "I could not believe it; could a mistaken reading make an effect on me similar to the one I experienced? Again, Monsieur, did Julie exist? Is Saint-Preux still alive? What country on earth does he inhabit?" Readers identified so intensely with the characters that they imagined becoming them: "My heart, still full of everything it has felt, becomes the very heart of Julie." Although Julie inspired the strongest reactions, the other characters also penetrated to the readers' core: "I will even confess that in reading these letters I felt all the sentiments they express; the characters they describe came alive in me, and I was successively Julie, Wolmar, Bomston, often Claire but rarely Saint-Preux, except in the first part."[11]

Having communed with the characters, the readers felt compelled to communicate with Rousseau. Their letters to him continued the epistolary exchanges in the novel, as if they were a sequel to it and as if nothing separated fiction from reality: "Oh Rousseau! My worthy friend! My tender father! Allow my heart, which you have penetrated and filled with the most profound estime, with the most vital and solid attachment to you, to address you in this way." The need to make contact with Rousseau became for some a compulsion to confess to him: "Oh, my good father ... I will confess to you all my faults and all my feelings; I will open my heart to you, and you will make it worthy of your lessons." Perfect strangers told him the story of their lives, revealed sins they had never confided to anyone, and resolved to convert to a virtuous way of life. Rousseau's novel, one reader confessed, made him love virtue more than any sermon he had ever heard in a church. *La Nouvelle Héloïse*, wrote another, was a religious experience, provided not by a book but by Providence. Yet another confided that his "sweet tears" had helped him apprehend the moral order inherent in nature: "At every page my soul melted. Oh, how beautiful is virtue." Not everyone reacted so strongly, but the main tendency in the letters showed that Rousseau's readers responded exactly as he had directed in his preface. "I felt the purity of Julie's feelings pass into my heart," wrote a woman who preferred to remain anonymous. "Her good works have lifted up my soul. I sense that I am better ever since I read your novel, which, I hope, is not a novel."[12]

La Nouvelle Héloïse conquered readers everywhere. It was the biggest best seller of the century and went through seventy-two editions by 1800. Despite its scorn for the sophistication of *le monde*, it took Paris by storm. Booksellers could not satisfy the demand and fell back on renting it out, by the day and sometimes by the hour: 12 sous for sixty minutes with one volume. Yet it offended Parisian critics, above all Grimm, who denounced its literary imperfections obsessively, in page after page of his *Correspondance littéraire*.[13] Although he despised Rousseau personally and spoke for the Encyclopedists whom Rousseau had offended, his reaction signaled something deeper—a shift in the sensitivity of the reading public, which was now extending to the middle classes. Earlier novelists, notably Prévost and Marivaux, had stirred sentiments, but most maintained an ironic distance between themselves and their characters, and they directed readers' reactions by deploying wit. Voltaire manipulated Candide like a puppet, pulling strings to make him act in accordance with philosophic themes. The virtues Voltaire advocated were those of *le monde*—decency along with luxury, toleration accompanied by good taste, liberty allied with the arts and sciences, civilization understood as a complex system developed at great cost over centuries and perpetuated by a small elite. When confronted with injustice, as we shall see in the next chapter, Voltaire rose to the occasion. He attacked France's institutional abuses, while Rousseau reached into hearts and spread sentiments powerful enough, even within *le monde*, to turn his readers against the established order. Whatever their status, they shared the same emotions and sensed a common equality beneath the artifice of social conventions.

To the astonishment of Paris, Rousseau was driven out of France a year and a half after publishing *La Nouvelle Héloïse*. He had offended the church, the state, and the Parlement by his next work, *Émile* (1762), a treatise on education that came across to readers as a provocative religious and political tract. It produced a tremendous scandal, according to the *Mémoires secrets*, because it contained "very daring things against religion and the government."[14] Now a super celebrity who dared to put his name on the title page of such a book, Rousseau openly challenged the orthodox values of the Ancien Régime. While the first parts of the four-volume work concentrated on the psychological development of Émile, Rousseau's specimen of an ideal education, the last part contained a "Declaration of faith of a Savoy vicar," which read like an attack on Catholicism, and also a condensed version of *Du Contrat social*, which idealized an egalitarian democracy. The *Contrat social* appeared in Paris a month after *Émile*, but readers did not know what to make of it. The *Mémoires secrets* declared it "impenetrable for the common run of readers."[15] *Émile*, on the other hand, was "in the hands of everyone." "All Paris has read it."[16]

In June 1762, the Parlement condemned *Émile* to be burned and Rousseau to be arrested. With help from powerful supporters, he fled from France. Gossip then located him everywhere—in England, Holland, the Rhineland, Switzerland, and Prussia. More condemnations followed, notably in Geneva, which also burned his books. Having found shelter in the principality of Neuchâtel, Switzerland, Rousseau responded by renouncing his Genevan citizenship. He also addressed a defiant letter to the archbishop of Paris, Christophe de Beaumont, who had damned *Émile* in an episcopal writ (*mandement*). The polemics continued, accompanied by more attempts by Rousseau to escape from persecution and by his increasing madness. For the next decade, Parisians followed his fate from reports in gazettes, because everything he did became news.

Rousseau suffered as a victim of his celebrity, whereas Voltaire luxuriated in it. They died within two months of one another in 1778. A popular print, hawked in the streets of Paris, showed them entering the Elysian Fields together. They had become a pair, linked inseparably by their mutual hostility.

12

Voltaire Occupies the High Moral Ground

LIKE MOST PEOPLE in the eighteenth century, Parisians viewed public executions as entertainment. They occurred every few weeks before enormous crowds. While the common people packed into the Place de Grève (or other designated locations) and waited, standing for hours, gentlefolk rented window seats and balconies to enjoy a comfortable view. According to the usual script, the condemned man (sometimes a woman) would first be forced to make amends (*faire amende honorable*) by falling to his knees in front of a church, holding a candle, barefoot and clothed only in a long shirt. Then he would be paraded in a cart past gawking onlookers to the Place de Grève. If he chose to die a Christian death, he would be led to a priest nearby in the Hôtel de Ville, and he would confess his crime, clearing his soul for the afterlife. Accompanied by the priest, he would emerge before the crowd and climb the stairs of the scaffold. A court clerk would read out the verdict that condemned him. The public executioner, an imposing figure known as the *exécuteur de la haute justice* or *maître des hautes oeuvres*, would place the noose around his neck, remove the support on which he stood, and send him dangling in the air. He usually died within ten to twenty minutes, and his body would be left hanging long enough for the public to get a good view.[1] Until 1760, corpses from hangings at the Gibet de Montfaucon in northern

Paris (now the Place du Colonel-Fabien) remained exposed to the public for months while their flesh rotted off. Such "fourches patibulaires"—tall stone towers connected by wooden beams —proclaimed the power of the king to administer justice.

If the convicted criminal were a nobleman, he had the privilege of being beheaded, as the axe was considered less degrading than the rope. In the case of particularly heinous crimes, the prisoner would be bound to a Saint Andrew's cross, and while the crowd watched, the executioner would break his limbs and rupture his internal organs by blows with an iron bar. Then he would be attached to a wheel, face to the sky, for two hours or until he died of his wounds. Often the executioner would curtail his suffering by strangling him. Finally, his corpse would be thrown on a bonfire, and its ashes would be scattered to the wind.

Although accustomed to such violence, Parisians were appalled by an execution that occurred far away, in Toulouse, on March 10, 1762.[2] It conformed to the usual scenario, but when information spread about the circumstances behind it, it turned into the greatest "affair" of the century: *l'Affaire Calas*. After a two-week trial, the Parlement of Toulouse convicted an elderly, respectable Protestant merchant, Jean Calas, of murdering his eldest son. Despite evidence of suicide, the judges credited rumors that Calas had killed the young man to prevent him from converting to Catholicism. Calas maintained his innocence through two sessions of torture. He made amends in front of the cathedral and was led to the Place Saint-Georges in front of a crowd of 20,000. After attaching him to a cross of Saint Andrew, the executioner smashed his body, then bound it to a wheel for the required two hours. With his last breath, Calas beseeched God to forgive his judges. His corpse was then thrown on a brazier.

The first account of Calas's fate appeared in *Pièces originales concernant la mort des sieurs Calas, et le jugement rendu à Toulouse*, a twenty-two-page pamphlet published anonymously. It consisted of two letters. The first, ostensibly written by widow Calas, was addressed to an unnamed friend. In simple, straightforward language, it told how she had experienced the death of her oldest son, Marc-Antoine, several months earlier. A young man named François-Alexandre-Gaubert Lavaysse had stopped by the Calas house on his way from Bordeaux to the country residence of his parents, who were friends of the Calas. Mme Calas's husband, Jean Calas, a cloth merchant in Toulouse, invited Lavaysse to join them for supper before retiring for the night in the house of another friend. During the meal in the family's quarters above the shop and storeroom, they engaged in small talk. Marc-Antoine left, as he often did, during dessert, passing through the kitchen and down the stairs to the rooms below. The rest of the party—Mme Calas, her husband, their youngest son Pierre, and Lavaysse—withdrew to the sitting room and continued chatting for about two hours.

When Lavaysse was ready to leave, Pierre escorted him downstairs with a torch. Suddenly, the Calas couple heard a frantic scream. Jean Calas rushed down the stairs. His wife remained behind, frightened and confused. Finally, she, too, began to descend the stairs, but Lavaysse stopped her and told her to return to the sitting room, where they would inform her about what had happened. After another long wait, she summoned their servant: "Jeannette, go see what is going on down there. I don't know what it is, and I am very upset."[3] Jeannette did not return, and therefore Mme Calas summoned up the courage to venture downstairs. To her horror, she saw Marc-Antoine's body on the ground. She ran to get some strong drink to revive him, but a surgeon who had been summoned told her he was dead. Her husband bent over a counter, so overwhelmed with misery that she feared he, too, would die. They were told to retire upstairs. There, soon afterward, they were arrested. Widow Calas ended her account at that point, imploring God to damn her if she had deviated in the slightest from the simple truth.

The story was continued in the second letter, written to her by another son, Donat, from the town of Chatelaine near the Swiss border. He had been away on a trip for a business in Nîmes, where he was an apprentice, when he learned of Marc-Antoine's death, and he did not dare return because of the religious hatred aroused by the tragedy and directed at his family. Donat learned that a crowd had gathered at their house, shouting that Jean Calas had strangled his son in order to prevent him from converting to Catholicism on the following day. A rumor had spread that Protestants like the Calas met in secret assemblies to plot the murder of anyone who planned to abjure their faith. People said that Lavaysse had been sent by an assembly to execute the crime. Donat knew that his brother had no intention of abandoning Protestantism; and if he did, Donat added, their father would have permitted it. In fact, a fourth brother, Louis, had converted; and instead of attempting to stop him, their father had supported him with a pension. Jean Calas was a gentle, elderly man who respected the principles of Protestantism: "Tolerance, that happy, saintly and divine maxim we profess, does not permit us to condemn anyone.... We follow the urgings of our conscience without upsetting the conscience of others."[4] Yet Toulousains spread the word that Marc-Antoine planned to join a Catholic confraternity, the Pénitents blancs. While his family was held prisoner in the Hôtel de Ville, his body was buried in the cathedral of Saint-Étienne as if he were a Catholic. Four days later the Pénitents blancs staged an elaborate ceremony in their chapel, treating him as a martyr.

Footnotes filled out the story. One explained that Marc-Antoine had been depressed in his last weeks, and must have killed himself. His father had claimed at first that he was murdered in order to preserve the family's honor. The bodies of suicides were dragged, face down, through the streets, and they left a permanent stain on the family name. But when he and the other members of his family were accused of the murder, Jean Calas admitted that Marc-Antoine had hanged himself. The notion that the father had killed the son was absurd, not merely because Jean was known for his mildness but also because a weak, sixty-eight-year old man could hardly overcome a strong twenty-eight-year-old.

Despite his obvious innocence, the lack of any motive, and the absence of evidence other than rumor, Jean Calas was found guilty by magistrates from the Parlement of Toulouse and subjected to torture, yet he maintained his innocence to the end. Donat did not describe the end itself—the breaking of his father's body, its exposure on the wheel, and its destruction by fire—because he spared his mother's sensitivity. Instead, he poured out his sympathy for her suffering: "Your children dispersed, your oldest son dead before your eyes, your husband, my father, expiring under the cruelest torture, your dowry lost, indigence and opprobrium replacing respect and wealth—such is your state! ... You undergo all the horrors of poverty, illness, and even shame in order to implore the king's justice from the feet of his throne."[5]

The last remark revealed the purpose of the letter. Donat tried to persuade his mother to seek his father's rehabilitation by requesting the Crown to evoke the case and to reach a new verdict after studying records deposited with the Parlement of Toulouse. A third document published separately, *Mémoire de Donat Calas pour son père, sa mère et son frère,* added details about the family. They were quiet, law-abiding people, who paid their taxes and loved their king, Donat stressed. Marc-Antoine, however, had a dark, melancholic temperament. He had been reading about suicide in Plutarch and Seneca and took to heart Hamlet's famous soliloquy. His jacket, left carefully folded on the counter, indicated there had been no struggle, yet the crowd that gathered around their house on the fatal evening shouted out accusations of a violent murder perpetrated by the entire family. One fanatic yelled that Marc-Antoine had been strangled to prevent his abjuration. Another replied that if Protestant children attempted to convert, their parents were required by their religion to kill them. A third claimed that Marc-Antoine's conversion was due to take place on the following day. A fourth asserted that Lavaysse had been dispatched from a cell of Protestants to execute the murder. The rumors reached such a pitch that they provoked a local official, notorious for his hatred of Protestants, to arrest everyone in the family and their Catholic servant. "That's just like the common people," Donat concluded. He warned that the tragedy exposed a danger that threatened everyone everywhere: "This horrible incident concerns all religions and all nations. It is vital for the state to know where the most dangerous fanaticism comes from."[6]

A final document was provided by Donat's brother Pierre. After condemning their father, the Parlement of Toulouse had sentenced Pierre to exile and had dismissed the case against Mme Calas, Lavaysse, and the servant woman, Jeanne Viguière, though without exonerating them. (They had been accused of collaborating as a group in the murder; so, after convicting Jean Calas, the court could hardly declare them innocent.) Pierre had joined Donat in Chatelaine and supported his story with a firsthand account of the tragedy, published as *Déclaration de Pierre Calas.* He confirmed that there were no signs of a violent struggle. The hair on Marc-Antoine's body was not even ruffled. Although more than fifty persons had testified during the investigation, they came up only with hearsay, much of it extravagant, none of it convincing. The Parlement of Toulouse refused to release its records, yet they should be made available, not merely for the rehabilitation of Jean Calas but for the sake of humanity, because "fanaticism, that execrable plague" threatened all human beings.[7]

All four of these documents were printed like pamphlets. All circulated widely and were presented as firsthand testimonies, yet none were written by the persons who signed them. They were composed by Voltaire. The artful exposition of the narratives, the simple but eloquent language, the carefully inserted footnotes, the delineation of character, the sense of tragedy (Voltaire's *Tancrède* had recently been a great success at the Comédie française)—everything revealed the hand of the master. As Parisians and all of Europe soon learned, Voltaire had taken on the case and turned it into a protest movement, "the Calas Affair." He had met with Donat and Pierre and had gathered information from Veuve Calas, who was living in seclusion in Paris. He had contacted other informants and investigated every detail of the events. Then, convinced of the innocence of the Calas and seized with fury about the suffering inflicted on them, he organized a campaign not merely to clear their name but to fight against what he called "l'infâme"—that is, religious bigotry, intolerance, and injustice in general. From this time on, he began to end letters with a battle cry: "écrasez l'infâme," crush the infamous thing.

Although Voltaire's fame had spread throughout Europe, few Parisians knew at first that he was masterminding the movement to rehabilitate Calas. While stoking public opinion with these preliminary pamphlets, Voltaire worked behind the scenes. He wrote letter after letter, aiming them at persons located at strategic positions in the power system, from salon ladies to courtiers and ministers, even Choiseul and Mme de Pompadour. Voltaire was no democrat. He believed in Enlightenment from the top down and therefore labored tirelessly to pull strings that would get the case, with the supporting documentation, transferred from the Parlement of Toulouse to the Council of the King.

Many of Voltaire's letters were copied and circulated in Paris, then reproduced by gazetteers and literary correspondents like Grimm. In one of the first, written to d'Alembert on March 29, 1762, Voltaire condensed the events into a few searing sentences:

The city of Toulouse, more foolish and fanatical than Geneva, took this hanged young man to be a martyr. No one thought to inquire whether he had hanged himself, as seems very likely. They buried him with pomp in the cathedral; some magistrates from the parlement, bare-footed, attended the ceremony. They invoked the new saint, and then the criminal court by a vote of eight to five had the father broken on the wheel. This judgment was all the more Christian in that there was no evidence whatsoever against their victim. He was a good bourgeois, a good father to his family of five children, including the one who was hanged. He wept for his son while dying; he maintained his innocence under the blows of the iron bar; he summoned the parlement to appear before the justice of God.[8]

To Parisians, the horrors of the religious wars had receded into the distant past, but memories remained vivid in Languedoc, where most of France's Huguenots (Calvinists) were located. After the revocation of the Edict of Nantes in 1685, they had no civil rights. Their marriages were not recognized; their children were considered bastards; they could not will and inherit property; and they were excluded from professions such as the law. In practice, their marriages were often validated by a superficial ceremony in a Catholic church, but they could not attend services of their own. Some worshipped secretly in remote, outdoor locations known as the "desert." It was a capital crime to be a pastor, and several pastors, some on underground missions from Switzerland, had been captured and hanged in the 1740s and 1750s. Less than three weeks before executing Calas, the Parlement of Toulouse had condemned a pastor, François Rochette, for preaching in the "desert," and it also passed a death sentence against three Huguenot brothers for attempting to rescue him. While he was hanged, they were beheaded, according to their privilege as members of the nobility.

A month earlier, a court in Mazamet, fifty-six miles from Toulouse, issued a warrant for the arrest of the family of Elisabeth Sirven, whose body had been found at the bottom of a well. Despite the likelihood that, like Marc-Antoine Calas, she had committed suicide (she was known to be insane), the magistrates suspected another case of a Protestant family murder, and her parents fled to Switzerland. While these three cases—Rochette, Sirven, and Calas—attracted enormous attention, the people of Toulouse were preparing the bicentenary of "la Délivrance," a ceremony to celebrate the massacre of 4,000 Huguenots on May 17, 1562. Many of them hoped that Calas would be executed on the same day.

In trying to rehabilitate Calas, therefore, Voltaire was attempting to turn back a wave of persecution. He also had to overcome formidable legal obstacles in order to get the case evoked to the king's council and reversed. With help from powerful allies, he recruited three of the best lawyers in Paris: Pierre Mariette, Alexandre Jérôme Loyseau de Mauléon, and Jean Baptiste Jacques Elie de Beaumont.

They wrote lengthy judicial memoirs, which were printed and reprinted in numbers large enough to reach a broad public. Each memoir discussed a different aspect of the case, relating it to rules of evidence going back to France's basic criminal ordinance of 1670 and judicial decrees since the reign of Charlemagne.

Yet they did not read like dry legal tracts. The lawyers wrote vivid accounts of the events, adhering closely to the narrative in Voltaire's pamphlets. Mariette supplied details about all the evidence, or lack of it, such as the state of the corpse, which had no bruises or other signs of a violent struggle. Loyseau and Beaumont began by describing the main characters—Calas, the honest bourgeois; Mme Calas, the loving mother, overwhelmed by suffering; Marc-Antoine, the tormented, suicidal son. They enlivened the story with snatches of dialogue, and emphasized episodes that illustrated the fanaticism of Calas's persecutors—notably the service in the chapel of the Pénitents blancs, which featured a skeleton loaned by a surgeon that was exposed on a catafalque holding a pen supposedly used to renounce Protestantism. All three lawyers insisted that the case against Jean Calas consisted only of unsubstantial and contradictory rumors, which originated among the lowest elements of the common people ("the dregs of the people," "the vilest populace") and revealed a climate of fierce bigotry.[9]

The memoirs created an enormous stir in Paris. Grimm and others noted that Loyseau's was especially moving because it broke with the conventional style of legal briefs and could be read like a novel, "very animated, very searing."[10] All of the memoirs were reprinted with Voltaire's original pamphlets in several anthologies such as *Recueil de différentes pièces sur l'affaire malheureuse de la famille des Calas*, which kept the case before the public. Many poems circulated, several of them in print.[11] Louis de Carmontelle did a drawing of Mme Calas and her daughters listening to her son Pierre read the memoir by Elie de Beaumont. After being reproduced as an engraving, it was sold in large numbers to raise money for the family. An etching by Daniel Nikolaus Chodowiecki showed Calas bidding farewell to his family and carried a caption, "I dread God . . . and have no other fear."

None of this material mentioned Voltaire. His notorious irreligion, as he understood better than anyone, could undercut the main purpose of his campaign—to get the sentence of the Parlement of Toulouse revoked and to have Calas declared innocent by a commission of the king's council (Tribunal des requêtes). The judicial procedure was a delicate affair that required a great deal of time and effort, especially as the Toulouse magistrates tried to withold their records. Although the case was formally evoked in June 1764, the Tribunal did not announce its decision until March 9, 1765. It fully rehabilitated Calas and declared his alleged accomplices to be innocent. In lieu of reparations, the king awarded the family a pension of 36,000 L.

By then, Voltaire could appear openly as the defender of Calas, and he brought the campaign to a close with a major work, *Traité sur la tolérance*, which fixed the place of the affair in the public imagination, not merely as the reversal of an injustice suffered by Calas but as the vindication of a general principle: tolerance. The *Traité* had been printed in Geneva in April 1763, but Voltaire held it back in order to avoid upsetting the negotiations for Calas's rehabilitation.

He began by telling Calas's story once again, this time in his own voice— direct, powerful, and laced with irony. The judicial murder of Calas, he argued, was but the latest tragedy in the suffering inflicted on humanity by religious fanaticism. A trail of atrocities led back to the religious wars of the sixteenth century and stretched all the way to antiquity. Drawing on the stock of esoteric information he had acquired in preparing his historical works, especially the *Essai sur les moeurs*, Voltaire recounted horror after horror in short chapters, which took up general questions, such as, "Is tolerance dangerous?" and "Is intolerance necessary?" By slaughtering subjects who did not accept the established religion, he argued, rulers had decimated their kingdoms. Yet the experience of the Greeks, Romans, Turks, Chinese, and Japanese proved that countries flourished when they permitted freedom of thought. Superstition continued to prevail, especially in Catholic Europe, where, for example, some priests still attempted to save harvests by excommunicating insects who ate grain. But the advance of philosophy was leading Europeans to abandon their absurd beliefs. "If someone took it upon himself today to be a *carpocratien*, or *eutychéen*, or *monothélite*, *monophysite*, *nestorien*, *manichéen*, etc., what would happen? He would be laughed at, like a man dressed in an outmoded style with a ruff and a doublet."[12]

By piling up esoteric references to doctrinal absurdities, Voltaire had undermined Christianity in his earlier works and in the *Dictionnaire philosophique*, published at about the same time as the *Traité sur la tolérance*. But the *Traité* struck a different note. While ridiculing Catholic practices—and reminding readers of the convulsionaries, the refusal of sacraments, and the expulsion of the Jesuits—Voltaire affirmed a spiritual commitment of his own, which had some affinity with the spirituality of Rousseau: "We must look upon all men as our brothers."[13] He ended the book with a prayer addressed to a God who presided over all creation, and he prayed with passion:

> Thou did not give us hearts to hate each other and hands for us to slit our throats. Let us help one another to mutually bear the burden of a painful, fleeting life. . . . May all men remember they are brothers! May they hold in horror tyranny exerted over souls, just as they feel loathing for brigandage that ravishes by force the fruit of labor and peaceful industry![14]

With the *Traité sur la tolérance*, Voltaire went beyond the disabused libertinism of his early works. He now occupied the high moral ground. As Grimm observed, "He dared to defend humanity and the cause of every citizen."[15] The *Traité* did not make as big a splash as the *Dictionnaire philosophique*, which was a *succès de scandale*, especially after the Parlement condemned it to be burned on March 19, 1765. But the *Traité* culminated Voltaire's campaign to transform an affair into a cause. For Parisians, it defined the larger meaning of a sequence of events that they had followed with enormous interest and that they celebrated as a victory when Calas was finally rehabilitated on March 9, 1765.[16] Even the common people, including those who did not read books, applauded Voltaire as "l'homme aux Calas."[17]

Voltaire's renown as a champion of the innocent and oppressed grew as he took on new causes, especially two, which also developed into full-scale affairs. After the Sirven family fled to Switzerland, they were condemned in absentia—the father to be broken on the wheel, the mother to be hanged, and the two other daughters to banishment. Voltaire intervened by pamphleteering and protests, and in November 1771 the family was exonerated by the very Parlement of Toulouse that had sentenceced Calas to death.

François-Jean, Chevalier de la Barre, was convicted of blasphemy and sacrilege in 1765. He had failed to take off his hat when a religious procession with the Eucharist passed by in a street in Abbeville, and according to a rumor, he and other feckless young men had desecrated a cross. When his bedroom was searched, the police found a copy of the *Dictionnaire philosophique*. He was condemned to have his tongue cut out, to be beheaded, and to have his body burned on a bonfire with the *Dictionnaire philosophigue* attached to it. Despite his protests, Voltaire could not save la Barre, who was spared only the amputation of his tongue. But those two affairs on top of the Calas case fired public indignation about religious persecution and miscarriages of justice.

Anyone inclined to dismiss *philosophie* as a game of scoring points in abstruse arguments now was faced with something formidable. Enlightenment could not be dismissed as fashionable freethinking. It meant commitment to a cause, opposition to injustice, engagement in a struggle to improve the lot of humanity; and it had enough moral force in the view of its partisans to displace the authority of the church on ethical issues.

13

Recycling Royal Mistresses

IN PARISIANS' IMAGINATIONS, there was nothing like peering into the *petits appartements* of Versailles, the private rooms where Louis XV relaxed with his mistresses and intimates—or, better yet, the Parc-aux-Cerfs, an area where he kept nubile women for one-night stands. Ordinary subjects never gained admission to such places, of course. They conjured them up from gossip and clandestine literature. The police monitored talk about royal love life and anything else that might sound seditious, but their spies mainly came up with trivia.[1] There was nothing unusual about extramarital sex in Versailles. Everyone expected kings to have mistresses, and everyone's favorite king, Henri IV, was admired for his womanizing. "Maîtresse en titre" was a title of respect in the court. Yet the rumormongering became increasingly nasty in the mid-century years, and by the time of the death of Mme de Pompadour on April 15, 1764, it expressed an attitude of hostility and contempt.

Versailles itself generated most of the rumors. Courtiers constantly snatched up information that could be used in the struggle to advance in favor or to block the rise of a rival, just as they had done under Louis XIV. When their talk fed "public noises" in Paris, however, it could be used as a political weapon. As we have seen, Maurepas was toppled by gossip reworked in songs coupled with court intrigue. And when the talk of the town was transformed into books, it could become an affair of state, verging on lèse-majesté.

An early example of this process shows how Louis XV's relations with his mistresses began to turn into a legend.[2] The story first broke into print as a novel in the form of a fairy tale written by Marie Madeleine Bonafon, a chambermaid to the Princesse de Montauban. It was a *roman à clé* published under the title *Tanastès* in 1745, and manuscript keys made it possible to identify the persons disguised by fantasy names. Tanastès (Louis XV), the king of the Zarimois (French), was a Jekyll-Hyde type. In his evil incarnation, he ruled despotically and took up three mistresses, one after the other. The third accompanied him to the front during a war, but her ambition led to a crisis and her death. The king then lacked an outlet for his lust, and the queen, who had fallen under the spell of power-hungry priests, refused to have sex with him. Fortunately, the king's better self then repossessed his spirit. At a masked ball to celebrate the wedding of the dauphin, he fell in love with a "grâce" (Pompadour), who became his fourth mistress, and the story ended with the hope—accompanied, however, by serious doubts—that she would help him reign happily ever after.

As the key revealed and as we saw in chapter 2, the first three mistresses were sisters, the daughters of the Marquis de Nesle. The third sister, the Duchesse de Châteauroux (Ardentine in the novel), did indeed follow Louis XV to the front during the War of the Austrian Succession. He fell seriously ill at Metz in August 1744, to the consternation of his subjects. The bishop of Soissons (Amariel in the novel) took charge of his confession, administered extreme unction and presided over his public recantation of adultery, while Mme de Châteauroux retreated to Paris. After recovering and despite the adulation that swept over the French and earned him the title of "the well loved," Louis had second thoughts. He agreed to restore Mme de Châteauroux to a position of dignity in Versailles, but she had contracted a fatal illness and died before she could reappear in court. Rumors then circulated about the queen's excessive religiosity and refusal to take Louis into her bed. He encountered Jeanne Antoinette Poisson, whom he later made Duchesse de Pompadour, on several occasions, including the ball to celebrate the dauphin's wedding. On September 14, 1745, she was formally presented to the court and became *maîtresse en titre*.

It made a great story: the king's first experience with mistresses, his brush with death, the tragic ending of Mme de Châteauroux, and the triumph of Mme de Pompadour. It also had shock value because some construed sex with sisters as incest. But it reached Parisians only in dribs and drabs. Mlle Bonafon brought it all together in a coherent narrative, and, even worse in the eyes of the authorities, she published it as a book. On August 27, 1745, she disappeared into the Bastille. In her interrogation, conducted by the lieutenant general of police, Claude Henri Feydeau de Marville, she said that she had adapted the story from gossip in Versailles. Marville did not believe her. How, he asked, could a servant, a female domestic servant, write a novel? She replied that she had written a great deal—the beginning of a second novel, a play, and many poems, though they had not been published. When interrogated about how she had managed to publish *Tanastès*, she said she had drawn on a network of fellow servants. A valet to the subgoverness of the dauphin arranged for the printing with a bookseller in Versailles (the palace was honeycombed with bookshops, and courtiers were avid customers of forbidden books), and the bookseller had it printed by a Widow Ferrand in Rouen. The printed copies were delivered to a secret entrepôt in Versailles, smuggled into Paris by sympathetic coachmen, stored by a concierge in the town house of a marquis, and distributed by the concierge to peddlers. Mlle Bonafon received two hundred copies as her share of the operation. She was kept in the Bastille for fourteen and a half months. Then her health deteriorated so badly that she nearly died and was transferred to a convent of Bernardines in Moulin, where she remained imprisoned for twelve years.

Although Mlle Bonafon excused herself by saying that she had merely drawn on rumors in the court, she admitted that her book had produced a strong reaction ("grand bruit") in the public. Her case illustrates the way information was amplified under the Ancien Régime—from talk to print and back to talk again—and it shows that the diffusion process involved intermediaries both at the top and near the bottom of the social order.

Other works followed the same pattern, spreading tales of royal mistresses to a large public. Two of them were also *romans à clé*. Like *Tanastès*, they required reading of a special kind, as a process of deciphering and puzzle solving. Many eighteenth-century readers were familiar with this approach to texts, because they solved puzzles regularly while going through the *logogriphes*, *énigmes*, and *bouts rimés* in literary periodicals like the *Mercure de France*. They also knew how to decode allusions in works by seventeenth-century authors like La Fontaine and Bussy-Rabutin. Yet the puzzles could be difficult, as one can tell from margin notes, which sometimes contained mistakes, and from the keys, which were often sold separately and occasionally gave contradictory answers.

Mémoires secrets pour servir à l'histoire de Perse (1745), possibly by Antoine Pecquet, an official in the ministry of foreign affairs, offered readers a long, complex history of Europe since 1715. It went through at least six editions before 1769, and its keys, which can be consulted in six copies from the Bibliothèque de l'Arsenal and the Bibliothèque municipale de Paris, varied greatly. One identifies 168 characters, and a dozen more identifications, written in what appears to be an eighteenth-century hand, are scattered through the margins of the text. Another printed key covers 208 characters, including 25 added by hand. Readers also had to decode place names. Some were easy: Persia was obviously France, and Japan was England. But what was Kabul? (Hanover) And Lahore? (Saxony). A guessing game about persons imposed on a geographical brain teaser challenged the capacity of the sharpest readers. But those who puzzled their way through the text could enjoy a rich view of the geopolitical environment. And even unsophisticated readers could take the measure of Louis XV as Cha-Sephi. He appeared as handsome and good-natured, but ineffectual, indecisive, allergic to work, given over to hunting and women, and incapable of ruling a kingdom—"in a word, a prince who lacked the soul essential for a king."[3]

Les Amours de Zéokinizul, roi des Kofirans (1746), probably written by Claude Prosper Jolyot de Crébillon, known as Crebillon fils, or by Laurent Angliviel de La Beaumelle, sets the same story in Africa and eliminates the diplomacy in order to concentrate on the erotic intrigues. It requires the reader to decode anagrams, most of them obvious: the Kofirans are the Français; Zéokinizul is Louis Quinze; and Mme de Pompadour has the amusing name of Vorompdap. It, too, attracted many readers and went through at least eight editions before 1789. Texts from four of the editions in the Bibliothèque nationale de France contain three different keys. One gives the solution to forty-four anagrams, another to fifty-eight, and a third to sixty-five. They disagree in places, and eighteenth-century readers occasionally rejected them, because marginal notes provide additions and corrections to the keys bound with the texts. One can imagine Parisian wits treating the book as a salon game or café contest, reading it aloud and laughing or applauding with each identification of a personage. It is all rather light-hearted, funny, bawdy, fast-paced, and told with considerable skill in the manner of Crébillon's racy novels, *Le Sofa* and *L'Ecumoire*. (Krinelbol, the name of the putative author that appears on the title page, is an anagram of Crébillon, but it could have served as camouflage for someone else.) Instead of high politics, the public got low intrigue, most of it directed by the clergy and turning on the king's libido. But this time the story carries an explicitly political message. The kingdom of the Kofirans has succumbed to the evil influence of imams, fakirs, and mullahs; and the king, stupid, ineffectual, and a victim of his passions, has turned into a tyrant: "The government, which had formerly been monarchical, became completely despotic."[4]

The public that deciphered *romans à clé* was relatively small. But the other genre that did most damage to the monarch and his mistresses was song, and songs, as explained in chapter 3, reached everyone in Paris. The songs that satirized Mme de Pompadour circulated in such number that, by way of a pun on her maiden name, Poisson (Fish), they became known as Poissonnades. Parisians considered them a genre, similar to the Mazarinades that accompanied the uprising of the Fronde in 1648–1652, although the Poissonnades did not call for a revolt. They mainly deplored the decadence of the court. Many originated from courtiers, yet they circulated widely among the common people of Paris, and, like the *romans à clé*, they made Louis XV look clueless and incompetent, "he who doesn't have a care." In mocking Mme de Pompadour, they struck a note of aristocratic haughtiness because she was the first *maîtresse en titre* to come from the bourgeoisie:

Si la cour se ravale,	*If the court degrades itself,*
Pourquoi s'étonne-t-on,	*Why should we be surprised:*
N'est-ce pas de la Halle	*Isn't it from the market*
Que nous vient le poisson?[5]	*That we get fish?*

Charles Collé, a gifted poet, noted in his journal that many Poissonnades were composed by courtiers because "the hand of the artist is not in them." He found their sentiments nasty and their versification faulty, as, for example:

Une petite bourgeoise,	*A little bourgeoise,*
Elevée à la grivoise,	*Raised indecently,*
Mesurant tout à sa toise,	*Judges everything by her own measure,*
Fait de la cour un taudis.	*Turns the court into a slum.*
Le roi, malgré son scrupule,	*The king, despite his scruples,*
Pour elle froidement brûle;	*Feebly burns for her,*
Cette flamme ridicule,	*And this ridiculous flame*
Excite dans tout Paris, ris, ris.	*Makes all Paris laugh, laugh, laugh.*

Whatever their origin, their destination was "all Paris," and Paris replied defiantly:

Il faut sans relâche	*We must without respite*
Faire des chansons;	*Make up songs.*
Plus Poisson s'en fâche,	*The more Poisson gets angry,*
Plus nous chanterons.[6]	*The more we will sing.*

After her installation as *maîtresse en titre* in Versailles, Mme de Pompadour occupied a central place in the media of Paris, not only by means of songs but also through prints, pamphlets, and especially rumor. Their cumulative effect can be followed through Barbier's journal and the *Mémoires secrets*. At first Mme de Pompadour fascinated the public from reports about her talent as an actress, dancer, and singer. Parisians learned that she staged plays and comic operas for the king and a small group of favorites in the palace. They grew into polished performances with elaborate costumes and scenery. Thanks to an excellent musical education and a pleasant, though thin singing voice, Mme de Pompadour was said to hold her own with professionals recruited from the Opéra and Comédie italienne. Louis was reputed to be "melancholic" and easily bored.[7] Therefore, Mme de Pompadour struggled hard to kept him diverted. In addition to the comic operas and plays, she organized all sorts of parties in the petits appartements and vacation-like sojourns in different royal châteaux, where he could enjoy changes of scenery and indulge his passion for hunting.

As to his passion for women, rumors constantly raised the possibility that Mme de Pompadour would be supplanted by another beauty sponsored by some enemy faction in the court. For a while, the Comtesse de Choiseul-Romanet was said to be a serious threat because she was aristocratic and well connected, but she overplayed her hand and was dismissed from the court in 1752, owing to the intervention of the Comte de Stainville, who would later become the Duc de Choiseul and Mme de Pompadour's most powerful ally in the government. There was also talk that the king, a sincere Catholic, would repent, confess, and receive absolution so that he could take communion. Easter week was deemed to be a dangerous time, because the king's confessors worked on his sense of sin, while his mistress withdrew into the background. Yet he could not bring himself to renounce adultery, even after he stopped sleeping with Mme de Pompadour, sometime in 1752, according to the gossip that reached Paris. By then, she reputedly tightened her hold on him by managing his schedule, filling it with diversions, and even encouraging him to have flings with beauties too young and guileless to threaten her position as *maîtresse en titre*.

One of the first, according to the rumors, was a pretty, plebeian girl, fifteen or sixteen years old, who may have been planted in his path in the gardens of the château de Choisy. Louis kept her for a while in a small house in the district of Versailles known as the Parc-aux-Cerfs. He soon moved on to others, one rumored to be only twelve. According to "stories" that made the rounds in Paris, a nude in a painting (later said to be an odalisque by Boucher, although the attribution is disputed) caught his eye. He asked to see the original, and soon installed her in what Parisians called his "harem." She turned out to be Louise O'Murphy, the daughter of an Irish shoemaker in Paris. To Parisians, who could not pronounce her name, she was "la petite Morphise." Gossips claimed that she would soon displace Mme de Pompadour, but they eventually learned that she had given birth to a baby girl, was married off with a dowry of 200,000 L., and disappeared into the provinces. Louis never recognized his bastards. He had their mothers provided with husbands and pensions, and maintained Mme de Pompadour as *maîtresse en titre*. Despite tales of other dalliances, which constantly leaked from Versailles, Parisians came around to the view that the official mistress had an unbreakable hold on the king's affections and even got on well with the queen, who agreed to have her appointed as a "dame du Palais de la Reine."[8]

Whatever they made of Louis's sex life—reactions varied from amusement to indignation—Parisians deplored its cost. They especially resented the extravagances showered on Mme de Pompadour—jewels, pensions, and property, beginning with the marquisat de Pompadour and continuing through the marquisat de Crécy-en-Brie and the marquisat de Ménars to the Elysée Palace and the exquisite Château de Bellevue.[9] Worse still, in the eyes of many, was her accumulation of political power. While accepting the inevitability of royal mistresses, Parisians thought the intrigues should be contained within the *petits appartements*. Soon they were exchanging horrified remarks about Mme de Pompadour's ability to make and unmake ministers. She was said to have engineered the downfall of Philibert Orry as controller general of finances and his replacement by Machault. Then, by ousting Maurepas, she began to control all appointments. She reportedly had François-Joachim de Pierre de Bernis made foreign minister and arranged for the Prince de Soubise to command France's largest army during the Seven Years' War. After the humiliating defeat of Soubise at Rossbach, the dauphine reportedly told Mme de Pompadour that she should limit herself to appointing the farmers general of taxes rather than generals of the army.[10] "It is said that the ministers report to her about all business before they come up in the Council," noted Barbier. "She is involved in military questions and all state affairs."[11] As she was known to be an enemy of the king's Jesuit confessor, the public attributed the dissolution of the Jesuits in large part to her influence. A popular epigram ended, "And Pompadour will get rid of the Jesuits"; and peddlers hawked a print that showed her and Choiseul shooting down a flock of Jesuits while in the background magistrates from the Parlement dug ditches for their burial.[12]

The only aspect of Pompadour's rule that pleased some in the public, or at least some of the gazetteers, was her role as a patroness of the arts and an ally of the *philosophes*. She had met many men of letters in Parisian salons during her youth and invited a select group including Montesquieu and Voltaire to a salon of her own during her early married life at Etiolles.

After her installation in Versailles, she made Quesnay, the leading physiocrat, her doctor, and she supported the *Encyclopédie*, which can be seen displayed clearly in a portrait of her by Maurice Quentin Delatour. When she died on April 15, 1764, the *Mémoires secrets* paid tribute to her as a "femme philosophe": "The striking protection with which she honored letters, the taste she had for the arts, prevent one from letting such a sad event go by in silence."[13]

Despite that note of sympathy, Parisians did not shed tears over the death of Mme de Pompadour. Nor did her disappearance put an end to Louis XV's run of mistresses. To Parisians, it merely marked a point in a downward trajectory, which led from the de Nesle sisters, who were courtiers, to Mme du Barry, who was a courtesan—and whom we shall meet in the following chapters.

PART THREE

The
Turning Point in Politics,
1770–1775

14

Enter Marie-Antoinette,
Exit Choiseul

W HAT TO MAKE OF Marie-Antoinette? Parisians had every
reason to be suspicious of her in April 1770, when she set
out for Versailles after having been married to the dauphin
by proxy in Vienna. To them she was *l'Autrichienne*—that is, a princess
from enemy territory who was destined to sit beside the future Louis XVI
on the throne of France. To be sure, the Habsburgs now were allies, having fought, though ineffectually, on France's side during the Seven Years'
War. But they had threatened to dominate Europe since the sixteenth century, when for a while they seemed capable of overwhelming France. The
long-term memory of that threat had probably dimmed among ordinary
Parisians, even though they had expressed no enthusiasm for the Austrian
alliance, which took them by surprise during the "diplomatic revolution"
of 1756, when France and England switched partners (France aligned
itself with the Habsburg monarchy while England replaced France as an
ally of Prussia.) In fact, only a few members of the public—mainly "les
politiques"—paid close attention to diplomacy. Aside from their inbred,
anti-Austrian sentiment, most people wanted above all to know what the
dauphine looked like. Louis XV expressed the general curiosity when,
according to some reports, he asked an emissary who had greeted her at
the French border, "Does she have much bosom?"[1]

The looks of royal personages fascinated their subjects, who studied their profiles on coins and their features in engravings sold in the streets. The first descriptions of Marie-Antoinette to reach Parisians were favorable. Only fourteen years old, she still had a girlish figure and was pleasantly attractive: dark blond hair, a dazzling white complexion, an oval face, vivacious blue eyes, a slightly pointed nose, and a small mouth, somewhat spoiled by a thick lower lip and a protruding jaw, typical of the Habsburgs.[2] Parisians took great interest in preparations for the celebration of her marriage with the dauphin, which would give the monarchy an occasion to exhibit its magnificence and to demonstrate largesse by providing the common people with free food, drink, and entertainment. For the royal aficionados among the public, every detail commanded attention, and plenty of information was available, not only from foreign journals like the *Gazette de Leyde* but also from the official *Gazette de France*, which specialized in court ceremony. Crowds came to marvel at the two magnificent carriages that the Duc de Choiseul had had constructed to convey the dauphine and her ladies in waiting from Vienna. Large yet light and flexible, their decorations—gold figures embroidered on a velvet background—dazzled everyone who inspected them in the shop of Francien, a master saddler, before they were shipped off to Austria.[3]

Thanks to extensive coverage in the journals, Parisians were able to follow the progress of Marie-Antoinette and her escort across Europe. On May 7 she arrived in Strasbourg, where she was joined by a large party of French dignitaries, including the Comtesse de Noailles, her *dame d'honneur*, a strict, elderly veteran of Versailles, who was appointed to instruct her in the etiquette of the French court. After a magnificent reception, the convoy of carriages continued to Nancy and more festivities. On May 14 at the Pont de Berne in the forest outside Compiègne, the dauphine was greeted by Louis XV and the dauphin. She knelt at the king's feet; he embraced her and presented her to the dauphin, who also gave her a formal embrace; and they escorted her to the château of Compiègne, where she dined with the princes of the royal blood (*princes du sang*). On the next day, the royal family and its entourage proceeded to the château de la Muette, where the dauphine met more courtiers and attended a banquet, bedecked in diamonds, which soon set the fashion for the finest taste in jewelry.

After that, Marie-Antoinette disappeared into Versailles. Few Parisians got a glimpse of her before her formal "entrée" into the city three years later, on June 8, 1773. They learned from the gazettes that although she had officially become the dauphin's wife at the proxy wedding, a marriage ceremony took place in the chapel of Versailles on May 16. It was followed by a magnificent banquet ("grand couvert") and the ritual bedding. The dauphin received his nightgown from the king; the dauphine received hers from the Duchesse de Chartres; and the couple slept together for the first time. Everyone hoped they would soon produce an heir to the throne, but Parisians were mainly interested in the festivities, spread out over nine days, to celebrate the marriage. Streets were adorned with lanterns, façades of houses illuminated, shops closed, masses celebrated, banquets organized, debtors released from prison, and all sorts of spectacles commissioned. (In a performance of Racine's *Athalie*, five hundred actors dashed across the stage during the last act.) The elite attended balls while the common people danced in the streets to music provided by bands in several neighborhoods. The revelers helped themselves to free wine, bread, and sausages. And the entire city was invited to the final event: fireworks, expected to be the grandest ever, set off from the new Place Louis XV.

Fireworks, as already mentioned, had developed into a particular art, perfected by firemasters ("artificiers"), in the eighteenth century. Although they included plenty of rockets, the "spectacles pyriques" took place primarily at ground level on structures designed to represent a motif such as a fortress or a mountain range. As the *Encyclopédie* explained, "It is necessary to paint."[4] Fiery pinwheels, cascades, and fountains lit up the scenery and dazzled the public, although, owing to the limitations of eighteenth-century chemistry, they lacked the vivid colors of fireworks today. The most famous masters spent months preparing a show, which went through a sequence of scenes, like a play. After the dauphine's wedding, two rival masters, Jean-Baptiste Torré in Versailles and Petronio Ruggieri in Paris, competed to produce performances that would bring the celebrations to a climax.[5] Torré's spectacle, which included 20,000 rockets and 3,000 firepots, went off so well in Versailles on May 19 that the king made him a knight in the Ordre de Saint Michel. Ruggieri planned to outdo him on May 30 with a "temple de l'hymen," 130 feet high, on the Place Louis XV. The temple's pediment, supported by six Corinthian columns, bore the arms of France and the Holy Roman Empire and the initials of the dauphin and dauphine. Its façade contained all sorts of decorations, which were to be set on fire at intervals throughout the carefully choreographed scenes. Behind the temple stood a bastion packed with rockets, including a spectacular "bouquet" timed to explode during the grand finale. By 9 o'clock in the evening, an enormous crowd had gathered. It included people from all sectors of the population, from beggars and pickpockets to aristocrats who watched the spectacle from the comfort of their carriages.

When the first rockets soared into the sky, one misfired. It landed on the "bouquet," which immediately burst into flame, spreading fire through the entire edifice, which exploded and collapsed. The spectacle was ruined as soon as it began.

As the disappointed crowd began to squeeze through the few available exits, some people pushed from the back. Those in front tripped into a gully that had been left unfilled. The mass in the middle stampeded, trampling over bodies and pushing more victims underfoot. Some carriage drivers tried to force their way through the chaos and were cut down by rioters armed with swords who also eviscerated their horses. The Gardes Françaises, undermanned and badly commanded (their commandant spent the evening playing cards), failed to restore order. In the end, 132 bodies were laid out in the nearby rue Royale. A police bulletin said the total killed was 367. Siméon-Prosper Hardy, the bookseller whose diary is the richest source of information about Parisian life at this time, thought that the number came to more than 500, as many died later of injuries. Manuscript notes circulated, giving a breakdown of the fatalities, which in one version included 22 "distinguished persons," 155 "bourgeois," 424 "little people," and 80 drowned, making 682 in all. A subsequent bulletin put the total at 1,200; Grimm made it 1,000; and the *Gazette de Leyde* reported that more than 3,000 had been killed or seriously injured. But those figures were shown to be exaggerated, and later estimates reduced the fatalities to the 132 from the rue Royale, who were buried in the churchyard of Magdaleine de la Ville-l'Evêque soon after the disaster, and 4 others, none of them drowned. Whatever the toll, Parisians took the tragedy as "one of those events that make a profound impression," as the Parisian correspondent of the *Gazette de Leyde* commented. "It occupies everyone's mind."[6] They blamed the authorities for having failed to take protective measures and commented bitterly on a marriage that had turned into a massacre. No one held the dauphin and dauphine responsible, but their wedding was a state occasion that remained stigmatized by tragedy. Hardy said that nothing comparable had ever happened: "Such a cruel event plunges everyone into consternation, and turns a day of joy into a day of mourning."[7]

Marie-Antoinette was one of the many factors that made the Duc de Choiseul the dominant force in the government. He first recognised her potential in 1757, when he arrived in Vienna as the French ambassador and was looking for ways to strengthen the new French-Austrian alliance. A marriage between a Habsburg archduchess and the dauphin would do wonders, he imagined, and he continued to pursue this idea after he became French foreign minister in 1758, although at that time Marie-Antoinette was only three years old. When the marriage took place in 1770, it consolidated Choiseul's power as the champion of the alliance, which had become the keystone of his foreign policy. Not that Marie-Antoinette, then a teenager, interfered in politics. She spent the last six months of 1770 learning her way around the court under the severe tutelage of the Comtesse de Noailles, and she was too much of a free spirit to accept the discipline—or at least that was the message that reached Parisians from gossips in Versailles. The underground press diffused a poem that mocked Madame de Noailles as an advocate of courtly insincerity and celebrated the dauphine for her naturalness:

Laissez-lui la sincérité;	*Let her keep her sincerity;*
En est-il un qui ne s'écrie:	*There is no one who does not say:*
Cette dauphine, en verité	*This dauphine, in truth,*
Nous l'aimons tous à la folie![8]	*We all love her madly!*

Attractive as it was to many Parisians, the picture of a naïve and natural Marie-Antoinette did not blend easily into reports about the power struggles in Versailles. The more astute observers—*les politiques*—assumed that the dauphine could not avoid entanglement in court politics and that she was coached about how to play her part by the shrewd Austrian ambassador, Florimond-Claude de Mercy-Argenteau, an advocate of the French-Austrian alliance. She was cast as a natural ally of Choiseul, who with his cousin César Gabriel de Choiseul, Duc de Praslin, occupied the ministries of foreign affairs, war, and the navy. As they also enjoyed the support of Mme de Pompadour, they seemed invulnerable.

But after Pompadour's death in 1764, Louis XV became enthralled with a beauty—oval blue eyes set off by ringlets of blonde hair—procured for him from the demimonde of casinos and brothels by his valet, Dominique Guillaume Lebel.[9] Louis became so infatuated with her that he decided to make her *maîtresse en titre*, a position of such importance that it required recognition as a member of the court. That took some doing. First, the woman—who went under the name of Mademoiselle Lange and was reputed to be the illegitimate daughter of a cook and a monk—had to be married off to an aristocrat. A wedding was arranged with Comte Guillaume du Barry, the brother of Jean-Baptiste du Barry known as "le roué," a casino owner who had kept her and rented her out to his clients. Then the new countess needed a sponsor to present her to the court. Following several refusals, the elderly Madame de Béarn agreed to do the job in return for having her gambling debts paid off. After Madame du Barry's presentation on April 22, 1769, she occupied a new locus of power in Versailles, despite her reputed lack of interest in politics.

Although the Parisian public learned of these details little by little over several months, it was immediately obvious that the new dauphine could not tolerate the *maîtresse en titre*. Marie-Antoinette would not speak to her, and Choiseul refused to court her, having attempted to install his own sister, the Duchesse de Gramont, as Louis's mistress. Choiseul's enemies, however, used Madame du Barry as leverage to gain influence with the king. They were led by René Nicolas Charles Augustin de Maupeou, who succeeded his father as chancellor at the head of the judicial system in 1768. Maupeou persuaded Louis to appoint abbé Joseph-Marie Terray as controller general of finances on December 22, 1769, and they immediately set about undermining Choiseul.

As always, this information seeped into Paris through rumors, which were amplified by poems, songs, and pamphlets. A typical poem, produced by partisans of Choiseul, made his enemies look like the incarnation of villainy:

Maupeou, plus fourbe que son père,	*Maupeou, more treacherous than his father,*
Et plus scélérat mille fois,	*And a thousand times more villainous,*
Pour cimenter notre misère,	*To consolidate our misery,*
De Terray vient de faire choix.[10]	*Has chosen Terray.*

Gazetteers portrayed Maupeou and Terray as the most hated government figures in living memory. In their reports, the chancellor appeared as insatiably power-hungry, while the controller general, aloof and inflexible, bled the country dry.

Rumor had it that Terray funneled enormous sums to Madame du Barry from the royal treasury and that the king showered her with luxuries, including a coach worth 60,000 L., which Parisians flocked to see in Francien's shop at the Place du Carousel. It outdid the dauphine's wedding coach by far, they remarked, and a drunk shouted out in the street that it was a shameful waste of the people's money at a time when they could not afford the price of bread.[11]

Hardy kept a record of the power struggle according to the information that arrived in Paris. The main subject of conversations in September, he noted, was the attempt of Choiseul and Maupeou to oust one another from the government. In November the talk focused on a violent session of the king's council in which Choiseul was said to have denounced Terray for ruining the state's credit. Many Parisians believed the controller general soon would be forced to resign. By December, however, power reportedly had shifted in favor of Terray and Maupeou because of a crisis on another front. As we shall see, a conflict between the Crown and the Parlement had escalated so severely that the public believed Maupeou was planning to destroy the Parlement by creating a whole new judicial system. The plan was not even submitted to the king's council, and therefore Choiseul, who had developed close relations with the *parlementaires* during the Jesuit Affair, appeared to be outmaneuvered. On December 6, Hardy wrote that the downfall of the Parlement looked inevitable: "All Paris was plunged into the deepest consternation."[12]

Although Maupeou did not consummate this coup until mid-January, the king dismissed Choiseul and Praslin on December 24 and sent them into exile. The public took their fall as a political "revolution" (the word did not yet have the power it acquired in 1789) and attributed it to Madame du Barry and Maupeou's "cabal."[13] Yet this view, fashioned by rumors and a notion of politics as little more than court intrigue, neglected a crucial aspect of the situation: foreign affairs. Hardy and other commentators did not even mention an international crisis that threatened to plunge France into a catastrophic war. While adhering to the Austrian alliance, Choiseul had concluded a "Pacte de Famille," which made the two Bourbon monarchies, France and Spain, close allies at a time when Spain was preparing to go to war against Britain over competing claims to the Falkland Islands off the coast of Argentina. Choiseul began to mobilize the French army and navy in the hope of making the British back down, but press reports indicated that they were ready to fight, and the superiority of their naval power, demonstrated during the Seven Years' War, indicated they would win. Moreover, France's debt, unrelieved since the end of the war, would make a new conflict impossible to finance, as Terray argued in meetings of the Conseil du Roi. For once, Louis XV intervened directly in the course of events and rejected Choiseul's policy. The war was avoided, and Choiseul was dismissed.

Parisians had no knowledge about the debates inside the Conseil du Roi, but they could follow the crisis in international affairs from the *Gazette de Leyde* and other journals.[14] Articles from London, Madrid, and Cadiz indicated throughout December that Spain and England were on the brink of war and that France was committed to fight on the side of the Spanish. Yet according to Hardy, public discussions concerned nothing other than the feuding in Versailles, the Parlement's resistance to the government, the increase in the price of bread—and the weather, because severe flooding in mid-December devastated several provinces, destroying at least thirty bridges and one hundred houses. Judging from the *Mémoires secrets*, the underground press reported at length on those topics but never mentioned the threat of war.

Modern historians, who have the benefit not only of hindsight but also of access to documents unavailable in 1770, may conclude that the Parisian public failed to understand the downfall of Choiseul.[15] From the perspective of the Parisians, however, the collapse of the mighty ministry fit into a pattern. Other ministers, like Maurepas and Machault, lost their grip on power as soon as they lost their footing in court, and court intrigues conformed to a general narrative about wickedness in Versailles: evil ministers conspired with depraved royal mistresses. Although sophisticates knew better, that view was beginning to harden into a hostile attitude toward the political system in general, one that would become deeply embedded during the next four years, when Maupeou executed a coup against the Parlement and crushed all opposition, confronting Parisians with what they saw as unmitigated ministerial despotism.

15

A Coup d'État

WITH CHOISEUL OUT of the way, Parisians directed their discontent at Maupeou, hated for his harshness, and Terray, abominated for ratcheting up taxes. The Duc d'Aiguillon joined them as foreign minister on June 6, 1771, and for the next three years pamphleteers, gazetteers, and café commentators deplored the rule of an oppressive triumvirate. Beyond the world of the cafés, most people usually went about their business without paying great attention to the comings and goings of ministers. It took a major event to shake them out of their everyday concerns, and on January 20, 1771, such an event occurred. Maupeou engineered a coup, or as some put it, a "revolution."

The trouble began early in the 1760s in Brittany, where the provincial estates and the Parlement of Rennes resisted an increase in taxation, arguing that it violated the province's autonomy. La Chalotais, the general attorney of the parlement who was famous for his tracts against the Jesuits, led the resistance, and d'Aiguillon, who was then *commandant* (governor) of Brittany, tried to bring the parlement to heel. The conflict escalated, touching off a torrent of pamphlets. Most of the magistrates resigned in 1765. La Chalotais, accused of sedition, was sent to jail, where he produced more tracts, writing with a toothpick, according to pamphlets that represented him as a martyr to the cause of liberty. Other Breton magistrates were arrested, and other parlements declared solidarity with them, claiming that they constituted "classes" in a single body, whose head was the

Parlement of Paris. The Parisian magistrates fanned the flames. Remonstrances, edicts, and protest literature of all sorts flooded Paris and much of France.[1]

On March 3, 1766, Louis XV declared that he had had enough. At a meeting of the Paris Parlement that he convoked in the Palais de justice, he gave the magistrates such a tongue-lashing that it became known as the "session of the flagellation." "What has happened in my Parlement of Rennes," he pronounced, "does not concern my other parlements. I treated that court as it was important for my authority, and I do not owe an accounting to anyone. In my person alone resides the sovereign power; from me alone my courts derive their existence and their authority; the legislative power belongs to me alone, without any dependence and any division."[2] This was stronger than any statement of absolute authority made by Louis XIV at the height of the age of absolutism. It took the Parlement and all of Paris by surprise. When printed versions of it began to circulate, the *Mémoires secrets* commented, "Those are principles of despotism established with the utmost audacity as opposed to those of natural law."[3]

Then, as so often in the past, the king began to back and fill. He recalled d'Aiguillon and restored the Parlement of Rennes to its previous state. It promptly turned on d'Aiguillon, whom it accused of abusing power. To defend his honor, he then asked to be tried by the Cour des pairs, a section of the Parlement of Paris with jurisdiction over the peerage. The trial, which took place in Versailles, soon got out of hand. Some testimony even suggested that d'Aiguillon had plotted with two members of an investigative commission (Jean Charles Pierre Lenoir and Charles Alexandre de Calonne, administrative officials who would play a crucial role during the crises of the 1780s) to have La Chalotais poisoned. Finally, in a *lit de justice* on June 27, 1770, the king quashed the trial and prohibited further discussion of it.

Far from complying, the Parlement continued to demand that d'Aiguillon be tried. It defied the government in declarations that circulated widely, whipping up public opinion. By December, further confrontations led to rumors that the government would exile the Parlement or even destroy it. Maupeou, who now led the government's effort to stifle "l'Affaire de Bretagne," as it became known to the public, engineered a *lit de justice* on December 7, which forbade the parlements to correspond among themselves, to claim to be classes of one body, and to go on strike by ceasing to administer justice. The Parlement of Paris riposted by issuing a defiant resolution and suspending its functions. When the king ordered it to resume, it flatly refused. Parisian lawyers also stopped work, and public opinion became so heated that the lieutenant general of police commanded the *maîtres de café* to forbid talk about the Parlement among their customers.

On the night of January 19–20, 1771, teams of musketeers banged on the doors of the magistrates, most of whom were in bed, and served them with a *lettre de cachet* requiring an instant answer to an ultimatum from the king: would they resume their functions, yes or no? Most refused. On the next night, more musketeers with more *lettres de cachet* sent 130 of them into exile. Others, including the Parlement's *premier président*, were exiled on the following days, and their offices, which they owned as a form of property, were declared forfeit. The venality of parlementary offices was considered the surest guarantee of the judiciary's independence, as Montesquieu had argued. Maupeou therefore seemed intent on destroying the entire judicial system, beginning with its highest court.

The coup, according to Hardy, sent shock waves through all of Paris—among the common people, "les petits," as well as "les grands."⁴ On January 24, Maupeou installed a new Parlement composed of administrative officials (*conseillers d'Etat* and *maîtres des requêtes*) to replace the old one. The ceremony struck Parisians as a military operation. Soldiers lined the streets as one hundred carriages transported Maupeou, accompanied by all the ministers and members of the Conseil du Roi, to the Palais de justice. Rows of soldiers closed off every entrance to the Palais. Squadrons of soldiers, guards, and police agents "armed to the teeth" held back the public while Maupeou and his retinue processed to the Grand'Chambre. Frightened by the threat of a riot, the chancellor reportedly called out to the guards, "Surround me, press close to me." Then, safely seated in the Grand'Chambre, he required the registration of a royal edict that appointed the members of the new Parlement, who were to serve until permanent replacements for them were selected. After a few speeches, the cortège exited under a heavy guard, leaving behind a sense of "desolation in the sanctuary of justice," as Hardy put it.⁵

When the new Parlement held its first sessions, soldiers and police agents continued to protect it from the public, which jammed into the Grand'Chambre and mocked the magistrates by jeering and volleys of loud coughing. No lawyers showed up to plead cases, so the court disbanded every day after a few formalities. Posters appeared on many street corners. One threatened the life of the king; another proposed replacing him with the Duc d'Orléans; and a graffito depicted Maupeou hanging from a gallows. Poems and epigrams circulated everywhere, along with a parodied Pater Noster: "Our father who is in Versailles; glorified be your name; your kingdom is shaken; your will is not executed, neither on earth nor in heaven; give us our daily bread, which you have taken from us; forgive your parlements, who have upheld your interests, as you forgive your ministers, who have betrayed them; do not succumb to the temptations of du Barry, but deliver us from that devil of a chancellor."[6]

While the temporary Parlement maintained the fiction that justice continued to be administered, Maupeou reconstructed France's judiciary. Edicts of February 23 and April 13 proclaimed changes that his partisans— and he had some vocal supporters, notably Voltaire—hailed as progressive reforms. Venality of office for the Parisian court was abolished; justice was to be administered free of charge in place of the fees known as *épices* collected in the old Parlement; and the jurisdiction of the new Parlement of Paris was diminished so that subjects no longer had to travel great distances to attend trials. Instead of owning their offices, magistrates would be appointed for life (and therefore be considered "inamovibles") and paid salaries. Members of the old Parlement were given six months to request the reimbursement of their offices—a provision that put them in a difficult position, because by receiving compensation they would acknowledge the legitimacy of their removal and by refusing it they would sacrifice payments that could be as much as 100,000 L. Six *conseils supérieurs* would take over most of the functions performed by the old Parlement of Paris in the area of its jurisdiction. The new Parlement would retain the right to register edicts and to remonstrate, but it lost most of its power as a court of appeals, and it was reorganized. The number of magistrates was reduced from 167 to 75 and limited to a Grand'Chambre and one *Chambre des enquêtes*. Although Maupeou considered replacing the provincial parlements with *conseils supérieurs*, in the end he retained all but four of them (Rouen, Metz, Provence, and Douai). But they lost their power to remonstrate, and their magistrates also became transformed into salaried civil servants, who charged nothing for their service. Maupeou purged the most militant leaders of the provincial parlements and abolished the Cour des aides in Paris, which handled fiscal matters and had vigorously opposed him.

The Crown had often taken harsh measures against the Parlement, but nothing like Maupeou's coup had ever occurred. However enlightened the reforms, the destruction of an ancient and deeply rooted system of justice was a shock to the whole body politic. It provoked ordinary people to question what they had taken for granted and, in many cases, to rethink fundamental principles of government. Not that the shock to the system made Frenchmen into philosophers, but it provoked the educated public to consider theoretical issues with a new urgency. Everyone was talking about "the nature and the constitution of our government," Mme d'Epinay wrote in a letter to abbé Galiani. "People of all sorts—female, rural, philosophical, poetic, prosaic, reasonable, unreasonable—have taken this up and are occupied with it. A war of the pen has begun, minds are in ferment, the dictionary is changing. One hears nothing but big words—'reason of state,' 'aristocracy,' 'despotism.'"[7] The general character of the public discourse can be appreciated by following arguments as they appeared at different levels of the information system: in theoretical treatises aimed at highly educated readers; official publications, which defined the lines of conflict and circulated everywhere; pamphlets, which proliferated on an unprecedented scale; and newssheets, which spread scandal and stimulated gossip.

Among the theorists consulted by relatively sophisticated readers, Montesquieu came first. Previous political philosophers, beginning with Aristotle, had distinguished three kinds of government according to the locus of power: the rule of one (monarchies), of several (aristocracies), and of all (democracies). Montesquieu transformed this approach by investigating the culture that characterized political systems—that is, their spirit, which could be described schematically as principles—and he made despotism one of the three main types. Monarchies were driven by the principle of honor, republics (whether aristocratic or democratic) by virtue, and despotisms by fear. As he explained in the chapter on "The General Spirit" in *De l'Esprit des lois*, nations were formed by many factors, from climate to history, customs, and manners. Moreover, they went through cyclical changes; so, political theory should be steeped in history, and history taught a lesson: Monarchies tended to degenerate into despotisms. Despotism was the supreme danger, as Montesquieu understood it, that threatened France under Louis XV. Intermediate bodies such as the parlements mitigated the threat by serving as channels to direct and check the flow of royal power, but as history also demonstrated, they could be worn down. To readers of Montesquieu in the 1770s, the message was clear: by destroying the ability of the parlements to restrain the legislative authority of the king, Maupeou was turning the monarchy into a despotism.[8]

Montesquieu's ideas were expressed, directly and indirectly, in many parlementary remonstrances, and they can be found everywhere in the pamphlet literature following the publication of *De l'Esprit des lois* in 1748. The other masterwork of political theory that is still celebrated today, Rousseau's *Du Contrat Social* (1762), did not have a comparable influence. Scholars have backed away from the view, made famous by Daniel Mornet in 1913, that Rousseau's treatise failed to reach a broad public before the Revolution, but references to it do not show up in protests from the Maupeou years. Phrases like "the general will" appear occasionally in pamphlets, but they are not accompanied by arguments for popular sovereignty. A strong version of social-contract theory, which asserted that the French people retained ultimate authority in legislation, appeared in *Extrait du droit public de la France* (1771) by Louis-Léon de Brancas, Comte de Lauraguais. However, it was weighed down and confused by a historical account of the French constitution, and it aroused little response by Maupeou's supporters or opponents. Rousseauistic arguments eventually surfaced, but not until Louis XVI had ascended the throne.[9]

Readers needed guidance from theoretical works that could be directly applied to the political crisis. Two Jansenist jurists, Louis-Adrien Le Paige and Claude Mey, met that need. Protected by the Prince de Conti, whose Parisian residence, le Temple, served as a buffer against police raids, Le Paige had directed the parlements' resistance to the Crown since the first conflicts over the refusal of sacrements. As a devout Jansenist, he did not share Montesquieu's religious views, but he accepted the argument in *De l'Esprit des lois* that liberty originated in the Germanic forest—that is, it derived from assemblies of the ancient Franks who elected their king and participated in the legislative process from the very beginning of the monarchy.[10] In *Lettres historiques sur les fonctions essentielles du parlement, sur les droits des pairs, et sur les lois fondamentals du royaume* (1754), Le Paige claimed that the Franks gathered every year at the Champ de Mars and authorized laws proposed by their king: they said yes by banging with their swords on their shields, and no by collective *murmures*. As we have seen, this vision of history supported an argument about fundamental laws that constrained the power of the king. Le Paige argued that the Parlement of Paris—or the body of all the sovereign courts, which he called "le Parlement de France"—descended directly from the original Frankish "nation." By functioning as "depository of the laws of the state," it acted as guardian of the fundamental laws of the kingdom, and therefore it could refuse to register any royal edict that violated them.[11] Le Paige traced the Parlement's lineage over 1,600 years, documenting it extensively through two thick volumes. The endless citations, mostly in Latin, made for heavy going. As he admitted, the argument could bore most readers,[12] but it provided an arsenal of ammunition for parlementary remonstrances and pamphlets against the government. Le Paige wrote many of them himself, and the Maupeou Parlement acknowledged his influence by decreeing his arrest. In January 1773 he went into hiding and operated underground until January 1774, when the Parlement cleared him of the charge of seditious pamphleteering, probably owing to Conti's intervention.[13]

Claude Mey, a fellow Jansenist and lawyer, expanded Le Paige's argument by modifying it and connecting it with natural law theory in *Maximes du droit public français* (2 vols., 1772, extended to 6 volumes in 1775).[14] Citing an equally dense corpus of documents, he traced the legislative authority of the French nation back to assemblies of the Estates General—assemblies of representatives of the clergy, nobility, and the Third Estate of commoners—rather than to the Parlement. Although the Parlement developed later from the king's court, Mey argued, it inherited the role of defending the fundamental laws of the kingdom when the Estates General ceased to meet. (It held its last cession in 1614.) He distinguished two kinds of these basic laws. "Natural fundamental laws" applied to all states and concerned inalienable rights such as liberty and property, as Grotius, Pufendorf, and other theorists had explained. "Positive fundamental laws" were peculiar to France. They included constitutional principles, which went back to the origins of the monarchy and had been acknowledged over the centuries. As the depository of these laws, the Parlement could resist legislation that violated them—for example, edicts that proposed new taxes in contradiction to the nation's right, established in the earliest Estates General, to consent to taxation. If the Parlement registered such edicts, it failed in its duty to prevent the monarchy from degenerating into a despotism. Despotism had advanced ever since the last meeting of the Estates General in 1614, Mey emphasized. Usually it took the form of an attempt by a minister to inflict an illegal measure on the nation by resorting to a *lit de justice*. No forced registration of an edict in a *lit de justice* could be legal, Mey concluded, and he cited a spectacular example: the edict of December 3, 1770, which opened the way to the destruction of the Parlement, and the *lit de justice* of December 7, which Maupeou staged to give the edict a specious legality.

Mey brought the full weight of his vast erudition—two volumes of 541 and 643 pages—to bear on the immediate crisis faced by ordinary Frenchmen. He did so, as he declared in his preface, to satisfy their need to come to grips with events that had no precedent in French history. "Everyone is following this great event [Maupeou's coup], and it is fitting that everyone should have a part in it." The conflicts between the ministry and the Parlement "... present to astonished citizens events that touch them, that concern them, that worry them."¹⁵ Despite its esoteric character, therefore, *Maximes du droit public français* presented itself as a response, at the level of theory, to sentiments felt by the general public. It was received that way, judging from Hardy's account. "No one had seen anything as well done or as interesting as this work, which seems to have been prepared with care by a man who is well versed in knowledge of the law and the true principles of government."¹⁶ The interim Parlement appointed by Maupeou recognized the danger of the treatise by taking action to have it condemned for *lèse-majesté*.

Whether most readers could wade through the two thick volumes seems unlikely, even if they could afford the price of 9 L. But the *Maximes du droit public français* and other treatises provided systematic historical and juridical arguments to bolster protests that Parisians encountered every day. Remonstrances and resolutions from the provincial parlements carried particular weight after the Parlement of Paris was silenced. They were copied by hand, passed around, printed, diffused clandestinely, and discussed widely. By April 1771, Parisians had access to edicts issued by the parlements of Rennes, Rouen, Aix, Grenoble, Besançon, Dijon, Bordeaux, and Douai. These formal protests stressed the same themes: the sanctity of fundamental laws, the need for free registration of royal decrees, the rights of citizens, the authority of the nation, and above all the danger of despotism. The protest from the Parlement of Rouen went furthest. In a resolution of February 5 and a letter to the king of February 8, it denounced the government's "despotism" in powerful language, supported by extensive citations of documents demonstrating "the original constitution of the monarchy." The state's fundamental laws, it claimed, represented "the general will" of the nation, and to restore legitimate rule, it called for the convocation of the Estates General. Hardy wrote that an underground edition in the form of a twenty-six-page pamphlet costing 24 sous was "devoured by the public" and created a "vivid sensation."[17]

Two other documents stood out in the official protest literature. On February 18, the Parisian Cour des aides, a "sovereign" court with ultimate jurisdiction over taxation, published remonstrances written by its first president, Lamoignon de Malesherbes. As explained in chapter 7, Malesherbes had relaxed the censorship when he served as director of the book trade from 1750 to 1763. He knew many of the *philosophes* personally and had intervened at critical moments to support Diderot and Rousseau. He also was a learned jurist, but he did not develop a historical argument about fundamental laws derived from the Champ de Mars. His remonstrances, written in clear, forceful French, used the language of the Enlightenment. They appealed to natural law, citing the rights to life, liberty, and property. They also invoked the "rights of the Nation" and therefore called for the convocation of the Estates General. Until the Estates General met, they claimed, the Parlement spoke for the nation and protected it by impeding the arbitrary authority of the government. The destruction of the Parlement removed the last barrier that prevented the monarchy from degenerating into a despotism, and the violence against the magistrates in "the horror of the darkness" during the night of January 19–20 showed how far Maupeou would go. (The remonstrances identified him clearly without using his name.) He would not be able to appoint credible judges to replace the members of the Parlement, because, moved by greed and ambition, they would lack legitimacy. In fact, Maupeou would have to rule by force, because he had destroyed the rule of law. Once a free people, the French were now being reduced to slavery.[18]

The remonstrances of the Cour des aides provoked a great deal of discussion in Paris. Before appearing in print, they were copied and recopied so often that manuscript versions existed in virtually every household, according to the *Mémoires secrets*. Parisians praised them as "sublime," a "masterpiece," which won Malesherbes a reputation as a leading patriot. The government did not reply to them. On April 9, it abolished the Cour des aides and sent Malesherbes into exile.[19]

The other document that aroused the most talk in Paris impressed the public less because of its content than because of the names attached to it. It was a memoir signed by the *princes du sang*, Louis XV's closest male relatives. Rumors had circulated since mid-February that they had tried to turn the king against Maupeou. By virtue of their birth, they were members of the Parlement, and on important occasions they sat with the dukes and peers of the realm in the Cour des pairs, an august sector of the Grand'Chambre. When they spoke out against the chancellor, they could expect to be heard—and they were. Their *Protestations des princes du sang*, declaimed before the substitute Parlement on April 12 and circulated as a fifteen-page pamphlet, produced "the greatest effect" and was said to have turned the tide of public opinion against Maupeou.[20] Although written in ponderous legalese, it unequivocally condemned everything he had done and invoked the "rights of the Nation" in the same way as the remonstrances from the Cour des aides. The princes also submitted their memoir to the king and reportedly requested him to have Maupeou put on trial as an enemy of the monarchy.[21] Instead, Louis banished the princes from the court. They spent the next two years in virtual exile.

By the summer of 1771, therefore, Parisians had at their disposal a body of theoretical literature and institutional protests that raised fundamental questions about the nature of the monarchy. As a gazetteer reported on April 23, politics had become the "constant subject of all conversation for four months."[22] How widely the treatises were read and how deeply the discussions extended is impossible to say, but the climate had changed, and an enormous flood of pamphlets brought the issues within the range of a broad reading public. Writing as "patriots" and appealing to the "nation," the supporters of the parlements produced at least 167 tracts. For his part, Maupeou organized a counteroffensive that came to eighty-nine pamphlets, by one count.[23] Taken together, the pamphlets constituted the largest political debate since the Fronde of 1648–1649.

Although Maupeou recruited a team of prolific pamphleteers, the most influential propagandist for the anti-Parlement side of the debate was a notoriously independent and provocative lawyer, Simon-Nicolas-Henri Linguet. Famous for his fiery rhetoric, Linguet had argued d'Aiguillon's case in court and published tracts that favored the absolute power of the king. He did not explicitly back Maupeou's measures. In fact, an endorsement of Maupeou could have backfired, because Linguet had become an advocate of "Asiatic despotism," which made him a dubious ally, despite his popular following. Rejecting notions of natural law and the fundamental laws of the French monarchy, he maintained that politics concerned nothing more than power. At the bottom of the social order, the common people suffered horribly, while those on top pursued their own interests. The absolute rulers of Asia—by which he meant Turkey, Persia, and Egypt but not China and Japan—actually promoted the welfare and even the liberty of their subjects, because it was in their interest to rule over a contented population. In Europe, by contrast, the common people suffered so terribly from socioeconomic conditions that they had become slaves. European monarchs could not provide relief because the wealthy elite, entrenched in antiquated institutions, blocked their way. Linguet scorned "intermediary bodies" and disparaged Montesquieu in a way that undercut the parlements' resistance to Maupeou, but his advocacy of despotism, however enlightened, had little appeal to a public primed to distrust the despotic tendency of its government.[24]

Unlike Linguet, the pamphleteers commissioned by Maupeou did not often engage their opponents at the level of theory, although a rebuttal to the *Protestations des princes* made a strong case for absolutism: The king's authority could not be resisted without violating its unity as the one and only "public will." By attempting to divide it, the parlements set themselves up as a rival authority, fomenting sedition and rebellion.[25] That argument echoed the "session of flagellation," and it reappeared in many pamphlets commissioned by the government. *La Tête leur tourne*, for example, directed the notion of undivided sovereignty against the parlements' claim to resist despotism by acting as intermediary bodies and guardians of the fundamental laws. It was written as a dialogue between a young enthusiast who equated the parlementary cause with liberty, and a wise old monarchist who warned that wild talk about liberty would actually promote despotism—not as an abuse of royal authority, which was inherently legitimate, but as an "absurd aristocracy" of magistrates. The old man won the argument and concluded, "I take the liberty to laugh in private at the foolishness of the public that believes all is lost. Before long, all of France will be laughing in the same way."[26]

Laughter was a crucial weapon in the polemics. Voltaire, the grand master of laughter despite the seriousness of the Calas Affair, intervened on Maupeou's side with several pamphlets. The best known, *Très-humbles et très-respectueuses remontrances du grenier à sel*, parodied parlementary rhetoric in a burlesque remonstrance supposedly written by officials from one of France's four hundred *greniers à sel*, salt depositories with tribunals to adjudicate disputes over the much-hated salt tax (*gabelle*). Declaiming like puffed-up *parlementaires*, the officials asserted that the state's monopoly over the sale of salt was another kind of Salic law and that the abolition of the *gabelle* would therefore violate the fundamental laws of the kingdom. Having run the pun (*sel, loi Salique*) into the ground, Voltaire went on to protest facetiously against Maupeou's reforms in a way that made them appear progressive.

Although the other *philosophes* shared Voltaire's scorn for the parlements, they did not join him in supporting Maupeou.[27] Their views varied, but they worried about the concentration of power in the hands of the government, which raided bookshops, dispatched writers to the Bastille, and repressed the press with greater ferocity than at any other time during Louis XV's long reign. While the *philosophes* stayed on the sidelines, many of the pamphlets were produced by lawyers and obscure hacks, who lived down and out in garrets and would scribble anything for a few livres. France's literary population expanded far beyond the capacity of the book market to sustain it in the 1770s. Paris developed its own version of London's Grub Street, and the writers who inhabited it, derided as "poor devils" by Voltaire, fed the enormous growth of pamphlet literature during the last decades of the Ancien Régime. Although they were as likely to write propaganda for Maupeou as against him, they probably wrote most of the libelous attacks on the chancellor.

That statement has to be hedged with a "probably," because the pamphlets were anonymous and cannot be connected with their authors, except for a few cases that appear in the archives of the Bastille. The most notorious example of a hack writer whose work can be identified is Charles Théveneau de Morande, an adventurer who avoided the Bastille by emigrating to London, where he churned out libels against Maupeou, the other ministers, and any grandee who made a good target. In his best seller, *Le Gazetier cuirassé, ou anecdotes scandaleuses de la cour de France* (1771), Morande reduced information that he received from informers in France to anecdotes in the form of short paragraphs, which he strung together in no particular order, so that the text read as a succession of news flashes. As illustrated by a frontispiece, he presented himself as a gazetteer who shot off cannonades at potentates, while they fired back with *lettres de cachet* that failed to pierce his iron-plated armor. One anecdote announced that Madame du Barry had infected the king with venereal disease; another that she kept her hold on him by using tricks picked up during her experience as a courtesan; and a third that she favored her former colleagues in brothels by ordering the police to keep out of them. Parisians were shocked at the audacity of this mudslinging, especially as so much of it splashed on the king.[28] Whether it inflicted severe damage on their respect for him is difficult to say, because they were already accustomed to rumors about Madame du Barry's past. *Nouvellistes* referred to her career as a prostitute as if it were common knowledge,[29] and a widely circulated epigram turned it into a half-serious joke:

France, tel est donc ton destin,   *France, such is your destiny,*
D'être soumise à la femelle!   *To be submitted to females!*
Ton salut vint de la pucelle,   *Your salvation came from the virgin [Joan of Arc],*

Tu périras par la catin.[30]   *You will perish by means of a whore [du Barry].*

The police treated the libeling as serious sedition. They sent an agent disguised as an umbrella merchant (it was said to rain a great deal in London) to kidnap Morande. The agent failed ignominiously, and his attempt provoked another libel, *Le Diable dans un bénitier*, which denounced the abuse of police power. Morande then set out to write a full-scale, tell-all biography of the *maîtresse en titre*, *Vie privée d'une femme publique*, which, as it turned out, he would use to blackmail the French government in 1774.[31]

More serious propaganda tended to be written by lawyers who could expound the legal case against Maupeou's coup. *Le Maire du Palais* (1771) attributed to a lawyer, Athanase Alexandre Clément de Boissy, reworked the parlements' arguments about the Champ de Mars and then denounced Maupeou as "the enemy of the nation," who should be driven from office and tried for "lèse-majesté." Though long and rambling, it read like a libel wrapped up in a dissertation about fundamental laws.[32] Hardy found it convincing, and its sequel, *Réflexions générales sur le système projeté par le Maire du Palais pour changer la constitution de l'Etat* (1771), was said to convey patriotic fervor so powerfully as to move the coldest readers.[33] Target, one of France's most famous lawyers by 1771, also invoked the shield-banging Franks in an equally forceful tract, *Lettres d'un homme à un autre homme* (1771). Yet he linked the historical development of France's fundamental laws to the "indestructible rights of mankind" and specifically to "the rights of the people." The Parlement spoke for the nation in resisting the arbitrary will of the king, he concluded, but only the nation itself, assembled in the Estates General, had the right to assent to taxation.[34]

A final genre, clandestine journals and newssheets, brought the general arguments down to street level by recounting events and spicing them with anecdotes, texts of songs, and *bons mots*. The most important of the *nouvelles à la main* circulated in manuscript from November 1770 until April 1775 and was published in seven volumes in 1776 as *Journal historique de la révolution opérée dans la constitution de la France par M. de Maupeou, chancelier de France*. It was written by Mathieu-François Pidansat de Mairobert, a marginal literary figure who was also the main author at this time of the *Mémoires secrets*. The same articles, word for word, can often be found in both works. But the *Mémoires secrets* was a grab bag of everything of interest in Paris, whereas the *Journal historique* concentrated on what it called the Maupeou "revolution." It covered events in enormous detail, frequently with a half dozen articles on the same day, and it treated them from the viewpoint of the "patriotic party," secular partisans of the Enlightenment who had no particular sympathy for the Parlement but abhorred despotism. Therefore, its readers could enjoy a running commentary on events while following them from day to day.

Some issues of the *Journal historique* showed how events spilled over from the Parlement's immediate environment to other parts of the city. On March 22, 1771, for example, the *Journal* reported on the "Réduction de Paris," a ceremony held every year to celebrate Paris's acceptance of Henri IV as the newly converted Catholic king of France. A great deal of parading in the center of the city always attracted crowds on this occasion. According to the standard protocol, a procession of cathedral canons accompanied by four sister chapters would march from Notre Dame to the chapel of the Convent of the Grands Augustins, where a high mass would take place. They were to be joined by a delegation of officials from the Hôtel de Ville and magistrates from the sovereign courts, who would process from the Palais de justice in red robes and in a prescribed order: the Parlement (then composed of placemen named by Maupeou), the Chambre des comptes (responsible for the king's accounts), and the Cour des aides. On March 22, an unusually large force of soldiers and police lined the streets, holding back the crowd that came to watch the processions and to attend the mass. When the Maupeou magistrates arrived, they took seats in the Parlement's appointed place, in the top row of the choir. After the Chambre des comptes marched in, its president glanced at the choir and asked the master of ceremonies, "Who are these gentlemen?" "The Parlement," was the reply. "The Parlement is in exile," the president retorted. "We do not recognize these gentlemen as the Parlement." And he led the magistrates of his court out another door. The Cour des aides (it had not yet been abolished) did the same thing, refusing to be seated in the presence of the substitute Parlement and exiting from the entrance where they had arrived. A great deal of commotion followed. A large candle was knocked over; a cross was dropped by a votary; and a balcony over the choir had to be cleared because spectators threw garbage down at the Maupeou placemen. While the mass continued, the two corps of rebellious magistrates marched back to their chambers in the Palais de justice, where they passed resolutions denying the legitimacy of the Maupeou magistrates. A large crowd welcomed them in the Palais, shouting, "There still are citizens! There still are Frenchmen!" In a city where parading and the acting out of ceremonies occupied the public's attention, a ceremony that failed on this scale was an important event—in fact, as Hardy noted in his journal, "an event that should find its place in the history of the nation."[35]

For the most part, however, the *Journal historique* informed its readers about intrigues in Versailles (it frequently reported that Maupeou was about to be overthrown, owing to feuds with d'Aiguillon and Terray) and politics in parlementary circles, both in Paris and the provinces. In covering sessions of Maupeou's Parlement, it stressed the incompetence of the magistrates, whom it referred to derisively as "unmovables." It described the *premier président*, Louis Jean Bertier de Sauvigny, as so ignorant of the law that when he presided over a session a bailiff had to whisper directions into his ear like a prompter in a theater. The other magistrates confused evidence so badly that they condemned innocent victims to be hanged and set notorious murderers free. Lawyers snickered at their stupidity, while the public sneered at them. After recounting the installation of the permanent Maupeou Parlement on April 13, the *Journal* listed all of its members and identified them with phrases such as "big usurer," "accused of monopolizing," "poor devil," "ruined by debt," "an unknown peddler," "does not know how to read." It described one *conseiller*, Sorhouet de Bougy, as "called the big soliciter by his colleagues," because Maupeou used him to recruit magistrates, a difficult job owing to the infamy attached to the court.[36]

At this point, the message of the *Journal historique* converged with the main theme of the most popular of the anti-Maupeou publications, *Correspondance secrète et familière de M. de Maupeou avec M. de Sorhouet, conseiller du nouveau Parlement*, attributed to Jacques Mathieu Augeard, a lawyer and *fermier général*. The *Correspondance secrète* pretended to be an exchange of letters between Maupeou and Sorhouet along with other personages from May 1771 to June 1773. It came out in four installments, and though obviously fictitious, it contained so much accurate information that it, too, could be read as a periodical. Sorhouet's letters show him to be a groveling sycophant, appointed not only to recruit "unmovables" for Maupeou's Parlement but also to serve Maupeou as a spy, reporting what Parisians were saying about him. The letters therefore recount endless *on dits*: it was said that Maupeou manipulated the d'Aiguillon trial to seize control of the government; that he was plotting to restore the Jesuits; that to assume absolute power he would abolish all the parlements and provincial estates; that he kept a stock of blank *lettres de cachet* so that he could dispatch opponents to the Bastille; that he was plotting to betray both Terray and d'Aiguillon; and that he had inflicted more suffering than any minister in the history of France. After insisting obsequiously on his total devotion to Maupeou, Sorhouet concluded, "I am constantly told that even if only half of all these rumors are true, you would be one of the blackest villains who ever existed."[37]

In reply, Maupeou wrote that he did not care a fig about what the public said; he had such a firm grip on the will of the king that he could get away with anything. Above all, he intended to destroy the parlements, because they were the only remaining obstacle to his power. In confiding his secret ambitions, Maupeou went over the historical and constitutional arguments and conceded that the nation had originally possessed the right to consent to taxation. The Parlement of Paris had pretended to represent the nation and to oppose taxes in its name. In fact, however, the Parlement had cooperated with the government in mulcting the French—to such an extent that Louis XV had collected more in taxation than all of the preceding kings combined. Now Maupeou was ready to drop the Parlement as a hidden collaborator and to replace it with a completely subservient body so that nothing would limit his arbitrary will.

Sorhouet's letters reported on his efforts to fill the Maupeou Parlement with yes-men and revealed what a sorry lot they were: "sixty slaves, for the most part dredged up from the scum of the populace, unknown men whom you enticed only by the lure of money, many of them ruined by debts and debauchery, without the slightest knowledge of the law and judicial procedure, whom you have made the arbiters of the life, honor, and wealth of the citizenry."[38] The *Correspondance secrète* served up so many anecdotes about their iniquities and debilities that it read like a collective *libelle* stretched out over two volumes. Through it all, Maupeou remained the main villain, convicted in his own words by the letters he confided to Sorhouet. In the end, Sorhouet found it impossible to continue with his role and informed Maupeou of a nightmare that made him decide to resign. He dreamt that the *princes du sang* burst into Maupeou's chambers, forced him to beg forgiveness from the people, and turned him over to a crowd, which tore him limb from limb and burned his remains on a bonfire.

The first installment of the *Correspondance secrète*, consisting of a dozen letters and costing 3 L. 10 s., appeared in early July 1771 and created a sensation, according to Hardy.[39] The second installment came out in September, causing an even greater stir. The *Mémoires secrets* praised its author as "a Demosthenes who thunders, demolishes, and crushes."[40] In February 1772, the third installment, a full, 173-page booklet featuring Sorhouet's nightmare, had an equally enthusiastic reception and sold out immediately.[41] On March 14, 1772, the Maupeou Parlement declared it seditious in an edict condemning it to be burned by the public executioner in the courtyard of the Palais de justice.[42] As always, a ceremonial auto-da-fe created great publicity, which was compounded in this case by a satirical tract directed at the author of the Parlement's edict, *À M. Jacques de Vergès et aux donneurs d'avis*. Written in the same style as the *Correspondance secrète*, the pamphlet also was a hit: 12,000 copies were sold immediately, and it triggered several sequels. A new fashion in coiffures, "À la Correspondance," confirmed the general view that the "patriots" had scored a decisive victory in the struggle to dominate public opinion.[43]

The fourth installment of the *Correspondance secrète* did not appear until the third week of May. It lacked the sharp edge of the earlier tracts, and it also was more expensive: it sold from 4 L. 10 s to 9 L. Hardy took it as a sign that the anti-Maupeou pamphleteering had lost steam. By that time, the output of tracts on both sides had slackened, and the public's attention had shifted to other subjects, such as the threat of a reduction in the payment of *rentes* in the Hôtel de Ville and the Morangiés Affair, a trial over a contested debt that involved crowd-pleasing oratory by Linguet. More important, the Maupeou Parlement and its subordinate courts had begun to operate quite effectively. Most lawyers, who had gone on strike, resumed their functions. Members of the old Parlement continued to refuse payment for the liquidation of their offices, but they remained impotent, stuck in exile. The *princes du sang* gave up their resistance and returned to the court. Terray had succeeded in imposing new taxes—an extension of the second *vingtième* and an increase in indirect taxation. And after noisy protests, the provincial parlements had lapsed into calm. In April 1773, Hardy noted that the public seemed lethargic and resigned to the continuation of the new legal system.[44] Everything suggested that Maupeou, firmly supported by the king, had ridden out the agitation and would govern indefinitely. He did so, despite quarrels with d'Aiguillon and Terray, until Louis XV's death on May 10, 1774.

By this time so many sequels and related pamphlets had been added to the *Correspondance secrète* that they were seen to constitute a distinct genre: "Maupeouana" (or, more rarely, "Maupeouânerie"). Various anthologies brought them together in book form from 1771 to 1773. *Maupeouana, ou Correspondance secrète et familière de M. de Maupeou avec M. de Sor**** came out in five volumes in 1775 and continued to be a best seller for the rest of the decade. Taken together, the protest literature—from treatises to remonstrances and pamphlets—fed into a general debate about the nature of the monarchy and spread a new way of talking about politics. Terms like "citizen," "nation," and "patriot" became part of a widely shared idiom. They reinforced older condemnations of ministerial despotism and conveyed new demands, including the right of the people to consent to legislation through the Estates General. Maupeou's "revolution" revolutionized general attitudes—not altogether or all at once, but it raised questions about the legitimacy of the political system that would not go away.

16

Beaumarchais Has the Last Laugh

B Y MID-1773 Parisians had resigned themselves to the fact that
the new Parlement was firmly installed, although, as the *Journal
historique* emphasized, Maupeou had difficulty in recruiting magistrates for it. It remained to be seen how well the recruits would perform
their duties. In June, the public was treated to a test case, which escalated
into a court battle, one of the greatest in a century when judicial "affairs"
had such a powerful effect on the ideological climate.

The "Goezman Affair" pitted a counselor of the Parlement, Louis Val-
entin Goezman, a former magistrate in the Conseil souverain d'Alsace,
against Pierre-Augustin Caron de Beaumarchais. By then Beaumarchais
had achieved a minor success with two plays at the Comédie française,
but he had not yet become a formidable public figure. When his name
appeared in the press, it often had a negative ring. On February 26, 1773,
he was sent to the prison of For-l'Évêque for having violated an order to
remain at home after a brawl with the Duc de Chaulnes, whose mistress
he had seduced. In its report on the event, the *Mémoires secrets* showed
no sympathy for Beaumarchais: "This individual is very insolent ... and
is not liked."[1]

Although Beaumarchais was permitted to leave the prison, accompanied by a guard, during the day, he had little room for maneuver in confronting a much greater conflict than the squabble with de Chaulnes. His
wealthy patron, Joseph Pâris Duverney, had died in 1770, willing the bulk

of his fortune to a nephew, the Comte de La Blache. By an earlier agreement, Duverney had promised to leave Beaumarchais 15,000 L. and to cancel a large debt, about 75,000 L., that Beaumarchais had accumulated. La Blache contested that agreement in a lawsuit, which Beaumarchais won. Then La Blache appealed the decision to the Maupeou Parlement, and Beaumarchais did everything possible in his sorties from prison to get his side of the case heard by the court's *rapporteur*, whose recommendation would determine its decision.

The *rapporteur* was Goezman. He first appeared in the *Journal historique* as one of many whom Maupeou plucked from penury and released to seek their fortune (while receiving a modest salary) by administering justice.[2] In 1772 Goezman acquired a name for himself as a champion of absolutism by leading the Parlement's attempt to suppress antigovernment pamphlets. He conducted investigations, directed raids on bookshops, and had suspects condemned to prison.[3] Then the La Blache appeal came into his hands. On April 6, 1773, following his recommendation, the court ruled against Beaumarchais, effectively ruining him. To pay off his debts, Beaumarchais had to sell his country house, vacate his Paris residence, and watch helplessly from prison, where he remained confined until May 8, while his creditors confiscated his furniture and assailed him with more bills.

While Beaumarchais seemed doomed to drown in debt, Parisians heard that he had tried to win the case by bribing Goezman. Spicy details seasoned the rumors. At first, working through a bookseller named Lejay and Goezman's wife, Beaumarchais reportedly had offered Goezman 50 gold louis (1,200 L.) wrapped neatly in a roll; then he doubled the bribe with a second roll of louis; then a gold watch studded with diamonds; and finally, as a sweetener, an additional 15 louis to be given to Goezman's secretary. The talk became so damaging that Goezman, perhaps prodded by his colleagues, brought a charge of attempted bribery against Beaumarchais. Lejay was arrested, Beaumarchais and Mme Goezman were summoned to testify, and "everyone," according to Hardy, was buzzing about the new lawsuit because it would provide a way to take the measure of Maupeou's judges. Were they genuine professionals, determined to do their duty, or were they worse than the magistrates from the old Parlement, who merely lined their pockets with *épices*?[4] The case became an affair. The Parlement itself was put on trial.

Throughout the summer of 1773, Parisians were treated to a flow of further rumors. Goezman was said to try to clear himself by blaming his wife and even to have attempted to get her locked up in a convent. She reportedly had returned the rolls of louis and the watch to Beaumarchais but had kept the supplementary 15 louis for herself. According to leaks from the court proceedings, she had testified for five hours, staggering from one contradiction into another. In his testimony, Beaumarchais reputedly denied that he had attempted to bribe Goezman. He had merely tried to get Madame Goezman to persuade her husband to grant him an audience. By September, the depositions of the witnesses had been completed. It remained for them to be cross-examined in "confrontations," a process in which they could interrogate one another, and then the court would be ready to reach a decision.

At this point, Beaumarchais published the first of four judicial memoirs, which he wrote himself, although he was not a lawyer. Parisians were electrified. Never in the history of court cases, even in the Calas Affair, had anyone known anything like it. It damned Goezman, Mme Goezman, their accomplices, and by implication the whole Maupeou system. Yet it did not simply succeed as an argument, nor could it be considered merely as a *factum*. It was a work of literature, written with incomparable talent, and it was very amusing. Meister, who rarely mentioned trials or politics in the *Correspondance littéraire*, treated the succession of memoirs as a masterpiece, which aroused "astonishment and admiration" everywhere.[5] The *Mémoires secrets*, which had disparaged Beaumarchais earlier, celebrated him as a superb satirist and his first memoir as a work that had created a "major ruckus."[6] Hardy noted that it was printed at a run of 4,000 copies, then reprinted immediately and avidly read by everyone.[7]

To contemporaries, the memoir and its sequels read more like a four-act play or installments of a novel than like a judicial *factum*. Narrating his experience in the first person, Beaumarchais recounted the succession of calamities that would have buried most persons in despair but inspired him to rise to the occasion and to demolish his enemies with wit. He addressed Goezman's accomplices, who were also implicated in the trial and published lengthy memoirs of their own, as if he were fighting duels: "your turn, M. Baculard," "now you, M. Marin," "now you, M. Bertrand." After dispatching them, he concentrated on the main target, Magistrate and Madame Goezman. To plead his case against La Bache, he explained, he had to gain access to the *rapporteur*. Therefore, he had to pay the 100 louis and to fight his way through intermediaries, one shadier than the other, including the lackies at the Goezmans' front door, who turned him away, time after time, while time was running out.

Finally, two days before the court's decision, Beaumarchais was accorded a brief conversation before the Goezmans sat down to dinner in their recently refurbished town house. He got nowhere but resolved to try again on the next day, when Mme Goezman let it be known that she would intervene once more in exchange for another present. Having nearly run out of louis, Beaumarchais came up with the gold and diamond-studded watch, which was delivered by Lejay. Even then, Mme Goezman insisted on the additional 15 louis as a gift she would transmit to her husband's secretary. When Beaumarchais turned up, the doorman refused to let him past the threshold. The only satisfaction he received was the assurance, sent later through another intermediary, that Mme Goezman would return the bribes if he lost the case.

Sure enough, he lost, probably, he surmised, because La Blache had outbid him. He received back the rolls of louis and the watch, but not the 15 louis, which became a leitmotiv in the last three memoirs. Goezman's secretary provided assurance that he had never been offered the money and would have refused it in any case. Mme Goezman must have kept it, Beaumarchais argued, yet she denied that she had received it while at the same time refusing to give it back. Although the 15 louis made up a comparatively small sum (360 L.), Beaumarchais insisted so relentlessly on them that they came to symbolize all the skulduggery. "Fifteen louis," "fifteen louis" reappeared throughout the text, and the refrain was repeated by the public. Because it evoked the name of the king, it lent itself to verbal play turned against the Maupeou Parlement: "Louis Fifteen established it, fifteen louis will destroy it."[8] Of course, the whole affair made the Parlement look bad by concentrating on the theme of bribery, but part of the memoirs' success came from Beaumarchais's skill in rhetorical tightrope walking. Although he wrote to win over the public, he formally addressed the Parlement, which would decide the case brought against him by Goezman. Therefore, Beaumarchais needed to sound respectful toward his judges, even though his opponent was one of them, and he had to argue that the inducements given to Goezman through his wife were not actually bribes because they were meant to give Beaumarchais access to an audience, not to sway the final verdict.

The second memoir appeared after the "confrontations," when the parties had an opportunity to challenge one another's testimony. Beaumarchais directed his strongest sallies at Mme Goezman—and again he kept a delicate balance, because he pretended to honor her as a lady while trapping her in damning contradictions. He was all gallantry; she, confusion; and their confrontation, written in dialogue, turned into sheer comedy.[9]

Beaumarchais began by quoting her first deposition in which, on sixteen occasions, accompanied by outbursts like "atrocious lie" and "abominable calumny," she denied receiving the 100 louis. Then he read from her second deposition, where she said Lejay had left the louis for her in a box with a bouquet of flowers and she had kept them safe in an armoire. Confronted with an obvious contradiction, she rambled on for a while and then explained that during her testimony she had been in "a critical time," meaning (though the transcription avoided the offensive term) she was having her period. "Believe me if you want to, Monsieur; but in truth, there are times when I don't know what I say, when I don't remember anything; the other day. . . ." Beaumarchais then added stage directions: Mme Goezman lost the defiant look in her eyes, lowered her voice, abandoned her insulting tone.[10]

Next, Beaumarchais took up the crucial subject of the 15 louis. Mme Goezman insisted that she had never heard of them: "Does it make any sense to offer fifteen louis to a woman of my station! To me, who had refused a hundred of them the previous day!" Then she recalled that she had just admitted receiving the hundred on the previous day and exclaimed, "Well! Of course, Monsieur, the previous day before. . . ." (She stopped short, biting her lip). At that point, she lost her composure. "Lay off," she said furiously, getting to her feet. "Or I will slap your face. . . . Sure, I had something to do with those fifteen louis! With your nasty, tricky little phrases, you are only trying to confuse me and undo me; but I swear by God that I will not utter another word in reply."[11]

The exchange over the 15 louis continued in this manner, as Mme Goezman kept tripping on contradictions and in the end fell back again on the menstruation defense. While tying her testimony in knots, Beaumarchais, ever the perfect gentleman, insisted on his admiration for the fair sex and paid homage to her delicacy. Next, he demolished the argument of her husband. Goezman had persuaded Lejay to write a letter, based on a copy provided by Goezman himself, saying that he had never transmitted the bribe to Mme Goezman. But the letter was full of florid language beyond the capacity of Lejay, who, as his wife testified, was a simpleton. (He had not been able to spell "signé" ("signed"), writing "siné" before his signature.) Later Lejay confessed that Goezman had led him by the nose, that the letter was a lie, and that he had indeed delivered the money and the watch to Mme Goezman. Yet Goezman maintained that Lejay's letter was authentic, and he claimed, further, that Mme Goezman had rejected the bribe "with indignation and contempt," despite the evidence to the contrary. Beaumarchais concluded that his testimony was as feeble as his wife's. After falsifying the evidence, Goezman had accused Beaumarchais of bribery while denying he'd been bribed.[12]

The second memoir delighted the public even more than the first. Readers found it so clever and amusing that they could barely wait to get the third installment and bought up a new edition of the first so that they could keep a complete collection. While valuing it as literature, they recognized that it had badly damaged the reputation of the Parlement. Rumors spread that several magistrates had threatened to resign if Goezman continued to sit with them. Beaumarchais's adversaries published memoirs of their own, but they fell flat. In December, his first two memoirs were adapted as a play, *Les proverbes, ou le meilleur n'en vaut rien*, performed before Louis XV, Madame du Barry, and members of the court. Préville (the stage name of Pierre Louis Du Bus), a star of the Comédie française, played Beaumarchais, and Dugazon (Jean Baptiste Henri Gourgaud), famous for comic roles, played Mme Goezman, squirming and grimacing hilariously during the exchanges about menstruation. The king was said to have laughed so hard he had to leave the room and ordered another performance for the following day. Gossips attributed the play to Beaumarchais himself, as seemed obvious, since the memoirs contained so much dialogue and could be read as a comedy.[13]

The third memoir, which appeared on December 22, was deemed to be as superior to the second as the second was to the first. Taken together, Hardy said, they constituted "a piece of literature worthy of being bound and preserved in libraries everywhere." The memoir was read aloud before a large crowd at the café de Foy—or rather, it was performed, as the orator had a booming voice, and he declaimed a text that ran seventy-eight pages.[14] It created a great stir because, in addition to heaping more ridicule on Beaumarchais's enemies (by then they had published six more memoirs against him), it revealed that Goezman had compromised himself in another scandal. Using a false name and address, he had acted as godfather to a baby, born to the wife of a baker, and he had not honored his promise to pay the cost of the wet nurse. While rumors spread that Goezman was the child's father, Beaumarchais denounced him in the last section of the memoir and brought a charge of fraud before the Parlement.

In January 1774 while Goezman, now transformed from judge to defendant, underwent interrogation in response to the accusation, Beaumarchais was "the toast of the town." Parisians celebrated him as "a citizen who is precious to the nation" and "the savior of the fatherland." They bought engravings of him and lionized him in popular poems:

Dans tes nouveaux écrits, courageux Beaumarchais
Ne lui donne pas de relâche;
En repoussant les traits de la perversité,
Citoyens et rieurs, tout est de ton côté.[15]

(In your new writing, brave Beaumarchais, / Do not give him any peace; / In deflecting the darts of perversity, / Citizens and laughter, everything is on your side.)

And in mid-February, they devoured his fourth memoir, which the *Mémoires secrets* praised as the best of all. An edition of 6,000 copies sold out at 2 L. 8 s. each in a few days.[16] At the same time, the other memoirs were reprinted yet again. Brought together, all four circulated as books, and they became best sellers.

The fourth memoir included more comic dialogue with Mme Goezman and piled more ridicule on Beaumarchais's adversaries, but it struck a new tone. He had argued his case with "gaiety," Beaumarchais wrote, and indeed gaiety, he added, was a main trait of his character. Yet the Affair was a serious matter, not merely for him but for all Frenchmen. Indeed, "My cause is that of all citizens." His trial had seized the attention of the entire nation, and the nation was the judge of judges.[17] Beaumarchais had to sound respectful of the Parlement, which was about to adjudicate both cases, Goezman's against him and his against Goezman, but he was using his new eminence to make the entire system look bad.

On February 26 after ten hours of heated deliberation, the Parlement announced its decision before a crowded courtroom. It condemned Beaumarchais and Mme Goezman to "blâme"—that is, to receive an admonishment, which would deprive them of their civic rights. (In Beaumarchais's case that meant the loss of some honorific offices and the possibility of accepting any state appointment.) Mme Goezman was required to surrender the famous 15 louis, which would be used to purchase bread for impoverished prisoners. Beaumarchais's memoirs were condemned to be lacerated and burned by the public executioner for defamation and disrespect to the magistracy. The case against Goezman and the others was dismissed, except for a few light fines.

But on March 17 the Parlement condemned Goezman in the separate case concerning his fraudulent role as a godfather. It expelled him from its bench and forbade him to hold any future office. By then he had run up so much debt that his creditors seized his furniture, and he disappeared. In fact, he was sent on a mission under a false name to England, probably owing to the intervention of his protector, the Duc d'Aiguillon. He had his wife, now known as "the lady of the fifteen louis," confined to a convent.[18]

Beaumarchais, as we will see, also left on a secret mission, which would ultimately lead to the restoration of his civic rights and the reversal of the court's decision in favor of the Comte de La Blache. Although the Parlement had decided against him, he won his case before the public, and he turned it against the Parlement itself. Songs, epigrams, and *bons mots* celebrated him as a hero. They also expressed the general implications of the Affair. As one poem put it, playing on the notion of *blâme*:

Le public seul juge suprême . . .   *The public, sole supreme judge . . .*
Blâme le Parlement lui-même.[19]   *Blames the Parlement itself.*

The Goezman Affair did not bring down the Maupeou judiciary, but it destroyed whatever remained of its legitimacy in the eyes of the public. Beaumarchais achieved this feat, using a tactic perfected by Voltaire and celebrated in the French saying we have already encountered: "One must get the laughter on one's side." He had the last laugh—although in the next few years laughter itself would come under attack.

17

The King Is Dead, Long Live Maurepas

W HEN LOUIS XV DIED at age 64 on May 10, 1774, Parisians were glad to see him go. He made a "good death," according to the rituals of the church and the bulletins that reached the capital. Although he needed help in opening his mouth to swallow the host, he took communion and received absolution for his sins for the first time in nearly three decades. The *grand aumonier* who administered the last rites reported that Louis expressed regret about the "scandal that he made to his people."[1] The people, however, were not impressed. Hardy commented on the general "indifference" of Parisians in contrast to their consternation when the king fell ill at Metz in 1744 and their horror at the assassination attempt by Damiens in 1757. A canon of Notre Dame remarked that in 1744 Parisians subsidized 6,000 masses to be said for the king's recovery; in 1757, they paid for six hundred masses; and in 1774, three.[2]

Although Parisians showed little affection for the king, they recognized that his death was a momentous event, and they followed his agony from printed bulletins that were posted twice a day on the front door of the Hôtel de Ville and outside shops in various neighborhoods. What at first had appeared to be severe indigestion was reported as a serious case of smallpox on April 30. From that time on, the bulletins informed Parisians on the progress of the disease in great detail: the eruption of pustules, the king's temperature, his pulse, the consistency of his urine, and the use of bleeding and *vésicatoires* (ointments to produce blisters). On April 30, the two great bells of Notre Dame began to ring, signaling a crisis. The clergy was summoned to conduct prayers nonstop for forty hours. The shrine of Saint Geneviève, the patron saint of Paris, was uncovered. All theaters were closed, all music forbidden in eating establishments. Spies circulated through cafés and public gardens, and they had many people arrested for disrespectful talk. One man was locked up after saying to a friend, who had informed him that the king was dying, "What does that matter to me? We can't be any worse off than we are."[3]

How had Louis contracted the disease? Parisians wondered. By May 9, the answer circulated as a devastating *on dit*. The king's procurers, aided by Mme du Barry, had come upon a lovely, sixteen-year-old peasant girl. They had the dirt scrubbed off her, dressed her enticingly, and served her to the king. Unknown to anyone, she had caught smallpox. She broke out with it on the day after her encounter with Louis and died three days later.[4]

After the king's death, the next question commonly asked was: What would become of Mme du Barry? She had remained at Louis's side during the first days of the disease. When he realized it was likely to be fatal and that he would have to take extreme unction, he dismissed her. Parisians heard several versions of their parting, which indicated Louis's desire to avoid the scandal that had followed his illness at Metz, when he took the last rites, dismissed his mistress, Mme de Châteauroux, and then, after recovering, recalled her. According to the simplest report, he said, "It is time, Madam, for us to be separated."[5] Mme du Barry left with the Duchesse d'Aiguillon to the d'Aiguillon estate at Rueil 10.5 miles west of Paris. Soon after his ascension to the throne, Louis XVI exiled her to the Abbey du Pont-aux-Dames in Brie, and three years later she was permitted to take up residence in her Château at Louveciennes.

On May 12, the king's body was transported in a double lead coffin (to prevent contagion from the putrefying carcass) by a simple convoy to the royal burial vault in Saint Denis. While a high mass was said for his soul in Notre Dame, Parisians vented their discontent in conversations and passed around epigrams, such as:

Louis a rempli sa carrière,	*Louis has ended his career,*
Il vient de finir ses destins;	*He has just fulfilled his destiny;*
Pleurez voleurs, pleurez catins,	*Weep, thieves, weep strumpets,*
Vous avez perdu votre père.[6]	*You have lost your father.*

The dauphin with members of the royal family and grand officers of the Crown had been kept at a safe distance from the dying king. As soon as they heard Louis XV had expired, everyone surrounding the twenty-year-old youth who instantly became Louis XVI sank to their knees and addressed him henceforth as "Sire" and "Your Majesty." The new king refused to meet with the old ministers. Instead, he left Versailles for the château de Choisy, where he planned to isolate himself for several weeks, studying plans for his new government. As he drove off with his new queen, crowds outside shouted "Vive le roi!" It all happened with such dizzying suddenness that Parisians found it difficult to get their bearings. After a fifty-nine-year reign, they expected big changes, but what would those be?

The first reports that came out of Choisy raised great hopes, though they concerned small matters. Louis announced that he wanted to have simple (if copious) dinners at one table accompanied by his family. He meant to cut back drastically on the expenses of the king's household, and he began by reducing the number of horses in his stables from 6,000 to 800. The reduction of dogs in "la grande Muette" only went from 138 to 100, but the number of carriages that followed the royal hunt was cut from twenty to two. Louis was known to be scrupulously pious, so Parisians did not expect to hear any more tales about mistresses. They could only guess about the fate of the ministers he had inherited, although one report provoked speculation. Three days after Louis XV's death the new king announced that he would make the Comte de Maurepas his principal advisor. In a letter to Maurepas, which soon circulated in Paris, he explained, "I am king; this name conveys many obligations, but I am only twenty years old, and I don't have the knowledge that is necessary for me.... The certitude that I have of your probity and of your profound knowledge of affairs makes me ask you to help me with your counsel."[7] Maurepas was then seventy-three years old. He had lived in exile since Louis XV had dismissed him in 1749, and he had memories that went back to the reign of Louis XIV, when he first served in the government.

Whatever might become of the ministerial triumvirate (Maupeou, Terray, and d'Aiguillon), the Parlement, and the enormous debt, Parisians reassured themselves that they need not fear any sudden or extreme change.

In fact, they enjoyed a brief period of optimism, if not euphoria, because the new reign promised to be the antithesis of everything they despised about the court of Louis XV. The government would be dedicated to virtue, thrift, and the welfare of the people. The king would become known as "Louis the Desired" or "Louis the Severe" by way of contrast to his predecessor.[8] The abuse of power would be eliminated. In reporting reactions to Louis XV's death, the *Mémoires secrets* remarked, "It seems as though the common people see this moment as one when they can take vengeance for all the calamities they have suffered," and cited an epitaph about the former king roasting in hell for having manipulated bread prices:

Ci gît le bien aimé Bourbon,	*Here lies the well loved Bourbon,*
Monarque d'assez bonne mine,	*A fairly good-looking monarch*
Et qui paie sur le charbon	*Who pays [by roasting] on coal*
Ce qu'il gagnait sur la farine.[9]	*What he earned from [monopolizing] flour.*

Hardy noted several poems on the same theme:

Ci gît Louis le fainéant,	*Here lies Louis the feckless,*
Qui donna papier en naissant	*Who produced paper [money] at birth,*
La guerre en grandissant,	*War as he grew up,*
La famine en vieillissant,	*Famine in aging,*
Et la peste en mourant.	*And the plague [smallpox] in dying.*

By contrast, the current poems identified Louis XVI with morality and prosperity:

Or écoutez petits et grands,	*Gather round, young and old,*
L'histoire d'un Roi de vingt ans,	*To hear the story of a twenty-year-old king.*
Qui va nous ramener en France	*Who will bring back to France*

Les bonnes moeurs et l'abondance.	*Good morals and abundance.*
D'après ce plan que deviendront,	*According to this plan, what will become of*
Tant de catins et de fripons?[10]	*So many strumpets and knaves?*

Despite the sunnier mood, however, Parisians remained confused by contradictory rumors about changes in the government, and they did not express unanimous fervor for their new king and queen. When the royal couple left Choisy for the château de la Muette, they deliberately passed through Paris and received loud cries of "Long live the king and the queen." But when the queen appeared in Paris two months later, she was greeted with a stony silence, and one onlooker called out, "Long live the king, provided that the price of bread goes down." The king had announced his determination to get the price of bread lowered, yet it had increased. Parisians remained silent again when the king and queen visited the capital on July 25.[11] The intensity of cries of "Long live the king!" served as a gauge of the enthusiasm for the monarch, and silence was taken as a measure of discontent. At the interment for Louis XV in Saint Denis, the bishop of Senez noted rather undiplomatically in his sermon, "The silence of the people is the shame of kings."[12] Louis XVI had not done anything to offend Parisians, but the price of bread continued to rise. On August 1 when traveling to Compiègne, he avoided Paris, just as Louis XV had done.[13]

Uncertainty over the future of the government added to the perplexity of Parisians. According to various reports, the king restricted his activities to daily conferences with Maurepas; and at the first meeting of the Conseil du Roi on May 21, he revealed nothing about which ministers he favored. Maupeou and Terray continued to run the government, while the *nouvellistes* spread contradictory rumors. The chattering and confusion reached such a pitch in July that the lieutenant general of police ordered all the cafés in Paris and its faubourgs to silence talk about the old and new Parlement, the old and new king, the ministers, and even the police themselves.[14] By then d'Aiguillon had resigned as foreign minister and had been replaced by Charles Gravier, Comte de Vergennes, yet the other two members of the triumvirate clung to power until August 24–25, when, after three months of hesitation, Louis dismissed them.

The news arrived in letters from the court, thrilling "the good citizens, the true patriots," who took it as a sign that a new political order had at last arrived, according to Hardy.[15] Parisians celebrated throughout the city with traditional, carnivalesque revelry. Crowds shot off fireworks and lit bonfires near the Palais de justice. They dressed a straw mannequin to look like Maupeou and set it on fire in front of the chancellor's hôtel near the Place Vendôme. By then he had gone into exile, pursued by people throwing stones and mud at his carriage. Straw men representing magistrates in the Maupeou Parlement were burned in the Place Dauphine and at several places along the quais on August 27. On the next day a crowd of 12,000 gathered at the Place Sainte Geneviève to cheer the condemnation of two mannequins outfitted as Maupeou and Terray, who were broken on an imitation wheel and hanged. Similar straw men were paraded in a coffin followed by a mannequin public executioner before 10,000 spectators in the quartier Saint-Antoine. They, too, were hanged after being broken on a model wheel. Two days later a large group of revelers in the Place Dauphine declared a straw man dressed as Maupeou guilty, burned it, and scattered the ashes. On September 1, a still larger crowd attempted to incinerate an elaborate mannequin of Maupeou—a straw body clothed in a robe beneath a sculpted wax head with a wig—on the Pont Neuf, but a detachment of six hundred soldiers prevented it by swinging sabers and closing off the bridge. A final burlesque ceremony took place late at night on September 12. Outfitted in black mourning dress and carrying torches, twenty journeymen goldsmiths held a mock funeral for Terray and buried an effigy of him in the Place Dauphine.[16]

Parisians seemed pleased by the ministry that replaced the Triumvirate. It included as controller general, Anne Robert Jacques Turgot, the intendant of Limoges, a contributor to the *Encyclopédie* and a champion of free trade; as keeper of the Seals (the effective head of the judiciary, because Maupeou refused to resign as chancellor, a lifetime appointment), Armand Thomas Hue de Miromesnil, *premier président* of the defiant Parlement of Rouen, which Maupeou had abolished; and, somewhat later, as minister for the Maison du Roi with responsibility for overseeing Paris, Malesherbes, who had won admiration for the remonstrances of the Cour des aides and who soon did everything possible to abandon the use of *lettres de cachet*. Turgot in particular got a warm welcome. Voltaire led the *philosophes* in praising him; the physiocrats greeted him as one of their own; an *Épître en vers à M. Turgot* described him as a humanitarian hero; and a *Lettre de M. Terray, ex-contrôleur général à M. Turgot, ministre des finances*, which presented itself as a sequel to the *Correspondance secrète*, celebrated him as the opposite of everything hateful about Terray.[17]

There remained the problem of the Parlement. By April 1773, three years after Maupeou's coup, Parisians had resigned themselves to the likelihood that his Parlement would last indefinitely. After Louix XV's death, they did not assume that it would be dissolved; far from it. Maupeou's magistrates paraded through Paris during the celebration of the Assumption of the Holy Virgin on August 15, in red robes, their heads held high, as if they expected to stay in office for the rest of their lives.[18] They continued to function as usual for ten weeks after the fall of Maupeou and the appointment of Turgot. But on November 12, 1774, after a great deal of hesitation, the king recalled the old Parlement. Although Parisians reacted favorably, they seemed happier to be rid of the "unmovables" than to see the old nobility of the robe restored to power. They also held conflicting views of many other issues. As factions regrouped in Versailles, the political *cognoscenti* in Paris favored various parties—free traders supported Turgot; Choiseulistes promoted the return of the exiled minister; and a *parti dévot* hoped to revive the Jesuits by rallying around the king's aunts. The state debt continued to be threatening, and there was no consensus on a strategy to overcome it.

Moreover, the ideological ferment from the Maupeou years did not suddenly dissipate. Key tracts from the patriotic opposition, notably the *Journal historique* and the *Correspondance secrète*, were reprinted and circulated in greater numbers than ever. A new run of libel literature was grafted onto the old. Parisians learned that Beaumarchais had left on a secret mission to negotiate with Morande, the most notorious libeler in the colony of French expatriates in London, for the destruction of a scandalous biography of Mme du Barry, *Mémoires secrets d'une femme publique*. In return for an enormous payment of blackmail, he got the entire edition incinerated. Back in Paris, Beaumarchais was rewarded with the restoration of his civil rights; he won his case against La Blache by getting the Maupeou Parlement's decision quashed; and he persuaded the government to lift its prohibition of *Le Barbier de Séville*, which became a hit at the Comédie française.

While Beaumarchais was rehabilitated, however, Mme du Barry continued to be the favorite target of libelers, even though she had withdrawn to her château of Louveciennes. A scurrilous biography, *Anecdotes secrètes sur Mme la comtesse du Barry*, traced her career from the brothel to the royal bed, filling the space left empty by the destruction of Morande's libel. It became a top best seller in the underground book trade of the 1770s, and it was supplemented by another best seller, *Vie privée de Louis XV*, a scandalous and cleverly narrated, four-volume history of Louis's entire reign. The public devoured this literature, and the police did everything possible to suppress it, because it conveyed a seditious message long after the reign had ended. To be sure, the vilification of Louis XV made Louis XVI look saintly by comparison, and sophisticated readers probably discounted the most extravagant episodes in the texts, but the libels' emphasis on the decadence of the court and the despotism of the government made the system itself seem rotten.

The libels repeated themes and lifted material from one another so extensively that they blended together, forming a coherent body of literature. The crucial unit in their narratives, as mentioned earlier, were short episodes known as anecdotes. In the eighteenth century, "anecdote" was a term applied to events that had truly taken place but had been suppressed by conventional accounts—or as the *Dictionnaire de l'Académie française* put it, a "secret feature of history that had been suppressed by previous historians." Far from being unreliable as we think of them today, anecdotes were understood as solid bits of information, which could be detached from one text and inserted into another like pieces of a mosaic. Having originated as gossip, they appeared in newssheets and pamphlets and then migrated so widely from book to book that they became fixed in the collective memory.[19]

That assertion, I confess, cannot be proven, but I believe that a variety of political folklore grew up around episodes familiar to an enormous public. Many Parisians, if not "all Paris," knew the anecdote about an incident in the "petits appartements" of Versailles, where Louis XV liked to retire with Mme du Barry. The king often amused himself by brewing his own coffee. One day when he was distracted, the coffee began to boil over, and Mme du Barry shouted, "Hey! France, look out, your coffee is buggering off." The anecdote required no comment. By dramatizing the vulgarity of the royal mistress, it captured what many took to be the debasement of the monarchy.[20] In another anecdote, Louis confided to one of his intimates, the Duc de Noailles, that after taking up with Mme du Barry, he had experienced pleasure that he had never before imagined. "Sire," the duke replied, "it's that you have never been in a brothel."[21]

While the libels fed the public's imagination about wickedness at the top of the power system, philosophical tracts challenged the legitimacy of the system at a theoretical level. On June 30, 1775, the Parlement condemned two anonymous works, *Catéchisme du citoyen* (attributed to a radical lawyer, Guillaume-Joseph Saige), and *L'Ami des lois* (attributed to another lawyer, Jacques-Claude Martin de Mariveaux) to be burned by the public executioner. Although published after Maupeou's fall, they belonged to the "patriot" literature that defended the Parlement against his coup. In fact, copies of both works were sent to the restored Parlement in the expectation it would welcome their support. Yet Antoine-Louis Séguier, the Parlement's main prosecuting attorney, denounced them in a fiery speech, and the assembled chambers declared them to be a seditious attack on the authority of the king.[22]

Like the treatises of Le Paige and Mey, the two tracts argued for restrictions on the power of the Crown by citing historical precedents going back to the assemblies of the Franks, but they built the argument around abstract concepts derived directly from Rousseau. Citing passages from *Du Contrat social*, they asserted that by virtue of the social contract, sovereignty inhered in the people, that it was expressed by the general will, and that it could never be alienated or divided. While maintaining legislative authority, the people entrusted executive functions to a government; and if the government violated the general will, it ceased to be legitimate and could even be overturned. The king of France, an "administrator" acting as the executive empowered by the French people, could not levy taxes without their consent. To do so, he would have to convene the Estates General, which spoke for the nation in the same way as the ancient assemblies on the Champs de Mars. *L'Ami des lois* was only a thirty-two-page pamphlet, but *Le Catéchisme du citoyen* developed the argument in a full-scale political treatise, which included demands for the liberty of the press and the abolition of *lettres de cachet*. It spoke respectfully about the par-lements as a bulwark against despotism, yet it treated them as a branch of the executive, which it described as "an aristocratic monarchy." In con-trast, it identified the third estate with the nation and expressed sympathy for "the plebeian class." Although it belonged to the crisis of 1771, it would be reprinted three times in 1788. It signaled the arrival of radical Rous-seauism as an ingredient in the political debate.[23]

Although the ideological climate remained heavily charged, the new king benefited from the goodwill that accompanied his accession. On June 11, 1775, his legitimacy was reinforced by an elaborate coronation ceremony in Rheims, and three days later, he exercised his thaumaturgic power by touching 2,400 persons afflicted by scrofula.[24] But the protec-tive layer of charisma did not make him immune from nasty rumors that continued to ferment in Versailles. In July 1774, Parisians learned that a note left on the king's plate warned him, "Sire, beware of the queen." Other notes that attacked the queen were said to have been slipped into the king's napkin. Gossips attributed them to a "cabal" led by the king's aunts, Madame Adelaïde and Madame Louise, and clerical potentates who wanted to alienate the king from the queen. By driving a wedge between the royal couple, they supposedly hoped to dominate Louis and open a way for the restoration of the Jesuits. Therefore, they sponsored scandalous talk about Marie-Antoinette's morals. According to one rumor, she was seen at sunrise returning from a tryst with a lover, and that information provided the basis for a libel, *La Belle Aurore*. The police reportedly arrested an abbé Mercier as its author and discovered a secret press that had printed it.[25]

Nothing suggests that these rumors seriously damaged Parisians' respect for the queen, but they turned out to be the first installment of scandalous reports that would pursue her throughout the reign. The king, unlike his grandfather, did not suffer from such slander. Yet his impec-cable morals exposed him to gossip of the opposite kind: He supposedly lacked virility. He had failed to father an heir to the throne for five and a half years by the end of 1775, when widespread rumors attributed the problem to a deficiency in his penis. The only hope for a dauphin, accord-ing to this talk, was surgical intervention.[26]

Whatever their concern for the king, Parisians worried most about feeding their families. Turgot did not intervene to stop the rise in the price of bread after he freed the grain trade on September 13, 1774. The standard, four-pound loaf, which had been costing 11 sous, rose to 13 sous 6 deniers. People complained so bitterly that extra guards had to be stationed in the marketplaces. Soon after the coronation, a man was arrested for saying, "Well then! The coronation ceremony has taken place, and the price of bread has not gone down! Therefore, the king must want to get himself assassinated."[27] And a report circulated that one of the king's most trusted domestic servants had given him some frank advice about the sentiments of the people. "Sire, no matter what you do," he supposedly said, "you will never be loved by them as long as bread is expensive."[28] To Parisians, the connection between their feelings for the king and the price of bread was self-evident. They expressed it in *émotions populaires*, riots that spread through much of France in the spring of 1775 and that became known as the Guerre des farines (Flour War).

18

Flour War

EDICTS ARRIVED in Paris from Versailles as if from on high, closing with the phrase, printed in capital letters, FOR SUCH IS OUR PLEASURE, for in an absolute monarchy the king's pleasure was law. Yet under Louis XVI edicts opened with long preambles in which the king explained the purpose of his legislation and even justified it. On September 13, 1774, an edict established free trade in grain throughout the kingdom. Its preamble, written by Turgot, read like a minitreatise on free-market economics. Turgot explained that state regulation stifled the grain trade and promoted dearth instead of alleviating it. By pursuing self-interest, merchants would satisfy need where it existed and would do so far more effectively than the police and other agents of the state, who made conditions worse by attempting to control prices. Free trade would establish a just price; thanks to competition, it would eliminate monopoly; and it would confirm the Crown's commitment to "the rights of property and of legitimate liberty." By invoking "reason and utility" as its basis, the edict distanced itself from the notion of law as the will of the king. Not, of course, that it renounced the traditional view, but it appealed to reason, and it argued its case as if it were a pamphlet addressed to the public— even, it could be claimed, as if it were seeking the public's approval.[1]

The edict got a warm reception—strong applause, as the *Gazette de Leyde* put it; appreciation for the forthright arguments in its preamble, as Hardy noted in his journal; and enthusiasm for a new tone in the way the government addressed the citizenry, as a *nouvelliste* emphasized: "In this edict the nation was delighted to read the words property and liberty, terms that had been eliminated for a long while from the dictionary of our kings."[2] Turgot himself received a great deal of applause when he succeeded Terray as controller general of finances, though not from the upper clergy and the *dévot* faction of the court. He was identified with the *économistes*, as the physiocrats were generally known, having worked closely with Vincent de Gournay, the intendant de commerce who reportedly coined the slogan "laissez faire, laissez passer." Turgot's long experience as an intendant in Limoges had also won him a reputation as a capable and civic-minded administrator, and he stood out, above all, in comparison to Terray, who was hated for his harsh measures and his disdain for the public's approval. A popular pamphlet, *Lettre de M. Terray, ex contrôleur général, à M. Turgot, ministre des finances,* pretended to be Terray's suggestions for policies Turgot should pursue. Instead of freeing the grain trade, he should tax the French to death, this fictitious Terray explained, because the secret to government was uninhibited oppression.[3]

Although the pamphleteers reduced the two administrations to a contrast of personalities, well-informed Parisians knew that Turgot's edict represented a profound shift in policy. They had lived through the same change a dozen years earlier. In fact, Turgot revived an edict of May 25, 1763, which removed all constraints to the internal grain trade, except for the provisioning of Paris, where increases in the price of bread sometimes aroused so much fury that they led to the riots known as *émotions populaires*. Before this radical break with past practices, grain could not flow freely from province to province, nor could farmers and millers intervene directly in the market. All sorts of middlemen, armed with exclusive privileges, negotiated ad hoc arrangements to store and supply grain and flour; and when the price of bread threatened to get out of hand, the police intervened by requisitioning supplies and capping price increases.[4]

The police and the common people shared assumptions about ethical limits to pricing. Parisians held to a vague notion of a "just price" and sometimes expressed it during crises by *taxation populaire* or raids on bakeries, where crowds seized bread and paid for it at a rate they considered equitable, such as 2 sous per pound or 8 sous for the standard, four-pound loaf. Their reasoning was moral rather than economic, because they believed they had a right to affordable bread and that the king, as father of the people, was bound to protect them from starvation. Although famine had not decimated France's population since the desperate last years of Louis XIV's reign, the poor often lacked adequate food, and they were haunted by the fear of dearth. Bread was the main ingredient of their diet. When he could find work, an unskilled laborer often made only 20 sous a day, supplemented by odd jobs picked up by his wife and children. A family of four normally consumed two four-pound loaves a day. During severe crises the price of one loaf reached 15 sous or more—and the family went hungry.[5]

The edict of May 1763 (formally a royal Declaration, confirmed by an edict of July 1764) followed ten years of good harvests in most of France. Registered, though with some hesitation, by the Parlement of Paris, it did not arouse much opposition. But bad harvests and poor provisioning forced the price of the four-pound loaf up to 13 sous in Paris by January 1767, then to a peak of 16 sous in December, and the price did not fall below 13 sous until the summer of 1769. Although the Parisians did not riot, they muttered angrily about a "famine plot"—that is, a conspiracy to monopolize grain and force up prices until it could be sold at an enormous profit. In some versions of this "bad talk" or "bad discourse," as the police called the hostile grumbling, the king himself or his ministers engineered the plot in order to pay off the debt accumulated during the Seven Years' War. In fact, the government had contracted with a company to stock grain for supplying Paris in a crisis, but the arrangement produced no relief and, when word of it got out, it confirmed suspicion of the Crown's complicity in a conspiracy.[6]

When Terray became controller general, he revoked the free-trade legislation of 1763 and restored the old policing measures, while creating an administrative body (*régie*) to build up an emergency supply for Paris. After three and a half years of state intervention, Turgot reversed Terray's policy, as he specified in the edict of September 13, 1774, which promised to establish "the just and natural price" in grain. Far from bringing down prices, however, free trade exposed them to fluctuations as severe as those of 1767–1768. They can be followed, week by week and sometimes day by day in the journal of Hardy, who considered bread prices crucial to the existence of the *menu peuple* (little people—artisans, shopkeepers, and laborers), though as a solid bourgeois he did not feel threatened himself.

On March 8, 1775, Hardy noted a danger signal: The price of the four-pound loaf in Paris, which had remained stable at 11 sous for the last ten months, had risen to 11 sous, 6 deniers. On March 15, it reached 12 sous, causing "huge grumbling among the common people, who were said to say quite openly in the marketplaces: 'What a rotten reign.'" On April 12, it rose to 12 sous, 6 deniers, and the *menu peuple* blamed the increase on the government. On April 15, it reached 13 sous. The bakers complained that they could not get enough flour, while the common people attributed the scarcity to a government plot. This was the beginning of the *soudure*, the period when last year's stock of grain was being depleted, and the new harvest had not yet arrived. On April 26, the price rose to 13 sous, 6 deniers, and Parisians learned that "emotions" had erupted in several cities. In Dijon, a crowd broke into the home of a miller who was believed to be a grain monopolizer. After smashing his furniture, the rioters stormed his mill and seized all the available grain and flour. Forty of them were arrested. Prices rose so drastically in Montauban that the intendant ordered farmers to supply the local market, in violation of Turgot's edict. And the high prices provoked such "fermentation" in Reims, where Louis XVI was to be crowned on June 11, that Hardy expected the coronation to be postponed. (It wasn't, although seditious posters appeared in the streets after a rumor spread that the king was hoarding bread in order to profit from the dearth.)

By May 1, word arrived that the epidemic of violence was approaching Paris.[7] Large crowds sacked grain from boats in Pointoise that were transporting provisions to the capital. Rioters in Saint Germain en Laye threw flour into the streets as a sign of defiance. And on May 2 an uprising in Versailles, a city of 50,000 inhabitants, seemed for a moment to threaten the king. According to some reports, Louis XVI appeared on a balcony of the palace and after failing to calm the crowd appeased it by ordering bread to be sold on the local market at 2 sous per pound. (In other versions the order was given by the captain of his guards.)

At eight in the morning on May 3, when the price of the four-pound loaf had reached 14 sous, rioting broke out in Paris. It spread quickly to every sector of the city and the faubourgs. Crowds swept bread off the stalls in all the marketplaces and dashed through the streets, looting bakeries. If they encountered any resistance, they smashed through doors with clubs and crowbars. They seized everything edible, although they did not sack entire shops. In some cases, they made payments at what they considered the just price—8 sous for the four-pound loaf. A few rioters claimed that the king had authorized *taxation populaire* at a rate of 2 sous per pound, but most of them simply helped themselves and tossed loaves out to others in the street. In addition to a thousand or so bakeries, the rioters broke into private houses, where they suspected bread was stored. Hardy had to let a crowd of sixty persons inspect his cellar to prove that he had no stock of his own. One group confiscated bread from the Abbey of Saint Victor in the Latin Quarter, promising to pay for it later at 2 sous per pound.

Despite rumors about brigands from outside the city, the crowds consisted of the Parisian "little people," including a great many women, who as a *nouvelliste* remarked, were "more dangerous than men in crises of this kind." The police did nothing to repress them because as Lieutenant General Lenoir later explained, no orders had arrived from Versailles. The Watch continued on its rounds, oblivious to the looting and incapable of suppressing it, so the rioters roamed through the city at will and effectively occupied it. By noon, not a loaf of bread was available anywhere, and, according to the *nouvelliste,* Paris looked like a city that had been sacked by an army. Yet he noted that the rioters had "a very gay demeanor," and there was relatively little bloodshed. A miller in Montmartre fought off a crowd, killing one person with a pistol shot, and twenty-three rioters were reportedly killed in a skirmish at the grain depot of Corbeil in the southern suburbs. But according to the abbé de Véri, the uprising, unlike earlier "emotions," was remarkably nonviolent: "It was all gaiety for the spectators, mildness and joviality for the perpetrators, and stupid or intentional inaction by those charged with maintaining public order."[8]

Turgot rushed to the scene from Versailles and after a confrontation with Lenoir, succeeded in rallying the police and the military forces. By the end of the day musketeers and troops from the Gardes Françaises and Gardes Suisses had restored order. Patrols of ten men, their bayonets attached to their rifles, marched through the streets; detachments of soldiers guarded all the marketplaces; and two troops were stationed in every bakery. Nearly two hundred persons were arrested. Parisians witnessed a group of eight "rebels," tied together, being marched to prison through the Place Maubert and three wagons full of prisoners being driven to the Bastille. On May 11, two men—a wigmaker and a laborer—were hanged in the Place de Grève, which was ringed with soldiers, who kept it closed to the public in order to prevent more violence. Many Parisians considered the condemned men as scapegoats, sacrificed to impress the public while the actual instigators of the uprising went free. But who were the true culprits?

Parisians discussed this question for weeks and never came up with an answer, although they remained convinced that some conspiracy must have been at work. The king himself encouraged this suspicion. On the night of May 3 he sent a courier to the Parlement with an order forbidding it to take any action because he had directed the government to investigate the uprising, "about which I know the secret causes."[9] The Parlement passed a decree nevertheless, forbidding all gatherings and requesting the king to reduce the price of bread to a level the people could afford. Printed copies of the decree were posted throughout the city on the evening of May 4, and groups of the common people flocked to read them by candlelight that night. On the next day, musketeers tore down the notices and in their place posted a contradictory ordinance of the king. It, too, outlawed gatherings and threatened the death penalty for anyone who interfered with the sale of bread, but it maintained the current price, which had reached 13 sous 6 deniers for the four-pound loaf. Two subsequent ordinances, cried out by peddlers and posted at street corners, reaffirmed the king's determination to repress disorder, although they withdrew the threat of summary execution. This information war, which pitted the Parlement against the king, resulted from the Parlement's claim to exercise "la grande police," including the right to investigate disturbances. Louis XVI prevented it from taking any such action in a *lit de justice* of May 5. At Turgot's urging, he replaced Lenoir as lieutenant general of police, and he continued to dispatch troops to Paris—50,000, of them, it was rumored, at a cost of 15 million L. On May 16, Louis sent a circular letter via the bishops to all the curates of the kingdom. It instructed them to maintain calm among their parishioners and warned that they soon would receive shocking news about the identity of those behind the uprising.

That revelation never took place. As time went by and the price of bread failed to drop, Parisians entertained all sorts of suspicions. Word spread that the conspirators were led by the Prince de Conti or the Prince de Condé or Louis XVI's aunts, Madame Adélaïde and Madame Louise, who were known to favor the Jesuits, or Maupeou and Terray, or the English. A Jesuit plot seemed credible to many observers, who thought it might be backed by Turgot's enemies among various financiers. The most extravagant rumor concerned a supposed Black heir to the throne born to Louis XV's queen Marie Leszczynska. (It did not explain how he came to be Black.) Having been kept in hiding abroad, he was said to have stirred up the insurrection in order to prepare the way for an invasion of France and the overthrow of Louis XVI.[10] All these "noises" were variations on the famine plot, which attributed the rise in the price of bread to conspirators who also wanted to provoke riots in order to get rid of Turgot—unless he himself was the archconspirator. A simpler explanation held that Turgot had brought on the uprising by letting grain find its own price. As a current poem put it, his free-trade policy had backfired:

Est-ce Maupeou, tant abhorré	*Is it much-hated Maupeou*
Qui nous rend le bled cher en	*Who has made wheat so dear in*
France?	*France?*
Ou bien est-ce l'abbé Terray?	*Or is it abbé Terray?*
Est-ce le clergé, la finance?	*Is it the clergy, the financiers?*
Des Jésuites est-ce vengeance?	*The vengeance of the Jesuits?*
Ou des Anglais un tour fallot?	*Or a foul deed by the English?*
Non, ce n'est point-là le fin	*No, the answer to the riddle isn't*
mot....	*those ...*
Mais voulez-vous qu'en confidence	*But do you in confidence want*
Je vous le dise? . . . C'est Turgot.[11]	*Me to tell you? . . . It's Turgot.*

Turgot held on to office for another year, but the Guerre des Farines, as it came to be known, undercut his support—in the ministry, where Maurepas turned against him; in the court, where the upper clergy rallied his opponents; in the public, where the early enthusiasm for him fizzled out; and finally with Louis XVI. The king himself suffered a loss of respect and perhaps of some of the sacrality that went with kingship. At the height of the crisis on May 2, he dashed off two letters, one in the morning, one in the afternoon, to Turgot, who was in Paris, attempting to contain the uprising. They had a decidedly unregal tone. At one point the king assured Turgot, "You can count on me to be firm." Copies of them circulated in Paris, where readers remarked that they made Louis sound as if he were a corporal reporting to his sergeant.[12] At the same time, just a month before Louis's coronation, hostile placards appeared in the streets of Paris:

> Louis XVI will be coronated on June 11 and massacred on the twelfth.

> If the price of bread does not decrease, we will exterminate the king and everyone of Bourbon blood.

> Henri IV was assassinated, Louis XV escaped [assassination], and Louis XVI will be massacred before being coronated.[13]

Of course, placards were meant to be provocative and should not be taken as an accurate measure of the general sentiment. But the Flour War certainly damaged Parisians' faith in their king, whom they took to be responsible for supplying them with affordable bread, and it destroyed whatever sympathy they felt for free trade. Turgot's rival, Jacques Necker, soon succeeded him—first as Directeur du Trésor Royal on October 22, 1776, then as Directeur général des finances on June 29, 1777. (Because he was a Protestant, he could not formally become a minister.) Just before the outbreak of the Flour War, Necker published *Sur la législation et le commerce des grains*, a long, carefully reasoned treatise that favored state intervention to control the price of bread and manage finances in general. Although less witty than another attack on the *économistes*, *Dialogues sur le commerce des bleds* (1770) by abbé Ferdinando Galiani, and less passionate than *Du Pain et du bled* (1774), the antiphysiocratic tract of Linguet, Necker's book was a great success, and it set an agenda for the next years of Louis XVI's reign. Like Terray, Necker would govern by immersing himself in the complex machinery of the state. Like Turgot, he would inform the public about his policies and cultivate its support. Whether pragmatic administration and careful public relations would restore the health of the Crown's finances remained to be seen. Yet Necker got off to a strong start and astounded Parisians by coming up with something undreamt of—a state budget.

PART FOUR

The Ideological Terrain, 1781–1786

19

The King's Secret Is Revealed

P ARISIANS SHARED the assumption, centuries old, that affairs of state were secret. They were the king's business, restricted to the king himself and his advisors. Although politics occasionally spilled into the street, they normally remained hidden in the distant world of the court, transacted behind closed doors, and determined in secret councils—a matter of *arcana imperii* (secrets of power, state secrets, *le secret du Roi*). In February 1781, Jacques Necker stripped away the secrecy by publishing his *Compte rendu au Roi*, a detailed account of the state's income and expenses and of his activities as director-general of finances.

Parisians were stunned. A revelation, in print, written by the official in charge of the state's finances, produced by the imprimerie royale, and available to everyone for a mere 3 L.—nothing like it had ever occurred. On the day of publication, they swarmed to the shop of Charles-Joseph Panckoucke, the most prominent bookseller in Paris, demanding copies. The entire stock of 3,000 was exhausted on the first day. (At that time pressruns typically came to about 1,000 copies and took many months or years to sell out.) The presses worked night and day on new editions. Reports arrived of amazing sales—12,000 in a few weeks; 42,500 within a month. Panckoucke expected to sell 100,000 copies, according to the *Courrier du Bas-Rhin*, whose Paris correspondent wrote that copies were to be found everywhere: "In all houses, on all toilettes, in cafés and promenades, one finds only the *Compte rendu*."[1] The *Correspondance littéraire secrète*, an illegal newssheet, piled on the superlatives in a long review, concluding that the *Compte rendu* was the greatest success in the history of publishing, the supreme work of the century. Translations into English, Dutch, German, Italian, and Danish appeared with amazing speed, while the French original, reprinted by Panckoucke and pirated frequently, spread everywhere in Europe. Although the text—116 pages about state finance—might appear rebarbative, readers gobbled it up. Hardy noted that it was "devoured . . . by a prodigious multitude." For weeks, Parisians talked about virtually nothing else, according to the *nouvellistes*. The sober *Gazette de Leyde*, which rarely reviewed books, said that no work had ever been received with more "avidity" and that the *Compte rendu* would leave an indelible mark on the history of France and indeed of all Europe. Week after week the *Gazette* printed long excerpts from the text, treating it as one of the most important publications ever to appear in print.[2]

Necker made the subject accessible by placing the statistics at the end of the book and expounding the administrative issues in clear detail. His critics found it overwritten and repulsively self-centered (the *Mémoires secrets* deplored its "stinking egoism").[3] But most readers seemed to have been taken with Necker's openness in explaining state affairs and the humanitarian tone of his determination to relieve the misery of the poor. The last section of the book included an emotional depiction of the suffering in France's prisons and overburdened hospitals. Necker explained his struggle to find enough money so that each hospital patient could have a bed of his own, and he paid tribute to his wife, who had founded a new hospital, which, he declared, would be supported by everything earned from the book's sales. The emphasis on humanitarianism hardly seemed appropriate to a budget report, but the *Compte rendu*, although formally addressed to the king, was actually aimed at the general public. Necker invoked public opinion in its first and final paragraphs. He made it clear that he intended to do away with the "mystery about the financial situation" and advocated that an account of the state's finances be published every five years. As a model, he cited the British practice of publishing an annual budget and submitting it to the approval of Parliament. Not that anything like a Parliament existed in France, of course.

Necker explained that by making regular reports, finance ministers would maintain "public confidence"—that is, they would always be able to float loans, just as he had done to finance the American war, which France entered as an ally of the American revolutionaries on February 6, 1778, without raising taxes. The loans could be paid off by maintaining a healthy balance of income over expenditure, all of it made manifest by open, honest "publicity."⁴

The *Compte rendu* demonstrated that such a system had in fact succeeded under Necker's administration, according to his calculations. In Part I, he showed how, after much labor, he had determined the actual state of France's finances—a difficult task, because the Crown disposed of many separate treasuries (*caisses*) administered by semiautonomous office-holders (all sorts of *receveurs* and *trésoriers*, aside from the *Ferme générale*, which collected customs and most indirect taxes). Far from constituting a civil service, these financiers owned their offices, and the accounts they generated had never been integrated in a single budget. By sorting through this vast undergrowth of offices and trimming much of it away, Necker determined to his satisfaction that the state was actually well off: In the last year, "ordinary" revenue exceeded "ordinary" expenses by 10.2 million livres. To be sure, the American war forced the government to raise "extraordinary" sums; but in the long run they could be covered by loans, without additional taxation, thanks to the built-in balance.

Part II explained how Necker had accomplished this feat. He had not played the game in the manner of his predecessors. Far from cultivating protectors in the court, he had refused to grant pensions and favors (*grâces*). He had retired many *receveurs* and *trésoriers* and had reduced the number of tax farmers from forty-eight to twelve, all of them supervised within a single organization. He had cut the expenses of the king's household by half and had saved money on transactions such as "exchanges" (trades of Crown land for less valuable estates of favorites) and the minting of new coins. In a word, he had eliminated all abuses. Although none of these reforms had been visible to the public, he brought them all to light in the *Compte rendu*, because the public deserved an accounting, and even more, it was entitled to a new kind of administration—severe, frugal, honest, and open. As the text made clear, those were the virtues of Necker himself, a Protestant and a Swiss, and they were the antithesis of the qualities embodied by most ministers, particularly the worldly, wily Comte de Maurepas, who was the dominant figure in the king's council and a secret enemy of Necker. According to the *Compte rendu*, government was ultimately a matter of "moral conduct," and therefore Necker's guardianship of the treasury served as testimony to his character, or as he himself put it, his "elevated soul."[5]

Part III showed how civic virtue would be built into a political program. Necker intended to transform France's taxation system, not by a direct assault on privilege (he said nothing about the exemptions of the church and nobility), but by readjusting it to correct the inequities that crushed the common people. He would reapportion the most fundamental tax, the *taille*, which varied enormously, whether levied on individuals or on land, by creating provincial administrations to distribute it more fairly. He would reassess the basis for payments of the *vingtièmes*, which had evolved into unequal taxes on all kinds of revenue. He would abolish the *corvée* (forced labor on roads and other public works by peasants). And although he could not rescind the much hated salt tax (*gabelle*) because it contributed so much to the treasury, he would make it fall more equally on everyone. He also would eliminate internal customs and lighten the load of indirect taxes by curtailing the power of the General Tax Farm. He even intended to standardize weights and measures. Above all, his program would bring relief to the poor, including the indigent in hospitals and debtors in prisons. He would heed the call of "suffering humanity."[6]

After proclaiming this program, Necker produced a budget, full of precise detail and numbers. Under revenue, he revealed the principal sources of the Crown's income, giving readers a view, for the first time, of sensitive subjects, such as the contribution of the church (the annual average of its *don gratuit*, voted on every five years by the general assembly of the clergy)— a mere 3.2 million livres in comparison with the 54 million raised by the salt tax. Under expenditures, he informed the French of how much of their taxes went to maintaining the household of the king (*maison du roi*)—25.7 million. If readers considered that extravagant, what did they make of the sum listed under "pensions"—28 million? Or the amount devoted to the police of Paris—1.4 million? Necker left the comparisons and evaluations up to them. At the end of the long run of statistics, he summarized it all in three numbers:

Revenue	264,154,000
Expenditure	*253,954,000*
	10,200,000

The secret was revealed. The state enjoyed a healthy balance in its budget. Necker had been a good steward.

Readers were inclined to accept those conclusions, judging from the reports on the book's reception. Yet they also had difficulty in assimilating Necker's argument because they had never before had access to such information, and French finances were extremely complex. How to make sense of it all? Pamphleteers rose to the occasion, especially among Necker's enemies. The most effective attack on the *Compte rendu*, according to the *nouvellistes*, was a tract titled *Les Comments*. It raised twelve objections to Necker's argument, each one beginning with *"Comment"* (*How*) in italics. It asked, for example, *how* Necker could claim that the budget had a surplus when he failed to take into account payments due on 350 million livres of accumulated debt. And *how* he could enter "anticipations" (advances on future revenue) at 5.5 million livres among the expenditures, when they actually came to 142 million. The anonymous author seemed to possess inside knowledge about the operations of the treasury, and he reached a disturbing conclusion: By pretending to expose the secret of state finances as if he were a British chancellor of the exchequer, Necker had egregiously misled the public. The royal treasury was suffering from a disastrous deficit. A supplement, titled *Les Pourquoi*, provided more figures and concluded that the deficit came to 19,580,000 livres.[7] And another attack, *Lettre d'un bon Français*, made a similar argument, with still more statistics, concluding that the deficit was 26 million livres.[8] Readers could be expected to favor a statesman known for his integrity over anonymous pamphleteers, but how could they sort out the bewildering numbers in order to know who was right?

A more popular work, *Lettre du marquis Caraccioli à M. d'Alembert*, which contemporaries attributed to Beaumarchais, also took Necker to task for failing to account for the heavy burden of his loans and "anticipations." For the most part, however, it mocked the pretensions of the "*Neckristes*," and readers took it to be "witty taunting" rather than reliable financial analysis.[9] Most of the other pamphlets against Necker also belonged to the genre of political satire that had long thrived in Paris, where, as the *Lettre du marquis Caraccioli* put it, "What is announced as very important in the morning is eliminated in the evening with a witticism."[10] That view coincided with the refrain that soon would be notorious from *Le Mariage de Figaro*: "Everything finishes with songs." While working on his play, Beaumarchais was said to be printing a collection of anti-Necker pamphlets on the presses in Kehl that were turning out his edition of Voltaire's works.[11] Necker's partisans scorned Voltairean ridicule. They replied with evidence about the state's income and expenditure, served up with indignation at the levity with which the anti-*Neckristes* treated serious questions of the public welfare.[12] The polemics continued for months, illustrating a growing opposition between sophisticated wit on one side and moralistic sentiment on the other—a contrast at the level of rhetoric that echoed the divergent appeals of Voltaire and Rousseau.

The attacks on the *Compte rendu* failed to stop the flood of enthusiasm that greeted it. Street singers belted out *chansons* that celebrated Necker as a champion of the people, and peddlers hawked prints that made him an easily recognizable hero, crowned with laurel, crushing the monster "envy," or triumphantly handing the *Compte rendu* to Louis XVI. One print showed Necker standing next to Lord North, the head of the British government. Necker held a copy of the *Compte rendu* in his hand; North held a copy of the British budget. Both smiled, and at their feet lay a cornucopia, indicating the abundance that would follow once peace was restored.[13]

Three months after the publication of the *Compte rendu*, Necker was dismissed. According to the reports that reached Parisians, he fell as a victim of court intrigue masterminded by Maurepas—and also because he overplayed his hand: he demanded that the king admit him to the royal council, a promotion that was then considered to be impossible for a foreigner and a Protestant. While lining up support among courtiers and ministers, Maurepas leaked a confidential memorandum that Necker had submitted to the king in 1778. Like the *Compte rendu*, it advocated a system of provincial administrations that would determine the amounts to be paid at the local level for key taxes, especially the *taille*. But it went further, because it recommended limiting the authority of the intendants and, more important, the parlements. Instead of exerting power to impede new taxes by refusing to register royal edicts, the parlements would be reduced to their judicial function, as under Maupeou. The government would set the amounts to be raised, and the provincial assemblies representing landowners would distribute the contributions among the local taxpayers, free of interference by the intendants.[14]

When it appeared in print, shortly after his fall, Necker's memorandum, *Mémoire sur les administrations provinciales*, was denounced by all his enemies—hostile ministers, courtiers, parlementary magistrates, clergymen, and financiers.[15] Yet it consolidated his support in the general public. Parisians reacted to Necker's fall with "consternation" and collective anger. For weeks, they talked of nothing else. They gathered in cafés, streets, and private homes to vent their resentment of Versailles. The Comédie française performed *La Partie de chasse de Henri IV*, a play that celebrated the people's favorite king and his minister Sully. In a scene where Henri discovered that an intrigue of courtiers had provoked him to dismiss Sully, he cried out, "They have deceived me"; and a voice from the audience answered, "Yes, yes!" Then the entire audience shouted "yes" over and over. The audience at a performance of *Le Misanthrope* also seized on a line to create a similar "brouhaha."[16] Necker remained more popular than ever, and his expulsion from the government enhanced a sentiment of solidarity that *nouvellistes* described as the opposition of "the people" to "the *grands*."[17]

After Necker's fall, his enemies among the financiers (*receveurs généraux, fermiers généraux*, and others) clawed back power; new taxes were levied; and the Contrôle général passed from one ineffective administrator to another until 1783, when it fell into the hands of Charles Alexandre de Calonne. The public saw Calonne as the antithesis of Necker. Sophisticated, witty, and well-connected in the court, he ruled over the state's finances with a light hand, dispensing pensions and favors until the end of 1786, when he revealed to an astonished Louis XVI that the Crown faced bankruptcy.

During those years, Necker continued to advocate his view of what had been and should be France's budget, drawing on the *Compte rendu*.

His tract of 1781 inspired *Neckriste* opponents of the government and remained enmeshed in polemics and politics. It also conveyed a message that resonated beyond the immediate circumstances. Far off in Berlin, the renowned geographer Friedrich Büsching celebrated it as the first time a monarch had revealed the "sacred mystery" of his finances to his subjects. In Besançon, the parlement hailed Necker as the first statesman to strip away the veil that had hidden "the mystery" of the state's finances and asked him to send a copy of the *Compte rendu* for it to keep in its archives.[18] In Paris, the public remained convinced that the *Compte rendu* "will mark an era forever memorable and glorious in the history of the monarchy."[19]

Whether or not readers understood the financial argument or agreed with the political program of the *Compte rendu*, they recognized that it represented a decisive break with the past. No longer would it be possible to keep the state's finances hidden. If future ministers tried to raise taxes, they would have to convince the public that the treasury required a new infusion of money. Even if he had got his calculations wrong, Necker had uncovered the mystery at the heart of France's system of government. The system itself was exposed to the examination of its subjects, who now were thinking of themselves as citizens. Once the king's secret was revealed, there was no turning back.

20

The Taste of Victory

THE NEWS OF the peace ending the American war reached most Parisians through their ears. As in 1748 and 1763, the peace of 1783 was "published" by a royal proclamation read aloud during elaborate ceremonies staged at fourteen locations scattered throughout the city. It was a noisy affair. The ceremonies began and ended with cannonades; the tocsin rang from church bells all day long; and the readings were accompanied by blasts of trumpets and drum rolls from a gigantic procession—seven hundred dignitaries and soldiers on horse and on foot. Three groups of musicians marched in the parade and performed at regular intervals, playing *cromornes* (a clarinet-like instrument), fifes, oboes, trumpets, and kettledrums. Although the proclamation merely announced that subjects of the French and British kings now could travel freely and do business in both countries, its "publication" left ears ringing.[1]

The event began on November 25 with breakfast at the Hôtel de Ville for the seven hundred participants, each dressed in ceremonial attire. Then each took his place in the formal "order of the procession," which displayed the status and dignity of the municipal officials. The lieutenant general of police, mounted on a splendid white horse, and the prévôt des marchands, in a gown of crimson felt, stood out, while detachments of the Watch and the Garde de Paris filled in the ranks. At each of the fourteen stops, after a burst of music, the Roi d'Armes called out three times "de par le roi" (by order of the king) and summoned a herald to read out the text of the peace *ordonnance*. Then the official commanded three fanfares, called out three times, "Long live the king!" and the procession moved on to the next stop. It continued in this fashion for eight hours and finally returned for a banquet in the Hôtel de Ville. Twenty thousand printed copies of the *ordonnance* were also distributed and posted. All of Paris knew that something momentous had occurred.[2]

What Parisians made of it is difficult to determine. Most of the fighting had ended two years earlier after the Battle of Yorktown. At that point, the diplomats took over; and while the negotiations dragged on, Parisians' attention shifted to other events. Most of them were more interested in the first public balloon flight, which took place on September 19, 1783, than in the details of the peace treaty, which was signed in Versailles on September 3. Wars always brought an increase in taxation, and sure enough, in August 1781, little more than a month after Necker's fall, the government levied a surtax on articles of consumption such as soap, sugar, and candles. Although it claimed to reduce the rate on some commodities, the surtax (an additional 2 sous for every livre paid at the previous rate) actually made life much more expensive for most Parisians, who complained bitterly. In Paris alone the tax raised at least 20 million L., and it was collected by agents of the much-hated Fermiers Généraux, who regained their hold on French finances after the disappearance of Necker. To many Parisians, the main result of the war was a crushing national debt, one so enormous that it could not be calculated, as illustrated by the conflicting claims of the pamphleteers.[3]

Peace certainly meant that France had regained its prestige as a great power, after the humiliating defeat of the Seven Years' War. The Parisian bookseller Nicolas Ruault expressed a common view when he wrote to his brother following the publication of the peace, "We have taken our revenge."[4] Although it produced satisfaction at the defeat of France's long-standing enemy, the peace did not release an explosion of joy. France did not gain any new territory, except Tobago and part of Senegal, which had no interest for most Parisians. True, France had helped detach territory from the British empire, but would the United States be a reliable ally? Ruault had his doubts because deep down the Americans were English—"That's all there is to say." Nonetheless, he rejoiced that an entire people had recovered its liberty. His recently published anthology of pro-American writing had introduced the French to some provocative documents, including a folksy essay from *Poor Richard's Almanac*, Ben Franklin's testimony about the Stamp Act before Parliament in 1766, and the Pennsylvania state constitution of 1776, which asserted the right of the people to disband their government and transferred power to a unicameral legislature elected by all taxpayers.[5]

Although rejoicing did not break out at the proclamation of the peace, official "réjouissances," as after the previous two wars, were organized by the Hôtel de Ville for the Parisian population. They took place on December 14, 1783, after a long delay, owing to lack of funds. The celebrations began at 7:00 in the morning with an artillery salvo and the ringing of the tocsin in the Hôtel de Ville. At 4:00 p.m., the archbishop of Paris officiated over a Te Deum in Notre Dame, which was followed by another salvo. At 6:00 a large crowd gathered in the Place de Grève to watch a fireworks display, which went off without much mishap. Then two gigantic buffets, one at 7:00 and another at 10:00, provided the crowd with a free meal of sausages, side dishes, and bread accompanied by wine dispensed from fountains. Food and wine were also distributed from seventeen other locations, as if the municipal officials had offered dinner to everyone in Paris. Ordinary Parisians were also invited to a dance in the Halle au bled, the grain market, which had been converted into a ballroom 120 feet in diameter. A huge dome had recently been built over the Halle, and from it hung a chandelier weighing 1,000 pounds and covered with mirrors reflecting the light of five hundred candles. A band played in the middle of the dance floor, and a gallery under the dome made it possible for people of distinction to watch the common folk below, who danced the night away.[6]

The *nouvellistes* found nothing unusual to report about the celebration. Some spectators got knocked over during the fireworks; a gentleman was slapped in the gallery of the Halle au bled; a police agent had his wig snatched. After getting permission, with much difficulty, from the archbishop, a masonic lodge called Le Contrat Social celebrated the peace on the following day with a Te Deum and music in the Congrégation de l'Oratoire of the rue Saint Honoré.[7] Meanwhile, having eaten their fill, gotten drunk, and danced, Parisians returned to their work. Apparently no one at the party had stopped to toast the new United States, but everyone was aware that the French monarchy had come to the rescue of a revolutionary republic, and Parisians in general were fascinated by this new species of humanity, the American.

What Is an American?

THE COMMON PEOPLE who danced away the night on December 14, 1783, had only a vague notion of the republic on the other side of the ocean, and the gentlefolk who watched them from the gallery probably could not picture it clearly on a mental map (reports often contained references such as "New-Haven dans la Nouvelle Yorck").[1] Yet a Frenchman, Michel-Guillaume-Saint-Jean de Crèvecoeur, was the first to ask, "What is an American?" That question opened up a set of subjects related to the new world, which provided opportunities to challenge old-world orthodoxies.

Born into a minor noble family in Caen, Crèvecoeur left France in 1755 at age nineteen to serve as a cartographer in the French army during the Seven Years' War. He eventually settled on a farm in Orange County, New York, adopted the name of J. Hector St. John, married an American woman, fathered three children, and prospered, while recording his experiences in a journal. In 1779, he returned to France in order, he said, to see his ailing father. While passing through London, he found a publisher interested in producing a book of essays adapted from the journal. It appeared in 1782 as *Letters from an American Farmer* and offered a new vision of the new world. Written in homespun English, it contained vignettes of life on the frontier, contact with Indians, and customs in exotic communities such as Nantucket whalers and Pennsylvania Quakers. Across the ocean, it revealed, there was a land of opportunity, free from the constraints of the old world, where immigrants from all countries and all levels of society could seek their fortune and find it, provided they were willing to work. They were the answer to the question, "What is an American?" True, slavery had spread misery in the South, creating a dissolute oligarchy in cities like Charleston; but a promising future awaited the main population of ordinary, hard-working folk such as Farmer James, Crèvecoeur's narrator and the quintessential American. *Letters from an American Farmer* was an early version of the American success story, and it was a success itself, a best seller, catering to the public's fascination with the way of life in the new republic.[2]

In Paris Crèvecoeur was taken up by Elisabeth Sophie Lalive de Bellegarde, Comtesse d'Houdetot, and the members of her circle—worldly aristocrats and men of letters. Mme d'Houdetot had helped set the fashion for *sensiblerie* and seized on Crèvecoeur as an unsophisticated soul who had arrived in her salon directly from the unspoiled wilderness.[3] Although intimidated by such attention from a countess, who, moreover, was believed to be the model for Julie in Rousseau's *La Nouvelle Héloïse*, Crèvecoeur submitted to her campaign to reintroduce him to French society—and also to get him named French consul in New York, a post he held from late 1783 to 1790 (he returned on leave to Paris in 1785–1787). With help from the writers in her salon, he produced a "translation" of his book, now dedicated to Lafayette and issued in two volumes, more than twice the size of the original, in 1784. Having spoken nothing but English for most of the last two decades, Crèvecoeur could not manage correct, literary French. But his helpers—fashionable luminaries such as Jean-François de Saint-Lambert, Pierre-Louis de Lacretelle, and Guy-Jean-Baptiste Target—provided the necessary polish, along with additional text. By subtracting, so to speak, the English edition of 1782 from the French edition of 1784, one can isolate the themes interjected for the benefit of a French audience and gain a view of this ideal type, the American, as it was construed in France.[4]

The French edition followed the English in celebrating the egalitarian character of life in America thanks to its freedom from feudal dues and ecclesiastical domination, but it outdid the original in emphasizing sentiment and morality. Key terms, such as "moeurs" (morals, customs), were inserted to bring out the peculiar virtues of Americans,[5] and long passages were added to show how those virtues shaped the social order. Like Farmer James, most Americans derived their sustenance from the soil. They lived simply, eschewed luxury, honored their conjugal vows, dedicated themselves to their children, sustained their neighbors in times of need, and worshipped the Supreme Being in sober country churches.[6] Because they lived close to nature, Americans developed a sensitivity to the spirit that infused creation. The English edition indicated that "natural religion" would become a peculiarly American doctrine, and the French edition bathed this deism in sentiment. It expanded a two-page English passage, mostly of observations about the habits of birds, into a six-page hymn to Nature. Crèvecoeur, in the person of Farmer James, sang along with the birds, prayed in his fields, and retired to a "temple of greenery," where he communed with the divine: "You come, carried on the wings of zephirs, thou sweet breath of Nature; already you are reasoning across the leaves that surround me everywhere."[7]

A Rousseauistic political message infused the descriptions of this idyllic society, and in a later edition, published in 1787 and expanded to three volumes, Crèvecoeur made its implications explicit. He pictured a group of Europeans discussing the nature of society in an American tavern. One had emigrated to escape monarchical wars, one "the oppressive tyranny of our seigneurial landlords," one religious persecution, and one the inhumane character of urban life. They decided to avoid those evils by carving their own society, "Socialburg," out of the wilderness. They agreed on plans for homesteads, roads, a school, and a church. And above all, they committed themselves to basic principles: agrarian virtues ("Honor the plow"), equality ("Consider all men as equal by birth"), a deistic civil religion ("The base of society must be founded on the cult we owe to the Supreme Being"), and the social spirit of "fraternal union." Socialburg would be run like the direct democracy idealized by Rousseau, and it would be created by an explicit social contract. Each immigrant signaled his commitment by drinking a toast, and on the following day they signed the contract composed of seventeen articles.[8]

Crèvecoeur's vision of America had enormous appeal to a reading public imbued with Rousseauistic *sensiblerie*. In fact, *Lettres d'un cultivateur américain* probably was the most influential book about America published in France before 1789.[9] Few books of any kind had such an enthusiastic reception. The *Journal de Paris* spread a rapturous review of the 1784 edition over three issues in 1785, a highly unusual treatment. The *Mercure* produced forty pages of extracts and the *Année littéraire* sixty pages. Three pirated editions were published by the end of 1785, and reprints continued to appear in subsequent years. Crèvecoeur succeeded better than anyone else who wrote about America, according to the *Journal de Paris*, because he knew how to "transmit his affections into the souls of his readers."[10] He also got across a political message, as Lacretelle explained in the *Mercure*, addressing his remarks rhetorically to the Americans: "In adopting democracy, you commit yourselves to strong and pure morals, and yet you do not separate yourselves from the rest of the universe, where political slavery and moral corruption triumph."[11] As United States ambassador to France, Thomas Jefferson received letters from enraptured readers of Crèvecoeur who intended to emigrate to America: "You are made to give us laws, because you illustrate for us the men of the Golden Age.... Ah, Monsieur, your land is the promised land.... How happy I would be to exist in such a good country. There I would be a man, whereas here I am nothing but a slave."[12]

The wave of enthusiasm for the French version of the *Lettres* buried a problem that could have blunted its radical message: Crèvecoeur had not supported the American Revolution. In fact, he had refused to take an oath of allegiance to the Patriots and left his farm to escape revolutionary violence in 1782. The last letter in the English edition suggested that he favored neutrality rather than commitment to one side or the other. After he departed for Europe, his wife's family fled to the Loyalist colony in Nova Scotia, and he expressed Loyalist sympathies in several letters. None of his aversion to the revolutionary cause came through in the French editions, however. On the contrary, they modified the text to justify the Americans' right to revolt, and they condemned British tyranny in suitably revolutionary rhetoric.[13] To the French, therefore, Crèvecoeur appeared as an American patriot, and after his makeover he occupied a prominent position in the ideological landscape that was radicalizing around him.

In January 1787 Crèvecoeur joined three other Frenchmen in founding the Société Gallo-Américaine, a philosophical club devoted to furthering close ties between France and America.[14] Although it was intended to develop branches throughout both countries, it ceased to meet after three months because its members were swept up in other activities, some of them seditious. Crèvecoeur himself did not contemplate any radical activism. He wanted the Society to promote commerce between the two countries in a way that would benefit his function as the French consul in New York. But the other three founders, Jacques-Pierre Brissot, Etienne Clavière, and Nicolas Bergasse, combined a passion for all things American with radical activism. Brissot, who would go on to become a leader of the Girondists during the French Revolution, had pursued a checkered career as a *philosophe* and pamphleteer, which led to four months in the Bastille in 1784. In one of his tracts, *Le Philadelphien à Genève*, he defended the Genevan revolution of 1782 (an unsuccessful uprising against a patrician oligarchy), writing from the perspective of a Rousseauistic American revolutionary. At several of the Society's meetings, he read selections from a book on French-American relations, *De la France et des Etats-Unis*, that he was drafting in collaboration with Clavière. They proposed ways to promote French-American trade with the proviso that France's exports reinforce American morals—that is, no luxuries of the kind favored by the decadent French elite: no jewelry, copper instead of silver cutlery, and woolens rather than silk. And they celebrated the American Revolution for teaching the rest of the world about the social contract and the right of citizens to overthrow despotic governments.[15]

Clavière had been a leader of the Genevan revolution, and after fleeing to France, speculated on the Paris Bourse in ways that, as we shall see, developed into a campaign against the French finance minister. While meeting with the Gallo-Americans, Bergasse was preparing to argue a case in an adultery trial that also would turn into an attack on the government. The minutes of the Gallo-American Society show that this odd variety of subjects—the evil of adultery, the dangers of the stock market, the threat of luxury goods—belonged to the admixture of elements that went into the French enthusiasm for America. Although the Society soon dissolved, it was a progenitor of the Société des amis des Noirs, an anti-slavery society founded by Brissot and Clavière in 1788, which included Crèvecoeur (then in New York), Lafayette, Condorcet, Mirabeau, Robespierre, Grégoire, and others who would play an important part in the French Revolution.

The mythical America conjured up in France should not be reduced to radical Rousseauism, however, because it contained contradictory elements and led to violent polemics. Jefferson frequented the circle of Marie-Louise-Nicole-Elisabeth de La Rochefoucauld, Duchesse d'Enville, where he enjoyed the company of well-bred champions of the United States who favored rational argument rather than sentiment. The duchesse's son, Louis-Alexandre de La Rochefoucauld had, at Franklin's suggestion, translated the American state constitutions into French, and her favorite, Condorcet, published radical but carefully reasoned pamphlets under the name of a Bourgeois de New Haven (or "BDNH"), New Haven having granted him honorary citizenship.

But Jefferson kept running into romantics inspired not only by Crèvecoeur but also by the reflections on America in Raynal's best-selling *Histoire philosophique et politique des établissements et du commerce des Européens dans les deux Indes.* Raynal actually took a somewhat critical view of the American Revolution that circulated as a pamphlet, *Révolution de l'Amérique,* extracted from the 1781 edition of the *Histoire philosophique.* Writing from Philadelphia, Thomas Paine attacked the pamphlet as a philosophical speculation uninformed by accurate information.[16] Jefferson shared Paine's distress about the errors in the depictions of America by the French. He spent many hours trying to correct the article on America that J.-N. Démeunier submitted to him before sending it to be published in the *Encyclopédie méthodique,* and in the end gave up: "He has left in a great deal of the abbé Raynal, that is to say a great deal of falsehood."[17]

Although Jefferson had some contact with the Gallo-Americans, two of his closest friends, François Jean de Beauvoir, Marquis de Chastellux, and Filippo Mazzei, were their enemies. In 1786 Chastellux, a major general under Rochambeau, friend of Washington, and member of the Académie française, published a two-volume account of the three years he had spent in America from 1780 through 1782. Brissot attacked it in a violent pamphlet, which condemned some ironic remarks about Quakers and the unsophisticated character of American manners, as "poison," the product of a desiccated soul. Mazzei, a Tuscan noble who had emigrated to Virginia and later joined Jefferson's circle in Paris, retorted in a letter to the *Journal de Paris* that Brissot's pamphlet demonstrated ignorance about the real life of Americans, notably Quakers, who were "Protestant Jesuits." Mazzei also announced the imminent publication of a book that would provide an accurate picture of America—his own four-volume *Recherches historiques et politiques sur les Etats-Unis de l'Amérique septentrionale par un citoyen de Virginie.*

This work debunked the fantasies about America conjured up by "novelists," beginning with Raynal and Mably, the *philosophes* who had helped launch the vogue, and culminating in Crèvecoeur. He warned readers that Crèvecoeur's *Lettres* had spread such an inaccurate and idealized notion of American life that they could provoke a wave of misinformed and unprepared immigrants. Though badly wounded, Crèvecoeur did not reply publicly, but Brissot vehemently denounced Mazzei in *L'Analyse des papiers anglais,* a journal edited by Mirabeau, who also had been savaged in the *Recherches historiques.* Condorcet, writing as "BDNH" in the *Journal de Paris,* then defended Mazzei's realistic account of America and castigated Brissot as a romantic enthusiast.[18]

For his part, Mirabeau promoted the radical view. In his *Considérations sur l'ordre de Cincinnatus* (1784), he assailed the Society of the Cincinnati, an association of officers from the Revolutionary War, as an attempt to create an aristocracy in the new republic because its membership was hereditary. Others, including Franklin, who had provided Mirabeau with material for his pamphlet, also deplored the aristocratic threat represented by the Society, but Mirabeau excoriated it in such violent language that his tract could be read as an attack on the sociopolitical order in France.[19] The polemics continued into the French Revolution, when Brissot published his *Nouveau voyage dans les Etats-Unis de l'Amérique septentrionale* (1791), an account of his tour of America in 1788, which contained more abuse of Chastellux and praise of Crèvecoeur.

Despite the success of Crèvecoeur's *Lettres* and the cross fire of books and pamphlets, nothing suggests that the general public took a great deal of interest in the polemics of the intellectuals. Information about Americans and their revolution spread among ordinary Parisians through reports on the war and talk about popular public figures, especially Washington, Franklin, and Lafayette. Franklin, who represented the American republic in France from 1776 to 1785, had a genius for appealing to the French. He impressed them as a canny diplomat, yet he adopted a man-of-the-people demeanor, appearing on occasion with his famous coonskin cap as if he had come from the frontier. His renown as a scientist led to his election to the Académie des sciences, and his experiments with electricity made him celebrated as the hero who had tamed lightning. He kept company with the *philosophes*, who applauded him when he embraced Voltaire at the masonic Loge des Neuf Soeurs in 1778. He was known for his wit, not the sardonic French variety but a generous, grandfatherly kind of humor that made him a favorite in salons, where he was known to some of the ladies as "cher papa." Common folk saw him as one of them, the Poor Richard or Bonhomme Richard of their almanacs, more folksy and down-to-earth than Crèvecoeur's Farmer James. Franklin's image appeared in prints, statuettes, and busts and on objects Parisians encountered every day—dinner plates, vases, mugs, snuffboxes, fans, and waistcoat buttons. The Franklin bric-à-brac was enormous and can be appreciated today from the hundreds of objects preserved in the Musée de l'amitié franco-américaine at Blérancourt near Soissons. It testifies to his presence everywhere in Paris.[20]

Franklin cleared a way for his successor, Thomas Jefferson, who, as mentioned, figured in the pro-American circles of the Duchesse d'Enville and Lafayette. Jefferson certainly won the respect of the French, but he did not touch their imagination as Franklin did, nor did he have as proficient a mastery of their language, though Franklin could not speak French fluently. It was Jefferson's young friend Lafayette who most embodied Franco-American friendship during and following the American Revolution. In 1777 Parisians learned that, despite orders to the contrary, Lafayette, then only nineteen years old, secretly sailed to join the American rebels. So determined was he to fight for their cause that he went into hiding and bought his own ship in order to escape capture by the French authorities, who had orders to prevent French army officers from enlisting with the Americans. News bulletins then informed the public of Lafayette's exploits in the war: heroic fighting at Brandywine, despite a leg wound; the terrible winter with Washington at Valley Forge; victories in three small battles (Gloucester, Barren Hill, and Monmouth in New Jersey and Pennsylvania); a leave in France in 1779 to win greater military support for the new American ally; and, back in action in 1780–1781, an important command that contributed to the final victory at Yorktown. The Hôtel de La Fayette, rue Bourbon, with two American Indian houseboys welcoming guests, became a conspicuous center for Americans in Paris during the peace negotiations. Lafayette went on a triumphal tour of the United States in 1784–1785, and his stops were covered with more bulletins. Parisians learned how he was feted with savage eloquence by the Iroquois, how four states made him a citizen, and how Washington treated him as both a hero and a son. Lafayette named his own son Georges Washington and one of his daughters Marie Antoinette Virginie, linking the American state with the French queen. Franklin joked that he hoped Lafayette would have enough children to honor all the American states, although "M. Connecticut" or "Mlle Massachusetts Bay" might not be pleased with their names.[21]

By the time they celebrated the peace, Parisians had received a great deal of news about the American war, but it came from an enormous distance and changed shape as it was relayed from one place to another. Typically it took form at first in colonial newspapers, then was worked over by the British press, and did not appear in French until it underwent translation, or rather adaptation, and censorship. When it finally reached Parisian readers, much of this news was inaccurate (Washington was reported dead at least four times), and all of it was late—that is, superseded by subsequent events known only to the fortunate few who received letters.[22]

Among French newspapers, *La Gazette de France* carried little more than official notices, and *Le Journal de Paris* printed nothing that might offend the government. *Le Courrier de l'Europe*, published in London, had plenty of material, most of it lifted from English papers, but it served up too much scandal and libel to be trustworthy, and it could not be distributed openly in France. The best information came from the French-language periodicals published in the Low Countries and the Rhineland. Among them, the *Gazette de Leyde* stood out, both for the professionalism of its editing and the savvy of its correspondents, including several from the American colonies. Its readers often were treated to articles under headings like "Extract from a letter from New York," although in fact the "letter" could have been compiled from the autonomous "paragraphs" that migrated from newspaper to newspaper in Britain and the Low Countries. Despite the disparity of its sources, the *Gazette de Leyde* made an effort to sort out information and to alert its readers to different and often contradictory sources. Its coverage of American affairs can be taken as a measure of the news that reached the reading public in Paris.[23]

Events during the climactic campaign of 1781 usually appeared in the *Gazette de Leyde* four to five weeks after they had taken place. At first the fighting in America received less coverage than that in other theaters of the war—Tobago, Minorca, Gibraltar, India, preparations to invade England from French ports, and naval engagements everywhere. At the beginning of September French readers learned that Washington, joined by French troops under Jean-Baptiste Donatien de Vimeur, Comte de Rochambeau, was preparing to attack New York City, then occupied by the main British force under Sir Henry Clinton. In late October, reports indicated a dramatic change of strategy. Washington had feigned the attack on New York in order to immobilize Clinton and then marched with Rochambeau to confront the British army under Lord Charles Cornwallis in Virginia. Harassed by American troops under Lafayette and Anthony Wayne, Cornwallis finally withdrew with 10,000 men to Yorktown behind embankments and redoubts, hoping he could hold out until relief arrived from Clinton. But the French fleet of twenty-eight warships under François Joseph Paul, Comte de Grasse arrived from the West Indies in time to defeat a smaller British fleet and to block access to Yorktown from the Chesapeake Bay.

From then on—events that occurred during the first weeks of October in America and that were reported during the last weeks of November in the *Gazette de Leyde*—readers followed the tightening of the noose around Cornwallis, his desperate appeals for help, the artillery exchanges, the storming of the key redoubts, and the appearance of the white flag behind a drummer on October 17, followed by the formal capitulation two days later. Contradictory letters from different sources sometimes blurred the sequence of events. (In the same issue, dated December 4, the *Gazette de Leyde* published one letter claiming that Washington had been wounded and captured and another announcing his victory with the terms of the British capitulation.) Yet each issue made dramatic reading because it soon became clear that a victory at Yorktown would determine the outcome of the entire war. Parisians were waiting impatiently for the latest news, the *Gazette* reported; and when "the great news" finally arrived on November 20, it caused "the most vivid sensation."[24] The police announced the victory in a bulletin, which Parisians copied in cafés and passed from hand to hand. An extraordinary ten-page supplement to the

Gazette de France on November 22 retraced the Virginia campaign, high-lighting the role of Lafayette. A Te Deum was celebrated in Notre Dame on November 27, and that evening all façades in the center of the city were illuminated.[25]

Although the Parisians welcomed the news of Yorktown as a decisive moment in the war, it did not provoke an enormous wave of enthusiasm for Americans and their revolution. Some *nouvellistes* did not even mention it. They filled their newssheets with information about the birth of the dauphin and the death of Maurepas, which also received greater coverage in the gazettes than the fighting far away in Virginia. Parisians complained about increased taxation, and some asked whether it was worth spending more than 6 million livres just to bring about the independence of some English colonies.[26] When the peace was finally celebrated, nearly two years after Yorktown, however, a sense of relief and satisfaction at the triumph over Britain produced a change in the atmosphere. By that time, the general public had warmed to the fashion for Americans and their revolution, which at first had been restricted to intellectuals and a few salons.

Aside from the cult that had grown up around Franklin and Lafayette, American themes appeared in the streets—the Mardi Gras parade of 1783, for example, featured a float depicting the thirteen American states with a statue of liberty in the middle.[27] Stylized Native Americans became stock figures in popular entertainments, notably in the down-market theaters frequented by working people as well as bourgeois. The Comédie française did its best to defend its monopoly of theatrical performances throughout the eighteenth century, but it kept losing ground—first to the Comédie italienne, which excelled in light comedies related to the Commedia dell'arte; then to the increasing appeal of the fair theaters, which produced farces during the commercial fairs of Saint-Germain in the spring and Saint-Laurent in the summer; and finally to the boulevard theaters, which proliferated in the 1770s and 1780s, offering something of everything—tightrope walking, juggling, marionettes, trained animals, vaudeville, dancing spectacles, pantomimes, *opera buffa*, *parades* (comic sketches), and melodramas.[28]

The biggest hit on the boulevards during the 1780s was *L'Héroïne américaine*, a three-act pantomime performed first at the Foire Saint-Germain and then at the Ambigu-Comique on the boulevard du Temple.

It went through fifty-seven performances, an extraordinary success at a time when runs rarely exceeded a dozen performances. Its plot, derived from an anecdote in Raynal's *Histoire philosophique*, went as follows. An English raiding party lands on the American coast, seeking to capture Indians to be sold as slaves. In a fierce battle—all done in pantomime without any dialogue—a tribe of "savages" defeats them, and they sail off, leaving behind Inkle, a handsome young man who hides in the forest. The beautiful Native American heroine, Jarika, finds him, feeds him, keeps him safe in her hut, and becomes his lover. A second ship arrives, followed by another battle in frenzied pantomime. This time the English win. Jarika leads Inkle through the forest to the ship, expecting to sail away with him. But the ship's captain, overcome with lust, offers to buy her from Inkle, and Inkle sells her into slavery for two bags of gold coins. Suddenly, a larger force of Indians, led by a noble chief, arrives; defeats the English in another battle (more pantomime filling the entire stage); and captures Inkle, while the surviving Englishmen escape in their ship. The "savages" are about to torture Inkle to death when Jarika persuades the chief to release him. Then, instead of reuniting with him, she chooses the chief as her spouse, and Inkle slinks off the stage. *L'Héroïne américaine* was published, a rarity for a melodrama (the text, which reads like a succession of stage directions, came to only twenty-five pages). And it inspired a sequel, *Le Héros américain*, next door at the Grands danseurs du Roi, which also was a success (fifteen performances), thanks to clever pantomime and the same, irresistible combination of stereotypes: wicked Englishmen and noble savages.[29]

Because of their experience in Quebec, the French had long been fascinated with Native Americans, who inspired the final act of Jean-Philippe Rameau's *Les Indes galantes* (1735–1736); but the fully formed noble savage did not appear on the stage before Rousseau inspired fantasies about an innocent state of nature. *Hirza, ou les Illinois* by Louis-Edme Billardon-Sauvigny, a friend of Rousseau, featured an Indian princess who outdid Jarika in heroism. ("I have the heart of a savage; I know how to die," she announced at the beginning of the play, and she died unflinchingly at the end.) A tragedy in classic alexandrines, it was first performed at the Comédie française in 1767 and revived in 1780.[30] The ballet *Les Sauvages* by Pierre Gardel brought Indians back to the Opéra in 1786, while they continued to attract audiences on the boulevards.[31]

When they appeared in print, Indians exhibited Rousseauistic sensitivity (*sensiblerie*). The *Journal de Paris* published excerpts from several books about America, favoring passages with "savage eloquence." In one of them, taken from François-Thomas-Marie de Baculard d'Arnaud's popular novel, *Les Epreuves du sentiment*, a European comes across an American Indian who has just lost his wife and expresses curiosity about the savage's feelings. "Am I sensitive, you ask, you monster from Europe?" the Indian replies indignantly. "Am I sensitive? You see me weeping like a woman, and you have doubts about my sensitivity!"[32] In its review of Crèvecoeur's *Lettres*, the *Journal de Paris* noted his description of heroic, wise, and sensitive Indians; and it concluded, "Judging from so many examples, Jean-Jacques Rousseau would have been certain to find the confirmation of his system, which has been so badly ridiculed."[33]

Many other stock figures—yeomen farmers, frontiersmen, minutemen, whalers, Quakers—populated the French fantasies of America. They appeared in novels, histories, travel books, and memoirs. The Comédie italienne even staged a "Ballet des Quakers" in November 1786. Songs, poems, and prints filled out the picture. Parisians sang about the American Revolution to a popular tune, "Qu'est qu'ça m'fait à moi!" They were informed that Houdon had gone to Mount Vernon to sculpt Washington; they flocked to see his bust of Lafayette in the Hôtel de Ville; and they could purchase inexpensive engravings of many American revolutionaries. Two prints, one of the battle of Lexington, the other of Lafayette at Yorktown, helped Parisians imagine the war at its beginning and its end. And they knew it came to a happy ending when they celebrated the peace on the dance floor of the Halle au bled.[34]

Far from being limited to an alliance against a common enemy, therefore, France's connection with America touched a cultural chord, and it went through several phases. At first, Parisians had little information about life in the new republic. Reports about the war were difficult to follow, even for sophisticated readers of the *Gazette de Leyde*, owing to the way news was refracted over space and time. By the time of the peace, images of Americans had begun to take shape around the figure of Franklin and "le bonhomme Richard." Crèvecoeur added other characters and placed them in an arcadia that was open to all and founded on egalitarian principles. Some intellectuals, like Condorcet, who had studied the Declaration of Independence and knew its principal author, Thomas Jefferson, contested the utopian view; yet they, too, read radical messages into the American experience. When Condorcet wrote as a "Bourgeois de New Haven," he adopted an identity at odds with Brissot, who wrote as a "Philadelphien"; but both challenged the fundamental orthodoxies of the church and state in France. And while the debate continued at the intellectual level, the stock figures proliferated, spilling onto the stage and into popular songs and prints. By 1789, they were everywhere. The French had been the first to ask, "What is an American?" Although they did not agree on an answer, the question continued to hover over them as they confronted the problems of their own identity.

22

Man Can Fly

ALL OF PARIS saw it but could hardly believe it—two men, in the air, 3,000 feet above the earth, flying! It was November 21, 1783, and the men, Jean-François Pilâtre de Rozier and François-Laurent d'Arlandes, were suspended in a basket beneath a hot-air balloon. As they rose into the air from a launching pad in the Bois de Boulogne, they waved their hats to a large crowd of spectators, gained altitude, crossed the Seine near the Invalides, and twenty-five minutes later landed in a field outside the faubourg Saint Jacques five miles from their point of departure. Although enormous (seventy feet high when fully inflated with hot air), the balloon looked like a small kite to the Parisians who followed it with their eyes. A crowd ran after it when it began its descent, and after it landed safely, Parisians hailed the "aéronautes" as heroes, the first men to fly.[1]

The event came as a climax to a series of scientific experiments that began nearly a year earlier. Parisians first learned of them in the summer of 1783, when reports arrived about balloons that the Montgolfier brothers, Joseph-Michel and Jacques-Etienne, had developed in Annonay in the Ardèche, where they ran the finest paper-making manufactory in France. They constructed a large globe made of sackcloth with layers of paper inside and a cover of netting outside from which they attached a basket. When suspended over a fire, the globe filled with heated air, lighter than the surrounding air, and took off. After the success of a test flight on

December 14, 1782, the Montgolfier brothers demonstrated their invention before a crowd in Annonay on June 4, 1783. The Academy of Sciences, duly informed of the invention, decided to sponsor a test flight, subsidized by the government, and Jacques-Etienne came to Paris to construct a balloon with the help of his friend Jean-Baptiste Réveillon, a wealthy wallpaper manufacturer in the faubourg Saint Antoine, who provided decorations (signs of the zodiac and other images used in wallpaper) for the outside surface.[2]

Excited talk about flying machines was circulating in Paris by the beginning of the summer. In August, a rival inventor, Jacques Alexandre César Charles, announced that he would beat Montgolfier by launching a balloon of his own, which he put on display in his workshop at the Place des Victoires. Having studied the research of Henry Cavendish and Joseph Priestley, he understood that "air inflammable" (hydrogen) could be controlled by valves and operate far more effectively than ordinary hot air. Unlike the Montgolfiers, he identified himself primarily as a scientist ("physicien"), and two of his students, Nicolas-Louis and Anne-Jean Robert, constructed a balloon made of rubberized silk. They financed their project by selling advance tickets to the launch at a cost of 3 L. each. The subscription was quickly filled and the money deposited at the fashionable Café du Caveau.[3]

So many people wanted to see Charles's spectacle that it was moved to the Champ de Mars, where the ticket holders could get a close look within a closed-off area, and the general public could watch from positions on both sides of the Seine. On the day of the launch, August 27, Jacques-Etienne Montgolfier arrived to take a place among the spectators, but Charles refused to admit him, insisting on the need to protect his secret and his claim to be the true inventor of the flying machine. Despite this nasty scene and a heavy rain, everything went off perfectly. The unmanned balloon shot up into the air before an enormous crowd, and it landed forty-five minutes later outside the village of Gonesse nineteen miles north of Paris. It terrified the local peasants, who took it to be a monster and tried to subdue it by pitchforks or, according to some accounts, by throwing stones. They were pacified after their curate spotted a notice on the balloon requesting that it be returned to Paris by anyone who found it. Its triumphant arrival gave Parisians an opportunity to laugh at the ignorance of country folk who did not understand the power of science. From then on, for many weeks, "all Paris" talked about nothing but flight, physics, machines, and the nature of air.[4]

The talkers soon distinguished between "Montgolfières" and "Charlières" in debates about the superior model of a flying machine. The Montgolfiers had an advantage—a much larger balloon, powerful enough to carry a man, and the backing of the Academy and the government. On September 19, they performed an experiment at Versailles before the king, queen, court, and a large public. In order to test the ability of living creatures to withstand flight, they placed a sheep, rooster, and duck inside a wicker basket attached beneath their gigantic balloon. It rose to a height of 1,278 feet and could be seen from as far away as Montmartre. Much to the disappointment of the spectators, it traveled only half a league (1.2 miles); but the sheep and duck survived. (The rooster had its neck broken from the impact of the landing.)

Jacques-Etienne Montgolfier and Pilâtre then went back to work in the residence of Réveillon. Jacques-Etienne actually took the first manned flight, but on a tethered balloon that went up only a few feet in the air. Then Pilâtre, as the primary "aéronaute," developed his skills, a matter of feeding the fire with enough hay to maintain the desired height, using sandbags as ballast, and letting the air inside the balloon cool gradually enough to make a soft landing. In a series of experiments from October 17 to 19, he ascended as high as three hundred feet, while his assistants struggled to hold the ropes that bound the "machine aérostatique" to earth. Enormous crowds, including laborers in nearby workshops and spectators in the Jardin du Roi across the Seine, witnessed the trial runs. Their excitement fed the "furor" and "frenzy" about manned flight that spread throughout the city after the machine was transported to the grounds of the château de la Muette in the Bois de Boulogne. On November 21, "all Paris" held its breath when the ropes were cut and Pilâtre and d'Arlandes soared up into the wind, visible to everyone in the city. Their success set off a wave of "general enthusiasm." Thrilled at having witnessed a historical event, Parisians opened a subscription to erect a monument on the spot where the craft returned to earth.[5]

Ten days later, Charles and Nicolas-Louis Robert, who had built an enlarged version of their hydrogen balloon, undertook a second manned flight, which attracted even more attention than the first. Charles had received permission to launch his balloon from the Tuileries Gardens, where the public could inspect his machine attached to two trees and guarded night and day. Parisians rushed to buy all of the 12,800 tickets that he sold at 3 L. each for places inside the enclosed area. Shortly before the launch, however, the king forbade it. He would permit two condemned criminals to take the places of Charles and Robert, but he would not allow his respectable subjects to risk their lives. Charles protested vehemently to the Baron de Breteuil, the minister in charge of the Department of Paris. It was an affair of honor, he insisted. He could not break his pledge to the ticket holders, and he would kill himself rather than suffer such a disgrace. Besides, success was a scientific certainty. Faced with another kind of danger—that of enraging an excited public opinion—Breteuil, backed by the Duc de Chartres, let the "experiment" take place.

It began with a scene that delighted the public. As a gesture of reconciliation, Charles invited Montgolfier to cut a ribbon, releasing a trial balloon to test the wind. It was a glorious day. The two "navigateurs aériens," seated in a "gondola" suspended nine feet below the balloon, ascended slowly into the air, waving white flags, then disappeared.[6] The flight lasted two hours and covered twenty-two miles. After landing in a field near Nesle to the north of Paris, Charles continued on his own for another two miles and reached an altitude of 9,800 feet, when his ears hurt so much that he released some "air inflammable" by means of a valve and again landed successfully. Hardy witnessed the flight from a spot on the quais, which were packed solid from the Pont Neuf to the Invalides. Aside from the crowd in the Tuileries Gardens, well over a hundred thousand Parisians must have had at least a glimpse of the balloon, and virtually everyone in the city heard about it.[7] Before Charles arrived back in Paris, the *Poissardes*—market women who traditionally celebrated royalty and important personages—had already prepared flowers and ballads in his honor. After his return, Lafayette fetched him to be feted by the Duc d'Orléans, who had followed the flight on horseback; and when Charles left the Palais-Royal, a crowd carried him on its shoulders back to Lafayette's carriage. A physicist as a popular hero—it was a new phenomenon. One of many poems expressed the general enthusiasm:

Vraiment chacun s'embarrasse	*Truly everyone is caught up*
D'honorer Charles en ces lieux;	*In honoring Charles at this spot;*
Sans nous, il a marqué sa place	*Without us, he has marked his place*
Entre les hommes et les dieux.[8]	*Between men and the gods.*

The balloon itself, deflated and folded, was paraded by torchlight from the faubourg Saint Denis to the Place des Victoires to cheers from the people who lined the streets.

From then on, the passion for balloons was unstoppable. Balloon designs appeared everywhere—engraved on prints, inlaid in furniture, sewn onto hats, designed as puffed-up sleeves, combed into coiffures, baked into candy, and carved as toys. When asked about the utility of balloons, Franklin, who had witnessed the first flights, fielded the question with his usual wit, "It is still a new-born infant. It may become an idiot, it may become a man of wit. Let's wait until it has passed the age of its early education."[9] A rumor spread that a balloon capable of lifting a house was being designed. Now willing to endorse manned flight, the king awarded Jacques-Etienne Montgolfier with membership in the Ordre de Saint Michel. He also granted a pension of 2,000 L. to Charles and pensions of 1,000 L. to Pilâtre and the Robert brothers.

As more flights took place, the public's enthusiasm turned into a frenzy. Hundreds of thousands of Parisians watched men ascend into the air under magnificent globes, beautifully decorated and painted. The spectators gasped, froze with fear, applauded, cheered, wept, and sometimes fainted.[10] According to one account, the common people were especially moved, and a woman who had witnessed a balloon being inflated and launched said it made her feel as if she had seen the origin of the cosmos: "On that day she believed she had been at the birth of creation, that she had seen matter separate from chaos, take form, grow, become animated and rise to form stars."[11] Science had provided a secular version of the creation myth: balloons showed how matter could be set in motion, and they demonstrated that man could master the force at work. Whether this view was shared by other spectators is impossible to say, but it was not liked by the church. A *nouvelliste* reported that priests considered ballooning "diabolical" and worried that manned flight would undercut faith in miracles such as the ascension of Christ.[12]

At the same time, Parisians learned that the enthusiasm threatened to get out of hand. People started flying balloons—"Montgolfières," "Charlières," "Robertines" (for the Robert Brothers), and improvised devices, most of them unmanned—all over the country; and as the vogue spread, accidents occurred. In October 1784 a small balloon used to amuse the crowd at the Foire Saint Laurent crashed into an enclosure of wild animals, which was being used for circus performances, and it nearly set the whole fairground on fire.[13] In May a flight made a crash landing in Strasbourg, causing a fire, though the two balloonists survived. The government forbade all unauthorized flights on May 1, but it could not stop the ambition of "aéronautes" to gain fame, honor, and even money, because most of them sold tickets for good views of the launching pad. When a manned flight was canceled at the last minute in Bordeaux on May 3, the spectators rioted; two were killed, the army intervened, and two of the rioters were hanged.[14]

A larger but less fatal riot occurred in Paris on July 11. An abbé Miolan, abbé Laurent-Antoine, who gave public lectures on physics, announced that he would build the largest balloon ever, one hundred feet high when fully inflated, and use it to take scientific measurements at a great altitude. For a price of 3 L., Parisians could enter a restricted area within the Luxembourg Gardens and watch the take-off. An enormous crowd waited and waited, as Miolan struggled to fill the Montgolfière with hot air. Finally he had to give up, and soldiers from the Watch announced that the event was canceled. Reinforced by an even larger mass of angry spectators from outside the Gardens, the crowd stormed the launching platform, tore the balloon apart, piled up its remains along with Miolan's tools and four hundred chairs, and lit a gigantic bonfire, which burned for four hours. As the Watch proved incapable of containing the violence, thirty army cavalrymen, brandishing sabers, finally restored order. Miolan escaped and went into hiding. For weeks afterward, prints and songs mocked him for his failure or reviled him as a swindler who had fleeced the public.[15]

Despite this disaster, two more successful flights by the Robert brothers dazzled Parisians in 1784, although they failed to solve the main problem that now challenged ballooning: how to steer a vehicle driven by the wind. The Roberts thought they could control their flight by rowing with specially designed "oars." On July 15, they took off, with the Duc de Chartres aboard, before another gigantic crowd, this time at Saint Cloud. Because the ascent began too slowly, they threw their ballast overboard, and the balloon shot up, then disappeared into a cloud. Tossed about by the wind and pummeled with hail, Chartres panicked and ordered a descent. Using a valve, the Roberts released enough "air inflammable" to bring the craft down after forty-five minutes. But they had not steered it, and to the delight of the Parisians, street singers ridiculed Chartres just as they had mocked Miolan.[16]

By now the craze for ballooning had begun to decline. The Roberts attempted to steer another flight on September 19, this time using "wings" instead of "oars." A somewhat smaller crowd gathered in the Tuileries Gardens—at a ticket price of 3 or 6 L., bringing in a total of 50,000 L.— and gasped collectively as the balloon rose to 3,800 feet and disappeared. The wives of the Robert brothers, sporting "balloon-style hats," began to be tormented by fear. But six hours later, news arrived from a field near Béthune in Artois, that the "aéronautes" had landed safely. They had traveled 173 miles and said they could have continued for three days and even crossed the Channel, although they had failed to direct the "Robertine" with its wings.[17]

While the balloonists continued to wrestle with the problem of steering, the prospect of a Channel crossing seized the imagination of the Parisians. Two "aéronautes"—Pilâtre and a "mechanic" named Jean-Pierre Blanchard—competed to accomplish this dangerous feat. Pilâtre personified the fascination with science among Parisians in the 1780s. Having taught chemistry and physics in Reims, he had won the patronage of the Comte d'Artois, and founded the Paris Musée, a club of scientists and inventors, who gave public demonstrations. As the first "aéronaute," he, like Charles, became a scientist-celebrity. Blanchard by contrast was a self-taught inventor who fascinated Parisians with proposals to construct a flying machine. In 1782, before balloons arrived in Paris, he informed the public that he had built a "flying boat," which he could propel and steer with oars and a rudder. He announced he would fly it to the top of a tower on Notre Dame, row in the air to Passy, and return, following the course of the Seine. He failed to get it off the ground, however, and dropped out of sight after being held up to ridicule in a popular farce at the Comédie italienne, *Cassandre mécanicien, ou le bateau volant*.[18] In 1784 the use of "inflammable air" in ballooning gave him an opportunity to convert his rowing machine into a gondola carried beneath a "Charlière." He impressed the authorities enough to receive permission to attempt a flight from the Champ de Mars on March 2. As he was about to ascend in front of a large crowd, who had paid the usual 3 L. admission fee, a student from the Ecole militaire drew his sword, jumped into the gondola, and demanded to be taken as a passenger. The police pulled him out, but the student, in a fury, slashed some wings attached to the oars so badly that they would not function. Blanchard took off, nonetheless, and used his rudder effectively enough during a two-hour flight, which reached a record altitude of 12,800 feet, to claim that he had steered his air boat. Having confounded his critics, at least to his satisfaction, he then set out to cross the Channel from Dover to Calais.[19]

Meanwhile, Pilâtre had received a commission from Calonne, the finance minister, to do a crossing in the opposite direction, despite a near crash during a flight from Versailles on June 23. Charles and the Robert brothers had withdrawn from the competition, and Pilâtre used a balloon that he called a "Carlo-Montgolfière," because it used both inflammable and hot air. By the end of the year, he had set up camp with sixty workers to construct a gigantic machine outside Boulogne and was waiting for a favorable wind. On January 10, 1785 news arrived in Paris that Blanchard, accompanied by an American, Dr. John Jeffries, had just landed successfully on the French coast near Calais. Parisians broke out in an "unbelievable brouhaha." America was the next stop, they shouted, certain that they had lived through a moment that would forever mark history. The citizens of Calais, equally enthusiastic, were permitted to keep Blanchard's balloon in their main church, so that they could celebrate it in the same way as Columbus's ship which had been kept in a church after his return from America. While Blanchard received a pension of 1,200 L. and a gift of 500 louis from the king, Pilâtre returned disconsolate to Paris.[20]

Having invested 40,000 L. in the Boulogne-Dover flight, however, Calonne insisted that Pilâtre attempt it. Weeks went by as he faced one difficulty after another: contrary winds, gas leaks, rats that ate connecting parts. Parisians followed all his tribulations from reports by the *nouvel-*

listes, although the drama had been drained from them, because Blanchard had already won the glory of the first Channel crossing. Finally, on June 15, Pilâtre set off with one of the workmen, Pierre Romain. Although the wind carried them over the sea, it reversed, and then something went wrong. Reports varied: Some said the hot air and inflammable air short-circuited; others that a valve misfunctioned. The machinery could have been deficient or badly designed. Whatever the cause, the spectators saw a column of flame shoot up above the balloon, which came crashing down to earth three miles from Boulogne and killed both men.[21]

Balloons now had their martyrs as well as their heroes, and they also had passed their peak in attracting public attention.[22] The news of Pilâtre's accident certainly created a sensation. It spread instantly through Paris, and the members of his Musée expressed the general sense of calamity in a ceremony to commemorate him. But his disaster confirmed the inability of inventors to overcome the difficulty of steering "machines aérostatiques," whatever their design. The flight of a "Charlière" with a new kind of wings from the Luxembourg Gardens on June 18, 1786, attracted a large crowd of spectators, and it could be seen for forty-five minutes from many parts of Paris. Yet it, too, could not be steered, and by then, after three years of widespread excitement, the novelty of ballooning had worn off.

The faith in science remained, however. Man had conquered the air. The natural world was ready to be dominated by those who could decode its inner laws. Perhaps even the laws governing society could be mastered. Reason seemed capable of anything.

23

Man Can Cure All Disease

"THE FRENZY FOR air balloons seems to be dying down," Hardy wrote in his journal on May 1, 1784, "and it is being replaced by animal magnetism invented by a sieur Mesmer, a German doctor." In fact, animal magnetism or mesmerism did not merely displace ballooning as the passion at the center of Parisians' interests, it caused more ink to spill and more tongues to wag than anything else during the craze for science of the 1780s. To call it a fashion would not do it justice. Like the vogue for balloons, it expressed something deeper—an underlying shift in the collective view of the world that had gathered force since the beginning of the century. Parisians witnessed what philosophers had preached: Reason could decipher the laws of nature. Man could fly. Mesmer taught them that man could cure disease; and as his cures accumulated, they began to believe that man could do anything.

Franz Anton Mesmer was a Viennese doctor who had written a dissertation on the influence of planetary bodies on human health and had established a practice using new techniques.[1] He claimed that he had discovered an invisible fluid that penetrated everything—all space, objects, and living beings. It exerted force in the same way that magnets attracted iron filings; and because it acted on animal life, he called his system animal magnetism. The human body, like magnets, had "poles," which directed the flow of the fluid from outside sources. When "obstacles" impaired the free flow of the fluid, a person became ill. Expert stroking—called "magnetizing" or, eventually, "mesmerizing"—broke down the obstacle, sometimes by inducing a "crisis" or convulsions, and restored "harmony."[2]

Despite its exotic terminology, Mesmer's theory was no more extravagant than many of the scientific theories that fascinated Parisians throughout the eighteenth century. After Newton's proof that all bodies attracted one another according to the same law, scientists discovered invisible forces at work everywhere, while ordinary people did their best to accommodate those discoveries in antiquated worldviews. For example, the *Journal de Paris* began an article on one of Lavoisier's fundamental experiments by invoking the venerable belief that the world was made of four basic elements, earth, air, water, and fire. Following Henry Cavendish and Joseph Priestley, however, Lavoisier had proved that water was not water but rather a combination of "air inflammable" (what he called hydrogen) and "air déphlogistiqué" (oxygen). The journal therefore concluded that instead of four elements, there were three.[3]

Difficult as it was to make sense of the science—what readers of the *Journal de Paris* could comprehend that Lavoisier was transforming chemistry?—it was also exhilarating. Scientists had discovered forces operating unseen at the heart of nature. Despite his aversion to hypotheses, Newton had speculated in the last paragraph of his *Principia* (1713 edition) about a "subtle spirit which pervades and lies hid in all gross bodies." Franklin envisioned electricity as a single, invisible fluid. Albrecht von Haller discovered "irritability" as an invisible, animating principle. Luigi Galvani reached a similar conclusion by experimenting with "animal electricity." Buffon believed that an imperceptible "moule intérieur" determined organic life. And doctors from the Montpellier school of medicine such as Théophile de Bordeu and Paul-Joseph Barthez understood health as the effect of an invisible, vitalistic force.

More popular writers like Etienne-Claude Marivetz, M. A. Thouret, and Jean-Louis Carra, claimed to be successors to Newton and published cosmologies full of forces that moved planets yet could not be detected by the human eye. Before throwing himself into the French Revolution, Jean-Paul Marat, a doctor-philosopher, propounded a revolutionary theory of fire, and Robespierre gained fame as a lawyer who defended the use of lightning rods. They belonged to a generation that turned to science for an explanation of all natural phenomena, and so did Mesmer.[4]

What set his system apart from the others was not so much its cosmological pretension as its practical application. Mesmer put himself "en rapport" with his patients, running his hands over their bodies in a manner that reinforced the flow of the fluid, particularly in places where they felt pain. One sensitive place was the "hypocondres" in the abdomen. As men often mesmerized women, this practice stimulated gossip about seduction—and made mesmerism all the more fascinating to Parisians. Yet Mesmer presented himself to the world as a respectable and cultivated physician. He knew the Mozart family well and was said to have made his garden available in Vienna for the first performance of *Bastien und Bastienne*, composed by Wolfgang Amadeus at the age of twelve. Having stayed in touch with Mesmer, Mozart later wrote a mesmerist episode into *Così fan tutte*.

When he appeared in Paris in 1778, Mesmer moved into an apartment in the Place Vendôme and soon acquired a devoted following of patients, who testified to his success in relieving them from all sorts of ailments. By then, however, his treatment included practices that quickly became notorious. Parisians were especially intrigued by his "baquet," a large circular tub filled with mesmerized minerals and water, covered on top, and pierced by holes through which movable iron rods protruded. Patients sat around the tub, applying the bent ends of the rods to the parts of their bodies where they suffered most. While absorbing fluid from the tub, they communicated it to one another through a rope that bound them together and by holding hands to form a "chain." When the fluid broke through an obstacle, a patient frequently fell into a "crisis" and was carried into a mattress-lined "crisis room" by Antoine, Mesmer's valet. Despite occasional shrieks from the crises, the treatments took place in a calm and muffled atmosphere, maintained in part by music—soothing pieces performed in the background by a pianist, a singer, or a master of the glass "harmonica." (It consisted of glasses filled to different heights with water, which emitted sounds when the musician rubbed their rims with his finger. Mesmer, who claimed that the fluid was transmitted by music, played the "harmonica" himself, and Mozart composed pieces for it.)

Although Mesmer kept the sessions closed and refused to divulge the deepest secrets of his science, information about his theory and practice leaked into the public. Everything about mesmerism stoked the curiosity of Parisians—its exotic staging, its paraphernalia, its whiff of scandal, and its open revolt against orthodox medical practices, which did little to cure diseases and often made them worse, as skeptics had insisted since the time of Molière. Although his theory could be compatible with deism, Mesmer did not attach a religious message to it. He described his theory as the science of sciences, one that explained gravitation, electricity, mineral magnetism, inflammable air, and all the natural wonders that had stirred the imagination of Europeans since the seventeenth century.

Parisians learned about mesmerism from gossip—What went on in the "salle des crises"? Why so much stroking on the "hypocondres"?—and then from reports about Mesmer's attempts to get his discovery endorsed by scientific bodies—first the Académie des sciences, then the Société royale de médecine, and finally the medical faculty of the University of Paris. In each case, he won over one or two individuals but failed to get a formal hearing and fell back on a request for a commission to verify his cures. Verification, however, turned on testimony by patients who had become deeply attached to the master, and it was never accomplished to anyone's satisfaction. Although Mesmer set up a tub for the poor, it got little use. He catered to the rich, who had to pay 10 louis (240 L.) a month, the equivalent of nearly a year's wages for an unskilled laborer, and his constant demand for money fed rumors that he was a fortune-seeking charlatan.

In *Précis historique des faits relatifs au magnétisme animal* (1781), Mesmer replied to his critics by presenting himself as a humanitarian and a victim of the scientific establishment. It was written for him—probably by Nicolas Bergasse, a lawyer from Lyon who was his most militant spokesman—because he never mastered much French. Indeed, Mesmer's formidable German accent added to the gravitas of his pronouncements before the patients in his clinic and the disciples he taught in private lessons. He had already outlined his theory in an earlier work, also published in French, *Mémoire sur la découverte du magnétisme animal* (1779). It summarized his system in twenty-seven propositions, which sounded as reasonable as many of the popular scientific treatises of the time. Yet he claimed to withhold the deeper truths that underlay the propositions. Society was not yet ready for their revelation, he explained in the *Précis historique*, and, moreover, they could not be reduced easily to words. He had imbibed them directly from nature during a three-month retreat in a bucolic setting. Cut off from humanity and surrounded by forests and fields, he developed a sublime sense of contact with ultimate reality: "Oh nature, I exclaimed in these trances, what do you want from me?"

While appealing to readers attuned to Rousseauistic *sensiblerie*, Mesmer claimed to base his science on a firm, empirical foundation, as demonstrated by lists of the patients he had cured.[5] The cures, also published in pamphlets and newspaper articles, attracted increasing attention, particularly after Mesmer converted a prominent doctor in the faculty of medicine, Charles Deslon. Deslon tried to convince his colleagues that Mesmer had revolutionized medical science. Having failed to win them over in several heated faculty meetings, he challenged them to a contest: each side would attempt to cure twelve patients, chosen by lot, and the winner would set the standard for medical practice throughout the kingdom. The faculty responded by voting to expel Deslon. After more meetings and extensive negotiations, it issued an ultimatum. He must sign an oath of allegiance to orthodox medicine or be stricken from the list of its members. "Sign or be expelled"—the word went out among the *nouvellistes*, for mesmerism now was news, and a schism among the leading doctors in Paris was the kind of event that attracted the public's attention.

In September 1779, twenty-eight doctors who had sympathized with Deslon caved in and signed, but Deslon remained faithful to the cause. He had developed a flourishing mesmerist practice of his own, and in 1780 he published *Observations sur le magnétisme animal*, which provided the public with an insider's account of Mesmer's secrets and the strange behavior rumored to take place behind closed doors in his clinic. Mesmer denied that Deslon had an adequate understanding of animal magnetism, and he refused to share the leadership of the movement. He and Deslon quarreled, made peace, quarreled again, and finally broke off relations in 1783.

Meanwhile, a group of Mesmer's patients resolved to guarantee his financial independence and to deepen their knowledge of his doctrine by creating a masonic-like association called the Société de l'harmonie universelle. They would limit it to one hundred members, all sworn to secrecy. In return for instruction in the ultimate truths that he had withheld from the public (and, as he claimed, from Deslon), they would each pay 10 louis as a membership fee. The money would go to Mesmer, who would give lessons and continue his practice in the sumptuous Hôtel de Coigny, rue Coq-Héron.

Bergasse and Guillaume Kornmann, a banker from Strasbourg (we will hear more about them later) founded the Société de l'harmonie universelle in the spring of 1781, and its ranks soon filled with wealthy and influential adepts, including Lafayette and two members of the Parlement of Paris, Jean-Jacques Duval d'Éprémesnil and Adrien Duport. Despite the limits imposed on its size, the society grew to include 430 members. It spawned a dozen provincial branches, and many of their members, duly instructed in theory and practice, set up treatments of their own. In April 1784, the *Mémoires secrets* observed, "Men, women, children, everyone is involved, everyone magnetizes."[6] The movement spread throughout the kingdom, to other countries, even to America, where Lafayette, on a visit, preached it to the American Philosophical Society and tried unsuccessfully to convert Washington.

Above all, mesmerism thrived on polemics. Every supposed revelation of Mesmer's secret and every conflict with outside bodies generated appeals to the public. Pamphlets poured out, more of them than on any other subject except the Maupeou coup before the political crisis of 1788–1789. A survey made in 1787 put their number at over two hundred, a reasonable estimate considering that one contemporary collection, now in the Bibliothèque nationale de France, includes 166 works, ranging from short tracts to lengthy treatises.[7] Mesmerist themes filled all the other media—poems, songs, prints, posters, gossip, and the stage (they were the subject of three plays). In his literary newsletter, Jean-François de La Harpe, who did not sympathize with mesmerism, described it as "an epidemic that has conquered all of France." In his *Correspondance littéraire*, Meister, who had doubts, observed: "Magnetism occupies everyone's thoughts. One is dazzled by its wonders. And at the very least one does not dare to deny its existence." The foreign French journals all agreed. "Everyone is now occupied with animal magnetism," wrote the Paris correspondent of the *Journal de Bruxelles*, and wondered whether it "will soon be the sole, universal medicine."[8]

The rage for mesmerism reached such a state that in the spring of 1784 the government decided it had to intervene. It commissioned a full-scale investigation to be conducted by four prominent doctors from the faculty of medicine and five members of the Académie des sciences, including the renowned astronomer Jean Sylvain Bailly, Lavoisier, and Franklin, who was to serve as chairman. Having learned about Mesmer's intractability from his earlier negotiations with scientific bodies, the commission decided not to deal with him and concentrated on the practice of Deslon, who agreed to cooperate fully. For five months the members of the commission studied mesmerist publications, interviewed Deslon, and observed his treatments. They felt nothing when mesmerized themselves, and then devised experiments to test the effects of Deslon's mesmerizing on his most sensitive patients. Following the committee's instructions, he mesmerized one of five trees in Franklin's garden. (Like the mesmerist tub, trees and ordinary objects could operate as batteries of mesmerist fluid.) A patient felt nothing when he touched the mesmerized tree and fainted at the foot of a tree that functioned as a placebo. Another patient was asked to drink water from five glasses, of which one had been mesmerized. She swallowed the mesmerized water with no effect and fell into convulsions after downing a glass of ordinary water. The committee's report, dated August 11, gave a vivid account of mesmerist practices and concluded that they had a powerful effect on the imagination but that Mesmer's fluid did not exist. Animal magnetism as a science was worthless, and as a way of treating diseases it could be downright dangerous.[9]

The report burst upon Paris at the height of the frenzy over mesmerism, sending tremors throughout France and the rest of Europe. The press described it as a devastating blow to Mesmer, although he refused to be bowed. He sent a defiant open letter to Franklin, protested that he could not be judged by the heretical practices of his student Deslon, and appealed to the Parlement of Paris for justice—that is, for another investigation by a less biased team of experts.[10] The time for committees had passed, however, especially as the findings of Franklin's commission were confirmed by a report from the Société royale de médecine, which had conducted an investigation of its own. Unable to win support from the Parlement, Mesmer finally reverted to the strategy he had adopted from the beginning: an appeal to public opinion.[11]

The public, however, seemed on the whole to be convinced by the commission's report, which became a best seller. Together with the report of the Société royale, it ran through several editions, totaling 80,000 copies. The tide of café conversations, reinforced by pamphlets, songs, and prints, turned against Mesmer, who was increasingly derided as a charlatan. On November 16, a one-act "comédie-parade," *Les Docteurs modernes*, brought down the house at the Comédie italienne. It featured a mesmerist doctor as a swindler who declares to his valet:

Mon enfant, conçois mon dessein:	*My child, understand my intention:*
Peu m'importe que l'on m'affiche	*What do I care if they spread it about*
Partout pour pauvre médecin,	*That I am a poor doctor,*
Si je deviens médecin riche.	*If I become a doctor who is rich.*

After working through a love story full of "vaudevilles" (light songs), it comes to a climax with a cast of patients who make a "chain" around a tub and then exit into the "crisis room" offstage. Mesmer's followers tried to disrupt the play by whistling and throwing pamphlets down from a balcony, but it went through twenty-six performances, an enormous success for such a light farce.[12]

The movement lost more ground in November 1784, when a schism broke out in the Société de l'harmonie universelle. Bergasse, Kornmann, and d'Éprémesnil demanded a revision in the society's statutes so that they could make Mesmer's full doctrine public. He refused and summoned a general assembly of his followers in May 1785, which voted to give him absolute control of the movement and to maintain the secrecy of his doctrine. While Mesmer continued to rule from the Hôtel de Coigny, the Bergasse rump withdrew to Kornmann's house, where it continued to meet as an informal discussion group and became increasingly involved in politics—for, as the "despotism" of the official bodies had taught them, there were plenty of obstacles to harmony within the body politic.

By the end of 1784, mesmerism seemed to be a spent force. In April 1785, however, the *Mémoires secrets* announced that it had become "more of a fashion than ever," owing to a discovery that revolutionized its practice.[13] While mesmerizing sick peasants at his country estate in Buzancy near Soissons, A.-M.-J. de Chastenet, Marquis de Puységur, found to his astonishment that a young shepherd fell into a kind of deep sleep and automatically obeyed his commands. Thanks to the powerful "rapport" between them, the youth became subjected to Puységur's volition, yet retained no memory of the experience after he regained consciousness.

News of this "artificial somnambulism," which later became known as hypnotism, created a sensation in Paris, where Puységur gave several demonstrations. Mesmer himself did not induce it in his patients, yet Puységur claimed only to be an orthodox mesmerist, who had learned to develop a particular kind of "crisis." He taught his technique to others, and it spread rapidly through the mesmerist networks.[14]

By the end of the century these practices were beginning to be absorbed into occultist movements that would eventually surface in the work of romantics like Victor Hugo and E. T. A. Hoffmann. But in the 1780s mesmerism, including its somnambulist variety, appealed to Parisians as a new kind of science. Mesmer's defenders tried to parry the blow from the Franklin committee by invoking philosophers whose ideas were analogous to their master's. One honor roll of Mesmer's predecessors went as follows: "Leibniz, Hume, Newton, Descartes, La Mettrie, Bonnet, Diderot, Maupertuis, Robinet, Helvétius, Condillac, Voltaire, J.-J. Rousseau, Buffon, Marat, Bertholon."[15] An anti-Mesmerist wit listed a succession of intellectual vogues, which evoked a similar context:

Autrefois Moliniste	*Formerly Molinist [Jesuit]*
Ensuite Janséniste	*Then Jansenist*
Puis Encyclopédiste	*Then Encyclopedist*
Et puis Economiste	*And then Economist*
A présent Mesmériste . . . [16]	*At present Mesmerist . . .*

Whether celebrated or derided, Mesmerism belonged to a climate of opinion formed in large part by the Enlightenment.

Parisians did not have to follow philosophical trends to absorb this outlook. They picked up scientific views from reports about exciting new discoveries and inventions that were as extravagant as Mesmer's tubs. On December 8, 1783, the *Journal de Paris* announced that a certain D . . . had discovered a new principle that would make it possible to walk on water. Based on the concept of ricocheting, it operated in a manner analogous to skipping stones on the surface of a river. If Parisians collected a subscription for 200 louis, D . . . promised to walk across the Seine on New Year's Day in "elastic clogs," a kind of shoe he had invented. The money was raised immediately, and the list of subscribers, which the journal printed, included many prominent figures, notably Lafayette, who gave one of the largest contributions. Shortly before the end of the month, the journal ran a notice that the shoes and the science were a hoax. Undeterred, however, it said that it would devote the collection to charity, and soon afterward it published a letter about a technique of seeing in the dark promoted by a group of balloon enthusiasts who believed in the affinity of "nyctalopes, hydrophobes, somnambulists, and water witchers."[17]

Water witching featured prominently among the latest vogues. Barthélemy Bléton, a peasant from the Dauphiné, used a divining stick to locate underground streams, and he succeeded well enough to convince many Parisians that he had stumbled upon a new technology. In a report on his ability to trace the underground water system that fed the fountains of the Luxembourg Gardens, the *Journal de Paris* concluded that he had demonstrated the existence of "terrestrial electricity."[18] Electricity itself was constantly on display before Parisians, both as an amusement in magic-like demonstrations and as a scientific principle that could cure disease. Nicolas-Philippe Ledru, Paris's best-known magician-physicist, cured thirteen epileptics by administering electric shocks, according to a committee of the faculty of medicine. Electricity as he understood it was "a universal fluid, the soul of the world and the principle of all movement."[19]

Aside from these highly publicized breakthroughs, periodicals constantly announced inventions based on the latest scientific principles: flying machines, submarines, a robot that played chess, a keyboard that could produce speech, an infallible fire extinguisher, an inextinguishable fire bomb, a liquid that would stop all hemmorhages, a telescope that would detect small objects on the moon, a perpetual motion machine that would grind grain forever, a kind of telegraph that would communicate messages over great distances. "A new invention is born every day," commented the Paris correspondent of the *Courrier du Bas-Rhin*. And the *Mémoires secrets* agreed: "We live in the century of inventions."[20] The message, confined at first to specialized publications like the *Journal de physique*, filled popular periodicals like the *Année littéraire*, which proclaimed, "We are surrounded by miracles. Genius is everywhere conquering nature and the elements."[21] The *Almanach des muses* waxed lyrical about the power of man's reason:

> Tes tubes ont de l'air déterminé le poids;
> Ton prisme a divisé les rayons de lumière;
> Le feu, la terre et l'eau soumis à tes lois,
> Tu domptes la nature entière.[22]

> *(Your tubes have determined the weight of the air; / Your prism has divided the rayons of light; / Fire, earth, and water submit to your laws; / You dominate all of nature.)*

In the 1780s, Parisians inhabited a world of wonderful, invisible forces, waiting to be discovered and harnessed for the benefit of humanity. Just as man had conquered the air, he was gaining mastery over disease and soon would control all of nature. There were no limits to the power of his reason. On the eve of the Revolution, many were convinced that anything was possible.

24

Does Everything End with Songs?

W HEN THE CURTAINS PARTED on opening night for
Le Mariage de Figaro, Paris was primed to be amused and
shocked. Beaumarchais had spent two years intriguing to
get his play permitted. It was reputed to be naughty, provocative, and very
funny. In the crush to get in the door of the Comédie française at the first
performance on April 27, 1784, there was an uproar. Women lost their
hats and shoes; coats were torn; two persons were said to have been killed;
and the hubbub continued long after the audience was seated.[1] *Figaro* took
Paris by storm. It was the biggest hit in the history of the theater under the
Ancien Régime, and it struck a chord of riotous gaiety that reverberated
throughout the city.

Aside from its quality as a great work of literature, *Le Mariage de
Figaro* can be considered as an event, or a series of events, which extended
until May 22, 1787, when the play was performed for the one hundredth
time. The applause, "heightened to transports,"[2] at the first performance
set off echoes in all the media of the time—gossip, polemics, newspaper
articles, caricatures, and especially songs. *Figaro* was a play full of zing-
ing one-liners and *coups de théâtre* in the tradition of Molière, and it was
also a musical comedy. At key points, the actors broke into song, accompanied by an orchestra. The last line of the play, "Everything finishes with
songs," was sung to a tune, known as "l'air de Figaro," that became a hit in
itself and served as a vehicle for verse about current events for the next five

years. Beaumarchais, who was also a musician, adapted a popular tune, "Malbrough s'en va-t-en guerre"("Marlborough goes off to war," known today as "For he's a jolly good fellow" and "The bear went over the mountain"), for the first song in the play—a plaintive love chanson performed by Chérubin, the naughty, lovesick page, who set the play's tone of erotic intrigue. According to contemporary reports, the tune became known to the upper classes after Marie-Antoinette heard it being sung by "Madame Poitrine," the wet nurse of her baby.[3] Having been worked into *Le Mariage de Figaro*, "Marlbrough s'en va-t-en guerre," also known as "la romance du petit page" ("the love song of the little page"), was sung all over Paris. It probably was the most popular tune of the 1780s. Carried by songs, as well as by the extraordinary run of performances, the spirit of *Figaro* touched a broad sector of the Parisian public. But how did Parisians react? Did they subscribe to the notion that everything ends in songs?

The theater occupied a more central place in the cultural life of Paris during the eighteenth century than it does today. Periodicals—not just literary journals like *Le Mercure de France*, but the daily *Journal de Paris*—devoted enormous space to plays, far more than to novels and other genres. Literary careers were built on scoring a success at the Comédie française. An author who had written a play that went through a dozen performances (thirty were considered an outstanding hit) would acquire enough prestige to win patronage and live off pensions and sinecures. Performances determined the rhythm of daily life among the elite, who, as we saw in chapter 11, finished their *dîner* in time to make the five o'clock curtain and postponed their *souper* until at least 10 o'clock. The theaters appealed to a wide variety of social groups—artisans, shopkeepers, clerks, apprentices, and domestic servants as well as nobles and wealthy bourgeois. While members of *le monde* paid high prices for seats in the loges and boxes, ordinary Parisians could afford the 20 sous charged for standing room (or, after 1782, seats) in the *parterre*. Usually six hundred or more spectators, half the total in the house, crammed into the *parterre*, and they constantly interrupted the action on the stage. They shouted, whistled, hurled insults at the actors, and demanded that favorite passages be repeated. Although a force of forty or more soldiers was always posted inside the Comédie française and the Comédie italienne to maintain order, fights often broke out and sometimes degenerated into riots.

Far from watching passively as they do today, audiences participated in performances. Their reactions determined which plays would succeed or fail, and the plays affected their responses to events outside the theater.[4]

A new play by Beaumarchais was an event in itself. *Le Mariage de Figaro* appeared as a sequel to his *Barbier de Séville*, which had been a big success (forty-six performances) in 1775, and in the interval he had become a celebrity. *Nouvellistes* had regaled the public with so many stories about him that they fit into a pattern, which went roughly as follows.[5] Having gained fame during the Goezman Affair, Beaumarchais went to England on a mission to buy off a libel against Mme du Barry. That led to adventures with Mademoiselle d'Eon, the woman or man (Londoners laid bets on his/her true sex) who served as a French agent, and to speculations on arms for the American rebels. "Beaumarchais l'Américain," as he called himself, became a champion of the revolutionary cause, while his enemies accused him of manipulating loans and furnishing deficient rifles. Back in France, he launched a gigantic enterprise to publish the complete works of Voltaire. He bought up nearly all the surviving manuscripts after Voltaire's death and created the largest printing operation in Europe—a type foundry, a bindery, and forty presses manned by more than 150 workers in Kehl, across the Rhine from Strasbourg. At the same time, he speculated on the Paris Bourse and wrote pamphlets to boost his bets on a bull market. All these imbroglios involved backroom intrigues, yet most of them resulted in publicity, for Beaumarchais, like Figaro, exulted in occupying stage center. As the *nouvellistes* remarked, he was "always eager to cause a commotion."[6] And as Suzanne, Figaro's fiancée, said to him in the play, "Intrigue and money, there you are in your element."[7]

Those themes stood out in a sketch of Beaumarchais's life that his enemies published in the form of a burlesque "Prospectus" for a fake, four-volume biography of him.[8] It denigrated his career as the adventures of a scoundrel, yet it had little effect, because Molière had taught the public to love scoundrels. From Molière's Scapin to Beaumarchais's Figaro, roguish servants were always duping their masters on the French stage. And as suggested by the autobiographical soliloquy in act five of *Le Mariage de Figaro*, Figaro could easily be identified with Beaumarchais. The soliloquy, with its attack on Figaro's master, the Comte d'Almaviva, could also be understood as an indictment of the Ancien Régime. Was the play essentially political, as later generations have interpreted it, or was it a farce with a happy ending—namely, that everything ends with songs?[9]

The controversies that preceded the opening of *Le Mariage de Figaro* and the polemics that followed it indicate the way it resonated with the public. Of course, most Parisians were not fully informed about Beaumarchais's intrigues to get the play performed, but reports appeared in newsletters and filtered into café conversations. In September 1781 the *Mémoires secrets* revealed that Beaumarchais had completed his new play and was attempting to persuade the Comédie française to stage it. A year later, it reported that he had got nowhere, mainly because the play was said to be "very libertine and filthy (ordurière)."[10] The term "ordurière" appeared often in subsequent articles, which mentioned rumors of private readings and performances. In June 1783 Beaumarchais arranged to have *Figaro* staged for members of the court. At the last minute, however, Louis XVI forbade the performance because, according to the rumors, he considered the play "unperformable" and "filthy."[11] Beaumarchais managed nonetheless to have a private performance executed before the Comte d'Artois and several influential courtiers at the château of the Comte de Vaudreuil. According to further rumors, they pronounced it "very immoral and absolutely inadmissible in a public theater."[12] Yet Beaumarchais pulled strings and perservered until he persuaded the Baron de Breteuil, who had authority over Parisian affairs as minister of the King's Household, to listen to a reading in the company of a half dozen influential men of letters. At that session Beaumarchais defended his play so effectively that Breteuil finally gave permission for public performances at the Comédie française.[13] The reports of all these obstacles and Beaumarchais's success in overcoming them served as powerful publicity. When *Le Mariage de Figaro* opened, it was sure to create a sensation.

The dominant reaction of the audience was laughter. "One laughs and laughs," wrote an underground journalist in reporting the response to the first performances.[14] Beaumarchais captured an element of eighteenth-century French culture that, as he himself put it, was currently under threat: gaiety as opposed to the trend of moralizing and sentimentality. Figaro personified gaiety, a term attached to him throughout the play, and he was something of a rogue, or at least a light-hearted schemer. In laughing at his intrigues and those of the other characters, the audience became complicit in the erotic naughtiness that pervaded the plot.[15]

Audiences today may be accustomed to sensuality on the stage, but it was shocking to Parisians in the eighteenth century. *Le Mariage de Figaro* is saturated with sex, beginning with the revelation that the Comte d'Almaviva plans to buy Suzanne's body by a modern version of the *droit du seigneur*, which supposedly gave a lord the right to deflower a peasant's bride on her wedding night. Nearly all the characters, including the Comtesse d'Almaviva, are swept up in libidinal intrigues. Chérubin, the incarnation of adolescent libido, envisions undressing the countess "pin by pin"[16] and then is partly undressed himself by the countess and Suzanne, who marvel at his flesh and dress him up again as a girl. Played by a woman, his role exudes sexual ambiguity, and his desire extends to everything around him, even the trees.[17] The sex play comes to a climax in the final act, where the count plans to make love with Suzanne in a pavilion on the stage (an episode that was particularly shocking to eighteenth-century theatergoers), only to be confounded by his wife disguised in Suzanne's clothes. Although earlier plays involved plenty of love intrigues, none exhibited sex so openly and without condemning it in the name of conventional morality.

Le Mariage de Figaro also provided other kinds of provocation. Its entire plot turned on the humiliation of a great aristocrat by his servant, and Figaro tossed off satirical remarks about many sensitive subjects. He derided and denounced censorship, the practices of diplomacy, the senseless killing in warfare, the justice system, and the Bastille. Audiences applauded the bravado of his soliloquy with its outburst against the count: "You took the trouble to be born." But Meister spoke for most theatergoers in dismissing the critical sallies as "a few gaities that at bottom can never be very dangerous."[18]

Contemporaries rarely mentioned the political message of the play. They concentrated on what they construed to be its immorality, although their indignation did not stifle the laughter it provoked or cut into the demand to get seats. Before the fifth performance, Beaumarchais's enemies threw a printed poem from a balcony into the *parterre*, causing a kerfuffle. It described the cast of characters as a collection of reprobates, showing how each one represented a vice and how all of their vices came together in Figaro, who embodied the character of Beaumarchais himself.[19] A similar poem circulated more widely because it was composed to be sung to the "air de Figaro." Epigrams, *bons mots*, articles in literary reviews, and letters to the editor of the *Journal de Paris* joined in the declamations against the play, which, as a gazetteer put it, could be summed up in one word: "immorality."[20] Beaumarchais replied that he had exposed immoral behavior, not endorsed it, and therefore announced (in what passed as an attempt to stir up publicity) that he had indignantly rejected a request from some great ladies to be seated in an enclosed loge so that they could see the play without being seen themselves.[21] In a speech to the Académie française, Jean-Baptiste-Antoine Suard deplored the immorality of the play, and then in an open letter accused Beaumarchais of degrading the French stage. The archbishop of Paris joined the chorus of critics in a proclamation (*mandement*) to the faithful at the beginning of Lent in 1785.[22] Normally the Lentine *mandement* accorded permission for some Catholics to eat eggs during the period of abstinence from meat before Easter. This time, however, in addition to permitting eggs, the archbishop took a swipe at *Le Mariage de Figaro* along with the Kehl Voltaire and the opera, where Beaumarchais was planning a new production. Beaumarchais riposted with a song:

Suivons tous les commandements	*Let us follow the commandments*
Des mandements ...	*Of the mandements ...*
Sur Figaro, sur l'opéra	*About Figaro, about the opera*
Et cetera.	*Et cetera.*
L'on y voit des conseils tout neufs	*One sees in them new advice*
A propos d'oeufs.[23]	*A propos eggs.*

While trying to keep the laughter on his side, he also attempted to shore up his reputation as a humanitarian by dedicating the revenue from the fiftieth performance of *Le Mariage de Figaro* to an "Institute of Humanitarianism," which would pay indigent wet nurses to nourish orphan babies.[24]

All these incidents kept Beaumarchais and his play at the forefront of the public's attention. Parisians who did not frequent the Comédie française attended down-market sequels to *Le Mariage de Figaro* in the boulevard theaters: *Le Voyage de Figaro en Espagne, Le Véritable Figaro, Le Repentir de Figaro, Figaro, directeur de marionnettes, La Romance de Chérubin, Les Amours de Chérubin,* and others. Then, when the play was published, the audience for it expanded even further. Readers were so eager to purchase copies that a Dutch publisher hired agents to cobble together an early version of the text by memorizing portions of the dialogue while attending performances. Three editions of the bastard *Mariage* sold out in two weeks, while the public waited for Beaumarchais's version "with unequaled impatience." When it appeared in print on April 1, 1785, 6,000 copies sold out within a week, and more editions followed.[25] In a long preface about "decadence in the theater," Beaumarchais declared his respect for the judiciary, the nobility, and the government, but he aimed his main argument against the accusation that the play corrupted morals. It actually reinforced ethical conduct, he insisted, by employing "frank and true gaiety" as a weapon to combat corruption, just as Molière had done.[26]

According to Ruault, Beaumarchais's Parisian bookseller, the publication was delayed because Louis XVI wanted to approve of the preface himself. Frustrated in his original effort to stifle the performance of the play, the king was determined to prevent any further offense to moral propriety. He found nothing objectionable in the preface, but decided to take action after Beaumarchais published a provocative letter in the *Journal de Paris* of March 7, 1785. In it, Beaumarchais replied to an earlier letter, dripping with irony, by a supposed clergyman (it was widely attributed to Suard), who facetiously praised Beaumarchais for his charity (noting that it served as self-promotion) and for the success of *Le Mariage de Figaro* (stressing that it celebrated immoral conduct in a way that would appeal to the lower classes by using their vulgar language). Badly stung, Beaumarchais retorted that his donations came to an impressive sum, 60,000 L., and that his play was a triumph. To get it performed, he wrote, "I had to vanquish lions and tigers." Parisian commentators took that phrase to be an insolent reference to Beaumarchais's success in overcoming the resistance of the king. Monsieur, the older of the king's two brothers, brought Beaumarchais's letter to Louis's attention, describing it as a personal insult. Louis, in a fury, declared that Beaumarchais should be packed off to Bicêtre. The Comte d'Artois, Louis's younger brother, who led the court faction that favored Beaumarchais, protested that Bicêtre was a prison reserved for the vilest criminals, whereas the prison of Saint-Lazare would be more appropriate, because it was used to punish misbehavior by respectable subjects. The king then dashed off a note to the lieutenant general of police: "Beaumarchais to St Lazare." The police arrested Beaumarchais at 11:00 in the evening while he was entertaining friends at supper in his Parisian *hôtel*. He did not protest, assuming he was headed for the Bastille and a short, symbolic kind of punishment, which would win the public's sympathy. As soon as he learned he was destined for Saint-Lazare, a house of correction located in a monastery, he gave in to despair.[27]

Saint-Lazare, though a cut above Bicêtre, had a terrible reputation. Noble and wealthy families used it to punish libertine sons who had behaved so outrageously that they were to be subjected to monastic discipline and even whipped. Unlike imprisonment in the Bastille, which could convey prestige in the case of persecuted writers, Saint-Lazare stigmatized its prisoners. Beaumarchais, then fifty-three, was being treated like a wayward adolescent. He stayed there only four days and was not (contrary to rumors) given a whipping, but he felt humiliated—so overcome by ignominy, in fact, that he shut himself up in his bedroom and refused to see visitors. Ruault, an intimate of the household, reported that Beaumarchais dismissed many of his servants, sold off his horses, and planned to spend the rest of his life in exile, probably in Switzerland.[28]

Parisians gossiped endlessly about the reasons for Beaumarchais's disgrace. *Nouvellistes* and the foreign press recounted every aspect of it because, as the *Gazette d'Amsterdam* put it, "Everything that concerns this extraordinary man is the subject of conversations in the court and town."[29] Beaumarchais's partisans tried to express support, but he would not receive them; and the public in general did not rally to his side. Far from arousing sympathy as a victim of arbitrary power, he was mocked by songs and epigrams. Having dealt in filth, they insisted, he deserved what he got—that is, a good whipping. Caricatures, which sold briskly for 6 livres, showed him, his bottom exposed, being flogged by a Lazarite monk, and a widely diffused song, sung to the "air de Figaro," elaborated on the same theme:

Coeurs sensibles, coeurs fidèles,	*Sensitive hearts, faithful hearts,*
Par Beaumarchais offensés,	*Offended by Beaumarchais,*
Calmez vos frayeurs cruelles,	*Calm your cruel fears,*
Les vices sont terrassés.	*Vice has been brought down.*
Cet auteur n'a plus d'ailes	*This author no longer has wings*
Qui le faisaient voltiger ...	*That made him soar ...*
Le public, qui toujours glose	*The public, which always takes note,*
Dit qu'il n'est plus insolent	*Says he is no longer insolent*
Depuis qu'il reçoit la dose	*Now that he has received a dose*
D'un vigoureux flagellant ...	*of a vigorous whipping ...*
Par ce châtiment horrible,	*By this horrible punishment,*
Caron est anéanti.[30]	*Caron is wiped out.*

Beaumarchais remained isolated for weeks in what he described as self-imprisonment. In an open letter to one of his supporters, he said he would not leave his residence until the king acknowledged his innocence, and rumors circulated that he wanted reparations in the form of an appointment to a position in the court. According to further gossip, Louis laughed off that idea and refused to make any gesture to relieve the opprobrium crushing Beaumarchais, whom he had always despised.[31]

Although Beaumarchais eventually received some "reparation" from Versailles and resumed his role in the theater, first as the author of the opera *Tarare*, a success in 1787, then by his play, *La Mère coupable*, a failure in 1792, he never won back the public's sympathy. His reputation suffered, as we shall see, from his speculations on the stock market and his involvement in a politicized divorce trial, the Kornmann Affair. While *Le Mariage de Figaro* continued to delight audiences until 1787, its off-stage *dénouement* turned into a disaster for Beaumarchais as a personage at the center of public affairs. He never recovered fully from the humiliation of Saint-Lazare. His play represented a final round of gaiety at a time when his opponents, particularly Mirabeau, were setting a new tone for public discourse. Laughter was giving way to anger, wit to moral indignation. By 1789, Parisians were convinced that everything did not end in songs.

25

The Dark Secrets of Despotism

TWO WRITERS, Simon-Nicolas Henri Linguet and Honoré-Gabriel Riqueti, Comte de Mirabeau, ranked with Beaumarchais among the best-known and most notorious public figures in France at a time when the cult of celebrities was first becoming a historical force.[1] In 1783, within a few months of one another, they published books on the same theme, the secret horrors of despotism, and they worked it over in the same way, stoking anger and indignation on the part of their readers. Like Beaumarchais, they thrived on scandal and provoked polemics; but instead of skewering their enemies with wit, they dealt in denunciation and moral opprobrium. Both spent years in prison as victims of *lettres de cachet* and then dramatized their personal experience in best sellers, which fed a growing sense of outrage at the arbitrary power of the state.

Linguet first made a name for himself as a barrister who took on highly visible cases—notably that of the Chevalier de la Barre, who was eventually executed for sacrilege—and turned them into spectacles by means of fiery orations.[2] In 1775 he directed his eloquence against the legal profession, and after attacking the most eminent barrister in Paris, Pierre-Jean-Baptiste Gerbier, he was expelled from the Paris bar. Linguet then took up pamphleteering and journalism, venting his resentments against a wide range of public figures and institutions—the *philosophes*, notably d'Alembert; the physiocrats, particularly Turgot; the Académie française, which he derided as a bulwark of elitist tyranny; and the Parlement of Paris, which he condemned for perpetuating corporate privilege.

Linguet excelled at going against currents and taking unpopular stands, which paradoxically stirred popular support. He luxuriated in paradoxes. While championing liberty and enlightened reform, he advocated absolutism and belittled the Enlightenment's greatest figures, including Newton and Montesquieu. He cast himself as a defender of the poor and therefore favored an alliance of the common people and the monarchy in opposition to corporate bodies and all forms of privilege. Yet he described the virtual slavery of the laboring classes as inevitable in a society based on private property. He opposed French intervention on the side of the American revolutionaries on the grounds of its cost to taxpayers, and in 1788 he went so far as to recommend royal bankruptcy: It would ruin *rentiers* and the state's credit, but it would eliminate the Crown's debt without increasing taxes on the poor. Linguet harrangued the public on those themes in *Annales politiques, civiles et littéraires*, a journal he created in 1777, edited from abroad (London and Brussels), and continued to publish, despite setbacks and interruptions, until 1792. Thanks to his talent—an instinct for selecting provocative subjects and dramatizing them in vivid language—he built the *Annales* into one of the most popular and prosperous journals in the French language. Although he made many enemies, he had powerful supporters, including Louis XVI and other members of the royal family, who reputedly considered his journal as their favorite source of information.

In September 1780, however, while on a visit to Paris, supposedly with a safe conduct, Linguet was imprisoned in the Bastille. Parisians speculated for weeks about the reasons for his arrest. Some attributed it to an insulting letter that he had sent to the *maréchal* Duc de Duras, while others blamed it on the cumulative effect of everything he wrote. As with all *embastillements*, there was no judicial procedure and no official report. Linguet merely disappeared from view, and he remained invisible for so long that he was rumored to have been secretly hanged by the public executioner. His fate stirred up angry talk among Parisians, who were eager to discover the true story behind it. When he was finally released in May 1782, he announced that he would recount his experience in a book, *Mémoires sur la Bastille*.[3]

Although Mirabeau eventually eclipsed Linguet in notoriety, he was not equally well known to the public at the time of his arrest three years earlier, in May 1777.[4] He had already acquired a formidable reputation, however. In fact, after his release in August 1782, a *nouvelliste* wrote that his life resembled a novel—and recounted the episodes as if they were chapters in a tale of romance and adventure, which went as follows.[5] Irresistibly ugly—or *beau-laid*, disfigured by smallpox—and exuding energy, Mirabeau broke rules, seduced women, and defied authority in every possible way. As a reckless young cavalryman, his misbehavior and love affairs led to imprisonment in the citadel of the Ile de Ré, thanks to a *lettre de cachet* obtained by his father, the Marquis de Mirabeau, famous in his own right as a physiocrat. After his release, he concocted a plot to marry an heiress who had been engaged to another man. He managed to marry her but not to collect her dowry, having alienated her father and his own by more riotous living. After running up 300,000 L. in debts, he separated from his wife and landed in prison again by another *lettre de cachet*. The lax treatment he received in the fortress of Joux made it possible for him to frequent the social elite in nearby Pontarlier. There he seduced the twenty-two-year-old wife of the seventy-year-old Marquis de Monnier. They ran off to Switzerland and then to Amsterdam, where Mirabeau earned a meager income by hack writing. Meanwhile, a court in Pontarlier condemned him to death for seduction and abduction, and the Paris police sent a secret agent to arrest the couple with the complicity of the Dutch authorities. In May 1777 they were seized and sent to confinement in France—his "Sophie" (Marie Thérèse de Monnier) to a convent and he, as directed by a third *lettre de cachet*, to the dungeon of Vincennes.

This version of Mirabeau's life, essentially accurate but enhanced here and there by extravagant details, circulated widely in Paris in 1783, but it told only half the story. He had received an excellent education, and during a period of exile imposed by his father in 1772, he wrote his first book, *Essai sur le despotisme*, which demonstrated both his talent as a writer and his hatred of arbitrary authority. He completed three works during his three years in Vincennes: *Erotika biblion*, a pornographic pseudotreatise, full of citations from biblical and classical sources about sex life in antiquity; *Ma Conversion* (later reprinted as *Le Libertin de qualité, ou confidences d'un prisonnier de Vincennes*), an account of his own erotic adventures; and *Des Lettres de cachet et des prisons d'état*, the two-volume treatise on despotism that made him famous.[6] He played the role of libertine-aristocrat-adventurer for all it was worth in subsequent years, while cultivating fame as a writer. After his release from Vincennes, he boldly turned himself in to the authorities in Pontarlier and then got his death sentence reversed, arguing his own case. Next, he tried but failed to get a court in Aix-en-Provence to force his wife to return to him, and he intervened in a suit between his own parents, who were also estranged. All this activity, accompanied by orations and publications, kept Mirabeau in the public eye. He continued to turn out tracts, mostly hack works written to make money, on all sorts of subjects until 1789. They sold well, because he infused them with energy and passion. Although hardly a man of the people, he appealed to a popular audience and loaded his writing with rhetoric that earned him the sobriquet of "Comte de la bourrasque" (the count of squalls).

Mémoires sur la Bastille and *Des Lettres de cachet et des prisons d'état* made a splash when they appeared, and immediately became best sellers.[7] They had many similarities. Both protested against the injustice of imprisonment without any legal procedure or any possibility of self-defense. Both attacked ministerial despotism epitomized by the use of *lettres de cachet*. And although they based their argument on general principles, both drove it home by detailed accounts of the author's personal experience. The details were virtually the same. Each author described the sensation of arriving in an alien world of stone walls, iron doors, and heavy locks. They were frisked, subjected to the confiscation of personal items such as watches, led through dark corridors, and shut up in a cell. There they remained for days, surrounded by silence, before being received by the commanding officer, who refused to listen to their protests or even to inform them of their supposed offense. Their cells had thick walls (twelve feet in the upper levels of the Bastille, sixteen feet in the dungeon of Vincennes); a narrow window with three rows of iron bars; and little furniture—nothing but a bed, a chair (two chairs in Vincennes), and a table. Although they had candles (eight a week in winter), the cells remained dark, glacial in the winter, stifling in the summer. The prisoners received two meals a day delivered by their turnkey, and the food was disgusting—rotten meat, vinegary wine, vegetables like sludge. Linguet thought he was being poisoned, and Mirabeau fell ill. Some prisoners were occasionally permitted to take walks, unaccompanied except by a turnkey, in a courtyard surrounded by oppressive walls—one hundred feet high in the Bastille, fifty in Vincennes. They were always isolated, forbidden to communicate with one another and the outside world. By special permission they might receive books and be allowed to write letters, although all correspondence was vetted and often confiscated. They remained defenseless before their autocratic keepers, the governor of the Bastille and the commandant of Vincennes, whom they rarely saw. Aside from unpleasant confrontations with those officials and occasional inspections by the lieutenant general of police, they had no contact with other human beings, except their turnkey, who was forbidden to converse with them.

Linguet and Mirabeau recounted these details in a manner designed to give the reader the impression of penetrating inside forbidden territory hidden in secrecy by an all-powerful state. Both also stressed that the worst effects of imprisonment were psychological—a combination of anxiety, deprivation, boredom, fear, despair, uncertainty about the future, lack of information about the present, and a sense of being cut off from everyone and everything outside the prison walls. They described their experience with similar rhetoric, appealing to the reader's passions with strong language strung out in Ciceronian cadences. Linguet brought a long sentence to a climax by invoking "those tortures of the soul, those prolonged convulsions, that perpetual agony, which stretches the pain of dying into an eternity without ever granting a moment of relief."[8] Mirabeau described a prisoner's suffering in the same way: "He lives in relentless pain: no correspondence, no human contact, no clarification of his fate. What a mutilation of existence! It is to cease living without enjoying the relief that comes with death."[9]

At the end of *Mémoires sur la Bastille*, Linguet appended a note stating that while his book was being printed he had received a copy of *Des Lettres de cachet et des prisons d'état* and that it confirmed his argument. It stripped away the secrecy hiding the horrors of Vincennes just as he had done in revealing the mysteries behind the walls of the Bastille. Yet the two books differed in fundamental ways. Linguet put his name boldly on the title page of his tract and devoted its first fifty pages to an account of his current situation. He had violated the condition of his release from the Bastille, which would have pinned him down in exile four leagues from Paris, and had fled to England in order to resume publishing his *Annales*. Mirabeau hid himself in anonymity, indicating at various points that he belonged to the military nobility, was twenty-eight years old, and expected soon to die in prison; hence the subtitle, "a posthumous work." He, too, began with a long preliminary argument—in fact with a separate volume of 366 pages. It was a political treatise, full of references to classical antiquity, the entire course of French history, English thinkers (Locke, Blackstone, Swift, and Hume), and a wide range of Enlightenment *philosophes*, particularly Montesquieu, Rousseau, and Raynal. While wandering through many subjects, it made a strong case for liberty as a natural right and for popular sovereignty as the sole legitimate source of law. Only after staking out this radical philosophical position did Mirabeau recount his personal experience in volume II, another 237 pages. Linguet, by contrast, did not philosophize, although he, too, presented himself as a champion of the common people. He had already become notorious as an opponent of ministerial despotism, but he was an ultramonarchist. He favored concentrating power in the hands of the king so that it could be used to benefit the poor at the expense of the privileged orders, especially aristocrats entrenched in the court.

Read in retrospect, *Mémoires sur la Bastille* and *Des Lettres de cachet et des prisons d'état* seem to have delivered a double blow to the legitimacy of the French state, but it is difficult to know how they were read in the 1780s. Although both books were illegal and could not be reviewed in the authorized press, their publication was recognised as an important event by letter writers and *nouvellistes*. Mirabeau was soon identified as the author of *Des lettres de cachet* and celebrated as a powerful new voice in the chorus of criticism against the regime, while Linguet, familiar as an agitator, received less favorable treatment. La Harpe praised Mirabeau's "energetic eloquence," despite its prolixity, and found Linguet's tract comparatively disappointing, although he complimented both authors for demonstrating the fundamental injustice of *lettres de cachet*.[10] Hardy was overwhelmed by Mirabeau's eloquence, much as he disapproved of its radical implications.[11] The *Correspondance littéraire secrète* exclaimed that Mirabeau's text was written "in letters of fire. One cannot read it without indignation." Linguet's tract, by contrast, was disappointing, although it made the same argument and had a wide readership.[12] The *Mémoires secrets* also noted that everyone was reading Linguet's text, although it seemed exaggerated and overwritten, whereas Mirabeau had created a sensation. His eloquence brought tears to the eyes; his argument, profound and erudite, made a convincing case against despotism; and the success of his book had transformed him into a formidable public figure.[13] Ruault's correspondence, unlike the newsletters, testifies to the effect of both books on an individual reader, in his case a sophisticated Parisian. Taken together, he wrote to his brother, they made a powerful impression of the horrors inflicted on citizens by the state. Although Ruault had little sympathy for Linguet, Mirabeau moved him deeply and reinforced his growing sense that France had degenerated into a despotism.[14]

The resonance of the books by Linguet and Mirabeau was reinforced in the following years by other accounts of suffering in state prisons. *Remarques historiques sur la Bastille* (1785) presented itself as a sequel to Linguet's book, which it criticized as too self-centered. It outdid him in describing the physical aspects of the Bastille and even in denouncing the suffering inflicted on prisoners, but it did not have a comparable success on the marketplace.[15] *Mémoires d'un prisonnier d'état* (1785) told an insider's story of the madhouse-prison of Charenton. Although it took the form of an epistolary novel, it was received as a credible description of the horrors inflicted on political prisoners as well as lunatics.[16] The first-person prison narratives culminated in *Histoire d'une détention de trente-neuf ans dans les prisons d'état. Ecrite par le prisonnier lui-même* (1787), attributed to Jean Henri Latude. It, too, focused on the suffering of the narrator, who did time (thirty-four years according to the text, although the title announced thirty-nine) in all of the nastiest prisons of Paris, and it recounted how he escaped from them, on three occasions, only to be plunged back into hideous *cachots* (underground cells). In his most dramatic story, Latude (or the author who wrote in his name) recounted how he and a cell mate broke out of the Bastille, using a rope they made from their old clothes and a ladder constructed from firewood. They climbed up the chimney of their cell, slid down the outside walls, and barely avoided drowning in the moat. How much fiction went into the tale, Parisians could not know, but a preface by the publisher made its moral clear: "The story of M. Latude is perhaps the best work that one could do to enlighten the nation and those who govern it about the useless atrocity of arbitrary punishments."[17]

The government itself seemed to acknowledge this message, because in 1784 it closed Vincennes as a prison and even permitted visitors to inspect it. Parisians poured in, shuddering at the iron rings attached to the wall of the torture room and the stone beds in cells where prisoners slept, shackled in chains. The public attributed the closing of the prison to the effect of Mirabeau's book. Mirabeau himself, now firmly established as a champion of liberty, gave some guided tours of the dungeon and commissioned an engraving to celebrate the end of its use for the victims of *lettres de cachet*. Contemporaries noted that the print resembled the frontispiece of Linguet's *Mémoires sur la Bastille*, which depicted a statue of Louis XVI gesturing toward the ruins of the Bastille. Linguet had imagined that in the future the king would order the Bastille to be destroyed and that he would be honored by the statue, bearing an inscription with his last words to the prisoners: "Be free and live."

Of course, Parisians had no idea of what the future would bring. Looking massive and indestructible, the Bastille dominated the eastern skyline of the city, and it also loomed large in the collective imagination, fixed in print as the embodiment of despotism.[18]

26

Did the Cardinal Try to Cuckold the King?

THE NEWS CAME pouring out, so unexpectedly and in such confusion that Parisians did not know what to make of it: the cardinal de Rohan, grand aumonier de France (the highest ecclesiastical position in the court), member of one of the wealthiest and most powerful families in the kingdom, dressed in his full robes and about to officiate over a mass to celebrate the Ascension of the Virgin, was arrested in Versailles on August 15, 1785, and imprisoned in the Bastille. Soon afterward, Parisians learned that a diamond necklace, valued at 1,600,000 L. and intended as a gift to the queen, had vanished—purloined, broken into fragments, and sold off secretly in the international market for stolen goods. Then rumors circulated about a nighttime rendezvous in the gardens of Versailles between the cardinal and the queen. As reports spread throughout the city, the cast of characters grew. It featured Jeanne de Saint-Remi, Comtesse de La Motte, an adventuress who pretended to be of royal blood; Nicole Le Guay, a beautiful courtesan passed off as the Baronesse d'Oliva and dressed up to imitate the queen; and Joseph Balsamo, Comte de Cagliostro, an alchemist, spiritualist, healer, prophet, and master of Egyptian freemasonry, who claimed to have bestowed eternal life upon himself. Around them gathered a supporting cast of swindlers, fortune seekers, and women of small virtue. The Diamond Necklace Affair, as it came to be known, provided endless material for gossip. For a while it outdid balloon flights and mesmerism in fascinating the public, and unlike them, it had the added attraction of scandal.

When word of the cardinal's arrest first reached Paris, some thought it involved court intrigue (Rohan was an enemy of the Baron de Breteuil, minister of the King's Household) or foreign affairs (Rohan had alienated Marie-Antoinette while ambassador to Vienna in 1772–1774). Within a few days, however, Parisians learned that it had to do with a swindle. Rohan had been implicated in a plot devised by Mme La Motte to purchase a fabulous diamond necklace from two Parisian jewellers and to present it secretly to the queen in order to win back her favor. He would pay for it in installments, authorized by the queen herself in a note signed "Marie Antoinette de France." When the first installment became due, Rohan could not come up with the money. The jewellers appealed to the queen, who denied any knowledge of the transaction, which was an obvious fraud, because she never added "de France" to her signature. Outraged at the insult to his consort's honor, Louis XVI met with Breteuil and the foreign minister, the Comte de Vergennes; summoned Rohan, who was about to officiate at the religious service in Versailles; and after hearing his confession, dispatched him to the Bastille. An agent was sent to capture Mme La Motte, who had run off with her husband and the remains of the necklace to Bar-sur-Aube. Although she was arrested, her husband escaped and disappeared with the diamonds across France's border.[1]

That much of the story eventually became clear, but the rest of it looked increasingly murky, as arrest succeeded arrest, and the Bastille filled up with prisoners—fifteen by the end of August and eventually thirty-five. The cardinal was not known for his sanctity. Fed by rumors about his extravagant expenditures, illegitimate children, and debts, Parisians initially expressed little sympathy for him.[2] Gradually, however, their sentiments shifted, because Mme La Motte, who figured in the gossip as one of his mistresses, began to look like the villain of the plot and he appeared as her dupe. Young, attractive, and posing as a descendent of a bastard son of Henri II, she pretended to have gained the confidence of Marie-Antoinette. When she met with Rohan in her Paris residence, she led him to expect that he could win the queen's favor. Cagliostro, who had gained an equal hold on the cardinal's highly suggestive imagination, reinforced that illusion. As a result, according to one report, Rohan had conceived for the queen "an audacious and criminal passion. He was easily persuaded that the homage of a necklace would be agreeable to her. It is said that Cagliostro, using occult operations, made him see that the queen was sensitive to his ardor."[3]

Cagliostro played an increasingly important role in the story as it was told in Paris after he was locked up in the Bastille with his wife on August 22. By a mixture of charm and charlatanism, he had succeeded in dominating Rohan and had lived in close contact with him in Strasbourg since 1781. Seduced by Cagliostro's claim that he had acquired knowledge of the deepest secrets of the universe from ancient Egyptian sources, Rohan believed that Cagliostro exercised occult power: he could cure disease, transform metal into gold, and see into the future. According to different reports about his origins, he might be the son of an Ottoman pasha, or the master of the knights of Malta, or an Egyptian ruler. He was at least 300 years old, perhaps even 2,000, for he was said to have dined at the table during the wedding of Cana. When asked during his interrogation in the Bastille whether he had any regrets about the life he had led, he replied that he still felt terrible about the assassination of Pompey (September 28, 48 BCE), although he had acted on orders.[4]

Anecdotes of this sort accumulated throughout the autumn of 1785, some leaked from depositions and interrogations, some fabricated.[5] Parisians could not sort out a coherent narrative until judicial memoirs began to appear. Granted a choice by Louis XVI, Rohan had elected to be tried by the Parlement of Paris rather than to put his fate into the hands of a special commission or to appeal to the king's grace. A parlementary trial, to be held before the senior magistrates in the Grand'Chambre, involved a complex procedure. During a preliminary phase, the prisoners gave depositions, and one of the magistrates, delegated to be a *rapporteur*, summarized the material in a report, which recommended that a trial be held. On December 15, when the court accepted the recommendation, the prisoners' status changed. They ceased to be held in the Bastille merely by order of the king—that is, by virtue of a *lettre de cachet*—and became prisoners charged with a crime and subject to the judgment of the court. At that point, Rohan began to lead a more restricted life. He had been allotted a large apartment in the Bastille, where he had given dinner parties for as many as twenty persons, including ladies, and Delaunay, the Bastille's governor, had taken him on tours of the boulevards in a carriage. Once constituted a prisoner by the Parlement, he had less access to visitors and, like the other prisoners, went through the formalities of a second phase. They were subjected to interrogations and confrontations—that is, exposed to one another and to the evidence against them in dramatic scenes—while the prosecuting attorneys prepared the state's case. Meanwhile, they continued to consult their lawyers, who published memoirs throughout the entire procedure. As in the case of Beaumarchais against Goezman and many other judicial affairs, the memoirs, though intended to function as legal briefs, turned into manifestoes that appealed to public opinion.

Mme La Motte's lawyer, who signed simply as "Doillot," published the first memoir on November 26, 1785. Although badly written and incoherent in places, it placed the blame for the crime on Rohan and especially Cagliostro, whom it presented to the public as a spectacular charlatan. Readers were treated to accounts of his mysterious origins—as a Portuguese Jew, a Greek, or an Egyptian—and his fabulous age, including the story of his presence at the wedding of Cana. They learned how he had seduced Rohan by summoning up spirits of dead and absent persons through rituals, which included a great deal of apparatus—swords, daggers, crosses, candles, and torches. In one ritual, a virgin girl saw the queen accompanied by an angel in a carafe of clear water while Cagliostro held a sword over her head and evoked Catholic and Egyptian spirits. The memoir discussed Mme La Motte's genealogy at length in order to assert the impossibility for a person of royal blood to become mixed up in a swindle, and it concluded that she had nothing to do with the purchase of the necklace or its supposed presentation to the queen. It also referred to allegations about a strange "interview" that Rohan was said to have had with the queen at midnight in the park of Versailles—only to dismiss them as an absurdity.[6]

Absurd or not, everything in the memoir seemed designed to appeal to a broad public. Parisians snatched up 4,000 copies of it overnight and discussed it avidly. The foreign French press—especially the *Gazette de Leyde*, which had informants among Rohan's supporters—covered the Affair extensively, week after week. The illegal newssheets also made it their lead story, churning out anecdotes, the more off-color the better. According to the *Mémoires secrets*, Mme La Motte persuaded a Parisian jeweller to design a device like a snuffbox that would contain a retractable portrait of the queen in a half-naked pose. He was horrified at the idea but complied after La Motte assured him that the queen herself wanted the work done so that it could be given to Rohan as a token of her "satisfaction." The *Correspondance secrète* dished up stories about Rohan's orgies, including a performance by actors who imitated the postures in the obscene sonnets by Pietro Aretino. But sensational anecdotes, accompanied by poems and epigrams, figured less prominently in the press than reports about the general character of the Affair and attempts to make sense of it. Parisians speculated endlessly about hidden causes, because they could not believe that a wealthy prince of the church could have been mixed up in a tawdry swindle. As they followed the unfolding of events, the Affair seemed to be increasingly "incomprehensible"—an "inextricable labyrinth," as the *Courrier du Bas-Rhin* put it. The city was flooded with "a thousand confused rumors," Hardy confided to his journal. None could be believed, yet all of them reinforced a general feeling that Rohan's arrest was an act of "despotism and arbitrary authority."[7]

Parisians began to get a clearer view of the case in December, when the *rapporteur* informed the Parlement about the depositions taken from the prisoners in the Bastille. On December 15, the Grand'Chambre decided to initiate procedures for the trial of four of them: Rohan, Mme La Motte, her husband (who had escaped to Ireland), and a "demoiselle Oliva." Although news about the arrest of Mlle Oliva had circulated in October, her name had not figured prominently in the rumors about the ramifications of the Affair. Once the prosecution began to prepare its case—a matter of interrogations and confrontations that continued until May 6—she appeared as a prime suspect. The proceedings were secret, however, and Parisians relied on gossip, which often seemed too far-fetched to be taken seriously, until March 20, when Mlle Oliva's lawyer published a memoir that added another, even more spectacular dimension to the Affair.[8]

The memoir, written in the first person as Oliva's plea for justice from a lonely tower in the Bastille, read like a novel. Born into a poor family, orphaned as a young girl, raised and then abandoned by family friends, Mlle Oliva supported herself—though she did not say so directly—as a courtesan in the Palais-Royal. The self-proclaimed "count" de La Motte picked her up, not for sex but, he said, for a service requested by the queen and organized by his wife, the "countess," a Valois who had become a confidante of Marie-Antoinette. The La Mottes took her to a rented room in Versailles, dressed her in a fine white costume, and instructed her in the role she was to play under the name of "baronne d'Oliva." She would meet a "great nobleman" late at night in the gardens of the palace. She would give him a letter they had prepared and a rose, saying only, "You know what that means." The queen would watch from a sheltered space and would reward her with a gift in addition to 15,000 L. to be paid by the La Mottes.

On an overcast night in August, Mlle Oliva was led by Mme La Motte to an arbor in the gardens and left in the darkness, trembling with fear. She saw a male figure approach. It inclined before her. She handed it the rose and stammered out her speech, but forgot the letter. Mme La Motte suddenly appeared and said, "Quick, quick, come," and then whisked her away while the figure withdrew. It was over in an instant, and it was a success, celebrated the next morning when Mme La Motte read her a letter, supposedly penned by the queen, expressing satisfaction and promising Mlle Oliva a happy future.[9]

In fact, Mlle Oliva's future turned out to be miserable. The La Mottes dropped her after paying only 4,268 livres. She ran up debts, left Paris for Brussels to escape from her creditors, and after three weeks was arrested in the middle of the night by a detachment of the local police, who passed her on to the French and the Bastille, where she awaited her fate, "surrounded by thick walls, which separate me from the rest of humanity, shut inside high towers where I can see nothing but my misery, where my soul feels only pain and consternation."[10] Mlle Oliva, or rather the lawyer who wrote in her name, drew on the mythology surrounding the Bastille, added plenty of sentiment—but not so much as to spoil an unadorned narrative by a woman of the people—and scored a hit. Parisians loved it. They bought up 20,000 copies of the memoir, at a cost of 24 sous each, within a few days. Moved by Mlle Oliva's candor and naïveté—and perhaps also by news that she gave birth to a baby during her imprisonment—grandees of the court competed to see who could claim her as a mistress after her release. To ordinary Parisians she demonstrated that an innocent "plebeian"—as well as a Linguet, a Mirabeau, and indeed a cardinal—could fall victim to the arbitrary power of the state.[11]

Meanwhile, more memoirs appeared, as several of the prisoners faced accusations of complicity in the crime, and they engaged lawyers to argue their case, appealing to the public as well as to the judges. The memoir that aroused the greatest interest came from Cagliostro, who drafted it himself in Italian, leaving his lawyer to turn it into French, unless, as some said, it was reworked by d'Éprémesnil, one of his most ardent supporters.[12] Parisians had waited eagerly for its publication, prompted for months by speculation and rumors. A scandalous tract, *Mémoires authentiques pour servir à l'histoire du comte de Cagliostro*, had prepared the way by spreading extravagant stories, such as Cagliostro's claim to have suppers with the dead (notably d'Alembert and Diderot, who revealed the secrets of the afterlife) and to make himself invisible. In fact, it maintained, he was a charlatan born into a poor Jewish family in Italy. He preached a bogus, supposedly Egyptian version of freemasonry, which his fake-countess wife adapted to the erotic tastes of some aristocratic ladies at a cost of 100 louis a head. Although Cagliostro had bamboozled Rohan for his own purposes, Mme La Motte had actually masterminded the diamond necklace swindle, and the whole Affair was likely to end undramatically with the exile of the main protagonists.[13]

Cagliostro proposed to set the record straight and to tell his own version of his story in a truly authentic memoir. In fact, the *Mémoire pour le comte de Cagliostro* had little to say about the criminal case but a great deal about the career of its hero, which he recounted in the first person as a "Confession," expressing enough *sensiblerie* to evoke Rousseau. He could not solve the mystery of his parents, he explained, although he knew they were distinguished nobles and Christians. At the age of three months, he was brought as an orphan to Medina, given the name of Acharat, and raised in the palace of Mufti Salahaym by a wise "governor" named Althotas, who gave him a superb education, especially in the medical sciences. He wore Arab clothes and learned many Eastern languages, but kept the "true religion" hidden in his heart..When he turned twelve, Althotas took him on travels to expand his education. First they went by caravan to Mecca, where the ruler treated him magnificently for three years. Next they traveled to Egypt, where ministers officiating at the pyramids revealed knowledge stored since the time of the pharaohs. They spent three more years traveling through Africa and Asia and finally came to a halt in Malta. The Grand Master of the Knights of Malta gave them a splendid reception, which suggested that he could have been the hero's father, although other possibilities had arisen, including the mufti of Mecca and the chérif of Trabzon. At that point, Althota died, and his charge, now a mature master of medicine, took the name "comte de Cagliostro" and adopted European clothing. Cagliostro continued to Sicily, Naples, and Rome, where he met and married Séraphine Félichiani, a beautiful young woman of noble blood who traveled at his side for the next ten years, visiting every country in Europe.[14]

The succession of exotic names and titles made Cagliostro's autobiography read like a tale from the *Arabian Nights*. But he gave it a believable twist by emphasizing his vocation as a doctor, empowered with knowledge from many civilizations and devoted to healing the poor. He let it be known that he possessed great wealth, although he kept its source secret, and he listed names of eminent persons scattered across Europe who could testify to his refusal to accept money or favors. His success had created enemies, of course. He had been attacked by libels, which made him out to be an alchemist, the Wandering Jew, or a 1,400-year-old wizard. He dismissed such slander as nonsense and admitted only to a mastery of animal magnetism, which he had employed in the séance with the young girl described by Mme La Motte. By that time he had settled in Strasbourg and had got to know Rohan. But he never dominated the cardinal, as Mme La Motte claimed; and as to her charge that he had been Rohan's accomplice in the diamond necklace swindle, it was obviously absurd. He had been in Lyon at the time when the negotiations to purchase the necklace had taken place, and he had never seen it.

The demand for the memoir was so great that Cagliostro's lawyer requested a detachment of eight soldiers to prevent its distributors from being overwhelmed by crowds. Booksellers sold 20,000 copies for 30 sous each within four days. Groups gathered to hear it read aloud. Many were moved because, as they observed, Cagliostro understood the human heart and knew how to "excite general pity." "Oh, how beautiful it would be, if everything were true," exclaimed one woman, and a "sensitive man" said that he let the emotion sweep over him while he read it as if it were a novel.

Hardy, more skeptical, noted that many considered the memoir "a kind of novel lacking any vraisemblance." Ruault, the Paris bookseller, dismissed it as absurd. But all commentators agreed that Cagliostro's account of his life had shifted attention away from the case itself, and the main interest of the public was now to see how Mme La Motte would reply.[15]

The rebuttal, written by La Motte's lawyer, went over Cagliostro's story point by point and dismissed all of it as a fabrication. Although he claimed to be a nobleman, Cagliostro was actually the son of a coachman named Thiscio who lived in the outskirts of Naples. He had been apprenticed to a coiffeur, worked for a while as a valet, and then took to the road with an adventurer known as Cosmopolite, who taught him the art of duping and swindling. Determined to seek his fortune on his own, he encountered one disaster after another until he finally succeeded in subjugating Rohan and draining off much of the cardinal's enormous wealth. The argument, however, was restricted to Cagliostro's biography and had little direct bearing on the case before the court. Some readers found it convincing as an exposure of a charlatan, while others considered it a "novel," every bit as fictitious as Cagliostro's own "confession." The general impression left by the debate was that Cagliostro had captivated the public's attention and had run away with the main narrative about the Affair.[16]

The final and most important memoir, a defense of Rohan and an attack on Mme La Motte, brought the debate about the case back to the central issue: who had engineered the theft of the diamond necklace and abused the name of the queen? The memoir was written by Target, now established as one of the most eminent barristers in France and a member of the Académie française, and it was published on May 19, 1786, after every scrap of information had been extracted from the prisoners by inter-rogations and confrontations. Having been approved by the government, the text of 146 pages was taken by the public to be the definitive account of the Affair.

Target turned it into the story of a swindle, conceived and executed by a supremely evil villain, Mme La Motte. Instead of discussing her sup-posed origins, he began his narrative by situating her with her husband in a miserable *chambre garnie* in Versailles, then in a shabby, two-room Pari-sian apartment, and later, as they began to plot schemes, in a residence that was staged to suggest gentility: furniture that looked impressive but had to be frequently pawned; a table setting of pewter, replaced on social occasions by borrowed silver; mirrors removed when threatened with confiscation by bill collectors; servants badly paid and frequently dismissed. Mme La Motte had enough money to keep up appearances, because in 1782 she began to borrow from Rohan. Having met her in Versailles, he took pity on her straitened circumstances and then showed serious interest when she let it be known that she enjoyed the confidence of the queen. By playing on his desire to regain the queen's favor, Mme La Motte persuaded him to advance funds for charitable projects that Marie-Antoinette wanted to promote while hiding in anonymity. She ingratiated herself so successfully that in August 1784 she was able to pull off the midnight rendezvous in Versailles, which Target described as the most outrageous fraud in French history. Overcome by indignation, he briefly dropped his lawyerly exposition of the facts and addressed Mme La Motte directly: "You are a monster of ingratitude and imposture."[17]

Having come to dominate Rohan, Target explained, Mme La Motte manipulated him unmercifully. Guillible but guiltless, naïve and blinded by the desire to win back a place in court, he let himself be duped by the greatest coup of all. Target described it in detail—the hoodwinking of the jewellers, the note with the queen's forged signature, and the transfer of the necklace to the La Mottes in a carefully choreographed scene. Until the end, Rohan believed it had reached the queen. He asked informants if she had been seen to wear it, while behind his back the La Mottes took it apart and sold off the diamonds. Then they went on a spending spree, which Target described at length: pearls, rings, and bracelets for Mme La Motte; two magnificent swords for Monsieur; horses, carriages, servants, great quantities of the most expensive furniture to outfit a new house in Bar-sur-Aube—all of it at a cost of 600,000 to 700,000 L.

Target treated his readers to an explanation of the dénouement, showing how the stories of all the prisoners came together during their interrogations in the Bastille. When questioned, Rohan held to his honest, straightforward account of the events; Mme La Motte became trapped in contradictions; and her key accomplice, a certain Rétaux de Villette, provided the final, crushing evidence of her guilt by confessing to his role in drafting fake letters, including the note with the queen's fake signature. As to Cagliostro, Target barely mentioned him, except to note that he had no connection with the swindle.

Target's memoir outdid Cagliostro's and Oliva's in stirring up Paris. The cardinal's supporters in his Paris residence, the Hôtel de Soubise, required people to register in advance to collect copies, yet they had to call in troops to prevent the crowd from rioting. Target's publisher distributed 60,000 copies within ten days; pirate publishers turned out at least three additional editions; journals printed long extracts; and Parisians talked of nothing else, as the *Correspondance littéraire secrète* noted, because the Affair now had something to interest everyone—"mystification, treachery, swindling, love, marriage, and perhaps a tragic catastrophe."[18]

Although the public derived most of its information from the judicial memoirs (at least eleven were published by the end of May), rumors fed on reports leaked from the interrogations and confrontations of the prisoners, which continued in the Bastille until May 6. According to the reports, Mme La Motte behaved like a wild animal. When confronted with Villette, she fell into a rage and had to be carried back to her cell after beginning to tear off her clothes. Upon hearing the testimony of the Baron de la Planta, a player in one of the Affair's subplots, she fainted and bit her turnkey when he brought her back to her cell. Later, she refused to eat, stripped off her clothes, and defied the jailers to bring her to her next confrontation naked. They got her back into a dress for subsequent scenes, but they could not control her. She punched Cagliostro in the stomach, tried to scratch out the eyes of Rohan, and again bit her turnkey, this time drawing blood. Parisians speculated that she was feigning insanity. Their sympathies shifted decidedly to Rohan, and they came to view Mme La Motte as Target had presented her: the incarnation of evil in female form.

The magistrates heard the evidence presented by their *rapporteur* from May 22 to 29. On May 30, they conducted the final interrogations of the accused, who were summoned before them in the Grand'Chambre and submitted to a grilling while seated on the *sellette*, a wooden stool. (In deference to his eminence, Rohan was permitted to sit on a bench.) According to reports that immediately began to circulate outside the courtroom, Cagliostro gave a spirited account of himself with a flood of exotic language, much of it incomprehensible, which kept the magistrates amused. Rohan maintained his dignity while adhering to his straightforward version of the events. And Mme La Motte, dressed properly with a newly made hat, managed to control her passions but not to present a convincing case. After deliberating from 5:00 a.m. until 9:30 p.m., with a break of ninety minutes for dinner, the court announced its verdict. It dismissed the cases against Rohan, Cagliostro, and Oliva. It condemned M. La Motte, who had escaped to a hiding place in the British Isles, to a life term in the galleys, and Mme La Motte to being whipped, branded on both shoulders with the letter *V* for *voleuse* (thief) while bearing a rope around her neck, and incarcerated for the rest of her life in the Hôpital de la Salpetrière, which was notorious as a prison for prostitutes.

Crowds surrounded the Hôtel de Soubise and cheered wildly in celebration of the cardinal, a free man and the hero of the day, although the king promptly exiled him to his abbey of Chaise-Dieu in Auvergne and stripped him of his position as grand aumonier. Cagliostro, equally applauded by crowds, also was exiled. Before leaving with his wife for London, he issued a statement expressing gratitude for the support of the French people; and as a last gesture, he bestowed a gift of 100 louis on Mlle Oliva, who had been left free but penniless, nursing the baby she had borne in the Bastille. Meanwhile, Parisians rented locations where they could get a good view of the punishment of Mme La Motte, which, according to rumor, would take place in the Place de Grève at noon on June 21. To avoid public disorder, however, the authorities decided to punish La Motte in a closed courtyard of the Palais de justice at 6 o'clock in the morning of the 21st. Although only a few persons witnessed the execution of her sentence, their accounts of it soon were circulating, and detailed descriptions turned up in letters and journals.

According to the reports, La Motte did not know what punishment awaited her, because she had been kept isolated in a cell of the Conciergerie prison. When led out to hear her sentence read by a clerk, she refused to kneel, as the ceremony required. Her jailers forced her to go down on her knees; and when she heard the court's decree, she screamed and flailed about so wildly that five hangmen had to pin her to the ground. They tied her hands, wound a rope around her neck, and dragged her to the Palais. She fought them off in the courtyard, rolling on the ground, kicking and screaming. While the principal executioner held the iron with the red-hot letter *V*, the others ripped open the back of her white déshabillé. She was nearly naked when he pressed the brand into her flesh, and she writhed so violently that it slipped, scorching most of her back, her armpit, and a breast. She bit one of her torturers, and flesh from his arm was still in her mouth when she finally passed out. Taken by coach to the Salpetrière, she regained consciousness, then fainted again. After her wounds were bathed, she was dressed in a ragged chemise and consigned to a collective dormitory that housed seventy-two women, mainly prostitutes.

Although the police ordered café owners to tell their clients not to discuss the crime and its punishment, Paris was flooded with talk about the Affair. Two persons identified by police spies were sent to the Bastille for "talk," and a great many pamphlets were confiscated. But the outpouring of pamphlets, caricatures, songs, and *bons mots* could not be contained. Parisians made collections of all the judicial memoirs and bought prints showing the twenty-two principal players to serve as frontispieces. Adding to the ferment, Cagliostro, resettled in London, published another memoir, directed this time against Delaunay, the governor of the Bastille, and a police agent whom he accused of ransacking his Paris residence after they arrested him and of failing to return cash and property worth 150,000 livres. It was written in a style of wounded *sensiblerie* and drew tears from readers who took it as evidence of further abuse of power. Backed by d'Éprémesnil, his champion in the Parlement, Cagliostro hoped to receive permission to pursue his claim in court, but the government rejected it.

In June 1787, Paris learned to its astonishment that Mme La Motte had escaped from the Salpetrière. Different versions of the story circulated in the gazettes. Some claimed that with the help of a fellow prisoner, she removed paving stones in a remote courtyard, dug under a wall, and disappeared, disguised as a man. Others noted that a carriage was waiting for her, and therefore some kind of conspiracy was at work. According to the most extravagant account, Mme La Motte's husband possessed compromising letters from the queen. He threatened to publish them, unless the government allowed her to join him in London. It succumbed to the blackmail and covered up its complicity by damaging the wall at the place of her ostensible escape.

The supposed letters appeared early in 1789 as a long appendix to a memoir purportedly written by Mme La Motte to justify herself and give her account of the Affair. The letters revealed that the cardinal and the queen had been lovers and co-conspirators in a plot to make him prime minister and to subject France to the dominance of Austria.[19] Although obviously fake, the memoir belonged to a growing body of scandalous literature, which by 1794 would make Marie-Antoinette appear as an oversexed monster, destined for the guillotine. Nothing suggests that Parisians held such wild ideas before 1789, but several scurrilous attacks on her were produced during the last years of the Ancien Régime. Two police inspectors, Jean-Claude Jacquet de la Douay and Pierre-Antoine-Auguste Goupil, who were assigned to repress the libels, actually collaborated in their publication. The inspectors ended up in the Bastille along with hundreds of copies of works like *Essais historiques sur la vie de Marie-Antoinette d'Autriche, reine de France*, which were successfully confiscated and kept as evidence or stored in preparation for pulping. In his journal entries about the Affair, Hardy mentioned a *"Vie de Marie Antoinette, a horrible libel aimed against the queen,"* and the arrest of booksellers and peddlers whose stock included slanderous attacks on the queen such as *Les Nuits d'Antoinette*.[20]

Although the police may have succeeded in stifling much of the printed slander, they could not stop the gossip. Parisians were horrified by reports about the queen's fantastic luxuries—the acquisition of diamonds worth 750,000 L. in 1781, earrings made for her at a cost of 800,000 L. in 1785, a porcelain service purchased for nearly a million in 1787. They exchanged stories about her extravagances, such as a loss of 300,000 L. in one evening of card games. The expense they most deplored was the king's gift to her of the Château de Saint Cloud at a cost of 6 million L. plus 1.6 million for an adjoining estate, whose owner was forced to sell. Calonne, the finance minister, was said to encourage her taste for luxury and to shovel money at her as a way to fortify his position in court. These "depredations," Parisians feared, were leading the state into bankruptcy. In 1787 when the queen was giving balls at the height of the financial crisis, they referred to her as "Madame Déficit."[21]

Paris had exploded with joy when Marie-Antoinette gave birth to a dauphin in 1781, and she always received applause when she appeared in the royal box at the Opéra. But during a formal visit in May 1785, the common people refused to shout "Long live the queen" while she traveled through the streets. Some attributed this slight to her failure to stop at the church of Sainte Geneviève, where she was expected to pray to the saint for relief from a drought, which greatly distressed the Paris poor. Others saw in it the effect of libels, songs, and hostile epigrams. In August 1787 Parisians actually booed and hissed the queen—that is, in French they called out "hou! hou!" and "tchi!"[22] By now, their resentment at her depredations had turned into hatred, according to some *nouvellistes*. The lieutenant general of police advised Versailles that it was unsafe for her to appear in the capital, and the king passed on the message, adding (the *nouvellistes* often quoted him as if they had been standing at his elbow), "Madame, I forbid you to go into the capital until I order otherwise." Deeply wounded, Marie-Antoinette canceled her public engagements in Versailles and withdrew to the privacy of her residence in the Petit Trianon.[23]

The hostility to the queen ran parallel to sympathy for the cardinal, according to reports about Parisians' reactions to the Affair. No one seemed shocked at the stories about Rohan's mistresses and illegitimate children, which came out in many of the memoirs. As one pamphlet put it, peccadilloes of that sort were expected from persons of his rank, and the most important thing about Rohan was his "good heart."[24] Parisians generally took the view that he had been duped. He might have been gullible or even ridiculous, but he was not guilty—and, like so many others, he was an innocent victim of arbitrary power. The king, who had sent him to the Bastille, received no sympathy. In his letters to his brother, Ruault wrote that while consummating the alienation of the queen from the people, the Affair had confirmed the incapacity of the king. He described Louis as well-meaning but stupid, bewildered, incompetent, timid, indecisive, constantly drunk, and unfit even to govern a German principality. "The public spirit has turned against him," Ruault noted at the height of the Affair, "because he inspires no respect, no fear, no confidence, and one throws away the people's money for all sorts of follies." By the summer of 1787, Ruault judged that the scorn for the king and queen had spread throughout the social order, reaching the "populace," who mocked them in the street, as well as "respectable people," who read and reflected. "It is completely debased, this royal family, and its authority, as well," he concluded.[25]

One aspect of the Affair seemed particularly to disturb the public imagination. Louis XVI had been unable to produce an heir to the throne during the first seven years of his marriage. He may have suffered from phimosis, a condition that impeded the retraction of his foreskin and impaired his ability to have sexual intercourse. Surgical intervention probably solved the problem, and the public knew nothing about it; but rumors of impotence had spread before Marie-Antoinette first became pregnant, and once she did, they cast doubt on Louis's paternity. A libel from 1781, *Les Amours de Charlot et Toinette*, claimed that Louis's brother, the Comte d'Artois, had taken his place with the queen. It showed no respect for the royal penis:

On sait bien que le pauvre Sire,	*It is well known that the poor Sire,*
Trois ou quatre fois condamné	*Three or four times condemned*
Par la salubre faculté	*By the salubrious faculty [of medicine]*
Pour impuissance très complète	*For complete impotence,*
Ne peut satisfaire Antoinette.	*Cannot satisfy Antoinette.*
De ce malheur bien convaincu,	*Quite convinced of this misfortune,*
Attendu que son allumette	*Considering that his match stick*
N'est pas plus grosse qu'un fétu;	*Is no bigger than a straw,*
Que toujours molle et toujours croche,	*Always limp and always curved,*
Il n'a de vit que dans la poche;	*He has no prick, except in his pocket;*
Qu'au lieu de foutre, il est foutu.[26]	*Instead of fucking, he is fucked.*

A secret agent, none other than Goezman, who had hired himself out to the foreign ministry after being humiliated by Beaumarchais in 1774, bought up the entire edition of this tract in London for 18,600 L. and delivered it to the Bastille.[27] A few copies probably escaped, however, and a great many were diffused along with new editions after July 14, 1789, when the Bastille's stock of confiscated literature was liberated. Slanderous rumors about Marie-Antoinette, many spread by songs and epigrams, had proliferated since 1774, according to Jeanne-Louise-Henriette Campan, her *femme de chambre*. The police worked hard to suppress them, yet some appeared in print. Hardy considered them so outrageous that he refused to mention their titles in his journal. By May 1786 when the court delivered its verdict on the Affair, the myth of an impotent king and a sex-starved queen had begun to take root. In 1789 during his travels in France, Arthur Young noted that ordinary people believed the most far-fetched stories about the wickedness of the queen: "There seems everywhere to be no absurdities too gross, nor circumstances too impossible for their faith."[28]

It was the nighttime rendezvous in Versailles that most aroused fantasies. *Nouvellistes* reported that it had been glossed over, by order of the government, during the trial.[29] The rose that Mlle Oliva presented to the cardinal, they imagined, could have signified acceptance of a liaison.[30] The diamond necklace, according to rumors, was intended to express Rohan's "audacious and criminal passion." And Cagliostro's séance convinced him that his "ardor" was acceptable to the queen.[31] Of course, such talk was nothing more than speculation, but that is what made it significant: The Affair stirred Parisians' imaginations. While sympathizing with the cardinal, they realized that he had dishonored the queen. As Ruault put it, he was a "bold and impudent fool . . . who imagined that the queen of France was in love with him and gave him a rendezvous at night in a grove."[32] By June 1786 some Parisians had thought the unthinkable: the cardinal had attempted to cuckold the king.

What sort of a regime was it whose greatest dignitaries behaved in such a fashion? Everything about the Affair—the cardinal, the queen, the king, the million-livre necklace, the mumbo jumbo of Cagliostro—worked on the imagination of Parisians in a way that sapped the legitimacy of the monarchy. At the very least, as expressed in the official charge against Rohan, the events had compromised "the respect due to royal majesty."[33]

27

The Poor March on Versailles

AMONG THE MANY kinds of poor—from the down-and-out *misérables* to the hard-up day laborers—*gagne-deniers* occupied a middle range. Parisians saw them everywhere, lugging boxes, hauling furniture, toting merchandise. They were porters, hired by the job and paid a pittance. They would carry anything, including people, who often needed help to get across the muck that flooded many streets. When business was bad, they didn't eat.

Business was terrible in the winter of 1785–1786, because it was so cold. For several days after December 25, the temperature fell far below freezing (to 10 degrees Fahrenheit, according to a report on January 4). Commerce slowed, and people stayed at home huddled by the fire, while the porters braved the cold, seeking work and finding little, aside from orders for firewood. Worse still, they faced a new kind of competition, a government-backed delivery service, which appeared out of nowhere on December 28. It employed men to operate like the carriers of the *petite poste*, making rounds, four times a day, to pick up packages that were deposited in two hundred locations scattered throughout the city. In addition to small items, the deliverymen handled large jobs, such as hauling furniture for people who were moving into new quarters. They received steady wages (30 sous a day) and worked in pairs, pulling small, red carts. Unlike the ragged porters, they wore smart-looking uniforms: green coats with red collars, grey breeches, hats well waxed to protect against the rain. Attached to the coats they sported metal badges bearing the royal coat of arms. Rumor had it that the company was backed by powerful courtiers in Versailles, including the queen's favorite, the Duchesse de Polignac, and the minister for the department of Paris, the Baron de Breteuil.[1]

On January 2, a group of porters in a wineshop of the rue Gallande near the Place Maubert worked themselves into a fury about the "parakeets of Breteuil," as they called the deliverymen, whose green coats were associated with the green in the livery of Breteuil's servants. They goaded one of their number, a certain Maréchal, known for his quarrelsome temper, to insult a deliveryman passing by in the street. Maréchal picked a fight; two pedestrians intervened; the other porters joined in; a crowd gathered; and the brawl had nearly turned into a riot when two squadrons of the Garde de Paris and the Watch arrived and restored order. The guards took two of the porters to be placed under arrest in the residence of a police *commissaire* named Dupuy nearby in the rue des Noyers. But the tumult had spread to workers in the faubourg Saint-Marcel, who mobilized to free the porters. A large crowd, armed with sticks from a cart carrying firewood, gathered outside Dupuy's house, which was protected by only a few guards. Before a full-scale insurrection could break out, a force of two hundred soldiers arrived in time to disperse the protestors, chasing them with bayonets. It captured five and killed two.

The soldiers cordoned off the rue des Noyers, then marched the seven captives to the Châtelet prison in what the *nouvellistes* described as an impressive show of force. Two cavalry troops led the way; then came a mounted brigade of the Watch; a large detachment of foot soliders marched in the next section; the prisoners followed, walking single file, attached to one another with a rope; next came another detachment of foot soldiers; and the procession ended with a second brigade of the mounted Watch. It later transpired that small riots had erupted in other parts of Paris and that groups of porters planned to rescue their comrades by ambushing the parade. Five hundred of them gathered at the Pont de la Tournelle under the mistaken assumption that the procession would pass that way en route to the prison of the Hôtel de la Force. Angry workers from the faubourg Saint Antoine gathered at the Pont Marie with a similar plan. When they learned that the prisoners had been led off by another route, they marched to the house of *commissaire* Dupuy and raised a tumult, which lasted late into the evening. They, too, had to be dispersed by force.

Force clearly would not work, not for the poor. During the next days, various incidents occurred, which suggested that the Parisians sympathized with the porters, or "Auvergnacs" and "Savoyards," as they were often called, because many of them came from those poor provinces. But the "parakeets" continued on their rounds, each of them escorted by four soldiers with their bayonets fixed. On January 11, porters streamed into the Place Louis XV from all parts of the city, bringing with them water deliverymen and other allies from the poor. Troops patrolled everywhere, having received an alert that trouble was brewing; yet they encountered no violence. When accosted by the commander of the Watch, one of the porters explained that they had no intention of doing anything illegal. They had gathered in the Place Louis XV in order to set off together for Versailles because they wanted to bring their misery to the attention of the king. They were peaceful and unarmed. All they had was a *placet*, a handwritten petition, but they knew that if they could present it to the king, he would save them from destitution.

At 6:00 in the morning, groups of porters set off from the Place Louis XV and other locations—the Place Maubert and various meeting places in the faubourg Saint Antoine—headed for Versailles, a twelve-mile walk, which usually took four hours. They were frequently stopped, first by soldiers of the Watch, then by troops dispersed along their route who tried to persuade them to turn back. They persevered, nonetheless, and when they arrived at the palace, their number had swollen to 1,500 or 2,000. At an outer barrier, a guard informed them they could go no farther, although he would permit a deputation of twenty-four to continue. At a first gate, a guard told the twenty-four that he would allow only twelve to pass. At a second gate, a guard permitted six to proceed. The six finally made it through an inner courtyard and to a gallery inside the château, where a servant said the king could not see them. He had gone hunting. Nonetheless, they waited there, clutching their *placet* and hoping that the king would return. After three hours, an officer of the *Garde du corps* took pity on them and promised he would deliver their petition to the *Premier gentilhomme de la chambre*, who would be sure to give it to the king. They should receive an answer within a week.

In fact, Louis had been forewarned, and decided to spend the day hunting. When he returned, according to one report, he seemed uninclined to favor the porters' appeal. He never answered it.[2]

On January 19, the Châtelet court announced its decision in the trial of the seven prisoners, which was printed and peddled everywhere. All were guilty of rebelling against the Garde de Paris. The first two received the harshest punishment: Blaise Chacel was to spend three days attached to a stake in public, to be branded on the right shoulder with the letters GAL (for *galérien*), and to be sent to the galleys for nine years. Jean Tailland was condemned to the same punishment but with a five-year term in the galleys. The Parlement commuted the punishment of both to nine years of banishment from Paris and a 3-livre fine, although it retained the provision for public exposure. The condemned were to be attached by an iron collar to a stake and to wear a sign on their chest and back saying "Violent rebel against the Guard." They would be exposed between noon and two o'clock on three consecutive days, first in the Place Maubert, then in the Place des Halles, and finally in the Place de Grève. The other five prisoners, who included Maréchal (his actual name was Antoine Clément), got off with an admonition and a 3-livre fine.

While parading Chacel and Tailland around Paris, the state again displayed a great deal of military power: several regiments of cavalry and foot soldiers escorted them to the stakes. Yet Parisians reacted with a great deal of sympathy for the condemned, which they expressed in a customary manner by leaving donations at the sites where they were exposed. After three days, the sum collected came to 236 L., the equivalent of a year's income for a porter, though not enough to keep a family alive.

While the poor sank deeper into poverty, the rich enjoyed "la douceur de vivre," as Talleyrand later put it in looking back on the last years of the Ancien Régime.[3] For many Parisians, the ballooning, the enthusiasm for America, the gaiety of Figaro, the promenades in public gardens, and the amusements of the boulevards cast a soft light over the early 1780s. But the atmosphere darkened in 1787, when the accumulated debt of the state produced a political crisis. The controller general, Charles Alexandre de Calonne, attempted to avoid bankruptcy by persuading an

Assembly of Notables to endorse new taxes. Their refusal led to his fall, the formation of a new government, and another attempt to raise taxes, which culminated in a desperate conflict between the Crown and the Parlement in 1788. To understand how Parisians experienced those events, it is necessary to suspend the political narrative and to set the scene by concentrating on two seemingly apolitical developments that obsessed the public in 1787: a battle on the stock market and a sensational adultery trial.

PART FIVE

Tremors,
1787

28

Battles on the Bourse

OR MOST PARISIANS, stockjobbing, insofar as they knew it
existed, took place in an incomprehensible "region of darkness."[1]
The poor spent too much time struggling to get bread on the table
to be concerned about the Bourse. Those with disposable capital invested
in *rentes* (annuites) or land or offices, which conveyed status as well as
income. To plunk down solid louis, *espèces sonnantes et trébuchantes*, for
a share in a stock company, an abstract entity that one had never seen,
was unthinkable. Although many Parisians knew there was a Bourse, few
would be able to find it, because it was not identified with a grand building
as in Amsterdam. It had occupied various sites since its origin as a "place"
for transactions among merchants in 1563. By 1780 it was located in the
Hôtel de Nevers opposite the stables of the Duc d'Orléans in the rue Vivienne, but a great deal of its business was transacted nearby in the Palais-
Royal, especially in the café du Caveau and "the camp of the Tartares," a
meeting place in the palace gardens.[2]

Having been burned by the collapse of John Law's system in 1720,
Parisians had no sympathy for seemingly modern and suspiciously British financial institutions. Law, a Scottish adventurer, had convinced the
Regent, the Duc d'Orléans, to back a project that combined a national
bank, paper currency, the state debt, tax collecting, and a stock company
with assets in the never-never land of Mississippi. A run on the stock created a bubble; the bubble burst; hundreds of people lost their fortunes;

and the state reverted to the old system of floating loans by selling *rentes*. Until the end of the Ancien Régime, the public looked upon paper money and joint-stock companies with deep distrust. Companies existed, of course, but they were private partnerships, often put together for a particular project (*sociétés en commandite*). The most conspicuous public company, the Compagnie des Indes, founded in 1664, was a relic from the age of mercantilism. Although it survived Law's system, it was a monopoly controlled by the Crown, and it collapsed in 1769. At that time, stockjobbing seemed to have no place in the public sphere.

This set of attitudes had changed by 1785, when a new Compagnie des Indes was created and public affairs had expanded to include activities on the Bourse. Although the trauma of Law's system had not vanished from the collective memory, a half dozen public companies had recently appeared, offering services that could affect everyday life, such as the supply of drinking water, insurance, and the provision of cash for bills of exchange. Parisians could read about fluctuations in the value of the shares every day in the *Journal de Paris*. The news had a fascination of its own, even for people who would never consider buying stock, because it told of fortunes made and lost by placing bets—millions of livres exchanged for shares in companies that seemed to come from nowhere and that remained mysteriously opaque. Speculation of this kind was known as *agiotage*, a term that was neutral in itself but had acquired a negative connotation, like stockjobbing in English. It suggested that the speculators dealt in imaginery assets—value imputed to shares that had no relation to their actual worth and that could be inflated or deflated according to their reputation on the Bourse.

Some speculations attracted special attention, because the players sold stock they did not own. They traded in futures, *marchés à terme*, agreeing to pay a certain price at a future date for shares in a company whose value might fluctuate wildly during the interim, depending on the general perception of its solidity. Bull speculators (*joueurs à la hausse* or *haussiers*) gambled that the price of particular shares would rise, and therefore they contracted with a rival speculator, who bet against a rise, to buy the shares at an agreed price on an appointed day. If the shares had increased in value when the date arrived, they could pay for them at the contracted price and sell them at the current, higher rate, pocketing the difference. Bear speculators (*joueurs à la baisse* or *baissiers*) employed the same strategy in the opposite manner. They agreed to sell shares to a rival speculator at the current or a relatively high rate; and if the value of the shares had decreased at the appointed date of sale, they could purchase them at a bargain price and sell them for the agreed amount.

Of course, only the wealthy—*agioteurs* or *capitalistes*, as they were known—could play this game, but the public could follow it as spectators. Millions of livres traded hands from one day to the next; and if this were not fascinating enough, rumors circulated about illicit maneuvers to manipulate the prices, even with the collusion of the government. Money and power—it all made excellent material for conversations in cafés and wineshops. The authorized press could not discuss the stockjobbing, although it could quote the prices, because the subject was sensitive and the government tried to exert some control over the Bourse. Financial affairs had been inseparable from politics since the time of Colbert. Calonne, as controller general, needed to maintain stability in the financial sector and also to prevent the new companies from diverting capital required for government loans. Moreover, the companies raised a threat of a different kind. The value of their shares depended on demand, and demand was ultimately determined by public opinion—a dangerous force, which could, under some circumstances, be turned against the government.

In 1785, Parisians began to get glimpses of activities in this shadowy zone, where finance and politics converged. The bulls and bears attempted to determine the future price of shares by the best weapon at their command: pamphleteering. From 1785 to 1788 they flooded the public with tracts designed to shape the perception of the value of the companies whose stock was being traded. They enlisted the most famous writers of the time—Mirabeau on the side of the bears, Beaumarchais for the bulls. The lines of fire could not be perceived clearly at first, and they kept shifting; but in March 1787 the public discovered what was ultimately at stake: the survival of the finance minister.

Nouvellistes began to report "great fermentation" on the Bourse in January 1785.[3] Conflict broke out over the Caisse d'escompte, a private bank that had a public function, because it discounted bills of exchange on a large scale and loaned money to the royal treasury. It had nearly gone bankrupt in 1783, when it was rescued by the state, which recapitalized its funds at 15 million livres. By 1785, it was operating profitably, and its shareholders met in January to vote on the amount of its semiannual dividend, which would determine the value of its shares and the outcome of *marchés à terme* riding on them. The meeting turned into the first of a series of conflicts between the bulls and the bears, all of them fueled by pamphleteering. A bull group pushed for a large dividend, 180 L. per share, and a bear group tried to hold it down to 140 L. As there were 5,000 shares, each worth 8,000 L. at the current rate, a great deal of money was at stake. Although the bulls dominated the meeting, the bears won the battle, because their leader, Isaac Panchaud, a Genevan speculator who had helped found the Caisse in 1776, enjoyed the support of Calonne. The government had the power to intervene in the setting of dividends, and Panchaud persuaded Calonne to produce an edict on January 16 that favored the lower rate. But the bulls refused to accept defeat. They protested with more pamphlets and raised a tumult in the Bourse. At one point, a bear speculator, Etienne Clavière (we have met him as a founder of the Gallo-American Society), took offense at a remark by a bull, Louis Pourrat, and slapped him in the face, and the Bourse dissolved into a punch-up.[4]

Undeterred by Calonne's intervention, the bull shareholders resorted to lobbying in Versailles and managed to get an audience with the king. They convinced him, according to most reports, that the Bourse had been taken over by a "spirit of *agiotage*," as bad or worse than the stockjobbing of London. Louis responded with another edict, dated January 24, which annulled the previous transactions, and Calonne intervened by setting the dividend at 150 L. This dénouement, confirmed at another meeting of the shareholders, left the public perplexed. A monumental battle had taken place, but who had won and who was favored by the government? The pamphleteers and *nouvellistes* gave conflicting accounts, full of arcane details, and it was difficult for outsiders to conclude anything, except that public affairs had entered strange new territory.[5]

The stockjobbing did not stop there, nor did the pamphleteering. In May a publication appeared that sent a jolt of new energy into the fights on the Bourse, because it was written by a powerful polemicist, the Comte de Mirabeau. As already explained, he had gained notoriety as a public figure, and he stirred up controversy with everything he wrote. His tract, *De la Caisse d'escompte*, blasted the *haussiers* and defended the *baissiers* in a 225-page account of the betting on the Bourse. Despite its obvious partisanship, Mirabeau claimed that he approached the subject as a *philosophe* and maintained strict neutrality. Insofar as he admitted any sympathies, they lay with the poor against the rich and with honest businessmen as opposed to "the aristocrats of commerce."[6] The Caisse d'escompte, he argued, was ultimately a public institution that required surveillance by the government. Unfortunately, the bull speculators had captured it and inflated the value of its stock by voting for absurdly high dividends at the semiannual meetings of the shareholders. Calonne had rightly overruled them by the edict of January 16, which lowered the dividend voted that month, but by pulling strings in Versailles the bulls had saved themselves from honoring their *marchés à terme*, as permitted by the edict of January 24. To explain these maneuvers while maintaining a pose of unbiased philosophizing required considerable dexterity—reinforced by one hundred pages of documents, which were obviously provided by Mirabeau's backers among the *baissiers*. After working through the esoteric details, Mirabeau arrived at a clear conclusion: the edict of January 24 should be rescinded, and henceforth the government should protect the public by reining in *agiotage*. Although he disclaimed any intention of flattering men in power, Mirabeau ended by singing the praises of Calonne.

De la Caisse d'escompte created a "sensation," according to contemporary reports. Whether or not readers could follow Mirabeau's argument, they were treated to the spectacle of a flamboyant adventurer taking on a new kind of public enemy. Soon, however, word spread that Mirabeau was acting as a propagandist for the *baissiers*, and critics noted a disparity between his celebration of Calonne and his reputation as an outsider who scorned the court and denounced despotism. In any case, a new area of public debate had opened up, and it was certain to expand because the betting shifted from the Caisse d'escompte to other joint stock companies, beginning with the Banque de Saint Charles, a Spanish bank whose shares were traded heavily on the Paris Bourse.[7]

In his next tract, *De la Banque d'Espagne dite de Saint-Charles*, Mirabeau attacked the bank as *agiotage* of the worst variety, every bit as bad as Law's system, because its inflated shares were tied to a Compagnie des Philipinnes, a pipe dream similar to Law's Compagnie du Mississipi. The pamphlet was timed to affect a new wave of speculation in June, and it succeeded in knocking down the price of the bank's shares on the Bourse.[8] But it confirmed the view that Mirabeau wrote as a hired gun for the bear speculators, despite the fact that, in a sequel he dashed off in July, he described himself as a "patriot" attacking "aristocrats of banking."[9] Moreover, Mirabeau's critics also detected a "secret motif" in his pamphleteering.[10] According to rumors, which by now were constantly fed by the activities of the Bourse, the stockjobbing had become a political issue, because Calonne needed to rescue the loan of 125 million livres that he had floated in December. Instead of subscribing to it, capitalists preferred to put their money on the shares currently booming on the Bourse. A drop in the market would shift capital to the loan, and therefore the government secretly supported the *baissiers*.

An edict of August 7, proclaimed and posted widely in Paris, exposed some of the issues in language that could be understood by ordinary Parisians. Warning against the epidemic of *agiotage*, it explained the nature of *marchés à terme* and outlawed them, including private deals negotiated in cafés. For several weeks, the jobbers disappeared from the café du Caveau, and the Bourse declined, although the government loan failed to attract more subscribers. In September the speculation resumed, more frantic than ever. Rumor had it that deals on futures, though prohibited, involved more shares than actually existed. Calonne responded on October 2 with another edict, which repeated the prohibition decreed on August 7 and named a commission to adjudicate the conflicts among the speculators. In a striking preamble, it warned the public that nothing like the current "frantic stockjobbing" had ever existed in France and that the king would not permit stockjobbers to "set traps for the public trust in selling what one does not have, what one cannot deliver, what may not even exist."[11]

Although some speculators deplored the edict as an "act of terrible despotism,"[12] it did not stop the agitation on the Bourse. On the contrary, the battles between the *haussiers* and the *baissiers* became fiercer, because they shifted to a high-stakes venture that had attracted a great deal of attention among Parisians for the last eight years: the Compagnie des eaux de Paris. Parisians drank the water of the Seine, either straight and laced with the sewage that had been dumped into it (if left to stand in a pitcher, much of the filth dropped to the bottom), or filtered by *fontaines sablées*. Porters carried water to the rich, while the poor fetched their own. In 1778 the Perier bothers, Jacques-Constantin and Auguste-Charles, launched a joint stock company based on a plan to distribute water from the Seine by means of steam pumps and networks of wooden pipes. Their Compagnie des eaux began to operate in 1782, using a pump located on the riverbank at Chaillot. By 1785 they were ready to expand it on a large scale, and the price of its shares shot up on the Bourse.

In October, Mirabeau fired off another tract, *Sur les actions de la Compagnie des eaux*, warning investors to avoid the company because the *agioteurs* were at it again. They had forced its shares up to four times the original price. Sheer arithmetic—based on information about consumption of water, pumping capacity, the cost of pipes, and returns on investments—proved beyond a doubt that the company could never yield more than a small fraction of the profits imagined by its backers.[13] Although this pamphlet created less of a sensation than its predecessors, it was received favorably, and it knocked 500 L. off the price of the company's shares. To rebut it, the bull players chose Beaumarchais, a veteran polemicist whose *Mariage de Figaro* was still setting box-office records at the Comédie française. Beaumarchais already belonged to their camp and had spoken up, although ineffectually, against the *baissiers* at a stockholder meeting of the Caisse d'escompte. The reading public was therefore treated to the spectacle of two famous writers slugging it out over what had become one of the hottest topics of the day: stockjobbing.

Although Beaumarchais did not put his name on the pamphlet, *Réponse à l'ouvrage qui a pour titre: Sur les actions de la Compagnie des eaux de Paris*, it was immediately attributed to him, and it bore the stamp of his style. He derided Mirabeau's rhetorical outbursts as "Mirabelles" (plums).[14] Then, mixing witticisms with economics, he went over all the information about the company's investments, costs, revenue, and potential for growth (more people will take baths, the streets will be kept cleaner), and concluded that the value of its shares corresponded to perfect fiscal health. Mirabeau's attack was merely an attempt to force their price down. While pretending to admire his "energetic pen," Beaumarchais dismissed Mirabeau as a hired hack of the *baissiers*. Like a lawyer desperate for clients, he would argue any case for cash.[15]

Mirabeau roared back with an all-out attack on Beaumarchais, his character and career, including the sale of deficient arms to the Americans and *Le Mariage de Figaro*, which had turned the theater into "a school of bad morals." In reply to the accusation that he wrote for the *baissiers*, Mirabeau retorted that he made no secret of it. Careful study of the evidence had convinced him that their cause was just. His friend Etienne Clavière had sold one hundred shares of the Compagnie des eaux for 1,600 L. each, deliverable in March 1787. As they were now selling for 4,000 L., Clavière, along with honest *pères de famille*, stood to suffer a huge loss, due entirely to *agiotage*. Beaumarchais, by contrast, wrote for the *haussiers*, rich financiers and courtiers. In fact, he had prepared a deluxe pressrun of his pamphlet for Versailles, and it had appeared with the approval of a censor, despite the declamation against censorship in *Le Mariage de Figaro*. As to Beaumarchais's backhand compliments about his character, they were libelous. Mirabeau would meet him and the administrators of the company in court.[16]

The trial never took place, except in the court of public opinion, where Mirabeau seems to have won. The *nouvellistes* praised his fiery eloquence. Even Hardy, who did not follow the Bourse closely, was swept away by Mirabeau's "patriotic zeal" and delighted to learn that it had produced a further drop in the shares of the Compagnie des eaux.[17] Some commentators worried, however, that the speculation had grown so wild that it could produce catastrophe far beyond the Bourse. "A frightening revolution is very near," Ruault wrote in a letter to his brother. "Everything is *agio*, finance, banking, discount, loans, usury, betting, depositing, etc. Everyone is obsessed with money and is crazy about these kinds of speculations."[18] The frenzy had political consequences, as Mirabeau made clear by revealing that he had attacked the *agiotage* at the invitation of Calonne. The government's policy seemed to be aligned with the betting of the bears.[19]

The lay of the land had shifted, however, by June 1786, when the shareholder assemblies met to determine the next round of dividends. Although the public could only guess at the machinations behind the fluctuations of the stock prices, it received reports about new outbreaks of "fervor" and "frenzy" on the Bourse, and they suggested that Calonne had switched camps.[20] Threatened by the drop in the value of its shares, the directors of the Compagnie des eaux announced that they would graft a fire-insurance and fire-fighting enterprise onto their system for supplying water. Mirabeau was not available to attack this scheme because he had left for Prussia on a special mission backed by the ministry of foreign affairs. But most of the pamphlets published under his name had been written by hired hands and allies of the *baissiers*, leaving Mirabeau to supply rhetorical passages.[21] Jacques-Pierre Brissot, the future Girondist leader who was then a protégé of Clavière and the most important of Mirabeau's ghostwriters, came up with the next tract, *Dénonciation au public d'un nouveau projet d'agiotage*. It claimed that Parisians, unlike Londoners, did not require fire insurance, because most of their houses were made of stone. And insofar as firefighters were needed, they should be volunteers, so as to reinforce civic spirit and strengthen the passion of empathy, which Rousseau had shown to be the basis of social life. To inject Rousseauistic ideology into a pamphlet about stockjobbing might seem far-fetched, but Brissot and Clavière were committed disciples of Rousseau, and their argument went over well with the journalists who reviewed it.[22]

At a general assembly on July 3, 1786, the shareholders of the Compagnie des eaux voted to merge the fire insurance company with the water company, which they expanded by issuing 1,000 new shares worth 4,000 L. each. Soon afterward, Calonne provided an edict permitting the merger and giving it the government's blessing. He also undermined a rival project to supply drinking water to Paris by diverting the Yvette river. Everything suggested, according to the *nouvellistes*, that he had thrown his support behind the Compagnie des eaux.[23] Brissot responded with another tract, *Seconde lettre contre la Compagnie d'assurances pour les incendies*, which he published under his own name (the first was anonymous). In addition to his previous arguments against the fire-insurance scheme, he claimed that the merger had transformed the Compagnie des eaux into an entirely new company and therefore that speculations on the old company were no longer valid—that is, although he did not make it explicit, Clavière could not be held to honor the *marché à terme* that bound him to provide the one hundred shares of the Compagnie des eaux that would mature in March 1787. Brissot went on to condemn the artificial inflation in the shares of all the companies that were then being traded on the Bourse. And he ended by denouncing the government's support of the *haussiers*, stopping just short of an open attack on Calonne.[24]

All these maneuvers received extensive coverage in newsletters and journals like the *Gazette de Leyde*. After three years of reports about drama and scandal on the Bourse, Parisians had become familiar with the idea that finance impinged on public affairs and that *agiotage* was ultimately political. Judging from contemporary accounts, readers could not follow the unfamiliar political arithmetic in the pamphlets, which contained dozens of pages of financial calculations, but they had no difficulty in assimilating the main point of the *baissiers*'s argument: *Agiotage* was wicked business. *Agioteurs* added fictitious value to shares, inflating them with spurious assertions about assets, and then dumped them on innocent investors. To expose the inflation was a patriotic duty assumed by writers like Mirabeau, and to bet against it by *baissiers* like Clavière was to act in the public's interest. What made the jobbery explosive was the intervention of the government because, by 1787, Calonne had taken sides with the bull speculators.

During the last six months of 1786, the speculations shifted back to the Caisse d'escompte and the Compagnie des Indes. The Caisse shares dropped spectacularly in October when a rumor spread that the government planned to make it into a national bank or to create a rival discount bank. They recovered just as abruptly thanks to intervention by Calonne, who assured the directors of the Caisse that no such plan existed.[25] To the public, now attuned to rumors of jobbery, the fluctuations looked like foul play, and an enormous rise in the shares of the Compagnie des Indes seemed even more suspicious, especially when it was connected with speculations by a priest, the abbé Marc-René-Marie de Sahuguet d'Espagnac. Beginning with only 20,000 L. in capital, he made a profit of 950,000 L. by betting on an unexpected increase in the dividend of Indes shares.[26] In October, Calonne permitted the company to issue 20,000 new shares, bringing its value up to 40 million livres and making it even more attractive to the bull speculators.

Both companies figured prominently in the climactic phase of speculation, which brought the Bourse to a paroxysm in the first months of 1787. By then Calonne faced a desperate deficit in the government's finances. Having failed to cover it with loans, he persuaded Louis XVI to convoke an Assembly of Notables, composed of prominent citizens from different estates, which (as we will see in chapter 30) would sanction a program to redesign the system of raising taxes and install various reforms. The Notables held their first session on February 22 amidst a deluge of pamphlets, placards, and *bruits publics*, most of it negative. Although fascinated by such an unprecedented event, Parisians generally regarded it as a ploy: The government needed to mobilize support by consulting a body that seemed in some undefined way to speak for the nation. The Parlement had adopted that role, but it had opposed tax reforms since the ministry of Machault in 1749. Calonne calculated that the Notables would be more compliant. Instead of acting as a rubber stamp, however, they insisted on a serious examination of the Crown's finances, and soon Calonne faced the greatest crisis of his career.

Although the Notables met behind closed doors, one aspect of the crisis was played out on the Bourse, where the public could get a partial view of the connections between finance and politics. At the beginning of February, Calonne attempted to get some relief from the hemorrhaging of the royal treasury by tapping the Caisse d'escompte. That prospect caused "panic and terror" and a drop of 2,500 L. in the shares of the Caisse. After meeting secretly with Calonne, the Caisse directors agreed to a rescue operation: they would create 20,000 new shares, which would bring in 80 million livres from investors, and they would loan the government 70 million in exchange for receiving a twenty-seven-year privilege for discounting notes.[27] The shares recovered quickly, but Calonne also had to cope with dangerous speculation on other stock, particularly that of the Compagnie des Indes, and this time his attempt to intervene was exposed by the most explosive of all the pamphlets published during the three years of polemics: *Dénonciation de l'agiotage*, which was dedicated to the king, addressed to the Notables, and written, at least ostensibly, by Mirabeau.

After returning to Paris in January 1787, Mirabeau took up again with Clavière, who needed a powerful pamphleteer, because he had uncovered information about one of the greatest scandals in the history of the Bourse. While the price of the Indes shares rose, the bull speculators had bought and sold them with abandon; and as the maturation date of the *marchés à terme* approached, they scrambled to divest their portfolios at peak prices. Abbé d'Espagnac obliged them by buying up everything available. In the end, he purchased 51,503 Indes shares, although only 37,000 existed (another 3,000 remained on deposit with the company). As nearly all the sellers had never possessed the shares they contracted to deliver, he could force them to settle on his own terms, exacting a spectacular profit, which he later put at 5,500,000 L. The bears, who also stood to lose, did not understand the full extent of d'Espagnac's coup, because its mechanism remained hidden in various syndicates and subcontracts. But Clavière or his allies had come up with a damning piece of evidence, a "Plan of the operations of abbé d'Espagnac," which they printed at the end of the *Dénonciation de l'agiotage*. Ostensibly written by d'Espagnac himself, it laid out his strategy for cornering the market on the Indes shares, complete with names and numbers. Mirabeau presented it as "the most audacious plan for a swindle that has ever been concocted."[28]

In fact, the Clavière-Mirabeau group had uncovered only part of a plot whose full story would not become known until after 1789, when the revolutionaries investigated the financial frauds of the Ancien Régime. Calonne had been secretly subsidizing the bull players with "assignations" (notes of credit) worth millions of livres from the treasury. Indeed, he personally stood to profit from the bull market, because he possessed a hidden portfolio of 1,000 shares in the Compagnie des eaux. Although the *Dénonciation de l'agiotage* did not reveal the full extent of Calonne's complicity in the stockjobbing, it emphasized that he had intervened to support the bull market. The most notorious *agioteurs*, it claimed, had inside access to the finance ministry—and even, in d'Espagnac's case, to "the revenues of the state." Although it did not refer to Calonne by name, it identified him clearly in key passages and brought its argument to a crescendo at the end with a description of a corrupt "administrator" who was responsible for the disasters facing France. There was no mistaking the message: a criminal conspiracy had manipulated the Bourse; the Notables should take action; and the king should dismiss his finance minister.[29]

Dénonciation de l'agiotage created a greater sensation than all the previous pamphlets. It appeared in Paris on March 12, at the most vulnerable moment of Calonne's struggle to overcome the opposition of the Notables. The government tried mightily to suppress it, and therefore it sold at first for the extravagant price of 24 L. But its price came down, and its readership expanded. The *nouvellistes* found Mirabeau's argument powerful and persuasive, although some suspected that he wrote as a partisan of the *baissiers*, Clavière in particular. They were convinced by his condemnation of *agiotage* and appalled by how much was at stake—47 million livres, according to the *Gazette de Leyde*, enough to ruin half the banks of Paris if a settlement were not reached. The journals reported that everyone recognised Mirabeau's portrait of Calonne, who was now being excoriated for corruption and immorality. The public wanted him dismissed. While the controversy raged, Mirabeau was said to have escaped to London or Prussia; Clavière went into hiding; and d'Espagnac got away with an order of exile to a country estate, pending a settlement of the claims and counterclaims produced by the jobbery.[30]

As a financial settlement was being negotiated, Louis XVI dismissed Calonne. No one attributed this dénouement to the *Dénonciation de l'agiotage*, although the pamphlet reinforced the opposition to Calonne within the Assembly of Notables. More important, Mirabeau's attack contributed to the growing sense of indignation among Parisians about corruption in Versailles. It brought to a climax a long run of pamphlets that had denounced foul play of a new kind, jobbery on the Bourse. Millions were made by sheer duplicity and with the backing of the government— that message resonated far beyond the small world of speculators in the rue Vivienne and the Palais-Royal. It revealed connections between money and politics undreamt of by ordinary citizens.

The *Dénonciation de l'agiotage* also demonstrated the power of rhetoric that appealed to the emotions and aroused moral indignation. While Beaumarchais had deployed wit with great success in the Goezman Affair, he failed to use it effectively in the financial polemics. Mirabeau scorned the witticisms—the "pitiful puns" and "flat epigrams"—of Beaumarchais's pamphlets.[31] He relied on denunciation, the *J'accuse* style of politics that would have a great future in the Revolution and the nineteenth century. That kind of rhetoric began to set the tone of public discourse in the 1780s. Its ability to stir the passions of Parisians became even more apparent during the next round of polemics, which took place in the wake of the Bourse scandals—the Kornmann Affair.

29

Despotism in the Marriage Bed

OON AFTER the arrival of Mirabeau's pamphlet, the Notables received another denunciation, one that caused an even greater storm but came from a surprising source. In a case before a Parisian court, an obscure citizen accused the authorities of complicity in an adulterous affair of his wife. He had the unfortunate name of Kornmann, which exposed him to puns about horns and the derision usually attached to cuckoldry. Yet Parisians did not laugh at his plight when they, too, received the printed account of his story. They reacted with a surge of moral indignation, and the Kornmann Affair turned into an indictment of the sociopolitical order at the very time when its legitimacy was threatening to unravel.[1]

After the Calas, Goezman, and Diamond Necklace Affairs, court cases had become established as the most effective way to mobilize public sentiment. They often featured innocent victims—"la fille Salmon," "les trois roués," "le Comte de Sanois"—who were threatened by being broken on the wheel or buried in prison. They were set pieces, similar to plays (particularly the sentimental melodramas known as *drames* or *comédies larmoyantes*), because they stirred emotions and conformed to histrionic patterns: an eloquent lawyer denounced an abuse; a judicial memoir translated it into a story of victimization and suffering; and the public reacted according to script, by outrage and "sweet tears," as innocence triumphed, if not juridically, at least in the court of public opinion. The Kornmann Affair represented the genre at the peak of its popularity.

Guillaume Kornmann was a wealthy banker from Strasbourg who took up residence in Paris, where he became one of the two leading disciples of Mesmer. The other was his close friend, Nicolas Bergasse, a lawyer from a family of merchants in Lyon. Kornmann's wife, born into a Protestant family in Basel, married him at age fifteen. Her relatives considered him a good match, although, according to the *mémoires* printed in her defense, she found him unattractive. In 1780, six years after their wedding and the birth of two children, she was seduced by Daudet de Jossan, a dashing man of the world and municipal official in Strasbourg with important connections in Versailles, notably the Prince and Princesse de Nassau and the Prince de Montbarrey, then war minister.

Kornmann told his version of the story in the form of a judicial *mémoire*, accusing his wife of adultery, Daudet of seduction, and two public figures, Beaumarchais and the former lieutenant general of police Jean-Charles-Pierre Lenoir, of complicity.[2] Mme Kornmann had no voice of her own throughout the affair. Everyone involved in it treated her as an easily manipulable object, and no one questioned the assumption that Kornmann held unrestricted authority over her, including the right to have her confined by a *lettre de cachet*. Bergasse wrote the text of the memoir, although he lacked the authority to make it legal, because he was not a member of the Paris bar. He fashioned it as a narrative of perfidy and intrigue, recounted by Kornmann himself in the first person.

The Kornmann-narrator explained that he and his wife had lived happily until Daudet insinuated himself into their household. Trusting in the sacred bonds of matrimony, it never occurred to him that his wife could fall under Daudet's spell. But when he took a trip to Spa, Daudet seduced her and made little effort to hide their affair. Upon his return, Kornmann realized that he had been betrayed, but he believed he could persuade his wife to resume her duties as spouse and mother by appealing to her better nature, for she was more naïve and capricious than wicked. Despite his offer of forgiveness, however, she continued to make secret trysts with Daudet—in the Bois de Boulogne, in the Parc de Vincennes, in their home with the connivance of his servants—and then began to siphon off

Kornmann's wealth, which was Daudet's ultimate goal. Knowing that Kornmann suffered from poor health, Daudet hoped to harrass him to death and marry his widow. When Kornmann blocked his wife's access to his cash box, she pawned her diamonds to come up with funds for Daudet. Still hoping for a reconciliation, Kornmann spent 10,000 L. to get the jewels returned. She was not moved; Daudet became more aggressive; and Kornmann's friends, worried about his safety, advised him to see the lieutenant general of police. At first, Lenoir obliged by setting his spies to work on the case and intercepting Mme Kornmann's mail. When he had accumulated enough material, including evidence of an assassination plot, he recommended that Mme Kornmann be confined by a *lettre de cachet*. Although that prospect filled him with horror, Kornmann consented, asking that, as a Protestant, she be put in a decent *maison de force*, rather than a Catholic convent.

At that point, according to the *mémoire*, a sinister figure intervened: Beaumarchais, an intimate friend of Daudet and an adventurer eager to take on new intrigues. He declared that he would take Mme Kornmann under his protection. Thanks to powerful contacts in Versailles, Beaumarchais gained entry into the *maison de force*, and soon it, too, was serving as a site for trysts. Next, Kornmann learned that Lenoir was secretly supporting his enemies and that his wife was pregnant. Beaumarchais and Lenoir procured an order from the king that she be transferred to another residence, where she would give birth and enjoy unrestricted freedom. Kornmann, who had never questioned the legitimacy of the state, was astonished that it could come between a husband and a wife. To remove his spouse from his authority and to support her infidelity by means of a royal decree was an act of "execrable despotism," which violated the most fundamental principle of morality.[3] When he protested, Lenoir answered that the order had the backing of the minister for Paris, the Prince de Montbarrey, the Prince de Nassau, and many other important persons. Kornmann realized that he was helpless, an isolated individual faced with the hostility of the police, the government, and the court.

Next, his enemies went after his fortune. He had 600,000 L. tied up in a complicated financial arrangement concerning the Quinze-Vingts, a hospice for the blind. By blocking its reimbursement, his enemies forced him into what loomed as unavoidable bankruptcy. They also placed spies among his servants, who reported on every move he made. One of them poisoned him. After thirty-six hours of unconsciousness, he woke up feeling desperate. He had lost his wife and stood to lose his fortune and even his life. He contemplated suicide but decided to make one more trip to Spa in the hope of repairing his nearly ruined health.

At Spa, Kornmann met Bergasse. After listening sympathetically to his tale of woe, Bergasse devised a rescue plan. By producing ample evidence, Kornmann could recover his 600,000 L., and by pursuing litigation for adultery, he could get his wife confined to her family in Basel, while he supported her with a pension and took custody of their children. It took several years—endless negotiations, near settlements, prevarications and refusals by his wife—before Kornmann brought the case to trial. At a critical juncture, when he was returning from a walk, an assassin seized him and aimed a pistol at his face. The shot only pierced a hat that he had been wearing pulled over his forehead, but it confirmed his belief that he would not survive much longer. Alone and unprotected except for the support of Bergasse, his last hope was to exact justice from the court, not merely for himself but for ordinary citizens everywhere.

The last section of the memoir spelled out those dangers in a philosophic discourse on morality and politics. All political systems, it argued (the narrator now spoke in another voice, clearly Bergasse's, in contrast to the confessional mode of Kornmann), were based on *moeurs*—the customs and values of society, which in turn were rooted in moral principles inherent in the order of nature. The most fundamental of those principles was the bond between man and woman in a state of permanent union designed for producing and nurturing children. The family was the foundation of society. In simple societies, the kind extolled by Rousseau, families maintained healthy *moeurs*, an equilibrium of equality and fraternity that promoted happiness, though not the blossoming of arts and sciences. Civilization flowered in advanced societies but at the cost of family life. Well-born and witty sophisticates cheated on their spouses, and the decline of *moeurs* provided ground for the growth of despotism. Adultery and the abuse of power went together—that was the moral of Kornmann's story, and therefore Kornmann submitted his memoir to the Assembly of Notables and published it as a summons to his fellow citizens. France needed to be redeemed; it needed a new constitution.

Kornmann's memoir was more than a tract of popular Rousseauism. (Although it echoed Rousseau's major themes, it criticized his failure to pay adequate tribute to matrimony in *Emile*.) It read like a novel, one episode succeeding another in rapid succession, and it bathed the action in sentiment. In the end, Kornmann took leave of the reader with a prayer to Providence as if he were expiring on the stage: "Eternal Providence.... You have subjected me to a terrible destiny." He expected to die as an expiatory victim of decadence and despotism, and his only hope was that his fate would awaken Frenchmen to the need for a moral and political revival.[4] After a long, action-packed narrative, the sentiment carried conviction; and instead of triggering derision, Kornmann's cuckolding read like a call to action, timed to stir passions at a moment of political crisis.

The publication of the memoir on May 12, 1787, transformed an obscure adultery trial into a spectacular affair. It set off a flood of pamphlets as the case worked through the courts, accumulating charges and countercharges and memoir after memoir. *Nouvellistes* devoted almost as much attention to it as to the Assembly of Notables. The *Mémoires secrets* published sixty-one articles about it in the last six months of 1787 and described Bergasse's original memoir as "the work that today attracts the most discussion, that one urgently tries to procure, that has alerted the entire police force... and that provokes debates for and against, according to the preconceptions of different groups."[5] When the case came to a climax with final arguments and a verdict in 1789, Hardy indicated that for a while it aroused more interest among Parisians than the debate about the composition of the Estates General. Beaumarchais claimed, probably with some exaggeration, that Kornmann's partisans published two hundred pamphlets in 1787 and 1788.[6] Bergasse wrote that within ten days of its publication, 4,000 persons had left their names at Kornmann's house, requesting copies of the memoir, which the government tried to suppress. By June 1788 he claimed to have distributed 10,000 copies, notwithstanding the government's persecution, and to have received 6,000 letters of support from readers. Bergasse and Kornmann gave their copies away free of charge, but Parisian publishers made a killing from thousands of reprints, which sometimes sold for as much as 48 L. As the case developed, Bergasse wrote several more memoirs, all of them enormously successful. One was so popular that waiters in the cafés of the Palais-Royal collected large sums by renting it out, a few pages at a time, to their customers. In the summer of 1788, Bergasse stated that more than 100,000 copies of his memoirs had been distributed and that a cause of such importance occurred only once a century.[7]

To follow the case to its conclusion will take us far beyond the spring of 1787, but its course should be recounted at this point in order to keep the continuity clear. Each of the persons accused of crimes in the Bergasse-Kornmann memoirs replied with memoirs of his own. The adulterous pair, Mme Kornmann and Daudet de Jossan, attracted plenty of attention, especially after their correspondence was published, with the term "obscene phrases" indicating deleted passages. But Beaumarchais and Lenoir became the main focus of the public's interest—Beaumarchais, because of his notoriety and the current success of both *Le Mariage de Figaro* and his opera *Tarare*; Lenoir, because of his former position as an all-powerful lieutenant general of police and his continued eminence as a member of the Conseil du Roi with an additional appointment as head of the royal library.

Beaumarchais was working feverishly on *Tarare* in May 1787, when the first Kornmann memoir appeared as if from nowhere and set off a passionate reaction among Parisians. The opera was to be the climax of Beaumarchais's career, a grand spectacle combining poetry with dramatic effects, both tragic and comic (the music, by Antonio Salieri, was considered of secondary importance). Set in an imaginary Oriental kingdom, complete with a cruel sultan and an exotic harem, it could be understood as an operatic sequel to Montesquieu's critique of decadent morals and despotism in *Lettres persanes*. But that message never got through to the public, because it was eclipsed by Bergasse's treatment of the same themes, applied to a real-life setting and an ordinary citizen overwhelmed by enemies in the government and the court, enemies led by Beaumarchais. In a three-page reply to the first Kornmann memoir, dashed off in between rehearsals for *Tarare*, Beaumarchais announced that he would sue Kornmann for slander. Yet he did not seem to take the attack seriously, treating it as an attempt to sabotage his opera and dismissing it with witticisms, which did not go over well with the public. "Beaumarchais . . . will joke mockingly all the way to the gallows," remarked the *Mémoires secrets*.[8]

Bergasse replied immediately in a pamphlet that acknowledged his authorship of Kornmann's memoir and denied having any knowledge of *Tarare*. Kornmann's cause could not be compared with the success or failure of an opera, he insisted. It raised profound issues of morality, which went to the heart of the sociopolitical order. On June 5, three days after the premiere of *Tarare*, Beaumarchais published a memoir of his own. Again, he wrote as a man of the world and paraded his intimacy with *les grands*, especially the Prince de Nassau, the epitome of "chivalrous goodness," who rallied the court and the government to rescue a lady in distress.[9]

Although this defense may have won over readers in Versailles, it did not please Parisians. A crowd in the Café du Caveau staged a mock trial, standing a copy of Beaumarchais's memoir on a table and accusing it of being a libel. After a unanimous vote, it was condemned to be lacerated and burned by a waiter, who played the role of public executioner.[10] In the memoir Beaumarchais had made a half-serious appeal to Parisians for support, "Oh Public, Public of Paris!"[11] Speaking in the name of the public, several pamphleteers answered with declamations against Beaumarchais's court connections, mockery of family virtue, and worldly wit. One, *Le Public à Pierre-Augustin Caron de Beaumarchais*, which went through at least three editions, denounced Beaumarchais so violently that some attributed it to Mirabeau.[12] Another emphasized that Beaumarchais's mundane immorality was confirmed by his style—"his puns, his trivial logic, his feeble play of words, his cynical pamphlets, his ambiguous sarcasm, his burlesque joking, his filthy equivocations."[13] A poem that made the rounds of the cafés and salons stressed the same connection between morality and rhetoric:

Les moeurs, l'honneur, la modestie	*Morals, honor, modesty*
Ne vaudront point dans ma patrie	*Will not in your world*
Le mérite de *Figaro*.	*Equal the merit of Figaro.*
Ah! Beaumarchais, bravo, bravo.	*Ah! Beaumarchais, bravo, bravo.*
Kornmann contre toi publie	*Kornmann publishes against you*
Un factum rempli d'infamie;	*A factum full of inculpations;*
Il est l'écho de Mirabeau.	*He is the echo of Mirabeau.*
Ah! Beaumarchais povero![14]	*Ah, poor Beaumarchais!*

Many other pamphlets echoed this repugnance at rhetoric based on wit. No longer was the cuckold a butt of jokes; he had become a victim of a depraved society and a hero of the struggle against despotism. The pamphlets described Kornmann as "an oppressed victim who invokes the most sacred rights of man, liberty and property." And therefore he spoke the language of the oppressed: "His language is that of sentiment, the accent of suffering, the expression of innocence."[15] The tone of public discourse had been transformed since 1772–1773, when Beaumarchais had buried Goezman under peals of laughter. Jean-François de La Harpe, an acute observer, noted that the public had turned against Beaumarchais in 1787 just as decidedly as it had supported him fifteen years earlier.[16]

Lenoir's role in the Affair was even more important than Beaumarchais's. After nearly ten years at the head of the police, he had learned to respect the power of public sentiment and the vulnerability of reputations to libels and public noises.[17] He wanted nothing more than to keep quiet and avoid publicity. But the government insisted that he answer Kornmann's charges in order to vindicate the reputation of the police. He complied with a brief memoir claiming that he had only carried out orders from his superiors in Versailles.[18] To the *nouvellistes*, however, that argument made the Affair especially interesting, because it confirmed that Kornmann's case was, at bottom, political.[19] As lieutenant general of police, Lenoir had embodied the absolute power of the Crown in Paris. He represented the long arm of the law, and it had delivered Mme Kornmann from one location, where she was confined at the will of her husband, to another, where she was made accessible to her lover.

Bergasse seized on this aspect of the Affair in a third memoir stressing the larger theme of despotism. To intervene between a husband and a wife, he charged, was the worst possible abuse of power, because it struck at the heart of the moral order that constituted the basis of society. Under Lenoir, the police had become an instrument of moral depravity, and after his retirement Lenoir continued to control his former agents, who did everything possible to suppress Kornmann's memoirs. Lenoir still spread terror among citizens who dared to protest against injustice, because he could bury them in the Bastille, where they would sink into oblivion, weeping bitter tears, lost to their families and forgotten by the outside

290 • THE REVOLUTIONARY TEMPER

world. Bergasse outdid Linguet in his description of the Bastille's horrors and concluded his memoir by announcing that Kornmann would take criminal action against Lenoir as well as Daudet and Beaumarchais.[20] The case was of such importance that it was being elevated from the Châtelet court to the Parlement, where (though Bergasse did not mention it) he and Kornmann could count on the support of an outspoken magistrate and fellow champion of mesmerism, Jean-Jacques Duval d'Éprémesnil.

Readers found this memoir as eloquent as the others, and the next wave of pamphlets turned public sentiment decisively against Beaumarchais and Lenoir, although in contrast to Bergasse's moralizing, many were crude libels.[21] They cast Beaumarchais as a social climber, who rose from "obscure watchmaker to impure courtier" ("horloger obscur" to "courtisan impur") and they made Lenoir look like the embodiment of depravity. One attack on him included a letter written from hell by the seventeenth-century libertine courtesan Ninon Lenclos, who congratulated Mme Kornmann for rejecting "the most absurd of prejudices, conjugal fidelity." The pamphlet ended by invoking Rousseau in a lament about the decline of morality and family solidarity.[22] A more damaging libel, *L'An 1787*, demanded that Lenoir be driven from his position as "despot" at the head of the Bibliothèque du Roi, where he had embezzled 310,000 L. from its funds and collections. His punishment should inaugurate a purge of everyone who had abused power in positions of authority, it argued. A later libel, *Apologie de Messire Jean-Charles-Pierre Lenoir*, caricatured Lenoir as a tyrant, who turned the police into a prostitution racket, recruiting victims and repressing honest fathers and husbands by means of *lettres de cachet*.[23]

No pleading had occurred in court before the summer of 1787, when the case was entered in the docket of the Parlement de Paris. But the Parlement had become embroiled with the government in a heated dispute over taxation, and on August 15 it was exiled to Troyes, leaving all cases suspended. A compromise agreement on the tax issue led to the lifting of the exile on September 21. On the next day, before cases could be resumed, the government issued an edict condemning the Kornmann memoirs as libels. It did not stifle the legal proceedings, however; and after the Parlement reinstalled itself in Paris, the Affair—a complex set of suits and countersuits—began slowly to work its way through the judicial machinery. At the same time, the Parlement renewed its opposition to the government; the conflict escalated into a major crisis; and on May 8, 1788, the government resorted to a coup. It destroyed the political powers of all the parlements in the kingdom by creating a new judicial system on the ruins of the old one, just as Maupeou had done in 1771. Yet this repression was more serious than Maupeou's because it took place at a time of near bankruptcy in the state's finances and of greater public hostility.

Bergasse had drafted a new memoir, every bit as impassioned as the old ones, before the destruction of the Parlement.[24] In it, he went back over the story of Kornmann's persecution, adding emphasis on the helplessness of an honest family man faced with the overwhelming power of the police, the government, and influential courtiers like the Prince de Nassau. Far from being a particular case, Kornmann's cause was the cause of every citizen, Bergasse wrote, and it epitomized the moral corruption that was destroying France. He capped his argument with a thirty-page disquisition on political theory, mixing ingredients from Montesquieu and Rousseau in a denunciation of arbitrary power. Others had exposed abuses like *lettres de cachet*, and rightly so, but Kornmann's suffering showed how despotism operated at another level, how it had penetrated into family life, corrupting society at its base. Morality (*moeurs*) had been the cement that held the political edifice together. That cement had eroded so badly that France's political system needed to be completely reconstructed.

Having reached this conclusion, Bergasse sent his text to the printer, but before the printing was completed, the coup of May 8 transformed the situation. He therefore added a preface, warning readers that justice had been driven out of the judicial system. Neither Kornmann nor Bergasse nor any citizen could have a fair trial in the new courts. The only hope was the king himself, because Louis XVI had a good heart and desired nothing more than the welfare of his people. In a dramatic appeal to the king, Bergasse declared that his enemies would try to crush him; he could flee; but he would stand his ground in Paris because he put his trust in Louis as the ultimate source of justice.

Hardy wrote that Bergasse's memoir had such an impact that it was certain to turn the public against his adversaries. It went through several editions, selling at first for 9 L. and then, after the initial rush to get copies, at 3 L. Hardy found the section on political theory persuasive, and he especially responded to Bergasse's presentation of himself as "the apostle of morality," ready to face martyrdom.[25] That, too, was the reaction of Louis-Sébastien Mercier, the popular author of *Tableau de Paris*, who described Bergasse as "the angel with a whip who drives away shameful sinners, naked, unmasked, but not contrite, alas!"[26] Beaumarchais sensed the tide of public opinion turning against him and replied with a short memoir, which, however, actually strengthened his opponents' case. He criticized Bergasse for speaking disrespectfully of men in power and played up his own connections in the court. Whereas Bergasse attacked the government, he defended it, using the inevitable pun on Kornmann's name: Bergasse and Kornmann were whipping up dangerous passions among the common herd, which, he warned, could use its horns as weapons against the state.[27]

Bergasse shot back with a final memoir, which hardly mentioned the trial—he and Kornmann refused to pursue it before the new courts—and concentrated entirely on the political crisis. By destroying the parlements, he argued, the government had eliminated the last barrier that protected the common people from ministerial despotism. The only hope now lay with the Estates General, which should restore a reformed judicial system, abolish *lettres de cachet*, destroy the arbitrary power of the police, free the press, apportion taxes equally, decree equality before the law, and, transforming itself into a permanent "national assembly," redesign the state as a constitutional monarchy. The French people had a right to revolt, as France had recognised by supporting the Americans. Yet the king would embrace their cause, if only this message could reach him, and his first step would be to banish the evil ministers, Etienne-Charles Loménie de Brienne and Chrétien-François de Lamoignon de Bâville, who had come to dominate the government after the fall of Calonne.[28]

This manifesto appeared on August 8 and created an enormous sensation. According to a contemporary report: "Everyone wanted to have it: one devoured it, one learned it by heart; one is still fighting to get hold of it."[29] Hardy agreed that it electrified the public and reinforced the cause of the people, although some Parisians considered it "incendiary."[30] Moderate commentators confirmed this view. In his *Correspondance littéraire*, La Harpe described Bergasse's open attack on the government as a political sermon perfectly calculated to arouse a strong response. Meister, writing in Grimm's *Correspondance littéraire*, maintained that Bergasse's last publication created greater fermentation than any of the pamphlets protesting against the coup of May 8 and that no government could permit such defiance to go unpunished.[31]

Bergasse expected to be dispatched to the Bastille by a *lettre de cachet*. On August 19, he fled from Paris and spent the next weeks in Switzerland and Lyon. He left behind a letter, describing himself as a martyr for the cause of liberty and repeating his denunciation of the ministers. Kornmann read it aloud to the crowds of Bergasse supporters that arrived at his house, and it was later printed as a pamphlet supplemented with eulogies of Bergasse and attacks on the government. Before fleeing, Bergasse also wrote an open letter to the queen, calling upon her to intervene in order to get the ministers dismissed. It circulated widely, first in manuscript, then in print. A similar appeal to the king, an open letter published under the title *Au Roi*, made the same demand in dramatic language that was actually lifted from the preface of Bergasse's last full-scale memoir.[32] These short pamphlets probably reached a larger audience than the memoir itself, because they cost only a few sous and ran through several editions, some as large as 12,000 copies. Bergasse later wrote that he had received 20,000 letters of support. Several different engravings of him were hawked in the streets, one with the following epigraph:

Fidèle à l'amitié, fidèle à la patrie,
Il apprit aux Français à rougir de leurs fers,
Et, fort de sa vertu, puissant par son génie,
Il fut l'appui du juste et l'effroi des pervers.[33]

(Faithful to friendship, faithful to the fatherland, / He taught the French to be ashamed of their chains, / And, strong in his virtue, powerful by his genius, / He was the bulwark of the just and the fear of the perverse.)

By the end of August Bergasse stood out as the greatest champion of resistance to the government (except for d'Éprémesnil, as we will see), and Kornmann's case had turned into an indictment of the regime.

Under unremitting financial pressure and violent opposition, both in Paris and the provinces, the government collapsed—at first with the dismissal of Brienne on August 25, 1788, which opened the way for the return of Necker, then with the fall of Lamoignon on September 14, which ended the attempt to impose a new judicial system on the kingdom. Bergasse returned in triumph to Paris, and the trial finally opened on December 20. It continued for more than three months, while lawyers from all the parties debated the complexities of the overlapping cases. Arguing his own case on March 19, 1789, Bergasse made a long declamation against despotism and immorality, which set off a great deal of weeping in the packed courtroom. He denounced the Prince de Nassau's role in the Affair as an abuse of aristocratic privilege, and made it clear that Kornmann's cause epitomized that of the Third Estate as it was then being championed in the debate over the composition of the Estates General. To Bergasse's opponents, his moralizing could be dismissed as ridiculous or sanctimonious, but to the general public it expressed anger—the righteous indignation of a commoner who defied the privileged orders. In concluding his case, Bergasse upbraided Nassau: "Learn from me that there is no distinction of birth, of rank, of standing before the law; that in free countries, the law establishes the equality of men."[34] He then repeated this theme in a pamphlet that favored the Third Estate, *Lettre de M. Bergasse sur les Etats-Généraux.*

On April 2, the court finally reached a decision. It cleared Kornmann's enemies of all charges and fined Bergasse and Kornmann 2,000 L. in damages. By this time, however, the Parlement had lost the support of Parisians, and the public's verdict, according to Hardy, declared Kornmann innocent. Radicals in the café du Caveau staged another mock trial and condemned the Parlement's judgment to be burned. While Beaumarchais and Lenoir were universally detested, Hardy concluded, Kornmann had won sympathy as a victim of the system that patriots hoped to abolish. Bergasse went on to be elected as a deputy to the Estates General, where he stood out as a leader of the Third Estate and soon would be collaborating on a new code of criminal law.

Although this dénouement takes us far beyond the spring of 1787, when Kornmann's case first seized the attention of Parisians, its course is worth following into 1789, because it illustrates the way events impinged on public attitudes. Abstract issues such as ministerial despotism were embodied by concrete figures like Lenoir, and they were played out in sentimental dramas, which pitted heroes against villains. Many other elements also contributed to the prerevolutionary climate, as we shall see. The point to be emphasized here is the power of denunciation to mobilize sentiment and sap the legitimacy of the regime. Bergasse's memoirs provided a moral indictment of the government, and they damaged it even more effectively than Mirabeau's denunciations a year earlier. They used the same kind of rhetoric, arousing indignation rather than employing ridicule. They treated wit itself as a symptom of decadence, a sign of aristocratic sophistication and sympathy for despotism. Beaumarchais, a master of witticism, served as a foil for both Bergasse and Mirabeau. He had demonstrated the effectiveness of laughter in the Goezman Affair, but fifteen years later he failed to make a cuckold's tale seem funny. The climate of opinion had undergone a fundamental change.

30

The Notables Say No

I T TOOK EVERYONE by surprise: the king announced that he would convoke an Assembly of Notables. As soon as the news was known—at first from the *Journal de Paris* of December 31, 1786, and then in all the gazettes—it dominated discussions of public affairs. No one attributed the king's decision to a crisis because everything seemed calm—no threat of war, no sign of sedition, no conflict between the Crown and the parlements. When Parisians tried to puzzle out the king's intentions, they had little to go on beyond the announcement itself, which referred to Louis's desire to promote "the good of the state and the relief of his subjects."[1]

As we have seen in the previous two chapters, the Notables provided a sounding board for public opinion. Before the Assembly convened, however, the public only knew that something important would take place—and soon, because the king proclaimed that he would preside in person over the opening session on January 29, 1787. The Notables would include more than a hundred of the most important persons in the clergy, the nobility, the judiciary, and municipal offices. No one knew much about the institution itself, although the announcement claimed that it went back to the reign of Charlemagne, when an Assembly of Notables had determined the fundamental laws of the kingdom. Since then, the announcement explained, it had been supplanted by the Estates General, but was revived in 1626, when it last met. Parisians speculated about its purpose for weeks. At first, according to several reports, their conversations favored four possibilities: the creation of provincial assemblies to distribute the tax burden more equitably, the reform of indirect taxes, the reduction of the royal domain, and the granting of civic rights to Protestants. Some attributed a pro-Enlightenment program to the king, who was said not only to favor Protestants but also to desire a reduction in the number of monks and even the construction of synagogues. Although opinions varied, many Parisians were convinced that the king meant to lower taxes and relieve the poor, not to raise new revenue. And his reference to fundamental laws led some to believe that the Notables would create a constitution for France, deliberating as a "National Assembly."[2]

For various reasons, the opening of the Assembly kept getting postponed—from January 29 to February 9, February 14, and finally February 22. Expectations and anxieties grew along with the delays. Parisians recognized that the government was trying to control public opinion, because they commented on "bulletins" that the police distributed in cafés in an attempt to tamp down "sinister conjectures."[3] As time went on, however, the public became increasingly convinced that the Crown intended to raise money, possibly by levying a new tax on landed property, perhaps even by taxing the clergy. The man behind the proposal soon was identified as Calonne, controller general since November 1783, who was known for his smooth talk and skill at playing politics in the court. He became the target of jokes, prints, pasquinades, songs, and *bons mots*, which spread throughout the city in the first months of 1787. They cast Calonne as a prompter who whispered lines for the Notables to speak on the public stage; as a theater director who was about to mount a production of "Les Fausses apparences" (a popular play by Jean-Claude-Gilles Colson, known as Bellecour); and as a cook who consulted the animals in his barnyard (the Notables) about the sauce they preferred him to use when he served them up as roasts. The cook conceit took many forms, some accompanied by prints.[4]

While providing good copy for *nouvellistes* and talking points for gossips, this material, despite its frothiness, conveyed a serious message: Calonne was expected to use the Notables as stooges to sanction a program for squeezing more money out of the general population. He selected the most prestigious possible cast of characters for the Assembly:

7 princes of the royal blood, 7 archbishops, 7 bishops, 12 dukes and peers, 8 military marshals, 6 marquis, 9 counts, 17 first presidents of the parlements, and 25 officers of municipalities among a total of 146 persons from the upper ranks of French society. If such eminent persons approved his tax proposals, he might be able to get around the inevitable opposition of the parlements. That was his strategy according to Parisian "agitators." Even Hardy, who was hardly a radical, diagnosed Calonne's purpose as "money, money, and more money."[5] Yet some *nouvellistes* assured their readers that the Assembly was not intended to raise money and that it would actually lower taxes for most people. On the eve of its opening, they reported that Parisians remained hopeful about a fundamental change in the political system. The Notables themselves had no idea of what was expected of them.[6]

Although the public was not admitted to the opening of the Assembly, it received full descriptions of the event in various gazettes. The ceremony took place on February 22 in the Salle des menus plaisirs of Versailles, which had been worked over for more than six weeks to provide suitable grandeur for the occasion. The main hall, 120 feet long, was designed for general assemblies, when the entire body of Notables would meet together. Hung with the Crown's finest tapestries, its ceiling freshly painted with allegorical designs, and its interior heated by four gigantic stoves, it made an impressive setting. The throne was elevated on a platform under a canopy in the middle of the hall with armchairs nearby for the king's brothers, banquettes for the princes of the blood and the peers, and seating for the others at appropriate distances. A dozen specially designed rooms provided space for the Notables to change into formal dress, get refreshments, and meet in committees, where they would do most of their work.

At 11:30 in the morning of the opening day, the king arrived in a superb carriage followed by a cortege, which included members of the royal family, assorted grandees, and 184 smartly dressed guards. He entered the hall by a special portal, then ascended the throne and delivered a short speech to the Notables, who had been waiting in their appointed seats. The next three speakers elaborated on the importance of the occasion. Of them, only Calonne gave some indication of its purpose. He outlined the program he intended to submit to the Notables for their approval, dividing it into four "sections," which would serve as an agenda for daily meetings that would continue until April 3, the tentative date for the adjournment. The Notables would deliberate in seven "bureaus," each presided over by a prince of the blood: the king's two brothers ("Monsieur," Comte de Provence, and "Monseigneur," Comte d'Artois), the Duc d'Orléans, the Prince de Condé, the Duc de Bourbon, the Prince de Conti, and the Duc de Penthievre.

Everything was to take place in secret. The Notables were housed and fed in Versailles, far from the rumor mills of Paris. Each of them received printed memoranda, which provided guidelines for the discussions. To prevent leaks, the printers were supervised carefully and permitted to work on only part of each job so they could not put together and pilfer complete texts. In fact, they were confined to their living quarters in Versailles as virtual prisoners for the duration of the meetings. By controlling information, Calonne seemed to have two purposes: to direct the Notables' response to his proposals and to insulate them, as much as possible, from the pressure of public opinion. That left the public starved for news. Although Calonne permitted a few texts, such as the speeches at the opening session, to be published, he insisted that the proceedings of the Notables, especially resolutions and accounts of debates, remain restricted to confidential records kept by secretaries. He also forbade all pamphleteering in Paris. The police inspected printing shops with unusual severity, and the Bastille was rumored to be full.[7]

Therefore, Parisians could only guess as to what went on behind the closed doors in Versailles. Judging from contemporary reports, they remained obsessed for weeks about the secret deliberations, as indicated among the well-dressed by a fashion for "waistcoats aux Notables," which had embroidered depictions of the king surrounded by the assembled delegates.[8] The only news that reached Parisians in March concerned the Duc d'Orléans, who abandoned his bureau one afternoon in order to go hunting. A deer escaped into the heart of Paris, and the hunt pursued it through the Place Vendôme and the rue Saint Honoré before subduing it in the Place Louis XV.[9] Why wasn't the prince tending to the nation's business? the public wondered, although it had no idea of what that business was. Of course there were leaks, an inevitable consequence of 146 individuals, all of them with extensive contacts, meeting to discuss crucial political issues. Yet despite the public's hunger for news, *nouvellistes* came up with only crumbs of information. The Assembly of Notables disappeared into silence for ten days after the opening ceremony.

Parisians generally assumed that the Notables would behave as expected, approving whatever Calonne put before them. The most important items from the first of the four sections, according to bulletins distributed by the government, were provisions for provincial administrations and an *impôt territorial* or general land tax. Parisians were familiar with the former, because Turgot and Necker had proposed creating provincial bodies that could administer taxation and other state business at the regional level. In fact, Necker had established provincial administrations in Berry and Haute-Guyenne and had planned to extend them to other provinces. The land tax, however, was an explosive issue. It had an even longer history, because it had been debated as a way of increasing revenue and equalizing the tax burden ever since Vauban's proposal for a *dîme royale* in 1707. The failed attempts by Machault in 1749 and Bertin in 1763 had demonstrated the power of privileged groups to defend their tax exemptions. According to rumors that reached Paris, the Notables told Calonne that they would not consider a tax increase until they had proof that it was necessary, because they had doubts about the accumulated imbalance between income and expenses in the state's finances. Calonne had claimed in his speech at the opening ceremony that the Crown suffered from a deficit of 80 million livres a year, and in March he increased his estimate to 100 million. He supported his argument by referring to sixty-three "*états*," or fiscal reports from the Contrôle général, but he refused to make them available. One Notable, from the Parlement of Aix-en-Provence, protested that no matter what the evidence, the Assembly had no right to sanction new taxes, nor did the parlements, nor the king. The only legitimate authority was the Estates General, which could speak for the nation.[10]

Moreover, many Notables were "*Neckristes*." In his *Compte rendu*, Necker had said that the state's finances enjoyed a surplus of 10 million livres in 1781. Calonne claimed that they were burdened by a deficit of 60 million at that time. If a deficit really existed in 1787, in the *Neckriste* view, it must have been Calonne's doing. He was notorious for ingratiating himself with courtiers by expensive favors and by draining funds from the treasury to reinforce support within the royal household. "Depredations," a byword for all sorts of embezzlement, became a rallying cry of Calonne's opponents, and it fit perfectly into a *Neckriste* version of France's financial history during the past ten years.

Necker himself requested permission from the king to publish a rebuttal to Calonne's assertions, which he considered an attack on his honor. He offered to sacrifice his entire fortune, 40 million livres, if he failed to vindicate his stewardship of the Crown's finances from 1777 to 1781. Although the government could not permit such defiance, word of it escaped; and Parisians also learned about the Notables' other objections to Calonne's program. Except for some of the clergy, they were not opposed, in principle, to the land tax, but they considered its mode of collection—a proportion of the harvest in kind rather than a fixed money payment—unfeasible and expensive. Similarly, the Notables approved of the proposal for provincial assemblies, but objected to the role that the *intendants*, who were considered to be all-powerful agents of the central government, would play in directing their deliberations because it raised the danger of domination by Versailles. As the arguments leaked into Paris, they were taken up in cafés and clubs. No one criticized the Notables for defending aristocratic privileges. On the contrary, as one *nouvelliste* remarked, Parisians developed an increasingly favorable opinion of them: "Our Notables, which were thought to be puppets or courtiers, are for the most part well informed patriots who know the true interests of the nation." According to another, they were "patriotic heroes."[11]

As the Parisians' view shifted in favor of the Notables, it turned against Calonne. A general assembly of the Notables on March 12 marked the turning point. Calonne presented them with the second section of his program, which concerned trade and indirect taxes. In summing up the deliberations on the first section, he congratulated the Notables for their support of everything he had advocated. Such objections as had arisen, he said, concerned merely the form, not the substance of his proposals. That contradicted the Notables' understanding of what had happened. They returned to their bureaus in a fury and then passed a series of resolutions declaring their fundamental opposition to Calonne's program. Far from being willing to paper over their differences with fine phrases, they proclaimed them openly, and the texts of their resolutions soon were circulating in Paris. The delegates in the Prince de Conti's bureau protested directly to the king in such vehement language that they became known in Paris as "the grenadiers of the Notables."[12]

Just as Parisians began to rally behind the Notables' defiance of Calonne, Mirabeau's *Dénonciation de l'agiotage* was published. It exploded like a bomb. By identifying the controller general with the scandals of the Bourse, it made his relations with stockjobbers appear as though they belonged to the same pattern as his handouts to courtiers—a tendency to siphon money from the royal treasury for his own purposes, or, in a word, depredations.[13]

The pattern, as Parisians perceived it, looked increasingly ominous during the last two weeks of March. Leaks from the bureaus of the Notables turned into a flood, and two new issues arose at the end of the month. One concerned a program to remint old louis, which were slightly deficient in gold, and to create new ones valued at the official standard of $21\,{}^{21}/_{32}$ carats. Because the old louis were valued at $21\,{}^{17}/_{32}$ carats, this operation required adding ${}^{4}/_{32}$ of a carat to each coin, and it led to suspicions about cheating in the royal mints. None of the rumors could be substantiated until news broke of a scandal in the mint of Strasbourg, which had allegedly received an order from Calonne to eliminate the additional infusion of gold. When this small fraction was multiplied by all the louis being reminted in the kingdom, according to reports in the underground press, it amounted to an embezzlement of 3,632,000 L. Although the government tried to hush up that scandal, rumors circulated that it was under investigation in the Paris Cour des monnaies.[14]

Other rumors concerned the embezzlement of Crown property. Calonne was said to cultivate allies in the court by granting them tracts of land owned by the Crown in exchange for their properties, which were worth much less, and even to appropriate land for himself, using others' names as cover.[15] Lafayette, one of the best-known Notables but one of the youngest and least familiar with administrative affairs, denounced the exchanges during a heated meeting in the bureau of the Comte d'Artois. Until then he had disappointed his admirers among Parisian radicals by failing to speak out against Calonne. They complained that he had been timid and even "servile," despite the bravery that he had demonstrated during the American war.[16] He finally broke his silence on April 1 with a devastating attack on Calonne, which marked his entry into French politics. Echoing Mirabeau's *Dénonciation*, he began by accusing the controller general of draining millions from the treasury to support stockjobbers and then described the exchanges as even more damaging than the evil inflicted by "the monster of stockjobbing." In the most notorious exchange, Calonne had alienated Crown land and forest evaluated at 5 to 6 million livres to the Comte d'Espagnac, brother of the stockjobber, in return for the Comté de Sancerre, which was barely worth a million and a half. Lafayette estimated that the exchanges had cost the Crown more than 45 million livres. "So many millions abandoned to depredation or cupidity are the fruit of the sweat, the tears, and perhaps the blood of the common people," he concluded, using a metaphor destined for a long life.[17] When he completed his speech, the other members of the bureau congratulated him for his courage. One of them said he had shown more heroism as a Notable than on the fields of battle in America. The written version of his denunciation was delivered to the king, copied by the *nouvellistes*, printed in several gazettes, and discussed avidly by Parisians.[18]

Although the Parisians could only guess at the rivalries within the government, they heard that by this time Calonne had lost the support of all the other ministers. His strongest backer, Vergennes, the minister for foreign affairs, had died only nine days before the Assembly opened. According to some rumors, Vergennes made a deathbed revelation to the king about depredations involving courtiers. According to others, Calonne, feeling isolated and exposed, had beseeched the king not to abandon him in the way that he had dropped Turgot; and Louis had replied: "Don't be afraid; I was a child then, now I am a man."[19] Of course, Parisians could not know what the king really said in the privacy of the royal apartments, but it enlivened conversations to quote him as if one had inside information. The pundits maintained that Calonne had reason to fear for his future because Louis was notorious for vacillating, and he frequently changed ministers in response to shifting pressures. Moreover, one of the Notables, Etienne-Charles de Loménie de Brienne, the archbishop of Toulouse, was said to be plotting to replace him and had won the backing of the queen.

Faced with the mounting threats and the intransigent opposition, Calonne resorted to a daring maneuver. On March 31, in a brazen attempt to turn public opinion against the Notables, he issued an appeal for support among the people of Paris. It took the form of an *Avertissement* published as a preface to the full text of his proposals to the Notables, and it was also distributed as a four-page pamphlet, which Calonne sent to all the curates in the city. They were to read it in their Sunday sermons and to diffuse copies among their parisioners. It was also reprinted in gazettes, hawked at street corners, and read aloud to crowds in les Halles. Far from proposing any new tax, Calonne asserted, he had meant to lessen the tax burden of the common people by requiring the privileged orders to share it. The land tax ("impôt territorial") was merely a new name for the old *vingtième* taxes, which now would be levied equitably on the clergy and nobility. He invoked "patriotism" and the "national will" in asking for the public's support. In fact, he claimed, all of his proposals had already received the sanction of the people, although the Notables had opposed them.[20]

The *Avertissement* created a sensation in Paris, and it backfired. Instead of turning against the Notables—its obvious intention according to most commentators—Parisians took it as a sign of desperation, possibly a last shot before dissolving the Assembly and trying to force the taxes through the parlements. The Notables reacted with a new outburst of fury, firing off one resolution after another and aiming them at Paris as well as the king. Far from equalizing taxes, they insisted, Calonne would saddle the common people with another 80 million per year. The Notables stood as a barrier protecting the people from a systemic abuse of power, and they would not relent until they had seen proof that the deficit—which Calonne now pretended to be 112 million—actually existed.

Their protests stirred more ferment in Paris, while in Versailles Calonne lost his hold on the confidence of the king. Louis's aunt, Madame Adélaïde, whom he greatly respected, informed him in a secret conversation that the rumors about the exchanges were true. Of course, the conversation itself was the subject of a rumor, but, as reported by the *nouvellistes*, it conformed to the Ancien Régime's mode of closed-door court politics, and it was enough to precipitate Calonne's fall on April 8. The reports also attributed Mme Adélaïde's intervention to the effect of Lafayette's denunciation, which they presented as the main cause of Calonne's disgrace. Therefore, as events appeared in the accounts that reached Paris, the Notables had brought down the government and defended the people in a momentous struggle at the apex of the power system.[21]

At first, Calonne's disgrace was relatively gentle. He was permitted for a few days to maintain his residence in the Hôtel du Contrôle général in Paris, where he gave a dinner for sixty guests and instructed his successor as controller, Michel Bouvard de Fourqueux, on the intracies of the state's finances. But he was exiled to his estate in Allonville near Amiens on April 15, and from then on he was vilified by a flood of rumors, songs, prints, and pamphlets. According to the *on dits*, Calonne had prepared thirty-three *lettres de cachet* so that he could dispatch the leading Notables to the Bastille and stage a coup; then, when he found it impossible to get rid of the opposition, he destroyed the incriminating evidence by burning his papers.[22] New versions appeared of the caricature casting him as the cook who consulted the barnyard animals about the sauce in which they preferred to be served. In "The Farmer and the Farm Yard," now a fable, the cook, transformed into a farmer, was upbraided by a turkey for exploiting the peasantry; and in another version the animals began to revolt, echoing a protest attributed to one of the Notables that they were not "sheep and beasts."[23] The most popular of the songs was a "Pot-pourri" in which a succession of nineteen verses, each to be sung to a different tune, characterized the players in the recent events. The king appeared as a simpleton who believed Calonne would improve the lot of the people; the queen celebrated Calonne for financing her extravagant whims; Calonne himself stated that he merely wanted to make money; the Notables lamented their inability to resist his power; and the common people saw clearly that his program would not produce prosperity—as in the famous "chicken in the pot" associated with Henri IV—but only more misery:

Quelle remise!	*What a reduction [of taxes]!*
On demande un nouvel impôt	*They are asking for a new tax*
Au lieu de la poule promise.	*In place of the promised chicken.*
Hélas! Nous n'aurons plus de pot	*Alas! We won't have the pot*
Ni de chemises.[24]	*Nor even shirts.*

According to the press, the dominant topic of conversation in Paris—indeed, the only topic, as some reported—was the transformation of the government. It involved more than the disappearance of Calonne, because the king kept shuffling ministers and department heads. The most important appointment, already mentioned, was Lamoignon as keeper of the Seals. Three controllers general succeeded Calonne within four months in 1787, multiplying the chaos in the finance ministry. The last of them, Claude Guillaume Lambert, was made subordinate to Loménie de Brienne, who became president of the Conseil des finances on May 1 and ministre principal on August 26, 1787, thereby consolidating his domination of the government, which continued for the next twelve months.

The coming and going of ministers provided endless material for political gossip, and the figure who most occupied Parisians' conversations was Necker, who seemed to be waiting in the wings for another opportunity to lead the government. Calonne's opponents in the Notables had based their stand on a *Neckriste* view of the budget. If, as Necker claimed, there had been a large surplus at the end of his ministry and not, as Calonne pretended, an enormous deficit, the current problems could be solved by raising loans and reducing expenses—unless Calonne's depredations had inflicted permanent damage on the treasury. The queen, who was said to favor Necker, announced that she would gladly give up her spendthrift habits, having had no idea of the state's financial difficulties, and she would begin by reducing the size of her stable to 162 horses.[25]

Necker himself took Calonne's version of the finances to be a vicious attack on his administration. After Calonne announced a structural deficit in his opening speech to the Notables, Necker prepared a reply. As mentioned, he requested permission to publish it, but the king refused. Nevertheless, Necker distributed it without authorization as a seventy-six-page pamphlet as soon as Calonne fell, and Parisians snapped it up.[26] Louis responded, rather mildly, by exiling Necker to a distance of twenty leagues (sixty miles) from Paris. Calonne had been exiled to Allonville five days earlier, and he immediately began drafting a justification of his administration. For the next year and a half, the two ex-ministers published wildly different accounts of the state's finances, while the reading public, fascinated but perplexed, avidly followed their debate.

Despite the general sympathy for Necker, Parisian commentators found it difficult to assess the arguments. Multiple accounts scattered over incompatible records from heterogeneous sources made it impossible for anyone to get a clear view of the situation. After resuming their sessions on April 15, the Notables got access to the sixty-three reports on revenue and expenditures that Calonne had cited to justify his demands, but they could not make much sense of them. Then, at the king's insistence, they moved on to other questions, following Calonne's original agenda. The taxation issue therefore remained unresolved, and it was compounded by a proposal for a stamp tax, which aroused opposition but nothing like the passion unleashed by the land tax. Brienne's appointment to the government on May 1 meant that a Notable had been put in charge of the state's finances. Despite his position as archbishop of Toulouse, he was known to sympathize with the ideas of the *philosophes*, particularly in economic matters, having been named by Turgot to investigate the problem of beggary in 1774. He also passed as a *Neckriste* and therefore a skeptic about the deficit.[27]

When he consulted the *premier commis*, or top civil servant in the Contrôle général, however, Brienne learned that revenues did not come close to covering expenses. In fact, when he announced his version of the deficit to the Notables on May 14, it came to a whopping 140 million livres. It would never be covered by loans and belt tightening, Brienne explained. There had to be new taxes. He opted for Calonne's solution, an egalitarian land tax, which he supplemented with the stamp tax, hoping that he could win the Notables' approval, because he pitched his argument as a former Notable, the antithesis of Calonne, a *Neckriste* at heart, and a Turgot-type reformer without a compromising past.

As Parisians learned from the gazettes, Brienne received a sympathetic hearing from the Notables, but in the end they would not budge. Their last resolutions, particularly from the "grenadiers" of the Prince de Conti's bureau, rejected both the land and stamp taxes, and they were dismissed by the king after a closing ceremony, full of pomp and circumstance, on May 25. By then, according to the *nouvellistes*, the Kornmann Affair occupied the public far more than the meetings of the Notables, which had lost their drama after the fall of Calonne.[28] Not that anyone in Paris believed the fiscal issues had been resolved. The tax proposals were now expected to be passed on to the Parlement, where Brienne would have to get them registered.

For most Parisian observers, the Assembly of Notables was a disappointment, although it led to the dismissal of an unpopular minister. It demonstrated the vulnerability of the government and the inevitability of a financial reckoning; but after raising hopes for fundamental change, it ended by leaving the impression that public affairs were stuck in a stalemate. As the *Mémoires secrets* put it, echoing the last refrain from *Le Mariage de Figaro*, perhaps after all everything would end by more taxes and more songs.[29]

31

A Minister Runs for Cover

PARISIANS WERE used to the rise and fall of ministers, especially during the reign of Louis XVI, when they came and went in rapid succession. But Calonne did not merely fall; he fled—and to France's enemy across the Channel. This was a spectacular event, reported in all the gazettes, discussed in all the public places. Parisians reacted with astonishment; they could find no precedent for it in French history, and it seemed to confirm suspicions that Calonne was guilty of horrendous crimes.[1] Whatever they were, his offenses had to be ferreted out and condemned, everyone agreed. Yet the Crown could not permit the Parlement to put Calonne on trial without abrogating its authority. Therefore, as soon as the Parlement began to take action, the king quashed its proceedings, and the case of Calonne was ultimately left to the tribunal of public opinion. Depredations, the all-purpose word used to cover his alleged crimes, became a leitmotiv of public discourse, while Calonne himself, the arch-*déprédateur*, acquired a place in the collective imagination as a villain, every bit as wicked as Maupeou.

At first, as mentioned, Calonne seemed to make a soft landing after his fall from power in April 1787. It was rumored that he ordered a thousand bottles of wine so that he could continue to give dinner parties in Paris. After briefing his successor Fourqueux on the complexities of the Contrôle général, he reportedly joked that he had become the *premier commis* of the ministry he once had headed. When he was exiled to his estate in

Annonville, however, things took a turn for the worse. A hostile crowd gathered around his carriage when he passed through Verdun. According to one account, the citizens wanted to force him to witness a hanging that was to take place that day so that he would see the fate in store for him. [2] Reports arrived in Paris that the peasants on his lands threatened to stone him. The bishop of Verdun protested that Calonne had manipulated the exchange of Sancerre to award himself extensive tracts of land adjoining his estate. A letter from the bishop, which was reprinted in the *Correspondance littéraire secrète*, claimed that Calonne also had had a road built to his château, damaging so much property of landowners along the route that they complained to the Parlement of Metz.[3] After he arrived at the château, Calonne received an order from the king to surrender his *cordon bleu*, the badge of membership in the prestigious Order of the Holy Spirit. This humiliation wounded him so badly that he appealed to Brienne, asking that the king's command be rescinded. He had nothing to be ashamed of, he claimed, beyond occasional errors that were inevitable in such a complex administrative role. They were not errors, Brienne replied, but "crimes" ("délits").[4] The news of this exchange confirmed rumors that the Parlement planned to press criminal charges. Faced with the danger of arrest, Calonne decided that the only safety was in London. Within three months, the minister who had been the most powerful man in France (except the king, who was notoriously weak of will) had become a fugitive.

Rumors of Calonne's flight reached Paris by July 3. Radicals in the Parlement had attacked him on the previous day; they did so again on July 30; and on August 10 Adrien-Jean-François Duport, a young magistrate with close ties to Lafayette and sympathy for the American Revolution, delivered a full-scale denunciation. He began with a discourse on political theory taken from Rousseau. Government is derived from a basic social contract, he emphasized, and it should be guided by the general will. But the government of France had degenerated into a despotism, which had culminated in the ministry of Calonne. Then Duport developed an argument about the deficit, attributing it entirely to Calonne's depredations. He concluded that the Parlement should bring Calonne to justice, and it complied by resolving to pursue five accusations: Calonne had robbed the Crown by means of exchanges; he had extended loans without authorization; he had embezzled funds in the reminting operation; he had drained the treasury to promote stockjobbing; and he had committed various abuses of authority.[5]

Although the government was now in the hands of Calonne's enemies, it prevented the Parlement from interfering with its authority (it could hardly permit the Parlement to try former ministers) by quashing the procedure on August 14. Yet denunciations of Calonne continued to wind like a red thread through the conflicts between the ministry and the Parlement during the summer of 1787. Brienne, adopting Calonne's proposal for a land tax and a stamp tax, tried to get the tax edicts registered, and the Parlement, inheriting the Notables' role, resisted them. In speeches, resolutions, and remonstrances, the magistrates kept invoking Calonne's depredations as grounds for opposing new taxation. The provincial parlements echoed those arguments, referring to Calonne scornfully as "le déprédateur." The Parlement of Grenoble claimed that his "dissipations" had cost France more in three years than everything Louis XIV had spent in seventy-two years, and that they were the most extravagant misuse of money in the history of the French monarchy. Calonne had declared himself guilty, according to the Conseil souverain de Roussillon, simply by taking flight. All of these pronouncements circulated in Paris and reinforced the argument already familiar from the resolutions of the Notables: if a deficit existed, Calonne had created it, and he had done so by raiding the treasury.[6]

The denunciations fueled resentment of the queen, whom Parisians took to be the main beneficiary of Calonne's crimes. Rumors put the total of his embezzlements at 26 million and claimed that Marie-Antoinette did not merely use her share to indulge her taste for luxuries; she sent most of it to her brother, the Habsburg emperor in Vienna. Nicolas Ruault, a keen observer of the climate of opinion, took this view. In his private correspondence, he reported that Parisians of all classes hated the queen and called her "Madame Déficit." Another version of the deficit appeared in *Ni emprunt, ni impôt*, a pamphlet by the Comte de Kersalaun. By compiling information from pronouncements of Calonne before 1787, he concluded that it came to only 27 million—all of it produced by Calonne, as the budget had a surplus of 33 million when he became minister in 1783—and that it could be covered simply by cutting expenses. Kersalaun was bundled off to the Bastille on September 3. Although he was released two weeks later, his arrest, at midafternoon in the middle of Paris, dramatized the government's attempt to stanch the flood of pamphleteering that accompanied the resistance of the Parlement, and it produced more hostile "public noises" about despotism.[7]

The Parlement's intransigeance provoked the government to exile it to Troyes on August 15, but it was back on October 1, having agreed to a compromise on the issue of taxation. Although by then it had abandoned its effort to try Calonne, he continued to occupy a place at the center of the agitation in Paris. Demonstrations broke out on September 28, two days before the Parlement resumed its functions in the Palais de justice. As had often occurred on similar occasions, they were led by the clerks of the *basoche* and other young men who set off fireworks to celebrate the Parlement's return. The celebrations led to riotous behavior, most of it good-humored and carnivalesque, and they were confined to the area around the Palais, especially the Place Dauphine. But they attracted large crowds, some estimated at 3,000, and threatened to get out of hand. Extra detachments of the Gardes Françaises reinforced the troops of the Watch. The youths taunted the troops, and at one point a soldier fired into the crowd, though without causing serious injuries.

On September 30, posters that mocked the king and queen appeared in several parts of the city, although the atmosphere remained festive near the Palais, where street singers accompanied by a fiddler performed on an improvised stage, celebrating the Parlement in new verses to old tunes. On the evening of October 1, however, the celebrations became more audacious. A large crowd gathered in the Place Dauphine, required an "illumination" of the surrounding houses (those who refused to display candles had their windows broken), lit a gigantic bonfire, and staged a mock trial of Calonne. He had already been burned in effigy on several occasions in the courtyard of the Palais. This time the law clerks playing as magistrates pronounced him guilty and decreed that punishment be executed on a mannequin being held as a prisoner in a nearby house. The dummy was a six-foot, wooden board with "Calonne" painted on it and two empty money bags attached in place of its hands, indicating the crime of draining the treasury. A pretend jailer threw the board out a window; the clerks tied it up with ropes; and they carried it with "great pomp" in a procession, forcing it en route to do *"amende honorable"* like a prisoner condemned to the gallows. Finally, they threw it on the bonfire, dancing around the flames and tossing their hats into the air. A poem attached beneath a nearby lantern implored the king to inflict the same punishment on the real criminal:

Il lui reste à punir du plus cruel supplice	*It remains for him to punish harshly*
De nos maux l'auteur détesté.	*The hated author of our ills.*
Qu'à nos yeux Calonne périsse!	*Calonne should perish before our eyes!*
Et de Louis chacun bénira l'équité.[8]	*And all will bless Louis for his equity.*

The failure to put Calonne on trial did not stop the pamphleteers' attacks on him, far from it; and two weeks after the Parlement's return, Parisians were astonished to find peddlers hawking a pamphlet by Calonne himself: *Requête au Roi*, a bold attempt to turn the tide of public opinion, written in the form of an open letter to the king. Calonne denied all the charges against him, rebutting them one after the other in the order of Duport's denunciation in the Parlement. The exchanges of land, he insisted, benefited the Crown; they had the king's approval; and some had been arranged before Calonne entered the government. He had indeed advanced 11.5 million livres to prevent a collapse of stock on the Bourse, but that was necessary for the good of the state, and it took the form of "assignations" on future revenue—short-term extensions of credit rather than payments from the treasury. The reminting accusation was false: he had never written any letter ordering the director of the mint in Strasbourg to withold the required supplement of gold. All the other charges lacked evidence. They were fabricated in order to brand him with "the horrible word Depredation," and they were based on a false view, not only of the deficit but of the state's finances in general. To correct the misinformation, Calonne provided a great deal of esoteric detail—his tract went on for 212 pages, including appendices—yet he enlivened it with personal touches. While reading the wildly exaggerated accounts of the deficit, he wrote, "My blood boiled . . . my hair stood on end." At times, he confessed, he had to interrupt his narrative while writing it "to let bitter tears flow,"[9] for he, too, was sensitive.

Never had French readers been addressed in such a manner by a former minister. Calonne gave them an insider's account of operations at the height of his power—his conferences with the king, his strategy sessions with the top civil servant in the Contrôle général—and he described his intimate thoughts and emotions. While maintaining a serene façade, he explained, he had suffered inner torment from anxieties about the state's survival. He had cultivated a confident and easygoing manner in public and drove himself relentlessly in private to prop up the Crown's faltering finance. His story as he told it was a tale of heroism, and it had a villain: Loménie de Brienne. While a member of the Assembly of Notables, Brienne had planted the calumnies about depredations in the form of a memoir distributed secretly to the other members. After his dismissal, Calonne had received a copy of the "infernal memoir," and therefore in his *Requête au Roi* he addressed the public as a victim of intrigue. (He did not mention his *Avertissement*, nor did he present himself as a reformer determined to destroy aristocratic privilege.) To right this wrong and inform the French about the true state of the Crown's finances, he asked the king to give him a public trial. The Parlement, including the peers of the realm, should act as an English type of grand jury; Calonne should be empowered to call all the witnesses he wanted; and while arguing his case, he should be protected by a safe-conduct decree.

As a polemical work, the *Requête au Roi* was a tour de force, bolder and better written than any of the pamphlets surrounding it—at least (speaking for myself), that is how it reads today. But it did not bowl over Calonne's contemporaries. Judging from what evidence exists, they reacted with hostility shading off into skepticism. Hardy considered some of Calonne's points valid but most of them offensive, and concluded, "All of France is revolted." The *Mémoires secrets*, which had a pro-Brienne bias, reported that the *Requête* had created a sensation at first but that readers got bogged down in its financial details and ultimately found it unpersuasive—in fact nothing but "lies, artifice, boasting, impudence." Nicolas Ruault dismissed it as the work of a charlatan who was lucky to have escaped from France without being tried and hanged. The *Gazette de*

Leyde, which remained neutral, said that most of the readers who favored Calonne were connected with the court. No one took seriously his request to appear before a special tribunal, which he also claimed would serve as the first step in a general reform of criminal law.[10]

Although it failed to win over public opinion, the *Requête au Roi* stood out as an important event, and it provoked another flurry of pamphlets. Most of them heaped scorn on Calonne without providing any new arguments or information. Two works, however, added substantial evidence to the case against him. *Observations de la ville de Saint-Mihiel en Lorraine sur l'échange du comté de Sancerre, en réponse à la requête de Monsieur de Calonne*, a well-documented, two-volume account of the most notorious of Calonne's estate exchanges, was taken by readers to prove Calonne a "scoundrel." *Mémoire justificatif pour le sieur Michel Rivage* gave an equally damning report on the reminting operation.[11]

Of all the other tracts, *Un Petit Mot de Réponse à M. de Calonne sur sa Requête au Roi* struck contemporaries as the most "damning." It was written by Jean-Louis Carra, a minor man of letters who specialized in the vehement style of invective popularized by Mirabeau. He had already published a violent attack on Lenoir, Calonne's "right-hand man," and he denounced Calonne in the same manner, elaborating on the five principal accusations that the Parlement had planned to pursue. In the case of the Sancerre exchange, for example, he claimed that Calonne had also awarded himself the estate of Hattonchatel near Sannonville in return for a pay-off to the estate's owner of a million livres stolen from the treasury. What made Carra's version of such abuses stand out, according to reviewers, was a revelation at the heart of it: he identified himself as the author of the "infernal memoir" that had been distributed to the Notables and that Calonne had identified as the main source of the campaign against him. Manuscript copies of the memoir had been circulating in Paris and created quite a stir. Carra reproduced it in full and supplemented its account of Calonne's depredations with a great deal of new material, rebutting the *Requête* point for point. He claimed to write as an independent patriot, but he mixed enough praise of Brienne into his vilification of Calonne for contemporaries to suspect that he wrote as a propagandist for Brienne's new ministry. Yet that suspicion did not undercut their conviction that Calonne was guilty, nor their appetite for more scandalous evidence, which Carra promised to provide, for his *Petit Mot*, he wrote, was only a first installment of a full-scale indictment, which he would publish a few months later.[12]

This work appeared under the title *Monsieur de Calonne tout entier* in April 1788. By then the pamphleteering had proliferated to such an extent that it formed a genre, "Calonniana," that resembled the "Maupeouana" of the 1770s. As in the attacks on Maupeou, the pamphlets against Calonne made political arguments by personal vilification. They dished up spicy anecdotes about his supposed immorality, embezzlement, and abuses of power, using the standard devices of libels, such as fake correspondence and imaginary dialogues. What set them apart from earlier pamphleteering was their emphasis on state finance. Several advanced a *Neckriste* view of the deficit: it had not existed in 1781, they insisted, and whatever it might be in 1787, it resulted from Calonne's depredations— the stockjobbing, land exchanges, reminted louis, and all the rest. Each abuse lent itself to supposedly new revelations, such as Calonne's gift to a mistress of candy wrapped in notes of the Caisse d'escompte, the expensive rosewood that he burned in her fireplace to create atmosphere for an orgy, and the banknotes that he used to light candles at their trysts. Larger sums went for pensions, sinecures, grants of land, and refurbished châteaux—the stuff of which patronage networks were built among *les grands*. Thus, after the Notables had extracted information about the deficit, the pamphleteers pretended to reveal its cause, writing in the familiar genre of the libel.[13]

Carra then compiled all the anecdotes, arguments, and financial data into an anti-Calonne epic, 406 pages long. He began by deploring the light, ingratiating style of Calonne's writings, a sure sign of aristocratic sympathies. In contrast, he adopted a tone of angry denunciation, like that of Mirabeau: "To upset the insidious maneuvers of scoundrels and rogues, one should not remove their masks with kid gloves; one should rip it off violently." And like Bergasse, he moralized indignantly, "The idiom of virtue makes no accommodation with that of vice." No term was too strong to describe the depravity of Calonne, that "monster," that "snake," that "pestilential miasma," "scourge of morality," "Pericles of libertinism." And Calonne's depredations revealed more than the evil of his character. As Carra construed them, they exposed the rot at the heart of the

Ancien Régime: arbitrary power monopolized by *les grands*, the men at the top, ministers and courtiers and their lackies in the administration and police.[14]

That message belonged to the literature of libel, which, as we have seen, used revelations about private lives to mobilize passions about public affairs. In the case of Calonne, the libeling was so effective that he ceased to be seen as an individual and came to personify an idea: ministerial despotism. By their nature, "isms" are abstract and often hard to grasp. Once attached to a public personage, however, they can acquire the power to move masses. Of course, other villains had haunted the collective imagination long before Calonne. They carried different ideological charges, depending on their context, yet they had common characteristics. The mythology of Calonne echoed that of Maupeou, and it would again be amplified in denunciations of Brienne. In fact, the idea of despotism, as embodied by villains, would resonate throughout the French Revolution and continue far into the nineteenth century.

32

The Parlement Plays Politics

WHILE EXCORIATING CALONNE, Parisians had to make up their minds about his successor, Loménie de Brienne, who became director of the Conseil des finances on May 1, 1787. Brienne could expect public support because he had been a Notable, known as a leader of the opposition to Calonne. He was said to have *Neckriste* sympathies and had championed the Notables' demand to see the government's confidential records ("*états*") of expenditure and income. Although the Notables had not endorsed any new taxes, the speeches at their last session, which were printed and circulated widely in Paris, suggested Brienne would enjoy a honeymoon period while he tried to get to the bottom of the state's fiscal problems. Like Necker, he was expected to strip away the veil that had hidden financial operations from the citizens. The *Gazette de Leyde* sounded optimistic when it reviewed the accomplishments of the Notables and the outlook for the new ministry. "The science of government," it concluded, was no longer a secret.[1]

Soon after assuming power, however, Brienne began to sound like Calonne. His estimate of the deficit, 140 million livres, was even higher than Calonne's. Others put it at 127 million, and some said it did not exist at all, or could be eliminated merely by cutting the expenses of the royal households.[2] Whom to believe? Parisians were confused, except about the one issue that touched them personally: they did not want to pay more taxes. Yet Brienne threw his weight behind the two tax proposals that he inherited from Calonne. The land tax, now reformulated as a *subvention territoriale*, was to be apportioned among all proprietors, whether they had held exemptions or not, and the stamp tax would fall heavily on nearly everyone engaged in commerce, because the stamp had to appear on all bills of exchange. The Notables had insisted that no new taxes could be levied without the consent of the nation assembled in the Estates General. Now Brienne's government intended to raise them in the traditional manner, by registration in the parlements.

Everyone who followed politics in Paris knew where that would lead. The Parlement would protest; the government would insist; and the struggle would conform to a familiar scenario: parlementary resolutions and remonstrances, ministerial admonitions and *lits de justice*. If things got badly out of hand, the Parlement could be sent into exile. Then there would be a new round of negotiations and a compromise solution—unless the conflict escalated so badly that the government resorted to extreme measures, as it had done under Maupeou. Although such affairs ignited passions in the neighborhood of the law courts, they did not usually interest artisans and laborers toiling in the faubourgs. In fact, the deficit did not seem urgent to most Parisians at the beginning of June, when Brienne was attempting to understand the financial crisis and to come up with a plan for bringing it under control. The hottest topic at this time was the Kornmann Affair, which had already become the dominant subject of public attention during the last sessions of the Notables but had not yet turned into an attack on the government.

Gossips in cafés also devoted a great deal of talk to international relations. The Republic of the Netherlands was descending into civil war, because the stadtholder, Wilhelm V, threatened to attack the oligarchy of Regents who controlled the government. France was committed to support the government, and the stadtholder had the backing of Prussia and England. Tensions came to a crisis after an incident in midsummer, when some radical republicans from the Dutch Patriot Party insulted the stadtholder's wife, who was the sister of the Prussian king, Frederick William II. Before the French could intervene, the Prussians invaded, routed the Patriots, and forced the government to accept a settlement that restored the authority of the stadtholder. In October, France formally abandoned its agreement to provide military support to its Dutch ally, having been outflanked by the Anglo-Prussian *entente*. The situation in the Austrian Netherlands also was unstable, but, Parisians wondered, how could France assert itself abroad if it lacked the funds to keep its government operating adequately at home? To those who followed foreign affairs, France had suffered a humiliating setback, which showed how much it had declined since its triumph over Britain only five years earlier.

While the pressure from the deficit continued to increase, the Parlement refused to come to the government's rescue. At first it argued that unlike the Notables, who were merely asked to give advice, it had the power to authorize new taxes by registering them. But like the Notables, it needed proof that the taxes were necessary, and therefore it demanded that the government submit financial records. The deficit, if it existed, might well be the result of depredations, and so, as explained, proceedings were also begun against Calonne. These demands were accompanied by so much defiant oratory that the Parlement of Paris looked like a small version of the Parliament in London, according to the *Mémoires secrets*.[3] The magistrates who spoke out strongest were identified by name and celebrated as patriots in discussions among Parisians, who followed the debates from rumors and reports in newssheets.

The news that received the greatest coverage concerned the debate about the stamp tax on July 2. The Parlement met in full session—that is, with all of its chambers gathered in the Grand'Chambre with the princes of the royal blood and the dukes and peers. According to the reports, the Comte d'Artois (the younger of Louis XVI's two brothers), stirred up a hornets' nest by stating that the king could levy any tax he wanted; such, he claimed, were the fundamental laws of the monarchy. D'Éprémesnil replied with a lecture about the fundamental laws, a favorite topic of the Parlement. They provided that the authority to raise taxes belonged exclusively to the French nation as represented in the Estates General, he argued. Any other attempt to tax the people, even by registering an edict with the Parlement, was an abuse. At the word "abuse," d'Artois rose to his feet and objected vehemently. D'Éprémesnil retorted that most of the expenses of the court, including the money spent on d'Artois's personal guards, were abuses. D'Artois, furious, said he would not be addressed in such a manner. Here in the Parlement, d'Éprémesnil shot back, you are only one of the peers, and you have only one vote, the same as the others.

At that point, Monsieur, the older of the king's brothers, tugged d'Artois by his sleeve and got him to sit down. Accounts of the scene soon were buzzing through the air in Paris, and the comments on it included remarks that it was a stamp tax that had triggered the American Revolution.[4]

That a young councillor in a lower division of the Parlement, the first Chambre des enquêtes, should give a dressing-down to a brother of the king was spectacular enough; but in qualifying the Parlement's registration of taxes as an abuse, d'Éprémesnil also signaled a shift in the grounds of the debate. Strictly speaking, he argued, the Parlement had no authority to legitimize taxation, although it had done so for centuries. He and other magistrates now began to insist that the Parlement should renounce its previous position and should base its opposition to taxes on a demand for the convocation of the Estates General. In adopting this argument, they made it clear that the Parlement was not defending the privileges of the clergy and nobility; they were speaking for the nation.

For the next three weeks, the Parlement and the government continued to quarrel, following the usual script. The Parlement protested against the taxes with formal "representations"; the government rejected its demands; the Parlement came back with "iterative supplications"; the government sent another refusal; and finally the Parlement decided to send "remonstrances." In the course of the exchanges, the magistrates turned up the volume of their speeches. While opposing the taxes, they demanded to see the state's financial records, expressed doubts about the deficit, denounced depredations of the court, threatened to try Calonne, called for the Estates General, and again reminded anyone who might be listening that the American Revolution had begun with a stamp tax. The remonstrances, voted on July 24, showed that the Parlement had now committed itself to a demand for the convocation of the Estates General. The government's response was equally uncompromising: the Parlement must register both taxes and abandon its attempt to sap the authority of the Crown.

By the end of the month, the conflict, which at first had been restricted to the political elite, resonated throughout Paris and everywhere in the kingdom. The provincial parlements, especially in Bordeaux, Rouen, and Besançon, passed resolutions that outdid the Parlement of Paris in the violence of their rhetoric. They were printed and disseminated widely, along with the Parisian remonstrances of July 24, which were "devoured" by the public and diffused everywhere in Paris, according to Hardy. Rumors reinforced their effect. In a favorite *"on dit,"* the queen remarked facetiously that she planned to give a ball but first would have to get permission from d'Éprémesnil. Other versions had her requesting his permission to buy a bonnet and to use a chamber pot.⁵ The theme of depredations continued to make the rounds. According to one story, the queen had recently spent a million livres on a banquet service. Another claimed that the Comte d'Artois had lost 800 L. in gambling—or 2 million in an angrier version—which the king had to cover.⁶ Ruault, who had criticized the Parlement in his correspondence, now wrote that it had become a "hero" to the common people. Its call for the Estates General echoed everywhere, and he had even heard talk of an extraordinary plot: appalled by the king's incompetence and chronic drunkenness, his brother (Monsieur, the Comte de Provence, who was said to be cunning, as opposed to Monseigneur, the Comte d'Artois, who was notorious for his erratic behavior) would seize the Crown, have himself declared regent, lock up Louis in a monastery with a good wine cellar, and send Marie-Antoinette packing to Vienna.⁷

After the failure of negotiations to reach a compromise, the government decided to resort to a *lit de justice.* The Parlement protested in advance on August 5 by a resolution that called for the convocation of the Estates General and cited Calonne's depredations as the epitome of everything that had gone wrong with the fiscal system. The Queen, who had been Calonne's strongest supporter, gave a ball that evening in Versailles, setting off complaints among Parisians that the depredations had not stopped.⁸ Early the next morning, the magistrates, dressed formally in red robes, set off for Versailles in forty carriages, pulled by teams of four or six horses and escorted by a detachment of cavalry. Seated under an imposing canopy (the *"lit"* of the *lit de justice*), the king ordered that the edicts for the stamp and land tax be entered on the Parlement's register. By 4 o'clock the procession had returned to Paris, and the magistrates resolved to take immediate action. On the following day, in a session filled with fiery speeches, they declared the forced registration of the taxes "null and illegal." That step sounded like open rebellion—"I know how to die if necessary," d'Éprémesnil declared—and it was applauded by an enormous crowd that filled the halls and courtyards of the Palais.⁹ The Parlement confirmed this stand on August 13 by passing an edict that pronounced the registration nullified. It had the edict printed immediately and mailed off to the courts under its jurisdiction in order to get the message out before the government could repress it. As the tension grew, Parisians expected a show of force. Sure enough, on August 15 the government dispatched *lettres de cachet* exiling all the magistrates to Troyes, 110 miles southwest of Paris.[10]

Exiles had occurred often enough for everyone to assume that a compromise would eventually be reached. This time, however, the conflict seemed to strike a chord deep within the Parisian population. To be sure, it is impossible to know exactly how such events reverberated, but one indication is furnished by peddlers, who hawked printed matter everywhere in the city and, as mentioned, functioned as town criers. When the Brienne ministry issued decrees, the peddlers "published" them by calling out a phrase or two that summarized their content, and the mode of their hawking served as a barometer of the climate of opinion. They were so reticent in distributing the edicts for the stamp and land taxes that the texts were not truly published, according to Hardy: "The peddlers did not publish them but walked through the streets announcing simply and with a great deal of reticence, 'Here is something new.'" Ruault noted that the peddlers disseminated the edicts "in a silent and almost shameful manner." Unwelcome as the texts were, a great many people bought them (they ran to thirty-two pages and cost 24 sous), in order to know exactly what to expect if the taxes were levied.[11] In its edict of August 13, the Parlement noted that the peddlers had not dared to raise their voices when distributing a printed account of the *lit de justice*. A few days later, the ministry issued edicts announcing cuts in the expenses of the king's household—that is, happier information, which the peddlers "published with infinitely more bluster."[12] But on August 16, two peddlers who continued to hawk the edicts for the taxes were attacked by a crowd of the "populace" and so badly beaten that they nearly died from their injuries.[13] The peddling, and the way it was done, disseminated news, news with a particular spin, everywhere in Paris, even among the poor and the illiterate.

News took many forms, of course. The peddlers also hawked printed copies of decrees issued by the Parlement of Paris and the provincial parlements, pamphlets, newspapers, prints, and judicial memoirs. Bergasse's memoirs, reprinted in many editions, were best sellers at this time. Kornmann's case had been moved from the Châtelet court to the Parlement and then was suspended during the Parlement's exile, but the flow of memoirs did not let up. Posters, handwritten or printed, appeared everywhere. Some attacked the king and queen so violently that Hardy could not bring himself to copy them into his journal.[14] Ruault noted the variation of their themes according to their locality. At the Place Maubert: "Long live the queen and the whores!" At the Place Vendôme: "Louis XVI known as the Stamped ["timbré"], the last king of France." At the Hôtel de la Monnaie: "Louis is nothing but a fat drunkard" ("Le Louis n'est plus qu'un gros sou," a double pun comparing coins, the louis with the sou, and "sou" with "soûl" for drunk).[15] Similar themes appeared in caricatures. One showed the queen mounted on a trojan horse (an allusion to Troyes, where the Parlement was confined), spitting out the tax edicts. In another, the king and queen gorged themselves at a table, while the common people surrounded them, begging for scraps.[16]

Because lawyers and attorneys refused to argue cases, legal proceedings came to a halt, freeing hundreds of clerks and minor officials to vent their anger in the streets. The Chambre des comptes and the Cour des aides, high courts that adjudicated financial and taxation matters, continued to meet as usual in the Palais de justice. Seeking further legitimation, the government forced them to register the tax edicts by *lits de justice* presided over by the king's two brothers. This unusual procedure provoked more formal protests by the courts and demonstrations by the crowds. When the Comte d'Artois arrived at the Cour des aides, he was jeered so fiercely that a riot nearly erupted and a massacre was barely avoided. The commander of the guards in the Palais ordered, "Ready . . . aim . . ." and the troops prepared to fire, when d'Artois countermanded the order and the crowd fell back. The *basoche* led protests in the neighborhood of the Palais, assaulting persons suspected to be police spies. In one incident a crowd of the "populace" chased a police agent into a wineshop and beat him to death. In another, some youths raided the headquarters of a police *commissaire*, forced him to free two clerks he had arrested, and smashed his furniture. Then the agitation spread to other parts of the city, including the faubourg Saint Antoine. To prevent an uprising, the government ordered regiments of the Gardes Françaises and Gardes Suisses to reinforce the troops of the Watch. They patrolled everywhere in groups of twelve, bayonets attached to their muskets. Some Parisians taunted them, calling out "carpes au bleu" at the Gardes Françaises whose blue uniforms suggested a fish dish.[17]

The fermentation in Paris was fed by remonstrances and resolutions turned out by the provincial parlements. Printed copies circulated widely, and Parisians gathered to discuss which made the strongest case against the government. Those of Bordeaux, Grenoble, and Besançon won the most admiration, Hardy wrote, although there was much to be said for the protests that came from Rennes and Roussillon. The Parlement of Grenoble argued effectively against the tax edicts by citing Montesquieu's *De l'Esprit des lois* and Necker's *Compte rendu*, and a decree from the Parlement of Besançon had everything to please the patriots: opposition to the taxes, a demand for the Estates General, condemnation of depredations, a plea to bring Calonne to justice, repulsion at stockjobbing, rejection of *lettres de cachet*, doubts about the deficit, hostility to the greed of courtiers, and horror at ministerial despotism.[18]

The government attempted to prevent the circulation of these protests and of scores of pamphlets that accompanied them. It also produced pamphlets of its own, which attacked the parlements for undermining the monarchy. The best known of the government publications, an anonymous tract titled *Observations d'un avocat*, rebutted the August 13 edict of the Parlement of Paris point by point. The edict, it argued, violated the legislative authority of the king so egregiously that it presented the French with a choice: either a monarchy as constituted by fundamental laws or a republic governed by the Parlement. Far from defending the two taxes as part of a radical program to destroy the privileges of the clergy and aristocracy, the pamphlet praised the government for taking a necessary measure to prevent bankruptcy. The radicals, it claimed, were the magistrates, who were fomenting sedition and rebellion.[19] When the pamphlet appeared, the law clerks were indeed behaving like rebels. They stormed through the corridors of the Palais with a copy of it, staged a mock trial, and burned it with the texts of the tax edicts at the foot of the Grand Staircase exactly as the Parlement had burned the publications it condemned. The tumult continued for several days until the government sent a detachment of sixty soldiers to occupy the Palais.[20]

By mid-September the government had regained control of the city.

It confiscated pamphlets, threatened *nouvellistes*, sent troops to maintain order in the Palais-Royal, and attempted to stifle political discussions by closing private associations, even a chess club. The Gardes Françaises patrolled everywhere, and the demonstrations ceased, in part because rumors began to circulate that the Parlement had entered into negotiations with the government. Despite the eagerness for the magistrates' return and for the resumption of court cases, some Parisians worried that the Parlement might concede too much.[21] The compromise, announced by an edict of September 19, satisfied many of them because the government abandoned the stamp and land taxes; but it alienated others because the Parlement agreed to accept a two-year extension of the *vingtième* tax, which fell, though unevenly, on most peoples' revenues. The peddlers hawked the edict with "a great show of satisfaction" and "lively elation."[22] Also, as we have seen, the crowds around the Palais greeted the news with joyful rioting and burned a dummy of Calonne. Yet even some of the *basoche* had reservations about the compromise. Having renounced its authority to approve new taxes, the Parlement seemed to contradict itself by agreeing to the prolongation of an old one. Indeed, some feared the government might redesign the *vingtième* in a way that made it, in effect, a substitute for the land tax. After months of contestation, Parisians had learned that ministers—with the notable exception of Necker—had an inexhaustible capacity for duplicity. They also had doubts about the Parlement. Although they had celebrated its patriotism when it went off into exile, many suspected that its main concern after it came back would be its self-interest. D'Éprémesnil, a hard-liner, warned his colleagues that the September 19 agreement meant the Parlement would return to Paris "covered with mud."[23]

The resolution of the government's conflict with the Parlement—which was only a truce in the view of some observers—did nothing to ease its financial difficulties. Gossips said the Dutch crisis meant France was certain to be drawn into a war, although it could hardly support its army. They also doubted that the government could take decisive action within the kingdom because it seemed to be paralyzed by intrigues among the ministers. (Even though he had been named "principal minister" on August 26, Brienne was said to be tied down by the opposition of his enemy, the Baron de Breteuil, minister for the king's household, who was supported by the queen.) The government failed to rescue its Dutch ally, but it finally came up with a plan to cope with the deficit: It would float a series of loans totaling 420 million livres spread over five years. By cutting expenses and increasing revenue, notably through the *vingtième,* it should be able to use the loans as a bridge to the recovery of its financial health. Edicts for loans had to be registered by the Parlement, however, and the Parlement, already stung by the disapproval of the September 19 compromise, seemed recalcitrant.[24]

On November 19, the king appeared in a session of the Parlement devoted to a discussion of the edict for the loans. To receive him, the magistrates gathered in full force—all of its chambers along with the princes of the blood, dukes, and peers. The convocation of such an assembly marked it as an important occasion, but its character was not clear. The king made a short speech, inviting the magistrates to give their opinions about the loan scheme. Then he took a seat in an armchair and listened—for seven hours, while their best-known orators (d'Éprémesnil, Robert de Saint Vincent, Fréteau de Saint-Just, Sabatier de Cabre) held forth about their favorite subjects: the fundamental laws of the monarchy, the nation's right to assent to taxes, and the necessity of calling the Estates General. Finally, after conferring with the Keeper of the Seals, the king ordered that the edict be transcribed forthwith on the Parlement's register. The Duc d'Orléans protested, saying that the session was either a *lit de justice,* in which case there had been no need for consultation, or a *séance royale,* which required a formal vote before the registration. If the latter, he said (the phrasing varied among the reports), the registration had been illegal. The king replied that everything he did was legal (according to one version, he said, "It is legal because I want it"), ordered the registration, and returned to Versailles. *Lettres de cachet* were issued that night, exiling Orléans to his château at Villers Cotterêts and sending Fréteau and Sabatier to prisons in the provinces. In a version of the events that circulated widely in Paris, the police agent who arrested Fréteau grabbed him by the collar and hustled him off before he could say good-bye to his wife and children.[25]

On the following day, the Parlement passed a resolution saying that it took no part in the forced transcription of the edict for the loan on its register. The king then summoned it to Versailles and required it to expunge the resolution from the minutes of its meeting. After returning to Paris, it voted "supplications," protesting vehemently against the exiling of Orléans and the imprisonment of Fréteau and Sabatier. The king rejected the protest in a curt reply, and the Parlement replied to the reply with "iterative supplications," which the king also rejected. All this back-and-forth did not impress the Parisians who followed it from gazettes and printed copies of the official texts. Most of this material circulated in the form of short pamphlets costing a few sous. When the peddlers "published" the text of the loan, it was taken to be a fait accompli, although Parisians wondered aloud whether a loan of such a size could ever be subscribed. They continued to snap up reprints of protests from the provincial parlements, including a resolution by the Parlement of Bordeaux that criticized the Parlement of Paris for having caved in to the government in order to end its exile.[26]

Parisians also appreciated burlesque edicts, which used parlementary legalese to get across radical ideas. A supposed "edict" of the Parlement of Aix cited Rousseau's *Contrat social* and Raynal's *Histoire philosophique* in declaring the monarch subject to "the will of the people." Hardy found this text persuasive, although he admitted that it "smells a bit of sedition." It circulated, he noted, among groups that gathered in private to discuss public affairs.[27] Clubs remained closed, provoking some burlesque "remonstrances" from the clubs of the Palais-Royal, which demanded their reopening along with "a constitution that frees us from oriental despotism."[28] Poems attacked the king more violently than anything that had circulated earlier, according to the *Mémoires secrets*. At the beginning of the new year, Hardy observed people copying the text of a poster that had been exposed in various parts of the city. It threatened an "uprising," a "general revolt," if the king failed to summon the Estates General.[29]

Hardy took those symptoms to indicate dangerous "fermentation."[30] Yet his journal and the underground gazettes may have exaggerated the extent of the danger. Hot spots like the Palais-Royal and the Palais de justice transmitted signals that sounded seditious, but there is little evidence that the rest of the city was ready to rise in revolt. The Parlement's radicalism sounded hollow to observers like Ruault, who suspected it of pursuing its own agenda while pretending to speak for the nation. It spent the last weeks of January debating the government's edict to extend civil rights to

Protestants and did not register the edict until January 29, after a great deal of hesitation, especially by reputed radicals like Robert de Vincent and d'Éprémesnil, who declaimed against heresy. By the end of 1787, many Parisians suspected that the Parlement was ready to make peace, since the government had accepted, in principle, its demand for the convocation of the Estates General. Whether that commitment could lead to a change in the constitution of the monarchy was a question to be resolved in 1788.

PART SIX

The
Collapse of the Régime,
1788

33

A New Coup, an Old Script

A S THE NEW YEAR BEGAN, hotheads in cafés continued to damn the despotism that they associated with the "royal session" of the Parlement on November 19, 1787. Louis XVI's reported outburst when he forced his edict down the throats of the magistrates —"It is legal because I want it"—seemed to announce that nothing could restrain the royal will. The Parlement always addressed the king respectfully, often obsequiously, and limited its protests to *ministerial* despotism, but the messages that appeared in the streets began to challenge the foundation of the king's authority. One poster, pasted on walls in several public places, accompanied the demand for the Estates General with a claim that sovereignty derived from the nation: "Kings have received their power from the people. . . . They owe an exact account of their revenue to the nation."[1] People made copies of the posters and passed them around, stoking the "fermentation" that Hardy noted fearfully in his diary. One author of a violent poem attacking the king and queen was discovered by the police and carried off to the Bastille. Parisians then memorized the poem and declaimed it publicly, so that it became lodged in "an infinite number of heads." Hardy also reported that the police had dispatched two persons to the Bastille for importing pamphlets that vilified the queen in connection with the Diamond Necklace Affair.[2]

To be sure, the *nouvellistes* who reported the agitation, sometimes with shock, sometimes with approval, frequented cafés, not working-class taverns, and they drew much of their information from salons and literary circles, not from the poorer neighborhoods of the faubourgs. Moreover, their reports indicated that the elite of "le monde" continued to pursue pleasures without any sense of impending doom. On January 7 the Baron de Breteuil, the powerful minister in charge of the king's household, gave an extravagant ball in his town house to celebrate the marriage of his daughter. True, he had to post one hundred guards to keep out violence from the street, but his guests, who included seven princesses and fifteen duchesses, danced the night away undisturbed by hostile demonstrations. Later that month, for the first time in many weeks, the queen ventured into Paris and called on the Princesse de Polignac without provoking an incident. Mardi Gras took place with the usual display of wealth and joie de vivre in the rue Saint Honoré, and in March the annual parade of "le monde" from the Place Louis XV to Longchamps was as grand as ever: 7,000–8,000 carriages. "Never has French frivolity equaled such splendor and charm," wrote a *nouvelliste*.[3]

By this time, the works of the *philosophes* circulated without much difficulty, although there were limits to the general atmosphere of tolerance. In January Pierre-Sylvain Maréchal, a minor writer and open atheist, published with the approval of a censor an *Almanach des honnêtes gens*, which featured Spinoza, Hobbes, and Voltaire in place of the saints that appeared at their appointed days in traditional almanacs. The Parlement condemned the book to be lacerated and burned by the public hangman. The censor was exiled, and Maréchal was imprisoned by a *lettre de cachet*. This was the last of the literary scandals under the Ancien Régime. It certainly scandalized Hardy, who expressed horror at the progress of irreligion and regret that the public burning made Parisians eager to snap it up at any price. According to another *nouvelliste*, the bonfire at the foot of the grand staircase at the Palais de justice made the price shoot up from 2 sous to 15 livres (i.e., 300 sous).[4]

Enlightenment principles also fixed the attention of the public when the Parlement took up a royal edict to convey civil status to Protestants. The king, tutored by progressive administrators like Lamoignon de Malesherbes, overcame his religious scruples, but many influential people objected. One was d'Éprémesnil, the fiercest opponent to royal absolutism in the Parlement, who embraced a militant variety of Catholicism tinged with Jansenism. Although he harrangued the Parlement vehemently, he failed to mobilize a majority against the edict. After agreeing to some modifications, the king resubmitted the edict, and the Parlement registered it on January 29. Hardy, who shared d'Éprémesnil's religious convictions, deplored the result. Despite its limitations (Protestants could not hold services publicly or obtain administrative offices), he saw the edict as the culmination of the Enlightenment—"the too sudden explosion that philosophy made in France during a span of thirty years."⁵ Religious toleration, the centerpiece of the secular campaign directed by Voltaire, had, at least to some extent, become the law of the land.

Meanwhile, the political tension continued to mount, driven by financial pressure, and state finances provoked more political debate. At issue was the dispute over the deficit, which had pitted Necker against Calonne and revived the debates from the Assembly of Notables. As we have seen, Calonne's *Requête au Roi*, written from his exile in London, caused a sensation when it began to circulate in Paris in early February. According to some reports, "It dragged M. Necker through the mud," and some of the mud stuck.⁶ According to others, it was not convincing.⁷ Indeed, it could have served as a weapon for Brienne, because by this time Brienne's hold on power was said to be threatened and Necker was the strongest candidate to replace him. However, the *Requête* ran to more than a hundred pages of esoteric detail about the royal accounts. Few Parisians could make sense of the arguments.⁸ Many "comptes rendus" had been published since Necker revealed the inner workings of the king's finances in 1781. In the spring of 1788, Brienne produced his own *Compte rendu au roi*, and it was accompanied by more confusing publications, including a *Collection des comptes rendus* and a *Compte rendu des comptes rendus*.⁹

What the reading public made of the polemics is impossible to say. Yet everyone agreed that the debate had important implications. If Necker was correct, he had left the government with a surplus of 10 million livres in 1781. If Calonne was correct, the Crown at the end of Necker's ministry was burdened with a deficit of 70 million. Of course, Calonne's version made him look good, because it indicated that the deficits went far back in time and could not be attributed to his own administration. Yet, as one reader observed, Calonne admitted that he had added 36 million to the former deficit while he was controller general during three years of peace, whereas Necker had run up the deficit by only 9 million during four years of war.[10] Those figures could be contested—and they were, in pamphlets and arguments around café tables—but however the costs were calculated, the bottom line looked monstrous. The Crown was staggering under an enormous financial burden, and the fault for it had to lie somewhere. What had gone wrong?

That question had hovered over the political struggles for more than a year, and an answer to it was beginning to emerge, distilled down to that key term, depredations. Bankruptcies bailed out, gambling debts paid off, mistresses subsidized, currency manipulated, a château here, an estate there, benefices, regiments, dowries, pensions, sinecures, emoluments, largesse of every kind (even, some said, the diamond necklace itself)—the profligacy had supplied gossips in *le monde* and pamphleteers in Grub Street with their favorite theme since the 1740s. Now it seemed to add up to something more than scandal. It accounted for the deficit, and the deficit derived from arbitrary power at the top.[11]

According to a typical argument in *Collection de comptes rendus*, the state debt amounted to 255 million livres, and most of it could be attributed to ministerial squandering. Not only was that correct, one reviewer observed, but it had an obvious implication for the current political crisis. The nation itself, represented in the Estates General, should take control of the state's finances "so that the revenues of the state will no longer be confided to depredators, who . . . are uniquely occupied with keeping themselves in power by handing over the substance of the people to avid and insatiable courtiers." It all came down to ministerial despotism, he concluded. To explain how that had happened, one need only read Montesquieu.[12]

While Montesquieu had discussed despotism in the abstract, as a general species of government, Linguet and Mirabeau had published testimony about the way it inflicted misery on individuals, and they stressed the use of *lettres de cachet* as its main weapon. The government used *lettres de cachet* in exiling members of the Parlement. It had recently employed them to send the Duc d'Orléans into exile and the parlementary magistrates Fréteau and Sabatier into prison. Nothing fit better into parlementary rhetoric than the general revulsion against this abuse of arbitrary power, even though most *lettres de cachet* were dispatched at the request of a family that needed to protect its honor by removing a prodigal son from exposure to the public.

On January 4, 1788, the Parlement issued a decree that elevated its defense of Orléans, Fréteau, and Sabatier into a general indictment of the monarchy. A printed version of the text circulated everywhere, and the passage that stood out in it, according to the reports of the gazetteers, challenged the fundamental legitimacy of the regime: "The monarchy clearly is degenerating into a despotism, since ministers use the king's authority to dispose of persons by *lettres de cachet*."[13] In discussing the Parlement's stand, Parisians identified it with "the cause of the entire society," and therefore they feared the worst. The government was said to be planning to destroy the independence of the judiciary just as Maupeou had done in 1771. It had prepared a new supply of *lettres de cachet*, and soldiers were standing ready to go into action.[14]

Instead of unleashing the troops, however, Louis XVI summoned a deputation of the Parlement to Versailles on January 17 and lectured them about the true nature of *lettres de cachet*, which, he insisted, belonged to the royal prerogative and were used to preserve the honor of distinguished families. The Parlement refused to see them as anything other than a weapon of despotism. It therefore resolved to expand its decree of January 4 into hostile remonstrances of the kind that had led to its exile to Troyes only a few months ago. The magistrates seemed to be hurtling down the path of self-destruction, some Parisians remarked. The future remonstrances could become their "death warrant."[15]

Meanwhile, remonstrances poured in from the parlements in the provinces. Most were printed and sold openly by "all shops with the latest publications" for affordable prices that varied from 12 to 24 sous.[16] Hardy noted their dates and transcribed their most inflammatory passages as if they served as a gauge of the mounting discontent. Protests arrived from Grenoble on January 3, from Bordeaux on January 12, from Toulouse and Rouen on January 25. They deplored the extension of the *vingtième* as well as the abuse of *lettres de cachet*. In fact, the only sovereign court aside from Paris to register the edict on the *vingtième* was the Parlement of Metz. The Parisian magistrates, prompted by their provincial colleagues, had second thoughts about their decision to accept the edict, which had restored peace with the government and ended their exile to Troyes on September

19. By manipulating newly established provincial assemblies, the Brienne ministry seemed determined to transform the *vingtième* into a new version of the land tax that had originally been proposed by Calonne.

Protests about taxation, outrage at the abuse of *lettres de cachet*, appeals for the Estates General, and rumors of impending violence ratcheted up the tension throughout February. Parisian "politiques" had dreaded a Maupeou-type coup since the beginning of the year. By March they considered it inevitable. The ministers were said to have consulted Maupeou himself (although disgraced in 1774, he held his position as chancellor for life) about the best way to replace the parlements with subservient courts. "The battle lines are being drawn: the authority and prerogative of the king on one side; hatred or rather fear of despotism on the other," remarked one *nouvelliste*. Although he had little sympathy for the Parlement and respected Brienne and Lamoignon, he thought the ministers had gone too far.[17] Hardy, who took the opposite position—he supported the Parlement and detested the ministers—came to the same conclusion. A line had been drawn. It was a matter of liberty versus despotism.[18] The Parlement took this position in the remonstrances it passed on March 11: *lettres de cachet* must be abolished; liberty must be defended. In a curt reply, the king demanded submission to his authority. The remonstrances and the reply were printed as a pamphlet of fifteen pages, which sold for a mere 8 sous. While the reading public studied the texts, the Parlement deliberated about how far it dared to push its resistance.

On April 11, it adopted further remonstrances, which rejected all compromise on the issue of *lettres de cachet* and the *vingtième* and which defined the principles at stake in the strongest possible terms: "Public liberty attacked at its root, despotism substituted for the law of the state, and the magistracy reduced to being nothing more than the instrument of arbitrary power. . . ."[19] This time, the king summoned a "great deputation" of the Parlement (forty-two of its members transported in thirteen carriages) to Versailles, and in upbraiding the magistrates, he (or the ministers who drafted his speech) struck a new note: the Parlement was attempting to turn the monarchy into "an aristocracy of magistrates."[20] Although Calonne had tried and failed to use a similar argument against the Notables, Brienne and Lamoignon now aimed it at the Parlement. Resistance to the Crown should be construed as a defense of aristocratic privilege. By framing the issue this way, the ministers were appealing over the Parlement's head to the court of public opinion. They also did so by commissioning pamphlets from ultraroyalist and anti-Enlightenment writers like Linguet and Jacob Nicolas Moreau, the royal historiographer. "Patriot" pamphleteers churned out propaganda in favor of the Parlement, just as they had done in the 1770s. Printed matter flooded the streets. Peddlers distributed the king's reply free of charge, and *bouquinistes* sold the Parlement's remonstrances as a twenty-four-page pamphlet for 10 sous. Every response by the Parlement was published and hawked at every street corner, according to Nicolas Ruault. The reaction, in all sectors of the city, was ominous "murmurs."[21]

Although Orléans was permitted to return to Paris in mid-April and Fréteau and Sabatier were freed, reports circulated everywhere of an impending coup. "The fermentation is growing from day to day," wrote a gazetteer on April 20. Hardy noted the constantly increasing "worry and agitation among the good patriots" on April 23.[22] A rebellious crowd hanged an effigy of Brienne, and several regiments were summoned to Paris in order to repress further disorder. Details were leaked about the new judicial system being prepared by Lamoignon. The Parlement of Paris would be deprived of its right to remonstrate, purged of the patriots in its lower chambers, and reduced to the most pliant members of its Grand'Chambre, while a set of subsidiary courts would assume many of its judicial functions. Similar measures would emasculate the provincial parlements. In fact, a team of compositors and pressmen under strict supervision in Versailles was said to be secretly printing the edicts that would destroy the old system of justice and create a new one. It seemed to be a matter of days before the Crown would eradicate the last barrier to its arbitrary rule.

Reinforced by the peers of the realm, who sat with it on important occasions, the Parlement deliberated for several days about how to make a final appeal, not to the king but to the nation. On May 3 it passed a resolution that sounded like a declaration of independence. Rejecting Louis-quatorzean absolutism, it advocated a constitutional system that seemed virtually British. Only the nation, assembled at regular intervals as the Estates General, could permit taxes, it asserted. The king's authority was limited by fundamental laws, which guaranteed the liberty of every citizen and subjected all royal decrees to registration by the parlements. In defending the rights of the nation, the magistrates accused the ministers of subverting the basic principles of the monarchy, and they swore that they would not sit in any body designed to replace the Parlement. According to one report, their "fulminating edict is in everyone's hands and makes the intensest sensation." It was printed and distributed to all the courts under the Parlement's jurisdiction, while the Parisians waited for "the big coup."²³

On the evening of May 4, the police, armed with *lettres de cachet*, attempted to arrest two of the most outspoken members of the Parlement, Duval d'Éprémesnil and Goislard de Montsabert, in their homes. When he heard a knock by a police agent on his front door, d'Éprémesnil fled out the back. Goislard escaped by climbing over a wall in his backyard garden, and both sought refuge in the Palais de justice. Once safely inside, they summoned all the magistrates along with the grandees. The full Parlement assembled in its Grand'Chambre the next morning. When the dukes and peers arrived, a large crowd applauded and cried "Bravo!" The doors of the Palais were thrown open to the public, which filled the entire building and followed the proceedings throughout the day and the following night. By a formal vote, the Parlement took d'Éprémesnil and Goislard under its protection and sent a deputation to Versailles to protest against this latest stroke of ministerial "despotism." While it remained in session waiting for the king's reply, a battalion of two hundred Gardes Françaises (troops attached to the king's household and stationed in Paris) marched into the Palais, sealed off the Grand'Chambre, occupied the corridors and galleries, and closed all the entrances to the building. Hundreds of additional soldiers, with bayonets attached to their muskets, surrounded the Palais from the outside. As the magistrates phrased it in drafting a protest, the Parlement had been subjected to a "military siege."²⁴

At two in the morning, the captain of the Gardes, Vincent d'Agoult, a rough-and-ready soldier who had no understanding of legal nicities, pounded on the closed entrance to the Grand'Chambre. He had stationed two rows of grenadiers outside the door, and they carried axes in order to break through it, if necessary. D'Agoult was admitted inside and demanded that the two magistrates be turned over to him. The presiding officer refused on the grounds that the Parlement was in session and would maintain its prescribed procedure. D'Agoult withdrew in order to get further orders from his commander, the *maréchal* de Biron. When he returned an hour and a half later, the elderly Duc de Luynes, one of the most distinguished peers sitting with the Parlement, upbraided him for entering the sanctuary of justice without being properly dressed. (D'Agoult was not wearing the *hausse-col* or collar piece expected of an officer). In some confusion, d'Agoult produced the collar piece from his pocket and announced that he had new orders specifying that he arrest councilors Duval d'Éprémesnil and Goislard de Montsabert. At that point, according to several accounts, all the magistrates replied with one voice, "We are all Duval and Goislard. It is all of us you must arrest."

Less dramatic accounts confirmed the Parlement's defiance and d'Agoult's increased confusion. Once again he withdrew and sought new orders. This time, Biron did not dare take it upon himself to resolve the deadlock. He sent to Versailles for instructions, while the entire Parlement, including the peers of the realm and about 2,000 spectators, remained confined in the Palais for the rest of the night. The magistrates were kept so heavily guarded that an armed escort accompanied them if they went to the toilet. At three in the morning, the deputation returned from Versailles with word that the king had refused to receive them. At seven, the Guards finally permitted the members of the public who had been sequestered with the Parlement to return to their homes. At eleven, d'Agoult reappeared with yet another set of orders and, at his side, a minor parlementary official named Archier. After being commanded to identify the two magistrates and in danger of arrest if he failed to do so, Archier said he could not recognize them among the crowd of men in black robes.

Finally, d'Éprémesnil came to Archier's rescue by identifying himself. He had not done so earlier, he said to d'Agoult, because he would not acknowledge the legitimacy of a *lettre de cachet*. Was d'Agoult determined to use brute force? he asked. Yes, came the reply; the soldiers were ready for action. D'Éprémesnil then said he would sacrifice himself "in order not to expose the sanctuary of the laws to a greater profanation." Before being carried off, he delivered an oration that left his colleagues in tears. He was ready to die for the cause of liberty, he asserted.[25] Goislard also accepted his fate heroically. D'Agoult then informed the magistrates that they were free to return to their homes. But first, after thirty hours of continuous session, they passed another resolution condemning the violation of law and liberty. It was "the last sigh of liberty on its deathbed," according to one commentator.[26] By now the government had withdrawn permission for parlementary protests to be printed, but manuscript copies along with detailed accounts of the "siege" circulated widely. They were then printed in defiance of the government's orders and also appeared in influential journals like the *Gazette de Leyde*. All the texts conveyed the same theme, using a standard set of symbols: the Palais was a "temple of justice," and it had been violated by "bayonets."[27] In his account of the "siege," Ruault borrowed terms from conventional descriptions of oriental despotism: D'Agoult was a "eunuch" commanding "janissaires" under the orders of the "sultan."[28]

The long-awaited and much-dreaded coup finally brought down the judicial system on May 8. Summoned to a *lit de justice* in Versailles, the Parlement had to listen mutely to its death sentence. The king gave it a scolding, and Lamoignon described the new judiciary to be established by royal fiat. As had been rumored, the Parlement would be replaced by a "Cour plénière" composed of members of the Grand'Chambre and other eminent personages—princes, peers, bishops, army marshals—who would be unlikely to oppose registering government decrees. The lower chambers of the Parlement, where hotheads like d'Éprémesnil and Montsabert had inveighed against the ministers, were abolished, except for one Chambre des enquêtes. Four new courts called "grands bailliages" were to take over the administration of justice in the large area of central France where the Parlement had had ultimate jurisdiction. Similar edicts transformed the judiciary in the rest of the kingdom. The provincial parlements were reduced to their judicial functions and stripped of the authority to register (and therefore resist) general decrees by the Crown. Although many progressive legal reforms were built into the new system, as in the Maupeou coup, it was purged of the political function that had made the parlements such an impediment to the control of the central government.

In the following days, the magistrates from the Grand'Chambre refused to participate in the Cour plénière; the inferior Châtelet court, which was to be recomposed as a *grand bailliage*, also announced its refusal; lawyers went on strike; the Palais de justice remained surrounded by troops; and justice was suspended. According to Hardy, all "true patriots" despaired, fearing that the nation was falling apart. To be sure, Hardy consistently identified patriotism with the Parlement. Yet other observers, who had little sympathy for the parlementary cause and had even expressed support for Brienne and Lamoignon, were horrified at the brutality of the repression.[29] The atmosphere had shifted decisively. The king seemed to be ruling by means of bayonets.

34

The Clergy Won't Pay

THE MONARCHY desperately needed money, everyone knew it, though opinions differed as to the size and the cause of the deficit. While the parlements blocked the way to more taxation, thoughts turned toward the church. It was enormously rich—that, too, was obvious to everyone. But it was a separate estate, which paid no taxes, ran its own affairs, and did not disclose information about its total wealth. The public had a general sense of the disparity between the lower clergy— priests with paltry incomes (the *portion congrue*, fixed at 700 L. a year for curates and 350 L. for vicars in 1786)—and the upper clergy, who lived like princes, moving from one rich benefice to another. An attempt to tap the wealth of those on top might well receive support from the public.[1]

Loménie de Brienne, in his dual capacity as principal minister and archbishop of Sens, understood better than anyone the potential for raising revenue from the church. He called a special General Assembly of the Clergy to come to the aid of the state in May 1788. General Assemblies normally met every five years. Their delegates, elected through diocesan gatherings, were dominated by the most powerful prelates. After discussing church business and negotiating behind closed doors with agents of the government, they normally voted "free gifts" (*dons gratuits*), which occasionally were considerable—as in 1780, when the General Assembly granted 30 million livres for help in the American war. In return, the government agreed to accept certain demands—often measures to suppress heresy, such as confiscation of books by the *philosophes*. What, Parisians wondered, would the General Assembly demand from Brienne, and what would he extract from it?

The sixty-four delegates, in splendid robes of red and black with staffs and mitres and other accoutrements, processed into the Couvent des Grands Augustins for the high mass that opened their deliberations on May 8. Located on the Left Bank of the Seine facing the Place Dauphine, the late-medieval abbey had often been the scene of important events, including the last meeting of the Estates General in 1614, an occasion that occupied the thoughts of public-minded Parisians as they began to contemplate the possibility of the Estates General gathering in 1789. The delegates deliberated in secret, debating propositions, taking votes, and adopting resolutions somewhat in the manner of the parlements. In fact, the fate of the parlements weighed heavily on the proceedings. The edicts that destroyed the independence of the judiciary were issued on the very day that the Assembly began to meet. Not that anyone expected it to take sides in the political crisis. Although, as required, its delegates included members from the lower clergy, it was controlled by the wealthiest and most privileged dignitaries of the Gallican Church, and they were not likely to support popular agitation. Hardy listed all of them with their titles in his journal, and at the end he observed that most of the prelates had held two or even three dioceses along with other offices, accumulating riches as they rose through the ecclesiastical hierarchy. The bishop of Valence, for example, received 14,000 L. a year from his see and 20,000 L. from two monasteries that paid him to do nothing as their *abbé commendataire* (absentee abbot).[2]

Because the transactions between the Assembly and the government took place behind closed doors, journalists pieced together stories as best they could from leaks. The Assembly's president, the archbishop of Narbonne, gave the first indication of its sentiments in a speech at a reception for the delegates in Versailles on May 12. Unfortunately, however, his remarks illustrated the difficulty of making sense of the situation, according to the Paris correspondent of the *Gazette de Leyde*.[3] Some detected in them hints of support for the ministry, and others heard nothing more than a determination to defend the clergy's privileges. That question dominated the first round of negotiations on May 19, when commissioners from the government arrived in the Couvent des Grands Augustins and announced what it wanted: 8 million livres to be paid over two years. While the Assembly considered its initial response, the commissioners waited in a separate room according to the established procedure. They waited and waited. After three hours they gave up and returned to Versailles. The session continued for seven hours. Evidently something had gone awry.

On the following day, the bishop of Blois rose to his feet and exhorted his colleagues to put aside their normal business. This was no time to talk about money, he insisted. "The entire kingdom is alarmed.... The constitution of France is threatened." Others echoed his remarks. The Cour plénière was illegal; the parlements should be recalled; the Estates General must be summoned. After another long debate, the Assembly voted to appoint a committee that would draft remonstrances to the Crown. Reports of the session created a sensation in Paris, where, according to Hardy, the bishop of Blois was celebrated as "the d'Éprémesnil of the clergy."[4] Whatever exactly had happened behind the closed doors, the Assembly apparently had decided to intervene in the political crisis.

The public got a clearer view of the Assembly's stance on June 15, when printed versions of the remonstrances began to circulate. Hardy got a copy of the second edition, a twenty-eight-page pamphlet, which was sold openly in the Palais-Royal for 15 sous. He said it had created a sensation among Parisians and rightly so, for it was one of the strongest statements ever produced by such a group of prelates (his sympathies lay with the lower clergy.)[5] The *Gazette de Leyde* reprinted the entire text, which occupied three issues. Although respectful in tone, the remonstrances made it clear that the payment of a *don gratuit* depended on the Crown's commitment to convoke the Estates General. Only such "national assemblies" had the authority to approve of taxes, the remonstrances argued. The parlements had spoken for the nation, and now that they were silenced, the only remaining body to express "the public outcry" was the clergy. If the Assembly failed in this duty, it would be condemned as criminal by the nation and posterity.[6]

The assembly submitted its remonstrances to the king on June 15. He replied two days later, enjoining the clergymen to restrict themselves to religious issues. That slap on the wrist did not stop the Assembly from holding more meetings and resolving to pass more remonstrances. However, rumors leaked that the archbishop of Narbonne, whose main concern was the privileges of the clergy, had secretly advised the king to send the delegates packing; and when they agreed on *itératives remontrances*, they shifted the emphasis from constitutional issues to the defense of their fiscal immunities. The ministry responded with assurances that the clergy's wealth would never be subjected to taxation and that the Crown would settle for a modest *don gratuit*. The negotiations dragged on for nearly three months. In a final audience at Versailles on July 27, Archbishop Narbonne presented the king with a record of the Assembly's deliberations, and the delegates seemed to be satisfied by the king's commitment, in principle, to convoke the Estates General. The exchanges between the Couvent des Grands Augustins and Versailles had come to resemble the sparring of the Parlement and the Crown: remonstrances were succeeded by a royal reply, by further remonstrances, by another reply, and then by negotiations that buried the conflict in a compromise.

Despite the early flurry of excitement, the General Assembly dissolved amid public indifference—or even hostility, because the main result was a successful defense of ecclesiastical privilege and a derisive *don gratuit* of 1.8 million livres to be collected over two years. As one *nouvelliste* observed, all the noise and fuss had only made the clergy appear "odious."[7]

35

The Provinces Take Fire

S OME PUT THE NUMBER killed at two hundred, some at six hundred. Later, when calm had returned, the best estimate was two or three. Whatever the count, all agreed that the catastrophe of June 7 in Grenoble was more than a riot. It was a revolt. Yet the disparities in the accounts of it exposed the gap that separated events in the provinces from the perception of them in Paris.[1]

According to reports that reached Parisian *nouvellistes*, the crisis began when the ministry attempted to impose the new judicial system on the provincial parlements. The Parlement of Grenoble took a strong stand against the edicts of May 8, and the ministry retaliated by *lettres de cachet* exiling the magistrates. Townspeople, enraged at the threat to the traditional autonomy of Dauphiné, swarmed to the magistrates' homes, compelling them to remain in the city and to continue their resistance. Troops under the Duc de Clermont Tonnerre, *commandant en chef du Dauphiné*, attempted to disperse the crowds. Fights broke out. Shots were fired. The tocsin signaling an emergency was rung from all the belfries of the city. Peasants heard the alarm and came running from the surrounding villages with whatever weapons they could find. Other peasants, who had come to sell produce in the market, joined the rioters. Although they failed to break into the Arsénal, they battled with the troops in the streets. Some of them climbed to the rooftops and hurled tiles down at the soldiers trapped below in the narrow streets—hence the "Day of Tiles," as the uprising came to be known. Other rioters stormed into the *commandant's* residence, where, according to some reports, he was having dinner with his family. They seized him, threatened to hang him from a chandelier, and then forced him to kneel and beg for "pardon from the people," while they brandished an axe over his head. According to other versions, he escaped, leaving the rioters to trash his house.

Eventually the soldiers withdrew to their barracks. The magistrates, who had gathered in the Palais de justice where the rioters demanded that they resume their functions, did not want to be identified with a popular insurrection. They quietly left the city during the next days and later issued an account of the events that minimized the violence and praised Clermont-Tonnere for his attempts to pacify the townspeople. The ministry, however, was furious at his failure to contain the uprising. It replaced him with the *maréchal* de Vaux and sent six regiments to reinforce the military's control of the city. A new gallows was erected to discourage further rioting, although the authorities decided not to use it later that month when faced with the threat of another uprising. The peasants who had returned to their villages reportedly said they were prepared to respond if they heard the tocsin ring again.

It had rung in the imaginations of the Parisians. Although they could not piece together a consistent account of the events, one thing was clear: the people—thousands of them, from all sectors of society—had risen in a violent insurrection against the armed forces of the Crown. The fragmentary character of the information as it arrived in letters from Grenoble left a great deal for the public imagination to mull over. Alerted by reports of special couriers arriving in Versailles, one after another, several on the same day, the Paris correspondent of the *Gazette de Leyde* realized that something momentous had occurred. When word leaked of a "revolt" in Grenoble, he wrote that the Parisians were alarmed. They imagined that the streets of Grenoble had filled with thousands of protestors, that hundreds had been killed, and that the violence was spreading to other provinces. He warned, however, that early reports were easily exaggerated. Four days later, after comparing different accounts, he reduced the estimate of casualties to a maximum of three killed and sixteen wounded, and four days after that he wrote that calm had been restored. Hardy, more susceptible to alarm, reported on June 16 that the supposedly authoritative account of the events, which was published by the magistrates of Grenoble and was being distributed in Paris for 4 sous a copy, probably *underestimated* the gravity of the situation, because the *parlementaires* wanted to avoid incriminating themselves and provoking sterner measures from Versailles. What was the truth? The only certainty seemed to be the threat of violence everywhere, especially in cities with parlements.

Letters from Rennes arrived at the same time as those from Grenoble and described an equally explosive situation.[2] After being forced to register the edicts of May 8 and to surrender the local Palais de justice to troops, a group of parlementary magistrates issued a defiant proclamation. The ministry retaliated with *lettres de cachet*, ordering them into exile. On June 3, the magistrates prepared to resist at a meeting in the town house of their *premier président*. All the shops were closed. Crowds gathered in the public squares. The *commandant* of Brittany, the Comte de Thiard, sent troops to surround the meeting and enforce the *lettres de cachet*. Soon, however, the soldiers themselves were surrounded by angry townspeople along with five hundred noblemen, ready for battle. Bloodshed was narrowly avoided by long negotiations, which led to the withdrawal of the soldiers and the departure of the *parlementaires* to their country residences. But it was a close call. The *commandant*, who had not dared to venture into the streets without an armed guard of fifty soldiers, ordered reinforcements and munitions from four other cities, and the ministry dispatched 12,000 troops to help maintain order. When the first 3,000 arrived, the townspeople refused to provide them with lodging, forcing them to sleep on straw in churches. Young men took control of the streets by organizing patrols. A crowd hanged an effigy of Thiard in a rowdy demonstration. Violence threatened to break out at any moment.

It never did, mainly because of skillful maneuvering in the negotiations by Thiard and a shift in tactics by the Bretons, who attempted to win the king to their cause by sending deputations to Versailles. Although Brittany's provincial estates were not in session, an executive body (the Commission intermédiaire des États de Bretagne) issued statements in its name, and groups of nobles assembled to pass resolutions and dispatch deputations. The message of the protests was the same as in the proclamations from Grenoble and other parlementary cities: Citizens in the provinces would not surrender to oppression from the central government;

their cause was the same as that of patriots everywhere in the kingdom—
a struggle of liberty against despotism. Far from insisting on the relatively
light load of taxation and other privileges they enjoyed, they spoke out as
citizens devoted to the nation. They demanded the calling of the Estates
General and the dismissal of the ministers in Versailles.

After the reports arrived in Paris, they were copied out, circulated,
and amplified. The Parisian correspondent of the *Gazette de Leyde* wrote
that the confrontation in Rennes had escalated into street warfare, causing several deaths. Hardy received reports that three hundred had been
killed, that the *commandant* had barely escaped lynching, and that Brittany had declared itself independent of France.[3] Letters from other cities reinforced a growing sense of catastrophe. On June 21, Hardy noted
accounts of angry crowds and incidents in Dijon, Aix, Toulouse, and Lyon
as well as Grenoble and Rennes. *Nouvellistes* filled their newsheets with
alarming information. The Parlement of Rouen had issued a defiant declaration. The common people in Toulouse were removing cobblestones to
build barricades. A riot in Dijon had been violently suppressed, leaving a
woman badly injured from a blow of a sabre. Riots in Pau had supported
the determination of the parlement to defy the government. As letter
after letter arrived with alarming news from Burgundy, Franche-Comté,
Languedoc, Guienne, Béarn, Brittany, and Dauphiné, a *nouvelliste* concluded that the entire kingdom could be swept up in a wave of rebellion.[4]
These views were not confined to newsmongers and gossips keen on sensa-
tionalism. The Marquis de Bombelles, a veteran diplomat residing in Versailles, wrote in his diary on June 21 that the king had been informed that
a wildfire had spread "to all corners of the kingdom."[5]

The most violent events took place in outlying provinces, the *pays
d'états*, which enjoyed particular privileges, and they were often led by
nobles, especially in Brittany. The *gentilshommes* of Rennes held meetings,
passed resolutions, and sent deputations to Versailles, hoping to present
their case directly to the king, for they refused to meet with the ministers
whom they declared guilty of abusing power. "Resistance to the despotism of the ministers" was their fundamental goal.[6] None of their protests
mentioned the privileges of the nobility. Instead they stressed "public liberty" and the common interests of the nation.[7] A deputation of "twelve
Breton *gentilshommes*" arrived in Paris early in July and attempted for

three weeks to gain access to the king. They got nowhere, although they won widespread sympathy among the Parisians.

Back in Rennes, the common people vented their hostility to the government by insulting the *intendant* whenever he appeared in public, although he was always surrounded by a guard. When some officials began to post a governmental decree condemning the provincial protests, crowds threw them off their ladders and burned all the copies of the decree in front of the *intendant's* residence. A day later, some commoners and peasants tried to storm the residence, and the *intendant*, threatened with assassination, fled from the city. The government then sent 1,200 more troops to restore order. It also decided to quelch the agitation of the Breton deputies in Paris. The "twelve *gentilshommes*" invited sixty fellow Bretons and some prominent public figures, including Lafayette, to a meeting on July 18. On the following night, a detachment of police took the Bretons off to the Bastille. The patriots in Brittany had prepared for this eventuality by choosing twenty-four substitute deputies—and forty-eight more in case the substitutes were imprisoned. In Paris, the *embastillement* of the deputies made them appear as victims and heroes. The government punished their supporters—Lafayette and the other dignitaries—by depriving them of honorific offices at the court. By employing the most hated modes of repression—the nighttime police raid, the *lettres de cachet*, the Bastille—the ministers reinforced the view that the resistance of the provinces was crucial for the liberation of the nation as a whole.[8]

The final phase of the events in Dauphiné, as they were reported in Paris, confirmed this view. There, too, assemblies of "*gentilshommes*" vowed to defend the province's liberty, and they were supported by armed groups of bourgeois and peasants. More blood was shed (some extravagant reports mentioned 2,000 dead) in late June when a crowd rioted in Grenoble to prevent the authorities from executing prisoners they had taken during the uprising of June 7.[9] The king issued a pardon, and *maréchal* Devaux, who had taken command of the 30,000 troops stationed in the city, restored order and favored peaceful measures. Although he had forbidden the provincial estates from holding meetings, he did nothing to oppose them when they assembled on their own authority in Vizilles, twelve miles outside Grenoble, on July 21. That meeting was soon celebrated as an indication of the direction events could take if the entire

nation met in the Estates General. The Third Estate had as many deputies as the first two combined, and the deputies met together as one body,
voting as individuals (by head) rather than by estate. Moreover, the resolution they adopted demonstrated that the Dauphinois were committed
to a national agenda. It denounced ministerial despotism in the strongest terms, asserted that only the nation assembled in the Estates General could consent to taxes, and grounded that assertion in language that
could have come directly out of Rousseau's *Social Contract*: "Law must be
the expression of the general will."[10]

The Vizille manifesto was but one of the many protests that poured out
of the provinces. They arrived in the form of letters, occasionally as oral
reports, and often as declarations by the parlements. Parisian *nouvellistes*
sifted through them, selected some items, omitted others, and reworked
them in their manuscript bulletins. Hardy's journal, for all its peculiari-
ties, exemplified the selection process. Scrupulously, laboriously, day after
day, Hardy copied parlementary remonstrances and proclamations, many
of them several pages long, into his journal. He entered them as soon as
they arrived in the mail or when they were passed on by others, who were
equally attentive to events and also made copies. "Everyone," he noted on
June 3, had made a copy of the Parlement of Besançon's "famous decree"
of May 26. Of course, "everyone" to him meant the sophisticated elite
that followed the news carefully. Yet printed versions of the documents
reached a broader public, usually in the form of short pamphlets that cost
about 6 sous. The same material circulated still more widely in newspapers
like the *Gazette de Leyde*, which published extracts and sometimes the full
texts of remonstrances.

None of this information came without spin. Although the *Correspondance secrète*, which was hostile to the government, had space only for a
brief summary of the Rouen Parlement's defiant proclamation of June 25,
it made the message of the "terrible edict" clear: the Parlement denounced
the ministers as "traitors to the fatherland." The *Gazette de Leyde*, which
tended to favor the government, published a slightly longer report on the
proclamation, noting, without mentioning the ministers, that the parlement attributed the treason preemptively to any magistrate who would
take up a seat in the new courts. Hardy, who detested the government,
copied the entire document, which declared both the ministers and the

potential magistrates guilty of treason and explicitly denounced Lamoignon, noting that he had contradicted the patriotic stance he had taken against the Maupeou coup in 1771.[11]

By choosing which documents to reproduce and which parts of them to emphasize, the *nouvellistes* conveyed the impression of a national uprising. When they reported events, they dwelt on dramatic details—bayonets brandished, the tocsin rung, the axe held over the head of the *commandant* in Grenoble. They did not suggest that the revolt had a social dimension. Peasants and commoners protested alongside *gentilshommes* in their narratives, and all citizens recognized the common enemy in Versailles. Not that they had a clear view of events. The *Gazette de Leyde* lamented that the repressive measures came so thick and fast, along with contradictory rumors, that no one knew what to expect.[12] The confusion was compounded by a deluge of pamphlets, according to the author of the *Correspondance littéraire secrète*, yet he had no difficulty spotting and deploring propaganda put out by the government[13]—nor did the author of a similar newssheet, who thought that the government's propaganda offensive would backfire.[14] Hardy had the same opinion and noted with disgust the pamphlets that defended the government's line. As an example, he singled out *Avis au peuple sur ses vrais intérêts*, a pamphlet distributed by the government.[15] It argued that the true interest of the common people lay with the ministers' program, whereas the parlements were defending the privileged orders.

Judging from contemporary reports, that argument did not stick. In fact, some "patriots" claimed that the government's coup against the parlements would actually reinforce the privileges of the nobility and the clergy.[16] No one contested the fact that the parlementary magistrates belonged to the highly privileged nobility of the robe. Instead of defending privileges, however, they cast themselves as patriots, who protected the nation against the arbitrary power of the ministers. In earlier conflicts with the Crown, as we have seen, the parlements had claimed to represent the nation by virtue of the authority they pretended to have inherited from the original assemblies of Franks. In their remonstrances and proclamations of 1788, the *parlementaires* abandoned that historical argument. Only the Estates General, they insisted, could speak for the nation and sanction laws proposed by the Crown, and the role of the parlements was merely to defend the nation by parrying the thrusts of despotism.[17]

Sensing its vulnerability to this attack, the government forbade the publication of all parlementary protests in an edict of May 20. It justified its action by listing the arguments of the parlements and trying to refute them, one after the other. There were eleven, each presented rhetorically with the phrase "comme si." For example, the edict said that the *parlementaires* had declared the ministers traitors to the fatherland *as if* they could speak in the name of the fatherland, and it said they had accused the ministers of transforming the monarchy into a despotism *as if* the monarch were capable of such an abuse. Posted on walls and hawked in the streets, the edict publicized the very arguments it meant to combat. Parisians mocked it as "the eleven Comme Si," and there was a brief fashion among well-dressed ladies of "bonnets Comme Si."[18]

Although no one could declare victory by the end of the summer, everything suggests that the government lost its attempt to control the general understanding of events. Many things combined to shape the public's perception, including even the fashion for bonnets. The texts of the remonstrances and other protests certainly had persuasive power. The way they were selected, parsed, and paraphrased by journalists magnified their effect. And finally, there was the impact of the events themselves, not in the form of isolated, rock-hard facts but understood as installments in a story that seemed to be pointed toward the collapse of power in Versailles and a shift to a new order that would emerge from the deliberations of the Estates General—when and if they were to meet.

36

Bayonets in the Streets

"**B**AYONETS INSTEAD OF BREAD"—that remark, scribbled in a manuscript gazette, summed up the mood of Paris during the summer of 1788.[1] Bayonets could be seen every day in the streets of Paris. After the "siege" of the Palais de justice, the government relied on regiments of soldiers (the Gardes Françaises and Gardes Suisses), not merely the forces of the police (the *guet à pied* and the *guet à cheval*) to put down protests and riots. The soldiers patrolled with their bayonets fixed—that is, primed to attack. Twenty-three inches long with a sharp blade and a triangular-shaped cross section, the bayonet extended a rifle's reach so far as to easily impale an opponent or, with a twist of the wrist, inflict a wound that would resist healing. Nothing caused more panic in a battle than a bayonet charge. Nothing stirred more fear and loathing among Parisians than the sight of bayonets in familiar places—before the Palais de justice, at the Châtelet, along the quais, in marketplaces.

Bayonets belonged to the symbolic landscape that filled reports in *nouvelles à la main*, journals, and letters. "The bayonet at the end of the musket," was the government's argument, Nicolas Ruault wrote to his brother.[2] Jacques Mallet du Pan expressed indignation in his diary at "bayonets overturning in one day bodies that have existed for centuries."[3] The authorities controlled Paris by "relying on bayonets," according to Hardy.[4] Yet the bayonets were more than a metonym for despotism, because the soldiers actually brandished them to keep order in the streets, and the streets constantly threatened to explode in violence.

Most of the incidents were mild, at least in comparison with the most violent uprisings in the provinces, but the atmosphere was tense. The lawyers went on strike, so the suspension of justice extended from the Parlement and the other high courts (the Chambre des comptes, Cour des aides, and Cour des monnaies) to the Châtelet and various inferior courts. Hundreds of unemployed law clerks, bailiffs, and minor officials milled around the Place Dauphine and other public spaces in the center of the city, taunting the troops, who continued to surround the Palais de justice and to patrol the nearby streets. Captain d'Agoult, the commander of the "siege," became the primary object of the public hostility, because he directed the patrols. Parisians referred to him as *gadoue* (excrement used as manure). On May 8 a group of youths spotted him walking unaccompanied across the Pont Neuf. They called out "get the cat," a signal to rally, and chased him with sticks, determined to pummel him to death and throw him in the Seine. He saved himself by ducking into a jeweller's shop, and the crowd was dispersed by the mounted police commanded by the *chevalier* Dubois, another officer reviled by the common people. At a demonstration a few days later, the clerks of the *basoche* burned one of the edicts aimed at the Parlement. Although alarmed by the seditious character of this incident, the gazetteer who reported it noted, "It's with bayonets that they promulgate laws intended, they say, to make the nation happy!"[5] Another *nouvelliste*, who favored the government, reacted in the same way while reporting on the anger in the streets: "The Châtelet is still surrounded by the Gardes Suisses and Gardes Françaises; the soldiers are even stationed in the court rooms. They dispense justice there from the end of a musket."[6]

The indignation took the form of verbal exchanges, caricatures, graffiti, and posters, some tinged with black humor. According to a popular joke, Brienne had arranged the marriage of "Monsieur Deficit" with "Madame Cour Plénière," who was the daughter of "Monseigneur Despotism," but the wedding had to be called off because it was incestuous—and furthermore, "Monsieur Deficit is monstruous, and Madame la Cour Plénière is deformed."[7] Journalists and pamphleteers seized on a contradiction implicit in the coup of May 8, because Lamoignon, as a magistrate in the Parlement of Paris, had led the opposition to Maupeou's coup in 1771. Now he was adopting Maupeou's measures in order to destroy the Parlement. Copies of a letter Lamoignon had supposedly written in 1771 circulated widely and were cited as damning evidence: he had been a patriot then; he was a tyrant today. The repression of 1788 seemed to be a replay of the tyranny of 1771 but worse, because it now involved military force deployed on a large scale.[8]

By May 19, the number of troops surrounding the Palais de justice had been doubled, and shelters for them had been erected in nearby streets, suggesting that the military occupation of the city center could last for a long time. Despite the armed guard, someone managed to paste a poster on the door of the Palais: "Palais for sale, magistrates for rent, ministers for being hanged, crown for being given away."[9] Copies of it circulated from hand to hand, while seditious talk spread by word of mouth. On May 26, d'Agoult, still on duty as commander of the Gardes Françaises, was taunted by a crowd, which threatened violence by again shouting, "get the cat." After calling for reinforcements, he managed to restore order, but he remained such a target of the public's anger that the authorities transferred him to another command. A riot broke out, nonetheless, on May 30. At a crucial moment, the Gardes were ordered to raise their rifles to their cheeks and prepare to fire. The crowd then dispersed, except for one woman, who lifted her skirts and exposed her bottom to the troops.[10]

The protests spread to the Châtelet on the Right Bank, where groups gathered to support the lawyers' strike. On June 3, when one attorney arrived in his formal attire as if he meant to argue a case, the crowd tore off his wig and gown, and it applauded an orator who advocated the halt of all litigation with such vehemence that Hardy predicted the inevitable response: more "bayonets."[11] Sure enough, three days later several hundred protestors jeered at a detachment of Gardes, a drummer sounded the alarm, and reinforcements, "bayonets at the end of their muskets," broke up the demonstration, which could easily have gotten out of hand, since some had talked of burning down the Palais de justice. Other incidents followed: a riot near the market of les Halles put down by three brigades of mounted police; a violent demonstration against the arrest of a clerk who had spoken out against the ministers; and a near riot of a crowd that had gathered around a street orator who defied some nearby soldiers by reading out antigovernment tracts. Hardy, who reported the disturbances, feared that an "explosion of the people" could break out at any moment.[12]

Hardy's alarm may have been exaggerated, because the agitation did not extend far beyond the city center. Yet a sense of outrage and indignation began to spread throughout the city. Aside from the common grumbling about abuses of power—*mauvais propos* and *bruits publics*—it had a theatrical character, which was often accompanied by violence. As explained earlier, theater audiences passed judgment on plays by noisy demonstrations, especially in the pit (*parterre*) of the Comédie française and the Comédie italienne, where performances were interrupted by catcalls and brawling. Companies of soldiers had been stationed inside both playhouses since 1751. They often intervened to repress violence—notably on December 26, when fifty troops put down a riot in the pit of the Comédie italienne. The pit exercised power. By applauding or hooting, it determined the success and failure of plays. Just as actors appealed to the pit, street-corner orators whipped up bystanders. Speeches in courts frequently sounded like harangues on the stage, and theaters served as a setting, both literal and figurative, for antigovernment protests.

A street poster made use of the theatrical idiom by announcing "Tomorrow there will be a performance of 'M. Deficit, grand pensionary of France,' with the fiftieth performance of 'The *Lits de justice*,' a grand pantomime preceded by 'The Piss House or the Siege of the Palais.'"[13] A similar burlesque notice informed the public that another play, *La Cour plénière* by Brienne and Lamoignon, would be canceled because the actors had refused to perform their parts and the pit threatened to revolt.[14] On May 12, the pit of the Comédie française went wild after an actor pronounced this verse from *Orphanis*, a tragedy by Adrien Michel Hyacinthe Blin de Sainmore:

Le dessein du tyran n'est que trop avéré.	*The tyrant's intentions are blatantly clear.*
Regardez ce palais de gardes entourés.	*Look at this palace surrounded by guards.*
De projets destructeurs ses ministres complices	*Ministers complicit in destructive projects*
Sèment partout l'exil, la terreur, les supplices.	*Foment exile, terror, and torture.*

Nothing could have fit current circumstances better. "Encore! Encore!" shouted the spectators. The actor repeated the lines amidst great excitement, and after the performance, the police carried him off to the Bastille.[15] In the Comédie italienne, a large poster was attached to the queen's box: "Tremble, tyrants. Your reign will soon end." Although removed, it left a visible mark, and soon all Paris was said to be talking about it.[16]

In reporting such incidents, the *nouvellistes* did not approve of them. Hardy deplored the incendiary notices, and the author of the *Correspondance secrète* remarked, "The time for songs and epigrams has passed. It has been succeeded by anguish and consternation."[17] The mood had shifted. Joking now seemed out of place; and placards adopted a declamatory tone. One posted on a parish church and other sites proclaimed: "The king is warned that a revolt has been planned for July 30. We are already fifteen thousand men, and perhaps at the end of the month we will be thirty thousand. The king had better increase the number of his troops."[18] It probably was not meant to be taken literally, no more than a harangue from a stage, yet the street and the stage seemed to be echoing one another.

Of all the pamphlets that passed through Hardy's hands, the one that moved him most was *Histoire du siège du palais par le capitaine d'Agoult*. It was an official report, produced by the Parlement of Paris, about the "siege" of the Palais de justice on May 5–6.[19] Although presented as a historical narrative within a legal protest, it read like a play and was written largely in dialogue. The entrances and exits of d'Agoult, the villain of the event, were noted as if they marked off scenes. The text described costumes (the dress of the magistrates and peers), props (the bayonets and axes carried by d'Agoult's troops), and stage directions (d'Agoult was said to have spoken "with a great deal of harshness"). The Grand'Chambre served as background scenery, which expressed the Parlement's significance as "the temple of justice, the sanctuary of the laws." By their speeches and gestures, the magistrates acted out the main theme of their remonstrances: the monarchy had degenerated into despotism.

When d'Agoult brandished his order for the arrest of d'Éprémesnil and Goislard, the magistrates were seized by "a shudder of horror." They responded, "We are all MM. Duval [d'Éprémesnil] and Goislard." At the climactic moment, d'Éprémesnil stepped to stage center and offered to sacrifice himself. "Forget me and devote yourselves to the cause of the public," he addressed his colleagues. "I recommend to you all that is dear to me. As to myself, I can swear that whatever fate is reserved for me, never will anything—promises, threats, the most horrible torments, death itself—make me abandon for an instant the principles of this body." As he was led off to prison, "the sacred vaults of the chamber resonated with sobbing and sounds of the most profound sadness. From the first to the last of the ministers of justice, young and old, peers, presidents, magistrates, bailiffs, ushers, everyone broke down in tears." Hardy responded in the same way while reading the text: "One could not read this work, as truthful as it is moving and well done, without shedding a torrent of tears. One felt moved simultaneously by sadness, indignation, and fear for the future."[20]

Melodrama requires villains. D'Agoult, an obscure officer unknown to the public before May 1788, appeared everywhere in the protests as the embodiment of villainy. One pamphlet mocked him for his prowess in arresting two unarmed magistrates with a force of 1,500 men.[21] Another facetiously announced a public subscription for a monument to celebrate his heroism. It would show him storming the Palais at the head of his troops and subduing the Parlement, each scene to be set off by a frame decorated with miniature bayonets.[22] In commanding the "siege," however, he was merely executing orders, which came from the ultimate source of the public's discontent: Brienne and Lamoignon, the two ministers who had planned the coup and were directing the repression of the protests. They came to personify the concept of despotism. In fact, they made such excellent villains in the public imagination that they were cast as antiheroes in an actual play, *La Cour plénière, héroi-tragi-comédie*, which reads like a sequel to *Histoire du siège du Palais*.

A preface to *La Cour plénière* says that it was performed in a château near Versailles on July 14, 1788. It may well have been staged or read aloud on other occasions, and its text circulated along with all the other protest literature during the summer of 1788. The printed version, which did not come out until September 9, sold very well.[23] It went through several editions, which varied in price from 24 L., when copies were hardest to procure (the police seized seven hundred in a raid on a bindery), to 3 L., when it was widely available. By the time Hardy got his hands on a copy, a new title page proclaimed that it was printed "in the shop of the Widow Liberty at the sign of The Revolution." (It also inspired a sequel, *Le Lever de*

Bâville, drame héroique en trois actes, pour servir de suite à la Cour plénière, which had a sardonic dedication to d'Agoult.)[24]

The play is set in Versailles. In act I, Brienne and Lamoignon discuss their plans to crush the Parlement and seize all power, while keeping the king—who desires nothing more than the good of his people—in the dark. Brienne is devious and scheming, Lamoignon impetuous and violent. Informed that d'Éprémesnil has escaped from the police agent they had sent to arrest him and that he had taken refuge in the Palais de justice, they order d'Agoult to storm the Parlement. They do not worry about provoking an uprising by Parisians: "When one disposes of two hundred thousand soldiers and fifty public executioners, one does not fear sedition," Lamoignon remarks.

Act II takes place fifteen days later. D'Éprémesnil has been confined to a miserable prison on the Île Sainte-Marguerite. The provinces are in open revolt, and the king (who never appears on the scene) remains unaware of the violence committed in his name. Lamoignon delivers a soliloquy: "Ambition! Vengeance! . . ." Then he and Brienne plan to send twenty regiments to suppress the revolts in the provinces. "Parbleu! The ministers of Louis XIV managed to make war against all of Europe and we have only France to combat." While scheming to annihilate all opposition, Lamoignon is visited by the old chancellor Maupeou, who comes to congratulate him for having adopted a more oppressive version of the same measures that had been used to crush patriots in 1771.

Act III places the dénouement in an imagined future. Deputies from the provinces have arrived in the royal antechamber to appeal directly to the king. Brienne and Lamoignon try to fend them off, but Breteuil, who is presented as a bluff but honest soldier-minister, intervenes in their favor. While Breteuil exits to present their case to Louis XVI, the head of a deputation from Brittany gives the two evil ministers a tongue-lashing. Then word arrives that the king has seen the light. The deputies cry, "Great God! The moment of vengeance has arrived." Both ministers are dismissed and exiled. Brienne goes off muttering about the cash he still hopes to extort from his clerical holdings, but Lamoignon flies into a rage, swoons, and wakes up ranting. Seized by "a deadly shudder," he gulps, "I . . . Ah! Ah! Ah! . . ." and dies as the curtain closes.

It is sheer melodrama, the acting out of the general theme in all the

antigovernment protests. Of course, sophisticated readers would have recognised the contrived nature of the plot. Yet when the play was performed,
according to its preface, the audience reacted as if it represented reality:

> The acting was so true, the illusion so complete, that at different
> moments the spectators, forgetting that they were at a play and by an
> error that demonstrated its effectiveness, hooted at the actors playing
> Brienne and Lamoignon, thinking they were jeering at the actual per-
> sons. Then, waking up as if from a dream, they stared at one another,
> laughed at their error, and made the room resonate with applause.

We cannot know whether this actually happened, but the account
certainly conforms to the nature of happenings that occurred throughout 1788. Whether listening to street orators or incinerating government
decrees, Parisians acted out the conviction that the monarchy had degenerated into a despotism—ministerial despotism, not the abuse of power
by the king. They cast Brienne and Lamoignon as the supreme villains of
a drama, just as they had cast ministers in the same role during earlier crises, in 1771 and 1787. The theatricality that pervaded public life directed
passions—anger, indignation, a desire for vengeance—against concrete
targets, not tyranny in the abstract but the tyrants in Versailles.

37

Hailstones Big as Eggs

THEY HIT AT 7 o'clock in the morning of July 13, hit hard, hail-stones big as eggs. According to some reports, they were as big as bottles—chunks of ice, "as hard as diamonds," weighing a pound and a half. A hailstone that was weighed in one village outside Paris came to eight pounds; one weighed in another village came to ten. The stones broke windows, smashed tiles on roofs, razed fields, destroyed vineyards, stripped bare fruit trees, struck horses dead, and even killed some peasants who were preparing to harvest what had promised to be an excellent crop of wheat. The "hurricane," as some called it, devastated crops in a vast area around Paris.[1]

The archbishop of Paris launched a charity drive to rescue the peasants who had lost their livelihoods in seventy parishes of his see. The king contributed 1,200,000 L., although the royal treasury was nearly empty. A lottery was organized to produce a relief fund of 12 million livres; and Parisians feared the worst was yet to come, because Paris bakeries depended heavily on the grain produced in the fields of the surrounding region. A steep increase in the price of bread seemed likely to spread hunger among the common people, and the hungry often rose in riots. Memories of the Flour War of 1775 were still alive in 1788.

The price of the standard, four-pound loaf of bread, normally about 8 sous, rose to 9 sous by the end of July and 9 sous 6 deniers on August 18, when rumors circulated about an incipient riot in the faubourg Saint-

Antoine, one of the most explosive parts of Paris. The authorities responded by doubling the size of the patrols inside the city and ordering new regiments to maintain order in areas outside it. Parisians grumbled about the Eden Treaty, signed between France and Britain on September 26, 1786, which permitted the export of grain. They complained about economic conditions in general. Twenty thousand workers were said to be unemployed in the faubourg Saint-Antoine in August, when the disaster of the harvest began to be felt in the price of bread.[2]

Hardy, who had been traumatized by the Flour War, noted every fluctuation of the price. On August 20 when he went to buy bread from his baker, he learned that the cost of the four-pound loaf had risen to 10 sous and was expected to go higher. An uprising of the *menu peuple*, he feared, might very well follow. Troops, with bayonets attached to their muskets, were deployed in all the city's marketplaces. On September 2, the price reached 10 sous 6 deniers. The danger of rioting increased proportionately, and still more troops were stationed in the markets. On September 7 the price reached 11 sous, touching off rumors about a future revolt among the poor in the faubourgs Saint-Antoine and Saint-Marcel. The government ordered cavalry regiments to help the Garde de Paris in maintaining order. Some of the tension was relieved on September 14, when word spread that Lamoignon had been dismissed, and workers from the faubourgs joined in the general rejoicing. But, as we will see, the celebrations became violent. Repression turned the public's anger against the Garde as well as the supposed speculators who hoarded bread in order to profit from the price increases. An edict of September 19, which prohibited the export of grain, did little to diffuse the resentment. Placards appeared in the faubourg Saint-Antoine and the faubourg Saint-Marcel warning of a "revolt" that would erupt on September 23 or 24. Nothing happened, although Hardy continued to worry about "the spirit of insubordination, rioting, and revolt."[3]

The rise in the price of bread, though an unavoidable result of the hailstorm, was connected to the political crisis in the minds of the Parisians. They had deplored the export of grain, which was favored by the liberal trade policy of Brienne, and they welcomed Necker's appointment as general director of finances on August 25, because he was known to be an opponent of the free-trade policies that had led to the grain shortage and Flour War. The common people counted on him to check the rise in bread prices, Hardy observed. Yet Necker might be overthrown as a result of machinations in Versailles, and his fall would probably provoke an uprising of the poor. Although Necker's hold on power seemed to be secure by the end of October, it did not prevent the price of bread from spiraling upward. On November 8 the four-pound loaf cost 12 sous. On November 25 it came to 12 sous 6 deniers. Hardy's baker said that no profit was to be had even at such a steep price. Forty of his fellow bakers had closed their shops. A woman from the lower classes who happened to be in the bakery at that time remarked angrily that bread at the current price meant starvation for the poor. They should march on Versailles, she said, and burn the palace down.[4]

38

The Ministers Are Roasted

WAS THE HAILSTORM a sign of divine anger? A century earlier that conclusion would have been obvious. Pierre Bayle's *Pensées sur la comète* (1682–1683) was an early attempt to persuade the public that natural phenomena had natural causes, despite the general view that occurrences like comets portended punishment from God. By 1788, when man had tamed lightning, flown through the air, and demonstrated that air itself was a compound of chemicals, Bayle's message had been assimilated. No clergyman (at least none on record) thundered from the pulpit that the hail was an icy form of brimstone, visited on the wicked to punish them for their sins and sent as a warning that greater disasters would rain down if the French did not mend their ways. Even the archbishop of Paris, when he announced the lottery to relieve the stricken, did not acknowledge "the anger of the All Power," according to a few of his old-fashioned parishioners.[1]

Parisians had come around to the view that most disasters were man-made, except for aberrations like the hailstorm; and when disasters occurred, they knew where to place the blame—on Versailles. Not on the king, however. Respect for Louis XVI had sunk to a low point,[2] yet according to the gazetteers, the public remained convinced that Louis desired nothing more than the welfare of his people and that their suffering was hidden from him by *les grands* in the court. Cabals in the court determined who would lead the government, and therefore the Parisians directed their anger at Versailles—that is, at the general system of power and, in particular, at the two ministers who monopolized power in the summer of 1788, Brienne and Lamoignon.

Not that Parisians had much information about who was plotting against whom in the world of *les grands*. Even a news-hungry observer like Hardy was reduced to conjectures. He noted rumors of plots against Brienne and Lamoignon and predicted their downfall a dozen times, only to conclude that nothing could be known for sure, and everything seemed ominous. *Nouvellistes* shared that view. "We live in consternation and alarm," one wrote.[3] While Versailles remained opaque, disasters were accumulating in plain sight. The government failed to install the new judicial system; the old courts ceased to function; lawyers continued on strike; and crimes went unpunished. The riots in Paris and the revolts in the provinces made some people imagine the possibility of a general insurrection. Some of the troops sent to suppress the violence declared that they would not fire on fellow citizens. Their duty, they said, was to defend the country against foreign enemies.[4]

And just when the soldiers were dispatched to Grenoble, Rennes, Rouen, Toulouse, Bordeaux, and Dijon, word arrived that they were urgently needed abroad. War threatened to break out in northern Europe, where France's enemies, Britain and Prussia, had enlisted its former ally, the Dutch Republic, in a coalition aimed against Russia and Austria. *Nouvellistes* speculated about plans to send an army of 60,000 men to reassert France's interests in the Low Countries and its support for Austria, but it was immediately apparent that the treasury could not bear the strain. France stood by helplessly in August as the Triple Alliance was formed and prepared for war. Although an open conflict was ultimately avoided, France remained on the sidelines, and its inability to intervene in the crisis consummated its humiliation as a great power.[5]

By that time, however, the Parisians who paid attention to foreign affairs worried more about the domestic economy than national prestige. The deficit in the state's finances had driven all the political conflicts since the Assembly of Notables met in February 1787, and it kept growing. Tax revenue declined. Loans were not subscribed. Notes on the royal treasury could not be negotiated on the Bourse, and the government's plan to redress its finances by means of the new land tax, the *subvention territori-*

ale, foundered in the face of opposition from the provinces. Maupeou and Terray had been able to ride out the crisis at the end of Louis XV's reign because they could rely on a minimal income stream from taxes. Brienne and Lamoignon could not fall back on a comparable source of revenue. They brought the state to the brink of bankruptcy.

On August 18, peddlers distributed a new edict decreed two days earlier by the Conseil du Roi.[6] Instead of hawking it openly, they kept their voices at a low pitch and moved with caution through the streets because they worried about being attacked as the bearers of bad news. The news was terrible, at least for Parisians who put their savings into annuities (*rentes viagères* and *rentes perpétuelles*), which provided them with a fixed income, paid in cash. The government decreed that two-fifths of most *rentes* (those representing an investment of more than 1,200 L.) would be paid in notes on the royal treasury. As those notes could only be exchanged for cash at an unfavorable discount from the Caisse d'escompte, the central bank in the rue Vivienne, a great many citizens were suddenly deprived of substantial income.[7] The state had declared partial bankruptcy.

In a long preface to the edict, the government explained that there was no other way to cover the gap between its revenue and expenses. Its attempt to float a graduated loan for 90 million livres had failed for lack of subscribers. Public confidence had collapsed, it admitted. But this measure, it claimed, was only a temporary expedient, which would provide relief until the Estates General met and took action to put the state's finances permanently on a firm basis.

Although no peddlers were assaulted, the edict produced outrage and panic. For three days and three nights, crowds converged on the Caisse d'escompte, trying desperately to cash notes for whatever they could get. Additional troops were summoned to restore order in the rue Vivienne. Even the king's guard in Versailles was reinforced because of the danger from the discontented. Far from being limited to *rentiers*, anxious talk about the partial bankruptcy spread everywhere in Paris, causing "universal consternation."[8] Rumors about the fall of the ministry increased every day and seemed more credible than ever. Finally, on August 25, Brienne— but not Lamoignon—was dismissed, and Necker, deemed to be the only one capable of restoring confidence in the credit of the state, was recalled as general director of finances.

As soon as word of Brienne's dismissal arrived on August 26, rejoicing erupted in the Place Dauphine, and the crowd burned an effigy of the fallen minister. On the next day, it paraded around the Place with a gigantic mannequin of Brienne, dressed in archbishop's robes. When it reached the Square du Vert-Galant, it forced the dummy Brienne to pay tribute on bended knee to the statue of Henri IV (the king idolized as the champion of the people). Back in the Place Dauphine, it condemned him to death by a burlesque edict; made him demand pardon to God, the king, and the nation; hoisted him high on a pole; and dropped him on an enormous bonfire. One of the demonstrators also read out an edict condemning Lamoignon to a similar fate. Firecrackers, rockets, and candles in all the windows of the Place Dauphine added to the festive air.[9]

On August 28, the Watch attempted to regain control of the Place Dauphine. Rioters from the neighborhood fought back late into the night, hurling stones and wielding clubs against sabers and bayonets. About fifty persons were injured and three soldiers were killed, according to Hardy. As fury spread against the Watch, Paris braced itself for large-scale street warfare on August 29. By nightfall, workers from the faubourg Saint-Antoine and the faubourg Saint-Marcel had joined the crowd in the Place. They tore down the recently built guardhouses, throwing the debris on a new bonfire, where a mannequin of Lamoignon was burned after being forced to beg forgiveness for its crimes. The rioters captured a few soldiers from the Watch, stripped them naked, and burned their uniforms on the fire. Fighting spread through several neighborhoods—around les Halles, Saint-Germain-des-Prés, and the Place Maubert. In the Place de Grève, the Watch opened fire on the crowd, killing three. Nearby, in the rue de la Mortellerie, the rioters beat two soldiers to death. The *Correspondance littéraire secrète* estimated the casualties at eighty wounded and twenty killed. Hardy merely registered his horror at the "open war" and his relief when reinforcements of 1,200 soldiers restored order on August 30.

The threat of another explosion did not dissipate, however. The price of bread continued to rise, the fate of the parlements remained uncertain, and Lamoignon clung to office, intent as ever to reconstruct the judiciary. Soldiers patrolled in groups of six, bayonets fixed. The size of the patrols was increased to twelve at the beginning of September, and cavalry regiments were dispatched to keep order in the faubourgs of Saint-Antoine and Saint-Marcel. Yet the common people continued to talk in the marketplaces of insurrection. Hopes for a solution to the crisis turned increasingly to a meeting of the Estates General. The government had promised to convoke a meeting in an edict of July 5, which the peddlers proclaimed loudly as a tiding of good news, but many Parisians dismissed it as an insincere attempt to pacify the public. On August 11, another edict, also hawked noisily, set May 1 as the date for the meeting to take place, and it also suspended plans to establish the Cour plénière. Yet as long as Lamoignon remained in office, rumors continued to circulate about his plots to destroy the parlements and perpetuate his hold on power. No one knew where power was really located in Versailles. On September 7, information leaked about a confrontation between Lamoignon and Necker at a meeting of the Conseil d'État. Although the public favored Necker, it could not shake off the fear that Lamoignon had prepared another "terrible coup."[10] Then at last, on September 14, word arrived that he had been dismissed.

Parisians reacted with an even greater explosion of joy and pent-up anger than after the dismissal of Brienne.[11] When the news arrived in the Palais-Royal, a hothead from the Café du caveau ran into the courtyard, jumped on a stool, and shouted to the onlookers, "Messieurs, that fucker Lamoignon has been dismissed." A clerk dashed into the Grand'Chambre of the Palais and belted out a solo Te Deum before the police arrived to drag him off. Groups of celebrators in the Place Dauphine shot off fireworks and required the residents to light up their windows with candles. On the next day they stopped all coaches crossing the Pont Neuf and required the passengers as well as the coachmen to doff their hats before the statue of Henri IV and cry out "Long live Henry IV, Go to hell, Lamoignon."

That night, a crowd paraded a large mannequin of Lamoignon dressed in a black robe, sash, neck bands, wig, and a square bonnet. After stopping regularly to force it to kneel and confess its crimes, the rioters staged a burlesque trial and pronounced a death sentence. Someone noticed a priest who was walking by and demanded that he take a final confession. In serious danger himself, the priest had the wit to turn an ear toward the mannequin's head and announce that it had so many sins to recount that the last rites would take all night. He was applauded and the dummy Lamoignon was pitched onto a giant *feu de joie*.

On the following day, youths continued to stop coaches before the statue of Henri IV while large groups gathered to witness the scene. Late that night an enormous crowd demonstrated joyfully around another straw-man Lamoignon in the Place de Grève. In the midst of the revelry, a tall man with a boy on his shoulders demanded silence. The boy then read out a placard: "A decree of the public judges and condemns the man called Lamoignon to do public penance, to have his fists cut off, and to be dragged through the gutter." The punishment was then executed on the mannequin.[12]

Soldiers from the Garde Française and the Watch stayed away from these demonstrations, trying to avoid a conflict of the kind that had occurred after the fall of Brienne. But on September 16 crowds carried two more mannequins of the dismissed ministers along with one of chevalier Dubois, the much-hated commander of the Watch, through the streets, staging the usual confessions. When they arrived at the town houses of the three, they attempted to set the mannequins on fire. At that point the soldiers of the Watch intervened, swinging their sabres. According to rumors, more than eighty protestors were killed or wounded, most of them near Dubois's residence in the rue Meslé by the Porte Saint-Martin, where the Watch staged an ambush. Thanks to reinforcements and extensive patrols, order was restored on September 18.

By then, the *émotion populaire* had died down. But the fate of France looked uncertain, the ministry had collapsed in ignomy, and the last attempt to raise taxes had demonstrated the impossibility of solving the financial crisis without transforming the state.

Necker to the Rescue

THE VILIFICATION OF Brienne and Lamoignon reinforced the appeal of Necker, who had cultivated an image that made him look like their opposite. He was not a courtier, not an aristocrat, neither of the sword nor the robe, not even French. He was Swiss—and, moreover, a Protestant. Protestants could arouse deep-seated hostility, of course. Although the wounds from the religious wars of the sixteenth century had mainly healed, most Parisians did not favor the edict of November 29, 1787, reluctantly registered by the Parlement, that gave non-Catholics minimal civic rights.[1] Yet Protestants had a reputation for integrity. Like Quakers and Americans, they lacked polish, but they worked hard and could be trusted. Those qualities were also thought to distinguish the Swiss. Parisians spoke admiringly of "helvetic openness," and they responded to a vogue for "helvétisme," which associated Switzerland's sublime mountains with the austere morals and republicanism popularized by Rousseau.[2] When the Paris correspondent of the *Gazette de Leyde* reported that Lamoignon was about to be dismissed, he wrote that, fortunately, "a man of upstanding character, of austere virtue" was waiting in the wings. That was Necker: "Public opinion, the assembled Nation, will be able to designate him."[3]

As we have seen, Necker cultivated this reputation in fashioning his public identity.[4] First in his *Compte rendu au Roi*, then in his polemics with Calonne, he had assumed the position of the honest outsider, answerable to public opinion and devoted to the welfare of the people, in contrast to the usual run of ministers, who rose to power by court intrigue. In *De l'administration des finances* (1784), he made a case for openness, exposing the vested interests hidden behind the secret operations of the state. Four years later, he published a sequel to his financial treatise in the unlikely form of a treatise on religion. Writing as "a citizen of France" (a citizen, not a subject), he argued in *De l'importance des idées religieuses* (1788) that no political system could sustain itself without a firm foundation of piety. He came to this conclusion, he explained, when, having been relieved from the burden of office and freed to reflect on the deepest truths, he had arrived at an appreciation of the religious ideas that linked mankind to "a Being that is powerful, infinite, the cause of everything, the universal motor of the universe." Lest that sound suspiciously Voltairean, he made it clear that, unlike some *philosophes*, he did not treat religious convictions as prejudices. He offered up a heartfelt prayer to the Supreme Being: "Oh unknown God... Sustain my determination." Readers might detect a whiff of Rousseauism in that language, but they would not suspect Necker of lacking piety.[5]

At the beginning of *De l'importance des idées religieuses*, Necker inserted a note saying that Calonne had just attacked him in a memoir, which he would refute as soon as possible. Calonne's *Réponse de M. de Calonne à l'écrit de M. Necker*, published in January 1788 in London where he lived in exile, was a full-scale assault on the *Compte rendu*. In 424 pages of texts and appendices, he contested every aspect of Necker's stewardship of the state's finances and came to the conclusion that he had announced to the Assembly of Notables: whereas Necker had claimed that there was a surplus of 10 million livres in 1781, there actually was a deficit of 46 million, and when further expenses were taken into account, the deficit amounted to 70 million. Moreover, the deficit was structural. Expenditure exceeded revenue going back to the reign of Louis XV. By 1787 it came to 115 million livres, and therefore Calonne could not be blamed for it. On the contrary, he had inherited the increased debt from the loans that Necker had used to finance the American war.

Despite the drubbing Calonne had received from pamphleteers after he fled France, his tract created a sensation, and many readers found it convincing. Others, however, dismissed it as an attempt, welcomed by the Brienne-Lamoignon government, to stanch the growing influence of Necker's partisans. The public—that is, the reading public and those who followed the affairs of state—seemed inclined to suspend judgment until Necker produced a rebuttal.[6] When at last it appeared under the title *Sur le Compte rendu au Roi en 1781. Nouveaux éclaircissements*, Necker was just about to reenter the government as general director of finances. It ran to 284 pages of esoteric detail, which, as he admitted, made difficult reading. Yet his basic argument was clear: he had trimmed expenditures and directed revenue in such a way as to leave the Crown in excellent fiscal health in 1781. If, as Calonne claimed, the government had run up a gigantic deficit by 1787, there must have been a great deal of mismanagement after Necker left the government. Fortunately, he argued, the *Compte rendu* had stripped away the secrecy that had kept the Crown's finances hidden, and he could make public enough information about the inner workings of the treasury to refute Calonne's argument point by point. The political arithmetic led to a happy ending, although it was left implicit. Having revealed the truth about financial administration, Necker could be trusted to take it over. He had the knowledge and, more important, the character to keep the government solvent until the Estates General met. Then the nation itself would assume responsibility for the state's finances and reorganize them as a core element in "a new order of things."[7]

What made this polemic so fascinating for the general public was not its substance—few people could follow it in detail—but its openness. Calonne published his tract as an appeal to the French nation. He agreed that the Crown's finances could no longer be kept secret, and tried to outdo Necker by presenting his *Réponse* as his own *Compte rendu*, more accurate and detailed than Necker's original. As a minister, he had respected public opinion, he claimed; and as an exile, he sought to win back its support, despite the attacks of libelers.[8] In his reply, Necker also invoked public opinion as a force that should determine the direction of affairs.[9] The public responded, as Hardy put it, by "devouring" the book. Although published at a huge pressrun of 20,000 copies, it was snapped up so quickly that some booksellers did not even have time to sew the gatherings together, and the publisher immediately began to prepare a new edition. Whether readers got through it all seems doubtful, because journalists and *nouvellistes* admitted they could not make sense of the baroque detail and statistics. Some, at least, remained unconvinced, but Necker's argument, as one reviewer remarked, left a general impression of honesty and virtue.[10] Riding on a tide of public enthusiasm, Necker came out on top of the debate. But it was the debate itself that mattered most. Two public figures, former directors of the royal treasury, hammered at one another in public, arguing opposite views of state affairs, openly, in print, and in enormous detail—nothing like it had ever taken place.

Openness had been crucial to Necker's success in floating loans while general director of finances from 1775 to 1781. They were built on "confidence," the public's faith that investments would be repaid at the promised rate—that is, in *rentes*, which by 1781 brought a return of 10 percent. The partial bankruptcy of August 16 damaged public trust so badly that the Brienne-Lamoignon government no longer had the option of raising loans. Far from being limited to the financiers of the rue Vivienne, the collapse of confidence was a matter of public opinion, and only Necker could restore it. He was, Hardy wrote, "the only man who at this moment, according to public opinion, can be the restorer of France."[11]

The appointment of Necker transformed the situation. When he assumed office, he found only 419,000 L. in the royal treasury, a derisory amount, according to press reports.[12] He revoked the edict of August 16 and declared that all notes on the royal treasury would be paid in cash. He had found sufficient revenue to finance government operations until the meeting of the Estates General, he declared. Once the representatives of the nation came together, they would determine a solution to the financial problem. Meanwhile, the public could be reassured that the direction of state affairs was in good hands. The payment of *rentes* did indeed resume. Calm returned to the Bourse. Taxes began to be paid as normal, even in the outlying provinces where the resistance to Brienne and Lamoignon had been most violent. Necker held his first public audience in Paris on October 10, and it was a triumph. Parisians from all sectors of society brought their problems to him, and he replied with courtesy and concern, striking a tone of Swiss openness.[13]

Despite this quick success, Necker had to overcome formidable difficulties. As explained in the last chapter, Lamoignon, backed by influential figures in the court, remained in office after the dismissal of Brienne on August 25, and he persevered with his determination to break the power of the parlements. Although the project for the Cour plénière had been shelved (it, too, was to be resolved by the Estates General), the government had not abandoned the general plan to reconstruct the judiciary. Rumors about a power struggle in Versailles circulated during the first two weeks of September. Parisians heard that a confrontation between Necker and Lamoignon took place at a meeting of the Conseil du Roi on September 3–4, but they did not know what to make of it. It seemed that Necker had prevailed, because he got the Conseil to approve an edict for the recall of the parlements. Yet Lamoignon remained in his position at the head of the judiciary. "Sinister rumors" raised fears of more catastrophes:[14] Necker was said to be ill; a new tax would be forced on the country; *rentes* payments would be reduced by one-third. The *lit de justice* that had been scheduled for the restoration of the parlements might turn into another coup, which would send the Parlement of Paris back into exile. Finally, however, at 5:00 p.m. on September 14, news arrived of Lamoignon's downfall, and, as we have seen, Paris erupted in joy.

Of course, the shift in power did not resolve the basic problems. All of them were left suspended, pending the meeting of the Estates General. The fate of the parlements, the payment of the deficit, and the future of the state's finances would not be settled until the deputies gathered on May 1, the date the king had finally set. Before then, however, a decision had to be reached about the most important problem of all, the nature of the Estates General itself.

40

The Cruelest Winter

IN NOVEMBER 1788, Parisians began to follow a new index to their misery. Having watched the price of bread increase from its normal level of 8 sous for the four-pound loaf to 12 sous 6 deniers, they also fixed their sight on the temperature: 7 degrees below freezing on November 26. Not that ordinary people had thermometers. They felt the cold in their bones, while the sophisticated consulted different kinds of devices, most of them calibrated to the Réaumur scale. In today's measures, minus 7 Ré (Réaumur) comes to 16 degrees Fahrenheit and to minus 8.75 Celsius.

There was also a heavy snowfall on November 26—an early start to winter. Reports on the temperature circulated in newspapers and by word of mouth. Hardy entered them nearly every day in his diary along with information on the price of bread and other necessities such as coal.[1] Paris was buried under a heavy snowfall on December 6–7, when the temperature sank to minus 10 Ré (9.5 Fahrenheit) and the price of bread rose to 13 sous 6 deniers. By then the Seine had frozen over. People crossed it on foot, although at first some fell through the ice and drowned. Frozen corpses were found in the streets. Several storehouses full of coal in the faubourg Saint Honoré caught on fire and burned for eight days, forcing up the cost of heating.

The price of all kinds of food in addition to bread increased drastically. A group of smugglers managed to drive a herd of sheep into Paris, where they could sell mutton at half the normal price (6 sous per pound instead of 12). Parisian butchers got the police to intervene, but a crowd drove the police agents away after a street battle. A few days later, the police arrested smugglers attempting to sell underpriced poultry. Soldiers were stationed in marketplaces to prevent rioting, and rumors circulated that three hundred bakeries had closed owing to the fear of violence as bread prices continued to escalate. Water mills along the Seine could not operate because the river remained frozen solid, cutting back on the supply of flour. It became impossible to wash laundry in the Seine and to fetch water from it. Although carts loaded with goods commonly crossed the river, a man leading a horse fell through the ice and disappeared on December 14.

Constant snow and a bitter north wind added to the misery. On December 15 thermometers registered minus 12 Ré (5 degrees Fahrenheit), and the price of bread had risen to 14 sous. At least 80,000 workers were unemployed, according to Hardy's estimate. The police hired some of them to clear snow from the streets at rates of 10 to 18 sous per day, although much of the city remained impassable to carriages and difficult to navigate by foot. Driven by hunger, the poor took to begging, and the beggars became aggressive. There were many reports of thefts and muggings. A favorite technique, according to one newssheet, involved a group: a mugger would fell a pedestrian and flee; then his companions would pretend to come to the victim's rescue and, while hovering over him, remove his purse. On December 16, the police arrested a gang of twenty-seven thieves in the center of the city at the rue de la Huchette. By this time, Parisians commonly said that the winter was the coldest that had ever occurred.

The snow kept falling, accumulating on roofs and clogging streets. Just before Christmas there were signs of a thaw, but on New Year's Eve the temperature fell to the lowest point ever recorded, according to scientists in the Observatoire who consulted a mercury thermometer: minus 18½ degrees Ré. (minus 9.6 Fahrenheit)—colder than the coldest days of the notorious winters of 1740 and 1709. Increasing numbers of half-dead, starving people were carried to the Hôtel-Dieu, which functioned more as a hospice for the dying than as a hospital and contained only 1,210 beds. Despite the cartloads of bodies, fifty to a cart, taken every night for burial in the unmarked ditches of the Cimetière de Clamart in the faubourg Saint-Marcel, the Hôtel-Dieu could no longer absorb any more of the poor at the end of the first week in 1789.

The temperature rose to zero Ré. (32 degrees Fahrenheit) on January 10. Although snow continued to fall, it melted rapidly, making the streets still nastier. The first rain since September poured down on January 18, when a thaw set in, but the price of bread, driven by the shortage of grain and flour, rose to 15 sous by February 4. The Parlement and police intervened to cap it at 14 sous 6 deniers, provoking a threat by bakers, who could not clear a profit at that rate, to close their shops. Detachments of the Watch (the *guet à pied* and the *guet à cheval*) were sent to keep order in marketplaces, because a popular revolt was expected to occur. According to one rumor, the royal princes were hoarding bread in order to provoke an uprising that would force Necker out of office. According to another, Necker himself was the hoarder, and he was supported by the king in the hope that they could exploit the rise in prices to rescue the state's finances. After noting the reports on conspiracies, political agitation, bread prices, and weather, Hardy concluded that a "horrible revolution" looked inevitable.[2] Yet Paris did not explode. Perhaps it was exhausted—and it was buried again on March 9 by another heavy snowfall, followed by still more on March 10, 11, 12, 13, 18, and 19. It was the longest, coldest, cruelist winter anyone had ever known.

PART SEVEN

The
Eruption of the Revolution,
1789

41

Summon the Nation

The Estates General must be summoned. Whatever their feelings about the rise and fall of ministers, Parisians agreed on that basic demand. The Parlement had called for the convocation of the Estates General in a declaration of July 6, 1787, and it had reiterated that demand several times as evidence of its commitment to the cause of the nation. Yet its exhortations lacked substance. They expressed a vague expectation, shared by the general public, that the assembled nation, whatever that meant, would bring the current conflicts to a happy conclusion, whatever it might be. Somehow, a new order of things would come into existence.

The public began to see the issues more clearly as the Parlement of Paris redefined its position during the spring of 1788. In its declaration of May 3, drafted by d'Éprémesnil, the Parlement redefined the kingdom's fundamental laws in a way that would virtually make France into a constitutional monarchy, and at the same time it renounced its claim to act as a surrogate for the Estates General by consenting to taxes. But it left hanging the question of how the Estates General would be composed, and that issue exposed it to an accusation raised by the government—namely (as explained in chapter 33) that the Parlement intended to establish an "aristocracy of magistrates" by dominating the new constitutional order.[1] That argument, however, was drowned in the charges of despotism and the frenzy produced by the siege of the Palais de justice.

While struggling to install the Maupeou-type judiciary, the government tried to win support by announcing on July 5 that the Estates General would indeed meet and that the public was invited to submit information about how it should be organized. By then, however, the Brienne-Lamoignon ministry had aroused so much hostility that the announcement got a cool reception. So many rumors swirled through Paris, according to Hardy, that no one knew what to believe, and some suspected the government of adopting a delaying tactic, designed to appease the public while the ministers attempted to find a way around the fiscal crisis.[2]

Nonetheless, the appeal for information touched off a new wave of pamphleteering. Pamphlets had proliferated "under the cloak" since March. From July onward, the flow turned into a flood, and a limited, undeclared liberty of the press opened up a public discussion of what, in practice, the Estates General ought to be. Although a royal edict of August 8 set May 1, 1789, as a firm date when the Estates General would convene, the public remained skeptical of the government's intentions. It was not until Brienne's ouster on August 25 that Parisians saw the meeting of the Estates General as a momentous event, certain to take place in the near future.[3]

At that point, the question of the Estates General's composition became urgent, and the public's attention turned increasingly to an answer provided by the provincial estates of Dauphiné, which had met in Vizille during the insurrection at Grenoble. The "model of Vizille," as it became known,[4] would require that the number of deputies from the Third Estate equal those of the first two and that voting take place "by head"—by counting the votes of individuals in a single assembly rather than by estates meeting separately. Proclamations from the assembly in Vizille circulated widely in Paris, and they were followed by manifestoes from later meetings of the Dauphiné estates, which demanded a doubling of the number of deputies from the Third Estate. "Doubling" and "by head" became the rallying cry of a movement to turn the Estates General into a "national assembly." In fact, the term "national assembly" had been widely used before the collapse of the Brienne-Lamoignon ministries. Other words—"patriot," "nation," "people"—filled café conversations, journal articles, and the growing mass of pamphlets, which the government tacitly permitted. The debate they raised was beginning to look like a struggle over power.

The question of power appeared as soon as the Parlement resumed its functions. On September 25 it registered a royal declaration convoking the Estates General for January (the date was later modified), and it specified that the convocation would take place "following the form observed in 1614."³ The implications of that seemingly casual remark did not sink in at first, but word soon spread that in 1614 the three estates had met separately and voted by estate. References to 1614 were then seen as a red flag, warning that the privileged orders intended to dominate the Estates General. The *Gazette de Leyde* noted that divisions began to appear among Parisians who had been united in their opposition to the Brienne-Lamoignon ministry. A new tone of discord spread through the city, amplified by epigrams, caricatures, and the continuous pamphleteering.

By November, the full implication of the Parlement's decision of September 25 had been assimilated by the public, and an open debate crystallized around two prescriptions for the Estates General: the model of Vizille vs. the model of 1614. It was fed by pamphlets, most of them hostile to the Parlement. As the atmosphere became more heated, the government had to take a position. Necker sought support by calling back the Notables who had assembled in 1787 and assigning them the task of recommending how the Estates General should be organized.

As in 1787, the public received only sparse reports about what went on behind closed doors in the meetings of the Notables, who were divided into six "bureaus," each presided over by a member of the royal family. The speeches given at the opening session on November 6 were published and circulated widely, although they revealed little, with the exception of the address by the first president of the Parlement, le Fèvre d'Ormesson, who advocated the 1614 model. Leaks over the next weeks suggested a growing tendency to favor the privileged orders. The Prince de Conti sent a letter to the other Notables warning that the pamphleteering had gone to such extremes that the monarchy itself was threatened. Lafayette, who was frequently advised by Jefferson at this time, spoke up for the freedom of the press, and most of the Notables endorsed the general principle of equality in taxation. But the dominant view, expressed in a declaration of the bureau of Monsieur (the oldest of the king's brothers), favored the model of 1614. The declaration based its case on historical precedents, citing documents from far-off dates—1355, 1438, 1560. If France were to have a new constitution, the bureau implied, it would be medieval.

As the discussions dragged on and no consensus was in sight, the public lost interest. Finally on December 12, the king dismissed the Assembly in a ceremony that attracted little attention. While the Notables dispersed, however, word spread about a memoir presented to the king by the princes who had directed the meetings. It began: "SIRE, the state is in danger. . . . A Revolution in the principles of government is being prepared." It went on to warn about agitation by pamphleteers, a breakdown of order, attacks on feudal rights, and a threat to property in general.[6] Copies of the *Mémoire des princes* circulated in Paris, provoking an angry reaction. At the same time, the Parlement condemned a pamphlet that favored the Vizille model, *Délibération à prendre pour le Tiers Etat*, to be burned, instructing the public executor to destroy it in private so as to avoid the publicity that would promote its sales.

The Parlement also opened an investigation of another pamphlet, *Pétition des citoyens domiciliés à Paris*, sponsored by the Six-Corps des marchands, a body that represented the city's main commercial corporations. The *Pétition* and a supplementary pamphlet, *Mémoire présenté au Roi par les Six-Corps de la ville de Paris*, argued that merchants and manufacturers had made enormous contributions to the kingdom since 1614 and therefore deserved a place in the Estates General, even though they had never been represented before, not even among deputies of the Third Estate. Although the pamphlets were anonymous, word spread that the *Pétition* had been written by a distinguished doctor from the Paris Faculty of Medicine, Joseph Ignace Guillotin (the Guillotin of the guillotine, which he did not invent but championed for causing less suffering than the usual measures of capital punishment). The *Pétition* made a strong case for the Vizille model by dismissing historical precedents and boldly invoking reason as the basis for establishing equality before the law. To the Parlement, which stood for historically based constitutionalism and had recently expressed sympathy for the *Mémoire des princes*, this kind of argument sounded like sedition. It was particularly threatening because printed copies of the *Pétition* began to circulate in late December and were made available by notaries for anyone to sign. The Parlement called Guillotin to the bar, evidently as a first step in a procedure that would lead to his imprisonment. He arrived in the Palais de justice, accompanied by a boisterous crowd of commoners, and defended himself with such eloquence that the Parlement dropped the case. Now a popular hero, Guillotin was feted by the Six-Corps at a grand banquet, and *nouvellistes* remarked that he was certain to be elected by the Parisians as a deputy to the Estates General.[7]

The Guillotin affair brought to a head passions among the common people that went beyond the dispute over the composition of the Estates General and were directed against the nobility in general. A remark by an aristocrat about the petition of the Six-Corps was cited as an example of what the people were up against: "What do these tradesmen think they are doing? They should be occupied with sweeping out their shops."[8] The magistrates of the Parlement now appeared to be defending the interests of the nobility, despite the role they had assumed as champions of the people during the coup of May 8. At the end of the year, they made a desperate attempt to regain the public's favor. On December 5, they passed a resolution intended to blunt the effect of their stand on September 25, though without renouncing it. In order to explain their "true intentions," they claimed that their earlier decree mainly concerned technicalities about how the deputies would be selected. As to the number of deputies from each estate, they would gladly leave that decision up to the king. Most of all, they emphasized, they wanted to stop the spread of sedition and anarchy.[9]

This vacillation impressed no one. When the crunch came, the Parlement had sided with the privileged orders. In fact, it aspired to lead them in the defense of their privileges. After months of protests in support of the Parlement's opposition to the ministry, Parisians came around to the view that the government itself had advocated—namely, that the Parlement threatened to turn the monarchy into an aristocracy dominated by *parlementaires* or what some saw as a "triple aristocracy" composed of the clergy and nobility under the lead of the magistracy.[10]

The shift in attitudes stood out clearly in the collapse of the public's admiration for d'Éprémesnil. After his defiant stand at the siege of the Parlement on May 5, he was celebrated as the most visible hero of the resistance to ministerial despotism. Although he disappeared into a prison on the Ile Sainte-Marguerite, he continued to be cited as the "Demosthenes" who had inspired the opposition to the government. After his release in October, Parisians prepared to welcome him on the day of his arrival with a grand ceremony. The street in which he lived was to be illuminated with candles. There would be speeches, poetry recitals, flowers, a laurel wreath, a cavalcade of clerks from the *basoche*, an honorary guard, a fife-and-drum band, and a delegation of *poissardes* to sing his praises. The celebration had to be called off because d'Éprémesnil was delayed en route. (He stopped in Roanne when his wife, who had joined him at the Île Sainte-Marguerite, gave birth to a baby.) But he returned in time to be applauded at a session of the Parlement on November 12. Engravings of him were still being hawked in the streets in late November, and printed songs in his honor were still on sale in early December. On December 11, however, d'Éprémesnil published *Réflexions d'un magistrat*, a tract that advocated the separation of the estates in the Estates General, the right of each estate to veto the resolutions of the others, and the maintenance of all the privileges of the nobility, except its exemption from taxation. The main issue before the public, as d'Éprémesnil defined it, was still "ministerial despotism," despite the public's admiration for Necker. By the end of the year, he had become notorious in Paris as an opponent of Necker and a defender of the privileged orders. In January a group of *poissardes*, hurling insults, tried to storm his house and was turned back only because it could not break through the front door. The popular hero had been transmogrified into an enemy of the people.[11]

After Necker became the effective head of the government, the issue of ministerial despotism no longer had immediate relevance in the debates about the future of the state. One pamphlet even argued that Necker should be made a "dictator" in the name of the king so that he could eliminate the privileges that oppressed the Third Estate.[12] Although no one took that proposal seriously, it indicated the shift that had occurred in the public's sense of its grievances. The enemy, for many Parisians, had become the privileged orders, not the government. Yet Necker had to proceed cautiously in resolving the problems connected with the Estates General. He had enemies, not only in the court, the nobility, and clergy, but among some Parisians who had favored the reforms of Brienne and Lamoignon. Finally, on December 27, Necker committed the government to the doubling of the Third Estate, but he did not dare take a stand on the more difficult question of the vote by head or by order. In a *Rapport fait au Roi*, he left that decision for the Estates General to determine. The *Rapport*, like the *Compte rendu au Roi* of 1781, was essentially an appeal for public support, even though it was addressed to the king. It circulated in printed form as if it were a pamphlet, and on the whole it was favorably received. Yet it gave the impression of a weak and vacillating government attempting to steer a course through rough waters. Meanwhile, hundreds of other pamphlets made the debate about the Estates General look like a struggle over the fate of France, and the atmosphere grew stormier.[13]

42

Pamphlets and Public Noises

ALTHOUGH THE WORDS were printed on paper, the messages of pamphlets flew through the air and mixed in the cacophony known as *bruits publics*. Pamphlets were bruited about. They were read aloud, performed, applauded, rebutted, and assimilated in the talk that filled *lieux publics*. Readers also pondered tracts in the quiet of their studies, but when they went outside they encountered other Parisians, in marketplaces, along the quais, in cafés, on the Pont Neuf, around the grounds of the Palais de justice, in the courtyard of the Louvre, on benches in the gardens of the Palais-Royal, the Tuileries, and the Luxembourg palace. Like smoke from thousands of chimneys gathering over the city, a climate of opinion gradually took shape.

The public noises in public places were best described, according to a gazetteer, in an impressionistic tract, *Les Entretiens du Palais-Royal* (1788).[1] Its author, Louis Sébastien Mercier, a sharp-eyed observer of Parisian life, recounted conversations—his imaginary reconstruction of them, not a literal rendering—among the people who gathered at the bookstands and wandered through the gardens of the Palais-Royal. The profusion of pamphlets and rumors belonged to the general "murmur" that enveloped Paris, Mercier explained.[2] In a sequel, *Les entretiens du Jardin des Tuileries* (1788), he described the way this "brouhaha" took place. Strollers in the Tuileries gardens improvised conversations as they encountered one another, shifting rapidly from topic to topic. Everyone was excited about

current events and public figures. Thus two men arguing about the financial crisis: "He's wrong," one of them said. "He's right," said the other.
What was it about? Two famous antagonists who recently were occupying the public scene in a debate about financial affairs. Everyone had read
their memoirs and had examined their calculations, and it was absolutely
necessary to take sides on this subject.³ A crowd gathered around the
debaters, interrupted, took sides, and moved on to other heated discussions. An abbé put on his glasses and read aloud an edict by the Parlement.
Listeners dashed into a nearby café to pick up more information. Strangers
accosted one another with reports on the latest news. Two men took up
the subject of the Estates General. The Assembly of Notables was nothing,
they agreed, in comparison with what was about to take place, because
the Estates General would certainly be convened. It was only a question
of when the first meeting would be held and who would be chosen as deputies. They had strong opinions on both topics. A general discussion followed, feeding hopes and fears of what the future held.

Although the crowds in the Luxembourg Garden tended to come from
the leisured classes, Mercier emphasized that the reading of pamphlets
and the discussing of public affairs extended through all orders of Parisian society. "Everyone wants to be an author or reader," he wrote. "Even
the coachman reads the latest work on his perch. Every person down to
domestic servants and water carriers is involved in the debating."⁴ To be
sure, Mercier often let his imagination run away with him, and his observations should not be taken literally. Yet much of what he wrote can be
confirmed by incidental remarks in journals and diaries.

"Everyone writes, everyone reads," commented the *Correspondance
littéraire secrète*.⁵ It described heated discussions around bookstalls in the
Palais-Royal, notably in the boutique of Desenne, where groups gathered
to cheer for the Third Estate and denounce the privileged orders.⁶ Nearby
in the café de Foy, pamphlets were read aloud, and "citizens work up a
frenzy in talking about the state." At a reading of a rebuttal to the *Mémoire
des princes*, the crowd shouted "Bravo!" after the strongest passages.⁷ On a
separate occasion, it burned a pamphlet that favored the nobility. A raucous crowd in the Café du Caveau, also located under the arcades of the
Palais-Royal, vented its outrage at an apology for the privileged orders in a
similar manner. The pamphlet was read aloud, condemned, lacerated, and

burned in a parody of the book burnings by the Parlement of Paris.[8] The Parlement condemned many tracts to be burned in 1788 and 1789. By then, however, it had learned that the traditional ceremony—an elaborate affair in which the *maître des hautes oeuvres* drove his sword through books and set them afire at the foot of the grand staircase in the courtyard of the Palais de justice—provided excellent publicity for the works it wanted to suppress, and therefore it had them destroyed outside the public view. After the Parlement's retreat from public book burnings, the curate of the Église de Saint-Sulpice staged his own, amateur auto-da-fe of an irreligious pamphlet that he considered especially offensive.[9] Whatever their message, pamphlets belonged to a world of spectacle, where texts spilled over the limits of private consumption and into noisy public gatherings.

The pamphleteering hewed closely to the course of events. Despite its enormous volume, it did not inject new elements into the ideological environment until the last months of 1788. When Necker entered the ministry, it shifted from constant attacks on ministerial despotism to issues connected with the Estates General, and several full-scale treatises began to dominate public discourse at the level of theory.

Nearly all of them argued the case for the Third Estate by contesting the historical-constitutional claims of the parlements. The most powerful of these, *Observations sur l'histoire de France*, by the well-known *philosophe*, Gabriel Bonnot de Mably, provided a six-volume survey of French history from the ancient Franks to Louis XIV. A primitive Champ de Mars had existed, Mably wrote, but it did not create a line of legitimate authority stretching from the original Franks to the early Estates General and the current parlements. France's history consisted mainly of power struggles among the *grands*, abuses by the nobility and clergy, and suffering among the common people. Mably died in 1785, and volume 6, which was not published until late 1788, closed with bitter reflections on the parlements and the Maupeou ministry rather than a hopeful prophecy about the Estates General. But the partisans of the Third Estate seized on it as a defense of the common people written with eloquence second only to Rousseau.[10]

Recueil de pièces historiques sur la convocation des Etats-Généraux et sur l'élection de leurs députés by Louis-Léon-Félicité de Brancas, Comte de Lauraguais, undid the argument in favor of the model of 1614 by a fine-grained analysis of historical precedents. Nothing, it concluded, justified the "odious and despicable privileges of the oppressive class of the privileged"—strong language coming from an aristocrat.[11] *Les Etats-Généraux convoqués par Louis XVI* by Target, now at the peak of his popularity, took the historical argument further, demonstrating that previous meetings of the Estates General were inconsistent in their organization and ineffective in their results. Instead of looking to a dubious past, Target emphasized, the French should prepare the way for a glorious future. That meant going beyond the Vizille model: instead of having a number of deputies equal to that of the first two estates combined, as advocated at Vizille, the Third Estate, Target argued, should have three deputies in relation to one each from the clergy and nobility. Above all, Target urged the French people to act in harmony as a unified nation: "Frenchmen, be united. . . . Be French, be only French." By appealing to a national spirit, Target avoided attacking the nobility and maintained a moderate tone. Yet his language confirmed that a revolutionary vocabulary had become embedded in political debate. He referred to the Estates General as a "National Assembly," which should express the "general will" of the French people and establish a constitution based on "the natural rights of man." A regenerated France would be a land of "liberty, equality, and fraternity."[12] (That was, as far as I can tell, the first use of what would become the rallying cry of the Revolution.)

Target's tract and its two sequels probably had the greatest impact on the reading public in 1788, judging from contemporary reviews, but several others stood out. *Mémoire sur les Etats-Généraux, leurs droits et la manière de les convoquer* by Louis-Alexandre de Launay, Comte d'Antraigues, another antiaristocratic aristocrat (he had close connections with the *philosophes*, particularly Rousseau), complemented Target's argument and supported it with a longer, emotionally charged overview of French history. When he invoked the Champ de Mars, d'Antraigues linked it to an argument for popular sovereignty. The French people retained the right to legislate, even to elect their kings, he claimed, and the people were identical with the Third Estate. They had never lost their legitimate authority, despite centuries of despotism. The ministry of Brienne and Lamoignon represented despotism at its most "odious"; yet its very abuses had triggered a reaction that would lead to a new constitutional order, in which the "general will" would dictate laws, although executive power would remain in the hands of Louis XVI.[13]

Mémoire pour le peuple français by Joseph-Antoine Cerutti, a minor man of letters trained as a Jesuit, argued the case for the Third Estate by dismissing historical precedents as inconsistent and irrelevant. Since 1614, Cerutti emphasized, everything in all sectors of French life had been contributed by commoners, yet they were nothing in the conduct of public affairs. If given their rightful place in the Estates General, they would pass reforms such as equality of taxation without threatening the superior status of the privileged orders. Cerutti's relative moderation—he invoked Montesquieu and the British model of a constitutional monarchy—pleased readers like Hardy, who copied out long extracts into his journal.[14]

Jean-Paul Rabaut Saint-Etienne, the most prominent spokesman for Protestants in France, produced a similar argument, although he adopted a more militant tone. In *Considérations sur les intérêts du Tiers-Etat*, he addressed the Third Estate directly, challenging it to stand up for its own interests, since they were the same as those of the nation. "You are the nation," he proclaimed. You pay the taxes, so you should have the vote. Consult your common sense, not the model of 1614; exert your sovereignty, never mind the parlements' self-serving argument about fundamental laws; take charge of the Estates General; force the clergy to pay taxes in proportion to its wealth; respect the honorific rights of the nobility, but make them, too, pay taxes. The privileged orders own more than half the land, yet they constitute a small proportion of the population (500,000 as opposed to 25 million) and exercise a disproportionate amount of power. You can do without them. You and you alone—the Third Estate, the sovereign people, the nation—in alliance with the king, can create a regime dedicated to the common good.[15] Rabaut's pamphlet went through at least four editions and was widely acclaimed. In March 1789, the Académie française awarded it a prize as one of the two most useful works among all recent publications.

The other was *Qu'est-ce que le Tiers-Etat?* by Emmanuel-Joseph Sieyès, published in January 1789. This tract of 127 pages, available in all bookstores at a cost of 30 sous, reprinted at least twice, and recognized instantly as outstanding in its persuasiveness, brought the debate about the Estates General to a culmination.[16] It echoed many of the preceding pamphlets.

In fact, it included few ideas that they had not discussed, although it combined them in an original manner. Sieyès cited his debt to "twenty writers" who had defended the Third Estate; praised authors from the nobility who attacked privileges; and joined the chorus of patriotic writers who took the *Mémoire des princes* as their main target.[17] What set his work apart was its rhetorical power. In its first paragraph, it distilled the complex issues that had been debated for months into three simple questions and answers:

> What is the Third Estate? Everything.
> What has it been until now in the political order? Nothing.
> What does it demand? To become something in it.

The "something" lured the reader into a seemingly straightforward argument that led to a radical conclusion. The Third Estate produced all the goods and services needed by society, and it paid all the taxes, yet it had no share in governing the country. Upon closer investigation, the share it demanded, the modest "something," turned out to be everything, because it was the source of all legitimate authority. It was the nation. The nobility and clergy were superfluous, parasitic, not part of the nation at all; and therefore the Third Estate should do without them, asserting its sovereignty by declaring itself as the nation and using the Estates General to create a new constitutional order in which all citizens, minus the privileged orders, would be equal.

Like Rabaut Saint-Etienne and Target, Sieyès based his argument on principle rather than historical precedents, and he took most of his principles from Rousseau, going back to the state of nature and the creation of a general will at the origin of society. He did not cite Rousseau by name, and he skipped over the complexities in Rousseau's concept of the general will, leaping to the conclusion, rejected by Rousseau, that the people, as citizens of an immense nation, could be represented by deputies in a national assembly.

But Sieyès did not go deeply into political theory. Above all, he offered a strategy for the empowerment of the Third Estate. He laid out a plan for elections; insisted that the privileged orders be excluded from the representatives of the Third; urged the deputies from the Third to convoke themselves (the king being but a "first citizen") as a national assembly; and warned them not to concede any fiscal reforms until they had established a constitution.[18] Having enshrined popular sovereignty in a constitutional order, they could retire and leave future assemblies to handle the ordinary business of government. The Third Estate would then have assumed its rightful place as a nation, not something but everything.

Looking back over the agitation of 1788, one can see a transformation of the climate. Public affairs at the beginning of the year appeared to Parisians as a continuation of the contests between the power of the government and the resistance of the Parlement. As the financial pressure increased, the confrontation looked at first like a replay of the troubles during the Maupeou ministry, but the uprisings in Paris and the provinces aroused a collective response that went beyond the indignation of "patriots" in 1771. Ministerial despotism, a familiar refrain from parlementary remonstrances, was now perceived as a threat to ordinary citizens and the nation as a whole. After the fall of Brienne and Lamoignon, the threat receded, although it did not disappear; and then things changed. Sieyès characterized the transformation of the political landscape with his usual astuteness: "The time has passed when the three orders, thinking only to defend themselves against ministerial despotism, were ready to unite against the common enemy." The Crown's commitment to convoke the Estates General set the terms for a new debate, and the Parlement's decision to favor the model of 1614 presented "political writers," as Sieyès called them, with a new target—not just the reactionary *parlementaires* but the privileged orders in general.[19] By the end of the year, the agitation had injected fresh passion into long-standing resentments. The pamphlets, amplified by "public noises," summoned commoners to identify themselves with the French people as a whole and to think of themselves as citizens of a nation determined to create a new political order.

This shift took place at the level of collective attitudes and passions, not merely from strains of public opinion. Parisians, or at least those who followed public affairs, had strong opinions about many issues that had cropped up during the previous decades and that had no connection with the Estates General. Some argued that the authorities should regulate the grain trade and control the price of bread; others favored free trade. Proposals for a land tax (*subvention territoriale*) attracted reform-minded partisans, yet some worried about the ability of the *intendants* or the privileged orders to dominate the provincial assemblies that were to assess it. Reformers wanted to abolish the *corvée* (labor or subventions for building roads), the *gabelle* (salt tax), and, in some cases, the General Tax Farm; but they hesitated about attacking provincial liberties (the *capitulations* preserving some autonomy among outlying provinces). Speculations on the Bourse, loans to the Crown, and the threat of royal bankruptcy continued to arouse polemics. Religious issues remained sensitive, especially in connection with the edict for the toleration of non-Catholics, which, as mentioned, was not popular among many Parisians. The legal system cried out for reforms, such as the abolition of torture, the redrawing of judicial boundaries, and reduction in the costs of litigation. Yet many opposed them, because they were embedded in Lamoignon's program for eliminating the power of the parlements. Foreign affairs (the Eden Treaty with Britain, the commitment to the Dutch Patriots), the military (the exclusion of commoners from the upper ranks of the army), and poor relief (the increase of beggars and of the sick and destitute in the *hôpitaux*) triggered debates. The abolition of the slave trade, and eventually of slavery, became a passionate cause with the founding of the Société des amis des noirs in February 1788, prompting opposition of slaveowners from Saint-Domingue, who would join forces in the Club Massiac, a powerful, pro-slavery lobby, in August 1789. In short, the ideological landscape was scattered with many issues, which activated different currents of public opinion and should not be confused with the overweening attitude of hostility to the government.

The public's opinions remained divided in large part because some of the causes were connected with the ministry of Brienne and Lamoignon, whose reform program included measures that looked progressive to some and repressive to others. Although an archbishop, Brienne was a worldly figure with contacts among the *philosophes*, notably abbé Morellet, a close friend from their student days. Morellet stood by him throughout the crises of 1787–1788 (he was cast as the chief pamphleteer among Brienne's "slaves" in *La Cour plénière*), not simply from friendship but also because Brienne's reforms corresponded with a strain of Enlightenment championed by Voltaire. Voltaire hated the parlements—for their book burning, their intolerance, their religious fanaticism, and their narrow esprit de corps. His *Histoire du Parlement de Paris* provided ammunition for all enemies of the parlements, especially fellow *philosophes* committed to tolerance and freedom of opinion.

One of these was Condorcet, whose writings in 1787–1789 illustrate a dissenting view from the mainstream of antiministerial pamphleteering.[20] A friend and biographer of Voltaire and an enemy of d'Éprémesnil,[21] Condorcet published a half dozen pamphlets about current events, writing anonymously and often, as mentioned, as a "bourgeois of New Haven" and a "citizen of the United States." In his capacity as an honorary citizen of New Haven, he adopted a radical republican approach to politics. His *Lettres d'un bourgeois de New Haven à un citoyen de Virginie* (1787) laid out his principles: all governments must respect the natural rights of man; all citizens should determine legislation by electing representatives to a general assembly; all landowners (including women) should qualify as citizens and pay an equitable share of taxes; and all public affairs should be protected from "all influence of the populace," meaning the lowest, poorest, and most irrational sector of society.[22]

Speaking as an American, Condorcet conceded that those principles had to be adjusted to the realities of French society and politics. His *Lettres d'un citoyen des Etats-Unis à un Français sur les affaires présentes* ("Philadelphie," 1788), written soon after the coup of May 8, summoned the French to support the Brienne-Lamoignon government and rebutted the prevailing argument about ministerial despotism. The true despots, Condorcet argued, were sitting in the parlements. They embodied an aristocratic order opposed to the natural rights of humanity: liberty, equality, security, and property. The ministers' policies, though imperfect, favored those rights, and Condorcet cited plenty of evidence for his argument: the egalitarian land tax, toleration of Protestants, measures to free trade, the commutation of the *corvée*, the abolition of torture, and other reforms of legal practices. The parlements stood for burning books and persecuting *philosophes*. Condorcet dismissed their claim of a right to register edicts as self-interested sophistry and their protests against despotism as cover for their own privileges as "a despotic aristocracy."[23]

Misconceptions about despotism worried Condorcet, because the campaign against the May edicts made the government's policies appear as a threat to liberty—no idle threat, either, because in the summer of

1788 the ministers dispatched troops to repress protests by ordinary citizens in favor of the parlements.[24] Condorcet rejected the idea that the soldiers should disobey their orders. He even condemned the protestors for enlisting "the populace" on their side, for the "populace," unlike "the people," could lead to anarchy and a worse variety of despotism.[25] Condorcet completed the *Lettres d'un citoyen des Etats-Unis* just as the government, on July 5, announced its commitment to convene the Estates General. Far from welcoming the announcement, he expressed concern that the Estates General would be dominated by violent demagoguery and, unlike the American constitutional convention, would not respect human rights.

In a sequel, *Sentiments d'un républicain sur les assemblées provinciales et les Etats-Généraux*, written soon afterward, Condorcet continued to argue that the Estates General could be manipulated by the aristocracy at the expense of the common people, but he no longer endorsed the ministry and did not refer to specific events. He retreated further in a last pamphlet, *Réflexions d'un citoyen sur la révolution de 1788*, which warned that the king might avoid an actual meeting of the Estates General by using the Cour plénière to sanction new taxes, even though it had no right to do so. Horrified by reports of hundreds of protestors killed by soldiers in Dauphiné, Condorcet now reversed his argument about despotism. He deplored current abuses of power by the government and advocated the recall of the parlements, which, he now claimed, represented the nation in accordance with a "solemn contract" between the nation and the Crown.[26] In a postscript added at the last minute, he wrote that circumstances had suddenly changed. He had relied on exaggerated newspaper accounts of violence and now believed the "National Assembly" really would meet. In the end, therefore, and after a good deal of backtracking, Condorcet came around to a position close to that of Sieyès.

Condorcet's contradictions provide an example of the fault lines and fractures in the ideological landscape at a time when it was overwhelmed by a tidal wave of opposition to the government. The hostility receded when Necker took power, although his ministry was essentially a holding operation cobbled together to keep the administration solvent until the Estates General could create a new political order, whatever that might be. To most observers, therefore, 1789 loomed as a decisive year. Yet a revolutionary change had already taken hold of France during the "revolution of 1788," as Condorcet called it. Although it did not upset institutions, it destroyed the sense of legitimacy that bound the people to their rulers, and it transformed the political environment. Whether or not they followed the arguments of the theoreticians, Parisians were swept up in the conviction of belonging to a nation, a sovereign body that would defy the privileged orders and take charge of its own destiny. This way of construing reality—the drawing of lines, the identification of a common enemy, the creation of collective self-awareness—can be understood as a process of radical simplification. Although it had origins that went far back in the past, it came together with unprecedented force in 1788 and underlay a revolutionary view of the world: us against them, the people against the *grands*, the nation against the aristocracy.

Although this revolutionary temper had emerged by 1789, its hold on Parisians was untested. In order to penetrate deeply into the population, it required the shock of more violence, which came quickly in the first months of the year. It also drew on the desperation caused by concrete circumstances—the coldest winter and the highest price of bread that Parisians had ever encountered.

43

~

The People Vote

WHILE THE POOR SHUDDERED and starved, Parisians located above the poverty line oscillated between great expectations and dread of catastrophe. Would the nation be reborn and a new political order be established, or would the kingdom collapse in violence, leading to a revival of despotism and aristocratic dominance? The people themselves would have a say in determining their fate, because they would elect representatives to a national body empowered to create some kind of constitution. But that, too, could end in disaster. For the first six months of 1789, hopes and fears were fixed on the Estates General.

As the Estates General had not met for 175 years and France had changed enormously during the interim, no one knew what to expect. Necker's *Rapport fait au roi*, which provided for the doubling of deputies from the Third Estate, was cheered in Parisian cafés as a "victory against the enemy."[1] Yet fears spread that this enemy, the nobility and clergy, would infiltrate the Third Estate and manipulate the electoral assemblies.[2] An edict of January 24 prescribed the procedures to be followed in the elections, which had to be adapted to the complexities of France's institutional landscape. All clergy and nobles (technically those nobles who had fiefs) were to vote in separate elections for their estates. In the elections of the Third Estate, the suffrage was extraordinarily broad. Every male over twenty-five who paid a minimal head tax (6 L. of *capitation*) would have a vote in primary assemblies located in districts (usually *bailliages*). Those assemblies would choose electors to general assemblies, where the deputies would be selected and the *cahiers de doléances* drafted, indicating the changes desired by the electorate. On May 5, after many disputes and delays, nearly 1,000 representatives of the three orders gathered in Versailles to determine the future of France.

A great deal had happened by the time they arrived. Despite the disappointment with the Parlement of Paris and the second Assembly of Notables, patriotic sentiment remained strong, and it often extended over class divisions. Many nobles announced their willingness to sacrifice their tax exemptions, if not their honorific and seigneurial prerogatives. Several of the most distinguished aristocrats—the Duc de La Rochefoucauld, the Duc de Luynes, the Duc d'Aiguillon, the Marquis de Lafayette—cooperated with commoners in clubs and gatherings such as the Société des Trente, which prepared programs for liberal reforms. Target, one of the Trente, published a model cahier: *Instruction, ou si l'on veut, cahier de l'assemblée du bailliage de* ***. Vote by head, equality before the law, abolition of *lettres de cachet*, freedom of the press, popular control of taxation, legislative power as the general will of the people expressed in regular meetings of the "National assembly"—it seemed to have everything an enlightened public could desire. It sold well at a price of 8 sous and was widely praised.[3] Yet it fell short of the reforms advocated by Sieyès, including the abolition of the nobility's honorific privileges. Above all, it advocated harmony and union among the three estates, recommending that they should meet together in one body. This position was rejected by patriots such as Rabaut de Saint-Etienne, who argued that the Third Estate should prevent a dilution of its power by declaring itself to represent the nation and by excluding the privileged orders.[4]

High-minded appeals for unity sounded increasingly hollow as France began to thaw out from the horrific winter, and they soon were outstripped by events. On January 26, violence erupted in Rennes. According to reports in the *Gazette de Leyde*, some Breton nobles who were hostile to the Estates General goaded their servants and day workers, described as *porteurs de chaises*, to pick a fight with students from the law faculty who favored the cause of the Third Estate and were discussing politics in a café. After a skirmish, the students withdrew, but they returned on the next day, reinforced by commoners beating a drum and crying, "Long live the Third!" In a furious street battle, the students began to get the upper hand until a force of nobles intervened with sabers and pistols. In the end, the students retreated, leaving several dead. A dozen persons including two nobles were killed and both sides suffered many casualties. Informed by a messenger from Rennes, seven hundred armed students set out from Nantes to continue the fight, but they turned back after the commandant in Rennes called in two regiments to restore order. Pamphlets and letters from both camps circulated in Paris, indicating that a line had been drawn in blood: on one side, noblemen determined to maintain their privileges; on the other, the Third Estate, intent on reversing the privileged order.[5]

Although nothing elsewhere approached the state of virtual civil war in Brittany, discord disrupted many provinces. In Dauphiné, which had provided a model of civil harmony, the nobility renounced the Vizille agreement, and the provincial estates gave way to squabbling. Riots connected with hoarding and the price of bread broke out in Reims, Saint-Quentin, and Vendôme in March, then spread throughout Provence in April. The rioters in Aix killed two soldiers, and two of them were hanged after the military restored order. The crowd in Marseille forced bakers to reduce the price of bread by 2 sous and sacked the town house of the *intendant*. Widespread pillaging took place in Avignon and Besançon; bread riots in Toulouse and Nancy led to bloodshed (the chroniclers did not provide details); reports of "uprisings" arrived in Paris from Sète, Orléans, and Caen. On May 5, the day the Estates General opened, the *Gazette de Leyde* concluded that a "revolutionary fire" had spread to "all the corners of the kingdom."[6]

Most of the violence was driven by the high price of bread, which peaked before the summer harvest could bring relief. The authorities of the Ancien Régime had plenty of experience in dealing with this kind of unrest. They stationed troops in the marketplaces of Paris and sent patrols of eight men each throughout the city. Yet the reports from the provinces unsettled Parisians, who worried about their location at the vortex of the political crisis. After noting rumors about conspiracies to hoard grain, Hardy wrote, "What horrible revolution must now be expected in the midst of the political fanaticism."[7] Newssheets indicated that rioters did not merely pillage for bread but directed their anger at nobles and the upper clergy. In Provence, they attacked the bishop of Sisteron with stones. In Toulon, they seized the bishop's carriage and threw it into the sea after disembowling its four horses. They sacked the episcopal palace in Belley en Bugey. In Provence, they gutted the château d'Oppède and went on to attack the nearby château of the Marquis de Montserrat. As the crowd approached, he fired into it with a musket and killed one of them. Then they stormed into the building, slit his throat, and hacked his body into pieces.[8]

Latent, long-term resentments against the privileges and overbearing manner of the nobility surfaced in less dramatic events, which fed the rumor mill of Paris. Although trivial in themselves, they caught the public's attention because of some peculiar twist or shocking detail. One such incident concerned the Marquis de Belzunce, who confronted his valet about a missing bank note. The valet insisted on his innocence; and when the exchange grew heated, the marquis slapped him in the face, then pulled out a pistol and killed him with a shot through the head. A few days later, a laundress found the bank note in a pocket of one of the marquis's waistcoats and returned it to him. His friends then advised him to leave Paris on a short trip while the affair was being arranged.[9] In Lisieux, a nobleman gave offense to members of the Third Estate by sporting a waistcoat with buttons inscribed, "Respect for the clergy, honor for the nobility, servitude for the Third." A commoner challenged him to a duel, which ended with only a few wounds but attracted a great deal of attention because it crossed class lines.[10] When aristocrats in Caen refused to allow commoners into their favorite café, a group of angry bourgeois drove them out and forced them to salute a flag that had been made to honor the Third Estate. After noting several occurrences of this sort, Hardy described them as "a kind of small war between the nobles and the Third Estate."[11] The Third also vented its anger against the upper clergy. In Lyon, a crowd burned a pastoral order (*mandement*) from the bishop that attacked the Third Estate.[12] A witticism of a farmer elected as a deputy from Falaise made the rounds in Paris. When asked what abuses he wanted to denounce in his cahier, he replied, "The pigeons, the rabbits, and the monks.... The pigeons eat our grain after we sow it, the rabbits as it is growing, and the monks when it is in sheaves."[13]

As the reports arrived from the provinces, the atmosphere became heavier in Paris. The *Mémoire des princes* had set the tone among the court nobility by warning that if the Estates General met, the privileged orders would lose everything, while the monarchy collapsed around them. The *grands* of the court had the ear of Necker's enemies in the administration, who included most or perhaps all of the other ministers, according to rumors that trickled down to Paris. Agitators in the Parlement, led by d'Éprémesnil (now labeled as "the most formidable enemy of the Third Estate and of M. Necker"), tried to take the lead in defending the nobility and the clergy.[14]

Then, seemingly out of nowhere, a new champion of the nobility appeared: Charles Alexandre de Calonne. In February he published an open *Lettre adressée au Roi*, warning Louis that the kingdom was slipping into anarchy, property (including feudal rights) was threatened, and the throne itself was endangered. Endorsing the *Mémoire des princes*, Calonne claimed that the Third Estate would destroy the king's authority by seizing legislative power in the Estates General, because wave upon wave of radical pamphlets had created a "revolution in people's minds."[15] To reverse the tide, the nobility and clergy should take charge of the Estates General and create a constitution that would empower them as the king's ally in an upper chamber like the English House of Lords.

Calonne made an unlikely leader of the privileged orders. Notorious for his attacks on the tax exemptions of the church and nobility in 1787, he had come to epitomize the abuses of ministerial despotism, and his pamphlet, published in London, where he remained in refuge, seemed to fly in the face of the prevailing national sentiment. But that was its point. To empower the Third Estate, Calonne argued, was not to resuscitate the nation but to sow anarchy, annihilating the monarchy and the privileges attached to it. The health of the state had deteriorated so badly under Necker that the Estates General should be constituted, not as an assembly of the people but as a rescue operation. Calonne himself would take on the job. He should be elected as a deputy from the nobility, invited to reveal the true nature of the deficit (while rebutting the slanderous attacks on his management of the state's finances), and accepted as the architect of a constitutional order that would benefit the people while maintaining a hierarchical social order with *les grands* on top.

Calonne's *Lettre* hit Paris at the height of the polemics surrounding the elections to the Estates General, and it created a splash. Nouvellistes reported that it was the talk of the town.[16] Although long (143 pages) and fairly costly (3 L.), it circulated widely and was taken seriously as a challenge to the prevailing arguments in favor of the Third Estate. It could not simply be dismissed as reactionary propaganda, because it advocated popular reforms, including limited freedom of the press and equality in taxation, and in some ways it sounded progressive. Calonne invoked Montesquieu, Adam Smith, William Blackstone, and "the progress of Enlightenment."[17] Even his enemies admitted that his tract was well written and, to some degree, persuasive.[18]

The best-known of the rebuttals, Cérutti's *Observations rapides sur la Lettre de M. de Calonne*, claimed that if Calonne set foot in France, he should be tried as a criminal, not welcomed as a defender of the monarchy. The king's authority would actually be enhanced by support from the Estates General, and Calonne's appeal to the privileged orders threatened to provoke a "civil war."[19] Calonne replied with a *Seconde lettre*, dated April 5. By then the violence in Brittany and other provinces had infused the debate about the Estates General with signals that a civil war might indeed erupt. Calonne took this view in a new appeal to the nobility, far more extreme than the first. He had actually attempted to get himself elected as a deputy from the *bailliage* of Bailleul, only to be driven back to his exile in London. Then, as he followed the agitation provoked by ever-wilder pamphleteering, he issued a warning and a prophecy: class hostility had reached such a point that the monarchy was doomed . . . unless the nobility took action to preserve a hierarchical order, which was the only kind suitable for a kingdom such as France.[20] The *Mémoires des princes* had alerted the privileged orders to the dangers that threatened them; Calonne's *Lettre* provided them with a program.

At the same time, an even more visible public figure, the Duc d'Orléans, appeared on the scene, offering another plan of action. Although first prince of the blood, Orléans had not signed the *Mémoire des princes* and had acquired a reputation for challenging the king's authority. In mid-March he published a widely distributed pamphlet, which instructed his agents in the sixty *bailliages* where he held property about the positions they should take in the electoral assemblies. In drafting cahiers, they should stand up for the principles that the duke endorsed—individual liberty, freedom of the press, equality of taxation, and the authority of the Estates General to approve all taxes and loans. He did not challenge the prerogatives of the nobility, nor did he come out in favor of voting by head, but he raised the prospect of an Orléanist party within the Estates General, because he directed his agents to vote for the candidates he would designate.[21]

Moreover, d'Orléans's pamphlet was printed with an adjoining tract, *Délibérations à prendre dans les assemblées de bailliages* by none other than abbé Sieyès. Although he retreated from the most extreme arguments of *What Is the Third Estate?* by envisioning collaboration with the nobility and clergy, Sieyès continued to equate the Third Estate with the nation and to insist on its authority to create a constitution based on civic equality. In his pamphlet, Orléans announced that he supported the principles proclaimed in Sieyès's *Délibérations*.[22] Taken together, therefore, the two publications suggested concerted action to push a radical program through the *bailliage* elections and the first sessions of the Estates General.

That is how they were understood in Paris, according to contemporary reports. Hardy wrote that the pamphlets created "an astonishing effect on everyone's mind," revealing Orléans's ambition to seize the leadership of the Third Estate and to transform the monarchy. Although some considered Sieyès's program "inflammatory," Hardy noted, others found it persuasive.[23] The most outspoken of the *nouvellistes* welcomed Orléans's intervention in the elections as a counterforce to Calonne's attempt to mobilize the nobility and clergy. The moderate *Gazette de Leyde* covered the two pamphlets and Calonne's *Lettre* extensively and without comment, except to note that public opinion had turned decisively against Calonne.[24]

This pamphleteering aroused a great deal of attention, because it stirred up debate just as the electoral assemblies were about to take place. Yet no evidence suggests that Parisians had come to see the elections as a choice between extremes—Sieyès and the commoners on one side, Calonne and the nobility on the other. Most voters—although we can only guess at their preferences—probably favored moderation of the kind recommended in the model cahier of Target, who soon would be chosen to preside over the assembly of the Parisian Third Estate. But whatever their views, they went to the electoral assemblies in an atmosphere charged with hostility between the newly assertive privileged orders and an increasingly aggressive Third Estate. Contemporary reports were full of language that suggested fear and foreboding: "murmurs," "fermentation," "tumult," "inflamed spirits," "confusion."[25]

The authorities made sure that all of Paris was informed about the elections. On April 16, official criers in markets, public places, and crossroads beat a drum and declaimed all twenty-seven articles of the edict convoking the three estates to draft cahiers and elect deputies to the Estates General in separate assemblies. Printed copies were posted throughout the city, and peddlers hawked them noisily in the streets. The edict, dated April 13, specified that Paris would have forty deputies—ten from the clergy, ten from the nobility, and twenty from the Third Estate. The clergymen were to meet in the great assembly hall of the archbishopric, the nobles in twenty specified locations, and the commoners in churches situated in sixty electoral districts. Even those excluded from the suffrage took interest in the impending event. Some porters, colliers, and other unskilled laborers who did not pay the minimal 6 L. in taxes protested because of their exclusion from the vote.[26]

Anticipating violence—whether in the form of political agitation or bread riots or both—the government sent extra detachments of the Gardes Françaises, each made up of eight soldiers, to patrol the city. It stationed cannon at key points and also kept a cavalry force of 1,200 troops ready to intervene. The first meetings of the nobility and clergy took place without incident on April 20. Paris was surprisingly quiet on the following morning when Parisians from the Third Estate gathered in their primary assemblies. The turnout was smaller than expected, according to the *Gazette de Leyde*, because of fear spread by rumors about an imminent uprising. In order to smother any spark of violence before it could spread, the battalion commanders were each allotted fifteen of the sixty districts to supervise. They dispatched agents into each district meeting; the agents sent reports every fifteen minutes (they kept tabs on the number of voters and on remarks they overheard); the reports were passed up the line of command; and bulletins were sent every hour by courier to Versailles.[27]

In each of the sixty districts, the citizens asserted their independence by rejecting the presiding officers named by officials in the Hôtel de Ville and electing their own presidents and secretaries. Then they debated principles, passed resolutions, discussed drafts of their cahier, welcomed delegations from other districts, sent out delegates of their own, accompanying everything with a great deal of oratory, and at last, after deliberating all night or even longer, chose their electors to the general assembly, which was to make the final choice of the Parisian deputies. Hardy, who attended the assembly of the District des Mathurins, described the activities in detail, expressing his fellow citizens' sense of exhilaration at taking charge of their own affairs. Having assembled at 9:00 on the morning of April 21, they did not complete their work until 8:30 a.m. the next day, and even then the district remained formally in session while its officers deposited the minutes and saw to various formalities at the Hôtel de Ville. Of 260 individuals who had appeared at the beginning of the meeting, 136 stuck it out to the end.[28]

The electors from the three estates, eight hundred in all, accompanied by a large crowd of spectators, gathered in the general assembly, which took place in the great hall of the archbishopric on April 23. They spent the entire session, fifteen hours, speechifying. The noise and confusion made it impossible to follow the debate, which turned on the question of whether to present one cahier for all of Paris or three from each estate. To make themselves heard, the orators had to shout over one another while the presiding officer tried in vain to maintain order. At one point, the Duc d'Orléans, who identified himself as a "bourgeois de Paris," stood on a chair and proclaimed his solidarity with the Third Estate. They finally adjourned at 10:00 p.m., having accomplished nothing except the verification of their powers (a formality commonly executed at the beginning of an assembly).

The king delayed the opening of the Estates General for a week so that the Parisian deputies could be elected in time to participate in it. But the electors in the Parisian general assembly got bogged down in negotiations—reported to the public as "cabals"—that lasted until May 19, two weeks after the Estates General went into session. Unable to act in unison, the electors broke up by estate into three separate assemblies. Each drafted a cahier and then proceeded to elect its deputies. The assembly of the Third Estate appointed forty-two of its members to go over the cahiers submitted from the sixty districts and condense them into a single cahier that would express the views of all the commoners in Paris.[29]

Just when public interest in the elections reached a peak, an explosion of violence transformed the atmosphere. All of Paris had been on edge for weeks, and reports of bread riots continued to arrive from the provinces, but the *émotion populaire* took everyone by surprise, because it did not break out in marketplaces. It erupted on April 27 in the faubourg Saint-Antoine, where an angry crowd of workers sacked the home and factory of Jean-Baptiste Réveillon, the manufacturer of wallpaper who had sponsored the first balloon flight, and the home of his neighbor, a saltpeter manufacturer named Henriot. Réveillon was an elector, and according to a rumor, he had remarked at a district assembly that a worker should be able to support a family on wages of 15 sous a day. Most of his employees expected to make 25 sous, and they had been unemployed throughout the winter. Driven wild with fury at their misery and joined by laborers from the faubourgs, they ran amok through much of the city for two days, battling soldiers after failing to capture Réveillon in the assembly of electors. As we shall see in the next chapter, the uprising touched off so much extravagant talk that it is difficult to know exactly what happened. Parisians believed that as many as six hundred persons had been killed and injured. Although order was restored by April 29, anarchy had seemed to overwhelm the city only a few days before the Estates General held its first meeting in Versailles.[30]

The meetings of the electors in Paris continued in this tense atmosphere, while Parisians, fearing another uprising, stocked up on provisions, and so many soldiers patrolled the city that it looked like a "battlefield."[31] The assembly of the Parisian noble electors passed a resolution in favor of equal taxation, although Hardy reported that it was an empty gesture, as most of them were determined to hold on to all of their privileges. The electors from the clergy came out openly against sacrificing any of their privileges and for maintaining the absolute power of the king. Meanwhile, on May 3, the assembly of the Parisian Third Estate began debating the one hundred articles in the draft of its cahier. The electors disagreed so vehemently, however, that they postponed a vote and spent the next days lining up supporters. After a great deal of caballing, they finally agreed on a text on May 11 and then began a new round of negotiations to elect the deputies. They took a full day to elect the first deputy, Bailly. More days passed in arguing and casting ballots for one candidate after another. As the debates wore on, some exasperated electors submitted facetious ballots, including one for "Monsieur Deficit to whom one is indebted for the convocation of the Estates General."[32] Finally, on May 19, the twentieth deputy was elected. He was Sieyès, who had been rejected by the clergy electors and welcomed by those from the Third Estate. (The electors from the Third had excluded candidates from the nobility but not the clergy.) By this time, the Parisian deputies from the clergy and nobility had already joined the Estates General, which had been meeting for two weeks.

Hardy reported some grumbling about the choice of the deputies from the Third Estate of Paris. They included too many lawyers, attorneys, and notaries (eight of the twenty), according to gossips who detected a cabal. Hardy also found little enthusiasm for the Third Estate's cahier, which was published on May 28.[33] It was actually an impressive pamphlet of sixty-nine pages, signed by the assembly's president, Target, and its three other officers, Camus, Bailly, and Guillotin, who were to accompany him as deputies to the Estates General. The cahier began with a Declaration of Rights, which included the principles advocated in most of the pamphlets, notably Target's, favoring the Third Estate: civic equality, personal liberty, freedom of the press, and a commitment to law as the expression of the general will. A section on the constitution demanded that the Estates General meet regularly and assume power over a new and equitable system of taxation, yet it did not challenge the prerogatives of the nobility or exclude some legislative function for the Crown, because it claimed that the authority to make laws belonged to the nation "conjointly with the king." Only in its last ten pages did the cahier advocate specific demands of the Parisians, and they, too, were moderate. Although it recommended an elected municipal assembly, it hedged on the question of abolishing guilds and did not mention the Parlement of Paris. It ended, however, with a demand that had great popular appeal: the demolition of the Bastille.[34]

44

Paris Explodes

THE VOTING IN PARIS took place in an atmosphere charged with violence and fear. Fear spread as reports arrived about violence in the provinces—bread riots, "uprisings," "seditions," "revolts" that seemed to break out everywhere.[1] Fear hung heavy over the marketplaces of Paris—notably at the Place Maubert, where two hundred troops stood guard as the price of bread peaked. And the threat of violence hung over the deliberations of the electors of the Third Estate. On April 27, rioters set out to storm the assembly hall of the archbishopric, where the electors were meeting, in order to seize and hang one of its members, Jean-Baptiste Réveillon, who, as mentioned, had enfuriated them by supposedly saying that they should be able to support a family on wages of 15 sous a day. Three of the electors, later celebrated as heroes, volunteered to confront the crowd and persuaded it to spare the assembly on the grounds that it was full of patriots defending the cause of the nation. On the following day, however, large sections of Paris dissolved into chaos. After a bloody battle with soldiers, rioters sacked Réveillon's house and wallpaper factory along with the house of his neighbor Henriot. But they failed to capture the main target of their attack, Réveillon himself. He had fled for safety—to the Bastille.

Hardy's entries in his journal show how the violence exploded and the shock waves spread. On the afternoon of April 27, he wrote, crowds of workers from Réveillon's factory in the faubourg Saint Antoine marched through the streets, armed with clubs and gathering supporters as they went. He encountered five to six hundred of them in his neighborhood on the Mont Sainte Geneviève. They were led by a drummer and a man carrying a replica of a gallows with a picture of Réveillon attached to it. They shouted, "Decree of the Third Estate, which judges and condemns Réveillon and Henriot to be hanged and burned in a public place." Shops had closed in anticipation of an uprising, but the men did not threaten anyone. When they passed a garrison in the rue Mouffetard, they told the soldiers not to worry: they only wanted to get their hands on Réveillon and Henriot.

A report in the *Gazette de Leyde* said that one group of rioters carried a mannequin of Réveillon and announced as it marched, "Here is the revolt. Close your doors, your shops." After winding through a large section of the Left and Right Bank, the procession halted at the Place de Grève, where, 3,000 strong, they set up the gallows and burned the mannequin.[2] Despite its menacing aspect, the uprising had a carnivalesque character, like the first rounds of the protests against Brienne and Lamoignon; and in the same way, it soon turned violent. That evening a crowd broke into the house of Henriot and destroyed nearly everything inside it. It failed to storm Réveillon's palatial town house and garden—the site where the Montgolfier brothers had constructed their balloon—because they were protected by a large detachment of troops.

The workers, supported by an enormous crowd of artisans and unemployed, reassembled in the faubourg Saint Antoine on the next morning. At first, they did not attempt to break through the military cordon surrounding Revéillon's house and factory, but when the soldiers made way for the carriage of the Duchesse d'Orléans (she took a route through the garden in order to attend a horse race in the bois de Vincennes), the crowd dashed for the house, beating off the soldiers with clubs and poles. Others joined them by climbing over the back wall from the ruins of Henriot's house next door. Then they began to loot, destroying and carrying off everything they could get their hands on, in the factory as well as the house. Mme Réveillon escaped with her jewelry, but she lost most of her possessions. An estimate of the damage included the loss of 500 louis (12,000 L.) in cash, smashed mirrors worth 15,000 L., and furniture valued at 50,000 L., the total loss coming to 150,000 L., aside from

50,000 L. that would be required for repairs. The rioters burned the furniture, woodwork, doors, linens, stocks of paper, carriages, and even some poultry in three gigantic bonfires. On the next day, seven of them were found dead in the cellar, having drunk poisonous liquids for wallpaper production that they took to be alcoholic beverages. Surprisingly, 2,000 bottles were left untouched in the wine cellar.[3]

The destruction took place in the midst of a pitched battle. Although they failed to protect the buildings, the soldiers stationed around them—Gardes Françaises and Gardes Suisses along with mounted and foot soldiers from the Watch—fought off the rioters as best they could and then summoned help from the nearby regiment of Royal Cravate de Cavalerie. At first, the cavalry held back, but after the crowd advanced, hurling stones, they charged, swinging sabers and leaving many dead. The rioters then climbed onto roofs and threw down tiles and bricks, as the crowd had done in Grenoble a year earlier. Several soldiers were wounded, and one was killed by a gunshot. The troops fired back, took prisoners, and finally dispersed the crowd, which broke up into groups and then went marauding through large sections of the city. Some stopped carriages and required the passengers to hand over money or cry out "Long live the king, Long live M. Necker, Long live the Third Estate." One group intended to break into the notorious Bicêtre prison and gain reinforcements by freeing the inmates. ("Escaped convict of Bicêtre" was a common insult, which alluded to the disreputable character of its prisoners who came from the poorest segments of the population.) Although that attack did not materialize, the government kept a large guard at Bicêtre for weeks afterward.[4]

Estimates of the casualties varied enormously, as in the case of earlier catastrophes. The *Gazette de Leyde* reported sixty killed and two hundred injured. Hardy initially put the number of killed and injured at five hundred to six hundred and later claimed that, according to police sources, 930 persons were killed.[5] Repression followed immediately. Two looters captured in Réveillon's basement, a roofer and a day laborer, were given a quick trial in the Châtelet court, paraded through the Right Bank, and hanged from gallows set up near the Porte Saint Antoine, where the riot had originated. The authorities executed the punishment in a show of force performed with great ceremony—perhaps the greatest ever meted out to criminals of such a low estate, according to the *Gazette de Leyde*.

The prisoners, each accompanied by a priest, were displayed in an open cart and escorted by detachments of foot soldiers and cavalry, followed by a great crowd. According to comments that circulated afterward, the roofer stared out insolently at the spectators along the route, refusing to pay attention to the priest, "who spoke to him of eternity," while the laborer, a younger man, tried to hide himself in the cart, overwhelmed with despair.[6] Although the police feared the execution could set off another uprising, the two men were dispatched without incident. Their bodies were left to dangle for an hour, then cut down, and the authorities set about punishing dozens of the prisoners they had captured.

The first lot were condemned by the Châtelet on May 18. They included a scrivener and a woman sentenced to hanging (her punishment was postponed because she was pregnant), five artisans condemned to the galleys for life, and twenty-three others whose sentencing was deferred. The punishments were conducted with elaborate ceremony on May 22. The condemned, each barefoot, carrying a candle, and clothed only in a smock, had to beg forgiveness before the façade of Notre Dame and then were paraded with a large military escort to gallows set up near the Porte Saint Antoine. The five galley slaves, proclaimed as looters by signs on their smocks, were attached by iron collars to poles set up in front of the gallows so that they had to witness the hanging. Although one burst into sobs, the others watched defiantly. After the execution, they were branded on both shoulders with the letters G.A.L. for *galérien* and then shipped off to the galleys in Brest. As after the previous hanging, troops fanned out throughout the city to prevent more rioting, and peddlers hawked printed copies of the sentences.[7] Virtually everyone in Paris heard or read some version of the uprising. Thousands took part in it or witnessed it, and many more followed its repression. While the Estates General held its first meetings, therefore, Paris became once again a theater of violence.

The military occupation continued for weeks, mainly in the form of patrols and of soldiers standing guard in public places. Hardy described them often—cavalry clomping through the streets in groups of thirteen, "a naked saber in the hand"; patrols of *Gardes*, bayonettes fixed to muskets, seven men thick; the Watch, on foot and horse, everywhere; even troops brought in from Germany and Hungary, who wore strange uniforms and sported frightening mustaches (the French were unaccustomed to seeing hair on faces).[8] Cannons loaded with grapeshot were ready to mow down demonstrators. Cavalry stationed outside the city stood poised to intervene at any moment. And far from abating, the fear grew thicker. Rumors spread that a new uprising would break out during the high mass to celebrate the opening of the Estates General on May 4 or the first session on May 5. Everyone expected the price of bread to remain disastrously high until after the summer harvest. On May 25 the police nearly provoked another uprising, when they rounded up a group of women who had come from country villages to beg for bread. As the women were being hauled off in a coach, an angry crowd of Parisians set them free and sent the police fleeing.[9]

Meanwhile, frightening news continued to arrive from the provinces. In addition to the revolts in Caen, Orléans, and Sète, a new revolt broke out in the town of Planchamp, near Uzès. A crowd sacked the house of the local seigneur, leaving him for dead. Then, after mounted troops arrived to arrest the ringleaders, it rose again, two hundred strong, and drove the troops away.[10] A large bread riot broke out in Rochefort, another in le Mans, and rioters in Marseille took over the city and reportedly proposed to declare it an independent republic. They were dispersed by a force of 10,000 soldiers; but as soon as army detachments stamped out rebellions in one place, they flared up in others. That, at least, was how the kingdom looked to Hardy, as he filled his journal with reports of violence: "One heard of nothing but uprisings and insurrections."[11] To be sure, he may have been more fretful than most Parisians, but even the sober Paris correspondent of the *Gazette de Leyde* emphasized the disorder—and the military presence meant to deter it. Paris looked like a war zone with soldiers everywhere, he wrote. Just when the Estates General set about restoring the kingdom, it seemed to be coming apart.

What, Parisians wondered, was behind it all? Word soon spread that Réveillon had never pronounced the fatal phrase attributed to him. Among the many versions that circulated, one had him saying that if the Estates General provided relief, a worker's family could get by on 15 sous a day, although he paid his men a minimum of 25 sous and often a great deal more. During the winter, when the cold made it impossible to manufacture wallpaper, he had given them 15 sous a day so they could survive. The local curate let it be known that Réveillon had contributed 50,000 L.

to relieve the poor in the parish. In fact, Réveillon became something of a hero to Parisians after they learned of his generosity as well as his losses. A pamphlet that he published from a safe place after the revolt made him sound like a solid citizen and a progressive entrepreneur—in fact, a self-made man, who had begun as a worker, had known hunger and destitution, and had devoted himself, as his business prospered, to the welfare of his employees, all of them well paid, all loyal. He did not believe that they had participated in the sacking, and he denied that he had ever said anything about wages of 15 sous.[12]

Although Réveillon ran a large manufacturing business, it never occurred to anyone to describe its destruction as a proletarian revolt against a capitalist boss. Nor did anyone attribute the insurrection to hunger, poverty, or the political agitation. True, allusions to the price of bread, Necker, and the Third Estate appeared here and there in accounts of the rioting. Yet the violence broke out at an unsuspected site—not a marketplace, nor a hot spot like the Palais-Royal—and it took Parisians by surprise. According to Hardy, they were horrified. Some despised the rioters as "the vilest populace, the last dregs of the nation" and imagined they had been manipulated by some kind of conspiracy.[13] But most Parisians did not know what to make of the uprising. Insofar as they came up with an explanation, they attributed it to the tension that had been building up for months. "It was an insurrection," remarked the *Gazette de Leyde*, "because one had become necessary."[14]

45

The Nation Seizes Sovereignty

AFTER VOTING for their deputies, Parisians fixed their attention on Versailles. Not that they ceased to worry about everyday realities in their own neighborhoods. On the contrary, each additional *denier* in the price of bread produced an outcry; and, as one pamphlet warned, the common people faced staggering increases in the cost of other basic necessities such as salt and wood. They also worried about instability in the streets, because the public order looked more fragile than ever after the Réveillon riots.[1] Yet the Estates General might give birth to a new order, if the patriots prevailed. Hope balanced fear as Parisians followed reports of the opening ceremony.

On May 4, a high mass prepared the way for the first business session of the Estates General, which took place on the following day.[2] The king, court, and deputies processed with the Holy Sacrament from the local church of Notre Dame to the church of Saint-Louis, where the mass was celebrated. Each person marched in ceremonial costume, each in his prescribed place, although the etiquette bruised some sensitivities, for France was still a society of orders, which put status on parade. The upper order of the clergy (bishops and cardinals) refused to mix with the lower (mostly curates), and the procession was delayed until the grand master of ceremonies, Henri-Évrard de Dreux-Brézé, resolved the dispute by separating the two with a phalanx of marching musicians. A quarrel over precedence also erupted within the Third Estate because the Burgundian deputies claimed that they should take the lead in place of the Parisian deputation, which had not yet been elected. They finally won on the grounds that Burgundy was the first province among the ancient Gauls to accept Christianity. Once the order of march was resolved, the procession filed out before an enormous crowd of spectators, including thousands from Paris.

First came monks from the local Recollet monastery, next a religious confraternity, then a company of Guards from the Hôtel de Ville and the deputies from the Third Estate. The crowd cheered its favorites, especially the Bas-Bretons, farmers who wore a traditional costume (brown coats and homespun breeches known as *culottes de bure*), but it refused to applaud some deputies of the Third who wore swords, indicating pretensions to nobility. Next came the Second Estate, where the Duc d'Orléans stood out and received much applause. The First Estate followed, with the musicians separating the lower from the higher order. Then came the sacred center of the procession, the Holy Sacrament and the king. The archbishop of Paris bore the Host, flanked by the king's brothers and the Grands Officiers of the court, who carried an elaborate canopy shielding the Host. The king, in a sober black costume, followed the archbishop with the Grand Aumonier on his right and the Premier Aumonier on his left. Behind him to the right marched the princes of the blood and the dukes and peers. To the left came the queen, followed by the royal princesses, carrying candles. As the royal couple passed, the spectators shouted, "Long live the king! Long live the queen!" Regiments of Swiss Guards filled out the end of the procession, and all the participants finally took their appointed seats in the Église de Saint Louis. The religious ceremony was suitably impressive, although the sermon was deemed to be too long (an hour and forty-five minutes). It was a beautiful day. When the crowds returned to Paris, they talked happily about having witnessed a grand spectacle. They did not know it, but they had had a last look at the top tier of the Ancien Régime as it put itself on display.

The opening session on May 5 took place in the Salle des menus plaisirs, an enormous hall, 120 feet by 57 feet, elaborately decorated. Directed by de Brézé, the deputies, approximately 1,150 in all, took their places, separated by estate, in benches at the center of the hall, and an enormous crowd of 3,000 occupied the galleries. After the ministers and certain *grands* of the court had been seated, the king and queen appeared. The king ascended the throne, took off his hat and put it on again. The deputies did the same, to the delight of the public, which admired the brilliant plumage of the nobles' headdress. Speaking in a resolute voice, the king urged the deputies to work together in the interest of his people. The Keeper of the Seals, Charles-Louis de Paule de Barentin, notorious as an enemy of Necker and also of the Third Estate, spoke next. He reportedly warned against "dangerous innovations," but nobody heard him. His voice was too weak, the hall too large. Necker then rose to address the assembly, but he, too, lacked an adequate voice. After struggling through the first part of his speech for fifteen minutes, he had to have a substitute read the rest, which went on for three hours. It was a disappointment, according to reports from the spectators: numbingly detailed descriptions of finances, including a somewhat enouraging account of the deficit (put at 56 million), yet no clear plan of action. The administration seemed to have left it up to the deputies to get on with their business.

Getting down to business turned out to be the assembly's greatest difficulty because it began with the *vérification des pouvoirs*, or confirmation of each deputy's papers authenticating his election, and that seemingly unimportant formality raised a fundamental question: would the verification take place separately by estate or jointly among all of the deputies? That issue, formulated as a choice between voting by order or by head, had been debated for months, and Necker had failed to take a position on it in his speech of May 5. Nothing could be accomplished until it was resolved. To many Parisians, however, the deputies seemed to get bogged down in the process of getting organized, and everything took place in the remote world of Versailles. Versailles was familiar territory to the aristocracy but alien to most Parisians. It lay nearly twelve miles from the city center, and in the unlikely event that they had business there, they would have to walk four hours each way, as we saw when the unemployed porters made their protest in 1786. Versailles impinged on the lives of Parisians mainly by the soldiers deployed throughout the city. On May 4 the administration doubled the number of troops stationed in marketplaces and increased the cavalry patrolling "sabers drawn," because rumors had spread that the opening of the Estates General would touch off another uprising. In fact, fear of a "popular insurrection" made many Parisians decide to remain in the safety of their homes on May 4 and 5.[3]

Nonetheless, wealthier Parisians, thousands of them, traveled by carriage to attend the sessions of the Estates General. When they returned, they filled the cafés and public places with talk about what they had witnessed.[4] Important speeches such as those of the king, Barentin, and Necker at the opening session were printed and distributed widely. Pamphlets contined to pour off the presses; and from May 5 France's only daily newspaper, the *Journal de Paris*, devoted a special rubric to reports on the Estates General. Although censored and minimal, the reports informed Parisians of nearly every session that occurred. More important, for the first time in French history, independent newspapers appeared openly, despite the administration's attempts to suppress them.

On May 2, Mirabeau, the loudest, boldest, and most notorious deputy in the assembly, broke through the barrier on news by publishing a prospectus for *États-Généraux*, a journal that was to appear three times a week without the approval of the government. Within a few days, 11,000 subscribers had deposited 9 L. each with the publisher, Le Jay fils, for a three months' supply. The first issues were as shocking and provocative as the readers had hoped. Mirabeau produced a caustic account of the preparations for the Estates General: the reception of the deputies by the king on May 2, which offended the commoners by absurd, courtly etiquette; the religious ceremony of May 4, which came to an anticlimax with a dreadful sermon; and the opening session of May 5, which exposed the incapacity of Necker to provide leadership. The government immediately banned the journal.[5] Mirabeau then launched another newspaper, *Lettre du comte de Mirabeau à ses commettants*, under the pretense that it was a report to his constituents. It, too, defied the government by denouncing the suppression of the previous newspaper as a blatant act of despotism and by attacking every effort of the first two estates to remain separate from the Third. Mirabeau had a talent for illustrating the abuses of privilege by details that captured the public's attention. One was the costume of the deputies. De Brézé had decreed that they must dress in black and follow distinctions according to estate: no lace or feathers on hats for deputies from the Third. Mirabeau came out for equality of costumes and scorned the pretension of a master of ceremonies to legislate a dress code as "the height of despotism."[6] In the end, the government gave up on its attempt to repress Mirabeau, and he chose to vent his passions as an orator rather than a journalist, leaving his newspaper to be continued by others at the end of July as *Le Courrier de Provence*. By May 24, four newspapers were reporting regularly on the Estates General. By the end of the year, one hundred had been launched. Although many foundered, newspapers exerted a vital force in politics, and the liberty of the press became embedded among the core principles favored by the leaders of the Third Estate.[7]

Whether they took their cues from newspapers or gossip or merely the patrols in the streets, Parisians knew that momentous events were taking place in Versailles; yet they could not make much sense of the information they received because, week after week, nothing seemed to happen. The deputies from the Third Estate refused to verify their powers unless the others joined them, and those from the clergy and nobility insisted on meeting separately. There was a great deal of speechifying, and a few orators—Mirabeau, le Chapelier, Mounier, Malouet, Barnave—began to make names for themselves, but the sessions produced nothing more than "useless chatter," according to the reports that circulated in Paris.[8]

After two weeks of inaction, each of the three orders named agents called *commissaires-conciliateurs* to confer on possibilities for cooperation. They got nowhere. On May 28 the king attempted to break the stalemate by inviting the agents to a summit conference in the presence of the keeper of the seals and other ministers. But the "Commons," as the Third Estate began to call itself, still refused to verify its powers separately, while the nobles decided to verify theirs on their own, and the clergy, who were divided evenly between the upper and lower orders, would not commit themselves. By June rumors circulated that the court and most of the ministers were determined to force Necker out of office. In fact, his supporters thought his life was in danger, and they worried that the stonewalling by the nobility was a maneuver intended to pressure the king to dissolve the Estates General.[9] D'Éprémesnil led the reactionaries in the Second Estate, warning them that Louis XVI could suffer the fate of Charles I of England. Mirabeau fired up the antiaristocratic passions of the Third, disowning his own title: "I don't care a fig for my title of count. I cast it off. Anyone who wants it can have it. I leave it for what it is worth—nothing."[10] The more the nobles and the commoners negotiated, the greater the split between them widened.

On June 4, after a long illness, the dauphin died at the age of seven.

Louis had left Versailles to be with his dying son in the château de Meudon and could no longer be an effective arbitrator. When he returned, consumed with grief, a deputation of the Commons, led by Bailly, attempted to appeal directly to him. He refused to see them, reportedly remarking, "So then there are no fathers in the chamber of the Third!"[11] The negotiations resumed on June 6 in order to consider a complex verification plan proposed by Necker, but they soon stalled.

Meanwhile, the situation in Paris became desperate. Posters appeared from anonymous sources, announcing that an insurrection would soon break out. The price of the four-pound loaf of bread rose to 14 sous 6 deniers. Some bakers charged 15 sous. Moreover, they were required to purchase flour from suppliers in Les Halles, who often mixed it with flour of a noxious, inferior grade, and rumors spread that the supply was about to give out. Beggars filled the streets. On June 11, the police, preceded by trumpeters, announced at street corners and public places that all beggars must leave the city within a week or be confined to "ateliers de charité"— workhouses, where the food was said to be inadequate. Everyone yearned for the summer harvest, still weeks away. Some desperate people were caught cutting young shoots of wheat in fields outside the suburbs. They were marched through the streets of Paris with their hands tied, bearing a sickle with stalks of green wheat on their shoulders—apparently headed for the gallows. (The *nouvellistes* did not say how they were punished.) Despite the continuous reinforcement of troops, Hardy expected a revolt to break out at any moment.[12]

On June 16 he went with his two brothers-in-law to attend a session of the Commons in Versailles. He got up at the crack of dawn and found a place in the gallery, amid 3,000 other spectators, at 8 o'clock. The hall appeared imposing—vast, well decorated, the deputies' benches covered in green cloth and arranged symmetrically around the president's desk in the middle. At 9 o'clock, when the deputies took their seats, Hardy was surprised at their dress. Some wore coats, some did not, and many had decked themselves out in colors. Bailly, as president, had enough voice to make himself heard over the general din. As the deputies spoke according to the alphabetical order of the places they represented, Mirabeau, from Aix-en-Provence, had plenty of opportunity to orate. Hardy, who had been appalled by Mirabeau's pamphleteering, found him as impudent in his speeches as in his written work. Although some speakers appealed to the galleries—Volney referred to the spectators as "my masters" and "my brothers"—Hardy was impressed with them in general. He listened intently until the session stopped for dinner at 2 o'clock, and waited until it resumed again at 6 o'clock. Much to his regret, he had to leave at 8 o'clock to make it back to Paris. The session went on until midnight and then adjourned for the decisive vote on the following day.

Hardy could not have picked a more dramatic moment. By June 16 the nobles had rejected all compromise, and the clergy, while still divided, had attempted to extract a concession from the Commons by suggesting they take action together to relieve the hunger in Paris. Radicals like Mirabeau denounced this as a "trap": if the Commons voted on any such measure, it would have acted as a body, virtually constituting itself as a separate estate.[13] Therefore, the deputies of the Commons declared that they would make the relief of Paris a top priority as soon as the other orders joined them to form a national assembly. By this time, most of them were ready to declare themselves the representatives of the nation, no matter what the privileged orders did. They had completed an informal process of verifying their powers and were poised to take the great leap that Sieyès had advocated in *Qu'est-ce que le Tiers État?*

Sieyès himself proposed this action on June 10, and the deputies debated it for several days. Finally, they reached a consensus about everything except a name for the new body they were about to create. Should it be "Assembly of the French People," "Legitimate Assembly of the Representatives of the Nation," "Assembly of the Known and Verified Representatives of the Nation," "Assembly of the Largest Part of the Nation in the Absence of the Smallest Part," or "Representatives of Twenty-Four Million Men"? The deputies had entered unknown territory. They weren't sure what to make of it, but on June 17 they broke decisively with the Ancien Régime and declared themselves the "National Assembly" by a vote of 480 to 89.[14]

The vote of June 17 did not come down to a play on words. It was a seizure of sovereignty. "Voilà, the word Estates General abolished," Ruault wrote to his brother. "That is much more important than you might think. In changing words, one changes ideas; and in changing ideas, one changes things. . . . June 17, 1789 will therefore be a great day in the history of our nation; it has caused a huge sensation in the capital."[15] To be sure, no one in the assembly hall thought the former Third Estate had declared the monarchy dead. There had been some loose talk, such as the remark attributed to a deputy that "the authority of the king ceases before that of the assembled nation."[16] A report also circulated that at the opening of the Estates General, Louis XVI had asked Necker whether he, as king, was to present a constitution to the deputies or whether they would deliver a constitution to him.[17] But the members of the Commons saw their enemy as the aristocracy, not the Crown. When they voted to assume power as representatives of the nation, they also suspended all taxes and then reinstated them for as long as they would continue to meet, assuming responsibility for the finances of the state and guaranteeing payment of the Crown's debt.

Moreover, the delegates of the newly proclaimed National Assembly knew they could count on the support of many deputies from the lower order of the clergy. Three curates had left the First Estate to join them on June 13; seven more dissenters had come over on June 14; and twenty had sat with them during the great debate on June 16. A minority of nobles also seemed ready to rally to their side. Orléans argued so vehemently in favor of joining the National Assembly on June 17 that he fainted, and he was later cheered as a patriot when he returned to the Palais-Royal. But a majority of the nobles supported d'Éprémesnil, who led the hard-core opposition to any cooperation with the commoners.[18]

Parisians followed these events avidly. They talked about nothing other than the Estates General, according to the *nouvellistes*.[19] When spectators, hundreds of them, returned from Versailles, they were surrounded by people eager to hear the latest news. Information spread from hot spots like the Palais-Royal, "the central point of the most zealous, the most ardent *nouvellistes*."[20] Along with the newspapers, pamphlets and posters warned in mid-June that the stalemate in the Estates General had reached a critical point, just as the price of bread reached a peak and rumors spread about a new uprising. The most frightening of the many *bruits publics* was talk about an imminent aristocratic coup. The Comte d'Artois was said to be conspiring with powerful courtiers and ministers behind the back of Necker and the king. The nobility would solve the financial problem by accepting the old proposal for a land tax; the Estates General would be dissolved; Necker would be dismissed; and a new government would be formed, perhaps with d'Éprémesnil at its head, to restore the old constitutional order.[21]

On June 20, a visitor to Versailles returned with the news that five hundred troops had surrounded the assembly hall, shutting out the deputies. A notice told them that all sessions were suspended until June 22, when they were ordered to report to a *séance royale* or meeting of the three estates to be conducted by the king. Paris reacted with consternation. If, as it appeared, the Third Estate's vote on June 17 was a revolutionary act, the new National Assembly seemed to be threatened with a counterrevolution.[22]

46

The Bastille Is Stormed

ROM THIRD ESTATE to Commons to National Assembly, the declension of the name conveyed a powerful message, but could it be transmuted into the kind of power that came out the barrel of a gun? Guns were everywhere in Paris after the Réveillon uprising, and more kept appearing, as the government sent regiment after regiment to patrol the streets and stand with bayonets fixed in marketplaces. Rumors of a violent military intervention had circulated in Paris for weeks. On June 20, it seemed likely to explode.

Although the majority of the clergy voted to join the National Assembly on June 19, a militant group of nobles in the Second Estate refused to yield any ground, and, more ominous, the Comte d'Artois, several princes, and the archbishop of Paris closeted themselves with the king in the nearby château of Marly on June 20. Louis, still stricken with grief at the dauphin's death, had withdrawn there from Versailles. According to reports that reached Paris two days later, Artois and the others persuaded him to dismiss Necker and dissolve the Estates General.[1] They were ready to use force, particularly the foreign troops, mainly German and Swiss, who were camped on the Champ de Mars and had no sympathy for French radicals.

Unaware of this threat, the deputies arrived to attend the National Assembly on the morning of June 20. They found the entry barred and soldiers posted all around the assembly hall. Bailly, their president, received a note from grand master of ceremonies de Brezé saying that the king had forbidden all sessions before the *séance royale* of June 22. Bailly then led the deputies to the Jeu de Paume or royal tennis court nearby in the rue St. François. They decreed that no power could prevent them from meeting and that wherever they met the National Assembly existed. Then, by pronouncing a "general Yes," they swore an oath not to disband before they had created a constitution. All of them signed the text of the oath, which began to circulate in manuscript that evening in Paris and was available in printed form the next day, when it was snapped up at 12 sous a copy.[2]

Parisians took the news of the closing of the assembly hall as a sign that the king meant to eradicate the National Assembly. "Soldiers at the door of an assembly of free men representing the people!" Ruault wrote to his brother. "That imprudent act revolts everyone here."[3] The Palais-Royal filled with furious protestors, who did not calm down until late on June 20, when the lieutenant general of police released a letter from Necker saying that the *séance royale* was intended to reconcile the three orders, not to disperse them. Nonetheless, word spread on the following day that conspirators soon would get rid of Necker himself, along with all the deputies. The archbishop of Paris, rumored to be a leader of the conspiracy, was openly despised as a "damn bugger." Persons who made deprecating remarks about the National Assembly were forced to beg the nation's pardon by falling to their knees and kissing the ground. Bulletins arrived regularly from Versailles and were read aloud to crowds, who applauded or disapproved noisily. A critical meeting of the king, his brothers (the Comte de Provence and the Comte d'Artois), and the ministers took place at 5 o'clock and lasted until 11 o'clock that evening. When Necker emerged from it, according to the reports in the bulletins, he looked disconsolate. Rumors immediately circulated that he had resigned and that the *séance royale*, postponed until Tuesday, June 23, would scuttle the National Assembly. Two additional regiments of artillery were dispatched to Paris in case the "prodigious fermentation" turned into a revolt.[4]

On Monday, June 22, the National Assembly gathered to continue its sessions, although the tennis court no longer had room for all of its members along with 4,000–5,000 spectators, who had arrived at 7 o'clock in the morning to provide support.[5] Trudging through continuous rain, the deputies sought a place to meet. At first, they gathered in the Recollet monastery, but it, too, could not contain everyone. Next, they went to their original assembly hall in the Menus plaisirs, having heard that it might now be open, but it remained shut tight and guarded by soldiers. Finally, soaking wet, they took refuge in the large church of Notre Dame. Soon after Bailly opened the session, 149 deputies from the clergy (or 145 according to some accounts) joined them, causing jubilation, because it now was clear that two-thirds of the members from the First Estate had thrown in their lot with the National Assembly, which would confront the king from a position of strength on June 23.

When the fateful day arrived, de Brezé seated the deputies from the first two orders in the rearranged assembly hall, leaving those from the Third Estate to stand outdoors for an hour in the rain. After they finally took their places, the king and ministers filed in—all except Necker whose seat remained ominously vacant. The king made a short speech, and left it to Barentin to announce his decision: the Crown annulled the Third's proclamation of June 17, and it reaffirmed the separation of the three orders. The proceedings lasted only half an hour. Then the king led the ministers out of the hall, and the deputies from the first two orders followed. The deputies from the Third Estate kept their seats, at first in a stunned silence, then with the determination to resume deliberating as the National Assembly. De Brezé reappeared and ordered them in the king's name to leave the hall.

Contemporary accounts of what happened next vary slightly, although all of them agree that everyone present was struck by one of those electrifying moments that transform the perception of events. Mirabeau rose to his feet and thundered at the master of ceremonies (according to his own version of his remarks), "I declare to you that if you have been directed to make us leave from here, you must get orders to use force, because we will only leave our places by the power of bayonets."[6] After de Brezé withdrew, Mirabeau made a motion, which was quickly adopted, that the deputies be deemed inviolable while serving in office. D'Éprémesnil had proposed in the assembly of nobles to declare the deputies of the Commons guilty of high treason and lèse-majesté for having attacked the sovereignty of the Crown, and Mirabeau's motion was meant to protect them from arrest.

Printed accounts of the session of June 23 were circulating in Paris by 7:00 in the evening of the same day: seven pages run off at top speed by Hardouin, the official printer of the National Assembly, and sold by peddlers everywhere for 4 sous. Handwritten bulletins continued to arrive from Versailles throughout the night, because Parisians hungered for every crumb of information they could get. Far from dispelling the tension, they learned, Mirabeau's bravado may have made it worse. A crowd in Versailles tried to stone the archbishop of Paris as he left the *séance royale* in his carriage. He was reputed to have implored the king, "a crucifix in hand," to dismiss Necker and dissolve the Estates General, and he was known to scorn Bailly, the president of the National Assembly, as "a modern philosopher."[7]

According to one rumor, the archbishop had actually succeeded, at least briefly. On the eve of the *séance royale*, so the Parisians heard, the king had signed a *lettre de cachet* to get rid of Necker and had appointed a new government bent on repression: the Prince de Conti had been named "principal minister"; the Prince de Condé was "generalissimo of all the troops of the kingdom"; and they were about to seize hostages from the deputies of the Third Estate, one from each *bailliage*, while dissolving the Estates General. Beds set up in the courtyard of the Bastille were prepared to receive the victims.[8]

Then, at midnight, the public massed in the Palais-Royal learned that the coup would not take place. A bulletin recounted that an enormous crowd of protestors in Versailles had swarmed into the palace, demanding to see the king. Conti and Condé ordered the guards to fight them off, but the guards refused—an act of blatant insubordination. Whether or not he was seriously in danger, the king restored calm by announcing that Necker would remain in office. Necker himself put in an appearance, and the crowd dispersed, pacified but confused, because no one knew if the National Assembly would continue to exist on the next day.[9]

As the events rushed past, they carried echoes of earlier events. The *séance royale* of June 23 conjured up the *séance royale* of November 19, 1787, when the king overcame resistance from the Parlement of Paris by asserting his absolute will. In both cases the reassertion of royal power had the trappings of a *lit de justice*. The tennis court oath of June 20 also sounded like the oath taken by the *parlementaires* on May 3, 1788, when they swore solidarity against the imminent coup of Lamoignon. Many Parisians expected a coup to occur at any moment during the military buildup of June and July 1789. Hardy had noted that well-informed people considered the opening ceremony of the Estates General to be a "brilliant pantomime" intended to impress the masses while the government prepared to restore absolute rule by force.[10] Parisians fretted about "ministerial despotism" in 1789 just as they had done in 1788, because they knew the National Assembly could be dismissed as readily as the Assembly of Notables.[11] It existed only in the form of a declaration by the deputies of the Third Estate.

The National Assembly resumed deliberations on June 24 as if the king had not abolished it. It now included a majority of the clerical deputies along with several nobles, and on the next day, forty-seven noble deputies, led by the Duc d'Orléans, joined its ranks. On June 27, the king reversed the position he had taken four days earlier and ordered all the deputies from the first two estates to sit with the Third, implicitly recognizing the transformation of the Estates General into the National Assembly. By then, 10,000 persons had been gathering regularly in the gardens of the Palais-Royal to hear readings of the bulletins sent from Versailles. When they learned that the National Assembly had survived, they celebrated with troops from the barracks of the Gardes Françaises, who assured them that they would never fire on their fellow citizens and were rewarded with rounds of drinks.

Soldiers and citizens caroused happily together on several occasions during the next few days. The tension that had increased inexorably since June 17 gave way to a brief period of festivity. Yet the king did not rescind a recent order to station six hundred additional troops in Saint Cloud and two hundred in Montreuil. Rumors spread that the queen had begged him, with the new dauphin (Louis Charles, their second son) in her arms, to restore the authority of the Crown. There was more talk of a famine plot, now attributed to Conti and Condé, who remained close to the king. Some said that troops stationed in the faubourg Saint-Marcel had planned to desert and that the National Assembly owed its salvation to patriotic soldiers, who had threatened to rebel if ordered to suppress the representatives of the people.[12]

The military aspect of the political struggle appeared increasingly critical as Parisians took stock of the situation at the beginning of July. While more of the soldiers stationed in Paris threatened to desert, new regiments arrived from outside to maintain order. Mirabeau, now the dominant voice in the National Assembly, allegedly fomented sedition by publishing a pamphlet, *Lettre d'un officier français au comte de Mirabeau*, in the form of a letter that he had actually written to himself. It claimed that the government had paid agents to destroy the future harvest in order to provoke a famine, an uprising, and chaos, which it would exploit to dissolve the National Assembly and install despotism. Every soldier's duty, it concluded, was to defend the fatherland by rebelling against the government.

At that time, eleven soldiers from the Gardes Françaises were awaiting trial for treason in a prison attached to the Abbaye de Saint Germain des Près. They were the guards who had refused to turn their weapons against the crowd that stormed into the palace of Versailles on June 23. A letter from one of their comrades arrived in the Palais-Royal on June 30, warning that two of the prisoners were to be hanged the next day and that the others were to await their fate after being transferred to the prison of Bicêtre. An enraged patriot from the Café de Foy, now known as "the current center of insurrections," climbed on a chair and read the letter aloud to about three hundred persons gathered in the garden. They rushed out, seizing clubs and other weapons, and their number grew to 6,000, as they dashed through the center of the city.[13]

When they arrived at the prison, they smashed through its outer door and liberated two dozen prisoners. A company of *hussards* (light cavalry) arrived, sabers drawn. "Down with your arms, friends," the crowd reportedly cried. The soldiers sheathed their sabers and shook hands with the rioters, who then demolished the interior of the prison. According to some reports, they intended to attack other prisons—Bicêtre, the Conciergerie, and Vincennes (the Bastille was considered impregnable). Instead, however, the crowd paraded the prisoners back to the Palais-Royal, feted them with food and drink, and provided them with housing in rooms above the Café de Foy. For the next two days, the liberated prisoners lowered a basket from a rope to collect donations, while their supporters applied pressure on the National Assembly to arrange an amnesty. A four-page printed account of the riot circulated widely.

Meanwhile, 28,000 more troops were ordered to encampments outside Paris and Versailles. The *maréchal* de Broglie took command of them and announced he would send patrols of 4,000–5,000 men each day to maintain order in Paris. Incidents continued to occur. On July 2 two soldiers were arrested for insubordination and then freed by a crowd. A rumor spread that two others were hanged for refusing to obey their officers, although it was later proven wrong.[14] The prisoners lodged above the Café de Foy turned themselves in, hoping to receive a pardon, which eventually arrived. But the crowds in the Palais-Royal grew angrier. Radicals often harangued them, standing on chairs and tables. After one young man made a violent speech against the nobility and clergy, someone shouted, "Get arms," and panic broke out. Although it died down, another orator spread an alarm on July 3 by reading aloud a letter that denounced a conspiracy of the nobles in the National Assembly to assassinate the deputies from the Third Estate. He called for 20,000 men to seize arms from the Invalides and the Ecole militaire and march on Versailles. Before violence erupted, a speaker who had just arrived from Versailles assured the crowd that no such plot existed, and the letter was exposed as a fake. Yet equally alarming news arrived from the Halles, where the supply of flour was said to have run out. According to Hardy, many Parisians now believed that the government was hoarding grain in order to cover its debt by selling its supply after the price rose to an exorbitant level.[15]

In fact, the bakeries continued to provide bread, though of an inferior quality, and calm returned to Paris for a few days. But on July 9 a crowd in the Palais-Royal seized a police spy and beat him so badly that he died a day later. At the same time on the Left Bank, several thousand workers broke into a prison to free two of their comrades who had been jailed for insulting an officer of the *hussards*. A cavalry regiment galloped across Paris to put down the riot, but the workers forced it to sheath its sabers and back off. They had had enough of soldiers pouring into Paris, they said, and enough of increases in the price of bread. Parisians suspected that the recent detachments of troops were intended to suppress them, not to protect them, and they talked darkly about an imminent "siege" of the city.[16]

Yet many of the soldiers seemed to sympathize with the people rather than their officers. On July 10, eighty cannoneers stationed in the Invalides defied the orders of their superiors by marching off, to the beat of a drum, to the Palais-Royal, where they were welcomed with food and a great deal of drink. After shouting "Long live the Duc d'Orléans, Long live the Third Estate," they announced that they wanted to dance. They marched to the Champs Elysées, formed a circle, and danced away with some women of the street while street musicians struck up tunes. Then they marched back to the Invalides in time to report for their evening duty. Although they were not punished, they were assigned the next day to a camp outside Paris.[17]

As reports of these incidents circulated through Paris, the tension reached an explosive level. On July 8, Mirabeau warned the National Assembly that the soldiers could set off a catastrophe and persuaded it to send a deputation to the king imploring him to withdraw the most recent reinforcements. Louis replied that he would not do so until calm had been restored. If the Assembly felt unsafe, he added, it could move to Noyon or Soissons. Meanwhile, a rumor spread in Paris that the king was about to call another *séance royale* in order to suspend the Assembly. Bread remained unbearably expensive, even when adulterated with poor-quality rye, while the harvest would not be ready for a few weeks. A pamphlet warned that the four-pound loaf, which had reached 15 sous, soon would soar to 20 sous; and when peddlers tried to hawk it in the faubourg Saint Antoine, they were driven away by angry crowds.

At noon on July 12, news arrived that the king had dismissed Necker. The Palais-Royal burst into a frenzy. Orators climbed on chairs and shouted, "Get arms! Get arms!"[18] Some dashed to alert the Parisian electors, who were meeting in the Hôtel de Ville. Others fanned through the boulevards, telling theaters to close. When they came to the wax museum of Philippe Curtius on the boulevard du Temple, they seized a bust of Necker, draped it in black crepe, and paraded it to the Place Vendôme, gathering a large crowd, which included sympathizers from the Gardes Françaises. As they entered the Place, some troops from a regiment of the Royal Allemand, foreigners notorious for their hostility to the patriot cause, tried to stop the crowd. Some threw stones; shots rang out; and a Garde fell to the cobblestones—the first casualty in what had now become an insurrection. Nearby, the Prince de Lambesc cut down another citizen while leading a detachment of Royal Allemand past the Tuileries Gardens. Soon afterward in the Place Louis XV, a corps of Gardes Françaises, backed by cannon, confronted more of the Royal Allemand and mowed down eleven of them. Throughout the night, crowds destroyed the much-hated customs barrier that surrounded the city. No one stopped them, because the Gardes Françaises had rallied to the Revolution, and the hostile troops were cowering in their camps or retreating outside the city. Yet powerful regiments still were stationed around Paris and also Versailles, where the fate of the National Assembly looked uncertain.

On July 13, Parisians woke to the ringing of the tocsin from all the city's churches. Citizens reported to the headquarters of the sixty electoral districts, bringing whatever arms they could muster. Then they formed patrols, joined by the Gardes Françaises, which quickly became a citizen militia designed to keep order. Although they captured a few looters, the city remained peaceful but throbbing with excitement. Everyone in the streets wore green cockades, a symbol of hope for the future. The districts sent representatives to join the electors in the Hôtel de Ville, and together they formed a Commune to coordinate the military action. Armed groups set off to free prisoners from Bicêtre, the Châtelet, and the Hôtel de la Force. Others went to the Congrégation de Saint Lazare in the faubourg Saint Denis, which was rumored to possess a store of grain. The monks claimed that they had provisions for only a few days, but the revolutionaries forced their way into a storeroom, where they discovered an enormous quantity of wheat—enough, according to some reports, to fill fifty-two wagons, which were summoned to transport it for sale at the Halle. The monks fled; the revolutionaries pillaged the convent; and the Commune dispatched more groups to requisition grain from other religious houses. It also summoned the lieutenant general of police, who reported that there were enough provisions to feed Paris for the next two weeks—and then disappeared, one of the first refugees to flee from the city. Meanwhile, word arrived that Necker had departed from Versailles, headed for Brussels, and that the king had named new ministers, all committed to restoring the old order. The National Assembly continued to meet. It requested the king to recall Necker, dismiss the new ministry, and order the hostile troops to leave Paris; but Louis remained adamant. In Paris that evening, the citizens applauded the patrols of the militia from their windows and went to bed, expecting the next day to be decisive.

The tocsin rang out early on July 14, summoning the new citizen militia to the Commune. Everyone discarded their green cockades and displayed new ones, composed of blue and red, the colors of Paris. Groups set off in search of arms. Some requisitioned caissons from the Ecole militaire and a load of gunpowder from a boat in the Seine, while the main force, 30,000 men, surrounded the Invalides, where the largest stock of weapons were stored. In order to avoid bloodshed, the governor of the Invalides opened its doors. The revolutionaries then seized 20,000 muskets and twenty or twenty-four cannon. At 2 o'clock the cry went out, "To the Bastille! To the Bastille!"

Meanwhile, the officers of the Commune found that Jacques de Flesselles, the *prévôt des marchands* or chief municipal official, was acting suspiciously. They had him seized and searched. A letter in his pocket turned out to be from Bernard-René de Launay, the governor of the Bastille. It read: "Hold out until 8 o'clock; you will then get troops and bombs. While waiting, I will distract the rabble"—the "rabble" being the revolutionaries who were then marching to the Bastille. The Commune turned de Flesselles over to a crowd of angry demonstrators who had massed outside in the Place de Grève. They tore him apart and cut off his head.

The first of the militia to arrive at the Bastille, a group of several hundred, announced that they had come to collect gunpowder and arms. Trusting a white flag that de Launay had exhibited, they crossed over a drawbridge to an outer court. Suddenly the drawbridge was raised, trapping them in the courtyard, and cannon fire rained down, killing about eighty. Crowds of citizen soldiers continued to mass outside the Bastille, although they had no leaders to direct them. Horrified at de Launay's treachery, they began to shoot at troops on the towers, who replied with cannonades that left many dead and sent the rest running for cover.

Reinforcements arrived with the cannon from the Invalides. They set a fire to cover their maneuvers with smoke, then managed to cut the chains holding the outer drawbridge. After crossing it, they discovered the bodies of their comrades and advanced, furious, to a second drawbridge, drawn up at the gate of an inner courtyard. They damaged it with cannon fire, but before it fell, they found a small bridge that led to another entrance. A few men dashed across the bridge, opened the way for the main force, and thousands of militia swarmed through the fortress. *Révolutions de Paris*, one of the first new journals, described the rout as if it were taking place before the eyes of the reader[19]: "The besieged forces defend themselves; the attackers slaughter everyone who tries to stop them; they mow down the [Bastille's] gunners; they dash forward, wreaking carnage; they charge, reach the staircase, seize prisoners, penetrate everywhere."

De Launay was captured by a grenadier of the Gardes Françaises as he was about to commit suicide. The Bastille's major, Antoine-Jérôme Puget, and some other officers were also captured, then led with de Launay through the streets to the Place de Grève past thousands of Parisians shouting insults at them. Although the militia intended to give them a summary trial in the Hôtel de Ville, the crowd could no longer contain its fury. It descended on de Launay and Puget, pummeled them to death, decapitated them, stuck the heads on pikes, and paraded them, streaming blood, through the streets. "Even ladies could be seen smiling and applauding the terrible spectacle," a witness noted.[20] The grenadier, rewarded with de Launay's cross of the Order de Saint Louis, and three of his comrades, who received civic crowns, were carried triumphantly in other processions. A prisoner who had spent thirty-two years confined to a cell was exhibited in the gardens of the Palais-Royal, barely able to walk and astonished at the light of day. Ruault wrote to his brother four days later, "Yes, the Bastille taken! . . . This beginning of a great revolution heralds incalculable consequences."[21] Joy exploded everywhere, and everyone celebrated the prospect of tearing down the Bastille, which was guarded that night by workers from the faubourg Saint Antoine in order to keep it safe for organized demolition.

The destruction did not begin immediately on July 15, however, because Parisians expected to be attacked by the 30,000 troops stationed outside the city. They erected barricades, set up cannon, and hauled paving stones to rooftops in readiness to hurl them at the invaders during battles in the streets. The *maréchal* de Broglie, in his capacity as commander of the royal forces and the new minister of war, ordered the regiments to march on Paris. But the men refused to move. Meanwhile, the executive committee of the Commune declared itself permanent. It ordered the militia, now commonly called the Garde bourgeoise, to take possession of the Ecole militaire and other strategic sites, including positions high up on Montmartre, which the enemy might use to bombard the city. The committee named Lafayette as colonel general of the Garde and Bailly as mayor of Paris. By the end of the day, it was clear to most Parisians that power had definitively shifted. It was now located in the revolutionary Commune, a political body organically connected to sixty local districts, and in the Garde bourgeoise, a military force capable of resisting invasion and keeping order in the streets.

After exiling Necker, the king remained determined to support his counterrevolutionary ministers, despite several appeals for Necker's return by the National Assembly. Louis retired to bed on the night of July 14–15, unaware of the events in Paris. By virtue of his position as Grand Maître de la Garde-Robe, the Duc de Liancourt entered the bedroom and informed the king, as later reported in the newspapers, that a "revolution" had erupted and that many troops had joined it. On July 15, Louis appeared before the National Assembly and supplicated, "Help me . . . assure the salvation of the state."[22] All the regiments dispatched to Paris, he announced, would be withdrawn—that is, there would be no repression. A delegation of deputies set off to bring the good news to the capital. It was received rapturously; a Te Deum was celebrated in Notre Dame; the entire city was illuminated by candles lit in windows; a salvo of musket fire gave the signal, and five hundred workers began to dismantle the Bastille.

The National Assembly persisted in requesting the recall of Necker on July 16. Late in the day, the king gave in. A courier galloped off after midnight to bring the summons to Necker, who by then had reached his château in Coppet, Switzerland. The newly appointed ministers resigned, and their leading supporters from the court—d'Artois, Conti, Condé, and others—took flight, many of them in disguise. Parisians delighted in swapping anecdotes about their escape—the Duchesse de Polignac dressed as a chambermaid and the Prince de Lambesc as a stable groom.

Louis confirmed the transfer of power by coming in person to Paris on July 17. He arrived without a military escort, despite warnings that his life could be in danger. The Garde bourgeoise, more than 100,000 men, lined the route from Passy to the city center and served as a barrier to protect the king from the crowds, which shouted "Long live the nation!" but not "Long live the king!" When the king arrived at the outskirts of Paris, Bailly presented him with the keys to the city. Then the royal carriage continued to the Hôtel de Ville, followed by a long procession: two cavalry units, several battalions of the Garde bourgeoise accompanied by cannon, other soldiers, Lafayette, and three hundred deputies from the

National Assembly. The Revolution, like the Ancien Régime, displayed itself on parade, yet in a different manner: it expressed power, not status.

When the king descended at the Hôtel de Ville, he passed under a vault made by the bayonets and swords of the Garde bourgeoise. Once inside, he ascended a throne and listened to speeches laced with patriotic *sensibilité*. Reports in newspapers said that tears ran down his cheeks and that he was at a loss for words. Bailly replied for him, attached a new cocade to his hat (blue and red separated by the white of the Bourbons), and showed him to a balcony, where the king looked out over many thousands, now shouting "Long live the king!" The air filled with their cries and with cannonades, fanfares, drum rolls, and general exhilaration. The king had accepted the new order. He departed for a Te Deum in Notre Dame and then returned to Versailles, where Necker was expected to form a new ministry and the National Assembly set about writing a constitution. "Everything will change, morals, opinions, laws, customs, usages, government," Ruault informed his brother. "In very little time, we will be new men."[23]

The Revolution did not end there, far from it. One astonishing event succeeded another during the next three months: the Declaration of the Rights of Man and of the Citizen; the peasant uprising known as the Great Fear; the abolition of feudalism; another threat of a military counterrevolution; and the march on Versailles led by market women, which brought Louis back to Paris and made him a potential hostage of an increasingly radical movement deep within the Parisian population. But by July 14, the Parisians had become revolutionaries. It was a long process, built up over the years by events and the perception of events. Although individuals experienced it in different ways, it took place collectively. It was the force that drove the storming of the Bastille, a revolutionary temper.

CONCLUSION

THE REVOLUTIONARY TEMPER

B Y THE END OF 1788, the outlook of most Parisians had been transformed. They had not adopted all the convictions that would prevail among the revolutionaries by the end of 1789 and that would develop into radical republicanism during the next five years, for those convictions also emerged in response to events. But the experience accumulated during the previous four decades made Parisians ready to overthrow the regime in 1789.

The foregoing chapters have provided a close reading of events and the perception of events as they were reported in the information system of eighteenth-century Paris. Abstracting from those details, the revolutionary temper can be said to have consisted of the following elements:

HATRED OF DESPOTISM. Parisians felt threatened by arbitrary power, primarily in the hands of ministers and the police rather than the king, which took various forms, such as troops patrolling the streets, *lettres de cachet*, and the forced registration of royal edicts. Although the Bastille contained only seven prisoners on July 14, 1789, and its attackers set out to capture its munitions, it loomed in the collective imagination as the supreme symbol of despotism. To be sure, the meaning of "despotism" was fluid, despite Montesquieu's attempt to fix it firmly in political theory and its constant use in parlementary rhetoric. The term could be applied to any perceived abuse of power, such as the restraints imposed on trade by corporations, the authority over doctors by the Parisian faculty of medicine, and the domination of literature by the Académie française. But "despotism" became a call to arms in 1789 because it was aimed at a crucial target, the power of the government embodied by the Bastille.

LOVE OF LIBERTY. The positive side of Parisians' hatred of arbitrary power was the desire to live free from the threat of its interference in their lives. "Liberty" like "despotism" could convey several meanings, depending on the context of its use. By 1789 it was employed increasingly in the singular, rather than the plural, which often referred to privileges such as the "liberties" enjoyed by the provincial estates. Instead of understanding liberty as a privilege (private law that favored some at the expense of others), Parisians came to think of it as a right that belonged to everyone (general law, which applied equally to all citizens). Liberty meant acting and speaking freely, without fear of police spies and *lettres de cachet*; reading independent journals, unhampered by censorship; and obeying laws determined by citizens, not proclaimed by Versailles.

COMMITMENT TO THE NATION. France's humiliation in foreign affairs, especially during the Seven Years' War, provoked disgust with the leadership of Versailles. Parisians came to feel that the nation should take charge of its destiny, that the nation was the source of legitimate authority, and that they owed fidelity to the nation as citizens rather than subjects. Therefore, they asserted the right to participate equally in the exercise of sovereignty, which they took to be inherent in the French people, not divided among estates or concentrated in the king. They infused this principle with passion, speaking and feeling as patriots. The *émotions populaires* that drove violence in the streets became absorbed in a sense of participating in a common, national destiny.

INDIGNATION AT DEPRAVITY AMONG THE ARISTOCRATIC ELITE. While objecting to the privileges of the nobility in general, Parisians directed most of their hostility at *les grands*, the upper aristocracy and the super-rich. They considered courtiers as parasites who inhabited an alien world of luxury and vice. In their view, decadence and despotism were joined in a system that drained wealth from the common people and spread corruption through the body politic.

DEDICATION TO VIRTUE. The ideal of virtue served as the positive counterpart to the scorn for decadent, aristocratic *moeurs*. Parisians valued personal integrity, devotion to domestic life, and humanitarianism (*bienfaisance*). While they celebrated virtue as the guiding principle of their private lives, Parisians especially revered it as a force in public affairs. It inspired commitment to the cause of the nation on the part of citizens and was the dominant quality they required in their leaders. It tended to be homespun, as exemplified by ideal types—Quakers, American farmers, noble savages, the Swiss—yet virtue inhered, at least potentially, in everyone, even noblemen and priests. Above all, it was patriotic.

MORALIZING. Parisians responded to sentimental appeals, which exalted virtue and condemned vice. Denunciation came to be seen as a patriotic duty, wit as a symptom of aristocratic worldliness. To be sure, Voltairean ridicule continued to be a powerful weapon, especially in attacks against religious dogmatism. Yet Voltaire himself set a tone of moral indignation in the Calas Affair, and Rousseau turned moral passion against the Voltairean ideal type of the *mondain*. In the balance of the passions, tears came to outweigh laughter. Among public figures, Mirabeau eclipsed Beaumarchais.

DISENCHANTMENT WITH THE MONARCHY. By the end of his fifty-nine-year reign, Parisians had lost faith in the sacred character of Louis XV, whose personal immorality made him literally lose the royal touch. Because he would not renounce his mistresses, he could not receive absolution for his sins, take communion, and cure subjects suffering from the King's Evil (scrofula) by touching them. He lost contact with Parisians in many ways after their outpouring of affection for him during his illness in Metz in 1744. After 1745, he avoided appearing in Paris and even built a road to circumvent it during his journeys from Versailles.

Much of the aversion to Louis XV derived from the notoriety of his mistresses. Although Parisians found nothing objectionable about royal mistresses in general, they were appalled by the increasingly negative mythology that surrounded the de Nesle sisters (perceived as a matter of incest), Madame de Pompadour (a commoner, unsuited for a king), Madame du Barry (a prostitute), and the supposed "harem" of the Parc aux cerfs. After his death—attributed to smallpox contracted by sex with an adolescent procured by his valet—Louis XV appeared to be a dirty old man.

Louis XVI, by contrast, was widely believed to be impotent, at least during the first seven years of his reign, when he failed to beget children. Although he resumed touching those who suffered from scrofula, he did not acquire charisma, and, in the rumors that accompanied the constant change of ministers, he was scorned for inconsistency and incompetence. Meanwhile, Marie-Antoinette fell victim to the rumor mill that made her out to be depraved, especially after the Diamond Necklace Affair. The public's hatred of the queen compounded the desacralization that sapped the power of the Crown and undercut the legitimacy of the political system.

BELIEF IN THE POWER OF REASON. While losing faith in the sacred power of the king, Parisians acquired faith in the ability of man to decipher the laws of nature. (I say man, because the world of science was exclusively masculine, despite the exceptions of some extraordinary women such as Voltaire's mistress, Madame du Châtelet.) At the beginning of the century, Newton had demonstrated that all bodies acted in accordance with an invisible force, known as gravity. The revolution in chemistry revealed that many such forces were at work in the world. To Parisians who assumed that the world was composed of four elements, earth, air, fire, and water, Lavoisier seemed to demonstrate that man could turn water into air, producing visible effects. The Montgolfiers harnessed some of that air to make man fly. Franklin demonstrated that man could tame lightning, a natural phenomenon driven by the invisible force of electricity. Scientific fads in the 1780s convinced Parisians, at least for a while, that man could cure all disease and even walk on water. It seemed credible that he could discover the laws governing society and, as Condorcet maintained, that he could adapt them to a new order of self-government.

DETACHMENT FROM THE CHURCH AND ATTRACTION TO THE ENLIGHTENMENT. The moral authority of the Catholic Church suffered from the Jansenist and Jesuit controversies. Sympathy for Jansenism ran deep, not merely among partisans of the Parlement but also among the common people who responded to the spiritual appeal of the

Jansenist convulsionaries. By supporting the upper clergy's persecution of Jansenists, the state alienated many Parisians, and it did not win them back when it abolished the Jesuit order. Instead, it reinforced older strains of anticlericalism, while resentment grew against the wealth and power of the upper clergy and Voltaire occupied the high moral ground in the Calas Affair.

Despite their differences, Voltaire and Rousseau stirred indignation at injustice and appealed to principles grounded in the empirical view of knowledge popularized by the *Encyclopédie*. The *philosophes* in general figured prominently in public life, spreading secular values such as tolerance, liberty, and equality before the law. How deeply those values penetrated society is difficult to measure, but they certainly undermined the commitment to orthodox beliefs among the educated classes, including many nobles and even priests. Whatever their ultimate beliefs, Parisians were conscious of living in an age of "*philosophie*" or "*lumières*," phrases that appear often in contemporary diaries and journals, long before their afterlife as "the age of Enlightenment" ("le siècle des Lumières") in cultural history.

POLITICAL ENGAGEMENT AND RESISTANCE TO TAXATION. At the beginning of the century, Parisians generally subscribed to the notion that politics was the king's business, *le secret du roi*. By 1789 they participated in politics, not directly but through the feedback mechanism of "public noises," which made them heard in Versailles. Ministers took increasing heed of public opinion after 1749, when it was a crucial element in the fall of Maurepas. By the time of Turgot and Necker, they wrote elaborate prefaces to royal edicts in order to justify their policies to the public. Necker's *Compte rendu* of 1781 exposed "the king's secret" in the form of a budget. From then until the end of Louis XVI's reign, the state's finances were subject to public debate.

The cumulative pressure of the state debt from the War of the Austrian Succession to the American war made increased taxation unavoidable, and quarrels over taxes took the form of conflicts between the Parlement of Paris and the Crown. The same scenario—remonstrances, *lits de justice*, exiles, and arrests—repeated itself, sharpening Parisians' awareness of political conflict. Taxation of all kinds compounded the hardships of the poor, and it was resented by all groups as unjust, unequal, and even unnecessary, because it was often attributed to the need to cover "depredations" in Versailles. Parisians did not express any deep attachment to the Parlement, but Maupeou's coup in 1771, accompanied by an enormous pamphlet literature, produced a shift in attitudes. Parisians began to think of themselves as "citizens" and "patriots" united in opposition to a despotic ministry. The state's debt precipitated a more serious crisis in 1787, when Calonne failed to rally public opinion behind a reform program that included new taxes. Parisians perceived his program as another threat of despotism, while the surrounding pamphlet literature repeated the themes of the "Maupeouana" of 1771–1774. The suppression of the Parlement by the Brienne-Lamoignon ministry in 1788 looked like a replay of the ministerial despotism of Maupeou-Terray seventeen years earlier. When Parisians took to the streets—and Frenchmen rose in revolt throughout the kingdom—they supported the Parlement's demand for the convocation of the Estates General. They did not promote the power of the Parlement per se, and abandoned it after September, when it committed itself to the 1614 format of the Estates General, which favored the privileged estates.

FAMILIARITY WITH VIOLENCE. Parisians were frequently exposed to violence, much of it meted out by the state in the form of hangings, beheadings, whippings, and the breaking of prisoners on the wheel. During political crises, troops patrolled with bayonets attached to their muskets, and on several occasions they fired into crowds. The crowds themselves turned violent, as in the stampeding and mauling of spectators after the fireworks of February 13, 1749, and May 30, 1770—official *"réjouissances"* (joyful celebrations) that left memories of massacres. The collective memory also kept alive scenes where the crowds turned against the authorities, notably the uprising of May 23, 1750, triggered by the rumor that the police were kidnapping children, and the "flour war" of May 3, 1775, ignited by the belief in a famine plot. On both occasions rioters briefly gained control of Paris, overwhelming the police.

The common term for riots, *émotions populaires*, suggests the collective passions they released. Many were provoked by devastating increases in the price of bread, which offended widely shared notions of a just price, and others were expressed in a carnivalesque idiom, which involved the trial and burning of mannequins designed as surrogates for ministers. The bonfire of a straw man Calonne on October 1, 1787, nearly provoked a riot, and the riotous burnings of straw Briennes and Lamoignons in August and September 1788 turned into uprisings that left many dead. The Réveillon riots of April 27–28, 1789, which also began in carnivalesque fashion and became even more violent, demonstrated the vulnerability of Paris on the eve of the opening of the Estates General. Although the troops restored order, the Gardes Françaises fraternized increasingly with the Parisian populace, and many of them joined the crowd that marched on the Bastille on July 14, a day when the price of bread had reached a new height. The storming of the Bastille was no aberration. It fit into a pattern that made Parisians accustomed to violence and even to welcome it, when there seemed to be no other solution to the political crisis.

For forty years and more (the collective memory went back for centuries; 1748 merely serves as a convenient starting point for this narrative), the experience of events and the cumulative responses to them had fashioned a revolutionary temper. It was fully formed by the end of 1788. Despite the variety of issues and the different strands of public opinion during the preceding decades, Parisians shared a common determination to intervene in the course of events and to take action, violent action, on July 14, 1789.

Although all these elements went into the formation of the revolutionary temper, the result was greater than the sum of its parts. Aside from the common notion of anger, the *Oxford English Dictionary* defines "temper" as the result of a process—both material ("the degree of hardness and elasticity or resiliency given to metal, especially steel, by tempering") and moral ("actual state or attitude of the mind or feelings"). To temper is to bring ingredients to a certain state, whether in the manufacture of metal or in the fixing of a "frame of mind."

The process that forged the revolutionary temper was exposure to information about events—"news," as we would put it today, "nouvelles" to eighteenth-century Parisians. Rather than being limited to a short time span, reports of events usually stretched into news cycles, which maintained the public's interest by means of a continuous narrative. Parisians learned that Prince Édouard was attempting to overthrow the King of England: would he succeed? The gazettes told of his defeat and his miraculous escape from Scotland: what would happen next? Gossips said that he had defied Louis XV's attempt to persuade him to leave France in accordance with the peace settlement of 1748, then that he was abducted outside the Opera, and finally that he had been sighted in various parts of Europe. By then the story was exhausted, and the cycle came to an end. Similarly, each judicial memoir of the Goezman Affair served as an installment in a narrative that kept the public fascinated for many months. The public's interest in the Diamond Necklace Affair and the Kornmann Affair followed the same pattern—a succession of shocking revelations and surprising twists and turns, ending with a verdict by the Parlement.

The Parlement itself generated news cycles by sparring with the government over issues like taxation and the refusal of sacraments, which kept the public guessing about the next installments: more radical remonstrances? A *lit de justice*? Arrests and exiles? The narratives unfolded in the same way, echoing one another and sustaining the collective memory. Disparate episodes such as the arrests of Édouard and of d'Éprémesnil—both done in public with enormous deployment of military might—struck the same chord. And the mutual reinforcement of the stories was compounded by the vilification of key players, because, as we say today, names make news, and the resentment of abuses of power crystallized around the villains. After being dragged through the mud by hundreds of pamphlets, they came to personify an abstract idea, despotism. They gave it legs; it ran everywhere in Paris, and it was reborn as villain succeeded villain in the literature of libel.

Royal mistresses appeared as successive reincarnations of a related motif: extravagant expenditure and immorality in the court. The queen herself came to embody this notion, which was taken, along with convictions about the perfidy of ministers, to explain the deficit. The attacks on Brienne replayed themes from the attacks on Calonne, which were replays of the attacks on Maupeou. Maupeouana from 1771 was reprinted in 1788. The same themes were also transmitted by seditious ceremonies such as the trial and burning of mannequins representing Terray and Lamoignon. Violence followed the carnivalesque revelry, and it, too, fell into installments of the same basic story: public protests against despotism and depredation in Versailles.

Once this master theme became fixed in the general temper, it left no room for views that favored the government. To be sure, ministers from Machault to Brienne proposed progressive reforms and commissioned pamphlets to support them. Different currents of public opinion about all sorts of issues can be traced from the mid-century to the outbreak of the Revolution. In the end, however, the differences were swamped by the flood tide of revulsion against ministerial despotism. Parisians shared a conviction that the system itself was rotten, that it had lost its legitimacy, and they were prepared to overturn it in 1789.

This argument can be sustained, I believe, by intense study of contemporary reports about events—a long, slow process of immersion in the sources, a kind of marination. It raises a problem, however, because I use the reports both as evidence of what happened and of what people thought was happening. I have tried to show how the perception of events inhered in accounts of the events themselves, and that raises problems of interpretation. In many cases, the evidence is straightforward. Marville and Hardy often recounted what people were saying about an occurrence while they reported it. They discussed the spread of "public noises," the multiple reprints of pamphlets, the reactions of audiences to orations, the reception of proclamations, and the public's horror at disasters like the stampede at the celebration of the dauphin's marriage to Marie-Antoinette in 1770. Diverse reports produced an overall impression, and the apparent concatenation of events confirmed convictions among Parisians about the general course of contemporary history.

Yet each report was subjective, and it is difficult to determine the degree of their inter-subjectivity, although that belongs to the story I have tried to tell. Biases can usually be identified. Hardy's sympathy for Jansenism and his dread of insurrection contrast with the anticlerical radicalism of Louis Métra (or the author of the gazette he published), and both differ from the disabused worldliness of Pidansat de Mairobert, the main author of the *Mémoires secrets*. One can also allow for differences in the nature of the narratives. While discussing events in his private journal, the Marquis d'Argenson attained a sophistication that is entirely absent in underground gazettes, and Ruault in his letters to his brother expressed a scorn for the monarchy that could never appear in print. Although we know a good deal about the *nouvellistes*, we cannot follow the chain of information that went into the *Correspondance littéraire secrète*, the *Correspondance secrète, politique et littéraire*, and the journal later published as *Correspondance secrète inédite sur Louis XVI, Marie-Antoinette, la cour et la ville, de 1777 à 1792*. The *Nouvelles ecclésiastiques* treated politics from a rabidly Jansenist perspective in contrast to the foreign French press, particularly the *Gazette de Leyde*, which attempted to maintain a neutral point of view. Because of their differences, the sources cannot be conflated and must be handled with care.

Moreover, they are limited in number. I have had to rely heavily on documents like Marville's correspondence and Hardy's journal. Rich as they are, they are exceptional; and even when supplemented by the thirty-six volumes of the gossipy *Mémoires secrets*, they do not necessarily represent the reactions of a typical cross section of the Parisian population. Yet major events touched everyone. It seems likely that the great majority of Parisians saw a balloon flight, heard a proclamation of peace, and knew about uprisings like the Réveillon riot and the protest against the abduction of children by the police. Paris functioned as a gigantic echo chamber of "public noises." Despite the imperfections of the evidence, it is still possible to pick up the undertones of that communication system and to know what events became lodged in the collective memory.

I therefore think it valid to situate my argument at the level on which information flowed. Instead of attempting to derive collective consciousness from the operation of the economy or the structure of the social system, I find it feasible to see how a frame of mind developed in response to the "public noises" and all the other reports about events. By studying Paris as an early information society, it is possible to construct a narrative of events as Parisians experienced them and to show how that experience, accumulated over four decades, came together in the formation of a revolutionary temper.

AFTERWORD

WHAT WAS REVOLUTIONARY
ABOUT THE FRENCH REVOLUTION?

L OOKING BEYOND the storming of the Bastille, a question arises: If the revolutionary temper existed before 1789, what was so revolutionary about the Revolution itself?

The short answer is everything: it was a total revolution, which aimed to transform the world. Most of us accept the world as it is and assume that it holds together firmly enough to constitute reality, the workaday world we normally inhabit. The revolutionaries—not just in Paris but everywhere in France—set out to create the world as it ought to be, in accordance with principles that they took to be inherent in a normative, natural order.

In 1789 the French confronted the collapse of a social order—the world that they defined retrospectively as the Ancien Régime—and struggled to fashion a new one out of the chaos surrounding them. They experienced reality as something that could be destroyed and reconstructed, and they faced seemingly limitless possibilities, for good and for evil, for raising a utopia and for falling back into tyranny. To be sure, a few seismic upheavals had convulsed French society in earlier ages—the bubonic plague in the fourteenth century, for example, and the religious wars in the sixteenth century. But in 1789, ordinary people began to take their fate into their own hands. For the first time, they participated in politics, both in the elections to the Estates General, which were based on something close to universal manhood suffrage, and by insurrections in the streets of cities and the parishes of the countryside.

Only a small minority of activists joined the Jacobin clubs, but everyone was touched by the Revolution, because the Revolution reached into everything. It re-created time and space. According to the revolutionary calendar adopted in 1793 and used until 1805, time began when the old monarchy ended, on September 22, 1792—the first of Vendémiaire, Year I.

By formal vote of the Convention, which was elected to replace the monarchy with a republican order, the revolutionaries divided time into units that they took to be rational and natural. There were ten days to a week, three weeks to a month, and twelve months to a year. The five days left over at the end became patriotic holidays, *jours sans-culottides*, given over to civic qualities: Virtue, Genius, Labor, Opinion, and Rewards.

Ordinary days received new names, which suggested rational, mathematical regularity: primidi, duodi, tridi, and so on up to décadi. Each was dedicated to some aspect of rural life so that the order of nature would displace the saints' days of the Christian calendar. Thus November 22, formerly devoted to Saint Cecilia, became the day of the turnip, and November 25, formerly Saint Catherine's day, became the day of the pig. The names of the new months also made time conform to the natural rhythm of the seasons. January 1 became the 12th of Nivôse, the month of snow, which was located after the months of fog (Brumaire) and cold (Frimaire) and before the months of rain (Pluviôse) and wind (Ventôse).

The adoption of the metric system represented a similar attempt to impose a rational and natural organization on space. According to a decree of 1795, the meter was to be "the 10,000,000th part of half the terrestrial meridian." Of course, ordinary citizens could not make much of such a definition. They were slow to adopt the meter and the gram, the new units of length and weight, and few of them favored the new week, which gave them one day of rest in ten instead of one in seven. But even where old habits remained, the revolutionaries stamped their ideas on contemporary consciousness by changing everything's name.

Fourteen hundred streets in Paris received new names because the old ones contained some reference to a king, a queen, or a saint. The Place Louis XV, where the most spectacular guillotining took place, became the Place de la Révolution; and later, in an attempt to bury the hatchet, it acquired its present name, Place de la Concorde. The church of Saint-Laurent became the Temple of Marriage and Fidelity; the cathedral of Notre Dame became the Temple of Reason; and Montmartre became Mont Marat in honor of the Revolution's most celebrated martyr. Thirty towns took Marat's name—30 of 6,000 that tried to expunge their past by name changes. Montmorency became Emile; Saint Malo became Victoire Montagnarde (an allusion to the Montagne or radical faction of the Convention); and Coulanges became Cou Sans-Culottes, (*anges* or angels being a sign of superstition).

The revolutionaries even renamed themselves. It wouldn't do, of course, to be called Louis in 1792 or 1793. The Louis called themselves Brutus or Spartacus. Last names like Le Roy or Lévêque, very common in France, became La Loi or Liberté. Children got all sorts of names foisted on them—some from nature ("Pissenlit" or Dandelion did nicely for girls, "Rhubarb" for boys) and some for current events ("Fructidor," "Constitution," "The Tenth of August," "Marat-Couthon-Pique"). The foreign minister Pierre-Henri Lebrun named his daughter "Civilisation-Jemappes-République."

Meanwhile, the queen bee became a "laying bee" ("abeille pondeuse"); chess pieces were renamed, because a good revolutionary would not play with kings, queens, knights, and bishops; and the kings, queens, and jacks of playing cards became liberties, equalities, and fraternities. The revolutionaries set out to change everything: crockery, furniture, law codes, religion, the map of France itself, which was divided into departments—that is, symmetrical units of equal size with names taken from rivers and mountains—in place of the irregular old provinces.

Before 1789, France was a crazy quilt of overlapping and incompatible units—fiscal, judicial, administrative, economic, and religious. After 1789 those segments were melted down into a single substance: the French nation. With its patriotic festivals, its tricolor flag, hymns, martyrs, army, and wars, the Revolution accomplished what had been impossible for Louis XIV and his successors: it united the disparate elements of the kingdom into a nation and conquered the rest of Europe. In doing so, the Revolution unleashed a new force, nationalism, which would mobilize millions and topple governments for the next two hundred years and has not yet spent its force.

Of course, the nation-state did not sweep everything before it. It failed to impose the French language on the majority of the French people, who continued to speak all sorts of mutually incomprehensible dialects, despite a vigorous propaganda drive by the revolutionary Committee on Public Instruction. But in wiping out the intermediary bodies, notably the parlements and the provincial estates, that separated the citizen from the state, the Revolution transformed the basic character of public life.

It went further: it extended the public into the private sphere, inserting itself into the most intimate relationships. Intimacy in French is conveyed by the pronoun *tu* as distinct from the *vous* employed in formal address. Although the French often use *tu* quite casually today, under the Ancien Régime they reserved it for asymmetrical or intensely personal relations. Parents said *tu* to children, who replied with *vous*. The *tu* was used by superiors addressing inferiors, by humans commanding animals, and by lovers—after the first kiss, or exclusively between the sheets. When French mountain climbers reach a high altitude, they often switch from the *vous* to the *tu*, as if all persons become equal in the face of the enormousness of nature.

The French Revolution wanted to make everybody *tu*. On 10 Brumaire Year II (October 31, 1793), a delegation of *sans-culottes* petitioned the National Convention to abolish the *vous*, except for use in the plural, as a result of which there would be "less pride, fewer distinctions, less enmity, more apparent familiarity, more of a penchant for fraternity, and consequently more equality."[1] That may sound laughable today, but it was deadly serious to the revolutionaries: they wanted to build a new society based on new principles of social relations. Also, they did not favor laughter. Some revolutionaries, like Desmoulins and Hébert, utilized irony or bawdy jokes, but the Revolution in general had no sense of humor.[2]

The revolutionaries redesigned everything that smacked of the inequality built into the conventions of the Ancien Régime. They ended letters with a vigorous "farewell and fraternity" ("salut et fraternité") in place of the deferential "your most obedient and humble servant." They substituted Citizen and Citizeness for Monsieur and Madame. And they changed their dress.

Dress often serves as a thermometer for measuring the political temperature. To designate a militant from the radical Sections of Paris, the revolutionaries adapted a term from clothing: *sans-culotte*, one who wears trousers rather than breeches. In fact, workers generally did not take up trousers, which were mainly favored by seamen, until the nineteenth century. Robespierre himself always dressed in the uniform of the Ancien Régime: *culottes*, waistcoat, and a powdered wig. But the model revolutionary, who appears on broadsides, posters, and crockery from 1793 to the present, wore trousers, an open shirt, a short jacket (the *carmagnole*), boots, and a liberty cap ("Phrygian bonnet") over a "natural" (that is, uncombed) crop of hair, which dropped down to his shoulders.

Women's dress on the eve of the Revolution had featured low necklines, basket-skirts, and exotic hairstyles, at least among the aristocracy. Hair dressed in the "hedgehog" style ("en hérisson") rose two or more feet above the head and was decorated with elaborate props—as a fruit bowl or a flotilla or a zoo. After 1789, fashion came from below. Hair was flattened, skirts deflated, necklines raised, and heels lowered. Still later, after the end of the Terror when the Thermidorean Reaction extinguished the Republic of Virtue, fast-moving society women like Mme Tallien exposed their breasts, danced about in diaphanous gowns, and revived the wig. A true *merveilleuse* or fashionable lady would have a wig for every day of the *décade*; Mme Tallien had thirty.

At the height of the Revolution, however, from mid-1792 to mid-1794, virtue was not merely a fashion but the central ingredient in a new political culture, purged of the aristocratic libertinism of the Ancien Régime and heavily tinctured with Rousseauism. To the revolutionaries, virtue was virile. It meant a willingness to fight for the fatherland and for the revolutionary trinity of liberty, equality, and fraternity. Although fraternity, like the rights of man, could be construed broadly, it left no room for women to participate in politics. Their place, as Rousseau had prescribed, was in the home, even though some feminists, notably Olympe de Gouges, demanded political rights for women.

At the same time, the cult of virtue produced a revalorization of family life. Taking their text from Rousseau, the revolutionaries sermonized on the sanctity of motherhood and the importance of breast feeding. They treated reproduction as a civic duty and excoriated bachelors as unpatriotic. "Citizenesses! Give the Fatherland children!" proclaimed a banner in a patriotic parade. "Now is the time to make a baby," admonished a slogan painted on revolutionary pottery. Saint Just, the most extreme ideologist on the Committee of Public Safety, wrote in his notebook: "The children belong to their mother until the age of five, if she has breast-fed them, and to the republic afterward, until death."[5]

With the collapse of the authority of the church, the revolutionaries sought a new moral basis for family life. They turned to the state, and passed laws that would have been unthinkable under the Ancien Régime. They made divorce possible; they accorded full legal status to illegitimate children; they abolished primogeniture. If, as the Declaration of the Rights of Man and of the Citizen proclaimed, all men are created free and equal in rights, shouldn't all men begin with an equal start in life? The Revolution tried to limit "paternal despotism" by giving all chldren an equal share in inheritances. It abolished slavery and gave full civic rights to Protestants and Jews.

To be sure, one can spot loophoes and contradictions in the revolutionary legislation. Despite some heady phrasing in the so-called Ventôse Decrees about the appropriation of counterrevolutionaries' property, the legislators never envisaged anything like socialism. The enslaved persons of Saint-Domingue (Haiti today) freed themselves by a successful insurrection. Although his troops failed to overcome the revolutionary government in Saint-Domingue, Napoleon reversed the abolition of slavery and the most democratic provisions of the laws on family life. Nevertheless, the main thrust of revolutionary legislation is clear: it substituted the state for the church as the ultimate authority in the conduct of private life, and it grounded the legitimacy of the state in the sovereignty of the people.

Popular sovereignty, civil liberty, equality before the law—the words fall so easily off the tongue today that we can hardly imagine their explosiveness in 1789. We also find it difficult to think ourselves back into the mental world of the Ancien Régime, where most people assumed that men are unequal, that inequality is a good thing, and that it conforms to the hierarchical order built into nature by God. Throughout the eighteenth century, the philosophers of the Enlightenment challenged those assumptions, and pamphleteers in Grub Street succeeded in tarnishing the sacred aura of the Crown. But it took violence to smash the mental framework of the Ancien Régime, and violence itself, the iconoclastic, world-destroying, revolutionary sort of violence is hard for us to conceive. The conquerors of the Bastille did not merely annihilate a symbol of despotism. One hundred fifty of them were killed or injured in the assault on the prison; and, as we have seen, the "conquerors of the Bastille" did not merely kill its governor. They cut off his head and paraded it through Paris on the end of a pike.

A week later, in a paroxysm of fury over high bread prices and rumors about plots to starve the poor, a crowd lynched an official in the war ministry named Foullon de Doué, who reportedly said about the malnourished, "Let them eat hay."

After hanging him from a street lamp, the rioters cut off his head, stuffed hay in its mouth, and paraded it on a pike. Another band of rioters seized Foullon's son-in-law, the *intendant* of Paris Bertier de Sauvigny, and marched him through the streets, holding Foullon's severed head in front of him and chanting, "Kiss papa, kiss papa." They murdered Bertier in front of the Hôtel de Ville, tore the heart out of his body, and threw it in the direction of the municipal government. Then they resumed their parade with his head on a pike beside Foullon's. "That is how traitors are punished," said an engraving of the scene.

Gracchus Babeuf, the future leftist conspirator, described the delirium in a letter to his wife. Crowds rejoiced at the sight of the heads on the pikes, he wrote. "Oh! How that joy sickened me! I was simultaneously satisfied and unhappy; I said to myself, so much the better and so much the worse. I understand that the common people take it into their own hands to execute justice; I approve of that justice when it is satisfied by the annihilation of the guilty, but could it not be less cruel? Punishment of all kinds, dismembering, torture, the wheel, public burnings, whips, gallows, public executioners proliferating everywhere have given us such terrible habits!"[4]

The violence subsided after 1789. For two and a half years of relative peace, the French redesigned their country. There were plenty of false starts, wrong turns, miscalculations, and human errors along the way. Contingency weighed heavily on the course of events, and factionalism multiplied the effects of unforeseen consequences. After the Civil Constitution of the Clergy and the loyalty oath required of priests in 1790; the king's attempted escape and his arrest at Varennes in 1791; and the commitment to wage war in 1792, first against Austria and eventually against most of the anciens régimes of Europe—after these and other fatal decisions, the Revolution entered a critical phase, and violence turned into Terror.

We can find plenty of explanations for the official Terror, the Terror directed by the Committee of Public Safety, as the period from September 1793 through August 1794 was retrospectively known. It was not extremely devastating, at least not by twentieth-century standards, if you make a body count of its victims and if you believe in measuring such things statistically. It took about 17,000 lives, counting those condemned by revolutionary tribunals, not the victims of massacres such as the *noyades* (mass drownings) in Nantes.⁵ There were fewer than twenty-five executions in half the departments of France, none at all in six of them. Seventy-one percent of the executions took place in areas where civil war was raging; three-quarters of the guillotined were rebels captured with arms in their hands; and 85 percent were commoners—a statistic that is difficult to digest for those who interpret the Revolution as a class war of the bourgeoisie against the aristocracy. Under the Terror, the word "aristocrat" could be applied to almost anyone deemed to be an enemy of the people.

Historians have succeeded in explaining much of it (not all, not the hideous last month of the "Grande Terreur" when the killing increased while the threat of invasion receded) as a response to the extraordinary circumstances of 1793–1794: the invading armies about to overwhelm Paris; the counterrevolutionaries, some imaginary, many real, plotting to overthrow the government from within; the price of bread soaring out of control and driving the Parisian populace wild with hunger and despair; the civil war in the Vendée; the municipal rebellions in Lyons, Marseille, and Bordeaux; and the factionalism within the National Convention, which threatened to paralyze every attempt to master the situation.

It would be the height of presumption for an American historian sitting in the comfort of his study to condemn the French for violence and to congratulate his countrymen for the relative bloodlessness of their own revolution, which took place in totally different conditions, while thousands of enslaved people suffered from the unrelenting violence of their daily lives. Yet what is he to make of the September Massacres of 1792, an orgy of killing that took the lives of more than 1,000 persons, many of them prostitutes and common criminals trapped in prisons like the Abbaye?

We don't know exactly what happened because the documents were destroyed in the bombardment of the Paris Commune in 1871. But the sober assessment of the surviving evidence by the most eminent specialist, Pierre Caron, suggests that the massacres took on the character of a ritualistic, apocalyptic mass murder.[6] Crowds of *sans-culottes* stormed the prisons in order to extinguish what they believed to be a counterrevolutionary conspiracy. They improvised a popular court in the prison of the Abbaye. One by one, the prisoners were led out, accused, and summarily judged according to their demeanor. Fortitude was taken to be a sign of innocence, faltering as guilt. Stanislas Maillard, a notorious conqueror of the Bastille, assumed the role of prosecutor; and the crowd, transported from the street to rows of benches, ratified his judgment with nods and acclamations. If declared innocent, the prisoner would be hugged, wept over, and carried triumphantly through the city. If guilty, he or she would be hacked to death in a gauntlet of pikes, clubs, and sabres. Then the body would be stripped and thrown onto a heap of corpses or dismembered and paraded about town on the end of pikes.

Throughout their bloody business, the massacrers talked about purging the earth of counterrevolution. They seemed to play parts in a secular version of the Last Judgment, as if the Revolution had released an undercurrent of popular millenarianism. But it is difficult to know what script was being performed in September 1792. We may never be able to fathom such violence or to get to the bottom of the other "popular emotions" that determined the course of the Revolution. After July 14 came the uprising of October 5–6, 1789, and a succession of other revolutionary "days"—August 10, 1792, May 31, 1793, 9 Thermidor Year II (July 27, 1794), 12 Germinal Year III (April 1, 1795), and 1–4 Prairial Year III (May 20–23, 1795). In all of them the crowds cried for bread and blood, and the bloodshed defies understanding.

It is there, nonetheless. It will not go away, and it must be incorporated in any attempt to make sense of the Revolution. One could argue that the violence was a necessary evil, because the Ancien Régime would not die peacefully and the new order could not survive without destroying the counterrevolution. Nearly all the violent "days" were aimed against men perceived as counterrevolutionaries, who threatened to annihilate the Revolution from June 1789 until November 1799, when Bonaparte seized power. After the religious schism of 1791 and the war of 1792, any opposition could be made to look like treason and no consensus could be reached on the principles of politics.

In short, circumstances account for most of the violent swings from extreme to extreme during the revolutionary decade. Most, but not all—certainly not the slaughter of the innocents in September 1792. For my part, I confess that I cannot explain the ultimate cause of revolutionary violence, but I think I can make out some of its consequences. It cleared the way for the revolutionary redesigning and rebuilding that I mentioned above. It struck down institutions from the Ancien Régime so suddenly and with such force that it made anything seem possible. It released utopian energy.

The sense of boundless possibility had built up before 1789, and it was not restricted to popular emotions in the streets. It could seize lawyers and men of letters sitting in the Legislative Assembly. On July 7, 1792, Antoine-Adrien Lamourette, a deputy from Rhône-et-Loire, told the Assembly's members that their troubles all arose from a single source: factionalism. They needed to respond to the principle of fraternity. Whereupon the deputies, who had been at each other's throats a moment earlier, rose to their feet and started hugging and kissing one another as if their political divisions could be swept away in a wave of brotherly love.

The "kiss of Lamourette" has been passed over with a few indulgent smiles by historians who know that one month later the Assembly would fall apart before the bloody uprising of August 10. What children they were, those men of 1792, with their overblown oratory, their naïve cult of virtue, their sentimentality, and their sloganeering about liberty, equality, and fraternity!

But we miss a great deal if we condescend to people in the past. The popular emotion of fraternity swept through Paris with the force of a hurricane in 1792. We can barely imagine its power, because we inhabit a world organized according to other principles, such as pay grades, bottom lines, and who reports to whom. We define ourselves as employers or employees, as teachers or students, as someone located somewhere in a web of intersecting roles. The Revolution at its most revolutionary tried to wipe out such distinctions. It really meant to legislate the brotherhood

of man. It may not have succeeded any better than Christianity christian-
ized, but it remodeled enough of the social landscape to alter the course
of history.

How can we grasp those moments of suspended disbelief, when anything looked possible and the world appeared as a tabula rasa, wiped clean
by a surge of popular emotion and ready to be redesigned? Such moments
pass quickly. People cannot live for long in a state of epistemological exhilaration. Anxiety sets in—the need to fix things, enforce borders, sort out
some version of "aristocrats" and "patriots." Boundaries soon harden, and
the landscape assumes once more the aspect of immutability.

Today most of us live in a world that we take to be not the best but
the only world possible. The French Revolution has faded into an almost
imperceptible past, its bright light obscured by a distance of more than
two centuries, so far away that we may barely believe in it. For the Revolution defies belief. It seems incredible that an entire people could rise up
and transform the conditions of everyday existence. To do so is to contradict the common working assumption that life must be fixed in the patterns of the common workaday world.

Have we never experienced anything that could shake that conviction?
Consider the assassinations of John F. Kennedy, Robert Kennedy, and
Martin Luther King Jr. Consider September 11, 2001. All of us who lived
through those moments remember how they exploded into our daily lives.
We suddenly stopped in our tracks, and in the face of the enormity of the
events, we felt bound to everyone around us. For a few instants we ceased
to see one another through our roles and perceived ourselves as equals,
stripped down to the core of our common humanity. Like mountaineers
high above the daily business of the world, we moved from *vous* to *tu*.

I think the French Revolution was a succession of such events, events so
terrible that they shook humanity to its core. Out of the destruction, the
French seized a new sense of possibility—not just of legislating liberty, but
of living by the values of equality and fraternity. Of course, those values
were limited by what was thinkable at that time. They excluded women
and failed to do justice to many inequities. Few historians would assert
that great events expose some bedrock reality underlying history. I would
argue the opposite: great events make possible the social reconstruction of

reality, the reordering of things-as-they-are so they are no longer experienced as given but rather as willed, in accordance with convictions about how things ought to be.

Possibilism against the givenness of things, those were the forces pitted against each other in France from 1789 to 1799. Not that other forces were absent, including something that can be called a "bourgeoisie" battling something known as "feudalism," while a great deal of property changed hands and the poor extracted some bread from the rich. But all those conflicts were predicated on something greater than the sum of their parts—a conviction that the human condition is malleable, not fixed, and that ordinary people can make history instead of suffering it.

Two centuries of experimenting with brave new worlds have made us skeptical about social engineering. Yet disillusion should not distort the view of 1789 and of 1793–1794. The French revolutionaries were not Stalinists. They were an assortment of unexceptional persons in exceptional circumstances. When things fell apart, they responded to an overwhelming need to make sense of things by ordering society according to new principles. Those principles still stand as an indictment of tyranny and injustice. The French Revolution was revolutionary in its struggle to realize the ideals that it proclaimed: liberty, equality, fraternity.

BIBLIOGRAPHICAL NOTE
AND ACKNOWLEDGMENTS

B ECAUSE THIS BOOK IS based on contemporary reports about events, it does not deal extensively with secondary literature. Yet I have relied on the work of many historians who have cleared the way for a new view of the primary sources, and I would like to acknowledge my debts to them.

Eighteenth-century France, the Enlightenment, and the Revolution have inspired an enormous literature, larger than any other historical field of study and too vast to be surveyed here. I have used this book to synthesize my own work, which goes back to my unpublished Oxford dissertation of 1964, but I owe a great deal to others. First, I would like to thank Roger Chartier and Daniel Roche, friends and collaborators over many years. Chartier's publications on the history of books and reading—notably *Histoire de l'édition française* (Paris, 1984), vol. 2, which he coedited with Henri-Jean Martin—have contributed greatly to the argument in the preceding pages about the power of the printed word. Roche's research is fundamental to the understanding of everyday life among Parisians, especially the common people and the material setting of their lives: *Le Peuple de Paris: essai sur la culture populaire au XVIIIe siècle* (Paris, 1981) and *Histoire des choses banales: naissance de la consommation dans les sociétés traditionnelles (XVIIe–XVIIIe siècle)* (Paris, 1997).

Expanding on Roche's work, David Garrioch has published a rich history of eighteenth-century Paris: *The Making of Revolutionary Paris* (Berkeley, 2002) and a fine-grained study of the city's complexion, *Neigh-*

bourhood and Community in Paris, 1740–1790 (Cambridge, 1986). Colin Jones has also supplemented Roche's views in two important articles about the emergence of a consumer culture: "The Great Chain of Buying: Medical Adverisement, the Bourgeois Public Sphere, and the Origins of the French Revolution," *American Historical Review* (1996): CIII, 13–40 and, with Rebecca L. Spang, "Sans-culottes, sans café, sans tabac: Shifting Realms of Necessity and Luxury in Eighteenth-Century France," in *Consumers and Luxury: Consumer Culture in Europe, 1650–1850*, ed. Maxine Berg and Helen Clifford (Manchester, 1999), 37–62. I have also benefited from Michael Sonenscher's deeply researched study of work and political concepts, *Work and Wages: Natural Law, Politics, and the Eighteenth-Century French Trades* (Cambridge, 1989).

Arlette Farge has studied Parisians up close in several excellent books, notably *Dire et mal dire: l'opinion publique au XVIIIe siècle* (Paris, 1992) and, with Jacques Revel, *Logiques de la foule: l'affaire des enlèvements d'enfants à Paris 1750* (Paris, 1988). Having worked in many of the same sources, particularly the archives of the Bastille, I have learned a great deal from her research and agree with her conclusions, which prove that vibrant strains of public opinion existed at street level, not merely in the world of the salons. That world is explored by Antoine Lilti in *Le monde des salons: sociabilité et mondanité à Paris au XVIIIe siècle* (Paris, 2005). I have also profited from his other publications, particularly *Figures publiques: l'invention de la célébrité 1750–1850* (Paris, 2014). And my discussion of bread crises and popular mentality relies on the fundamental work of Steven L. Kaplan, *Bread, Politics, and Political Economy in the Reign of Louis XV* (The Hague, 1976), 2 vols.

Among the studies of finance and administration, I owe a great deal to Herbert Lüthy, *La Banque protestante en France de la révocation de l'Édit de Nantes à la Révolution* (Paris, 1961), 2 vols., and John Bosher, *French Finances 1770–1795: From Business to Bureaucracy* (Cambridge, 1970). I also have benefited from Michael Kwass, *Privilege and the Politics of Taxation in Eighteenth-Century France: Liberté, Égalité, Fiscalité* (Cambridge, 2000). It successfully revises the standard view of taxation and politics in Marcel Marion, *Histoire financière de la France depuis 1715* (Paris, 1919). Connections between finance and political history can be traced through the entire century, culminating in the ministries of

Necker, which provoked enormous waves of pamphleteering, as discussed astutely by Léonard Burnand: *Necker et l'opinion publique* (Paris, 2004) and *Les pamphlets contre Necker. Médias et imaginaire politique au XVIIIe siècle* (Paris, 2009).

I have indicated my debts to monographs and biographies in footnotes to the chapters on ministers, public figures, and episodes such as the abduction of "Prince Édouard" Stuart and the Diamond Necklace Affair, but I should acknowledge studies on the erosion of the Crown's legitimacy and the desacralization of the monarchy: Jeffrey W. Merrick, *The Desacralization of the French Monarchy in the Eighteenth Century* (Baton Rouge, 1990) and the excellent series of articles by Thomas E. Kaiser, notably "Madame de Pompadour and the Theaters of Power," *French Historical Studies* XIX (1996), 1025–44. I also have profited from Sarah Maza's superb study of judicial affairs, *Private Lives and Public Affairs: The Causes Célèbres of Prerevolutionary France* (Berkeley, 1993).

I need not repeat my acknowledgment in the Introduction to the fine work on eighteenth-century journalism by Pierre Rétat, Jean Sgard, François Moureau, Jack Censer, Jeremy Popkin, Gilles Feyel, and Elizabeth Bond; but I should stress its importance for the understanding of politics, because the monarchy, although absolute in principle, became increasingly vulnerable to the pressure of public opinion during the second half of the century. Two key essays on public opinion are: Keith Michael Baker, "Politics and Public Opinion under the Old Regime: Some Reflections," in *Press and Politics in Pre-Revolutionary France*, ed. Jack Censer and Jeremy Popkin (Berkeley, 1987), 204–46, and Mona Ozouf, "L'Opinion publique" in *The Political Culture of the Old Regime*, ed. Keith Michael Baker (Oxford, 1987), 419–34.

In interpreting political history, I have relied on the masterful work of Michel Antoine, particularly *Louis XV* (Paris, 1989). For the prerevolutionary reign of Louis XVI, John Hardman has supplied a close analysis of ministerial rivalries: *French Politics, 1774–1789. From the Accession of Louis XVI to the Fall of the Bastille* (London, 1995). British historians have also done excellent research on the relations between the Crown and the parlements, a main ingredient of politics under the Ancien Régime, and I have especially profited from the work of William Doyle, beginning with *The Parlement of Bordeaux and the End of the Old Regime, 1771–1790* (New

York, 1974). I have also drawn on Julian Swann, *Politics and the Parlement of Paris under Louis XV, 1754–1774* (Cambridge, 1995) and the vivid and thoroughly researched account of the legal profession in David Bell, *Lawyers and Citizens: The Making of a Political Elite in Old Regime France* (Oxford, 1994).

I have profited greatly from work on the ideological dimension of politics under the Ancien Régime. In several articles and books—my favorite is *The Damiens Affair and the Unraveling of the Ancien Régime 1750–1770* (Princeton, 1984)—Dale Van Kley has demonstrated the importance of Jansenism as a political force in eighteenth-century politics. Although he has corrected the secular bias in much historical writing, I remain convinced that anticlericalism, reinforced by the works of the *philosophes*, was a powerful ingredient in political culture, particularly during the last two decades of the Ancien Régime. I also owe a great deal to the work of Keith Baker, who with Van Kley, has transformed our understanding of political culture in the eighteenth century. I find the essays in *Inventing the French Revolution: Essays on French Political Culture in the Eighteenth Century* (Cambridge, 1990) persuasive, particularly those on relatively unknown figures such as Jacob-Nicolas Moreau and Guillaume-Joseph Saige. In contrast to historians like Jonathan Israel, who treats ideas as autonomous, self-sufficient forces (notably in *Radical Enlightenment: Philosophy and the Making of Modernity, 1650–1750* [Oxford, 2001]), Baker successfully dissects the competing claims of thinkers as elements in an ongoing political discourse. While admiring his approach to political culture, I do not accept his argument that the course of the Revolution was determined by a Rousseauistic discourse of will as opposed to a discourse of reason and that the turning point came when the Constituent Assembly voted for a suspensive royal veto on September 11, 1789. My own view coincides with that of Timothy Tackett, who sees many turning points in the Revolution and allows for the importance of contingency as well as ideology: Tackett, *Becoming a Revolutionary: The Deputies of the French National Assembly and the Emergence of a Revolutionary Political Culture (1789–1790)* (Princeton, 1996). After demolishing Marxist interpretations of the Revolution, François Furet shifted the interpretation of it to the transfer of legitimacy by means of the "magistère de la communication": *Penser la Révolution française* (Paris, 1978), 81. My own emphasis on communication is compatible with his, although I disagree with his view that "l'imaginaire démocratique" (p. 79) determined the course of the Revolution from 1788 to 1794.

The ideological issues stand out in the literature on the "Pre-Revolution" of 1787–1788. According to classical histories of the Revolution by Albert Mathiez, Georges Lefebvre, and Albert Soboul published from 1922 to 1962, the Revolution was triggered by a "révolte nobiliaire" of the privileged orders, who opposed the reforms of Calonne and Brienne. Alfred Cobban, an anti-Marxist, also subscribed to that interpretation, making the opposition of reform and privilege the central theme of France's history in the eighteenth century. Although I do not dispute the importance of reforms, I have found that Parisians rose in revolt against what they construed as ministerial despotism. If that is true, how is one to explain the disparity between their views and those of the historians? It was not, I think, that Parisians failed to perceive what in retrospect appears as political reality but rather that they constructed reality in line with their experience of events during the previous forty years. In fact, I do not believe that a "révolte nobiliaire" took place.

Jean Egret exposed deficiencies in the "révolte nobiliaire" argument in *La Pré-Révolution française 1787–1788* (Paris, 1962), and Vivian Gruder dispatched with it entirely in an excellent monograph, *The Notables and the Nation: The Political Schooling of the French, 1787–1788* (Cambridge, MA, 2007). My research confirms Gruder's and profits from the recent revival of interest in political history. Although I have uncovered plenty of evidence about resentment against aristocratic privileges, I believe that the hostility to the nobility was directed primarily against *les grands*—that is, the court aristocracy, power brokers, and government ministers.

As to the relevance of social science theory to interpretations of the Revolution, I have learned a great deal from the work of William H. Sewell Jr., particularly *Logics of History: Social Theory and Social Transformations* (Chicago, 2005). I also admire Sewell's synthesis of the secondary literature in *Capitalism and the Emergence of Civic Equality in Eighteenth-Century France* (Chicago, 2021). But I cannot accept his argument that the concept of civic equality derived from the experience of commercial capitalism and did so somehow by a process of abstraction that made persons analogous to commodities.

Finally, I would like to acknowledge the help of friends and editors who gave critical readings to several drafts of this text. Steve Forman, my longtime editor at W. W. Norton, made many helpful suggestions. Stuart Proffitt at Penguin Books in London nurtured the book since its incubation many years ago, when our common tutor, Harry Pitt of Worcester College, Oxford, encouraged me to write it and to adopt *The Revolutionary Temper* as its title. David Bell generously went over a first draft, which I modified according to his recommendations, although I alone am responsible for its shortcomings. Pascal Bastien kindly made available prepublication transcripts from Hardy's journal, and Marie Suzanne Fleur Prunières provided valuable help in the preparation of the illustrations and the map of Paris.

NOTES

Abbreviated References for Frequently Cited Sources

I have relied only on sources written soon after events occurred, not on memoirs written long afterward. Because works like the *Mémoires secrets* appeared in several different editions, quotations are identified by the date rather than by the page, except in the case of Grimm's *Correspondance littéraire*, which has monthly rather than daily installments.

Arsenal: Bibliothèque de l'Arsenal
Barbier, *Chronique*: Edmond-Jean François Barbier, *Chronique de la Régence et du règne de Louis XV (1718–1763)* (Paris, 1857–1885), 8 vols.
Bibliothèque historique: Bibliothèque historique de la ville de Paris
BnF: Bibliothèque nationale de France
Correspondance secrète: *Correspondance secrète inédite sur Louis XVI, Marie-Antoinette, la cour et la ville de 1777 à 1792*, ed. Mathurin de Lescure (Paris, 1866), 2 vols.
D'Argenson, *Journal*: René Voyer, Marquis d'Argenson, *Journal et mémoires du marquis d'Argenson*, ed. E. J. B. Rathéry (Paris, 1857–1858), 2 vols.
Grimm, *Correspondance littéraire*: Friedrich Melchior Grimm, *Correspondance littéraire, philosophique et critique par Grimm, Diderot, Raynal, Meister, etc.*, ed. Maurice Tourneux (Paris, 1877–1882), 16 vols.
Hardy, *Journal*: Siméon-Prosper Hardy, "Mes loisirs, ou journal des événements tel qu'ils parviennent à ma connaissance (1764–1789)," 8 vols., Bibliothèque nationale de France, Manuscrits Français, 6680–87, currently being edited by Pascal Bastien and others and published by Hermann Éditeurs (Paris, 2012–2019). Vols. 1–7 have appeared as of this writing.
Journal historique: Mathieu-François Pidansat de Mairobert, *Journal historique de la révolution opérée dans la constitution de la monarchie française par M. de Maupeou, chancelier de France* (London, 1776–1777), 7 vols.
Luynes, *Mémoires*: *Mémoires du duc de Luynes sur la cour de Louis XV (1735–1758)*, ed. L. Dussieux and Eud. Soulié (Paris, 1860), 17 vols.
Mémoires secrets: Louis Petit de Bachaumont, Mathieu-François Pidansat de Mairobert

and others, *Mémoires secrets pour servir à l'histoire de la république des lettres* (London, 1777–1789), 36 vols.

Métra, *Correspondance: Correspondance secrète, politique et littéraire, ou Mémoires pour servir à l'histoire des cours, des sociétés et de la littérature en France depuis la mort de Louis XV* (London, 1787–1790), 18 vols.

Ruault, *Gazette*: Nicolas Ruault, *Gazette d'un Parisien sous la Révolution. Lettres à son frère 1783–1796*, ed. Anne Vassal (Paris, 1976).

Véri, *Journal: Journal de l'abbé Véri*, ed. Jehan de Witte (Paris, 1928–1930), 2 vols.

Introduction

1. The readiness of historians in the Annales school to reconsider events goes back to an article by Pierre Nora published in 1972. See the reworked version of it, "Le retour de l'événement," in *Faire de l'histoire. Nouveaux problèmes*, ed. Jacques Le Goff and Pierre Nora (Paris, 1974), 210–28. See also François Dosse, "L'Événement historique: une énigme irrésolue," *Nouvelle revue de psychosociologie*, no. 19 (2015), 13–27; Paul Ricoeur, "Événement et sens," *L'Événement en perspective*, ed. J. L. Petit (Paris, 1991), 41–56; Pierre Laborie, *Penser l'événement, 1940–1945* (Paris, 2019); and Hayden White, "The Modernist Event," in *The Persistence of History: Cinema, Television, and the Modern Event*, ed. Vivian Sobchack (New York, 1996), 17–38. For a view of events that connects history and anthropology, see Marshall Sahlins, *Historical Metaphors and Mythical Realities: Early History of the Sandwich Islands Kingdom* (Ann Arbor, 1981) and the interpretation of Sahlins's theory by William H. Sewell Jr., *Logics of History: Social Theory and Social Transformation* (Chicago, 2005), chap. 7. Sewell applies a related concept of structure to the fall of the Bastille in chap. 8.

2. This definition derives from the *Oxford English Dictionary* and is discussed more fully in the Conclusion at the end of this book.

3. Among the many monographs on Paris, I have drawn on the work of Daniel Roche, especially *Le Peuple de Paris: essai sur la culture populaire au XVIIIe siècle* (Paris, 1981) and *Histoire des choses banales: naissance de la consommation dans les sociétés traditionnelles (XVIIe–XIXe siècle)* (Paris, 1997); David Garrioch, *The Making of Revolutionary Paris* (Berkeley, 2002); and several books by Arlette Farge, especially *Dire et mal dire: l'opinion publique au XVIIIe siècle* (Paris, 1992).

4. I have sketched these themes, drawing on police archives, in "An Early Information Society: News and the Media in Eighteenth-Century Paris," *The American Historical Review* 105 (February 2000): 1–35.

5. Planted at the beginning of the century and cut down during the remodeling of the Palais-Royal in 1781, the Tree of Cracow was such a well-known institution that it was celebrated in a comic opera by Charles-François Panard, *L'Arbre de Cracovie*, performed at the Foire Saint Germain in 1742. Its name probably derived from the groups of *nouvellistes* who gathered around it during the War of the Polish Succession, 1733–1735. See François Rosset, *L'Arbre de Cracovie: le mythe polonais dans la littérature française* (Paris, 1996).

6. See Gilles Feyel, *L'Annonce et la nouvelle. La presse d'information en France sous l'Ancien Régime (1630–1788)* (Oxford, 2000) and the excellent monograph by Elizabeth Andrews Bond, *The Writing Public: Participatory Knowledge Production in Enlightenment and Revolutionary France* (Ithaca, N.Y., 2021), which concentrates on letters to the editor.

7. Jack R. Censer, *The French Press in the Age of Enlightenment* (New York, 1994), 7 and 215–17.

8. Among the many monographs on the press, I am indebted especially to Pierre Rétat, *Gazettes et information politique sous l'Ancien Régime* (Saint-Étienne, 1999); Jack R. Censer, *The French Press in the Age of Enlightenment* (New York, 1994); Jeremy D. Popkin, *Press and Politics in Pre-Revolutionary France* (Berkeley, 1997); and the superb volumes edited by Jean Sgard, *Dictionnaire des journaux* (Oxford, 1991), 2 vols., and *Dictionnaire des journalistes* (Oxford, 1999), 2 vols.

9. Although written for a popular audience, the work of Frantz Funck-Brentano contains much original research on the Doublet salon and the *nouvellistes*: *Les Nouvellistes* (Paris, 1905). But it is superseded by the studies of François Moureau, *De Bonne main: la communication manuscrite au XVIIIe siècle* (Oxford, 1993) and *Répertoire des nouvelles à la main: dictionnaire de la presse manuscrite clandestine XVIe–XVIIIe siècle* (Oxford, 1999).

10. Darnton, *Poetry and the Police: Communication Networks in Eighteenth-Century Paris* (Cambridge, MA, 2010).

11. I have summarized my research on these subjects in *The Business of Enlightenment: A Publishing History of the Encyclopédie 1775–1800* (Cambridge, MA, 1979); *A Literary Tour de France: The World of Books on the Eve of the French Revolution* (New York, 2018); and *Pirating and Publishing: The Book Trade in the Age of Enlightenment* (New York, 2021).

12. Darnton, *The Devil in the Holy Water, or the Art of Slander from Louis XIV to Napoleon* (Philadelphia, 2009); see especially pp. 269–99.

13. Steven L. Kaplan, *Bread, Politics and Political Economy in the Reign of Louis XV* (The Hague, 1976), II, 701.

14. See, for example, Bronislaw Baczko, *Les Imaginaires sociaux. Mémoires et espoirs collectifs* (Paris, 1984), especially pp. 30–35. Many historians use similar phrasing. Thus "âme collective" and "conscience sociale" in Jean Nicolas, *La Rébellion française. Mouvements populaires et conscience sociale (1661–1789)* (Paris, 2002), 541; "imaginaire collectif" in François Furet, *Penser la Révolution française* (Paris, 1978), 108; "modes collectifs de pensée et de sensibilité," in Laborie, *Penser l'événement*, 89; "collective psychology" and "revolutionary consciousness" in Timothy Tackett, *Becoming a Revolutionary: The Deputies of the French National Assembly and the Emergence of a Revolutionary Culture (1789–1790)* (Princeton, 1996), 302 and 309; "social imagination" and "collective memory" in David Garrioch, *The Making of Revolutionary Paris* (Berkeley, 2002), 71, 131; and "collective consciousness" in Michael Kwass, *Privilege and the Politics of Taxation in Eighteenth-Century France* (Cambridge, 2000), 26.

15. *De la Division du travail social* (Paris, 1960; 1st edition, 1893), 46. All translations in this book are mine.

16. Gabriel Tarde, *L'Opinion et la foule* (Paris, 1901) and *Les Lois de l'imitation* (Paris, 1890).

17. Benedict Anderson, *Imagined Communities: Reflections on the Origin and Spread of Nationalism* (revised edition, London, 1991). See especially pp. 35–36, where the argument closely resembles Tarde's thesis.

18. Erving Goffman, *Frame Analysis: An Essay on the Organization of Experience* (Boston, 1986; original edition, 1974), 10. See also Goffman, *The Presentation of Self in Everyday Life* (New York, 1990; original edition, 1959).

19. Darnton, "Theatricality and Violence in Paris, 1788," in *Voltaire: An Oxford Celebration*, ed. Nicholas Cronk, Alison Oliver, and Gillian Pink (Oxford, 2022), 9–29. A shortened version of this essay was published in *The Times Literary Supplement*, March 25, 2022, pp. 7–9.

20. Max Weber, *Wirtschaft und Gesellschaft. Grundriss der verstehenden Soziologie* (Tübingen, 1980; first edition, 1922), 2.

21. Clifford Geertz, *The Interpretation of Cultures* (New York, 1973), 5 and 131.

Chapter 1

1. To appreciate the disparity between the reports of events that circulated in Paris in 1747 and the version of events reconstructed by historians, compare the account that follows with standard histories such as Walter L. Dorn, *Competition for Empire 1740–1763* (New York, 1940), 161–62, vol. 9 of *The Rise of Modern Europe*, edited by William L. Langer; and Henri Carré, *Louis XV (1715–1774)* (Paris, 1911), 153–54, vol. 8 of *Histoire de France*, edited by Ernest Lavisse. A more recent history of the war treats Lawfeld as a French victory: Reed Browning, *The War of the Austrian Succession* (Phoenix Mill, UK, 1994).

2. Bibliothèque nationale de France (henceforth BnF), ms. fr. 13705, fo. 149. This is the text of the note according to a bulletin from the salon of Mme Doublet. A different version appeared in the *Courrier d'Amsterdam* of July 14, 1747.

3. Ibid., fo. 156. The *Courrier d'Avignon* of July 14, 1747, also contains a different version of this note. On July 2, 1747, Louis XV also ordered the bishop of Bayonne to conduct a Te Deum in his cathedral: Michèle Fogel, *Les Cérémonies de l'information dans la France du XVIe au XVIIIe siècle* (Paris, 1989), 342–46. On rumors in relation to the war, including reports about Lawfeld, see Tabetha Leigh Ewing, *Rumor, Diplomacy and War in Enlightenment Paris* (Oxford, 2014).

4. The reports are scattered through the *nouvelles à la main* in BnF, ms. fr. 13705. The quotation comes from a letter from Tongres dated July 3, 1747, fo. 154.

5. *Gazette d'Amsterdam*, July 7, 11, 14, 18, and 21, 1747, in Bibliothèque de l'Arsenal, Paris (cited henceforth as Arsenal), Quarto H.8, 929. The reports on casualties varied enormously from issue to issue. On July 18, 1747, the *Gazette d'Amsterdam* printed a letter from London dated July 11, which stated, "Notre perte est peu considérable en comparaison de celle des ennemis." The *Courrier d'Avignon*, which strongly favored the French, published articles that made the battle look more decisively like a French victory. See its issues of July 14, 18, 21, 25, and 28, 1747.

6. Thus the report of a police spy dated December 2, 1747, Arsenal, ms. 10169, fo. 222: "Tout Paris commente beaucoup sur la réponse des Hollandais contenue tout au long dans leur gazette d'hier." See also the spy report of November 24, 1747, Arsenal, ms. 10169, fo. 114.

7. On public opinion and police *nouvellistes*, see Arsenal, ms. 10022, fos. 45–47 and ms. 10169, fo. 112.

8. Arsenal, ms. 10022, fo. 46.

9. Barbier, *Chronique de la Régence et du règne de Louis XV (1718–1763), ou Journal de Barbier, avocat au Parlement de Paris* (Paris, 1857; cited henceforth as Barbier, *Chronique*), IV, 250.

10. Louis Sébastien Mercier, *Tableau de Paris*, ed. Jean-Claude Bonnet (Paris, 1994), I, 377.

11. This personalization also characterized the language of peace treaties, such as the one that ended the War of the Austrian Succession: *Traité de paix entre le Roi, le Roi de la Grande Bretagne, et les Etats Généraux des Provinces-Unies des Pays-Bas* (Paris, 1750).

12. See the police reports on conversations in cafés and public places in Arsenal, ms. 10169. Similar references occur in *Lettres de M. de Marville, lieutenant général de police, au ministre Maurepas (1742–1747)*, ed. A. de Boislisle (Paris, 1905), III and Barbier, *Chronique*, IV.

13. In *Privilege and the Politics of Taxation in Eighteenth-Century France: Liberté, Égalité, Fiscalité* (Cambridge, 2000), Michael Kwass has corrected the standard view that the nobility generally managed to avoid direct taxes. That view derives mainly from the work of Marcel Marion, particularly *Les Impôts directs sous l'Ancien Régime, principalement au VIIIe siècle* (Paris, 1910).

14. Barbier, *Chronique*, IV, 289.

15. The *Dictionnaire de l'Académie française* (Nîmes, 1778; edition of 1762) defined "publier" as "rendre public." The dictionary also defined "Publication" as "action par laquelle on rend une chose publique et notoire." Among the examples it cited was "la publication de la paix."

16. The following account is based on BnF, ms. fr. 12719, p. 185; *Courrier d'Avignon*, Feb. 25, 1749; and Barbier *Chronique*, IV, 350–52.

17. Barbier, *Chronique*, IV, 350.

18. *Journal et mémoires du marquis d'Argenson*, ed. E.-J.-B. Rathery (Paris, 1862), IV, 391. For reports of police spies, see François Ravaisson, *Archives de la Bastille* (Paris, 1881), XVI, 19.

Chapter 2

1. The following account is based primarily on "Dossier du Prétendant Charles Édouard" in the archives of the Bastille, Arsenal, ms. 11658; the *nouvelles* connected with the salon of Mme Doublet, BnF ms. fr. 13707–13710; and Barbier, *Chronique*, IV, 329–41. See also the excellent article by Thomas E. Kaiser, "The Drama of Charles Edward Stuart, Jacobite Propaganda, and French Political Protest, 1745–

1750," *Eighteenth-Century Studies* XXX, no. 4 (1997): 365–81; and L. L. Bongie, *The Love of a Prince: Bonnie Prince Charlie in France* (Vancouver, 1986). On the general issue of the desacralization of the monarchy, see Jeffrey W. Merrick, *The Desacralization of the French Monarchy in the Eighteenth Century* (Baton Rouge, 1990).

2. Barbier, *Chronique*, IV, 161.

3. *Courrier d'Avignon*, Dec. 10, 17, 20, and 27, 1748.

4. In addition to the sources cited above, note 1, this account draws on reports in *Courrier d'Avignon*, Dec. 20, 1748; *Gazette d'Utrecht*, Dec. 27, 1748; *Gazette d'Amsterdam*, Dec. 27, 1748; and *Journal inédit du duc de Croÿ, 1718–1784*, ed. Vicomte de Grouchy and Paul Cottin (Paris, 1906), 114.

5. The following quotations come from Bibliothèque historique de la ville de Paris (henceforth Bibliothèque historique), ms. 649, pp. 13, 16, 31, and 60.

6. Ibid., p. 60. "Français, rougissez tous, que l'Ecosse frémisse; / George d'Hanovre a pris le roi à son service, / Et Louis devenu de l'Electeur exempt, / Surprend, arrête, outrage indignement / Un Hannibal nouveau, d'Albion le vrai maître, / Et qui de l'univers, mériterait de l'être."

7. See BnF, ms. fr. 13710, fos. 65–66; *Courrier d'Avignon*, Aug. 22, 1749; Barbier, *Chronique*, IV, 440 and V, 121; and *Mémoires du duc de Luynes sur la cour de Louis XV (1735–1758)*, ed. L. Dussieu and E. Soulié (Paris, 1862), IX, 147–55.

8. Louis XV's supposedly incestuous affairs with the de Nesle sisters provoked gossip and reports by police spies and underground gazettes throughout the early 1740s. See, for example, Arsenal, ms. 10029, fo. 129: "Les gens d'affaires, les officiers retirés, et le peuple gémissent, murmurent contre le ministère et prévoient que cette guerre aura des suites fâcheuses. Les gens d'Eglise, Jansénistes surtout, sont de ce dernier sentiment et osent penser et dire que les malheurs qui sont à la veille d'accabler le royaume viennent d'en haut en punition des incestes du roi, et de son irreligion." On the king's early mistresses and his loss of the royal touch, see the excellent biography by Antoine Michel, *Louis XV* (Paris, 1989), 484–92. The definitive work on the royal touch is Marc Bloch, *Les Rois thaumaturges, études sur le caractère surnaturel attribué à la puissance royale particulièrement en France et en Angleterre* (Strasbourg, 1924).

9. Ravaisson, *Archives de la Bastille*, XII, 212.

10. BnF, ms. fr. 12720, p. 367.

11. BnF, nouvelles acquisitions françaises (henceforth n.a.fr.), 10781.

12. D'Argenson, *Journal*, V, 464 and 468.

Chapter 3

1. Chamfort himself attributed the remark to "un homme d'esprit": Sébastien-Roch Nicolas de Chamfort, *Chamfort. Oeuvres principales* (Paris, 1960), 213. Patrice Coirault has explored the history of folk songs in several works, notably *Notre chanson folklorique* (Paris, 1941). For a detailed study of the material discussed in this chapter, see my *Poetry and the Police: Communication Networks in Eighteenth-Century Paris* (Cambridge, MA, 2010).

2. D'Argenson, *Journal*, V, 343.

3. Hélène Delavault, accompanied by Claude Pavy on the guitar, has recorded twelve of the songs, which are freely available online at www.hup.harvard.edu/features/darpoe. See "An Electronic Cabaret" in *Poetry and the Police*, 174–88.

4. *Poetry and the Police*, 158–61.

5. *Portefeuille d'un talon rouge. Contenant les anecdotes galantes & secrètes de la cour de France* (Paris, n.d.), 22.

6. The original version is in *Clef des chansonniers, ou recueil de vaudevilles depuis cent ans et plus* (Paris, 1717), I, 130: "Réveillez-vous, belle dormeuse, / Si mes discours vous font plaisir. / Mais si vous êtes scrupuleuse, / Dormez, ou feignez de dormir." The attack on the duchess is in BnF ms. fr 13705, fo. 2: "Sur vos pas, charmante duchesse, / Au lieu des grâces et des ris, / L'amour fait voltiger sans cesse / Un essaim de chauve-souris." Although it had no political message, it prepared the way, by means of association, for the attack on Mme de Pompadour, which appeared in several sources and is quoted here from d'Argenson, *Journal*, V, 456. See also BnF, ms. fr 13709, fo. 42.

7. Barbier, *Chronique*, IV, 366, and for a general account of Maurepas's fall, pp. 361–67. See also Bibliothèque historique, ms. 649, pp. 121 and 126; d'Argenson, *Journal*, V, 456; and Charles Collé, *Journal et mémoires de Charles Collé*, ed. Honoré Bonhomme (Paris, 1868), I, 48–49, 62–64, and 71.

8. D'Argenson to Berryer, June 26, 1749; Arsenal, ms. 11690, fo. 42.

9. D'Argenson to Berryer, July 6, 1749; ibid., fo. 55.

10. D'Argenson, *Journal*, V, 343. See also Barbier, *Chronique*, IV, 377–78 and Collé, *Journal*, I, 121.

11. Abbé André Morellet, *Mémoires inédits de l'abbé Morellet* (Paris, 1822), I, 13–14; *Vie privée de Louis XV, ou principaux événements, particularités et anecdotes de son règne* (London, 1781), II, 301–2. See also *Les Fastes de Louis XV, de ses ministres, maîtresses, généraux et autres notables personnages de son règne* (Villefranche, 1782), I, 333–40.

12. Bibliothèque historique, ms. 649, p. 123.

13. Ibid., p. 53.

14. Ibid., p. 59.

15. Bibliothèque historique, ms. 650, p. 261.

Chapter 4

1. *Nouvelles ecclésiastiques, ou Mémoires pour servir à l'histoire de la Constitution Unigénitus,* July 10, 1749. This underground Jansenist journal provides much information for the following account, as do the foreign newspapers published in French, especially the *Gazette de Leyde* (it began publication on Jan. 1, 1750), and the sources mentioned in the previous chapters, particularly d'Argenson, *Journal* and Barbier, *Chronique*. In his *Journal*, V, 491–92, d'Argenson, like the *Nouvelles ecclésiastiques*, estimated the number of mourners at 10,000. In his *Chronique* IV, 373, Barbier stressed that many Parisians considered Coffin a "saint." Drawing on the large literature on Jansenism, I have relied especially on the excellent studies by Dale Van Kley: *The Jansenists and the Expulsion of the Jesuits from France, 1757–1765* (New

Haven, 1975); *The Damiens Affair and the Unraveling of the Ancien Régime, 1750–1770* (Princeton, 1984); and *The Religious Origins of the French Revolution: From Calvin to the Civil Constitution, 1560–1791* (New Haven, 1996). For other aspects of this subject, see Monique Cottret, *Jansénisme et Lumières. Pour un autre XVIIIe siècle* (Paris, 1998); Catherine-Laurence Maire, *De la cause de Dieu à la cause de la nation: le jansénisme au XVIIIe siècle* (Paris, 1998); and B. Robert Kreiser, *Miracles, Convulsions, and Ecclesiastical Politics in Early Eighteenth-Century Paris* (Princeton, 1978). For the general religious context, see Jean Delumeau and Monique Cottret, *Le Catholicisme entre Luther et Voltaire* (Paris, 1997) and John McManners, *Church and Society in Eighteenth-Century France* (Oxford, 1998), 2 vols.

2. Among the many studies of the parlements, see especially Jean Egret, *Louis XV et l'opposition parlementaire* (Paris, 1970); François Bluche, *Les Magistrats du Parlement de Paris au XVIIIe siècle* (Paris, 1960); J. H. Shennan, *The Parlement of Paris* (Ithaca, 1968); Julian Swann, *Politics and the Parlement of Paris under Louis XV, 1754–1774* (Cambridge, 1995); John Rogister, *Louis XV and the Parlement of Paris, 1737–55* (Cambridge, 2002); and William Doyle, *Venality: The Sale of Offices in Eighteenth-Century France* (Oxford, 1996). The most important documents are collected in Jules Gustave Flammermont, *Remontrances du Parlement de Paris au XVIIIe siècle* (Paris, 1888–1898), 3 vols., although in the following pages they will be quoted from the texts—parlementary publications and journal articles—that reached Parisian readers.

3. On the milieu of the Palais de justice, see the excellent monograph by David A. Bell, *Lawyers and Citizens: The Making of a Political Elite in Old Regime France* (New Haven, 1994), and on robe-sword relations, Franklin L. Ford, *Robe and Sword: The Regrouping of the French Aristocracy after Louis XIV* (Cambridge, MA, 1953).

4. The following account relies primarily on Kreiser, *Miracles, Convulsions, and Ecclesiastical Politics.*

5. *Courrier d'Avignon*, Aug. 8 and 19, 1749.

6. Barbier, *Chronique*, IV, 379; d'Argenson, *Journal*, VI, 1–2 and 9–10; de Luynes, *Mémoires*, IX, 454–56.

7. Barbier, *Chronique*, IV, 500–507 and V, 1–2 and 8; *Gazette de Leyde*, Jan. 12, 15, and 22, 1751.

8. The following account is based on reports in the *Gazette de Leyde*; Barbier, *Chronique*; and d'Argenson, *Journal.*

9. D'Argenson, *Journal*, VII, 29.

10. Barbier gives the fullest account of this crisis: *Chronique*, V, 176–213. See also *Nouvelles ecclésiastiques*, May 7, 1752, and April 17, 1753. On Jan. 2, 1753, the *Nouvelles ecclésiastiques* noted in connection with the Parlement's decree of April 18, 1752, "Le plus simple artisan quitte son travail pour acheter et pour lire le nouvel arrêt."

11. Barbier wrote in May 1752 (*Chronique*, VI, 220), "Tout Paris est Janséniste, à peu de gens près." But that remark probably indicated sympathy for the victims of the persecution rather than theological convictions.

12. *Nouvelles ecclésiastiques*, March 6, March 27, and April 3, 1753.

13. Quotations from d'Argenson, *Journal*, VII, 193 and 227. See also Barbier, *Chronique*, V, 259–64, 338–49, and 393–400.

14. *Remontrances du Parlement au Roi du 9 avril 1753*, quotations from pp. 2 and 10.

D'Argenson considered the remonstrances to be "un appel au peuple . . . destinées à la nation." *Journal*, VII, 464.

15. Barbier, *Chronique*, V, 386.
16. Barbier, *Chronique*, V, 386 and VI, 11.
17. D'Argenson, *Journal*, VIII, 343.
18. D'Argenson, *Journal*, VIII, 153.

Chapter 5

1. The main sources for the following account are Barbier, *Chronique*, IV–V, covering the period from Nov. 1749 through Oct. 1750; d'Argenson, *Journal*, VI, 202–44 from June 1749 through Sept. 1750; de Luynes, *Mémoires*, X, from May through August, 1750; and *Gazette de Leyde*, Jan. 9 to Aug. 18, 1750. This chapter is intended only to supplement the definitive study by Arlette Farge and Jacques Revel, *Logiques de la foule: l'affaire des enlèvements d'enfants, Paris 1750* (Paris, 1988). See also Lisa Jane Graham, *If the King Only Knew: Seditious Speech in the Reign of Louis XV* (Charlottesville, 2000).
2. D'Argenson, *Journal*, VI, 204; Barbier, *Chronique*, IV, 454. See also de Luynes, *Mémoires*, X, 268.
3. D'Argenson, *Journal*, VI, 206.
4. Barbier, *Chronique*, IV, 437.
5. *Gazette de Leyde*, June 26 and July 3, 1750.
6. *Gazette de Leyde*, Aug. 14, 1750. The *Gazette* identified thirty-one of the arrested as belonging to "le bas peuple."
7. D'Argenson, *Journal*, VI, 213 and 219.

Chapter 6

1. Pierre Goubert and Daniel Roche, *Les Français et l'Ancien Régime* (Paris, 1984), vol. I, *La Société et l'État*, 338–39.
2. On reactions to the *vingtième*, see Barbier, *Chronique*, IV, 367–71. On the distinction of ordinary and extraordinary taxes, see Pierre Goubert and Daniel Roche, *Les Français et l'Ancien Régime* (Paris, 1984), I, 338–39. And among works on taxation and state finance, see Marcel Marion, *Les Impôts directs sous l'Ancien Régime, principalement au XVIIIe siècle* (Paris, 1910) and J. F. Bosher, *French Finances, 1770–1795* (Cambridge, 1970).
3. Michael Kwass in *Privilege and the Politics of Taxation in Eighteenth-Century France* (Cambridge, 2000) has demonstrated that the nobility paid considerable amounts in direct taxation, although he stresses that the tax burden fell more heavily on commoners.
4. Accounts of this gossip are in d'Argenson, *Journal*, IV, 466; VI, 222, 251, 262, and 276; and VIII, 3 and 7.
5. Ibid., VII, 23. See also similar passages in V, 343, 393, 410, 416, 433, and 443.
6. Ibid., IV, 480. See also Barbier, *Chronique*, IV, 369 and de Luynes, *Mémoires*, IX, 410–16.

7. *Gazette de Leyde*, Sept. 1, 1750; Barbier, *Chronique*, IV, 467–70; de Luynes, *Mémoires*, X, 318; d'Argenson, *Journal*, VI, 17, 39, 94, 99, 107, 136, and 162.

8. De Luynes, *Mémoires*, X, 434.

9. *Gazette de Leyde*, Sept. 8, 22, and 29; Oct. 6 and 20, 1750; De Luynes, *Mémoires*, X, 435; Barbier, *Chronique*, IV, 470–71 and 481–82; d'Argenson, *Journal*, VI, 258, 262–63, and 266.

10. D'Argenson, *Journal*, VI, 272.

11. Voltaire, *La Voix du sage et du peuple* (Amsterdam, 1750), 4. Although this pamphlet was anonymous, it was immediately attributed to Voltaire.

12. *Gazette de Leyde*, Nov. 15, 1750.

13. D'Argenson, *Journal*, VI, 364. See also pp. 367–78.

14. Ibid., VII, 23.

15. The government did not publish the text of the edict, a tangle of verbiage that avoided the term *don gratuit*, but copies of it circulated, and it was printed in the *Gazette de Leyde* of Jan. 18, 1752. Barbier included a copy, which he dated as Dec. 22, 1751, in his *Chronique*, V, 143. D'Argenson described the edict as "une reculade prodigieuse d'autorité": *Mémoires*, VII, 65–66.

16. D'Argenson, *Mémoires*, VII, 49.

Chapter 7

1. Diderot, "Encyclopédie" in *Encyclopédie, ou dictionnaire raisonné des sciences, des arts, et des métiers, par une société de gens de lettres* (Paris, 1751–1772), 1st edition, V, 642. Of the many works on the Enlightenment, a perceptive, recent assessment is Antoine Lilti, *L'Héritage des Lumières: ambivalences de la modernité* (Paris, 2019).

2. This chapter incorporates work I have published as *The Business of Enlightenment: A Publishing History of the Encyclopédie 1775–1800* (Cambridge, MA, 1979); "Philosophers Trim the Tree of Knowledge," in *The Great Cat Massacre and Other Episodes in French Cultural History* (New York, 1984); and "Les Encyclopédistes et la police," *Recherches sur Diderot et l'Encyclopédie*, no. 1 (Oct. 1986): 94–109. Among the many studies of the *Encyclopédie* and Diderot, see Jacques Proust, *Diderot et l'Encyclopédie* (Paris, 1967) and Arthur M. Wilson, *Diderot* (New York, 1972).

3. "Discours préliminaire," *Encyclopédie*, I, xv.

4. Herbert Dieckmann, *Le Philosophe: Texts and Interpretation* (St. Louis, 1948).

5. *Mercure de France*, July 1751, 112 and 114.

6. *Journal des savants*, Sept. 1751, 626.

7. On reactions to the de Prades scandal, see Barbier, *Chronique*, V, 146–48, 149–53, 157–60, and 174–75.

8. Barbier, *Chronique*, V, 153.

9. D'Argenson, *Journal*, VII, 56–57, 63, 68, 71–72; *Nouvelles ecclésiastiques*, March 19 and April 2, 1752, and Jan. 3, 1753. See also Grimm, *Correspondance littéraire*, I, 94.

10. *Arrêt du Conseil du Roi du 7 février 1752*.

11. D'Argenson, *Journal*, VII, 102, 110, and 122; Malesherbes, *Mémoires sur la librairie. Mémoire sur la liberté de la presse*, ed. Roger Chartier (Paris, 1994), 61, 67–73.

12. *Déclaration du Roi . . . donnée à Versailles le 16 avril 1757:* "Tous ceux qui seront convaincus d'avoir composé, fait composer et imprimer des écrits tendant à attaquer la religion, à émouvoir les esprits, à donner atteinte à notre autorité et à troubler l'ordre et la tranquillité de nos états, seront punis de mort."

13. Darnton, *The Business of Enlightenment*, 33–37. Since the publication of this book, I have slightly corrected the statistics. I now estimate that a total of 24,400 copies were produced and that about 11,200 were sold in France.

Chapter 8

1. For typical remarks, see Grimm, *Correspondance littéraire*, IX, 132 and 149.

2. Quotations from Barbier, *Chronique*, VIII, 78. See also *Chronique*, VIII, 65–66; *Mémoires secrets*, June 6 and 20, 1763 (references to the *Mémoires secrets* are given by date because there were many editions with different pagination); and *Gazette de Leyde*, March 4, 1763.

3. *Gazette de Leyde*, May 20, June 10, and June 21, 1763; Barbier, *Chronique*, VIII, 76–77.

4. Barbier, *Chronique*, VIII, 81–82. *L'Orage du 20 juin 1763*, a contemporary pamphlet, dated June 21, 1763, described (p. 1) the downpour as so sudden and violent that the festivities had to be abandoned: "Le temps se charge, les éclairs partent, le tonnerre gronde, l'ondée survient. . . . Sauve qui peut! Robes, coiffures, habits, frisures, et tout étalage est en proie aux insultes de l'intempérie subite."

5. Barbier, *Chronique*, VIII, 82–84; *Gazette de Leyde*, July 5 and 8, 1763; *Mémoires secrets*, July 2 and 4, 1763.

6. *Mémoires secrets*, July 2, 4, and 7, 1763.

Chapter 9

1. See James C. Riley, *The Seven Years War and the Old Regime in France: The Economic and Financial Toll* (Princeton, 1986), especially 194–220.

2. *Richesse de l'Etat* (n.p., n.d.), p. 6.

3. Barbier, *Chronique*, VIII, 77. In a sequel to his pamphlet, *Développement du plan intitulé Richesse de l'Etat*, reprinted in *Richesse de l'Etat à laquelle on a ajouté les pièces qui ont paru pour et contre* (Amsterdam, 1764; henceforth *Richesse* anthology), 18, Roussel claimed that his pamphlet had "fait la matière de toutes les conversations" in Paris and that seven-eighths of Parisians favored it.

4. *Mémoires secrets*, June 12 and July 5, 1763.

5. *Gazette de Leyde*, June 24, June 28, July 1, 19, 22, and 29, 1763. Grimm, *Correspondance littéraire*, X, 252–61, 342–43, 363, 513.

6. The quotations in the order of their appearance come from *Mémoires secrets*, April 3, 1764; *Tout n'est pas dit* in *Richesse* anthology, 188; *La Patrie vengée*, in *Richesse* anthology, 288; and *L'Orage du 20 juin*, in *Richesse* anthology, 2.

7. The quotations in the order of their appearance come from *Résolution des Doutes modestes sur la possibilité du système établi par l'écrit intitulé Richesse de l'Etat*, in

Richesse anthology, 189; *Le Patriote français, ou l'heureuse vérité* (n.p., 1763), 2, evoking "les esprits échauffés à l'arbre de Cracovie"; *Idée d'un citoyen sur l'administration des finances du Roi*, *Richesse* anthology, 205; *Le Bien de l'Etat*, in *Richesse* anthology, 270; *Examen des richesses de l'Etat*, in *Richesse* anthology, 286–87.

8. *Idée d'un citoyen*, in *Richesse* anthology, 201. The physiocratic treatise by Victor de Riqueti, Marquis de Mirabeau, *Philosophie rurale, ou économie générale et politique de l'agriculture, réduite à l'ordre immuable des lois physiques et morales, qui assurent la prospérité des empires* (Amsterdam, 1763), 3 vols., appeared in the midst of the debate stirred up by *Richesse de l'Etat* but did not refer to it.

9. See the excellent study by Keith Michael Baker, "Controlling French History: The Ideological Arsenal of Jacob-Nicolas Moreau," in Baker, *Inventing the French Revolution: Essays on French Political Culture in the Eighteenth Century* (Cambridge, 1990), 59–85.

10. Moreau, *Doutes modestes sur la Richesse de l'Etat, ou Lettre écrite à l'auteur de ce système par un de ses confrères* (Paris, 1763). The tax proposal of *Richesse de l'Etat*, Moreau warned (p. 3), would create "la plus parfaite égalité entre tous les individus."

11. *Mes rêveries sur les Doutes modestes à l'occasion des Richesses [sic] de l'Etat*, *Richesse* anthology, 94 and 96.

12. Roussel, *Développement*, 29.

13. *Mémoires secrets*, July 5, 1763; Barbier, *Chronique*, VIII, 76–77.

14. See Kwass, *Privilege and the Politics of Taxation*, 155–212.

15. *Objets de remontrances arrêtés par le parlement séant à Rouen, toutes les chambres assemblées, le 16 juillet 1763*, (n.p., n.d.), see especially 5–7; Barbier, *Chronique*, VIII, 90–91 and 95–100; *Mémoires secrets*, July 22, 1763. The Parlement's decree of August 18 was printed with other documents related to its defiance of the Duc d'Harcourt in *Relation de ce qui s'est passé au parlement séant à Rouen, au sujet des édit et déclaration du mois d'avril 1763* (n.p., n.d.).

16. Barbier, *Chronique*, VIII, 112.

17. *L'Anti-financier, ou relevé de quelques unes des malversations dont se rendent journellement coupables les Fermiers-Généraux et les vexations qu'ils commettent dans les provinces* (Amsterdam, 1763), 5 and 71.

18. Barbier, *Chronique*, VIII, 116.

19. *Mémoires secrets*, April 3, 1764.

Chapter 10

1. The best study of the expulsion of the Jesuits is Dale K. Van Kley, *The Jansenists and the Expulsion of the Jesuits from France, 1757–1765* (New Haven, 1975).

2. See Roger Chartier, Dominique Julia, and Marie-Madeleine Compère, *L'Education en France du XVIe au XVIIIe siècle* (Paris, 1976).

3. Barbier, *Chronique*, VII, 133.

4. Ibid., VII, 358 and 362.

5. Ibid., VII, 382.

6. Chauvelin, *Discours d'un de Messieurs des Enquêtes au Parlement, toutes les chambres assemblées, sur la doctrine des Jésuites, du huit juillet mil sept cent soixante-un*

(n.p., n.d.), 92. This edition of Chauvelin's speech was published with the damning but more moderate *Compte rendu des constitutions des Jésuites*, which the *procureur général* Jean Omer de Fleury submitted to the Parlement on July 8, 1761. See also the anonymous tract written by Chauvelain, *Réplique aux apologies des Jésuites* (n.p., n.d.), p. 14, which stressed that documents published by the Jesuits "disent ces horreurs [crimes including regicide] en termes formels de façon à faire dresser les cheveux sur la tête."

7. Barbier, *Chronique*, VII, 399 and Grimm, *Correspondance littéraire*, VIII, 145.

8. *Arrêt de la cour de Parlement du 6 août 1761* (Paris, 1761), 7. Barbier discussed the "arrêts foudroyants" at length: *Chronique*, VII, 391–95.

9. Ibid., VII, 397.

10. Ibid., VII, 404–5 and 421.

11. *Gazette de Leyde*, May 18, 1762.

12. Events connected with the Jesuits were covered extensively in the *Gazette de Leyde*, April and May 1762, and Barbier discussed them at length in his *Chronique* for February through April 1762.

13. Barbier, *Chronique*, VIII, 58.

14. Grimm, *Correspondance littéraire*, IX, 145–46.

15. *Extraits des assertions dangereuses et pernicieuses en tout genre que les soi-disants Jésuites ont, dans tous les temps et persévéramment, soutenues, enseignées et publiées dans leurs livres* (Paris, 1762), 455–56.

16. Ibid., 3.

17. Grimm, *Correspondance littéraire*, VIII, 145.

18. Ibid., IX, 144.

19. *Compte rendu des constitutions des Jésuites* (n.p., 1762), 77.

20. *Mémoires secrets*, April 13, 1762.

21. *Sur la destruction des Jésuites en France* ("Edinbourg," 1765), 129. D'Alembert, writing anonymously, dedicated this work to La Chalotais as a magistrate moved by "patriotisme vraiment philosophique." In replying to La Chalotais's attack, a Jesuit tract, *Remarques sur un écrit intitulé Compte rendu des constitutions des Jésuites* (n.p., n.d.) by Henri Griffet, accused him (p. 12) of courting the "nouveaux philosophes" and the "disciples de l'*Encyclopédie*."

22. *Balance égale* (n.p., 1762), 11.

23. *Mémoires secrets*, Jan. 26, 1762.

24. There were several versions of *Les Trois Nécessités*, including some that included a fourth necessity: the separation of France from the papacy. See *Mémoires secrets*, Aug. 19 and Oct. 1, 8, and 15, 1762; and Grimm, *Correspondance littéraire*, IX, 356.

Chapter 11

1. Quotations from "Le Mondain" in Voltaire, *Mélanges* (Paris, 1961, Bibliothèque de la Pléiade), 203–6. In later editions of the poem, the last line appeared as: "Le paradis terrestre est où je suis." Among the many books on Voltaire and Rousseau that provide background information for this and the next chapter, I should particularly acknowledge René Pomeau, *Voltaire en son temps* (Paris, 1995), 2 vols., and

Jean Starobinski, *Jean-Jacques Rousseau, la transparence et l'obstacle, (suivi de) sept essais sur Rousseau* (Paris, 1976).

2. On the development of celebrity as a cultural phenomenon and Rousseau's place in it, see Antoine Lilti, *The Invention of Celebrity* (Cambridge, 2017), especially chap. 5.

3. *Discours sur l'origine de l'inégalité parmi les hommes* in *Oeuvres choisies de J.-J. Rousseau* (Paris, 1960, Classiques Garnier), 72.

4. Quoted in Pomeau, *Voltaire*, I, 807–8.

5. *Lettre à d'Alembert* in *Oeuvres choisies de J.-J. Rousseau*, 142 and 150.

6. *Julie, ou la Nouvelle Héloïse*, Seconde Préface in *Oeuvres complètes* (Paris, 1964, Editions Gallimard), II, 12.

7. Although the definitive edition of Rousseau's correspondence was published by Ralph Leigh—*Correspondance complète de Jean Jacques Rousseau* (Geneva and Oxford, 1965–1998), 51 vols.—for reasons of convenience I will quote the letters as they appear in Raymond Trousson, *Lettres à J.-J. Rousseau sur La Nouvelle Héloïse* (Paris, 2011). The following discussion draws on my essay, "Readers Respond to Rousseau: The Fabrication of Romantic Sensitivity" in *The Great Cat Massacre*, chap. 6.

8. The quotations appear in the following order in Trousson, *Lettres*: pp. 70, 86, 12, and 73.

9. Of course, many authors and especially playwrights provoked tearful reactions long before Rousseau. A performance of Voltaire's *Tancrède* produced widespread weeping, even by the sophisticated Duc de Choiseul: Pomeau, *Voltaire*, II, 82.

10. Trousson, *Lettres*, pp. 121, 110, 186, 131, 186, 88, 91, 110.

11. Ibid., 166, 150, 157.

12. Ibid., 185, 183, 182, 129, 182, 140, 118.

13. Grimm, *Correspondance littéraire*, VII, 21–27 and 40–44.

14. *Mémoires secrets*, May 26, 1762.

15. Ibid., Sept. 3, 1762.

16. Ibid., Aug. 28 and June 30, 1762.

Chapter 12

1. There are many descriptions of executions in Hardy's journal. For example, see the entry for April 2, 1771, on a hanging and August 29, 1772, on breaking on the wheel. See also the article "Exécuteur de la haute justice" in the *Encyclopédie*. Among secondary works, see the excellent study by Pascal Bastien, *L'Exécution publique à Paris au XVIIIe siècle: une histoire des rituels judiciaires* (Seyssel, 2006).

2. The following account is based primarily on *Recueil de différentes pièces sur l'affaire malheureuse de la famille des Calas* (n.p., n.d.). For background information, see David D. Bien, *The Calas Affair: Persecution, Toleration, and Heresy in Eighteenth-Century Toulouse* (Princeton, 1960) and Pomeau, *Voltaire*, II, 110–33.

3. *Pièces originales concernant la mort des Srs. Calas, et le jugement rendu à Toulouse* (n.p., n.d.), 5.

4. Ibid., 10.
5. Ibid., 14.
6. Ibid., quotations from pp. 8 and 18.
7. Ibid., 30.
8. This letter was reproduced by Grimm, *Correspondance littéraire*, IX, 156. It was also reprinted in the *Correspondance littéraire de Karlsruhe* and four British journals.
9. Mariette, *Mémoire pour Dame Anne-Rose Cabibel, veuve du Sieur Jean Calas* (n.p., n.d.), 82.
10. *Mémoires secrets*, Dec. 13, 1762; Grimm, *Correspondance littéraire*, X, 19–20.
11. *Mémoires secrets*, Jan. 12 and Aug. 28, 1763.
12. *Traité sur la tolérance*, ed. John Renwick (Oxford, 1999), 23.
13. Ibid., 91.
14. Ibid., 94.
15. Grimm, *Correspondance littéraire*, X, 111.
16. "Article nouvellement ajouté," *Traité sur la tolérance*, 104.
17. Pomeau, *Voltaire*, 132.

Chapter 13

1. The richest run of spy reports is in the Bibliothèque de l'Arsenal, mss. 10155–10170. And the best study of rumors and other "public noises" is Arlette Farge, *Dire et mal dire: l'opinion publique au XVIIIe siècle* (Paris, 1992).
2. The following account draws on my essay, "Mlle Bonafon and the Private Life of Louis XV: Communication Circuits in Eighteenth-Century France," *Representations* (Summer 2004), 102–24.
3. *Mémoires secrets pour servir à l'histoire de Perse* (Amsterdam, 1745), 31.
4. *Les Amours de Zeokinizul, roi des Kofirans* (Amsterdam, 1746), 17.
5. BnF, ms. fr. 13709, fo. 71.
6. Charles Collé, *Journal et mémoires de Charles Collé*, ed. Honoré Bonhomme (Paris, 1868), 49–50 and 62.
7. Barbier, *Chronique*, VI, 246.
8. Ibid., V, 360–61.
9. Ibid., IV, 149, 315, 338; VI, 36, 69; VII, 77, 270.
10. Ibid., VI, 603.
11. Ibid., VII, 17.
12. *Mémoires secrets*, May 17 and 18, 1762.
13. Ibid., April 15, 1764.

Chapter 14

1. Quoted in *Grand dictionnaire universel du XIXe siècle* (Paris, 1865), II, 450.
2. "Portrait de Madame la Dauphine" in *Mémoires secrets*, May 27, 1770.
3. Ibid., Jan. 30, 1770.
4. "Feu d'artifice," *Encyclopédie*.

5. *Mémoires secrets*, May 21, 1770.

6. *Gazette de Leyde*, June 15, 1770.

7. Hardy, *Journal*, May 31, 1770.

8. *Mémoires secrets*, June 14, 1770.

9. On Mme du Barry's career as a "prostituée de luxe," which was followed closely by the Parisian police, see Erica-Marie Benabou, *La Prostitution et la police des moeurs au XVIIIe siècle* (Paris, 1987), 257–58.

10. *Mémoires secrets*, March 10, 1770.

11. Hardy, *Journal*, Sept. 27, 1770; *Mémoires secrets*, Sept. 30, 1770. See also ibid., Jan. 9, March 10, and April 29, 1771.

12. *Mémoires secrets*, Dec. 6, 1770.

13. Ibid., Dec. 24, 1770.

14. See especially the issues of the *Gazette de Leyde* for Dec. 7, 11, 14, and 21, 1770, and Jan. 1, 1771.

15. For a well-balanced, recent account, see Antoine, *Louis XV*, 916–26.

Chapter 15

1. Luc Daireaux, *"Le Feu de la rébellion"? Les imprimés de l'Affaire de Bretagne (1764–1769)* (Paris, 2011), covers the pamphleteering exhaustively. Jules Gustave Flammermont, *Le Chancelier Maupeou et les parlements* (Paris, 1883), still holds up well, and John Rothney, *The Brittany Affair and the Crisis of the Ancien Régime* (New York, 1969) brings it up to date with more recent research. Durand Ecchevaria, *The Maupeou Revolution: A Study in the History of Libertarianism: France, 1770–1774* (Baton Rouge, 1985), surveys the polemics from the viewpoint of political theory. They are studied in relation to public opinion in Shanti Singham, "'A Conspiracy of Twenty Million Frenchmen': Public Opinion, Patriotism, and the Assault on Absolutism during the Maupeou Years, 1770–1775," unpublished PhD diss., Princeton University, 1991. On the transformation of the legal world in Paris during the Maupeou revolution, see Bell, *Lawyers and Citizens*, chap. 5. Julian Swann, *Politics and the Parlement of Paris under Louis XV, 1754–1774* (Cambridge, 1995), gives a fine-grained view of the parlementary politics. The following account relies primarily on reports in the foreign French journals, the *Mémoires secrets*, Hardy's *Journal*, and the pamphlets themselves.

2. This is the most common version of the king's statement as quoted in Lavisse, *Histoire de France*, VIII, 383. A somewhat different version circulated in Paris, according to Hardy, *Journal*, March 3, 1766.

3. *Mémoires secrets*, March 4, 1766.

4. Hardy, *Journal*, Dec. 6, 1770, and Jan. 21, 1771.

5. Ibid., Jan. 24, 1771.

6. *Mémoires secrets*, Jan. 17, 1771. See also Hardy, *Journal*, Jan. 19–31, 1771.

7. Mme d'Épinay to Galiani, April 5, 1771, *La Signora d'Épinay e l'abate Galiani. Lettere inedite (1769–1772)* (Bari, 1929), 165; Echevarria, *The Maupeou Revolution*, 27.

8. See *De l'Esprit des lois*, book 19, chap. 4. From Aristotle through Bodin and Gro-

tius, political philosophers had referred to despotism, but they generally favored tyranny as a key term. See Melvin Richter, "Despotism," in *Dictionary of the History of Ideas* (New York, 1973), II, 1–18.

9. On Mornet's argument and the controversy surrounding it, see my *The Literary Underground of the Old Regime* (Cambridge, MA, 1982), 167–68. The passages closest to Rousseau's *Du Contrat social* appear in Louis de Brancas, Comte de Lauraguais, *Extrait du Droit public de la France* (London, 1771), 26 and 31–32. On the reception of Brancas's tract, see *Journal historique de la révolution opérée dans la constitution de la monarchie française par M. de Maupeou, chancelier de France* (London, 1774; henceforth cited as *Journal historique*), II, 20–23. The Rousseauian strain in the parlementary polemics appears most clearly in *L'Ami des lois* by Claude Martin de Marivaux and *Catéchisme du citoyen* by Guillaume-Joseph Saige, but both were published in 1775 after Maupeou's fall. The term "general will" was used quite widely and did not necessarily coincide with the meaning attributed to it by Rousseau.

10. See *De l'Esprit des lois*, book 11, chap. 6; book 18, chaps. 26 and 30.

11. *Lettres historiques sur le Parlement, sur le droit des pairs, et sur les lois fondamentales du royaume* (Amsterdam, 1754), quotations from I, 73 and II, 300.

12. Ibid., II, 4 and 251.

13. Hardy, *Journal*, Jan. 20, 1773, and Jan. 29, 1774. On Le Paige's anonymous pamphleteering, see Dale K. Van Kley, *The Religious Origins of the French Revolution: From Calvin to the Civil Constitution of the Clergy, 1560–1791* (New Haven, 1996), 262–65.

14. I have followed most authorities in attributing the *Maximes* to Mey, but he could have had collaborators, and the six-volume edition of 1775 probably included contributions by Gabriel-Nicolas Maultrot and André Blonde: see Van Kley, *The Religious Origins*, 265.

15. *Maximes du droit public français* ("en France," 1772), I, 10.

16. Hardy, *Journal*, Aug. 17, 1772. Of course, Hardy may have responded to an implicit Jansenist bias in favor of the Parlement that agreed with his own view.

17. See the text and comments in Hardy, *Journal*, Feb. 10, 1771, and the remarks in *Mémoires secrets*, Feb. 27, 1771.

18. *Remontrances de la Cour des Aides du 18 février 1771*. The quoted passages were copied by Hardy into his *Journal* of Feb. 22, 1771.

19. *Mémoires secrets*, Feb. 21 and 26 and March 7, 1771.

20. Ibid., April 29, 1771. See also Hardy, *Journal*, April 7, 1771.

21. Hardy, *Journal*, April 7, 1771.

22. *Journal historique*, I, 271.

23. Echevarria, *The Maupeou Revolution*, 23, and *Mémoires secrets*, Dec. 4, 1771.

24. Linguet, *Réponse aux Docteurs modernes, ou apologie pour l'auteur de la Théorie des lois et des Lettres sur cette Théorie*, 2 vols. (Paris, 1771), quotations from II, 257 and 278. See also Linguet, *Observations sur l'imprimé intitulé "Réponse des Etats de Bretagne au Mémoire du duc d'Aiguillon"* (Paris, 1771).

25. *Observations sur l'écrit intitulé: Protestations des princes* (n.p., n.d.), quotation

from p. 6. Unlike the *Protestations des princes*, this twenty-three-page pamphlet formulated its argument in pithy phrases, for example (p. 6), "Le Roi seul est Roi, par conséquent absolu" and (p. 11) "Ceux qui demandent la liberté demandent le pouvoir."

26. *La Tête leur tourne* (n.p., n.d.), 21 and 48.

27. Grimm's criticism of Voltaire for supporting the Maupeou Parlement probably indicated the views of Diderot and his circle: Grimm, *Correspondance littéraire*, X, 81. See also *Mémoires secrets*, May 15, 1771.

28. *Mémoires secrets*, Aug. 10 and 15, 1771.

29. *Journal historique*, III, vi.

30. *Mémoires secrets*, April 22, 1771.

31. I have recounted these episodes in *The Devil in the Holy Water, or the Art of Slander from Louis XIV to Napoleon* (Philadelphia, 2010), chaps. 1–3.

32. *Le Maire du Palais* (n.p., 1771), quotations from 3 and 118. By referring to Maupeou as "le maire du palais," the tract accused him of usurping the king's authority just as the "maires" of the king's household had displaced the Merovingians in the eighth century.

33. Hardy, *Journal*, June 5, 1771, and *Mémoires secrets*, Sept. 20, 1771.

34. *Lettres d'un homme à un autre homme sur les affaires du temps* (n.p., n.d.), quotations from 18 and 39.

35. *Journal historique*, I, 166–68; Hardy, *Journal*, March 22, 1771.

36. *Journal historique*, I, 283–86.

37. *Correspondance secrète et familière de M. de Maupeou avec M. de Sor***, conseiller du nouveau parlement*, 2 vols. (n.p., n.d.), I, 37.

38. Ibid., I, 9.

39. Hardy, *Journal*, July 8, 1771. See also *Mémoires secrets*, July 9, 1771.

40. *Mémoires secrets*, Sept. 14, 1771.

41. Hardy, *Journal*, Feb. 14, 1772; *Mémoires secrets*, Feb. 19, 1772.

42. Hardy, *Journal*, March 14, 1772; *Mémoires secrets*, March 17, 1772.

43. Hardy, *Journal*, April 2, 1772; *Mémoires secrets*, March 17 and 23 and April 3 and 7, 1772.

44. Hardy, *Journal*, April 6 and 23 and May 18, 1773.

Chapter 16

1. *Mémoires secrets*, March 1, 1773. The most recent and extensive biography of Beaumarchais is Maurice Lever, *Pierre-Augustin Caron de Beaumarchais*, 3 vols. (Paris, 1999).

2. *Journal historique*, I, 286.

3. Hardy, *Journal*, July 14, Aug. 3, 5, and 12, Oct. 24 and 27, 1772, and Jan. 20, 1773.

4. Hardy, *Journal*, July 10, 1773.

5. Grimm, *Correspondance litteraire*, X, 329.

6. *Mémoires secrets*, Sept. 8 and 16, 1773.

7. Hardy, *Journal*, Sept. 7, 1773.

8. Ibid., Dec. 28, 1773.

9. The following account is based on Beaumarchais's memoires as they appear in his *Oeuvres* (Paris, 1988, Pléiade edition), 675–927.

10. Ibid., quotation from 720–21.

11. Ibid., quotation from 723.

12. Ibid., quotation from 755.

13. Hardy, *Journal*, Nov. 21 and 22, 1773, and *Mémoires secrets*, Nov. 19, 1773.

14. Hardy, *Journal*, Dec. 22 and 23, 1773.

15. Ibid., Jan. 19, 1774.

16. *Mémoires secrets*, Feb. 15 and 18, 1774.

17. Beaumarchais, *Oeuvres*, 887 and 870.

18. Hardy, *Journal*, Feb. 26, 1774. On Goezman's subsequent career, see my *Pirating and Publishing: The Book Trade in the Age of Enlightenment* (New York, 2021), 248–53.

19. Hardy, *Journal*, Feb. 26, 1774.

Chapter 17

1. Hardy, *Journal*, May 7, 1774.

2. Ibid., May 5, 1774.

3. Ibid., May 9, 1774. See also *Gazette de Leyde*, May 17, 1774.

4. Hardy, *Journal*, May 9, 1774. The *Mémoires secrets* of June 13, 1774, hinted at this version of Louis XV's death without making it explicit. Libels about Louis XV later recounted his death in scabrous detail. See *Vie Privée de Louis XV* (London, 1781), IV, 268–69.

5. Hardy, *Journal*, May 4, 1774.

6. Ibid., May 11, 1774.

7. *Gazette de Leyde*, May 27, 1774. On the reports that reached Parisians, see Hardy, *Journal*, May 13 and May 19, 1774; *Mémoires secrets*, May 15, 1774; and *Gazette de Leyde*, Sept. 6, 1774.

8. *Mémoires secrets*, May 26, 1774; Hardy, *Journal*, May 13 and 16, 1774; Grimm, *Correspondance littéraire*, X, 423.

9. *Mémoires secrets*, June 3, 1774.

10. Hardy, *Journal*, May 22, 1774 (the remark on "papier" referred to the use of paper money during Law's System, 1716–1720) and June 10, 1774.

11. Ibid., May 18, July 22, and July 25, 1774.

12. Ibid., July 30, 1774, and *Gazette de Leyde*, Aug. 30, 1774.

13. Hardy, *Journal*, Aug. 1, 10, and 27, 1774.

14. Ibid., July 8, 1774.

15. Ibid., Aug. 25, 1774. See also *Gazette de Leyde*, Sept. 9 and 13, 1774.

16. Hardy, *Journal*, Aug. 27 and 30, 1774; Louis Métra (sometimes given as Mettra), *Correspondance littéraire secrète*, cited henceforth as Métra, *Correspondance*, Aug. 29 and Sept. 29, 1774.

17. The subtitle of *Lettre de M. Terray, ex-contrôleur général à M. Turgot, ministre des*

finances (n.p., n.d.) made its affinity clear: *Pour servir de supplément à la Correspondance entre le sieur Sorhouet et M. de Maupeou.* Unlike the *Correspondance*, however, it made Terray the main villain and claimed that he suggested the destruction of the Parlement to Maupeou.

18. Hardy, *Journal*, April 21 and Aug. 15, 1774; *Gazette de Leyde*, Sept. 20 and 23, 1774.

19. Darnton, *The Devil in the Holy Water*, 269–99.

20. *Anecdotes sur Mme la comtesse du Barry* (London, 1775), 215, and *Vie privée de Louis XV*, IV, 266.

21. *Vie privée de Louis XV*, IV, 159.

22. Hardy, *Journal*, June 30, 1775; *Mémoires secrets*, July 3, 1775.

23. *Catéchisme du citoyen, ou éléments du droit public français, par demandes et réponses* ("en France," 1788), quotations from 24, 27, and 86. See Keith Baker, "A Classical Republican in Eighteenth-Century Bordeaux: Guillaume-Joseph Saige," in Baker, *Inventing the French Revolution: Essays on French Political Culture in the Eighteenth Century* (Cambridge, 1990), 128–52.

24. *Gazette de France*, June 16 and 19, 1775; *Mémoires secrets*, June 16, 1775.

25. Hardy, *Journal*, July 11, 12, 13, 15, and Aug. 24, 25, 29, and 30, 1774; Métra, *Correspondance*, Aug. 29, 1774.

26. *Mémoires secrets*, Nov. 4, 1775.

27. Hardy, *Journal*, June 22, 1775.

28. *Mémoires secrets*, Aug. 3, 1775.

Chapter 18

1. *Arrêt du Conseil d'Etat du Roi du 13 septembre 1774.* This kind of edict, as opposed to more formal *lettres patentes*, did not carry the phrase "CAR TEL EST NOTRE PLAISIR." In legal usage, "plaisir" connoted will rather than caprice. In discussing the edict with his friend, abbé Joseph-Alphonse Véri, Turgot explained, "J'ai voulu le rendre si clair que chaque juge de village pût le faire comprendre aux paysans. C'est une matière sur laquelle l'opinion populaire peut beaucoup." *Journal de l'abbé de Véri*, ed. Jehan de Witte (Paris, 1928–1930; cited henceforth as Véri, *Journal*), I, 201.

2. Quotation from Métra, *Correspondance*, Nov. 9, 1774; *Gazette de Leyde*, Sept. 23, 1774; Hardy, *Journal*, Sept. 21, 1774.

3. *Lettre de M. Terray, ex contrôleur général, à M. Turgot, Ministre des finances, pour servir de supplément à la Correspondance entre le Sr. Sorhouet et M. de Maupeou.* The *Lettre* received favorable notices in *Mémoires secrets*, Jan. 18, 1775, and Métra, *Correspondance*, Feb. 9, 1775.

4. The following account draws on the masterful work of Steven L. Kaplan, *Bread, Politics, and Political Economy in the Reign of Louis XV*, 2 vols. (The Hague, 1976). A good analysis of the Flour War, which concentrates on the regions outside Paris, is Cynthia A. Bouton, *The Flour War: Gender, Class, and Community in Late Ancien Régime French Society* (University Park, PA, 1993).

5. The literature on sustenance and bread riots has been inspired primarily by the

work of George Rudé, which he summarized in his *The Crowd in History, 1730–1848* (Oxford, 1964). For information on expenditure among the common people, see Michel Morineau, "Budgets populaires en France au dix-huitième siècle," *Revue d'histoire économique et sociale* 50 (1972): 203–36 and 449–81. The crucial role of women in the "makeshift" economy of the poor is discussed in Olwen Hufton, *The Poor of Eighteenth-Century France, 1750–1789* (Oxford, 1974). In the large literature on rioting and popular rebellion, the fundamental work is E. P. Thompson, "The Moral Economy of the English Crowd in the Eighteenth Century," *Past and Present*, no. 50 (1971): 76–136. Among subsequent studies, see Colin Lucas, "The Crowd and Politics Between *Ancien Régime* and Revolution in France," *Journal of Modern History*, 60 (1988): 421–57, and the vast treatise on all kinds of rebellion by Jean Nicolas, *La Rébellion française. Mouvements populaires et conscience sociale, 1661–1789* (Paris, 2002).

6. Steven L. Kaplan, *The Famine Pact Persuasion in Eighteenth-Century France* (Philadelphia, 1982).

7. In addition to Hardy, the following account is based on Métra, *Correspondance*; *Mémoires secrets*; *Gazette de Leyde*; and Véri, *Journal*.

8. Métra, *Correspondance*, May 3, 1775; Véri, *Journal*, I, 286.

9. Hardy, *Journal*, May 3, 1775.

10. Ibid., May 9 and 14, 1775; *Mémoires secrets*, May 30, 1775.

11. *Mémoires secrets*, May 30, 1775.

12. Hardy, *Journal*, May 4, 1775.

13. Ibid., May 6, 1775.

Chapter 19

1. *Courrier du Bas-Rhin*, March 10, 1781. See also *Gazette de Leyde*, March 2, 1781; *Correspondance secrète inédite sur Louis XVI, Marie-Antoinette, la cour et la ville de 1777 à 1792*, ed. Mathurin de Lescure, 2 vols. (Paris, 1866; cited henceforth as *Correspondance secrète*), Feb. 21, 1781; Hardy, *Journal*, Feb. 19, 1781; and *Lettre du marquis Caraccioli à M. d'Alembert* (Paris, 1781), 9.

2. Quotation from Hardy, *Journal*, Feb. 19, 1781. On the reception of the *Compte rendu*, see Métra, *Correspondance*, March 7 and 14, 1781; *Gazette de Leyde*, March 2, 20, and 27, 1781; *Correspondance secrète*, Feb. 21 and March 8, 1781. The *Mémoires secrets* was one of the few periodicals to review the *Compte rendu* negatively, but treated its publication as a major event: Feb. 23, 24, and 27, March 5, and April 28, 1781.

3. *Mémoires secrets*, Feb. 27, 1781.

4. *Compte rendu*, 2–3.

5. Ibid., 43 and 59.

6. Ibid., 137.

7. *Les Comments* and *Les Pourquoi* in *Collection complète de tous les ouvrages pour et contre M. Necker* (Utrecht, 1782), vol. II. Accounts of these pamphlets and the reactions to them appeared in *Mémoires secrets*, March 5, 6, 7, and 15, 1781; Hardy, *Jour-*

nal, March 24, 1781; and Métra, *Correspondance,* June 13, 1781. On these polemics, see the excellent studies by Léonard Burnand, *Les Pamphlets contre Necker. Médias et imaginaire politique au XVIIIe siècle* (Paris, 2009), and *Necker et l'opinion publique* (Paris, 2004).

8. *Lettre d'un bon Français à M. Necker,* dated March 15, 1781, and signed "Bourboulon." Bourboulon had been employed in the Contrôle général and therefore may have had inside information. According to the *Mémoires secrets,* March 15, 16, and 26, 1781, Necker considered his attack serious enough to try to get him sent to the Bastille, but the Comte d'Artois intervened to protect him.

9. *Lettre du marquis Caraccioli à M. d'Alembert,* dated May 1, 1781. On its reception, see *Mémoires secrets,* April 7, May 25 and 28, 1781; Métra, *Correspondance,* June 13 and 27, 1781.

10. *Lettre du marquis de Caraccioli,* 1.

11. *Mémoires secrets,* Aug. 29, 1781.

12. See *Observations modestes d'un citoyen sur les opérations de finances de M. Necker et sur son Compte rendu* (1781), and *Mémoires secrets,* Aug. 22, 1781.

13. *Correspondance secrète,* March 23 and May 25, 1781. On other prints and songs celebrating Necker, see *Mémoires secrets,* April 22 and 28, May 6, June 5, and July 13, 1781; Hardy, *Journal,* May 17.

14. *Mémoire sur l'établissement des administrations provinciales présenté au roi par M. Necker, directeur général des finances* (1781); see especially pp. 23 and 35.

15. *Correspondance secrète,* April 23, May 1 and 10, 1781; *Gazette de Leyde,* May 1, 8, and 29, 1781; *Mémoires secrets,* April 25, 1781.

16. *Mémoires secrets,* May 23 and 26, 1781.

17. Hardy, *Journal,* May 20, 1781; *Correspondance secrète,* May 30, June 1 and 5, 1781; Métra, *Correspondance,* June 13, 1781. On the complex history of this underground gazette, which is usually attributed to Louis Métra, see Jean Sgard, ed., *Dictionnaire des journaux, 1600–1789* (Oxford, 1991), II, 255–62.

18. *Gazette de Leyde,* April 17, March 27, 1781. See also *Correspondance secrète,* May 30, June 1 and 5, 1781; Métra, *Correspondance,* June 13, 1781; and Hardy, *Journal,* May 20, 1781.

19. *Mémoires secrets,* Feb. 27, 1781.

Chapter 20

1. Like many edicts, the *Ordonnance du Roi pour la publication de la paix,* dated Nov. 3, 1783, specified that "la présente sera lue, publiée et affichée où besoin sera."

2. Hardy, *Journal,* Nov. 25, 1783; *Mémoires secrets,* Nov. 26, 1783.

3. Hardy, *Journal,* Aug. 3 and 12, 1781; *Mémoires secrets,* Aug. 19, 27, and 29, 1781.

4. Nicolas Ruault, *Gazette d'un Parisien sous la Révolution. Lettres à son frère,* ed. Anne Vassal (Paris, 1976; henceforth cited as Ruault, *Gazette*), 33.

5. Ibid., 33. See *La Science du bonhomme Richard* (Paris, 1778) published by Ruault.

6. Hardy, *Journal,* Dec. 14, 1783; *Mémoires secrets,* Dec. 15, 1783.

7. Hardy, *Journal,* Dec. 15 and 18, 1783.

Chapter 21

1. *Journal de Paris,* July 11, 1785.

2. Among the many studies of Crèvecoeur, see J. P. Mitchell, *St. Jean de Crèvecoeur* (New York, 1916); H. C. Rice, *Le Cultivateur Américain* (Paris, 1933); and Gay Wilson Allen and Roger Asselineau, *St. John de Crèvecoeur: The Life of an American Farmer* (New York, 1987). Among studies of French-American relations, see Durand Echeverria, *Mirage in the West: A History of the French Image of American Society to 1815* (Princeton, 1968).

3. Brissot described Mme d'Houdetot's sponsorship of Crèvecoeur as follows: "Fière de posséder un sauvage américain, elle voulut le former et le jeter dans le grand monde." Although he did not frequent such elevated company, Brissot himself regarded Crèvecoeur as "l'homme de la nature." *Mémoires de J.-P. Brissot (1754–1793), publiés avec étude critique et notes,* ed. Claude Perroud, 2 vols. (Paris, 1911), II, 48–49.

4. The following account is derived from my unpublished PhD dissertation, Oxford University, 1964, "Trends in Radical Propaganda on the Eve of the French Revolution (1782–1788)," chaps. 3 and 4.

5. For example, a phrase in the English edition described American society as based upon "health, temperance, and a great equality of conditions." In French it became "la santé, la tempérance, la pureté des moeurs, l'égalité des conditions." *Letters from an American Farmer, describing certain provincial situations, manners and customs not generally known and conveying some idea of the late and present interior circumstances of the British colonies in North America, written for the information of a friend in England* (London, 1782), 148; *Lettres d'un cultivateur américain écrites à W. S. Ecuyer, depuis l'année 1770 jusqu'à 1781,* 2 vols. (Paris, 1784), II, 128.

6. In one of the many passages praising the Quakers, the English edition stressed, "The same simplicity attends the worship they pay to the Divinity." The French translation construed it as, "Tout semble, parmi eux, être analogue à la simplicité du culte qu'ils rendent à l'Etre Suprême; ils ne paient ni dîmes, ni salaires, ni aucuns droits d'Eglise." *Letters from an American Farmer,* 191; *Lettres d'un cultivateur américain,* II, 180.

7. *Letters from an American Farmer,* 38–40; *Lettres d'un cultivateur américain,* I, 71–76.

8. *Lettres d'un cultivateur américain adressées à Wm. S . . . on Esq., depuis l'année 1770 jusqu'en 1786,* 3 vols. (Paris, 1787), III, letter 5.

9. See *Journal de Paris,* Aug. 17, 1787.

10. Review reprinted in R. Crèvecoeur, *Saint John de Crèvecoeur,* appendix.

11. Excerpt from the *Mercure* printed in 1787, *Lettres,* I, xxiii–xxiv.

12. Le Mau de l'Ecossay to Jefferson, Oct. 27, 1787, in *The Papers of Thomas Jefferson, Digital Edition.*

13. For example, the English text sounded ambivalent about the war: "And after all who will be the really guilty? Those most certainly who fail of success." The French translation of 1784 read: "Et après tout, quel est le plus grand coupable? Celui qui

traverse l'océan, pour venir m'imposer des taxes injustes par le moyen de sa bayonette." *Letters* of 1782, 276; *Lettres* of 1784, II, 250. Several Loyalist letters that Crèvecoeur wrote and later hid are published in *Sketches of Eighteenth-Century America: More "Letters from an American Farmer,"* ed. Henri L. Bourdin (New Haven, 1925).

14. See "Trends in Radical Propaganda," chap. 4.

15. Brissot and Clavière, *De la France et des Etats-Unis, ou de l'importance de la révolution de l'Amérique pour le bonheur de la France, des rapports de ce royaume et des Etats-Unis, des avantages réciproques qu'ils peuvent retirer de leurs liaisons de commerce, et enfin de la situation actuelle des Etats-Unis* (London, 1787); see especially xxi, xxx, 55, 64, 95, 130, and 149.

16. Paine's reply to Raynal appeared in French under two titles, *Lettre adressée à l'abbé Raynal sur les affaires de l'Amérique septentrionale . . .* ("Philadelphie," 1782) and *Remarques sur les erreurs de l'Histoire philosophique et politique de M. Guillaume Thomas Raynal . . .* (Amsterdam, 1783). Paine, a friend of Franklin and Jefferson, made a short trip to France to collect funds for supporting the American forces in March–August 1781, and he returned for a few months in 1787; but he did not spend a great deal of time in France until 1790, when he became deeply involved in the Revolution.

17. Jefferson to David Humphreys, Aug. 14, 1786, *The Papers of Thomas Jefferson Digital Edition*.

18. For a detailed discussion of these polemics, see "Trends in Radical Propaganda," 154–61.

19. *Considérations sur l'ordre de Cincinnatus, ou imitation d'un pamphlet angloaméricain* (London, 1784); see especially 15–18.

20. In the enormous literature on Franklin, see especially Claude-Anne Lopez, *Mon Cher Papa: Franklin and the Ladies of Paris* (New Haven, 1966) and Alfred Owen Aldridge, *Franklin and His French Contemporaries* (New York, 1957).

21. *Mémoires secrets,* Sept. 29, 1782. Of the many books on Lafayette, see especially Louis R. Gottschalk, *Lafayette between the American and the French Revolution, 1783–1789* (Chicago, 1950).

22. William Slauter, "News and Diplomacy in the Age of the American Revolution," PhD dissertation, Princeton University, 2007, 199–201; and Slauter, "The Paragraph as Information Technology: How News Traveled in the Eighteenth-Century World," *Annales: Histoire, Sciences Sociales* no. 2 (April–June 2012): lxvii, 253–78.

23. According to the *Mémoires secrets,* March 8, 1785, the *Gazette de Leyde* was "la plus recherchée" of all the foreign journals. The following account relies primarily on it but also draws on the *Gazette d'Amsterdam* and the *Courrier du Bas-Rhin*.

24. *Gazette de Leyde,* Nov. 30, 1781.

25. Hardy, *Journal,* Nov. 20 and 27, 1781.

26. *Correspondance secrète,* Oct. 1, 1781.

27. Métra, *Correspondance,* March 12, 1783.

28. Robert M. Isherwood, *Farce and Fantasy: Popular Entertainment in Eighteenth-Century Paris* (New York, 1986); Michèle Root-Bernstein, *Boulevard Theater and*

Revolution in Eighteenth-Century Paris (Ann Arbor, 1984); Emile Campardon, *Les Spectacles de la foire* (Paris, 1877). For a salty, contemporary account of boulevard theater, see François-Marie Mayeur de Saint-Paul, *Le Désoeuvré, ou l'espion du boulevard du Temple* (London, 1781).

29. Jean-François Arnould, *L'Héroïne américaine, pantomime en trois actes* (Paris, 1786). Arnould, a specialist in melodramas, codirected the Ambigu-Comique with its founder, Nicolas-Médard Audinot. I have not been able to locate the text of *L'Héroïne américaine*, which, according to the *Journal de Paris* of June 17, 1786, offered "danses, musique . . . et combats." See also *Journal de Paris,* April 9 and June 25, 1786; Oct. 9, 1787; and Jan. 8 and June 17, 1788.
30. *Hirza, ou les Illinois, tragédie* (Paris, 1774), 5. See also *Journal de Paris,* Jan. 23, 1780.
31. *Mémoires secrets,* Nov. 5, 1786.
32. *Journal de Paris,* May 19, 1781. See also the issues of Dec. 16, 1782, and May 31, 1784.
33. Ibid., Feb. 7, 1785.
34. Ibid., April 10, 1782; Oct. 12, 1782; Dec. 18, 1783; June 26, 1784; Nov. 5, 1786; and Dec. 16, 1786.

Chapter 22

1. *Mémoires secrets,* Nov. 22, 1783; Hardy, *Journal,* Nov. 21, 1783. On the scientific aspect of ballooning, see Charles C. Gillispie, *The Montgolfier Brothers and the Invention of Aviation 1783–1784: With a Word on the Importance of Ballooning for the Science of Heat and the Art of Building Railroads* (Princeton, 2014).
2. *Mémoires secrets,* Aug. 2, 5, 17, and 24, 1783.
3. Ibid., Aug. 24 and 25, 1783.
4. Ibid., Aug. 28 and 29, 1783; Hardy, *Journal,* Aug. 27, 29, and Sept. 16, 1783; *Gazette d'Amsterdam,* Sept. 12, 1783. In addition to the above sources, the public's fascination with ballooning can be followed from the *Journal de Paris,* which published regular accounts of flights throughout 1783 and 1784.
5. Quotations from Hardy, *Journal,* Oct. 17, 1783, and *Mémoires secrets,* Nov. 22, 1783.
6. Hardy, *Journal,* Dec. 2, 1783.
7. Contemporary sources do not contain estimates of the size of the crowd, but a flight in Lyon was reportedly seen by 300,000: *Gazette d'Amsterdam,* Feb. 3, 1784.
8. *Mémoires secrets,* Dec. 8, 1783.
9. *Gazette d'Amsterdam,* Sept. 26, 1783.
10. As a typical account of the experience of witnessing balloon flights, see *Journal de Bruxelles,* Jan. 31, 1784.
11. *Courrier du Bas-Rhin,* July 3, 1784.
12. *Mémoires secrets,* March 1, 1784.
13. *Courrier du Bas-Rhin,* Oct. 6, 1784.
14. *Journal de Bruxelles,* May 29, 1784; *Mémoires secrets,* May 17, 1784; Hardy, *Journal,* July 11, 1784; *Mémoires secrets,* July 8, 10, 11, and 27, 1784.
15. Hardy, *Journal,* July 11, 1784; *Mémoires secrets,* July 8, 10, 11, and 27, 1784.
16. Hardy, *Journal,* July 13 and 15, 1784; *Mémoires secrets,* July 16, 1784.

17. Hardy, *Journal,* Sept. 19 and 21, 1784; *Mémoires secrets,* Sept. 19 and 23, 1784.

18. *Courrier du Bas-Rhin,* May 18, 1782; *Mémoires secrets,* Aug. 1 and 3, 1783.

19. *Mémoires secrets,* Feb. 4, March 1, 2, 3, and 9, 1784.

20. *Mémoires secrets,* Nov. 29, Dec. 7 and 30, 1784, Jan. 10 and 14, 1785, and Feb. 10, 1785; Hardy, *Journal,* Jan. 10, 1785.

21. *Mémoires secrets,* June 17, 19, and 25, 1785; Hardy, *Journal,* June 17, 1785; *Courrier du Bas-Rhin,* June 26 and 29, 1785.

22. The *Journal de Paris* of Sept. 4, 1785, noted that the public's interest in balloon flights had died out: "Aujourd'hui à peine se permet-on d'en parler."

Chapter 23

1. The following discussion draws on my *Mesmerism and the End of the Enlightenment in France* (Cambridge, MA, 1968), which contains extensive references to primary and secondary sources.

2. Because Mesmer had a poor command of French, the works attributed to him were drafted by his French disciples, either from dictation or as adapted from the lessons he gave to the initiate. The most important of these publications are *Mémoire sur la découvete du magnétisme animal* (Geneva, 1779); *Aphorismes de M. Mesmer dictés à l'assemblée de ses élèves* (Paris, 1785); and *Précis historique des faits relatifs au magnétisme animal* (London, 1781).

3. *Journal de Paris,* April 30, 1784.

4. The *Journal de physique* published favorable reviews of works by Marivetz, Thouret, and Marat; but it expressed skepticism about Carra's *Nouveaux principes de physique,* noting in its issue of December 1781, "Jamais il n'a paru autant de différentes théories de l'univers que depuis quelques années." In its issue of March 1784, the *Journal des savants* praised Robespierre's argument for lightning rods in a legal case.

5. *Journal des savants,* March 1784, 21–22.

6. *Mémoires secrets,* April 9, 1784.

7. *Appel au public sur le magnétisme animal* (n.p., 1787), 11. The collection, which includes many manuscript notes, is in the BnF, 40Tb62.1. By way of comparison, the number of political pamphlets during the first six months of 1787, including the crisis surrounding the Assembly of Notables, came to 108: R. W. Greenlaw, "Pamphlet Literature on the Eve of the French Revolution," *Journal of Modern History* 29 (1957): 354.

8. Jean-François de La Harpe, *Correspondance littéraire, adressée à Son Altesse Impériale Mgr. le grand-duc, aujourd'hui empereur de Russie, et à M. le comte André Schowalow, chambellan de l'impératrice Cathérine II, depuis 1774 jusqu'à 1789,* 6 vols. (Paris, 1801–1807), IV, 266; Jacques-Henri Meister (successor to Grimm) in Grimm's *Correspondance littéraire,* XIII, 510; *Journal de Bruxelles,* May 1 and 22, 1784. The *Courrier de l'Europe,* which had reported on February 27, 1784, that mesmerism obsessed "tout Paris," noted on October 5, 1784, "Le grand objet des entretiens de la capitale est toujours le magnétisme animal."

9. *Rapport des commissaires chargés par le roi de l'examen du magnétisme animal* (Paris, 1784), 63–64.

10. *Gazette de Leyde,* Sept. 3, 1784; Mesmer, *Lettres de M. Mesmer à Messieurs les auteurs du Journal de Paris et à M. Franklin* (Paris, 1784); *Journal de Paris,* Aug. 31, Sept. 1, 5, and 6, 1784; *Mémoires secrets,* Sept. 2 and 6, 1784.

11. Mesmer, *Précis historique,* 40: "C'est au public que j'en appelle."

12. *Les Docteurs modernes, comédie-parade, en un acte et en vaudevilles, suivie du baquet de santé, divertissement analogue, mêlé de couplets* (Paris, 1784), quotation from p. 5. On the performances and polemics, see *Journal de Paris,* Nov. 17, 18, and 27, 1784; and *Mémoires secrets,* Nov. 17, 18, 24, and 30, and Dec. 13, 1784.

13. *Mémoires secrets,* April 18, 1785.

14. A.-M.-J. de Chastenet, Marquis de Puységur, *Mémoires pour servir à l'histoire et à l'établissement du magnétisme animal* (n.p., 1784).

15. *Appel au public sur le magnétisme animal, ou projet d'un journal pour le seul avantage du public et dont il serait le coopérateur* (Paris, 1787), 49.

16. *Mémoires secrets,* May 25, 1784.

17. *Journal de Paris,* Dec. 8–26, 1783; quotation in *Journal de Paris,* Feb. 7, 1784. See also *Mémoires secrets,* Dec. 8, 1783.

18. *Journal de Paris,* March 24 and May 21, 1782; *Mémoires secrets,* Dec. 8, 17, 21, 23, and 25, 1782. The *Journal de Paris* ran articles about Bléton nearly every week in the spring and summer of 1782. See also *Mémoire physique et médicinal montrant des rapports évidents entre les phénomènes de la baguette divinatoire, du magnétisme et de l'électricité* (London, 1781).

19. *Journal de Paris,* Jan. 22, 1784; *Mémoires secrets,* June 24, 1783.

20. *Courrier du Bas-Rhin,* May 10, 1782; *Mémoires secrets,* May 7, 1782. For examples of supposed inventions, see *Courrier du Bas-Rhin,* May 3 and 10, 1783; *Journal de Paris,* April 11, 1784; and *Mémoires secrets,* May 15, 1783.

21. *Année littéraire* (Paris, 1784), I, 6.

22. *Almanach des muses* (Paris, 1785), 51.

Chapter 24

1. Ruault, *Gazette,* 42; La Harpe, *Correspondance littéraire,* IV, 227–32.

2. *Journal de Paris,* April 28, 1784.

3. *Mémoires secrets,* March 9, 1783.

4. Among works on the theater, see Jeffrey S. Ravel, *The Contested Parterre: Public Theater and French Political Culture* (Ithaca, 1999); John Lough, *Paris Theatre Audiences in the Seventeenth and Eighteenth Centuries* (London, 1957); and Henri Lagrave, *Le Théâtre et le public à Paris de 1715 à 1750* (Paris, 1972).

5. In addition to Maurice Lever, *Pierre-Augustin Caron de Beaumarchais* and the sources cited in chap. 16, see the excellent, older biography by Louis de Loménie, *Beaumarchais et son temps: études sur la société en France au XVIIIe siècle,* 2 vols. (Paris, 1873), and the more recent study of Beaumarchais's relations with the Comédie française: Gregory S. Brown, *Literary Sociability and Literary Property*

in France, 1775–1793: Beaumarchais, the Société des auteurs dramatiques and the Comédie française (Aldershot, Eng., 2006). On Beaumarchais and the chevalier d'Eon, see Gary Kates, *Monsieur d'Eon Is a Woman: A Tale of Political Intrigue and Sexual Masquerade* (New York, 1995).

6. *Mémoires secrets*, Sept. 19, 1781. See also La Harpe, *Correspondance littéraire*, IV, 227.

7. Beaumarchais, *La Folle Journée ou le mariage de Figaro* in *Oeuvres*, 384.

8. The text appears in Grimm, *Correspondance littéraire*, XI, 398–402. It was a parody of Beaumarchais's elaborate prospectus for his edition of Voltaire. See also *Mémoires secrets*, June 23 and July 3, 1783.

9. Although I do not want to minimize the radical elements in the play, I think that most current interpretations of it wrongly claim that the public reacted above all to its political message in the 1780s. In fact, the reaction mainly concerned the play's treatment of sex. As an example of the common misinterpretation of the play's meaning for eighteenth-century audiences, see *"Marriage of Figaro"* in Wikipedia.

10. *Mémoires secrets*, Oct. 23, 1782.

11. Ibid., April 19, June 12, 13, and 14, 1783; Grimm, *Correspondance littéraire*, XI, 398–402.

12. Grimm, *Correspondance littéraire*, XII, 110; La Harpe, *Correspondance littéraire*, IV, 122.

13. Grimm, *Correspondance littéraire*, XII, 111–12; *Mémoires secrets*, Feb. 29 and April 24, 1784.

14. Métra, *Correspondance*, May 12, 1784. Also, *Mémoires secrets*, Oct. 6, 1784.

15. In the preface to the published version of his play (*Oeuvres*, ii), Beaumarchais defended it as an expression of "la franche et vraie gaieté qui distinguait de tout autre le comique de notre nation." He emphasized the play's success in capturing the audience by "flots d'une inaltérable gaieté," and he described Figaro's character as "la raison assaisonnée de gaieté et de saillies."

16. *Mariage de Figaro*, 391.

17. Ibid., 24.

18. This remark and the fullest account of contemporary reactions is in Grimm, *Correspondance littéraire*, XII, 110–20, which was then being continued by Jacques-Henri Meister. La Harpe, like Meister, emphasized the play's supposed immorality and also pointed out the audacity of its satire: *Correspondance littéraire*, IV, 122–23 and 227–30.

19. *Mémoires secrets*, May 8, 1784. Beaumarchais himself sent a copy of the poem to the *Journal de Paris*, treating it as a way to "s'emparer de l'opinion publique": *Journal de Paris*, May 14, 1784.

20. Métra, *Correspondance*, Oct. 6, 1784. This article noted, "Les partisans de cet écrivain [Beaumarchais] conviennent un peu de l'immoralité de sa pièce; les autres fondent sur cette immoralité toutes leurs clameurs et leurs injures." See also *Mémoires secrets*, May 31 and June 1, 1784; Hardy, *Journal*, June 15, 1784; and *Journal de Paris*, Nov. 22, 1784.

21. *Mémoires secrets*, July 19, 1784; Grimm, *Correspondance littéraire*, XIII, 530.

22. Métra, *Correspondance,* Dec. 8, 1784 and Feb. 10 and 17, 1785; Grimm, *Correspondance littéraire,* XIV, 92.

23. *Mémoires secrets,* Feb. 26, 1785.

24. *Journal de Paris,* Aug. 15, 1784.

25. Quotation from Métra, *Correspondance,* Nov. 10, 1784. See also *Gazette d'Amsterdam,* Aug. 20, 1784; Hardy, *Journal,* April 6, 1785.

26. Préface, *Mariage de Figaro,* 352 and 354.

27. The letter by the "ecclésiastique" appeared in the *Journal de Paris* of Feb. 21, 1785. "Le bruit de votre nom et de vos succès a retenti jusqu'aux Halles et au port S. Nicolas," it claimed ironically. "Il n'y a pas un gagne-denier, ni une blanchisseuse un peu renforcée qui n'ait vu au moins une fois le *Mariage de Figaro* et qui n'en ait retenu quelques traits facétieux qui égaient à chaque instant leurs conversations." Ruault interpreted this provocation as a trap, which led Beaumarchais to publish his letter in the *Journal de Paris* of March 7, 1785. This account is based on Ruault, *Gazette,* 53–58; Grimm, *Correspondance littéraire,* XII, 291–96; and *Mémoires secrets,* March 9 and 11, 1785.

28. Ruault, *Gazette,* 53–57. See also *Correspondance secrète,* March 14, 1785, and *Courrier du Bas-Rhin,* March 19, 1785.

29. *Gazette d'Amsterdam,* March 22, 1785. See also *Courrier du Bas-Rhin,* March 19, 1785.

30. Grimm, *Correspondance littéraire,* XIV, 121–22.

31. *Mémoires secrets,* March 23 and 25, 1785. However, Grimm reported in September 1785 that Calonne, the controller general, made "réparation" to Beaumarchais by giving him a letter assuring him of the king's "satisfaction" at Beaumarchais's service to the state during the American war. Calonne also arranged for the state to pay off its debt to Beaumarchais for his activity during the war, and there was a rumor he had been given a pension. Also Beaumarchais was permitted to be present at a private performance of *Le Barbier de Séville* at Versailles in which the queen played the role of Rosine and d'Artois that of Figaro: Grimm, *Correspondance,* XII, 418–19.

Chapter 25

1. Antoine Lilti, *Figures publiques: l'invention de la célébrité 1750–1850* (Paris, 2014).

2. Darline Levy, *The Ideas and Careers of Simon-Nicolas-Henri Linguet: A Study in Eighteenth-Century French Politics* (Urbana, Illinois, 1980). Grimm, *Correspondance littéraire,* X, 341, noted Linguet's general appeal, "surtout dans les cafés de Paris, où la violence de sa plume intéresse la malignité, amuse les oisifs, et le fait admirer des sots comme un des plus sublimes modèles de l'éloquence française."

3. *Mémoires secrets,* Nov. 21, Dec. 19 and 21, 1780.

4. Among the many works on Mirabeau, the old biography by Louis de Loménie is still fundamental: *Les Mirabeau: nouvelles études sur la société française au XVIIIe siècle,* 5 vols. (Paris, 1889–1891).

5. *Mémoires secrets,* March 31, 1783.

6. Mirabeau's pornographic works have been reprinted in *Oeuvres érotiques de Mirabeau,* ed. Charles Hirsch (Paris, 1984).

7. Among works on the Bastille and the symbolic representation of despotism, see Hans-Jürgen Lüsebrink and Rolf Reichardt, *The Bastille: A History of a Symbol of Despotism and Freedom* (Durham, 1997).

8. Linguet, *Mémoires sur la Bastille* (London, 1783), 57.

9. Mirabeau, *Des Lettres de cachet et des prisons d'Etat,* 2 vols. (Hamburg, 1782), I, 97.

10. La Harpe, *Correspondance littéraire,* XII, 84–85 and 116–18.

11. Hardy, *Journal,* June 23, 1783: "On se sentait entraîné, pour ainsi dire, par la force de ses raisonnements, à penser comme lui." Hardy also was moved by the "énergie" of Linguet's style but distrusted his revelations: *Journal,* June 9, 1783.

12. Métra, *Correspondance,* Jan. 29, 1783. On Linguet, see Métra, *Correspondance,* Feb. 26 and Apr. 9, 1783.

13. *Mémoires secrets,* Jan. 29, March 9, 12, and 31, 1783. On Linguet, *Mémoires secrets,* April 6 and 7 and Sept. 10, 1783.

14. Ruault, *Gazette,* 21 and 34.

15. *Remarques historiques sur la Bastille* (London, 1783); see especially the description of "cachots" and "calottes," 24–26. The *Mémoires secrets,* Nov. 30, 1785, found its "affreuses vérités" undercut by exaggeration.

16. *Mémoires d'un prisonnier d'Etat, ou correspondance de M. le vicomte de B . . . avec . . . la marquise de St. L et plusieurs autres personnes de distinction* (London, 1785), 43. On its reception, see *Mémoires secrets,* Dec. 20, 1785.

17. *Histoire d'une détention de trente-neuf ans dans les prisons d'Etat* (Amsterdam, 1787). Another version, published in the same year, went under the title *Le Donjon de Vincennes, la Bastille et Bicêtre, mémoire de M. Masers de Latude, gentilhomme languedocien, détenu dans les prisons d'état pendant trente-neuf ans; avec la lettre du marquis de Beaupoil à M. de Bergasse sur l'histoire de M. de Latude et sur les ordres aribitraires* (1787). Latude disavowed both of these works in the book he published with the help of a lawyer named Thiéry in 1790 and that became an enormous success: *Le Despotisme dévoilé, ou Mémoires de Henri Masers de la Tude, détenu pendant trente-cinq ans dans les diverses prisons d'état* (Amsterdam, 1787). See Claude Quétel, *Les évasions de Latude* (Paris, 1986), 205.

18. *Mémoires secrets,* Jan. 8 and 26, Aug. 13, and Sept. 25, 1784; Hardy, *Journal,* Sept. 14 and 21, 1784; *Courrier du Bas-Rhin,* Jan. 24, 1784.

Chapter 26

1. Scholarship on the Diamond Necklace Affair extends from Frantz Funck-Brentano, *L'Affaire du collier* (Paris, 1903) to the recent monograph by Jonathan Beckman, *How to Ruin a Queen: Marie-Antoinette, the Stolen Diamonds and the Scandal That Shook the French Throne* (London, 2014).

2. *Correspondance secrète,* Sept. 13 and 15, 1785.

3. Ibid., Oct. 12, 1785.

4. Ibid., Feb. 24, 1786.

5. The *Courrier du Bas-Rhin* claimed to have procured leaks about Rohan's interrogation and quoted them extensively in its issue of Feb. 11, 1786.

6. *Mémoire pour Dame Jeanne de Saint-Remy de Valois, épouse du comte de La Motte* (Paris, 1786), 44. For a description of Cagliostro's rituals, see 29–30.

7. Quotations from *Mémoires secrets*, Oct. 23, 1785; *Courrier du Bas-Rhin*, Aug. 31 and Oct. 19, 1785; and Hardy, *Journal*, Aug. 18 and 30, 1785. See also *Correspondance secrète*, Sept. 13 and 15, 1785; Hardy, *Journal*, Nov. 26, 1785; and *Mémoires secrets*, Nov. 28 and Dec. 1, 1785.

8. Hardy, *Journal*, Oct. 12 and Nov. 25, 1785; *Courrier du Bas-Rhin*, Jan. 11, 1786.

9. *Mémoire pour la demoiselle Leguay d'Oliva, fille mineure émancipée d'âge* (Paris, 1786), 18.

10. Ibid., 45.

11. Ibid., 26; Hardy, *Journal*, March 22, 1786; *Mémoires secrets*, March 20, 23, and 26, 1786.

12. *Mémoires secrets*, Feb. 20 and March 7, 1786.

13. As in the memoir for Mlle Oliva, Cagliostro's *factum* stressed the horrors of the Bastille: *Mémoire pour le comte de Cagliostro, accusé, contre M. le procureur général, accusateur* (Paris, 1786), 6. The *Mémoires authentiques pour servir à l'histoire du comte de Cagliostro* (n.p., 1786), 47–69, described a supposedly Egyptian ritual for ladies, which featured a nude Cagliostro, who descended on a rope from a dome.

14. *Mémoire pour le comte de Cagliostro*, quotation from p. 9. Cagliostro's "Confession" occupies the first half of the memoir, pp. 8–22.

15. Quotations from Métra, *Correspondance*, Feb. 22, 1786, and Hardy, *Journal*, Feb. 20, 1786. See also Ruault, *Gazette*, 68–69; *Mémoires secrets*, Feb. 20, 1786; and Métra, *Correspondance*, March 1, 1786.

16. *Mémoire pour Dame Jeanne de Saint-Remy de Valois, épouse du comte de la Motte*. *Mémoires secrets*, April 1, 1786; Hardy, *Journal*, March 30, 1786; Métra, *Correspondance*, April 5, 1786.

17. *Mémoire pour Louis René Edouard de Rohan, cardinal de la Sainte Eglise Romaine* (Paris, 1786), quotation from the separate section titled "Résumé et réflexions," 8.

18. Métra, *Correspondance*, May 2, 1786. The following account is based on Métra, *Correspondance*; *Mémoires secrets*; Hardy, *Journal*; *Correspondance secrète*; *Gazette d'Amsterdam*; and *Gazette de Leyde* for March through July, 1786.

19. *Mémoires justificatifs de la comtesse de Valois de La Motte, écrits par elle-même* (London, 1789); see pp. 43 and 52–53 on the queen's purported sexual adventures and the political plot. A woman who ran a dress shop in Paris was sent to the Bastille in January 1789 for importing La Motte's memoir hidden in copies of clothing material: *Correspondance secrète*, Jan. 19, 1789; Métra, *Correspondance*, Jan. 25, 1789.

20. Hardy, *Journal*, Aug. 31, 1785, and Feb. 8, 1786. On the police and libels against the queen, see *Mémoires secrets*, Feb. 11 and 26, 1786; Ruault, *Gazette*, 67; and *The Devil in the Holy Water*, 114–22 and 397–421. On the vilification of Marie-Antoinette, see Chantal Thomas, *La Reine scélérate: Marie-Antoinette dans les pamphlets* (Paris, 1989); Lynn Hunt, "The Many Bodies of Marie-Antoinette: Political Por-

nography and the Problem of the Feminine in the French Revolution" in *Eroticism and the Body Politic,* ed. Lynn Hunt (Baltimore, 1991); and Jacques Revel, "Marie-Antoinette dans ses fictions: la mise en scène de la haine," in *De Russie et d'ailleurs: feux croisés sur l'histoire,* ed. Martine Godet (Paris, 1995).

21. *Correspondance secrète,* Feb. 24, March 4, April 17, May 18, 1785; Jan. 22, Aug. 1, and Sept. 15, 1787; *Mémoires secrets,* May 28, 1785, and Aug. 9, 1787.

22. *Mémoires secrets,* May 26, June 1 and 3, 1785; *Correspondance secrète,* June 8, 1785; Ruault, *Gazette,* 88–89.

23. Ruault, *Gazette,* 89 and 90–91; *Mémoires secrets,* Aug. 12 and 20, 1787.

24. *Lettre d'un garde du roi, pour servir de suite aux Mémoires de Gagliostro* [*sic*] (London, 1786), 11.

25. Ruault, *Gazette,* 68 and 97. See the similar remarks on pp. 84 and 89.

26. *Les Amours de Charlot et Toinette, pièce dérobée à V.........* ("à la Bastille," 1789), 4.

27. On this episode and related rumors, see *The Devil in the Holy Water,* 398–402.

28. Arthur Young, *Travels in France During the Years 1787, 1788 and 1789,* ed. Constantia Maxwell (Cambridge, 1950), 209.

29. *Correspondance secrète,* June 4, 1786.

30. Ibid., April 17, 1786.

31. Ibid., Oct. 12, 1785.

32. Ruault, *Gazette,* 71.

33. The wording occurred in the decree directing the Parlement to investigate the case, which was registered in the Grand'Chambre on Sept. 6, 1785. Quoted in *Mémoires secrets,* Sept. 9, 1785, and Hardy, *Journal,* Sept. 6, 1785.

Chapter 27

1. The following account is based primarily on the *Journal* of Hardy, entries from December 1785 through January 1786; *Gazette de Leyde,* Jan. 20, 24, 27, and 31, 1786; and *Mémoires secrets,* Jan. 2, 3, 12, and 20, 1786.

2. *Mémoires secrets,* Jan. 20, 1786.

3. Jean Tulard, *Talleyrand, ou la douceur de vivre* (Paris, 2010).

Chapter 28

1. Métra, *Correspondance,* Jan. 13, 1785.

2. The *Mémoires secrets,* June 8, 1786, described the camp des Tartares, a cluster of barracks in the northern section of the garden, as "le rendez-vous de tous les crocs, escrocs, filous, mauvais sujets." The following discussion is based on my PhD dissertation, "Trends in Radical Propaganda," chap. 5, and among secondary works draws on Hubert Luethy, *La Banque Protestante en France de la révocation de l'Edit de Nantes à la Révolution,* 2 vols. (Paris, 1959); Jean Bouchary, *Les Manieurs d'argent à Paris à la fin du XVIIIe siècle,* 3 vols. (Paris, 1939); Robert Bigo, *La Caisse*

d'Escompte (1776–1793) et les origines de la Banque de France (Paris, 1927); and Paul-Jacques Lehmann, *Histoire de la Bourse de Paris* (Paris, 1997).

3. *Mémoires secrets*, Jan. 16, 1785.

4. Ibid., Jan. 21, 23, 25, 1785; Métra, *Correspondance*, Jan. 27, 1785.

5. *Gazette de Leyde*, Feb. 1, 4, and 8, 1785; *Mémoires secrets*, Jan. 29 and 30, Feb. 16 and 19, and April 1, 1785; *Correspondance secrète*, Jan. 26, Feb. 3, and March 10, 1785.

6. Mirabeau, *De la Caisse d'escompte* (n.p., 1785), 85. As an example of Mirabeau's moralistic rhetoric, see p. 8: "Nous savons que la manie ou plutôt la fureur du jeu [stockjobbing] infeste tous les rangs, trouble le repos, souille les moeurs, isole et dessèche les hommes."

7. Quotation from *Gazette de Leyde*, June 3, 1785. See also *Mémoires secrets*, May 25 and June 7, 1785. In its issue of July 21, 1785, the *Mémoires secrets* reversed its earlier favorable reaction to Mirabeau's tract. The *Gazette de Leyde*, June 10, 1785, named Isaac Panchaud and Clavière as the *baissiers* behind the tract but reported that it continued to be a brilliant success and praised Mirabeau for his eloquent denunciation of cupidity.

8. The following account is based on the extensive coverage of the Bourse in the *Gazette de Leyde* and the *Mémoires secrets*, supplemented by the *Correspondance secrète* and Métra, *Correspondance*, from July 1785 until April 1787; and it draws heavily on the pamphlet literature.

9. Mirabeau, *Lettre du comte de Mirabeau à M. le Coulteux de la Noraye sur la Banque de Saint-Charles et sur la Caisse d'escompte* (Brussels, 1785), quotations from pp. 4 and 87. In *De la Banque d'Espagne dite de Saint-Charles* (n.p., 1785), x, Mirabeau claimed that he was exercising his "métier du citoyen" by denouncing speculation, but he did not convince his critics.

10. *Mémoires secrets*, July 31, 1785.

11. The text of the edict with commentary appeared in the *Gazette de Leyde* of October 18, 1785, and Métra, *Correspondance*, October 12, 1785.

12. *Mémoires secrets*, Oct. 9, 1785.

13. Mirabeau, *Sur les actions de la Compagnie des eaux de Paris* (London, 1785). Mirabeau claimed, p. 26, that the company's shares could not be worth more than 2,135 L., although they had climbed to 3,800 L.

14. *Réponse à l'ouvrage qui a pour titre: Sur les actions de la Compagnie des eaux de Paris, par M. le comte de Mirabeau* (Paris, 1785), 11. Beaumarchais's pamphlet seemed to bear an official stamp of approval, because unlike the preceding pamphlets, it was published "avec approbation et privilège." It appeared under the name of "les administrateurs de la Compagnie des eaux de Paris."

15. Ibid., 53.

16. *Réponse du comte de Mirabeau à l'écrivain des administrateurs de la Compagnie des eaux de Paris* (Brussels, 1785), quotation from p. 12.

17. Hardy, *Journal*, Jan. 25, 1786. See *Mémoires secrets*, Dec. 7, 17, and 20, 1785, and *Correspondance secrète*, Dec. 22, 1785.

18. Ruault, *Gazette*, 79.

19. *Réponse du comte de Mirabeau*, 10: "Le ministre des finances m'y avait appellé, invité, encouragé." See also *Mémoires secrets*, Nov. 8 and Dec. 10, 1785.

20. *Mémoires secrets*, June 8, 1786; *Correspondance secrète*, May 29, 1786; *Journal de Leyde*, June 16, 1786.

21. "Trends in Radical Propaganda," 196–209; J. Bénétruy, *L'Atelier de Mirabeau. Quatre proscrits genevois dans la tourmente révolutionnaire* (Geneva and Paris, 1962).

22. *Dénonciation au public d'un nouveau projet d'agiotage, ou lettre à M. le comte de Sxxx sur un nouveau projet de compagnie d'assurance contre les incendies à Paris et en général sur les inconvénients des compagnies par actions* (London, 1786), see especially 31–48. On its reception, see *Mémoires secrets*, July 18, 1786.

23. *Correspondance secrète*, July 4, 1786; *Mémoires secrets*, Aug. 28, 1786.

24. Brissot, *Seconde lettre contre la compagnie d'assurances pour les incendies à Paris et contre l'agiotage en général, adressée à MM. Perier & compagnie* (London, 1786). See especially p. 67.

25. *Mémoires secrets*, Oct. 25, 26, and 29, 1786; *Gazette de Leyde*, Nov. 7 and Dec. 8, 1786.

26. *Gazette de Leyde*, June 16 and July 14, 1786.

27. Ibid., Feb. 13 and 16, 1787.

28. *Dénonciation de l'agiotage au Roi et à l'Assemblée des Notables* (n.p., 1787), 38. Information about d'Espagnac's success in cornering shares at the expense of the *baissiers* had circulated in January: *Gazette de Leyde*, Jan. 26, 1787, and *Mémoires secrets*, Jan. 19 and 24, 1787.

29. *Dénonciation de l'agiotage*, key passages on pp. 40, 57, 66, and 132.

30. *Gazette de Leyde*, March 23, April 3 and 13, 1787; Métra, *Correspondance*, March 18 and 24, April 6 and 13, 1787; *Correspondance secrète*, March 15, 1787; *Mémoires secrets*, March 12, 22, and 23, 1787; Hardy, *Journal*, March 18 and 20, 1787. Unlike the other gazettes, the *Mémoires secrets* claimed that Mirabeau could have written under the patronage of Calonne, because he attacked Necker, who was Calonne's enemy, even though he made negative comments about the government.

31. *Réponse du comte de Mirabeau*, 13.

Chapter 29

1. The following account derives from "Trends in Radical Propaganda," chap. 8. For an excellent survey of judicial affairs, see the aforementioned study by Sarah Maza, *Private Lives and Public Affairs*, which also discusses the Kornmann case, pp. 295–311.

2. *Mémoire sur une question d'adultère, de séduction et de diffamation, pour le sieur Kornmann contre la dame Kornmann, son épouse; le sieur Daudet de Jossan; le sieur Pierre-Augustin Caron de Beaumarchais; et M. Le Noir, conseiller d'Etat et ancien lieutenant-général de police* (n.p., 1787).

3. Ibid., 42.

4. Ibid., 142.

5. *Mémoires secrets*, May 22, 1787. Hardy made the same observation: *Journal*, May 20, 1787. As an example of the endless gossip produced by the memoir, see *Mémoires de la baronne d'Oberkirch*, 2 vols. (Paris, 1853), I, 380.

6. Beaumarchais, *Troisième mémoire, ou dernier exposé des faits qui ont rapport à P.-A. Caron de Beaumarchais dans le procès du sieur Kornmann contre sa femme* (Paris, 1789), 66.

7. Bergasse, *Observations de M. Kornmann sur un écrit de M. de Beaumarchais* in *Pièces intéressantes relatives au Mémoire de M. Kornmann* (n.p., n.d.), 16; *Observations du sieur Bergasse sur l'écrit du sieur de Beaumarchais ayant pour titre, Court mémoire* (n.p., 1788), 58; *Mémoire pour le Sieur Bergasse dans la cause du Sieur Kornmann* (n.p., 1788), 17 and 137. The remark on the waiters in the Palais-Royal comes from *Lettre à Milord XXX au sujet de M. Bergasse et de ses Observations dans l'affaire de M. Kornmann* (n.p., 1788), 3.

8. *Mémoires secrets*, May 23, 1787.

9. *Mémoire de Pierre-Augustin Caron de Beaumarchais en réponse au libelle diffamatoire signé Guillaume Kornmann, dont plainte en diffamation est rendue, avec requête à M. le lieutenant-criminel et permission d'informer* (n.p., 1787), 48.

10. *Mémoires secrets*, June 5, 1787; Hardy, *Journal*, June 5, 1787.

11. *Mémoire de Pierre-Augustin Caron de Beaumarchais*, 57. See Métra, *Correspondance*, June 23, 1787.

12. *Le Public à Pierre-Augustin Caron de Beaumarchais* (n.p., 1787). See especially p. 11 and, for the public's response, Hardy, *Journal*, June 22 and 23, 1787, and *Mémoires secrets*, June 12, 1787. This pamphlet was by Antoine-Joseph Gorsas, a marginal pamphleteer who turned out many tracts against Beaumarchais and Lenoir and later became a revolutionary journalist associated with the Girondists.

13. *Le Public pour la seconde fois à Pierre-Augustin Caron de Beaumarchais* (n.p., 1787), 9. The many pamphlets that continued to attack Beaumarchais in this manner are discussed in "Trends in Radical Propaganda," 343–47.

14. Grimm, *Correspondance littéraire*, XV, 71.

15. *Seconde lettre du public Parisien à Beaumarchais* (n.p., 1787), 14.

16. La Harpe, *Correspondance littéraire*, IV, 190.

17. Darnton, "The Memoirs of Lenoir, Lieutenant de Police of Paris, 1774–1785," *The English Historical Review* (1970), LXXXV, 532–59, and Vincent Milliot, *Un Policier des Lumières* (Seyssel, 2011).

18. Jean-Charles-Pierre Lenoir, *Mémoire présenté au Roi, par M. Lenoir, conseiller d'Etat* (n.p., n.d.).

19. *Mémoires secrets*, May 20, 1787. Lenoir was notorious for his close connection to Calonne, going back to the Brittany Affair.

20. Bergasse, *Observations du sieur Kornmann en réponse au mémoire de M. Lenoir* (n.p., n.d.), see especially pp. 7–8 and 33–34.

21. Hardy, *Journal*, July 9, 14, and 20, 1787; *Mémoires secrets*, July 6 and 23, 1787.

22. *Ninon Lenclos à M. S . . . d, de l'A.A.E.IE F.A.C.I.E.* (n.p., 1787), 1.

23. *L'An 1787. Précis de l'administration de la bibliothèque du Roi sous Mr. Le Noir. Seconde édition, assurément plus correcte que la première; avec un petit supplément* (Liège, 1788); *Apologie de Messire Jean-Charles-Pierre Le Noir par son très-humble et très-obéissant serviteur Suard, l'un des quarante* (n.d., 1789).

24. *Mémoire pour le sieur Bergasse dans la cause du sieur Kornmann, contre le sieur de Beaumarchais et contre le Prince de Nassau* (n.p., 1788).

25. Hardy, *Journal*, July 19, 1788.

26. *Tableau de Paris*, II, 925.

27. *Court mémoire, en attendant l'autre* (n.p., n.d.), 5–6 and 37.

28. *Observations du sieur Bergasse sur l'écrit du sieur de Beaumarchais ayant pour titre Court mémoire, en attendant l'autre, dans la cause du sieur Kornmann* (n.p., 1788); see especially pp. 22–26, 28–31, and 51–52.

29. *Lettre à Milord*, XXX, 2–3.

30. Hardy, *Journal*, Aug. 21, 1788.

31. La Harpe, *Correspondance littéraire*, V, 290–93; Grimm, *Correspondance littéraire*, 295–96.

32. Hardy, *Journal*, Aug. 28, 1788; Bergasse, *Au Roi* (n.p., 1788).

33. BnF, Bureau des Estampes, N2. The BnF has twenty-seven different engravings of Bergasse from 1788 and 1789, an indication of his extraordinary standing as a celebrity.

34. *Plaidoyer prononcé à la Tournelle criminelle le jeudi 19 mars 1789 par le sieur Bergasse dans la cause du sieur Kornmann* (n.p., 1789), 49–50. See also Bergasse, *Observations sur le préjugé de la noblesse héréditaire* (London, 1789).

Chapter 30

1. *Journal de Paris*, Dec. 31, 1786. Jean Egret, *La Pré-Révolution française 1787–1788* (Paris, 1962), opened the way for a reinterpretation of the Assembly of Notables and the prerevolutionary crisis. His work has been superseded by the excellent study by Vivian Gruder, *The Notables and the Nation: The Political Schooling of the French, 1787–1788* (Cambridge, MA, 2007).

2. *Gazette de Leyde*, Jan. 9, 1787. See also the reports in the *Gazette de Leyde* of Jan. 12 and 16, 1787.

3. Hardy, *Journal*, Jan. 11 and 24, 1787.

4. *Mémoires secrets*, March 6, April 14 and 27, 1787.

5. Hardy, *Journal*, Feb. 22 and 28, 1787.

6. *Gazette de Leyde*, Feb. 16, 1787; Métra, *Correspondance*, Feb. 8, 1787; *Mémoires secrets*, Feb. 17, 1787.

7. Métra, *Correspondance*, March 5, 1787; Hardy, *Journal*, Feb. 15, March 1 and 15, 1787.

8. *Mémoires secrets*, March 26, 1787.

9. Ibid., March 17, 1787.

10. Ibid., Jan. 18, March 5 and 6, 1787.

11. Métra, *Correspondance*, March 24, 1787; *Correspondance secrète*, March 18, 1787. On reports about the Notables at this time, see also *Gazette de Leyde*, March 13 and 16, 1787; *Correspondance secrète*, March 3 and 9, 1787; *Mémoires secrets*, March 4, 1787; and Hardy, *Journal*, March 2, 4, and 5, 1787.

12. *Mémoires secrets*, March 17, 1787.

13. *Correspondance secrète*, March 15, 1787; *Mémoires secrets*, March 12, 16, and 22, 1787; Métra, *Correspondance*, March 18, 1787; Hardy, *Journal*, March 18, 1787.

14. *Mémoires secrets*, March 30, 1787; Hardy, *Journal*, April 16, 1787.

15. Hardy, *Journal*, April 4, 1787.

16. Ibid., March 19, 1787. In sketches of the Notables, the *Mémoires secrets* wrote off Lafayette on February 20, 1787, as "d'un caractère doux et timide, peu instruit; il n'y a pas grand'chose à en attendre."

17. Métra, *Correspondance*, May 11, 1787.

18. *Gazette de Leyde*, April 20, 1787; Métra, *Correspondance*, May 11, 1787; *Mémoires secrets*, April 30, 1787.

19. *Correspondance secrète*, March 9, 1787. See also *Correspondance secrète*, March 22, 1787, and *Mémoires secrets*, April 4, 1787.

20. *Gazette de Leyde*, April 10, 1787. See also *Correspondance secrète*, March 5, 1787, and Hardy, *Journal*, April 1, 1787.

21. *Mémoires secrets*, March 31, April 1, 2, and 3, 1787; *Correspondance secrète*, April 12, 1787; *Gazette de Leyde*, April 13 and 17, 1787; Hardy, *Journal*, April 5, 1787.

22. *Mémoires secrets*, April 13 and 22, 1787.

23. Ibid., Feb. 4, March 6 and 28, and April 14 and 27, 1787.

24. Ibid., April 13, 1787. What made the verses especially effective, as the *Mémoires secrets* noted on April 11, 1787, was their association with well-known tunes, which resonated in different ways, making "une espèce de petit drame, où l'on parodie la première séance de l'Assemblée des Notables et ce qui s'est passé depuis." See also Hardy, *Journal*, April 19, 1787.

25. *Mémoires secrets*, April 5, 1787; *Journal de Leyde*, May 29, 1787.

26. Hardy, *Journal*, April 14, 1787. The pamphlet included some letters exchanged between Necker and Calonne and therefore was titled *Correspondance de M. Necker avec M. de Calonne* (n.p., 1787). It included a great deal of esoteric discussion about finances along with a protest (p. 4) about Calonne's address to the Notables of February 22, 1787, even though he had not mentioned Necker: "Tout à coup je me suis vu attaqué, ou pour mieux dire assailli, de la manière la plus injuste."

27. Hardy, *Journal*, April 14, 1787; *Mémoires secrets*, Feb. 21 and May 13, 1787.

28. *Correspondance secrète*, June 10, 1787.

29. *Mémoires secrets*, May 20, 1787.

Chapter 31

1. As an example of the public reaction, see Hardy, *Journal*, July 16, 1787, and *Réponse catégorique et sans réplique à la Requête au Roi, adressée à Sa Majesté par M. de Calonne, ministre d'Etat* (n.p., 1787), 4: "C'est le premier exemple depuis la fondation de la monarchie française qu'on ait vu un de ses premiers ministres qui s'enfuit, et où? Chez qui? Chez une nation rivale, ennemi naturel de la France."

2. *Mémoires secrets*, May 8, 1787.

3. Métra, *Correspondance*, May 24 and June 15, 1787; Hardy, *Journal*, June 14, 1787.

4. *Mémoires secrets*, July 5, 1787; Métra, *Correspondance*, July 7, 1787.

5. *Mémoires secrets*, Aug. 10, 1787; Hardy, *Journal*, Aug. 10, 1787. The text appears in *Journal pour servir à l'histoire du XVIIIe siècle, contenant les événements relatifs aux impôts de la subvention territoriale et du timbre* (n.p., 1787).

6. *Mémoires secrets*, Aug. 8, Sept. 16 and 21, 1787; Métra, *Correspondance*, Sept. 1, 1787; *Journal de Leyde*, Sept. 18, 1787; Hardy, *Journal*, Aug. 4, 10, and 13, 1787.

7. *Mémoires secrets*, July 22, Aug. 9 and 12, 1787; *Correspondance secrète*, July 4 and Aug. 1, 1787; Ruault, *Gazette*, 83 and 91; Hardy, *Journal*, June 25, Sept. 4 and 19, 1787. These sources, along with Métra, *Correspondance*, and the *Gazette de Leyde* provide the basis for the following account.

8. Métra, *Correspondance*, Oct. 2, 1787; Hardy, *Journal*, Sept. 28, 29, 30, and Oct. 1 and 2, 1787.

9. Calonne, *Requête au Roi, adressée à Sa Majesté par M. de Calonne, ministre d'Etat, avec les pièces justificatives* (n.p., 1787), quotations from pp. 60, 79, and 105.

10. Hardy, *Journal*, Oct. 21, 1787; *Mémoires secrets*, Oct. 25 and 30, 1787; Ruault, *Gazette*, 88; *Journal de Leyde*, Oct. 19 and Nov. 16, 1787.

11. In addition to the above works, see *Procès de M. Calonne, ou réplique à son libelle* (n.p., 1787). On reactions to them, see *Mémoires secrets*, Nov. 2, 30, and Dec. 7, 1787; and Hardy, *Journal*, Oct. 29, 1787.

12. Carra, *Un Petit Mot de réponse à M. de Calonne sur sa Requête au Roi* (Amsterdam, 1787); see especially pp. 53–67. For reactions to it, see *Mémoires secrets*, Nov. 15, Dec. 14 and 17, 1787. Carra also denounced Lenoir as an accomplice of Calonne's despotic rule: *L'An 1787. Précis de l'administration de la Bibliothèque du Roi sous Mr. Le Noir* (Liège, 1788).

13. Among the many pamphlets published against Calonne in 1787, see *Lettres surprises à M. de Calonne*; *Correspondance familière de M. de Calonne à ses amis, échappée de son portefeuille*; *Réponse d'un ami de la vérité à M. de Calonne*; *Réplique au mémoire justificatif de M. de Calonne*; *Suite de la Conférence d'un ministre avec un conseiller*; and *Réponse catégorique et sans réplique à la Requête au Roi*.

14. *M. de Calonne tout entier, tel qu'il s'est comporté dans l'administration des finances, dans son commissariat en Bretagne, etc., etc. Avec une analyse de sa Requête au Roi et de sa réponse à l'écrit de M. Necker* (Brussels, 1788), quotations from vii, 28, 30–32, 35, and 369–70.

Chapter 32

1. *Gazette de Leyde*, June 15, 1787.

2. Ibid., May 18, 1787. In addition to the sources cited in the preceding chapters, this account is based on *Journal pour servir à l'histoire du dix-huitième siècle* (Paris, 1788), a contemporary collection of documents, and *Lettres d'André Morellet*, ed. Dorothy Medlin and Jean-Claude David (Oxford, 1994). Morellet was a friend and supporter of Loménie de Brienne. He attributed the deficit to Calonne's depredations and also to the failure of Brienne's ministry to win the support of public opinion.

3. *Mémoires secrets*, July 3, 1787.

4. Ruault, *Gazette*, 85–86; *Mémoires secrets*, July 3 and 6, 1787; Hardy, *Journal*, July 4, 1787.

5. *Mémoires secrets*, July 27, 1787; *Correspondance secrète*, Aug. 13, 1787; Ruault, *Gazette*, 90–91.

6. *Correspondance secrète*, Sept. 13 and 24, 1787.

7. Ruault, *Gazette*, 87–89.

8. *Mémoires secrets*, Aug. 9, 1787.
9. Hardy, *Journal*, Aug. 7, 1787.
10. The texts of the relevant documents were reprinted in *Journal pour servir à l'histoire du dix-huitième siècle*, 95–134.
11. Hardy, *Journal*, Aug. 11, 1787; Ruault, *Gazette*, 91.
12. Hardy, *Journal*, Aug. 14, 1787. The *Mémoires secrets*, Aug. 16, 1787, noted that the peddlers had received instructions from the authorities on the manner of their hawking: "On a affecté de faire crier hier par les colporteurs à haute et intelligible voix le règlement concernant la réforme de la maison du roi."
13. Hardy, *Journal*, Aug. 16, 1787.
14. Ibid., Aug. 16, 1787.
15. Ruault, *Gazette*, 98.
16. *Mémoires secrets*, Aug. 27, 1787.
17. Hardy, *Journal*, Aug. 22, 1787. See also *Mémoires secrets*, Aug. 21, 1787, and Métra, *Correspondance*, Sept. 8, 1787.
18. Hardy, *Journal*, Sept. 10, 1787.
19. *Observations d'un avocat sur l'arrêté du Parlement de Paris du 13 août 1787* (n.p., n.d.); see the remarks on pp. 21 and 23, which noted that the two taxes would bring relief to the common people but did not construe the privileges of the clergy and nobility as abuses to be destroyed.
20. *Mémoires secrets*, Aug. 21 and 28, 1787; Hardy, *Journal*, Aug. 18, 20, and 28, 1787.
21. *Mémoires secrets*, Aug. 28 and Sept. 8, 1787; *Journal de Leyde*, Aug. 31, 1787; Hardy, *Journal*, Sept. 18, 1787.
22. Hardy, *Journal*, Sept. 24 and 26, 1787.
23. *Mémoires secrets*, Sept. 22 and 27, 1787. See also Hardy, *Journal*, Sept. 22, 24, and 27, and Oct. 1, 1787; and Métra, *Correspondance*, Oct. 14, 1787.
24. *Gazette de Leyde*, *Mémoires secrets*, and Hardy's *Journal* for October 1787.
25. The events are recounted in *Journal de Leyde*, Nov. 30, 1787; *Mémoires secrets*, Nov. 19 and 22, 1787; and Hardy, *Journal*, Nov. 21, 1787.
26. *Mémoires secrets*, Nov. 30, 1787.
27. Hardy, *Journal*, Oct. 13, 1787.
28. *Mémoires secrets*, Dec. 29, 1787.
29. Hardy, *Journal*, Jan. 2, 1788; *Mémoires secrets*, Dec. 21, 1787.
30. Hardy, *Journal*, Jan. 2, 1788.

Chapter 33

1. *Correspondance secrète*, Jan. 9, 1788.
2. Hardy, *Journal*, Jan. 2 and 24 and Feb. 3, 1788.
3. Métra, *Correspondance*, March 29, 1788.
4. Hardy, *Journal*, Jan. 9, 1788; Métra, *Correspondance*, Jan. 12 and 18, 1788.
5. Hardy, *Journal*, Jan. 16, 1788. Although the author of the *Correspondance secrète* was a partisan of the Enlightenment, his account (Jan. 31, 1788) agreed with Hardy's. See also Véri, *Journal*, II, 1537, Jan. 10, 1788.
6. *Correspondance secrète*, Feb. 8, 1788.

7. Hardy, *Journal*, Feb. 13, 1788.

8. *Correspondance secrète*, March 8, 1788: "Le public ne sait encore que penser des discussions de M. Necker et M. de Calonne." See also *Correspondance secrète*, Feb. 20, 1788.

9. Métra, *Correspondance*, Feb. 16, April 5, and May 3, 1788.

10. *Correspondance secrète*, March 8, 1788.

11. On November 17, 1788, Ruault noted in his *Gazette*, p. 119: "Versailles coûte trop cher à l'État; on y dépense sans compter; il y a trop de luxe, trop de gaspillage surtout, trop de somptuosité, trop d'officiers, trop de maîtres et de valets, trop de maisons de princes et de princesses. Les dépenses sourdes et inconnues surpassent les dépenses écrites et sues de tout le monde. Versailles dans l'état où il est monté, coûte au royayume plus que le quart de ses revenus."

12. Métra, *Correspondance*, April 5, 1788.

13. *Correspondance secrète*, Jan. 9, 1788; Hardy, *Journal*, Jan. 4, 1788.

14. Hardy, *Journal*, Jan. 8 and 9, 1788; *Correspondance secrète*, Jan. 11, 1788.

15. *Correspondance secrète*, Jan. 19, 1788.

16. Hardy, *Journal*, Jan. 3, 1788.

17. *Correspondance secrète*, March 5, 1788. See also *Correspondance secrète*, March 8, 1788; and Métra, *Correspondance*, March 7, 1788.

18. Hardy, *Journal*, March 9 and 16, 1788.

19. The full text was published along with other documents from 1788 in *Réimpression de l'ancien Moniteur* (Paris, 1840–1845), I, 278, and key parts of it were quoted in Hardy, *Journal*, April 17, 1788.

20. *Réimpression de l'ancien Moniteur*, 284; Hardy, *Journal*, April 17, 1788.

21. Ruault, *Gazette*, 106–7.

22. *Correspondance secrète*, April 20, 1788; Hardy, *Journal*, April 23, 1788.

23. *Correspondance secrète*, May 4, 1788; Hardy, *Journal*, May 3, 1788.

24. Accounts of the "siege" of the Parlement differ only in minor details. See *Gazette de Leyde*, May 13 and 16, 1788; Hardy, *Journal*, May 3, 5, and 6, 1788; *Correspondance secrète*, May 7, 1788; Ruault, *Gazette*, 109–11; and *Réimpression de l'ancien Moniteur*, 288–94.

25. *Réimpression de l'ancien Moniteur*, 292. Hardy, *Journal*, May 6, 1788, mentions a "procès-verbal très circonstancié" of this session that circulated in Paris.

26. *Réimpression de l'ancien Moniteur*, 293.

27. Ibid., 293–94; Hardy, *Journal*, May 5 and 6, 1788.

28. Ruault, *Gazette*, 108–9.

29. Hardy, *Journal*, May 13, 1788; Métra, *Correspondance*, May 9 and 18, 1788.

Chapter 34

1. See Michel Perronet, "L'Assemblée du clergé de France tenue en 1788," *Annales historiques de la Révolution française*, no. 273 (1988), 227–46.

2. Hardy, *Journal*, May 8 and July 3, 1788.

3. *Gazette de Leyde*, May 30 and June 3, 1788. The *Gazette de Leyde* is the main source for the following account.

4. Hardy, *Journal*, June 26, 1788.
5. Ibid., June 26, 1788.
6. *Gazette de Leyde*, July 1, 4, and 8, 1788.
7. Métra, *Correspondance*, Aug. 10, 1788. Hardy recounted the last phases of the exchanges between the government and the Assembly in his journal entries for late June and July.

Chapter 35

1. For differing accounts of the provincial upheavals, see *Gazette de Leyde*, June 20 and 24, 1788; Métra, *Correspondance*, June 15, 1788; *Correspondance secrète*, June 15 and 19, 1788; Hardy, *Journal*, June 12 and 16, 1788; and Ruault, *Gazette*, 114–17. On the Journée des Tuiles and its resonance in the press, see Jean Sgard, *Les Trente récits de la Journée des Tuiles* (Grenoble, 1988).
2. The main sources of the following account are those cited in the previous note, especially the *Gazette de Leyde*.
3. *Gazette de Leyde*, June 13 and 17, 1788; Hardy, *Journal*, June 15, 1788.
4. *Correspondance secrète*, June 30, 1788.
5. Marquis de Bombelles, *Journal*, ed. Jean Grassion and Frans Durif (Geneva, 1977), II, 207.
6. *Gazette de Leyde*, July 25, 1788.
7. Ibid., July 13 and 15, 1788.
8. The *Gazette de Leyde* provided the most extensive coverage of the Breton protests during the summer of 1788.
9. *Correspondance secrète*, June 30, 1788; Hardy, *Journal*, June 27, 1788; *Gazette de Leyde*, July 25, 1788.
10. *Gazette de Leyde*, Sept. 5, 9, and 12, 1788.
11. *Correspondance secrète*, July 5, 1788; *Gazette de Leyde*, July 8, 1788; Hardy, *Journal*, June 28, 1788.
12. *Gazette de Leyde*, Aug. 12, 1788.
13. Métra, *Correspondance*, June 1 and 29, 1788.
14. *Correspondance secrète*, July 5, 1788.
15. Hardy, *Journal*, July 18, 1788.
16. This was the theme of *Réclamation du Tiers-Etat au Roi* (n.p., n.d.). See also Métra, *Correspondance*, June 15, 1788.
17. The Parlement of Paris made this position especially clear in its declaration of May 3, 1788, which Hardy copied into his journal on May 18. As an example of how this argument was taken up by the provincial parlements, see *Journal de Leyde*, July 15, 1788.
18. Hardy, *Journal*, July 2, 1788; *Correspondance secrète*, July 19, 1788.

Chapter 36

1. *Correspondance secrète*, Aug. 7, 1788.
2. Ruault, *Gazette*, 113.

3. Mallet du Pan, *Mémoires et correspondance de Mallet du Pan pour servir à l'histoire de la Révolution française*, ed. A. Sayous (Paris, 1851), I, 150.

4. Hardy, *Journal*, May 30, 1788.

5. *Correspondance secrète*, May 12, 1788. On these incidents see the entries for May in the *Correspondance secrète* and in Hardy's *Journal*.

6. Métra, *Correspondance*, June 15, 1788.

7. *Correspondance secrète*, May 22, 1788; Hardy, *Journal*, May 19, 1788.

8. Métra, *Correspondance*, June 22, 1788; *Correspondance secrète*, May 5, 1788; Hardy, *Journal*, May 27, 1788; and *Gazette de Leyde*, May 16, 1788.

9. Hardy, *Journal*, May 25, 1788; *Correspondance secrète*, May 30, 1788.

10. *Correspondance secrète*, June 4, 1788; and Hardy, *Journal*, May 26, 1788.

11. Hardy, *Journal*, June 3, 1788. See also *Gazette de Leyde*, June 13, 1788.

12. Hardy, *Journal*, July 2, 1788. See also the entries of June 6, 16, and 18, 1788.

13. Hardy, *Journal*, June 1, 1788. I have discussed this theme in "Theatricality and Violence in Paris, 1788," in *Voltaire: An Oxford Celebration*, ed. Nicholas Cronk, Alison Oliver, and Gillian Pink (Oxford, 2022), 9–29.

14. Hardy, *Journal*, May 28, 1788.

15. Métra, *Correspondance*, June 1, 1788; Grimm, *Correspondance littéraire*, XV, 250; Hardy, *Journal*, May 16, 1788.

16. Hardy, *Journal*, July 1, 1788.

17. *Correspondance secrète*, June 19, 1788.

18. Hardy, *Journal*, July 3, 1788.

19. *Histoire du siège du Palais par le capitaine d'Agoult à la tête de six compagnies de Gardes Françaises et deux compagnies de Gardes Suisses, sous les ordres du maréchal de Biron* (n.p., n.d.). The text was reprinted as an official report by the Parlement in the *Réimpression de l'ancien Moniteur*, which noted (I, 288) that many different versions of the text had circulated.

20. Hardy, *Journal*, May 30, 1788. On June 3, Hardy noted that the *Histoire du siège du Palais*, which at first had been available in manuscript, was circulating everywhere as a printed pamphlet, accompanied by copies of the remonstrances of May 4, which were written by d'Éprémesnil.

21. Métra, *Correspondance*, June 1, 1788; Hardy, *Journal*, May 26, 1788.

22. Bibliothèque historique de la ville de Paris, ms. 713: "Obélisque ou souscription patriotique pour l'élévation d'un monument à la gloire de l'immortel d'Agoult, capitaine aux Gardes Françaises dans la Place Dauphine."

23. Hardy, *Journal*, Sept. 22 and 23, 1788; Métra, *Correspondance*, Sept. 21, 1788; Mallet du Pan, *Mémoires et correspondance*, I, 156.

24. Judging from its context, *Le Lever de Bâville* appeared in late September. It was a cruder work in which Lamoignon was put on trial by the Parlement de Paris, condemned as "infâme," and sentenced to prison with a fine of 1,500,000 L., representing the funds he had drained from the treasury.

Chapter 37

1. *Gazette de Leyde*, Aug. 12, 1788; Hardy, *Journal*, July 13, 1788. Further details are in BnF, ms. fr. 2225, and Bibliothèque historique de la ville de Paris, ms. 1204. At that time the French pound (livre, poids de marc) equaled 1.07 current U.S. pounds.

2. *Correspondance secrète*, Aug. 5 and 7, 1788; *Gazette de Leyde*, Aug. 15, 1788; Hardy, *Journal*, Aug. 17 and 18, 1788.

3. Hardy, *Journal*, Oct. 1, 1788. Hardy discussed the previous events in entries throughout September.

4. Ibid., Nov. 25, 1788. See also the entry for Oct. 19, 1788.

Chapter 38

1. Hardy, *Journal*, July 27, 1788.

2. See, for example, Ruault's letter of May 19, 1788, in his *Gazette*, 110–11: "Le roi se perd, ou on perd le roi pour mieux s'exprimer, par de très mauvais et très perfides conseils, par des actions insensées qui irritent le peuple contre la maison royale. Ce malheureux prince ne sent point le danger de sa situation envers ses sujets qui se détachent de lui chaque jour."

3. *Correspondance secrète*, May 10, 1788.

4. Hardy, *Journal*, June 5, 1788: "On était dans les plus vives alarmes sur les événements futurs. . . . L'on pouvait bien dire que le feu était actuellement dans presque toutes les provinces du royaume." See also *Correspondance secrète*, June 7, 11, and 19, 1788.

5. Hardy noted the state's problem with foreign affairs and finances in journal entries throughout June and July.

6. The *Gazette de Leyde* for August and September, supplemented by Hardy's journal, is the main source for the following account.

7. The text of the edict of August 16 was published in the *Gazette de Leyde* of August 29. The edict also required that *rentes* from investments of 500 L. to 1,200 L. would be paid at a rate of 3/8 in notes rather than specie. Two additional edicts dated August 18 authorized the Caisse d'escompte to pay off its notes in other bills of exchange rather than in cash. As already explained, the Caisse was a private institution, although it sometimes received assistance from the state. The *Gazette de Leyde* of August 25 said the government's action was the equivalent of a forced loan for 140 million livres.

8. Hardy, *Journal*, Aug. 18 and 19, 1788.

9. The celebrations and rioting are described most fully in *Correspondance secrète*, September 7, 1788; Hardy's journal, entries for August 26–30, 1788; and *Gazette de Leyde*, Sept. 9 and 12, 1788.

10. Hardy, *Journal*, Sept. 14, 1788.

11. The most detailed accounts of these events are in *Correspondance secrète*, September 21, 1788, and Hardy's journal, entries for September 15–17, 1788. Additional details are in *Gazette de Leyde*, Sept. 26 and 30, 1788; Grimm, *Correspondance littéraire*, XV, 312, and Bombelles, *Journal*, II, 236.

12. Grimm, *Correspondance littéraire*, XV, 312.

Chapter 39

1. On the hostility to the edict, see Mallet du Pan, *Mémoires et correspondance*, I, 137, and Hardy, *Journal*, Jan. 20, 22, and 29, 1788.

2. On the vogue for all things Swiss, see Charly Guyot, *De Rousseau à Mirabeau. Pèlerins de Môtiers et prophètes de 1789* (Neuchâtel, 1936) and *La Vie intellectuelle et religieuse en Suisse française à la fin du XVIIIe siècle* (Neuchâtel, 1946).

3. *Journal de Leyde*, Sept. 2, 1788.

4. See Léonard Burnand, *Necker et l'opinion publique* (Paris, 2004).

5. *De l'importance des idées religieuses* (Liège, 1788), quotations from pp. 4, 16, and 24.

6. *Correspondance secrète*, Feb. 8, 16, 20, and March 8, 1788; Hardy, *Journal*, Feb. 13, 1788.

7. *Sur le Compte rendu au Roi en 1781. Nouveaux éclaircissements* (Paris, 1788), 277.

8. *Réponse de M. de Calonne à l'écrit de M. Necker publié en avril 1787* (London, 1788); see especially pp. 112, 191, and 201.

9. *Sur le Compte rendu*; see especially pp. 13, 25, and 207.

10. *Correspondance secrète*, Sept. 15, 1788; *Gazette de Leyde*, Sept. 23, 1788; Hardy, *Journal*, Sept. 11, 1788.

11. Hardy, *Journal*, Sept. 15, 1788. See also *Correspondance secrète*, Aug. 21, 1788, and, as an example of the view of a well-informed courtier at this time, *Mémoires du baron de Besenval sur la cour de France*, ed. Ghislain de Diesbach (Paris, 1987), 478–80.

12. *Journal de Leyde*, Sept. 9, 1788. See also Hardy, *Journal*, Sept. 1, 1788.

13. Hardy, *Journal*, Oct. 10, 1788.

14. Ibid., Sept. 12, 1788.

Chapter 40

1. The following account is based on Hardy's *Journal*, supplemented by Métra, *Correspondance* (especially Dec. 4 and 11, 1788) and *Gazette de Leyde* (especially Dec. 9, 19, and 30, 1788).

2. Hardy, *Journal*, Feb. 13, 1789.

Chapter 41

1. The phrase was used in the king's rejection of the Parlement's outspoken remonstrances of April 11 and was quoted by Hardy in his journal entry of April 17, 1788.

2. Hardy, *Journal*, July 8, 1788.

3. *Correspondance secrète*, March 5 and Aug. 16, 1788; Métra, *Correspondance*, Aug. 17, 1788; *Gazette de Leyde*, Aug. 5, 1788; and Hardy, *Journal*, Aug. 8 and 11, 1788.

4. *Gazette de Leyde*, Sept. 5, 1788. On Sept. 12, the *Gazette* noted a widespread conviction that the principles of Vizille should "servir de modèles à tout le royaume." The following account is based primarily on the *Gazette de Leyde* supplemented by the *Journal politique de Bruxelles*.

5. *Gazette de Leyde*, Oct. 3, 1788.

6. Ibid., Dec. 26, 1788. At this time the word "révolution" connoted sudden change or upheaval but not the violent, systemic transformation that it came to mean in 1789. See Keith Michael Baker, "Inventing the French Revolution," in Baker, *Inventing the French Revolution*, chap. 9.

7. *Pétition des citoyens domiciliés à Paris* in *Résultat du Conseil d'Etat du Roi et très-humble adresse de remerciement présenté au Roi par les Six-Corps de la ville de Paris* (n.p., 1789), 10–11 and 14; and *Mémoire présenté au Roi par les Six-Corps de la ville de Paris* (n.p., 1788). See also *Gazette de Leyde*, Dec. 30, 1788; Métra, *Correspondance*, Dec. 26, 1788; *Correspondance secrète*, Dec. 20, 1788; and Hardy, *Journal*, Dec. 16, 1788.

8. *Correspondance secrète*, Dec. 27, 1788. In its issue of December 25, the *Correspondance secrète* remarked, "La fermentation règne dans toutes les classes des citoyens d'un bout du royaume à l'autre; les écrits nombreux que le gouvernement a tolérés échauffent les têtes, et les gens honnêtes sont très alarmés sur les événements de l'année 1789."

9. *Gazette de Leyde*, Dec. 16, 1788; Hardy, *Journal*, Dec. 5, 1788.

10. *Correspondance secrète*, Nov. 20, 1788. See also the issues of Dec. 13 and 16, 1788.

11. Métra, *Correspondance*, Nov. 1 and 22, Dec. 11, 1788, Jan. 9 and 16, 1789; Hardy, *Journal*, Oct. 29 and Dec. 11, 1788.

12. Métra, *Correspondance*, March 29, 1789.

13. Although Necker expressed deference to the views of the privileged orders, he emphasized, "La cause du Tiers-Etat aura toujours pour elle l'opinion publique": *Rapport fait au Roi dans son conseil par le ministre des finances, précédé du Résultat du Conseil d'Etat du Roi tenu à Versailles le 27 décembre 1788* (n.p., n.d.), 19. On the reception of Necker's decision and the sharpened sense of crisis, see *Correspondance secrète*, Jan. 2, 3, and 11, 1789, and Hardy, *Journal*, Jan. 2 and Feb. 1, 1789.

Chapter 42

1. Métra, *Correspondance*, Feb. 14, 1789.

2. Mercier, *Les Entretiens du Palais-Royal de Paris* (Paris, 1788), 75. See the similar remarks on pp. 41, 57, and 157–65. This edition contained a "Seconde Partie," which greatly extended the remarks in the first edition of 1786 and the reprint of 1787.

3. Mercier, *Les Entretiens du Jardin des Tuileries de Paris* (Paris, 1788), 4.

4. Mercier, *Tableau de Paris*, I, 185.

5. Métra, *Correspondance*, Dec. 26, 1788.

6. Ibid., March 22, 1789.

7. Ibid., Jan. 2 and 9, 1789.

8. Hardy, *Journal*, March 18, 1789.

9. Métra, *Correspondance*, Jan. 25, 1788. See the issues of March 8 and 22, 1789, on the hidden book burnings by the Parlement.

10. Métra, *Correspondance*, Jan. 9, 1789. In announcing "le grand ouvrage de Mably" on October 28, 1788, the *Correspondance secrète* reported that the king had ordered the police to repress it as "incendiaire et dangereux." See Keith Michael Baker, "A

Script for a French Revolution: The Political Consciousness of the Abbé Mably," in Baker, *Inventing the French Revolution*, chap. 4.

11. *Recueil de pièces historiques sur la convocation des Etats-Généraux et sur l'élection de leurs députés* (Paris, 1788), 99.

12. Target, *Les Etats-Généraux convoqués par Louis XVI* (n.p., n.d.), quotations from pp. 7, 16, 21, and 25.

13. De Launay, *Mémoire sur les Etats-Généraux, leurs droits et la manière de les convoquer* (n.p., 1788), 222 and 246.

14. Cerutti, *Mémoire pour le peuple français* (n.p., n.d.); see especially pp. 30 and 57. On its success, see Hardy, *Journal,* Dec. 17, 1788, and Métra, *Correspondance,* Jan. 9, 1789.

15. Rabaut Saint-Etienne, *Considérations sur les intérêts du Tiers-Etat, adressées au peuple des provinces par un propriétaire foncier* (n.p., n.d.), quotation from p. 37.

16. In his *Journal,* Feb. 3, 1789, Hardy discussed Sieyès's pamphlet at length and concluded, "On pensait que cet ouvrage devait être distingué singulièrement dans la prodigieuse multitude de ceux que tant de citoyens zélés pour la cause commune et vraiment attachés à la chose publique avaient déjà composés en faveur du Tiers Etat." See the excellent study by William H. Sewell Jr., *A Rhetoric of Bourgeois Revolution: The Abbé Sieyès and "What Is the Third Estate?"* (Durham, NC, 1994).

17. Sieyès, *Qu'est-ce que le Tiers Etat?* (n.p., n.d.), quotation from the Paris reprint of 1888, p. 30.

18. Ibid., 66.

19. Ibid., quotations from pp. 36 and 67.

20. Among the many works on Condorcet, see especially Keith Michael Baker, *Condorcet: From Natural Philosophy to Social Mathematics* (Chicago, 1975).

21. See Condorcet, *Un ami de Voltaire à M. d'Éprémesnil* (London, 1780).

22. Condorcet, *Lettres d'un bourgeois de New Haven à un citoyen de Virginie* (1787) in *Oeuvres de Condorcet,* ed. A. Condorcet O'Connor and M. F. Arago (Paris, 1847), IX, 58.

23. Condorcet, *Lettres d'un citoyen des Etats-Unis à un Français sur les affaires présentes* ("Philadelphie," 1788), "Seconde lettre," 11.

24. In a later work, *Idées sur le despotisme à l'usage de ceux qui prononcent ce mot sans l'entendre* (1789), Condorcet stressed that the despotism of a privileged minority was more oppressive than the concentration of power in the hands of a monarch and that a nation could be misled into seeing its oppressors, the parlements, as its protectors. Thus a nation could suffer from despotism "sans le savoir": *Oeuvres,* IX, 150.

25. *Lettres d'un citoyen des Etats-Unis,* 20–21; *Idées sur le despotisme,* 160–62.

26. Condorcet, *Réflexions d'un citoyen sur la révolution de 1788* (Paris, 1788), 37–38.

Chapter 43

1. Métra, *Correspondance,* Jan. 2, 1789; Hardy, *Journal,* Jan. 2, 1789.

2. Hardy, *Journal,* Jan. 9 and 10, 1789. The fear was stoked by pamphlets such

as *Prenez-y garde, ou avis à toutes les assemblées d'élection qui seront convoquées pour nommer les représentants des trois ordres aux Etats Généraux* (n.p., 1789), and *Mémoire à consulter et consultation pour les habitants de la ville de Paris* (n.p., n.d.)

3. Hardy, *Journal*, March 4, 1789.

4. In his *Instruction, ou si l'on veut, cahier de l'assemblée du bailliage de* *** (n.p., 1789), p. 22, Target defended the "prérogatives de rang, d'honneur et de dignité" along with feudal dues. In *Prenez-y garde*, Rabaut warned the Third Estate to exclude the nobility from its electoral assemblies in order to avoid being manipulated by it.

5. *Gazette de Leyde*, Jan. 16, Feb. 3, 13, and 27, 1789. Although it received many reports from Rennes, the *Gazette* warned its readers that it could not confirm the details of this important incident. See also *Correspondance secrète*, Jan. 31, Feb. 2 and 15, 1789; and Hardy, *Journal*, Jan. 30, Feb. 3 and 5, 1789.

6. *Gazette de Leyde*, May 5, 1789.

7. Hardy, *Journal*, Feb. 13, 1789.

8. Métra, *Correspondance*, April 26, 1789.

9. Hardy, *Journal*, Feb. 25, 1789.

10. Métra, *Correspondance*, April 12, 1789.

11. Hardy, *Journal*, March 3, 1789.

12. Ibid., March 5, 1789.

13. Métra, *Correspondance*, April 19, 1789; *Gazette de Leyde*, April 24, 1789.

14. Hardy, *Journal*, Jan. 9, 1789, and entries for Jan. 2 and 5, 1789.

15. *Lettre adressée au Roi par M. de Calonne* (London, 1789), 7. The *Lettre* was dated Feb. 9, 1789, but it did not circulate in Paris until March.

16. *Correspondance secrète*, March 8, 1789; Métra, *Correspondance*, March 15, 1789.

17. *Lettre adressée au Roi*, 103.

18. *Gazette de Leyde*, March 20 and April 14, 1789; Hardy, *Journal*, March 15 and 18, 1789.

19. Joseph-Antoine-Joachim Cérutti, *Observations rapides sur la Lettre de M. de Calonne au Roi* (Paris, 1789), 17.

20. Calonne's *Seconde lettre adressée au Roi par M. de Calonne* (London, 1789), dated April 5, 1789, reads like a prophecy of doom, foreseeing civil war, anarchy, and the emergence of a dictatorship. It described the current conflicts as "une lutte entre la classe oisive et la classe laborieuse" (p. 29); warned that the Estates General would be polarized into two factions "sous les noms de patriotes et de royalistes" (p. 47); lamented that "on anéantit toute autorité qui n'est pas populaire" (p. 30); and excoriated the partisans of the Third Estate as rabble rousers: "Au milieu du tumulte général on n'entendra qu'un cri, *liberté, liberté*" (45). On the reactions to it, see *Gazette de Leyde*, April 14 and 21, 1789, and *Correspondance secrète*, April 4, 1789. On April 28, the *Gazette de Leyde* reported that Calonne made a secret, three-day visit to Paris in order to prepare the way for his election as a deputy from the nobility.

21. *Instructions données par S. A. S. Monseigneur le duc d'Orléans* (n.p., n.d.); see especially pp. 7–9.

22. *Délibérations à prendre dans les assemblées de bailliages* (n.p., n.d.). In allowing for collaboration with the nobility and clergy, Sieyès nonetheless adopted a defiant

tone (p. 14): "C'est au Tiers à rendre la liberté à la nation, de concert avec les deux ordres, s'ils se montrent dignes d'un si grand bienfait." It should be noted, however, that Sieyès, a canon of the Chartres cathedral, opposed the abolition of the *dîme* collected by the church.

23. Hardy, *Journal*, March 15, 1789.

24. *Correspondance secrète*, March 12 and 22, 1789; *Gazette de Leyde*, March 20 and 24, 1789.

25. See, for example, *Correspondance secrète*, April 19 and 23, 1789; *Gazette de Leyde*, May 5, 1789; and Hardy, *Journal*, April 18 and 19, 1789.

26. *Gazette de Leyde*, April 26, 1789. For a general account of the elections, see François Furet, "La monarchie et le règlement électoral de 1789," and Ran Halévi, "La monarchie et les élections: position des problèmes," in *The Political Culture of the Old Regime*, ed. Keith Michael Baker (Oxford, 1987), chaps. 19 and 20. Also, as an excellent overview of the issues discussed in this and the following three chapters, see Timothy Tackett, *Becoming a Revolutionary: The Deputies of the French National Assembly and the Emergence of a Revolutionary Culture (1789–1790)* (Princeton, 1996).

27. *Gazette de Leyde*, May 5, 1789; Hardy, *Journal*, April 22, 1789.

28. Hardy, *Journal*, April 21 and 22, 1789.

29. *Journal de Leyde*, May 5, 1789; Hardy, *Journal*, April 23, 1789.

30. Hardy, *Journal*, April 29, 1789.

31. *Gazette de Leyde*, May 12, 1789.

32. Hardy, *Journal*, May 13, 1789.

33. Ibid., May 23 and 28, 1789. See also *Gazette de Leyde*, May 29, 1789.

34. *Cahier du Tiers-Etat de la ville de Paris* (Paris, 1789), 7 and 69.

Chapter 44

1. *Gazette de Leyde*, May 5, 8, and 12, 1789. The *Gazette* and Hardy's *Journal* are the main sources for the following account.

2. *Gazette de Leyde*, May 5, 1789.

3. Hardy, *Journal*, May 14, 1789. Réveillon gave his estimate of his losses in *Exposé justificatif pour le sieur Réveillon, entrepreneur de la manufacture royale de papiers peints, faubourg Saint Antoine* (n.p., n.d.), 23–24.

4. Hardy, *Journal*, April 28, 29, 30, and May 1, 1789.

5. *Gazette de Leyde*, May 8, 1789; Hardy, *Journal*, April 29 and May 5, 1789.

6. Hardy, *Journal*, April 29, 1789; *Gazette de Leyde*, May 12, 1789.

7. Hardy, *Journal*, May 22, 1789.

8. Ibid., May 4 and 13, 1789.

9. Ibid., May 25, 1789.

10. *Gazette de Leyde*, May 12, 1789.

11. Hardy, *Journal*, May 12, 1789.

12. Réveillon's pamphlet, *Exposé justificatif pour le sieur Réveillon*, told the story of his life from, as he claimed, his humble beginnings, as an attempt to defend the honor of his name. He said he was proud to have been an "ouvrier et journalier," and he

described the way he built his business, step by step, until he achieved success (p. 15): "J'ai joui de cette satisfaction inexprimable qu'éprouve un homme honnête, laborieux, qui s'est créé lui-même."

13. Hardy, *Journal,* April 29, 1789, and *Gazette de Leyde,* May 12, 1789.
14. *Gazette de Leyde,* May 12, 1789.

Chapter 45

1. *Idées patriotiques sur les premiers besoins du peuple proposées à l'assemblée des Etats-Généraux* (n.p., n.d.), and Hardy, *Journal,* May 2, 4, and 17, 1789.
2. The following account is based on *Gazette de Leyde,* May 15, 1789; Hardy, *Journal,* May 4, 1789; *Correspondance secrète,* May 5 and 6, 1789; Métra, *Correspondance,* May 17, 1789; and the reports in *Réimpression de l'ancien Moniteur.*
3. Hardy, *Journal,* May 4, 1789.
4. Métra, *Correspondance,* June 6, 1789.
5. Mirabeau, *Etats-Généraux,* reprinted in *Lettres du comte de Mirabeau à ses commettants,* articles covering May 2, 4, and 5, 1789. Hardy, in his *Journal* of May 5, 1789, deplored Mirabeau's "ton d'impudence et de liberté."
6. *Lettres du comte de Mirabeau,* 22.
7. Target came to Mirabeau's defense and attacked censorship at a meeting of the Paris electors on May 8: Hardy, *Journal,* May 8, 1789.
8. *Correspondance secrète,* May 23 and 29, 1789.
9. Hardy, *Journal,* May 30, 1789.
10. *Gazette de Leyde,* June 9, 1789.
11. *Gazette de Leyde,* June 19, 1789.
12. Métra, *Correspondance,* June 20, 1789; Hardy, *Journal,* June 6, 10, 11, and 13, 1789.
13. Mirabeau, *Lettres du comte de Mirabeau,* 113–14.
14. The votes are given as reported in the *Journal de Paris* and Hardy, *Journal,* June 19, 1789. The *Gazette de Leyde* of June 26, 1789, gave the vote as 491 in favor of Sieyès's motion and 90 against, and the *Correspondance secrète* made it 481 to 119.
15. Ruault, *Gazette,* June 21, 1789.
16. *Gazette de Leyde,* June 12, 1789.
17. *Correspondance secrète,* May 5, 1789.
18. *Gazette de Leyde,* June 30, 1789.
19. Métra, *Correspondance,* June 6, 1789.
20. Hardy, *Journal,* June 30, 1789.
21. Ibid., June 15 and 16, 1789.
22. Ibid., June 20, 1789; *Gazette de Leyde,* June 30, 1789; *Correspondance secrète,* June 21 and 25, 1789.

Chapter 46

1. Hardy, *Journal,* June 22, 1789.
2. Ibid., June 20 and 21, 1789. The full text of the oath appeared along with an account of the day's events in *Gazette de Leyde,* June 30, 1789.

3. Ruault, *Gazette,* June 21, 1789.

4. Hardy, *Journal,* June 22, 1789; *Gazette de Leyde,* July 3, 1789.

5. The main source for the following account is the *Gazette de Leyde,* July 3, 1789, supplemented by Hardy's *Journal,* entries for June 23, 24, and 25, 1789.

6. *Lettres du comte de Mirabeau à ses commettans,* 272, thirteenth letter dated June 23, 24, and 25. The *Gazette de Leyde,* which gave a full account of the *séance royale* in its issue of July 7, reported Mirabeau's speech as follows: "Monsieur, il n'y a que la force qui puisse nous faire sortir d'ici. Quant à moi, on ne me mettra dehors que percé de baïonnettes." More standardized versions, including a reference to the "volonté du peuple," have passed into revolutionary mythology.

7. Hardy, *Journal,* June 24, 1789.

8. Ibid., June 23, 1789.

9. Ibid. The *Gazette de Leyde* published a somewhat different account on July 7, 1789.

10. Hardy, *Journal,* May 14, 1789.

11. Ibid., July 6, 1789.

12. Ibid., June 25, 26, and 28, 1789. Hardy observed on June 28 that the National Assembly had survived only because of "l'insubordination militaire commandée par le patriotisme."

13. This account is based on Hardy, *Journal,* June 30, 1789, and *Gazette de Leyde,* July 10, 1789.

14. *Gazette de Leyde,* July 10 and 14, 1789.

15. Hardy, *Journal,* July 2, 3, and 6, 1789.

16. Ibid., July 9, 1789.

17. Ibid., July 10, 1789.

18. Tradition has it that the future revolutionary leader, Camille Desmoulins, was the first to issue the cry from a table outside the Café de Foy, but his name does not appear in the contemporary papers that are the source of the following account, which is based primarily on *Révolutions de Paris,* the journal of Elisée Loustalot, who participated in many of the events and witnessed most of them. Its reports for the period July 12 to 17, 1789, were reprinted in August 1789 by its publisher, Louis Marie Prudhomme, as a pamphlet, *Révolutions de Paris, dédiées à la nation et au district des Petits Augustins.* I have supplemented it with other contemporary sources, notably articles in the *Gazette de Leyde.* The journalistic version of events provides evidence about the way Parisians saw them, which is what I intend to convey. It differs somewhat from the standard versions of historians, which I have not attempted to blend into my narrative. Among them, the most authoritative is Jacques Godechot, *La Prise de la Bastille: 14 juillet 1789* (Paris, 1965). See also Munro Price, *The Fall of the French Monarchy: Louis XVI, Marie-Antoinette, and the Baron de Breteuil* (London, 2002) and the astute essay by William H. Sewell Jr., "Historical Events as Transformations of Structures: Inventing Revolution at the Bastille," *Theory and Society* XXV (1996), 841–81.

19. "Détails du mardi 14 juillet," *Révolutions de Paris,* 17.

20. *Gazette de Leyde,* July 24, 1789.

21. Ruault, *Gazette,* July 16, 1789.

22. *Gazette de Leyde,* July 24, 1789.

23. Ibid., July 30, 1789.

Afterword

1. *Réimpression de l'Ancien Moniteur depuis la réunion des Etats-Généraux jusqu'au Consulat* (Paris, 1841), XVIII, 314.

2. In his *Fragments sur les institutions républicaines* (published posthumously, Paris, 1831), 42, Louis-Antoine de Saint Just wrote, "Celui qui plaisante à la tête du gouvernement tend à la tyrannie."

3. Saint Just, *Fragments,* 57. Saint Just added that girls could remain at home, but boys were to be raised in boarding schools with Spartan discipline until the age of sixteen.

4. Babeuf to his wife, July 23, 1789, *Oeuvres de Babeuf,* ed. V. Daline, A. Saitta, and A. Soboul (Paris, 1977), I, 340.

5. Donald Greer, *The Incidence of the Terror during the French Revolution: A Statistical Interpretation* (Gloucester, MA, 1966).

6. Pierre Caron, *Les Massacres de septembre* (Paris, 1935).

ILLUSTRATION CREDITS

(BnF: Bibliothèque nationale de France)

Insert I

Page 1: A group of *nouvellistes* in the Luxembourg Garden. *BnF*

Page 2: (top) The Tree of Cracow. *BnF.* (bottom) Engraving after M. Peyrotte's "Council of Monkeys." *BnF*

Page 3: (top) Gossips in a café. *BnF.* (bottom) Street singer. *BnF*

Page 4: (top) The publication of the peace in 1763. *BnF* (bottom) A pro-Jansenist depiction of miracles. *BnF*

Page 5: (top) The disaster at the fireworks. *BnF.* (bottom left) Madame de Pompadour. *BnF.* (bottom right) Mme du Barry. *BnF*

Page 6: (top) Rousseau and Voltaire. *BnF.* (bottom) A condemned man being broken on the wheel. *BnF/Bridgeman Images*

Page 7: (top) Scene from "The Marriage of Figaro." *BnF.* (bottom) Pierre Calas reads the judicial memoir by Elie de Beaumont. *BnF*

Page 8 (top left) Louis XV. *Louvre, Paris, France; photo © Photo Josse/Bridgeman Images.* (top right) Chancellor Maupeou. *BnF.* (bottom left) Louis XVI. *BnF.* (bottom right) Marie Antoinette. *BnF*

Insert II

Page 1: The second manned flight of a balloon, December 1, 1783. *BnF*

Page 2: (top) The contemporary faith in science. *BnF*. (bottom) A satirical print showing Mesmer treating fashionable women at his tub. *BnF*

Page 3: (top) A purportedly accurate representation of the diamond necklace. *BnF*. (bottom) Cagliostro. *BnF*

Page 4: The official celebration of the peace after the American war on December 14, 1783. *BnF*

Page 5: (top) Louis XVI protesting to Calonne that the treasury is empty. *BnF*. (bottom) An anti-Necker print that shows him performing a conjuring trick before Louis XVI. *BnF*

Page 6: (top) The Assembly of Notables. *BnF*. (middle) The *Lit de justice* of August 6, 1787. *BnF*. (bottom) The arrest of d'Éprémesnil and Goislard on May 6, 1788. *BnF*

Page 7: (top) The burning of a guardhouse on the Pont Neuf during the uprising of August 29, 1788. *BnF*. (bottom) Camille Desmoulins urging the crowd to seize arms. *BnF/Bridgeman Images*

Page 8: (top) The storming of the Bastille. *BnF*. (bottom) The crowd in the Place de Grève before the Hôtel de Ville on July 14, 1789. *BnF/© Archives Charmet/Bridgeman Images*

INDEX